Publications of The Perry Foundation for Biblical Research
The Hebrew University of Jerusalem

THE TEN COMMANDMENTS

IN HISTORY AND TRADITION

Edited by
BEN-ZION SEGAL

English Version
Edited by
GERSHON LEVI

THE MAGNES PRESS, THE HEBREW UNIVERSITY OF JERUSALEM

First published in Hebrew, Jerusalem 1985

ISBN 965-223-724-8

Printed in Israel
by "Graph-Chen" Press Ltd., Jerusalem

THE TEN COMMANDMENTS
IN HISTORY AND TRADITION

The Holy Ark at Trino Vercellese, Italy (Middle of 18th century) Courtesy of David Cassuto, Jerusalem

CONTENTS

LIST OF PLATES

CONTRIBUTORS

Ephraim E. Urbach   Emeritus Professor of Talmud and Midrash at the Hebrew University of Jerusalem and former President of the Israel Academy of Sciences and Humanities

Moshe Weinfeld   Professor of Bible at the Hebrew University of Jerusalem

Alexander Rofé   Professor of Bible at the Hebrew University of Jerusalem

Meir Weiss   Emeritus Professor of Bible at the Hebrew University of Jerusalem

Moshe Greenberg   Professor of Bible at the Hebrew University of Jerusalem

Yehoshua Amir   Emeritus Professor of Jewish Thought at Tel-Aviv University

Ezra Zion Melammed   Emeritus Professor of Bible at the Hebrew University of Jerusalem

David Flusser   Emeritus Professor of Comparative Religion at the Hebrew University of Jerusalem

Nathan Rotenstreich   Emeritus Professor of Philosophy at the Hebrew University of Jerusalem and Vice-President of the Israel Academy of Sciences and Humanities

Shalom Albeck   Professor of Talmud at Bar-Ilan University

Mordechai Breuer   Professor of Jewish History at Bar-Ilan University

Amnon Shiloah   Morris and Dena Wosk Professor of Musicology and Provost of the Rothberg School for Overseas Students at the Hebrew University of Jerusalem

Aharon Mirsky	Emeritus Professor of Hebrew Literature at the Hebrew University of Jerusalem
Joshua Blau	Max Schloessinger Professor of Arabic Language and Literature at the Hebrew University of Jerusalem and President of the Israel Academy of Hebrew Language
Yehuda Ratzaby	Professor of Hebrew Literature at Bar-Ilan University
Gad Ben-Ami Sarfatti	Emeritus Professor of Hebrew Language at Bar-Ilan University
Bezalel Narkiss	Nicolas Landau Professor of History of Art and Director of the Center for Jewish Art at the Hebrew University of Jerusalem

PREFACE

This volume of studies on "The Ten Commandments in History and
Tradition" is dedicated to the cherished memory of Silas Shalome
Perry, founder of the Perry Foundation for Biblical Research at the
Hebrew University of Jerusalem. Born in Bombay in 1891, he was the
son of Samuel Shalome Perry ז״ל, originally of Baghdad, and of Leah
Mendelowitz ז״ל, who was born in Hebron and returned to live in
Jerusalem after the death of her husband.

Business concerns took Silas Perry to Hong Kong, London and
Johannesburg where he lived from 1949 until his death in 1972.

Love of Zion was a guiding principle in the life of Silas Perry. He
visited this country frequently, and bequeathed a large part of his estate
to Israeli institutions, including the Keren Hayesod, the Jewish National
Fund, the Hebrew University and the Perry Foundation for Biblical
Research. He expressly directed that the Perry Foundation should
serve as a means of stimulating the publication of commentaries and
monographs on the books of the Bible, as well as on the beliefs and
ethics of Judaism. Since its inception in 1946, the Perry Foundation
has published, through the medium of the Hebrew University-Magnes
Press, works by leading scholars in these fields.

Silas Perry often spoke of the fundamental place of the Ten
Commandments in human civilization as a revelation of eternal truths.
By the publication of these studies, therefore, the academic committee
of the Perry Foundation is acknowledging a debt of honour and
gratitude to a dear and unassuming man who held the values of
Judaism close to his heart.

Mr. Ben-Zion Segal, secretary of the Perry Foundation since its
inception, has displayed a great deal of devotion in stimulating the
production of these studies and in editing them in consultation with a
special committee consisting of Professors Y. Dan, A. Rofé and
Y. Sussman. The former director of the Magnes Press, Mr. Ben-Zion
Yehoshua, and its present director, Mr. Dan Benovici, took care of all

XI

the details of printing and publication. To all of these we offer our thanks.

The Perry Foundation also acknowledges with thanks permission by Mosad Bialik to reproduce plates 2 and 3, and by Mosad Harav Kook to reproduce plate 4.

Ephraim E. Urbach
Chairman, The Perry Foundation for
Biblical Research

Jerusalem, The Hebrew University
Eve of Shavuot 5745

INTRODUCTION

It seems hardly necessary to explain the importance of the Ten Commandments in both Judaism and Christianity. It may be equally superfluous to point out that the status of the Decalogue in these two traditions is not at all the same. However, it might surprise many readers to learn that even within Judaism there have been varieties of interpretation — and still are, as the essays in this volume will show.

In the original Hebrew of this collection, eighteen of Israel's leading contemporary scholars contributed of their learning, their insights and opinions to a wide-ranging discussion of "The Ten Words" as these have been viewed throughout centuries of Jewish thinking and commentary, with more than a glance at Christian views as well. The fact that such a project could have been brought to fruition is attributable to the wisdom, patience and skill of the original editor, Ben-Zion Segal, longtime Secretary of the Perry Foundation for Biblical Research.

This book should be seen for what it is — a collection of essays as distinct from a unitary structured whole, in which each contributor would have been restricted to one limited aspect of the central theme. Nevertheless, and as was only to be expected, a certain amount of natural selection has taken place. That is to say, the historians have focused on the historical background, the Bible scholars on the text and its variations, the philosophers and the theologians on levels of meaning, and so on. It is therefore in no way surprising that the liturgists have dealt with the Commandments in the hymnology of the Synagogue, the grammarians and musicologists with the traditional Torah chants, and the art historians with graphic representations of the Tablets and associated themes.

But at the same time, considering the freedom given each contributor, it was only to be expected that there would be a certain amount of overlapping, some repetition in the exposition and in the quotation of sources — and even some disagreement in the substantive interpretation. For the reader who wants to follow up comparisons and contrasts in these matters, this English version attempts to provide a reasonably complete index.

And who might that reader be? The scholarly specialist, or the member of the general public? The answer will have to be somewhat equivocal. It can be said that this book is addressed to a wide spectrum of readers of English, Christian as well as Jewish. Nevertheless, we have tried as much as feasible to adhere to the standards and conventions of academic discourse. Inevitably, this has led to certain compromises.

Probably the most noticeable of these — a problem from which the original authors were exempt — is the matter of transliteration. A language with as many historical levels as Hebrew can scarcely be forced into the straitjacket of a single system. We have adopted a two-track method, using "scientific" transliteration only when the discussion involves specific details of ancient Semitic languages (including Hebrew). Even then, we have been sparing with diacritical signs. The English reader does not really need to know, for example, the value of each Hebrew vowel; while the Hebrew scholar does not need to be told. On the other hand, the doubled consonant reflecting a *dagesh forte* is retained when (and only when) it might help the reader to an approximately correct pronunciation.

Certain conventions have been arbitrarily adopted. Terms in common use in one or another part of the English-speaking world (Torah, mitzvot, etc.) are treated as naturalized loan-words. Most of these are to be found in recent lexicons such as *The International Heritage Dictionary*; but for greater convenience, a short glossary has been provided.

The word "Commandment" always refers to one of the Ten (*dibberot*). The same word, spelled lower case, is used to translate the Hebrew *miṣwah*, quite often rendered here "mitzvah, mitzvot". And since the order of the Ten Commandments is not the same in the different sources and traditions (see "Order" in the Index), it should be noted that in the present volume the Ten are invariably numbered in accordance with the now standard Jewish practice.

Quotations from the Hebrew Bible follow the renderings of *Tanakh*, the New Translation of the Jewish Publication Society, unless the context calls for a different treatment. For passages from the New Testament, the Revised Standard Version has been used.

Unspecified references to Talmudic tractates (see the key) always refer to the Bavli. Otherwise the prefixes M. (Mishnah) Tos. (Tosefta) and Yer. (Yerushalmi) are employed.

When this translation was first mooted, it was thought to exclude the four chapters dealing with liturgical poetry ("Piyyut", mostly medieval) on the grounds that the form does not lend itself to translation, and that the scholarly analyses are too technical. But further consideration led to the conclusion that some aspects of these essays might prove of general interest if presented in abridged form along with specimen translations of selected excerpts of the hymns themselves. It is this method which has been adopted in part, with one notable exception. Prof. Ezra Fleischer, a leading authority in the field, felt that his study "An Ancient Piyyut on the Ten Commandments — Model and Replicas" was far too specialized to bear inclusion in an English version. His wishes have been respected, so that this volume is launched with seventeen of the original eighteen chapters.

The editor wishes to thank the authors of these essays, all of whom patiently reviewed the translations of their work. He also wishes to thank the translators, who labored at no easy task. Their names appear at the end of each of the chapters.

Finally he must express his gratitude to Prof. Ephraim E. Urbach, who took a special interest in this project; to Mrs. Yvonne Glikson, daughter of the founder of the Perry Foundation, who took an active part in bringing it to fruition; and especially to Mr. Ben-Zion Yehoshua and Mr. Dan Benovici of the Magnes Press for their constant and cheerful encouragement.

Jerusalem   Gershon Levi
Hanukkah 5748

1. THE UNIQUENESS OF THE DECALOGUE AND ITS PLACE IN JEWISH TRADITION

MOSHE WEINFELD

Every single commandment in the Decalogue can be found in more or less the same terms elsewhere in the Pentateuch — except for "You shall not covet" about which more later. The prohibitions against idol worship[1] and false oaths[2]; the commands to keep the Sabbath[3] and to

---

1   See Ex. 20.20; 23.24; 34.14, 17; Lev. 19.4; 26.1; Deut. 4.15 ff; 6.14; 12.29–31; chaps. 13, and 17. 2–7. The expressions in the above verses which denote defection from monotheistic worship resemble those found in the first two Commandments: "(gods of silver) you shall not make for yourselves" (Ex. 20.20); "you shall not bow down [to their gods] or serve them" (ibid. 23.24); "You shall not bow down to any other god" (ibid. 34.14); "[molten gods] you shall not make for yourself" (ibid. 34.17); "[molten gods] you shall not make for yourselves" (Lev. 19.4); "you shall not make idols for yourselves."(Lev. 26.1).

   The admonitions in Deut. 4.15 ff. against the making of any image or likeness (see verses 16, 23 and 25) as well as the expressions "bow down and worship" and "serve other gods" which appear over and over in this book, are apparently due to the influence of the Ten Commandments on Deuteronomy. See M. Weinfeld, *Deuteronomy and the Deuteronomic School*, 1972, p. 321. In the opinion of N. Lohfink, *Das Hauptgebot*, 1963, pp. 100 f., the term "house of bondage" in the Book of Deuteronomy comes from the Ten Commandments. On the dependance of the former on the latter, see S.A. Kaufman, "The Structure of the Deuteronomic Law," *Maarav*, A Journal for the Study of the Northwest Semitic Languages and Literatures, vol. 1, no. 2 (1979), pp. 105–158. This article contains some pretty far-reaching statements, but the thesis it maintains is instructive.

2   Lev. 5.22 (in a casuistic context); ibid., 19.12, "You shall not swear falsely by my name"; cf. Psalm 24.4. It should be pointed out that "false" and "vain" are nearly synonymous, but not completely so; compare the Ninth Commandment in Exodus (*'ed šāqer*) with the version in Deuteronomy 5 (*'ed šaw*). See Dillman, *Die Buecher Exodus und Leviticus*³, Kurzgefasstes Exegetisches Handbuch zum AT, 1897, p. 233.

3   See Ex. 23.12; 31.14–15; 34.21; 35.1–3; Num. 15.32–36.

1

honor one's parents[4]; the ban against murder[5], adultery[6], theft[7], and false witness[8] — all these are repeated several times over in various legal summaries included in the Torah.

For example, the ancient code of laws known as the Book of the Covenant, occurring in Exodus shortly after the Ten Commandments, begins with the prohibition of idolatry: "You shall not make any gods of silver, nor shall you make for yourselves any gods of gold" (Ex. 20. 20). The same code goes on to list almost all the other laws found in the Decalogue — the Sabbath (23. 12); honoring one's parents (21. 15–16 — couched to be sure in the negative[9]); murder (21. 12); theft of persons[10] and property (21. 16 and 22. 1–3); and false witness (23. 1).

---

4   See Ex. 21.15, 17; Lev. 19.4; 20.9; Deut. 21.18 ff.; 27.16. About honoring one's parents, see below.

5   See Ex. 21.12; Lev. 24.21; Num. 35.30; Deut. 19. 11–13; 27.16.

6   Lev. 18.20; 20.10; Deut. 22.22 ff.

7   See Ex. 21.16, 37 ff.; Lev. 19.11; Deut. 24.7.

8   See Ex. 23.1; Deut. 19. 16-21. There is a connection between the Ninth Commandment (false witness) and the Third (taking God's name in vain). Compare "You shall not utter a false report" (Ex. 23.1). See the essay by S.A. Kaufman quoted above (n. 1) pp. 125–126.

9   For the contrast between cursing one's parents (NJPS="revile", "repudiate") and honoring them, cf. an Akkadian document from Ugarit: "Whoever among my children dishonors (*ša uqallil*)...his mother...and whoever of them honors (*ša ukabbit*)... his mother", Thureau-Dangin, in *Syria*, 18 (1937), p. 249:19. Comp. Matt. 15.4: "For God commanded 'Honor your father and your mother', and 'He who reviles his father or mother, let him surely die'". As a general rule in biblical usage the *pi'el* form of the verb *qll* means "to revile", "to utter an explicit curse" (see my article *qelalah* in *Encyclopedia Miqra'it*, VII, pp. 186 ff.), as opposed to the *niph'al* and *hiph'il* which mean "treat with contempt" (see, e.g., I Sam. 2.30; II Sam. 6.22; ibid., 19.44; Ezek. 22.7). Compare the use of the verb *qlh* in Deut. 27.16 and my remarks in *Deuteronomy and the Deuteronomic School*, pp. 277–278. At the same time, there is something to be said for the view expressed by H.Ch. Brichto (*The Problem of the Curse in the Bible*, 1963) that the root meaning of *qll* is the same as in Akkadian *qullulu* and *gullulu*, namely "to treat with contempt". It seems to me that this is the most likely meaning in the story of Naboth (where, to be sure, the euphemism *brkh* replaces *qll*; see I Ki. 21. 1–13). In that context, the accusation is not that of explicit cursing, but of committing lèse majesté against God and the King. See also *qilelath elohim* in Deut. 21. 22–23, and Weinfeld, *Deuteronomy* etc., p. 51, n. 4. Compare now also Y. Yadin, *The Temple Scroll*, II, p. 74, 7–13, in a context dealing with traitors: "He despised (*wa-yěqallel*) his people and the sons of Israel," and then: "those dishonored (*měqollělē*) by God and men".

10 The rabbinic Sages took "You shall not steal" in the Decalogue to refer to the theft of persons - kidnapping (Sanh. 86a). Some modern scholars take the same line: A.

What then is unique about the commandments in the Decalogue? How did they come to be regarded as the crowning point of the encounter between the God of Israel and the people of Israel? What entitled this particular collection of imperatives to be the one spoken directly to the people by the Deity (Ex. 20. 1 and 15 and 18; Deut. 4. 12; 5. 4 and 12)? Or to be written by the finger of God on stone tablets which were placed in the Ark of the Covenant (Ex. 31. 18; 32. 16; 34. 1 and 28; Deut. 4. 13; 5. 19; 9. 10; 10. 1–4)?

If it be suggested that these things came about because of the greater antiquity of the Decalogue, the answer is that there is no proof that the Ten Commandments are older than any other laws in the Torah, whether the criterion be content or style. The terse "Thou shalt not's" are not unique. There are similar laconic formulations in Leviticus 19 (verses 11 and 13) and elsewhere. Likewise, there is nothing unusual about the diversity of content in the Ten Commandments. Similarly heterogeneous collections of laws occur in Leviticus 19 as well as in the Book of Deuteronomy.

But just as there is no proof of the special antiquity of the Decalogue, so are there no grounds for postdating it. The contention that the Ten Commandments bespeak a prophetic morality and are therefore the product of a later age has been discarded for some time now, ever since Hugo Gressmann submitted the theory to critical analysis in 1913, in his book *Mose und seine Zeit* (pp. 473 ff.).

Great importance attaches to the unique theophany that accompanied the promulgation of the Ten Commandments. As is well-known, Judaism celebrates the event annually on the festival of Shavuot, which is also called "The Time When Our Torah Was Given". The question arises whether in ancient times as well this Feast of the First Fruits also celebrated the giving of the Torah. And what was the role of the Decalogue in the worship service? The Mishnah tells us that the Ten Commandments were read together with the Shema in the Temple during the time of the Second Commonwealth (M. Tamid V:1). Indeed, we learn that we would still be doing the same were it not for the misleading claims of the *Minim*[11]. The fact is that certain

---

Alt, "Das Verbot des Diebstahls in Dekalog", in *Kleine Schriften*, I, pp. 333 ff.; M. Goshen-Gottstein, *Theologische Zeitschrift*, 9 (1953), pp. 394 ff. But see now H. Klein, "Verbot des Menschendiebstahls im Dekalog", in *Vetus Testamentum*, 26 (1976), pp. 161–169.

11   Bavli Ber. 12a; Yer. Ber. I:5. 3c: "Properly speaking the Ten Commandments

prayer-rites found in the Cairo Genizah include the Decalogue[12]; and to this day there are some pious folk who append the Ten Commandments to their daily prayers after concluding the formal morning service.[13]

This essay will attempt to answer such questions. We shall rely on a variety of sources, biblical and extra-biblical, insofar as these tend to enlighten us regarding the meaning of the Ten Commandments.

THE DECALOGUE: A BASIC FORMAL OBLIGATION IN THE RELIGION OF ISRAEL

We begin with an outline of the special aspects which characterize this group of commandments, and set them apart.

A. By contrast with many laws and commands, the performance of which depends on special circumstances in the life of the individual or his social group; for example sacrifices, which depend on the obligations of the person (a vow to fulfill, a sin to expiate) or of the community (maintenance of the sanctuary), or other laws that flow from the incidence of certain events, like the laws of ritual purity and impurity, the Sabbatical and Jubilee years; the civil law and the laws of marriage and divorce; the laws affecting tithes and priestly offerings, and so on, and so on — by contrast the commands in the Decalogue obligate *everyone*. Every single individual, regardless of his condition or the circumstances in which he finds himself, is required to observe them. Every Jew undertakes not to worship idols, not to perjure himself, to keep the Sabbath, to honor his parents, not to commit murder, adultery or theft, not to bear false witness and not to covet.

B. The Ten Commandments are formulated in basically *negative* terms. Even the two apparently couched in positive language[14], namely observing the Sabbath and honoring one's parents, have a negative thrust. The Sabbath commandment is explicitly interpreted as a

should be recited every day. Why then are they not? Lest people say, as the *Minim* do, that these Commandments alone were given to Moses at Sinai". See L. Ginzberg, *Perushim ve-Ḥiddushim bi-Yerushalmi*, I, p. 166.

12   J. Mann, *HUCA*, 2 (1925), pp. 283, 295.

13   See the end of daily morning service in various prayerbooks, e.g., Baer (Rödelheim 1868, p. 159); Yavetz (Berlin 1922), p. 118. And see *Tur, Oraḥ Ḥayyim*, para. 1.

14   This is what lies behind the unjustified attempt to emend the text of these two Commandments; see, e.g., K. Rabast, *Das apodiktische Recht im Deuteronomium und im Heiligkeitsgezetz*, 1949, pp. 34 ff.

prohibition: "Six days you shall labor...but the seventh day is a sabbath...you *shall not* do any work" (Ex. 20. 9–10). As for the command to honor one's parents, its main purpose is to prohibit harming them in their person or in their dignity. This becomes clear when we examine other laws on the same subject found elsewhere in the Torah. They deal with striking one's parents (Ex. 21. 15), reviling or treating them with contempt (Ex. 21. 17; Lev. 20. 9; Deut. 27. 16) or disobedience and rebelliousness (Deut. 21. 18–21). Actually in Leviticus 19, which bears a special relationship to the Decalogue (see below), the commandment is put in negative terms: "You shall each fear (*tira'u*) his mother and his father" (19. 3).[15]

This tendency towards negative formulation stems from the very nature of these laws, whose purpose is to establish fundamental terms of agreement which will be readily acceptable by the people. The terms are mediated to them by the prophet, who informs them concerning the will of the Deity. The list spells out what acts must be avoided by every person who allies himself with the unique community of the LORD.

The same sort of thing can be seen in the list of prohibitions laid down by Jonadab the son of Rechab, founder of the Rechabites, for the guidance of his followers: "You shall drink no wine...nor shall you build houses...or sow fields or plants vineyards...so that you may live long upon the land" (Jer. 35. 6–7)[16]. Here too, the regulations are in the negative. Later on we shall cite a parallel from the Hellenistic world, where everyone who wishes to enter a certain shrine must bind himself by oath to observe a list of prohibitions which the god had laid down to the founder of the sanctuary.

---

15   In documents from the ancient East the duty of a son to his parents is expressed, to be sure, equally by the verbs "honor" (*kabātu*) and "fear" (*palāhu*). See M. Schorr, *Urkunden des altbabylonischen Zivil — und Prozessrechts, VAB*, 5 (1913), 13a (*CAT*, II, 35), 8; (*ipallah ukabassi* = let him fear and honor). In that context the matter is connected with support of the parent in his lifetime, and honoring his memory after death ("he should clothe him and feed him, and when he dies, mourn for him and bury him"). Comp. Qid. 31b: "What is meant by honor [of parents]? One supplies him with food and drink, helps him go out and go in." For a comparative study of honoring parents in the Bible and in ancient eastern cultures, see A. Rainer, "Hintergrund und Bedeutung des Elterngebots im Dekalog", *ZAW*, 90 (1978), pp. 348–374; G. Blidstein, *Honor thy Father and Mother — Filial Responsibility in Jewish Law and Ethics*, New York 1975, p. 173.

16   The Rechabites, too, follow the rule of their order because it is the command of their ancestor (Jer. 35.14, 16, 18). See E. Gerstenberger, *Wesen und Herkunft des apodiktischen Rechts*, 1965, p. 17.

C. The Commandments of the Decalogue are phrased *concisely* and to the point. They are arranged in a set formal number (ten). Long ago people noticed that their original form had been gradually worked over and expanded, a fact most apparent in the Sabbath Commandment. The version of that Commandment in Deuteronomy gives an entirely different reason for observing it from the version in Exodus.[17] But even aside from this detail, one senses revisions and additions to what must have been the original text.[18] We may perhaps reconstruct the original Decalogue as follows:[19]

1.   I the LORD am your God. You shall have no other gods beside me.[20]

---

17   The Sabbath Commandment in Exodus is grounded on God's rest from Creation, in accordance with the Priestly tradition. Critics of the Wellhausen school who postdated the Priestly Code took great pains to prove that the Decalogue in Exodus is later than the version in Deuteronomy; (cf. most recently F.L. Mossfeld, *Der Dekalog*, Göttingen 1982). However, long ago K. Budde, in *Die Biblische Urgeschichte*, 1883, pp. 493 f., sensed that Exodus 20.11 reflects an ancient tradition. Nevertheless, his loyalty to the Wellhausen theory led him to argue that the Priestly Code, though late, was influenced in this matter by the Decalogue. See my comment in *Tarbiz*, 37 (1968), p. 109, n. 22. On the reason for the Sabbath given in Deuteronomy, see my *Deuteronomy*, p. 222.

18   About which, see Stamm-Andrew, *The Ten Commandments in Recent Research*, 1967, pp. 18 ff. For Deuteronomic expressions in the Exodus version, see my *Deuteronomy*, p. 318, n. 2.

19   See M. Greenberg in the present volume.

20   The arrangement here suggested was put forward long ago by Philo (*De decalogo*) 12, etc.) and Josephus (*Ant.*, III, 91–2). In normative Jewish sources, the accepted way of arranging the Decalogue is as follows: Verse 2 ("I am the LORD") constitutes the First Commandment, while verses 3–6 (against idolatry) make up the Second Commandment. (Thus *Mekhilta de R. Ishmael, Baḥodesh*, 5, ed. Lauterbach, II, p. 229 ff.; so too *Mekhilta de R. Simeon bar Yoḥai* and the medieval commentators.) Nevertheless, traces of the subdivision according to Philo and Josephus are not entirely absent from rabbinic tradition. For example, *Sifre Numbers*, 112: " 'Because he has spurned the word of the LORD' — that is, he has spurned the First *Commandment* spoken to Moses by the Almighty (saying) 'I the LORD am your God, you shall have no other gods beside me' "(ed. Horovitz, p. 121). The rabbinic saying "'I am the LORD', and 'You shall have no other', we have heard directly from the Almighty", also seems to treat these as one Commandment. See Hor. 12a, where this is quoted in the name of a Tanna of the school of R. Ishmael; and comp. Mak. 24a.
    The division expressed by Philo and Josephus is also reflected by some of the various Masoretic traditions concerning the Decalogue; cf. M. Breuer in the present volume on the *lower accentuation*, and the division into sections (*parashiot*).

2. You shall not make for yourself a sculptured image.

3. You shall not swear falsely by the name of the LORD your God.

4. Remember[21] the Sabbath day.

5. Honor your father and your mother.

6. You shall not murder.[22]

7. You shall not commit adultery.

8. You shall not steal.

9. You shall not bear false witness against your neighbor.

10. You shall not covet the house of your neighbor.

See also J.S. Penkower, *Textus*, 9 (1981), pp. 116–117.

For the various methods of subdividing the Decalogue, with particular reference to mss. of the *Peshitta*, see M.D. Koster in *Vetus Test.*, 30 (1980), pp. 468 ff.

Even according to the plain sense of the text, "I, the LORD am your God" is introductory to the prohibition that follows it: compare especially Judg., 6. 8–10: "I the LORD am your God; you must not worship the gods of the Amorites". See also Hosea 13.4, and Ps. 81. 8–10. For a study of the opening words of the Decalogue, and the significance of *anokhi* and *ani* at the beginning of sentences in ancient semitic inscriptions and in the Bible, see A. Poebel, "Das appositionell bestimmte pronomen der 1 Pers. sing. in den westsemitischen Inschriften und im Alten Testament," *Assyriological Studies,* No. 3, Oriental Institute, Chicago 1932. Poebel argues that such a form should not be understood as a self-introductory sentence ("I am the one who, etc."); but rather as an appositional clause "I, who brought you out, command you etc."

21 The version in Deuteronomy reads "observe" (*šamor*). Deuteronomy takes *zakhor* (=remember) in a purely historical sense; cf. the usage in the same Commandment: "Remember that you were a slave in the land of Egypt" (verse 15). The Tetrateuch, particularly Leviticus, takes *zakhor* in a sacral sense ("commemorate"). In Exodus 20, the Sabbath is grounded on a sacral commemoration, the purpose of which is to re-enact the Divine rest on the seventh day; whereas in Deuteronomy 5, the Sabbath is grounded on historical recollection: "that you were a slave in the land of Egypt." The author of Deuteronomy makes a distinction, then, between *zakhor* ("remember") and *šamor* ("observe"). He uses the latter term for fulfilling commandments, reserving the former word for the historical idea. See my *Deuteronomy*, p. 222.

22 Philo (*De decalogo*, 36, 121 et passim) puts "You shall not commit adultery" before "You shall not murder", as does the Septuagint. The Septuagint in Deuteronomy has the order: "adultery, murder, theft"; but in Exodus, "adultery, theft, murder". The Nash papyrus also puts adultery before murder (see M.Z. Segal, *Tradition and Criticism* (Hebrew), p. 230). The same is true for Luke 18.20 and Romans 13.9. On the other hand, Josephus follows the masoretic order (*Ant.*, III, 91–92). In the opinion of M. Weiss in his article in the present volume, Jeremiah 7.9 deliberately cites the Decalogue in inverse (chiastic) order. If that be so, then Jeremiah had a text like that of LXX and of the Nash Papyrus: adultery, murder, theft.

Moshe Weinfeld

Granted, in Hebrew this version lacks uniformity of rhythm. By that criterion the Commandments fall into three rhythmic groups:[23] a) those with four beats or more, namely the first, second, third, ninth and tenth; b) those with three beats — the fourth and fifth; and c) those with two beats — the sixth, seventh and eighth. Nevertheless, there is no justification for supposing that the collection as we have it is a secondary composition, artificially put together. The length and rhythm of each sentence are dictated by its content. There are some subjects that just cannot be disposed of in two words.

In addition, it must be said that mere heterogeneity of form is no indication that we are dealing with a secondary, re-edited piece of work, as some scholars have suggested. Original collections of apothegms of varying length are not uncommon in the Bible and in the literature of the ancient Near East.[24] Hence there is no justification for turning the two positive Commandments into negatives, in order to force them to conform with the rest.[25] On the other hand, there are unifying aspects in the Ten Commandments, such as the characteristically terse form, and the stylized number ten, which in turn is evenly divided into two fives: a) religious duties ("between man and God"), and b) ethical obligations ("between man and his fellow").

These characteristics point to the unitary nature of the collection. The form and structure lend themselves to incision on stone tablets and to easy memorization. Our conclusion may well be that we are dealing with a fundamental set of regulations which every Israelite was required to know, and to commit to memory.

D. These commands are "categorical imperatives" universally applicable, timeless, not dependent on any circumstances whatsoever.[26] They are stated without sanctions, without elaboration or definition. Hence they can scarcely be thought sufficient for the jurist, or even for

---

23   See G. Fohrer, "Das sogenannte apodiktisch formulierte Recht und der Dekalog", in *Kerygma und Dogma*, 11 (1965), pp. 49–74; idem, *Einleitung in das Alte Testament*[12], 1979, pp. 73–74.

24   See H. Cazelles, "Les origines du Décalogue", in *Eretz Israel*, IX (W.F. Albright Volume, 1969), p. 16, n. 27.

25   See n. 14 above, and the attempt in this direction by Cazelles in the article just cited. Cazelles thinks the original form of the Sabbath Commandment was "You shall do no work on the Sabbath day". He also believes the Commandment to honor parents was added later, under the influence of wisdom literature.

26   See A. Alt, "Die Urspruenge des Israelitischen Rechts", in *Kleine Schriften*, I, pp. 321–322.

the ordinary citizen. He may well ask: What does the Commandment mean by "stealing?" What is to be done with the thief? So too with the other laws.

But such questions are not relevant. This is not a code of detailed laws. This is a formulation of those conditions required for membership in the community. One who does not adhere to the imperatives here laid down excludes himself from the community of believers. This is the purpose of the Decalogue. Specific laws and the sanctions attached to them come later, in the various legal collections in the Torah. But these do not belong in the Decalogue, which simply sets down the fundamental obligations which the Deity imposes on His people.

Especially instructive in this connection is the command "You shall not covet". As B. Jackson[27] has shown, there is no reason to question the commonly accepted meaning of this Commandment, namely that it refers to a state of mind. Obviously, then, it deals with a prohibition that cannot be enforced, since sanctions cannot be applied to mere thought.[28] It must therefore be admitted that this is no statute in the ordinary sense, but rather a demand, subject to Divine judgment alone.

As a matter of fact, the Hebrew Bible itself does not call the Ten Commandments "laws", or even "commandments". It calls them "words". They are referred to as *'asereth ha-devarim* — "The Ten Words" (Ex. 24. 5; Deut. 4. 13 and 10. 4).[29] Even more striking is the Rabbinic usage *'asereth ha-dibberoth*, which uses the plural of the noun *dibber*, a term for "the Word" revealed to a prophet, as in Jeremiah 5. 13: "The prophets shall prove mere wind, for the Word is not in them."[30]

27　B. Jackson, "Liability for Mere Intention in Early Jewish Law", in *Essays in Jewish and Comparative Legal History*, 1975, pp. 202–234. After reading Jackson, I retract what I wrote in *Reflections on the Bible, Selected Studies in Memory of Yishai Ron*, II (Hebrew), Tel Aviv 1977, p. 109, n. 1. A. Rofé in the present volume does not refer to Jackson's study.

28　The Sages, who wanted to make this law conform to halakhic rules, interpreted this Commandment as forbidding actual appropriation; see *Mekhilta de R. Ishmael*, ed. Horovitz, p. 235; ed. Lauterbach, II, p. 266: "Perhaps the Commandment forbids expressing [envious desire] in words? Not so; for the Torah states 'You shall not covet the silver and gold on them and take it for yourself'. Just as in that instance one is culpable only after acting, so too in the present case". Cf. also *Midrash Tannaim* (ed. D.H. Hoffman, 1908) on Deut. 5.25.

29　See A.B. Ehrlich, *Randglossen zur hebraischen Bibel*, 1908, p. 340.

30　See M. Gruber, *Beit Miqra*, 88 (1982), pp. 16–21.

In the light of all this we must conclude that the rules of the Decalogue were understood to be in a different class from the other commandments and statutes in the Torah, such as are subject to the judgments and sanctions of human courts. They were perceived rather as uniquely revealed imperatives, demands made by the Deity directly on the individual human being.

E. The Commandments are couched in the second person singular, as though addressed personally to each individual member of the community. As Philo points out, when rules are addressed to the group as a whole, the individual can evade responsibility by hiding himself in the crowd (*De decalogo* 39). But when he is addressed personally, there is no escape. In saying this, Philo brings out the I-Thou relationship elucidated in modern times by Martin Buber.[31] Actually, Buber developed the concept against the background of the Ten Commandments,[32] but he did not make as much use as he might have of the findings of modern biblical research regarding the role of the apodictic mode in biblical legislation.

The distinction drawn by Alt between the apodictic and the casuistic styles of expression has deepened our understanding of biblical legal language[33] and has made us aware of the special quality of the apodictic mode, specifically of the uniqueness in biblical law of commands couched as "Do!" (thou shalt) and "Don't!" (thou shalt not).[34] This contrasts with the casuistic style which is normal in the codes of the ancient Near East, and which continues to be true of modern legal parlance. In the language of jurisprudence the categorical directness of the apodictic mode is out of place. It now appears that it originated in a formal ceremonial context: a king imposing obligations ("covenant") on his subjects.[35] In fact, this was exactly the way in which the Ten

---

31   *Ich und Du*, 1923. On the history of this idea, see Horvitz, "Aspects of the Development of Buber's 'I and Thou' " (Hebrew), *Proceedings of the Israel Academy of Sciences and Humanities*, 5.8, 1975.

32   In his *The Way of Scripture* (Hebrew), 1964, pp. 100–102.

33   See n. 26.

34   Under the heading "apodictic" Alt included commands couched in the third person and also pronouncements beginning with a verbal noun (e.g. "he who strikes", etc.). Subsequent studies have sharpened the distinctions, so that we now know there is a difference between such injunctions and the clear imperatives "You shall", "You must not". See my article "The Origin of the Apodictic Law", *VT,* 23 (1973), pp. 63–75.

35   See my article cited in the previous note.

Commandments were perceived — as the orders of a divine King who had appeared before His subjects.

F. At the same time it should be pointed out that the Decalogue does not include any generalized or abstract moral laws such as "Love your neighbor" (Lev. 19. 18), "Befriend the stranger" (Deut. 10. 19)[36] or "Justice, justice shall you pursue" (Deut. 16. 20). Hence there is no justification for the statement that the Ten Commandments represent the highest moral achievement of ancient Israel.

The Decalogue is to be seen, then, as a basic list of concrete imperatives applicable to every individual Israelite. They represent a distillation, so to speak, of the core demands made by the God of Israel on those covenanted to him. These demands fall naturally into two parts. The first half includes commandments that are a consequence of the special relationship between the people of Israel and the God of Israel, implying exclusive allegiance to Him. Multiple loyalties, such as are acceptable to idol worshippers, are ruled out. So we have the ban on graven images, and on taking God's name in vain; and the obligations to keep the Sabbath and respect one's parents.[37] The second half bears a socio-ethical character, and includes prohibitions against murder, adultery, theft, false witness and covetousness.

A list of commands similar to those laid down in the Decalogue is

36 Deut. 10.19, drawn apparently from Lev. 19.34: "The stranger who resides with you shall be to you as one of your citizens; you shall love him as yourself, for you were strangers in the land of Egypt".

37 This command is the one best suited to be the transition from those "between man and God", and those "between man and his fellow". After all, parents are in a position of superior authority, like God and the King. Compare Philo, *De decalogo*, 107. Indeed, offenses against all these three are declared to be capital crimes; compare the case of Naboth (who was accused of contempt of God and the King); and the sanction on one who reviles father and mother (Ex. 21. 16–17; Lev. 19.9). Compare also the rabbinic teaching: "It is written 'You shall each revere his mother and his father' (Lev. 19.3) — and it is also written 'You must revere the LORD your God' (Deut. 10.20). Thus, Scripture makes reverence for parents comparable to reverence for God. It is written 'Honor your father and your mother' and it is also written 'Honor the LORD', etc. (Prov. 3.9). Thus Scriptures makes honoring parents comparable to honoring God. Further, Scripture says 'He who reviles (*meqallel*) his father or his mother shall be put to death' (Ex. 21.17); and also 'Anyone who blasphemes (*yeqallel*) his God shall bear his guilt' (Lev. 24.15). Thus, reviling of father and mother is made comparable to reviling the All Present" (*Sifra, Qedoshim*, 1).

found in Leviticus chapter 19.[38] This is the only place in the Priestly Code where we encounter an intermingling of cultic and ethical laws, such as we find in the Ten Commandments. This kind of heterogeneity does not occur in any other section of that code, each of which deals with one specific law.

To be sure it must be admitted that the variety in Leviticus 19 has a common factor — the idea of holiness.[39] Nevertheless, it is obvious that the background for this chapter is the Decalogue. Indeed, from the proem to that chapter (verse 2: "Speak to the whole community" (*kol 'adath*) the rabbinic Sages concluded that this passage was spoken in full assembly (*behiqahel*).[40]

It should also be noted that the gathering at Mount Sinai itself is called *yom haqahal* (Deut. 9.10; 10.4; 18.16; see below, note 113). The same midrashic context[41] speaks of the connection between Leviticus 19 and the Decalogue:

> Why was this chapter *Qedoshim* spoken at the Assembly? Because most of the principal elements of the Torah depend on it.[42] Rabbi Levi says, because the Ten Commandments are included in it.[43]

And indeed, Leviticus 19 does begin with the Fifth, Fourth and Second Commandments of the Decalogue, in that order (honor of parents, keeping the Sabbath, the ban on idolatry). To quote: "You shall each revere his mother and his father[44] and keep my Sabbaths: I the LORD am your God. Do not turn to idols, or make molten gods for yourselves: I the LORD am your God" (verses 3–4). The arrangement is chiastic, i.e. in reverse order, a practice not uncommon when quoting, or adverting to, well-known established texts.[45] The author opens with

---

38 For a recent analysis of this chapter, see B. Schwartz, *Leviticus 19 — A Literary Analysis*, MA thesis, Hebrew University, 1980.

39 On this, see B. Schwartz, above, n. 38.

40 *Sifra, Qedoshim*, 1:1 and *Leviticus Rabbah*, 24:5, where this is attributed to R. Hiyya. The homiletical basis is Lev. 35.1: "Moses then convoked (*wayaqhel*) the whole Israelite community (*kol 'adath*)". See B. Schwartz, n. 38 above, p. 26.

41 See *Sifra* and *Leviticus Rabbah*, as in preceding note.

42 Cf. Matt. 22.40, referring to love of neighbor and love of God: "On these two Commandments depend all the law and the prophets."

43 *Lev. Rabbah*, 24.5.

44 For the relationship between "fear" (= revere) and "honor" see above, n. 15.

45 See M. Zeidel, *Ḥiqre Miqra*, 1979, 1–97.

the Fifth Commandment, moves on to the Fourth and ends up with the Second. Even within the sentence he inverts the subject and the predicate: "Each one his mother and his father shall you revere." He uses the same sort of inversion when speaking of the Sabbath — not "observe my Sabbaths", but "my Sabbaths observe"; and even inverts two predicates "his mother and his father".

The same three topics, in slightly altered form, recur towards the end of the section (verses 30–32): observance of the Sabbath, the ban on divination and respect for the aged.[46] Finally, two of these subjects, idolatry and the Sabbath, mark the conclusion of this Book of Holiness at Leviticus 26. 1–2. This shows how central these matters were in the outlook of the author.[47]

Reverting to the beginning of the code, we find laws against theft, false witness and false oaths (verses 11 and 12). The rabbinic Sages also detected references to the prohibition of murder in "Do not stand against the blood of your neighbor" (verse 16) and to adultery in "Do not degrade your daughter, making her a harlot" (verse 29).[48] It is also a reasonable assumption that the Commandment "Do not commit adultery" is intended to include the laws against mixing incongruous species of plant, animal or clothing; the law of the designated slave-woman; and the ban on the fruit of trees during their first three years (*'orlah*=lit. "foreskin", verses 19 to 25). A similar association of topics can be seen in the passage in Deuteronomy beginning with 22.9, where the laws of mixed species are followed by laws dealing with adultery and rape.[49] The law of *'orlah* gets into this context, it would appear, by the sort of associative concatenation not uncommon in legal codification in the ancient East.[50] And if the assumption is correct that

46 For the structural similarity between verses 30–32 and verses 3–4, see B. Schwartz, n. 38 above, pp. 92–94. Philo too (*De decalogo*, 165–167) includes respect for the aged along with respect for parents, in the Fifth Commandment.

47 Note that these two themes (idolatry and violation of the Sabbath) predominate in the denunciation by Ezekiel in chapter 20 (verses 16, 18–20, and 24).

48 Lev. 24.5.

49 In the opinion of S.A. Kaufman (art. cit. n. 1 above, pp. 138–139) the entire group of laws in Deut. 22.9, 23.19 is an elaboration on "You shall not commit adultery". According to him, all these laws (including mixture of species and admissibility into the community) are sex-related.

50 On this, see S.M. Paul, *Studies in the Book of the Covenant in the Light of Cuneiform and Biblical Law* (*VT*, Suppl 18, 1970, pp. 106 ff). So too S.A. Kaufman, art. cit. n. 1 above p. 115.

sees a connection between counterfeit weights and measures, and the
Commandment "Do not covet",[51] then the passage in Leviticus 19.
35–6 closes on a note similar to that which concludes the Ten
Commandments.

Let us add that, just as the Decalogue opens with a declaration of
identity by the Deity, a declaration which gives force to the commands
that follow, so too the commandments in Leviticus 19 begin with the
declaration: "I the LORD am your God" (verse 2). This formula is
repeated in connection with other laws in the same chapter.

All this makes it appear that Leviticus 19 was intended to fill a lacuna
in priestly literature. Unlike the Book of Deuteronomy, which repeats
the Decalogue of Exodus, the Priestly Code does not contain the Ten
Commandments, even though the code declares explicitly that it is
setting forth "the laws, norms and directions that the LORD established,
through Moses on Mt. Sinai, between himself and the Israelite people"
(25.46; and see 27.34). The absence in the Priestly Code of any reference
to the Decalogue leaves the impression that the centerpiece is missing.
The lack is overcome by Leviticus 19, which provides a sort of decalogue
in revised and expanded form.[52]

It should be remembered, however, that the chapter is presented as a
variation on the Ten Commandments, but not as a substitute for them.
It differs from them completely in the form and manner of presentation.
The Ten Commandments are characterized by the fact that they are
imposed on every individual, entirely without regard to any condition
or circumstance. This is not true of Leviticus 19, apart from the several
laconic commands which do match. As for the rest, they are governed
by the special circumstances in which the person affected finds himself.
For example, the law of the "offensive sacrifice" (*pigul*: verses 5 to 8)
applies only to a person who is bringing an offering of well-being; the
law of gleanings and corners of the field applies only to one who owns a
field (verses 9 and 10). The warning against unfair judgment is directed
solely to judges (verses 15 and 16). The laws affecting mixed species

---

51   S.A. Kaufman, art. cit., above n.1, pp. 143–144.

52   Note Abarbanel's comment on Leviticus 19: "No doubt the Blessed One ordered
     Moses to gather the entire community of Israel and admonish them concerning the
     mitzvot and remind them of the Ten Commandments and of the main fundamentals
     of the mitzvot; because all of this was preparation for concluding the covenant
     mentioned at the end of this Book of Leviticus. The Ten Commandments as spoken
     to the Israelites are not repeated here, since the intention here is to explain them,
     not to rehearse them."

(verse 19) concern the owner of a field or vineyard or the like. The same sort of thing applies to the designated slave-woman (20–22) and *'orlah* (23–25).

The remaining statutes which outlaw a variety of pagan practices are cited against the background of circumstances, in which respect they differ from the tone of "categorical imperative" characterizing the Ten Commandments, as pointed out in section 4 above.

As for the injunctions to love your neighbor, and to harbor no grudge or hatred (17–18) — these belong to the realm of homiletics. They are addressed to the conscience, and as such have no place in the Ten Commandments, which deal with concrete matters, and not with abstract generalizations, as we have already pointed out.

Finally it should be observed that Leviticus 19 contains cultic laws (verses 5–8, 21–22, 24–25) in contrast to the Decalogue, which contains no such matter whatsoever. Hence this chapter cannot be placed on the same level as the Ten Commandments.

Research on the Ten Commandments has led many scholars to compare them with other collections of commands and directives in the Bible.[53] In the last analysis, however, it appears that the Decalogue remains unique. Let us, nevertheless examine the more striking of those collections which show some resemblance to the Ten Commandments.

1. First, there is chapter 27 of Deuteronomy. Here we have a set of admonitions against certain acts, each beginning with the words "Cursed be he who...". The prohibited acts bear a certain resemblance to some of the Ten Commandments (idolatry, sex crimes, murder, degrading one's parents). But this passage differs both in form and purpose from the Decalogue.

The warnings in Deuteronomy 27. 14-26, do not represent obligations which bind everybody in the community. They are directed rather at those who commit forbidden acts *under the cover of secrecy*. The medieval Bible scholars Abraham ibn Ezra and Samuel ben Meir pointed out long ago that this is the common denominator of these verses. The sins here enumerated are usually committed by stealth, or in such a manner that it is difficult to prove them. Examples are the sex offenses listed in verses 20 to 23; moving a neighbor's landmark (17);

53 See Stamm-Andrew, *The Ten Commandments in Recent Research*, pp. 22–75, where there is a detailed list of the laws involved.

misdirecting a blind person (18); degrading parents (16);[54] subverting justice (19) and taking bribes (25). Even the two crimes which do not lend themselves readily to concealment (idolatry, verse 15, and murder, verse 24) are explicitly spoken of as having been committed "in secret" so that the culprits cannot be apprehended and punished.

Hence we must conclude that this passage in Deuteronomy deals with a solemn ceremony by which the community purifies itself from transgressors over whom it has no control. That is why the execution of punishment is turned over to the Deity. Calling down a curse on the hidden sinner expels him from the community, thus freeing the group, so to speak, from collective punishment on his account.[55]

All this is a far cry from the categorical commands of the Decalogue, where there is no mention of circumstances or sanctions, while here, on the other hand, the offenses are defined in detail, and the sanction is specified: "Cursed be he!" The warning against these transgressions is directed to property owners (17) and judges (19 and 25) whereas the Ten Commandments are addressed to every single individual. It is also obvious that there is a great difference in form and style between the admonitions in Deuteronomy 27 and the Ten Commandments. The latter are phrased apodictically: "Thou shalt, thou shalt not" whereas in Deuteronomy 27 the admonitions are couched in present participles — "he who does" preceded by the sanction "cursed be". This form corresponds to the style of Exodus 21. 12 to 17, as in "He who strikes a man shall be put to death:" a present participle active plus the punishment.[56]

2. A collection of fundamental religio-ethical obligations reminiscent of the Ten Commandments is to be found in Ezekiel 18, beginning with verse 5. This is a description of the just man, who does what is lawful and right. He does not practice idolatry, not commit adultery, nor lie with a menstruant. He pays his debts, does not steal or cheat, does not

54   On the difference between *qll* and *qlh* see my *Deuteronomy etc.* pp. 277 ff.
55   Conceptually, the ceremony is most congruent with the ancient, pre-monarchic period, when the entire community felt itself collectively responsible for the preservation of religious norms, so that the presence of a transgressor among them constituted a threat to the whole social entity. Compare the episode of Achan (Josh. 7) and see I Sam. 14.36 ff. For a discussion of the problem, see my article "Zion and Jerusalem as Religious and Political Capital" in *The Poet and the Historian*, Essays in Literary and Historical Biblical Criticism (ed. R.E. Friedman), 1983, p. 81 ff.
56   See my article in *VT*, 28 (1973), p. 63 ff. Cf. n. 34 above.

practice usury, and will not touch any shady deal. He brings about a just settlement between two who are in dispute, and what is more, shares his bread with the hungry and helps clothe the naked.

Now, while certain of these items correspond to some of the Commandments (idolatry, adultery and theft) we cannot overlook the fact that Ezekiel mentions several moral attributes which are not dealt with in the Decalogue, such as sharing one's food and clothing with the needy, more reminiscent of Isaiah (58.7). The same applies to usury, and to effecting justice. These messages were directed at property-owners and judges, not at the ordinary person. The opposite is true of the Ten Commandments, all of which obligate every single person.

Another difference is that the passage in Ezekiel includes, beside its ethical topics, certain ritual and cultic elements, such as eating "upon the mountains" or intercourse with a menstruant woman (verse 6), matters totally absent from the Decalogue.

The list in Ezekiel is characterized by its opening and closing phrases, which more or less define the distinction of one who abstains from these transgressions: "If a man is righteous and does what is just and right" (verse 5); "he is righteous, such a man shall live" (verse 9). The subject under discussion is the attributes of the just man, who not only avoids evil deeds, but does what is proper, and does right by the poor.

Note that there is no mention at all of murder, which is additional evidence that we are not dealing with basic human obligations, such as are set forth in the Ten Commandments. Rather, the passage in Ezekiel is more like the list of religio-ethical attributes set forth in Psalms 15 and 24. Those psalms are addressed to individuals who want to enter the sanctuary. They list in definite and specific terms what is required of anyone who wants to penetrate the holy precincts or handle sacred things,[57] and they do so in a manner that differs sharply from the categorical style of the Ten Commandments.

The Book of Ezekiel also contains, in chapter 22. 6–12, another similar list which resembles the Decalogue even more strongly. That chapter includes the Sabbath and honoring one's parents (verses 7–8), as well as the prohibition of bloodshed and illicit sex (9–11). But alongside these there is also reference to cheating and bribery (7 and 12)

---

57   See my "Instructions for Temple Visitors in the Bible and in Ancient Egypt," in *Scripta Hierosolymitana*, XXVII (1982), *Egyptological Studies* (ed. S. Groll), pp. 224–250.

usury (12) and matters relating to ceremonial and sacred things (8 and 9) as well as ritual purity and impurity. Actually all the subjects correspond remarkably to the content of Leviticus 19.

Note that the list opens with the honor due one's parents, as does Leviticus 19. It goes on, after denouncing violence done to the alien, and wrong wreaked on the widow and the orphan (compare Lev. 19. 33–34) to say: "You have despised my sacred things and profaned my sabbaths" — (verse 8) — an almost exact echo of Leviticus 19.30: "You shall keep my sabbaths and venerate my holy things."[58] Then comes verse 9, "Talebearers have been in you to shed blood" — which amounts to an explanation of the sequence in Leviticus 19.16: "Do not go about as a talebearer among your people, do not profit by the blood of your neighbor." We are given to understand that what is being denounced is slander which costs lives.

It becomes apparent that the list in Ezekiel 22 cannot be classified with the Ten Commandments. It is more like the Holiness Code, which includes matters of worship and ceremonial, and of ritual purity and impurity. It also resembles Ezekiel 18 when it mentions usury and bribe-taking. Quite obviously it is addressed to men of substance and to public figures, not to ordinary individuals, as the Ten Commandments are. Actually, Ezekiel says explicitly that he is talking about "the princes of Israel" (verse 6). It is scarcely necessary to add that his words are not couched in the categorical, absolute terms of the Decalogue.

To be sure, it is a fair assumption that the Ten Commandments lie behind this list in Ezekiel, and behind the Code of Holiness in Leviticus, too. However, in the present instance the prophet has greatly expanded on the theme, suiting his words to the special situation of his time, namely the conduct of the "princes of Israel" for whom his message was intended.[59]

---

58   *Miqdaš* is not necessarily a House of God. Frequently it means simply "sacred objects" in general, as in Lev. 21.23, Num. 18.29 and elsewhere.

59   The "bloodshed" Ezekiel speaks of is not actual murder. It refers to acts by those in authority which lead, in the end, to the loss of human life. Particularly instructive is verse 9: "Talebearers have been among you to shed blood", which parallels Lev. 19.16, where the sentence stands in the context of laws addressed to judges (verses 15–16). The intent is apparently to warn judges who rely on slanderous hearsay, and then stand by while their careless judgment takes effect. For the connection between *śar* ("officer") and *šofēt* ("judge") in the Bible, see my "Judge and Officer in Ancient Israel and in the Ancient Near East," in *Israel Oriental Studies*, 7 (1977), pp. 65–88.

3. Mowinckel proposed a connection between the Decalogue and Psalms 15 and 24, as well as Isaiah 33. 14–15. He calls these passages "entry liturgies".[60] They make admission into God's house, and the privilege of dwelling therein, conditional on the fulfillment of ethical norms: clean hands and a pure heart, abstention from slander, from false oaths and from reviling friends and neighbors, respect for those who fear the LORD, refusal to take bribes or usury. These lists begin with the question: "Who may go up on God's mountain?" (Ps. 24); and "Who may dwell in your tent?" (Ps. 15) and "Who of us can dwell with the devouring fire?" (Isa. 33. 14). All these resemblances led Mowinckel to believe that the passages reflect ceremonials of admission into the sanctuary.

He proposes that in later times, under the influence of the prophets, the ethical elements were separated from the ritual, thus paving the way for the Decalogue as we know it.

Actually, however, there is no real reason for comparing the passages cited from Psalms and Isaiah with the Ten Commandments. These passages speak only of refined ethical requirements. They make no mention whatever of murder, adultery and theft. They differ from the Ten Commandments in another respect: they contain no religio-national rules, but are on a completely universalistic plane. As I have shown elsewhere,[61] the purpose of these psalms is to define the "righteous man" who is entitled to dwell in God's tabernacle; they do not refer to the ordinary individual. Similar rules have been found on the portals of Egyptian temples.[62] This explains the questions with which the passages begin: "Who shall go up?" "Who shall dwell?" What we are dealing with here are general ethical requirements, and not a list of obligations incumbent on every Israelite, in the manner of the Decalogue, or even of the parallel regulations laid down in Leviticus 19 and Ezekiel 18 and 22. The format and style of the psalms quoted are altogether different.

4. It is customary to compare the commandments in the Decalogue with the "negative confession" included in chapter 125 of the Egyptian Book of the Dead,[63] and also with the Mesopotamian list of

---

60   M. Mowinckel, *Le décalogue*, 1927, pp. 141 ff.
61   See my article cited in n. 57.
62   Ibid.
63   Now see M. Lichtheim, *Ancient Egyptian Literature*, vol. II. 1976, pp. 124–132.

incantations called *Šurpu*.[64] However, these texts are very different from the Ten Commandments, both in form and in content. As to form, the Book of the Dead is a sort of confession of the departed before he enters the next world. *Šurpu* is a series of incantations intended to free a sick person from every conceivable sin, so as to cure his illness.

With respect to content, the differences can be enumerated as follows: The Book of the Dead includes, to be sure, such sins as murder, adultery and robbery, but also such lesser transgressions as false weights and measures, talebearing and insulting others. Also included are purely cultic sins, such as blasphemy, neglect of divine worship, profanation of sacred things and misappropriation of holy objects. Similarly, the sins mentioned in *Šurpu* include murder, adultery, robbery, false oaths, talebearing, hypocrisy, wrongful acquisition, counterfeiting weights and measures, boundary encroachment and failure to clothe the naked. Here too we find sins of a cultic nature, such as eating forbidden foods, profanation of the sacred, having contact with the outcast, and so on. It scarcely needs to be pointed out that we are dealing with every possible kind of transgression, which sets these lists sharply apart from the Decalogue.

In fact, the Decalogue is *sui generis*. It differs from every other list of commandments. What makes it different is that it brings together a distilled short list of the basic prerequisites laid down for each member of the Israelite community who wants to be party to the special covenant of the people with its God. It serves as a sort of Israelite catechism. In that respect it resembles the Shema, a declaration consisting of one sentence easily committed to memory, summarizing the monotheistic principle, and readily available as a recognition password for those who believe in One God. It was no accident that the Shema and the Ten Commandments were recited together every morning in the ancient Temple (Mishnah Tamid V:1).

Just as the monotheistic principle embodied in the Shema is spelled out in various statutory requirements, such as smashing idols, the proscription of anything connected with them, the law of the seducer to idolatry, the judgment on the subverted town and similar laws in various codes to be found in the Torah — in the same way, the religious

---

64   M. Reiner, *Šurpu, A Collection of Sumerian and Akkadian Incantations, Archiv für Orientforschung*, Beiheft 11, 1958, Tablet II, pp. 13 ff.

and ethical principles contained in the Decalogue find expression in laws set down elsewhere in the Torah. Indeed, we have seen that there are attempts to put together legal summaries corresponding more or less to the Ten Commandments. But the truth of the matter is that they are really not parallels of the Decalogue, but rather explanatory commentaries on it. In the same way, Jewish thinkers like Philo and Saadiah sought to show that all the commandments in the Torah derive from the Decalogue.[65]

In their role as the fundamental demands made by the God of Israel on the Community of Israel, the Ten Commandments were familiar to every Israelite loyal to his heritage. They became the crowning point of his religious and ethical tradition. Nor is it surprising that this short list of commands, out of all the others, should have been seen as basic and primary in establishing the bond between God and Israel. For it was only the Ten Commandments that Israel was privileged to hear directly spoken by the Deity. Therefore they are the token and testimony of the people's relationship to its God.

RENEWING THE PLEDGE: THE DECALOGUE IN WORSHIP

For the past fifty years or so, biblical scholarship has been giving more and more credence to the idea that the theophany at Mount Sinai was understood in Israel not as a one-time event, over and done with; but rather as an occurrence that repeated itself every time the people assembled to renew the covenant and swear allegiance to their God.

The idea was first put forward in 1927 by Mowinckel in his book *Le décalogue*. Basing himself on a close examination of Psalms 50 and 81, he came to the conclusion that assemblies were held in ancient Israel to re-enact and celebrate the revelation at Mount Sinai.

Psalms 50 and 81, which hint at covenant-ceremonies and at festive gatherings, quote the opening of the Ten Commandments: "I the LORD am your God" and "You shall have no other gods" (Ps. 50.7 and 81.10–11). In addition Psalm 50 mentions the later Commandments: theft, adultery and false witness (18–20). The background for this psalm is the revelation of the LORD at Zion (verse 2), where he appears in a storm, pronouncing righteous judgment[66] upon the upright who

---

65   See the discussion by E.E. Urbach, *The Sages*, Jerusalem 1975, pp. 360 ff.

66   "Then the heavens proclaimed His righteousness, for He is a God who judges; selah"(verse 6). In this covenantal nexus, righteousness and judgment are connected with the giving of the Torah. Comp. Ps. 99.4, where "You who worked righteous

have made a covenant with him by sacrifice (verses 5–6). All this is reminiscent of the proclamation of the Torah at Mount Sinai and of the covenant concluded there (Ex. 19. 1–8).

The background for Psalm 81 is a festive gathering accompanied by blasts of the shofar and the declaration that God has set up statutes, laws and ordinances for Israel (verses 4–5). Putting together the elements in these two Psalms, which quote the Ten Commandments and include references to the promulgation of laws and statutes at a solemn festive gathering, one is impressed by Mowinckel's theory that we are dealing with a festive assembly celebrating the giving of the Torah.

But on second thought, it is important to note that the thrust of these two Psalms is *not* the celebration of the covenant renewed, but rather a message of reproof. Psalm 50 denounces those who offer many sacrifices but do not obey God's commands (verses 8–13). It also reproves the hypocrite, who constantly mouths the words of the covenant, but fails to fulfil them (16–21).[67]

Similarly, Psalm 81 cites the giving of the Law and the Ten Commandments, and then goes on to reprove the people for not obeying God's commands, for straying from his ways (verses 12–16). Denunciations of this sort based on the Ten Commandments can be found in the prophecies of Hosea and Jeremiah. Both these prophets complain of violations of the fundamental laws of the Decalogue, and go on to lash out at the priests, and at the stress on the sacrificial ritual. Hosea complains of the lack of knowledge of God in the land (4.1) which results in "(false) swearing, dishonesty and murder, theft and adultery" (Hos. 4.2). Then he proceeds to denounce the priests who have despised knowledge of the LORD and forgotten the teachings of God, while they eat the flesh of sin-offerings (Hos. 4. 6–8). In the same way, Jeremiah reproves the people who come into the sanctuary to prostrate themselves (Jer. 7.2) calling their attention to five of the Ten Commandments (verse 9): "Will you steal and murder, and commit adultery, and swear falsely, and sacrifice to Baal, and follow other

judgment in Jacob" appears alongside the "decrees" and "law" given to Moses and Aaron (verses 6–7). In this connection, see M. Weinfeld, *Judgment and Righteousness in Israel and Other Peoples* (Hebrew), Jerusalem 1985.

67   See B. Schwartz, "Psalm 50, Its Subject, Form and Place", *Shnaton* (Annual for Biblical and Ancient Near Eastern Studies), III (1979), pp. 77 ff.

gods?"[68] After which he launches into a diatribe against sacrifices: "Thus said the LORD of hosts, the God of Israel: Add your burnt offerings to your other sacrifices, and eat the meat! For I did not speak to your ancestors, nor did I command them when I brought them out of the land of Egypt, concerning burnt-offerings or sacrifices. But this is what I commanded them: Do my bidding, that I may be your God, and you may be my people" (7. 21–23).

In another context[69] we have called attention to the fact that Jeremiah's declaration that the Israelites were not commanded to bring sacrifices at the time of the exodus from Egypt can only be understood on the assumption that Jeremiah was talking about the Ten Commandments, which make no mention of sacrifices. According to Deuteronomy (5.18 ff.) it was only the Decalogue that God spoke to Israel at Sinai, whereas the rest of the laws were imparted to Moses alone, and he transmitted them to the Israelites on the Plains of Moab, shortly before his death.

We see, therefore, that Psalms 50 and 81, which do indeed mention the revelation at Sinai, are really psalms of reproof, like the words of rebuke spoken by Jeremiah and Hosea, both of whom also invoke the Ten Commandments. It seems that the connection between the theophany and the rebuke can be explained in the following manner: The authors of these remonstrances deliberately chose to address their words to the people on the festival celebrating the event at Mount Sinai. On such an occasion, when the Ten Commandments were read in public, these prophets and psalmists took the opportunity to denounce the hypocrisy of those who preach fine principles which they ignore in practice (compare Ps. 50. 16–21). For the same reason they decried the multiplicity of sacrifices, pointing out that these are not mentioned in the Ten Commandments.[70]

The difference between the prophets and the psalmists is this: the main concern of the prophets was exhortation, so they paid little or no attention to the ceremonies at which they pronounced their messages of reproof. The psalmists, on the other hand, were the bards of the

---

68   See M. Weiss in the present volume.

69   *Jeremiah and the Spiritual Metamorphosis in Israel*, ZAW, 88 (1976), pp. 17–56. David Kimhi's comments on the verse are quoted there (p. 54).

70   Compare Amos 5.25: "Did you offer sacrifice and oblation to Me those forty years in the wilderness?" This is said in the context of "I loathe, I spurn your festivals" (verse 21).

sanctuary, very much involved in the liturgy. Hence they describe the ceremonial renewal of the covenant in glowing terms, and then go on to denounce those who are unfaithful to the covenant. Thus we find Psalm 50 opening with the revelation at Zion in language that echos the theophany at Sinai,[71] from which it is apparent that the locus of the revelation had been transferred from Sinai to Zion. The fire and the storm (verse 3) are characteristics of the theophany. The saints who make the covenant by sacrifice (verse 5) are reminiscent of the covenantal scene at Sinai (Ex. 24).

Psalm 81 lights up another aspect of the picture. It looks to the historical background of the festival which commemorates the bestowal of statute and law on Jacob, and "a decree upon Joseph".[72] It describes the exodus from Egypt, and the wanderings of the people in the desert,[73] until they have arrived at the Waters of Meribah.[74] Then comes a quotation from the Ten Commandments. The sounding of the shofar, mentioned in connection with the giving of statute and law (verses 4–5) is apparently an echo of the blasts of the shofar heard at Sinai when the Torah was given (Ex. 19. 16 and 19). It seems that the shofar was sounded at ceremonies renewing the covenant, as would appear from II Chronicles 15.14.[75]

The sequence of events described in Psalm 81 corresponds to the

---

71   Contrast Deut. 33.2: "The LORD *came* from Sinai/He shone upon them from Seir/He *appeared* from Mount Paran" with Psalm 50.2: "From Zion...God *appeared*/Let our God *come*!" etc.

72   Compare S.E. Loewenstamm, "A Decree Upon Joseph"(Hebrew), in *Eretz Israel*, 5 (Mazar Volume) pp. 80–82.

73   Verse 8: "I answered you from the secret place of thunder" means that the response came from the cloud accompanying the Heavenly lightning and thunder. Compare Ps. 18. 12–14: "He made darkness his screen/Dark thunderheads, dense clouds of the sky.../Then the LORD thundered from heaven" and so on. The answer from the cloud can be interpreted as God speaking to Moses out of the cloud (see Ex. 19. 18–19: "Now Mount Sinai was all in smoke...and the whole mountain trembled... As Moses spoke, the LORD answered him in thunder." Compare Ps. 99.7: "Moses and Aaron... When they called to the LORD He answered them./He spoke to them in a pillar of cloud;/they obeyed His decrees, the law He gave them."

74   There is a dual meaning to the experience at the Waters of Meribah: on the one hand, God puts Israel to the test; and on the other, the Israelites try Him. On this, see Loewenstamm, op. cit. (n. 72 above).

75   Late Jewish tradition has, to be sure, connected Psalm 80 with Rosh Hashanah (R.H. 8a–b; 34a and elsewhere) but this is homiletic midrash. In the same way, the blasts of the shofar at Sinai (Ex. 19. 16–19) made their way into the *shofarot* section of the Rosh Hashanah service; see below, n. 123.

sequence of events in Book of Exodus. There the giving of the Torah comes after the Waters of Meribah — i.e. Exodus 19 comes after Exodus 17. That being the case, it seems that the celebration described by the Psalmist points to the Festival of Shavuot (Pentecost).

As for the style of the exhortation connected with the renewal of the covenant, particular importance attaches to the wording used by these psalms when speaking of the theophany involving the Ten Commandments:

Psalm 50.7	*Psalm 81. 9–10*
Hear, O my people	Hear, O my people
and I will speak;	And I will admonish you;
O Israel, and I will	O Israel, if you would
arraign you;	but listen to me!
I am God, your God.	There shall be no foreign
	god in your midst...
	I the LORD am your God,
	Who brought you out of
	the land of Egypt.

The expressions "Hear, O my people" and "Israel" preceding "I the LORD am your God" and "I am God, your God" are reminiscent of the declaration "Hear O Israel, the LORD is our God, the LORD alone" (Deut. 6.4), and may well cast light on the close connection between the Shema and the Ten Commandments, a connection which we know about from liturgical practice at the time of the Second Commonwealth.

However, for present purposes the most instructive element is the adjuration, the calling to witness, where the verb *he'id* is followed by the preposition *be*, such as we find in Psalm 81.6.[76] This usage occurs in II Kings 17.15 and in Nehemiah 9.34, where the sense is "the bestowal of laws and statutes" (by a process of adjuration). Indeed, from recently published studies it appears that the verb *ha'ed*, apart from its ordinary meaning "to warn" also signifies both "to legislate"[77] and "to instruct".[78]

---

76 The rabbinic Sages regarded the recitation of the Shema as an act of affirmation, or bearing witness; see Ber. 14b.

77 T. Veijola, "Zu Ableitung und Bedentung von He'id I im Hebräischen", *Ugarit Forschungen*, 8 (1976), pp. 343 ff.

78 B. Couroyer, "Un Egyptianisme dans Ben Sira IV, 11", *Rev. Bib.*, 82 (1975), pp. 206 ff.

All of this throws light on the connection between reproof, admonition, and the laying down of laws, as demonstrated in Psalms 50 and 81. It should be added that the verb *hizhir* (=warn) also displays a similar duality of meaning: "promulgating a law" (e.g. Ex. 18.20); and "warning" (II Ki 6.10).[79] The semantic connection between promulgating a law and enjoining obedience to it is not without logical basis, since the practical application of a law is its enforcement ("You have been warned").

No wonder, then, that in Psalms 50 and 81, admonition goes hand in hand with the commands, This close connection is clearly visible in Jeremiah 11 where the prophet, who has been told to broadcast the terms of the covenant in Jerusalem (verse 6) couches his message in menacing language: "Cursed be the man who will not obey the terms of this covenant" (verse 3). To be sure, we read in this connection (verse 7) "For I earnestly *enjoined (ha'ed ha'idothi)* upon your ancestors on the day that I brought them out of the land of Egypt, telling them early and often, 'Hearken to my words'". In the light of Psalms 50 and 81, the usage *ha'ed be-* in this sentence is not intended to convey "threaten, warn", but rather "give commands", which are in themselves admonitions. Compare in this connection the words of Moses in Deut. 32.46: "Take to heart all the words with which I have charged you *(me'id bakhem)*. Enjoin (command) them upon your children, so that they may observe faithfully all the terms of this teaching." All of this tends to show that the giving of the Torah, and the admonition, are two sides of the same coin. Hence in Psalms 50 and 81 they go hand in hand.

We shall see as we proceed that the pilgrim festival Shavuot served during the Second Commonwealth as the occasion for a great public assembly (*'aẓereth*) at which the covenant of Sinai was ratified and renewed. We may assume, therefore, that the celebration of this festival was the background for the two Psalms just mentioned. It is highly likely that Mowinckel sensed that these Psalms were associated with the ceremonies of a festival, but because he was eager to find intimations of Rosh Hashanah at every turn, he did so in this instance too, although there are no grounds for his assumption.

---

79   The Septuagint uses the same verb (*diamartúromai*) for both *we-hizharta* (Ex. 18.20) and *ha'id be-* in the Psalms under discussion. It is interesting that the medieval liturgical composition connected with the reading of the Ten Commandments bears the name *'azharot*: the name seems to be based on old tradition. See I. Elbogen, *Der jüdische Gottesdienst*, p. 217.

In our opinion, Psalms 50 and 81 indicate that they were connected with the Festival of Shavuot. To be sure, this festival is not assigned a precise date in the Torah, but according to the Book of Jubilees, as well as the documents of the Qumran sect, it was observed on the 15th of the month (see below). Consequently, the "full moon of our festival" in Ps. 81.4[80] may well correspond to the Festival of Shavuot, the occasion for the annual renewal by the people of its covenant with its God. The phenomenon of annual renewal of a covenant is documented for the ancient East, from the second pre-Christian millennium up to the Hellenistic and Roman periods.[81] It is mentioned specifically in the Dead Sea Scrolls in connection with the annual covenantal ceremony of the members of the Qumran sect (*Manual of Discipline*, page 2, line 19).

It should be observed that the attempt by Albrecht Alt to postulate a septennial ceremony for the renewal of the covenant (a theory based on Deut. 31. 10–13) does not stand up to close analysis. That passage deals with the assembly called *haqhel*, at which the nation's leader was required to read the Torah to his people. The Sages called this "The Section of the king" (M. Sot. VII: 2 and 8); it has no connection with renewal of the covenant. I have demonstrated elsewhere that this practice has to do with the rules for the king in the Ancient Near East.[82]

THE TRADITION OF THE TEN COMMANDMENTS THROUGH THE AGES

When we attempt to reconstruct the development of the tradition concerning the Ten Commandments, we arrive at the following:

1. At the dawn of Israelite history the Ten Commandments were received in their original short form as the basic constitution, so to

---

80   The word *keseh* in this verse means "the day of the full moon", as we now know from Phoenician (*Diso*, 129) and Akkadian, where *kasiu* means "the lunar corona" (AHW 515a). It is apparently derived from *kasû*, which means "binding" (the crown). See the Kohler-Baumgartner dictionary. It has recently been maintained that the calendar of the Pentateuch, especially that of the Priestly Code, corresponds to the calendar of Jubilees and of the Dead Sea sect. See e.g., A. Jaubert *VT*, 3 (1953), 250 ff.; *VT*, 7 (1957), pp. 35 ff. Cazelles even suggested that *keseh* and *ḥodeš* in Ps. 81.4 be regarded as parallel synonyms, both meaning "the day of the full moon" (H. Cazelles, *Biblica*, 43 (1962), p. 206).

81   See my article in *VT*, 23 (1973), p. 72 (above n. 34), and also my article "The Loyalty Oath in the Ancient Near East", *Ugarit Forschungen* 8 (1976), pp. 393–394.

82   M. Weinfeld, "The Temple Scroll or King's Law", *Shnaton*, 3 (1979), pp. 220 ff.

speak, of the Community of Israel. The words were chiselled or written on two stone tablets that came to be known as "The Tablets of the Covenant (*berith*)" or "The Tablets of the Testimony (*'eduth*)".[83] The tablets served as evidence of the pledge given by the People of Israel to fulfil the commands inscribed on them. These tablets were placed in the Ark of the Covenant which, together with the cherubim, symbolized the dwelling-place of the Deity. The cherubim were thought of as the throne of God, and the Ark beneath them as his footstool.[84] In fact, we now know from Hittite documents contemporary with Moses that it was customary among the peoples of the region to place at the feet of the deity the written treaties which he had sanctioned.[85]

   This analogy with the customs connected with treaties in those days helps us understand why Moses broke the tablets when he saw the Israelites worshipping the golden calf. We have learned that among the peoples of the ancient Middle East, especially those of Mesopotamia, breaking the tablet meant nullifying the commitment. The classic Mesopotamian expression for this was *ṭuppam ḫepû*, i.e. "break the tablet".[86] (Compare the Roman *tabulae novae* which were written after

---

83   *Berith* and *'eduth* are congruent terms. Etymologically, the word *'eduth* is cognate
      with Aramaic *'adin* and the Akkadian *adê*, both of which mean "covenant"; see my
      article s.v. *"berith"* in *Theologisches Wörterbuch zum Alten Testament*, 1, 1972, pp.
      781 ff.

84   See M. Haran, "The Ark and the Cherubs" (Hebrew), in *Eretz Israel*, 5 (Mazar
      Volume), pp. 87–88.

85   For example, Rameses II writes to King Mira in the north: "Behold, the text of the
      treaty (which I concluded) on behalf of the great King of the Hittites has been
      deposited at the feet of the (Storm) god. Let the great gods be witness thereto... and
      behold, the text of the treaty which the great (king of the Hittites) contracted on my
      behalf has been placed at the feet of the god Ra. Let the great gods be witness
      thereto" (B. Meissner, *ZDMG*, 72 (1918), p. 58 = *KBo* 1.24 Rs. 5 ff. For additional
      references, see V. Korošec, *Hethische Staatsverträge*, 1932, pp. 100 f.

86   See *Chicago Assyrian Dictionary*, VI, H, pp. 171–172. I would suggest that this is
      the origin of the word *shobhar* ("receipt", "quittance") in talmudic legal parlance,
      in the sense of cancelling a promissary note or a marriage contract. In certain
      contexts the term can still be taken literally, as in "She breaks her marriage
      contract and leaves" (M. Sot. I:5), i.e., she breaks the ostracon on which the
      contract was written. As time went on, and it became customary to write receipts
      or quitclaims as a separate document, the term *shobhar* was transferred to that
      document. Later the form *shobher 'al* came to mean "annul" as in Tos. Ket. 4.11
      and 9.1. It is well known that the terminology used in the Mishnah for legal
      instruments derives from Akkadian: witness *šṭar, geṭ*, etc. After I had called
      attention to the origin of the term *shobhar* I found that Asher Gulak in *Das
      Urkundenwesen im Talmud*, 1935, p. 148, n. 1, had come to the same conclusion,

the old debts were cancelled.) The conclusion is that Moses did not break the tablets out of weakness or anger, but deliberately and of set purpose.[87] The making of the golden calf was a violation of the First Commandment of the Decalogue, and necessarily led to the breaking of the tablets of the pact, to show that it was no longer valid.

The import of this act was correctly understood by Abraham Ibn Ezra in his comment on Exodus 32.19: "In his great zeal Moses broke the tablets which he carried as the document of agreement, like one who tears up a deed of contract; and this he did in the presence of all Israel (*the other contracting party*) as is written (Deut. 9.17) 'I smashed them before your eyes'."

2. It can be assumed that the Ten Commandments were read in sanctuaries[88] at ceremonies of renewal of the covenant. Each time, those present undertook once again to obey everything commanded, something we can derive from the custom prevalent in the ancient Near East of renewing pacts annually.[89] Indeed, Psalms 50 and 81 imply renewal ceremonies of this sort, as we have tried to show above. In our opinion, these ceremonies were conducted on the Festival of Shavuot, the Festival of the Giving of the Torah.

3. During the Second Commonwealth, the Ten Commandments were read together with the Shema every day in conjunction with the daily morning sacrifice (M. Tamid, V:1). The Nash papyrus, which was discovered in Egypt, shows the Ten Commandments followed by the Shema in what is clearly a liturgical text.[90] The phylacteries found at

---

    even though supporting evidence from Akkadian literature was not yet available to him.

87   Comp. Yer. Taan. 4.7 (68c) and parallels: "Moses reasoned a fortiori: If the paschal lamb, the eating of which is a single mitzvah, is forbidden by the Torah to the uncircumcised, how much more the Torah as a whole which contains all the mitzvot." Also ibid: "It was taught in the school of R. Ishmael: The LORD told Moses to break the tablets."

88   Psalm 50 originated in Jerusalem, witness verse 2 ("from Zion") whereas Psalm 81 belongs to a northern tradition ("a decree upon Joseph", verse 6). Apparently it stemmed from one of the northern sanctuaries. For a study of north-country psalms that were transferred to Jerusalem after the fall of Samaria, see N.M. Sarna, "The Psalm Superscriptions and the Guilds", *Studies in Jewish Religious and Intellectual History, Presented to A. Altmann on his Seventieth Birthday*, 1980, pp. 288 ff.

89   See n. 81 above.

90   See M.Z. Segal, *The Nash Papyrus*, in *Tradition and Criticism*, (Hebrew), 1957, pp. 227–236.

Qumran[91] also have the Ten Commandments alongside the Shema. According to Jerome, this liturgical practice persisted in Babylonia until a rather late period.[92] With respect to the reading of the Decalogue, Josephus tells us: "We are not permitted to pronounce them explicitly to the letter" (*Antiquities*, III.90). He probably means that they were not to be read as written in circumstances or places unsuitable to their holiness.

4. Some light may be shed on the origin of this religious custom through a comparative study of cultic practices in antiquity. The foundation inscription of a private shrine dating from the first century BCE has been discovered at Philadelphia, in Asia Minor.[93] The inscription details the commands of the goddess Agdistis, in whose honor the shrine was built. The man responsible for the inscription, one Dionysius, tells how Zeus appeared to him in a dream, and imparted to him the commands engraved on the inscription. These obligate everyone who enters this sanctuary, or belongs to this house (*oikos*) to swear that he will obey the list of commands, which are as follows:[94]

> Not to destroy a fetus, or cause an abortion.[95]
> Not to commit robbery.[96]
> Not to murder.

91   See Y. Yadin, "Tefilin from Qumran", *Eretz Israel*, 9 (1969), pp. 60 ff.
92   See A.M. Haberman, "The Phylacteries in Antiquity", *Eretz Israel*, 3 (1964), pp. 174 ff.
93   O. Weinreich, *Stiftung und Kultsatzungen eines Privatheiligtums in Philadelphia in Lydien*, in the *Sitzungsberichte* of the Heidelberg Academy of Sciences, 1919, phil-histor. Klasse, Abhandlung 16.
94   For a parallel in *The Teachings of the Twelve Apostles (didache)* see my article "Comparative Study of Abortion in the Traditions of Israel and Other Peoples" (Hebrew), *Zion*, 42 (1977), pp. 129–142.
95   See article in preceding note.
96   Based on reading *m[ē harpagmon mē] phonon*. However, the lacuna is filled differently by F. Sokolowski, *Lois sacrées de l'Asie mineure*, (1955), no. 20, pp. 11.20 ff; *m[ē allo ti paido] phonon*. If we adopt that reading, then the whole sentence deals with infanticide. However, the generally accepted reading is the one proposed by Keil-Premerstein, which forms the basis of Weinreich's thoroughgoing study cited above, n. 93. See also A.D. Nock, "Early Gentile Christianity and its Hellenistic Background", *Essays on the Trinity and the Incarnation*, ed. A.E.J. Rawlinson, 1928, pp. 72 ff. (=A.D. Nock, *Essays on Religion and the Ancient World*, ed. Z. Stewart, I, 1972, pp. 65 ff.).

Not to steal anything.

To be loyal (*eunoein*)[97] to the sanctuary.

If anyone commits a transgression, or plans one, he (*the communicant*) will not allow him, but will expose him,[98] and bring him to punishment.

No man will lie with a strange woman other than his wife...nor with any boy or maiden.

The inscription goes on to say that any man or woman who commits one of these sins

> shall not enter this shrine, for here sit enthroned mighty gods who keep an eye on all these transgressions and will not tolerate sinners.[99] ...The gods will look with favor on those who obey, and will grant them blessings, but will hate those who transgress, and will inflict on them great punishments.[100] ...Men and women who are sure of their integrity — let them touch this inscription[101] once a month or once a year at the time of offering the sacrifice.

Without drawing any comparison to the Decalogue, Nock[102] noted the similarity between this inscription and the Epistle of Pliny to Trajan,[103] where we read about those Christians who rise before the dawn (*ante lucem*) to sing hymns responsively (*invicem*)[104] after which

97 On this verb with the sense of "to be faithful", "loyal" see my article in *Ugarit Forschungen*, above, n. 81.

98 On clauses in covenant-documents demanding the exposure of violators and those who incite to violation (cf. Deut. 13), see my article in *Ugarit Forschungen* (above, n. 81), pp. 389–390.

99 Compare the Decalogue: "an impassioned God, visiting guilt"..."for the LORD will not clear one", etc.; and Josh. 24.19. "For He is a holy God, He is a jealous God, He will not forgive your transgressions and your sins."

100 Note the promise and the threat in Ex. 20. 5–6, Deut. 5. 9–10: "visiting the guilt... upon...those who reject Me...but showing kindness to...those who love Me."

101 This is a symbolic act, like "taking hold of an object", a customary accompaniment to swearing under oath in the ancient Near East and in Greece. See my remarks in *Leshonenu*, 38 (1977), p. 232 and n. 5.

102 A.D. Nock, *Classical Review*, 38 (1924), pp. 58 ff. In his article cited above (n. 96), Nock mentions that the parallel to Pliny's letter had been noticed by O. Casal in *Jahr. f. Liturg.*, IV, 285, no. 261.

103 *Epist. ad Traianum* x. 96. 7, written in the year 112 C.E. See A.N. Sherwin-White, *Pliny*, 1966, pp. 327 ff.

104 I believe these were a sort of morning hymns (*pesuqe de-zimra*) such as are recited preceding the Shema and its benedictions, the latter being the *yoẓer* and the

they put themselves on oath (*sacramentum*)[105] not to steal, commit adultery, violate a trust nor to embezzle.[106] After Nock had made this point, there were those who suggested that Pliny was referring to the Ten Commandments.[107] As a matter of fact, we know that the reading of the Ten Commandments and the Shema every morning was regarded as "taking on oneself the yoke of the Kingdom of Heaven" which amounts to a commitment under oath.[108]

Although the shrine at Philadelphia in Asia Minor dates from the first pre-Christian century, there can be no doubt that the practices it reflects are rooted in more ancient religious traditions of the Near East.[109] These can help us to a better understanding of the traditions in Israel concerning the Ten Commandments.

We are justified in assuming that these customs began in circumstances not very different from those found at Philadelphia in Lydia. The Congregation in Sinai was gathered around the Ark in which were deposited the Tables of the Covenant. These two Tables contained the Ten Commandments which had been revealed to Moses, founder of the Congregation and of its cultus, and which the faithful

---

ahavah. The *ahavah* constitutes a "taking on oneself of the yoke of the Kingdom of Heaven (the Shema and the Ten Commandments)". See my "Traces of Kedushat Yoẓer and Pesuqey de-zimra in the Qumran Literature and in Ben Sira"(Hebrew), *Tarbiẓ*, 45 (1976), pp. 23 ff. A good example of responsive or antiphonal recitation of the morning Psalms is to be seen in the Qumran scrolls, where Psalm 145 has the congregation responding after each verse "Blessed be the LORD and blessed His name for ever and aye". See art. cit.

105 For the use of *sacramentum* in the sense of "oath of fealty" in a religious context, see my article "Loyalty Oath" (above, no. 81), pp. 406–407.

106 *ne furta, ne latrocina, ne adulteria committerent, ne fidem fallerent, ne depositum apellati abnegarent.*

107 C.J. Kraemer, *Classical Philology*, 29 (1934), pp. 293 ff.; S.L. Mohler, ibid., 30 (1935), pp. 167 ff.; C.C. Coutler, ibid., 35 (1940), pp. 60 ff. The last two items on the list seem to correspond to the last two Commandments of the Decalogue (false witness and coveting). To be sure, Mark 10.19 reads, instead of "you shall not covet" *me aposteréses* ("do not defraud") as in Lev. 19.13, where the entire passage has the Ten Commandments as its background. Compare Lev. 5.21, where the subject is misappropriation or deceitful statement regarding an object left for safekeeping. On this see C.C. Coutler art. cit.

108 See the discussion in my article "The Loyalty Oath" (above, no. 81), pp. 406 ff.

109 See Nock's *Early Gentile Christianity etc.* (n. 96 above), pp. 74 ff. Also H. Pettazzoni, "Confession of Sins and the Classics", in *Harvard Theological Review*, 30 (1937), pp. 1–14. On confession in Egypt see my remarks in *Tarbiẓ*, 48 (1979), pp. 196–197, n. 56; also my "Instructions for Temple Visitors" (above, n. 57).

swore to observe. Dionysius of the Philadelphia shrine occupies a role parallel to that of Moses.

Thus the Tables of the Covenant, with the Ten Commandments inscribed on them, formed, so to speak, the basic constitution which was binding on the Congregation of Israel. After the Tables disappeared, and the Ark of the Covenant in which they were kept was no more, the tie between the Commandments and these tangible symbols to which they had been attached ceased to exist. But at festive assemblies and at the morning worship in the Temple each day, it became customary to read the Ten Commandments aloud, and all present bound themselves to observe them by covenant, and under oath.[110]

As an addendum to the importance assigned to laws inscribed on stone by the sources we have quoted, it is worth mentioning what Pausanius writes about a shrine in Greece (Arcady) where the sacred writings were kept between two stones (compare the "Book of the Torah" placed "beside the Ark of the Covenant" which contained the stone tablets, Deut. 31.26) and the faithful would swear by these stones (Pausanius, VIII.15.2).

Despite the external resemblance between traditions associated with the Decalogue and the oath taken by the faithful at the shrine in Philadelphia, it is important to take note of the profound inner difference between the position of the Ten Commandments in Israel, and the superficially similar commands among the communicants at the Lydian shrine. By contrast with the Israelite conception of the Ten Commandments as obligating every Israelite, wherever he might be, the pagan tradition thinks of the obligations as binding only on those persons who enter the sanctuary. They must take care not to profane the holy place. It is only in this respect that the conditions for entering the sanctuary in Israel can be compared to the rules customary in the ancient orient (see above, at note 60).

It is also noteworthy that the resemblance between the Decalogue and the commands on the Philadelphia inscription is confined to the last five Commandments, which deal with moral and criminal transgressions. Actually, the Jewish Sages distinguished between the

---

110 *Emet Ve-yaziv* which was recited in the Temple after the Decalogue and the Shema
     is a sort of affirmation under oath of intention to fulfil the demands of those two
     biblical passages; see my article "The Loyalty Oath" (above, n. 81), pp. 405 ff. pp.
     40.

first five Commandments, which were addressed to the Israelites alone, and therefore use the Tetragrammaton — and the last five Commandments, which were addressed to the nations of the world, and therefore do not mention God's name. This is hinted at in the Midrash:

> The Emperor Hadrian, that wicked man, asked Rabbi Joshua ben Hananiah: Why is it that God associated his name with the first five Commandments he gave Israel...but did not associate His name with the last five Commandments, which he gave to the Gentiles? (*Pesiqta Rabbati*, 21, **'eser devarim**; ed. Ish Shalom, p. 99).

THE THEOPHANY AT SINAI
AND THE FESTIVAL OF GIVING THE TORAH

1. The festival at which it became customary to call up the memory of the scene at Mount Sinai and so to speak receive the Torah anew with an oath of loyalty was the Festival of Shavuot. In our opinion, the ceremonies on that occasion are reflected in Psalms 50 and 81. During the Second Commonwealth this festival was given the name *'azereth* (="assembly")[111]. That is the designation used by Josephus.[112] The very names signifies that Shavuot was a day of public gathering, or in biblical language *yom ha-qahal* — "the Day of the Assembly". This was the occasion when the people at large gathered to hear the word of the LORD, as expressed in the Ten Commandments (Deut. 9.10; 10.4; 18.16).[113] It appears that on this festival of *'azereth* they re-enacted in a special ceremony the great event of "The Stand at Mount Sinai", and renewed the covenant and the oath to keep the Ten Commandments.

It is stated in Exodus 19.1 that the Israelites arrived in the Wilderness of Sinai in the third month. Immediately we are plunged into a description of the preparations to receive the revelation. Since Mowinckel it has been assumed, and rightly so, that the rites of purification and the sounding of the shofar, as described in Exodus,

---

111 See Onkelos and Targum Jonathan on Num. 28.26 (*beshavu'othekhem = be'azartheikhon*); also the Neofiti Targum for Num. 16.10.

112 *Ant.*, III.252: *asartha*.

113 See the thoroughgoing analysis by D.Z. Hoffman in his commentary on Leviticus, II, pp. 258 ff. Note that Jonathan and the Neofiti Targum render *beyom ha-qahal* as "the day of the public assembly" and in Deut. 18.16 as "the day when the tribes gathered to receive the Torah".

reflect the customary ceremonial procedure for the renewal of a covenant. The preparations for the scene at Sinai are actually the accepted procedures for an encounter with the Deity, such as takes place at every assembly in the sanctuary. The self-purification, washing of clothes and abstention from sex, described in Exodus chapter 19 as preparatory steps before the revelation (verses 10, 15) are paralleled in the Book of Genesis (35. 1–3), where Jacob commands his household to purify themselves and change their clothing before going up to Beth-El.[114] The setting up of bounds around the mountain and keeping the people away from the holiest area, as described in Exodus 19 (verses 12–13; 21–24) are also typical of the customary limitations regarding access to sacred areas.[115] The blast of the shofar was indicative of a gathering involving oaths of fealty.[116] In support of this see II Chronicles 15.14, where the shofar is sounded along with the oath at the covenant ceremony in the fifteenth year of the reign of Asa, in the third month. This led Ehrlich to conclude[117] that the long established custom of accompanying oath-taking with the sound of the shofar is rooted in the Bible.[118]

Just as the Festival of the Paschal lamb and the unleavened bread re-enacted the exodus from Egypt, and the Feast of Tabernacles dramatized the booths in which the Israelites had lived in the wilderness, so the Festival of Shavuot marked the theophany at Mount Sinai.

114　Similar restrictions on sanctuary visitors existed in Greece; see M.P. Nillson, *Geschichte der Griechischen Religion*, II³, 1974, p. 74. The inscription on the shrine of Zeus Kintheus is instructive. It insists that the visitor have clean hands, be dressed in white, and be barefoot. He must also have undergone a period of abstinence from sex and from contact with corpses. On similar regulations governing entrance to the Temple in Jerusalem, see Shmuel Safrai, *The Pilgrim in the Days of the Second Temple* (Hebrew), p. 143; on the wearing of freshly laundered clothing, ibid., p. 144.

115　Nahmanides already noticed the resemblance between the restrictions laid down in Exodus 19 on approaching Mount Sinai, and the warnings against approaching the Tent of Meeting; see his introduction to the Book of Numbers, and his preliminary remarks to Exodus 25. Now see J. Milgrom, *Studies in Levitical Terminology*, I, 1970, pp. 44 ff.

116　So, for example, at a coronation, during which the people swear fealty to the new king; see II Sam. 15.10; I Kings 1.49; II Kings 9.13; 11.14 (with the sounding of trumpets). On the sounding of the shofar as an accompaniment to oath-taking, see *Aruch Completum*, s.v. *heseth* (p. 229).

117　*Miqra Kifshuto* on II Chron. 15.

118　See n. 116 above.

That this was so — that Shavuot came to be the time when throngs gathered in the Temple — is evidenced by what we read in Josephus as well as in the Acts of the Apostles. Josephus makes two references to mass gatherings in Jerusalem on Shavuot. One was at the time of the incursion of the Parthians in the year 40 BCE:

> When the feast called Pentecost came round, the whole neighborhood of the Temple and the entire city were crowded with country folk (*Bellum*, I.253).

The second time was during the uprising following the death of Herod. When Shavuot came,

> a countless multitude flowed in from Galilee, from Idumaea, from Jericho and beyond the Jordan. But it was the native population of Judaea itself which, both in numbers and ardor, was predominant (*Bellum*, II.43).

To be sure, the mass gathering served as a cover for the rebels, but the original reason for it was the tradition of a great public assembly on Shavuot (see also *Bellum*, II.73).

That tradition is also reflected in Acts 2, where we are told that the assembly who witnessed "the great things" (*ta megaleia*)[119] that took place on the Feast of Pentecost included

> Parthians and Medes and Elamites and residents of Mesopotamia, Judaea and Cappadocia, Pontus and Asia, Phrygia and Pamphylia, Egypt and the parts of Libya belonging to Cyrene, both Jews and proselytes, Cretans and Arabians (Acts 2. 9–11).

The fact that Shavuot (Pentecost) was of special importance to pilgrims is apparent also from Acts 20.16, where Paul makes an effort to reach Jerusalem in time for Shavuot. One is reminded of what is told of Judah Maccabeus in II Maccabees 12. 31–32.

Philo speaks of Shavuot as a festival celebrated in an especially

---

119 Acts 2.11. (AV/ RSV = "wonderful"/"mighty works of God"); compare Deut. 4.34 (*mora'im gedolim*) and Deut. 26.8 (*mora'gadol*), which the Septuagint renders *en horamasi megalois* (= "great visions"), and the Aramaic targumim take to mean "revelation" (*hezwanin ravrevin*). So too the rabbinic midrash: "*mora' gadol* — that is to say the revelation of the Shekhina" (*Midrash Tannaim*, ed. D.Z. Hoffmann, Berlin 1909, p. 133).

popular manner (*heortē dēmotelestatē*) (*De legibus I, 183*). When he describes the observance of this festival by the Therapeutai, he calls it "the greatest festival" (*heortē megistē*).[120]

Other sources as well testify to the celebration of Shavuot as the Festival of the Giving of the Torah, and as the occasion for ceremonial renewal of the covenant:

1. In II Chronicles 15. 8–15 we read that in the fifteenth year of the reign of Asa in the third month,[121] there gathered in Jerusalem men of Judah and Benjamin, of Ephraim and Menasseh, and Simeon, for the rededication of the altar. They brought sacrifices, and entered into the covenant to seek the LORD with all their heart and all their soul. They took an oath to the LORD in a loud voice, with shouting and trumpets and with horns. The oath which they took was an oath of the covenant,[122] reminiscent of the covenant at Sinai, which was also accompanied by offerings and sacrifices (Ex. 24.3 ff). It was taken willingly and joyfully, which makes the undertaking all the more binding.[123] The joy also underscores the fact that we are dealing here with a festival at which there was a public ceremony renewing the covenant.[124] The repetition of the root *šb'* three times in this passage (verses 14 and 15) is no doubt intended to stress the connection of *šebu'oth* (="oaths") with *šebūoth* (="weeks"). Thus the festival gains a

---

120 *De vita contemplativa*, 65.
121 The Targum adds (v. 11) *beḥaga diševu'aya* = "on the Feast of Weeks" (ed. A. Sperber, p. 45).
122 *beryt/shevu'ah* (verses 12, 15). These terms are congruent with *beryt* and *'alah* (Deut. 29.11, 13, 20) which constitute a hendiadys for "covenantal oath". See my article "Covenant Terminology in the Ancient Near East and its Influence on the West", in *JAOS*, 93 (1973), pp. 190–191.
123 The joy and willingness express the full and free consent of the covenanted person, and show that there has been no pressure or coercion. There is evidence for such elements in ancient contractual documents; see Y. Muffs, "Joy and Love as Metaphorical Expressions of Willingness and Spontaneity in Cuneiform, Ancient Hebrew and Related Literatures", in *Morton Smith Festschrift*, III, 1975, pp. 1 ff. Cf. *Mekhilta Baḥodesh*, ed. Lauterbach, II, p. 230, "When all the people stood together at Mount Sinai to receive the Torah, they all made up their minds alike to accept the reign of God joyfully". See also the benediction following the evening Shema: "They willingly accepted His sovereignty over them...with great joy, etc." For a similar formulation in swearing loyalty to Roman emperors, see my article "The Loyalty Oath" (n. 81, above), pp. 406 f.
124 For joy on the Shavuot festival, see Deut. 16.11. In relation to the Sinaitic covenant, see the targumim on Ex. 24.11: "They rejoiced in their sacrifices".

twofold significance: the first fruits celebration after seven weeks of harvest, and the occasion for renewing the covenant.[125]

The twofold meaning of Shavuot appears in the Book of Jubilees (6.21):

> For it is the feast of weeks and the feast of first-fruits: this feast is twofold and of a double nature.[126]

The same is evident from the Temple Scroll, where it is said of this holy day: "It is the festival of Shavuot, and the festival of the First Fruits, for an everlasting memorial (page 19, 9)".[127] In my opinion, the last (added) phrase is intended to stress the special importance of this festival.

The sounding of the shofar at the ceremony recorded in II Chronicles 15 was an accompaniment to the oath-taking. In accordance with the position set forth by this paper, the same holds good for the sounding of the shofar in Psalm 81.3.[128]

2. The Book of Jubilees gives us a very clear description of the Festival of Giving the Torah. It tells us that the heavenly tablets determined that Shavuot should be observed in the month of Sivan as

---

125 On the tendency for dual interpretation of names in Chronicles, see Y. Zakowitz, "Duality of Name Interpretation", thesis submitted to the Hebrew University of Jerusalem, 1971, pp. 166 ff.

126 On this passage, see R.H. Charles, *The Book of Jubilees*. In n. 21, p. 53, Charles writes: "Why this festival should be said to be 'of a double nature' I do not see." But as we have explained, the duality consists of the agricultural-cum-historical meaning of Shavuot. It should be added that in the Book of Jubilees, this festival is related to the various covenants which the Deity made with the Patriarchs (see below). Thus there is an additional duality — the commitment which God made on this day to the patriarchs, on the one hand, and the commitment which the Israelites made to God on this day, on the other.

127 See Yadin's note to *The Temple Scroll*, I, p. 84.

128 Philo (*De legibus*, II, 188) says that the purpose of sounding the shofar on Rosh Hashanah is to remind us of the Giving of the Torah. In this he was apparently influenced by the liturgy of the *shofarot* section on Rosh Hashanah. ("You revealed Yourself in Your cloud of glory...and appeared in the sound of the shofar"). The truth, however, is that the shofar symbolized the proclamation of God's sovereignty (see above, n. 16). It was Mowinckel who originally called attention to this fact. Compare Ps. 47.6 ff. — the actual Psalm which is recited before the sounding of the shofar. The Sinaitic shofar is mentioned in the *shofarot* liturgy simply as one of the ten biblical verses on this theme, assembled with no necessary connection to Rosh Hashanah itself.

the occasion for the annual renewal of the covenant (6.17). Indeed, according to the author of Jubilees, the covenant with Noah was also made in the month of Sivan, and Noah was the first to celebrate Shavuot; and the covenant with Abraham "between the pieces" (Gen. 15) also took place in the middle of the month of Sivan:

> On the day we made a covenant with Abraham, like unto the covenant which we made with Noah in that same month; and Abraham renewed the festival and its statute for all time (Jubilees 14.20).

On the fifteenth of the month of Sivan, the date of Shavuot according to the Book of Jubilees[129] as well as in the calendar of the Qumran sect,[130] the LORD appears to Abram and promises him in a solemn covenant that he will have descendants. It is then that Abram is commanded concerning circumcision, and he immediately complies (chapter 15). Subsequently Isaac is born on Shavuot (halfway through the month of Sivan) and is circumcised on his eighth day (16.13). To Jacob, too, God appears in the middle of Sivan (Chap. 44). The covenants with Noah and Abraham are solemnized by sacrifices (6.3; 14.19), just like the covenant at Sinai (Ex. 24.3 ff; cf. Ps. 50.5) and the covenant in Asa's reign (II Chron. 15.11).

3. It was the practice of the Qumran sect to renew the covenant every year (Manual of Discipline, col. I, 16f.). According to a text from cave IV, not yet published, this ceremony was conducted on the Festival of Shavuot.[131]

4. The Therapeutae in Egypt, who are described by Philo in his *De vita contemplativa*, bear strong resemblances to the Qumran sect, and they regard Shavuot as the most important festival (*megistē heortē*).[132] They observe the night preceding it as a "watch-night", singing songs of praise. As we shall note a little later, similar activities are standard

---

129 See Charles, op. cit. n. 126 above, p. 52.
130 See S. Talmon, "The Calendrical System of the Qumran Sect" (Hebrew), *Essays in Memory of A.L. Sukenik*, 1957, pp. 77 ff.
131 See J.T. Milik, *Ten Years of Discovery in the Wilderness of Judaea*, 1959, pp. 113 ff.; also M. Delcor, 'Pentecôte,' in *Diction. Bibl. Suppl.*, 1966, pp. 870–871.
132 To be sure, it is not specifically stated that the fiftieth day mentioned is the fiftieth day after the Omer offering; but the phrase "after seven weeks" (*di' hepta hebdomadon*) and the above-quoted "most important festival" strengthen the assumption that Shavuot is meant.

Jewish practice. We are not told how the day itself was observed, but it is reasonable to assume that the Therapeutae conducted a covenant renewal ceremony, just as the members of the Qumran sect did.

5. Shavuot as the Festival of the Giving of the Torah is the background for the description in The Acts of the Apostles, chapter 2, of the meeting of the first congregation of Christians. We read that when Pentecost (Shavuot) arrived, all the Apostles were gathered together. Suddenly there was a loud sound from heaven, like a rushing storm, and it filled the house. Then tongues of fire appeared, and rested on each of them. They were filled with the holy spirit, and began to speak in tongues, as the spirit moved them (verses 1–4).

The essential elements of this account derive from traditions associated with the Giving of the Torah at Mount Sinai:

a. The sound from heaven and the tongues of fire come from aggadic descriptions (dating from the last years of the Second Commonwealth) of the theophany at Horeb. The midrashim, the Aramaic Targums and Philo Judaeus all describe the words heard at Sinai as burning flames, based on the text, "All the people *saw* the voices (*qoloth*) and the flames (*lapidim*)" (Ex. 20.18). R. Akiba commented:

> They saw something fiery coming out of the mouth of the Almighty and hewing on the tablets, as it is written (Ps. 29) "The voice of the LORD heweth out flames of fire" (*Mekhilta de R. Ishmael, Baḥodesh*, 9, ed. Lauterbach, II, p. 266).

In the same vein Philo writes that the flame turned into articulate speech which could be understood by the listeners but seemed to be seen rather than heard (*De decalogo*, 46). Similar descriptions can be found in Targum Pseudo-Jonathan, in Targum fragments from the Genizah and in the Neofiti Targum:

> When a work had issued from the mouth of the Holy One, blessed be His Name, in the form of sparks or thunderbolts or flames like torches of fire...then a flame on the right and a tongue of fire on the left would fly through the air and return and hover over the heads of the Israelites, and then return and incise itself into the tablets.[133]

---

133 About versions in various targumim, see J. Potin, *La fête juive de la Pentecôte, Etude des textes liturgiques*, II, pp. 37 ff.

This description also derives from Deut. 33.2: "At his right hand was a fiery law for them," on which the Sifre comments:

> As each Commandment proceeded from the mouth of the Holy One, blessed be He, it went forth from the right side...to the left of Israel, and circled around the Israelite camp...and the Holy One, blessed be He, would receive it back and etch it on the tablets as it is written: "the voice of the LORD heweth out flames of fire" (*Sifre Deut.*, ed. Finkelstein, p. 399).

b. What we are told in Acts about the flames which separated into tongues, in whose train the Apostles began to speak in various tongues, has its origin in a midrash, according to which each commandment divided into seventy tongues, i.e., into the languages of all the nations.[134] Thus, we have a tradition quoted in the name of R. Johanan:

> What is the meaning of the verse "The LORD giveth the word proclaiming tidings to a great host" (Ps. 68.12)? Every word that proceeded from the Holy One, blessed be He, divided itself into seventy tongues (Shab. 88b).[135]

A little later in the same context we read:

> It was taught in the school of Rabbi Ishmael: The verse "My word is like fire, says the LORD, and like a hammer that shatters rock!" (Jer. 23.29) can be taken to mean that just as the hammer throws off a shower of sparks, so too every word that emanated from the Holy One separated into seventy languages.

What is especially significant for present purposes is the correspondence between the phrasing of the midrash "the word (like fire) separated into seventy tongues", and the phrasing in the Acts of the Apostles: "There appeared to them tongues as of fire, distributed and resting on each one" (*kai opthesan autois diamerizomenai glossai hosei puros*: Acts 2.3).

In the aggadic tradition, the Word is divided into seventy tongues, so that it might be spread among all the nations. So too, the Mishnah says

---

134 On the existence of seventy nations in the world, see Gen. 10 and my brief commentary on Genesis (Hebrew), Masada, 1975. For rabbinic midrash on the theme, see L. Ginzberg, *Legends of the Jews*, V, pp. 194–195, n. 72.

135 See *Midrash Tehillim*, ed. Buber, p. 22. For other sources, L. Ginzberg, *Legends of the Jews*, III, p. 97, and n. 214.

that on the stones of the altar on Mount Ebal (Deut. 27) were inscribed all the words of the Torah in seventy tongues — i.e. all the languages of mankind (M. Sot. VII:5).[136] In the same way, the Christian tradition has tongues of fire which separate and settle upon those present at the revelation, giving each of them the power to spread the new teaching in all the languages of the world, as described in the sequel.[137]

It should be added that the *Sifre* on Deuteronomy 33, quoted above in connection with the Word as flame (ed. Finkelstein, p. 399), also speaks of the Torah having been given in several languages:

> When the Holy One, Blessed be He, revealed Himself in order to give the Torah to Israel, He did not speak to them in one language only, but in four, as it is written (Deut. 33.2) "The LORD came from Sinai" — in Hebrew; "He shone upon them from Seir" (Edom) — that is, in Roman; "He appeared from Mount Paran" — that is, in Arabic; "And approached from Ribeboth-kodesh" — that means, in Aramaic (*Sifre,* ed. Finkelstein, p. 395).

c. The tongues of fire which came to rest[138] on the heads of the disciples (Acts 2.3) are reminiscent of the coronets with which the Israelites are said to have been crowned at Mount Sinai.[139] These crowns are simply the luminosity of the Shekhinah over their heads.[140]

---

136 See Tos. Sotah, VIII, 6–7; also *Mekhilta Deut.* as published by Schechter in *Israel Lewy Festschrift* (1911), p. 189. For a full discussion, S. Lieberman, *Tosefta Kifshuto*, part 8, pp. 699–701.

137 See Potin, n. 133 above, pp. 310 ff.

138 *ekathisen.* The verb *kathixo* is used by the Septuagint to translate "rested" (i.e., the Ark), in Gen. 8.4.

139 See *Pesiqta d'rav Kahana* on *nahamu*, ed. Mandelbaum, p. 268, and the parallels cited there; also Shab. 88a. Note the discussion by Urbach in *The Sages*, pp. 148 ff. He distinguishes between the older sources, which have God himself placing the coronets or haloes on the heads of the Israelites, and the later sources which assign the task to the angels.

140 Compare "You have adorned him with glory and majesty" (Ps. 8.6) which refers to divine radiance around the head (cf. the Akkadian *melammu*). See also Job 19.9, "He has stripped me of my glory / Removed the crown from my head". The "chaplet of glory" placed on Moses' head (*kelil tifereth*, Ben Sira 45.5, corresponding to the Psalmist's "glory and majesty") as mentioned in the Sabbath morning liturgy refers to the radiance around his head (Ex. 34.29 ff.). In the Dead Sea Scrolls it is called *kelil kavod (Temple Scroll* 4, 1.8; *Qumran Hodaya*, 9, line 25). In Hellenistic literature this crown is called *diadema tes doxes*. See

Elsewhere[141] I have dealt with the fact that this tradition about people[142] on whom tongues of fire descend, and who are then filled with the holy spirit, all derive from Numbers, chapter 11. That context speaks of the elders upon whom the spirit rested, whereupon they became the leaders of the congregation.

The institution of the seventy elders corresponds to the seventy members of the Sanhedrin, who were required to know seventy languages.[143] In Acts this tradition is transferred to the founding assembly (the Mother Church) of the Christian community. According to the Christian tradition, the Holy Spirit also rested on the leadership of that community as once it had on the Elders of Israel, and like the Sanhedrin they too were able to speak in many tongues, on account of the tongues of fire which rested on them.

The time of Israel's first revelation — the one at Sinai — became the focus for the development of traditions about other revelatory experiences of a mystical nature which were said to have occurred on Shavuot. Josephus tells us that on the night of that festival before the destruction of the Temple, priests in the Temple heard heavenly voices as of a host (saying) "we are departing hence" (*Bellum*, IV.299).[144] In sixteenth century Safed, Rabbi Joseph Karo and his associates sat together at the night-long *tiqqun* of Shavuot. Suddenly he uttered sounds in a voice not his own. The entire company fell into a swoon.[145]

On another Shavuot night the holy spirit was supposed to have descended on Nathan of Gaza, the faithful messenger of Shabbetai Zevi. He too fell into a swoon and uttered sounds which were later interpreted to mean that Shabbetai Zevi was worthy of becoming King of Israel.[146]

R. Reitzenstein, *Hellenistische Mysterienreligionen*, 1927, pp. 359–360. This is identical with the crown which adorns "the heads of the righteous who bask in the affulgence of the Divine Presence" (Ber. 17a). On the subject of glory as a crown, see my article *"Kabod"* in *Theōlogisches Wörterbuch zum AT*, ed. Botterweck-Ringgren, IV, pp. 23–40.

141 In my article in *Immanuel*, 8 (1978), pp. 16 ff.

142 It is not clear whether Acts 2.4 refers to the 120 persons mentioned in 1.15, or only to the 12 apostles.

143 See Tos. Sanh. 8.1; Yer. Sheq. V:1 48d; Bavli Sanh. 17a and Men. 65a.

144 Comp. Tacitus, *Historia*, V:13.

145 On this see R.J.Z. Werblowsky, *Joseph Karo*, 1962, pp. 19–21.

146 G. Scholem, *Shabetai Zevi*, I (Hebrew), Am Oved 1975, p. 178. To my mind, the fainting on Shavuot night is connected with the tradition that all present at the

Vestiges of this special status of this festival, in the form of various customs, persist up to the present day. There are, for example, certain liturgical and halakhic rules connected with the "three days of circumambulation." There is the long watch-night of study on the festival night (*tiqqun*). There is the reading of the Ten Commandments on the day of the festival, together with special liturgical introductions, such as the reading of *Aqdamut*, and the recitation of *azharot*. Finally, there is the special form of cantillation in which the Ten Commandments themselves are read while the congregation rises to its feet.

Translated by Gershon Levi

theophany at Mount Sinai lost consciousness. Comp. Shab. 88b: "Each time a Commandment issued forth from the Holy One, the Israelites fainted, as it is written 'I was faint because of what he said' " (Cant. 5.6). See also the text published by Mann in *HUCA*, 2 (1925), p. 330, from a genizah version of *shofarot* for Rosh Hashanah: "His children quailed in the presence of the Almighty, and could not receive the Commandments from the Divine effulgence that rested on them. They recoiled and fainted, all of them, and fell on their faces and lost consciousness at the sound of the Commandments." J. Mann, *HUCA*, 2 (1925), p. 330.

2. THE TENTH COMMANDMENT IN THE LIGHT OF FOUR DEUTERONOMIC LAWS

ALEXANDER ROFÉ

I

The exact meaning of the Tenth Commandment has been disputed by both ancient and modern interpreters of the Bible. Does "You shall not covet" (Ex. 20. 14)[1] simply forbid envious desire for what is not ours? Or is it more concrete, prohibiting the *taking of steps* to satisfy that desire?

The latter interpretation is the one followed by the ancient halakhic midrashim. The *Mekhilta de Rabbi Ishmael* says:

> Perhaps the Commandment forbids coveting in words? Not so; for the Torah states (Deut. 7. 25) "You shall not covet the silver and gold on them and *take* it for yourself". Just as in that case one is culpable only on committing an act, so too in the present instance.[2]

The *Mekhilta de Rabbi Simeon bar Yoḥai* is even more explicit:

> The Commandment here reads "You shall not covet", but the text in Deuteronomy (5.18) goes on to say "nor shall you crave". The purpose is to make craving a separate offense, and coveting a separate offense. For if a person craves, he will end up by coveting.... Craving is in the heart, as Scripture says "if your soul craves" (Deut. 12. 20) while coveting is an actual deed, as in the verse "You shall not covet the silver and gold on them and *take* it for yourselves" (Deut. 7. 25).[3]

---

1 Hebrew *ḥmd* is here translated by "to covet", although the ambiguity of the Hebrew verb does not show in this English equivalent.

2 *Mekhilta de Rabbi Ishmael*, ed. Horovitz–Rabin, Jerusalem 1960, p. 235; cf. Lauterbach ed. and transl., Philadelphia, II, p. 266.

3 *Mekhilta de Rabbi Simeon bar Yoḥai*, ed. D. Hoffmann, Frankfurt-on-Main 1905, p. 112.

45

This interpretation, according to which coveting involves action, became the standard halakhic ruling. Maimonides lists it as prohibition number 265, and elaborates in some detail:

> This Commandment admonishes us not to contrive schemes for acquiring what belongs to someone else. That is what the Exalted One means by saying "You shall not covet your neighbor's house". As the *Mekhilta* puts it, "Perhaps the Commandment forbids coveting in words? Not so; etc." Thus it is made clear that this injunction warns against developing stratagems for getting hold of what belongs to someone else, even if we are prepared to buy it at a high price. Any action of this sort is a violation of "You shall not covet".

Similarly, in the next prohibition on his list (number 266) which deals with craving, Maimonides writes:

> One's desire for the object may grow stronger, to the point of devising a scheme to obtain it, and one will not stop begging and pressing the owner to sell it, or give it in exchange for something better or more valuable. If a person has his way, he breaks not only this prohibition (of craving) but "You shall not covet" as well, since by his persistence and scheming he has acquired a thing with which the owner did not want to part.[4]

Liberal Protestant theologians, unaware of the halakhic sources but eager to find differences between the Hebrew Bible and the New Testament, also interpreted the Tenth Commandment in this way.[5] So too did later scholars and commentators, although not necessarily motivated by the same considerations.[6] Today this is the interpretation

4   *Sefer ha-Miṣwot*, ed. J. Kafeh, Jerusalem 1971, nos. 265, 266; cf. transl. by C.B. Chavel, London-New York 1967, II pp. 250–251. Maimonides makes it clear that one does not violate this precept unless and until he *takes* the object coveted. See also his *Mishneh Torah, Torts*: Theft and Loss, I. 10. He defines coveting, in contrast to craving, as engaging one's thoughts and devising schemes to acquire the desired object, including putting pressure on the owner. However, it seems that further steps are needed to consummate the transgression.

5   Ernst H. Meier, *Die ursprüngliche Form des Dekalogs*, Mannheim 1846, pp. 70–74; L. Lemme, *Die religionsgeschichtliche Bedeutung des Dekalogs*, Breslau 1880, pp. 107–112.

6   R.H. Kennett, *Deuteronomy and the Decalogue*, Cambridge 1920, pp. 67–68; J. Herrmann, "Das zehnte Gebot", *Sellin Festschrift*, Leipzig 1927, pp. 69–82; A Alt,

most widely accepted by non-Jewish scholars, on the basis of the following reasons:

1. In a series of commandments that refer to deeds, one that forbids thoughts seems oddly out of place.

2. But if thoughts *are* to be forbidden, why choose a mere craving for property which may only lead to theft or robbery? Would it not be more appropriate to forbid jealousy which, like Cain's, can lead to murder (Gen. 4)?

3. The root *ḥmd* originally denoted a feeling that inevitably leads to a certain action. This is apparent in the frequent occurrence of the sequential pair *ḥmd* : *lqḥ* ("take"), as in Deut. 7. 25: "You shall not *covet* the silver and gold that is on them and *take* them for yourselves". The same sequence occurs in Joshua 6. 18: "But as for you, keep away from the devoted things, lest you *covet* and *take* of the devoted things" (reading *taḥmedu* with the Septuagint).[7] So too Joshua 7. 21: "I saw among the spoils...and I *coveted* and *took* them".

A similar sequence is formed by *ḥmd* : *gzl* ("rob", "seize"), as in "They *covet* fields and *seize* them (*we-gazalu*), houses and take them away" (Micah 2. 2). The description in Proverbs of the fate that awaits the adulterer says: "Do not lust (*taḥmod*) for her beauty nor let her captivate you (*tiqaḥakha*) with her eyes" (Prov. 6. 25).

The sequential relationship between *ḥmd* and the resulting action is so close that at times the act is not even mentioned. For example: "I will drive out nations from your path and enlarge your territory. No one will covet your land when you go up to appear before the LORD your God three times a year" (Ex. 34. 24). This verse is not meant to allay supposed fears of the pilgrims that the nations will merely eye the land of Israel with desire or will envy the Israelites because of their territory. The promise is that the nations will not *endanger* the land's borders.

"Das Verbot des Diebstahls im Dekalog", *Kleine Schriften zur Geschichte des Volkes Israel*, I Munich 1953, pp. 333–340; J.J. Stamm, *The Ten Commandments in Recent Research* (transl. with additions by M.E. Andrew), London 1967, pp. 101–105; E. Nielsen, *The Ten Commandments in New Perspective* (Engl. transl.), London 1968, pp. 13n., 43; B.S. Childs, *Exodus:A Commentary* (OTL), London 1974, pp. 425–428.

7   M. Weinfeld, "The Ten Commandments as Interpreted in Jewish Tradition" (Hebrew) in: *Reflections on the Bible: Selected Studies in Memory of Yishai Ron*, Tel Aviv 1977, pp. 109–121, n. 1; see also N.H. Tur-Sinai, "*Metatheses in the Biblical Text*" (Hebrew) in: *Ha-Lashon ve-ha-Sefer*, II, Jerusalem 1951, p. 111.

That is to say, coveting here implies the adoption of measures to satisfy a desire.[8]

4. Another proof is that in Phoenician the root *ḥmd* has the semantic value of "desiring and seizing", as proven by the Karatepe inscription. There, to be sure, the noun *ḥmdt* means "lust", "desire"; however, the verb *yḥmd* expresses both "wanting" and "taking possession" as well.[9]

According to this interpretation, then, the Commandment "You shall not covet your neighbor's house" forbids not mere thoughts and feelings, but rather practical schemes and real actions aimed at acquiring the property of someone else. If so, what it forbids does not merely relate to illegal acts, but rather, as Maimonides explains: "This injunction warns against developing stratagems for getting hold of what belongs to someone else, even if we are prepared to buy it at a high price. Any action of this sort is a violation of "You shall not covet".[10]

The other interpretation of the Commandment appears for the first time in the Septuagint, which translates "You shall not covet" as *ouk epithumeseis*. The verb *epithumeo* means to "crave", "desire", "long for". It is derived from *thumos*, which connotes "spirit", "soul", "desire", "longing". Here the Commandment is understood as forbidding envious thoughts or feelings about what belongs to someone else, even if unaccompanied by schemes or actions to obtain the desired object. This interpretation was greatly developed and elaborated by Philo,[11] who detached the prohibition from the object "your neighbor's house", and read it as forbidding *epithumia*, i.e. desire and appetite in general. He specified: lust for lucre, love of honor, craving (sexual) for a beautiful body, pleasure-seeking and gluttony.[12] In his view,

---

8   In my view, we must leave out of consideration such passages as Ps. 68. 17: "the mountain God desired (*ḥamad*) as His dwelling / The LORD shall abide there forever". When God is the subject, there is of course no distinction between desire and its actualization; see the discussion below on Psalm 132. 13–14.

9   H. Donner–W. Röllig, *Kanaanäische und aramäische Inschriften*, I–III, Wiesbaden 1962–1964, Nr. 26.

10 *The Book of Commandments*, No. 265 (see above, n. 4). According to this interpretation, the woman of valor in the Book of Proverbs, about whom it is said: "She sets her mind on an estate and acquires it; she plants a vineyard by her own labors", disregarded the Tenth Commandment. There is a similar discrepancy between Deuteronomy 24. 10–11 and Proverbs 22. 26–27, on which see below.

11 Philo, *De decalogo*, 142–153; *De specialibus legibus*, IV, 79–131, apud: *Philo, with an English Translation*, by F.H. Colson, VII-VIII, Cambridge, Mass. 1937–1939.

12 *De specialibus legibus*, IV, 79 ff.

All the wars of Greeks and barbarians between themselves or against each other, so familiar to the tragic stage are sprung from one source — desire (*epithumia*) whether for money, glory or pleasure. These bring disaster to the human race.[13]

Philo maintains that the curtailment of desire in the Tenth Commandment is the general rule, while Moses through particular statutes chose to focus his battle against desire on one single appetite, namely gluttony, which he fought by means of the dietary laws. Such laws are intended to teach self-restraint with regard to all the other appetites as well.[14] This is in keeping with Philo's general approach. He regarded the statutes laid down by Moses as particulars derived from the general principle, namely the Ten Commandments — which had been given to Israel directly, in God's own voice.[15]

Philo's midrashic interpretation remained an exception in Jewish exegesis. However, beginning in the Middle Ages Jewish commentators, the first of them unwittingly, returned to the interpretation offered by the Septuagint, explicitly rejecting that of the *Mekhilta*. We find this in Ibn Ezra, Sforno, Luzzatto,[16] and more recently in B. Jacob, M.D.U. Cassuto, N. Leibowitz and M. Greenberg.[17]

This reversal, with Christian commentators today holding to the original halakhic interpretation, while Jewish authorities dissociate themselves from it, is no doubt related to the basic approaches of the two sides. At least some of the Christian scholars, predisposed by the

---

13 *De decalogo*, 153.
14 H.A. Wolfson, *Philo, Foundations of Religious Philosophy in Judaism, Christianity and Islam*, Cambridge, Mass. 1947, pp. 225–237. According to Wolfson, Philo was influenced by Aristotle, who called the conquest of inordinate desire *enkrateia*.
15 Ibid., IV. 132. The idea that all the mitzvot are dependent on the Ten Commandments also appears in Sa'adiah Gaon and in Judah Halevi; see M. Stein, *Philo of Alexandria: His Works and His Philosophy* (Hebrew), Warsaw 1937, pp. 124–132.
16 In their commentaries on Ex. 20.17.
17 B. Jacob, "The Decalogue", *JQR*, n.s. 14 (1923–4) pp. 141–187; U. Cassuto, *Commentary on Exodus* (Hebrew), Jerusalem 1952; idem, "*Dibberot, 'Aseret ha-dibberot*", in *Encyclopedia Miqra'it* (Hebrew), Vol. 2, Jerusalem 1952, p. 595; N. Leibowitz, *New Studies in the Book of Exodus* (Hebrew), Jerusalem 1970², pp. 248–255; M. Greenberg, "Decalogue", *Encyclopaedia Judaica*, Jerusalem 1972, 5, cols. 1435–1446.

sermon on the Mount,[18] expect to find in the Decalogue, as the basic document of the Mosaic religion, those elements of the legalistic approach which they ascribe to Judaism.[19] Whereas some of the Jews, taking up the challenge, try to prove that God's concern with intentions is already found in the Ten Commandments.

However, this kind of debate does little to advance our understanding of the Scriptures. Concern with intentions does play an important part in ancient Israelite religion, as can be seen for example in the liturgies of entrance into the Sanctuary (Is. 33. 14–17; Psalms 15 and 24) which resemble the Ten Commandments.[20] These liturgies declare that one who ascends the mountain of the LORD must have, not only "clean hands", but "a pure heart" as well (Ps. 24. 4). However, the meaning of these passages does not at all affect the interpretation of any one of the Ten Commandments.

II

One may argue that an interpretation of the Tenth Commandment antedating those of the Septuagint and the *Mekhilta* is already present within the Scriptures themselves. When the Decalogue is repeated in Deuteronomy (5. 18) the Tenth Commandment is formulated as follows:

> You shall not covet (*thmd*) your neighbor's wife, nor shall you crave (*tt'wh*) your neighbor's house or his field or his male or female slaves or his ox or his ass, or anything that is your neighbor's.

To be sure, it is only in the Masoretic text that this reading is attested with any certainty. Other texts such as the Samaritan Pentateuch,[21] the manuscript of Deuteronomy from Qumran Cave IV,[22] and the two

---

18   Matt. 5. 27–28: "You have heard that it was said, 'You shall not commit adultery.' But I say to you that every one who looks at a woman lustfully has already committed adultery with her in his heart".

19   Note 5, above.

20   See S. Mowinckel, *Le décalogue*, Paris 1927, pp. 141–156.

21   On this point the Samaritan tradition is perfectly consistent; see A. von Gall, *Der hebräische Pentateuch der Samaritaner*, Giessen 1918, ad loc.

22   *Scrolls From the Wilderness of the Dead Sea — A Guide to the Exhibition Arranged by the Smithsonian Institution*, London 1965, Pl. 19.4Q Deut[m](Scil[n], vide p. 31).

phylacteries from Qumran which contain the text of Deuteronomy 5[23]
— all these use the same verb twice: "You shall not covet (*ḥmd*) nor
shall you covet (*ḥmd*), when rendering Deuteronony 5.18.[24] In the
Nash Papyrus there is a peculiar variant that makes sense only as an
attempt to alter *tḥmd* so as to bring it into line with the reading *tt'wh*.[25]

Even though the Masoretic reading has so little support on this
point, it is unlikely that scribes from the fifth century onward would
have been so bold as to amend the Ten Commandments by changing
"covet" to "crave". To the extent that they did make emendations, it is
more reasonable to suppose that they tried to bring the text of the
Decalogue in Deuteronomy into line with its primary formulation in
Exodus 20. That is what was done in other passages in the Qumran
Cave IV document, and what was attempted in the Nash Papyrus. It
may be concluded, therefore that the Masoretic text of Deuteronomy
5. 18, though unsupported by any other sources, transmits an ancient
reading from late pre-exilic or early postexilic times.

What does the variant "You shall not crave" reveal about the meaning
of "You shall not covet"? Under the rules of philology, the variant
cannot provide us with a decisive interpretation. We can suppose that
the formulator of the Decalogue as we now have it in Deuteronomy 5
had before him an early version of the Ten Commandments, like the
one in Exodus 20. He saw "You shall not covet" and replaced it with
"You shall not crave". Why?

Perhaps he thought the two verbs could function as synonyms.
(Compare, for example, the verbs *zbḥ* and *šḥt* in the parallel verses
Ex. 23. 18 and Ex. 34. 25). But he may also have felt *ḥmd* was too

23   Y. Yadin, *Tefillin from Qumran (XQ Phyl. 1–4)* Jerusalem 1969 (transl. from
     Eretz Israel, 9, W.F. Albright Volume); J.T. Milik ed., *Qumran Grotte 4 II
     (Discoveries in the Judaean Desert* VI), Oxford 1977, p. 65.

24   The Septuagint cannot serve as evidence here, for it translates both *ḥmd* and *'wh*
     (and their derivatives) by *epithumeo*. The order of the predicates in LXX is the
     same as in the masoretic text, which uses two different verbs — *lō taḥmōd* and *lo
     tit'aweh*. However, the same order is followed by the Qumran phylacteries, which
     use only the verb *ḥmd* (twice).

25   The reading is *l'ttmwh*: the *ḥeth* has been changed to a *taw*, the *daleth* to a *he'*; only
     the *mem* remains unchanged. A good photograph of the Nash Papyrus appears in
     N.H. Tur-Sinai, *Ha-Lashon ve-ha-Sefer*, I, Jerusalem 1954[2], facing p. 12; see also
     the comments by M.Z. Segal, "The Nash Papyrus", in: *Tradition and Criticism*
     (Hebrew), Jerusalem 1957, pp. 227 ff.

ambiguous and wanted a more precise term. (Compare a similar change
as between II Ki. 20. 7 and Is. 38.21: *wys 'ymw > wymrhw*.)[26] Or he may
have thought that *ḥmd* had a connotation inappropriate in this context.
(Compare, for example, the replacement of "The anger of the LORD
again flared up against Israel" in II Sam. 24. 1, by the phrase "Satan
arose against Israel" in I Chron. 21. 1.) In other words, "You shall not
crave" may be an ancient interpretation of "You shall not covet'",
although its antiquity would be no proof that it reflects the original
meaning. On the other hand, the phrase may be a revision of the Tenth
Commandment, one that sought to give that Commandment a meaning
it did not originally have.

In any event, what is the meaning of *lo tit'aweh*? It has recently been
argued that it means the same as *lo taḥmod*, and that in biblical
Hebrew, as in Akkadian, verbs that express a feeling or desire develop
a secondary meaning, and come to denote also the deed that actualizes
the feeling.[27] For example, *śn'* ("detest") when applied to a woman
sometimes means "to divorce"; and in the Elephantine papyri, the noun
śn'h means "divorce".[28] To this we may add an instance relating to the
opposite sentiment: Biblical Hebrew and Ugaritic *'rś* (cf. Akkadian
erēšu) meant "to desire". It developed the meanings "to ask" (a wife)
and "to betroth".[29] Allegedly, this linguistic process can be observed in
Proverbs 23. 6, which cautions: "Do not eat of a stingy man's food",
and in the parallel strophe adds "Do not crave for his dainties". The
craving to eat is here presented as a parallel to the act of eating itself.

But none of this can decisively determine the meaning of the verb *'wh*
and its derivatives as used in the Bible. In all genres of biblical literature
— law (Deut. 12. 20, 14. 26), narrative (II Sam. 23. 15), prophecy
(Amos 5. 18; Micah 7. 1), poetry (Ps. 10. 17) and wisdom (Prov. 13. 12)
— in all these *'wh* connotes desire only without any accompanying

26   *mrḥ* is a Second Commonwealth term; see the Ben Yehuda Dictionary, s.v.
27   W.L. Moran, "The Conclusion of the Decalogue (Ex. 20. 17 = Deut. 5. 21)", *CBQ*,
     29 (1967), pp. 543–554. Moran relies on Pedersen's studies about the thought
     patterns of the ancient Hebrews; see p. 545 of his article.
28   C.F. Jean–J. Hoftijzer, *Dictionnaire des inscriptions Sémitiques de l'ouest*,
     Leiden 1965, p. 34. These documents were republished by B. Porten (in
     collaboration with J.C. Greenfield) in *Jews of Elephantine and Arameans of
     Syene: Aramaic Texts with Translation*, Jerusalem 1976.
29   W. Baumgartner, *Hebräisches und aramäisches Lexikon zum Alten Testament*,
     Lief. I, Leiden 1967, pp. 88–89.

action. The proverbs about the sluggard are particularly instructive on this point:

> A lazy man craves, but has nothing; the diligent man shall feast on rich fare (Prov. 13. 4).
> The craving of a lazy man kills him, for his hands refuse to work. All day long he is seized with craving, while the righteous man gives without stint (Prov. 21. 25–26).

In the latter proverb, *hit'aweh ta'awah*, does not imply the satisfaction of desire (as would be the case if *ḥmd* and *'wh* were synonymous) but implies the exact opposite — desire left dangling.

Only when the subject is God, the Absolute Sovereign, does the distinction between the wish (expressed by *'wh*) and its realization fade. Take Psalm 132. 13–14:

> For the LORD has chosen Zion / He has desired it for his seat /
> "This is my resting place for all time /
> Here will I dwell, for I desire it".

In one verse only (Prov. 23. 6) can *'wh* possibly be understood to denote both a desire and its satisfaction; and even then, only if the parallel strophe is regarded as perfectly synonymous — which is not necessarily the case. For the most part, the appearance of absolute synonymity is only superficial.[30] The second strophe in a biblical parallelism serves one of several possible purposes; it may underscore an idea or buttress it, or perhaps carry it one step further. Accordingly, the proverb should be understood as saying,

"Do not eat a stingy man's food; do not *even* crave his dainties".

In the last analysis, our understanding of the semantics of biblical Hebrew ought to be derived above all from the usages of the people whose language it was — that is, from the Bible itself as well as from contemporary Hebrew-Canaanite sources. These should be given priority over similar phenomena in other languages, and over generalizations about the thought-patterns of the ancient Hebrews.

An examination of the root *'wh* and its derivatives in the Bible indicates that the Deuteronomic author, in using the words "You shall

---

30   J.L. Kugel, *The Idea of Biblical Poetry — Parallelism and Its History*, New Haven 1981, p. 8: "Now by its very afterwardness (the) B (clause) will have an *emphatic* character...".

not crave", went beyond the original prohibition against coveting, adding even longing thoughts for the property of one's fellowman.[31] The original prohibition, as we have interpreted it, applied only to actual machinations and deeds — legal as well as illegal — aimed at acquiring control of someone else's property.

III

It appears to me, however, that another — and different — interpretation of the Tenth Commandment is to be found elsewhere in Deuteronomy. Embodied as it is in statutes, this interpretation is practical and illustrative, rather than conceptual, and cannot therefore be suspected of being a theoretical innovation, aimed at re-interpreting the original law. Admittedly, this interpretation is not necessarily correct, for the statutes could have been formulated as illustrations of a later understanding of what this Commandment means. Yet if these statutes do reflect an interpretation of the Commandment, it would be the most ancient interpretation we have of *lo' taḥmod*.

The statutes to which I refer are the following four which are, as can be seen, similar in language and in content.

1.   You shall not move your neighbor's landmarks, set up by previous generations, in the property that will be allotted to you in the land that the LORD your God is giving you to possess (Deut. 19. 14).
2.   When you enter your neighbor's vineyard, you may eat your fill of the grapes, as many as you want; but you must not put any in your vessel (Deut. 23. 25).
3.   When you enter your neighbor's standing grain, you may pluck ears with your hand; but you must not put a sickle to your neighbor's grain (Deut. 23. 26).
4.   When you make a loan of any sort to your neighbor, you must not enter his house to seize his pledge. You must remain outside, while the man to whom you made the loan brings the pledge out to you (Deut. 24. 10–11).

Each of these four statutes employs the term "your neighbor" (*re'akha*), one of them (23. 26) even twice. Moreover, the internal rhythm with

---

31   Jacob (n. 17 above), Moran (n. 27 above) and others are correct when they observe that *'wh* is a state of mind, while *ḥmd* refers to visual attraction.

which they unfold, especially the first three, is similar to that of the Tenth Commandment. The similarity is most apparent in Deuteronomy 19. 14: negation, followed by a verb in the imperfect, followed by a direct object, followed by "your neighbor". The structure in Deut. 23. 25 and 26, both cast in pseudo-casuistic form,[32] is similar: a particle *ki* instead of *lo'*, a verb in the imperfect, a noun in the construct state followed by "your neighbor". Only Deuteronomy 24. 10–11 diverges somewhat from this pattern. Counterbalancing that, as it were, the concluding statement of 23. 26 ("you must not put a sickle to your neighbor's grain") has the very same structure as the Commandment "You shall not covet your neighbor's house".

This similarity is even more striking in view of the fact that these four statutes are the only places in Deuteronomy where the term *re'akha* is used in laying down norms for interpersonal behavior. True, the term occurs in Deuteronomy 13. 7, but there it has a specific, limited meaning, different from the usage in the four statutes quoted above. In that context — a law directed against idolatry — *re'akha* means, not just anyone, but rather "bosom friend". This is evident from the other individuals mentioned — brother, son, daughter, wife. But as a general rule the statutes in Deuteronomy use different terms to designate one's fellow: "your brother" (*'ahikha*, 15 times): "his brother" (*'ahiv*, 4 times) and "his neighbor" (*re'ehu*, 10 times). Thus, the term "your neighbor" in these four statutes cannot be regarded as either a typical Deuteronomical usage, or as synonymous with "your brother".[33] A reason must be sought for the use of the term in these particular statutes — in them only and nowhere else in Deuteronomy.

Still, the distinctive features just enumerated might be regarded as coincidental were it not that these four statutes also have a similar

32 The pseudo-casuistic formulation is reflected in two features: 1) The conditional clause is not cast in the third person, as is the case in Israelite and ancient Near East casuistic statutes. 2) Whereas in casuistic laws the protasis contains an action, usually a transgression, and the apodosis contains the punishment, in this case the protasis describes an occasion ("when you enter") and the apodosis contains an apodictic commandment. This has been noted by H.W. Gilmer, *The If-You Form in Israelite Law* (SBL, DS 15), Missoula, Mo. 1975, pp. 45 ff.

33 For a similar conclusion, see J. Fichtner, "Der Begriff des 'Nachsten' im Alten Testament", *Gottes Weisheit (GSAT)*, herausg. von K.D. Fricke, Stuttgart 1965, p. 101. On the other hand, as Fichtner correctly observes, in Lev. 19. 16–18 the terms עמך, רעך, אחיך, עמיתך, בני עמיך, are fully synonymous.

content: they are all laws protecting property from seemingly minor infringement. In legal terms, they can be considered laws against various forms of trespass, and hence related to the prohibition against coveting as interpreted in the *Mekhilta*, namely, when action is involved. The relation between "You shall not covet" and these statutes appears to be, that the former is a comprehensive general rule, while the latter are specific instances which concretize that rule. The concretizations here are: the neighbor's field, his vineyard, his standing grain, and the pledge that is within his house.

The relationship we have pointed out between the Tenth Commandment and these four statutes corresponds to some extent to the basic conception in Moses' second address to the people (Deut. 4. 44–26. 19).

In that address the Ten Commandments and "the instruction, laws and norms" (5. 28; 6. 1; etc.) are spoken of as integral parts of the covenant made in Horeb, the only difference being that the Decalogue was given to Israel directly by God, whereas the other laws were mediated to them through Moses, because the people feared God's direct revelation (Deut. 5. 1–6. 4).[34]

Now if these are indeed different parts of one covenant, we might expect the author to let them correspond one to the other. But what correspondence can there be between a brief passage delivered first by God and called "words" (Deut. 5. 19) and a lengthy address delivered by Moses defined as "instruction, laws and norms"? In part, at least, it would be the correspondence that exists between a general rule and its particularizations, between the principle and its applications. This is how Philo, Saadiah and Judah Halevi conceived of the relationship between the Decalogue and the other laws of the Torah. In the instances at hand, then, the resemblances in both language and content between the four statutes quoted above and the Tenth Commandment, are not merely coincidental, but reflect an ancient attempt to concretize and exemplify the meaning of "You shall not covet".[35]

---

34   Cf. A. Rofé, "Deut. 5. 28–6. 1 — Composition and Text, etc.", *Henoch* 7 (1985), pp. 1–14. Nielsen, in his book on the Ten Commandments (n. 6 above), completely missed the thrust of Deut. 5.

35   L'Hour likewise perceives groups of statutes in Deuteronomy as attempts to establish a social order on the principles of the Ten Commandments: the prohibition of idol worship in the Second Commandment is expanded in 17. 2–7 and 13. 2–19;

These general conclusions are reinforced by a detailed examination of the four statutes in terms of their meaning, their relationship within biblical literature, their position among the Deuteronomic laws and their relationship to each other.

The statute in Deuteronomy 19. 14 warns against moving landmarks, chiefly stones, into a neighbor's field in order to enlarge one's own.[36] Similar warnings are found in Greece and Rome.[37] There is also a Mesopotamian analogue in the *kudurru*, the sacred boundary stone bearing the names and symbols of the gods, which was not to be moved.[38]

In my view, the notion of property boundary in the present passage differs from that which prevailed in Mesopotamia. There, the boundary marker was under the direct protection of the god, as expressed by the inscriptions on the stone. For example: "The name of the stela is *Nabu*, guardian of the *kudurru* of the fields".[39] By contrast, the boundary in the biblical passage does not enjoy any such protection. The moving of the marker is forbidden by God, but the boundary derives its authority from the division of the land carried out at the time when the land was first settled.[40] So this statute does not appear to have been shaped under the influence of, or in any relation to, the Mesopotamian ambience.

---

the honor due to parents in 21. 18–21; the prohibition of murder in 19. 1–13 and 21. 1–9; of adultery in 22. 13–29; of theft in 24.7; of false witness in 19. 16–19. All of these conclude with the phrase, "Thus you will sweep out evil from your midst", as befits criminal legislation. See J. L'Hour, "Une législation criminelle dans le Deutéronome", *Biblica*, 44 (1963), pp. 1–28.

36   The quotation is from Rashi.

37   See S.R. Driver, *A Commentary to Deuteronomy* (ICC), Edinburgh 1902³, ad loc.

38   The material collected by L.W. King in: *Babylonian Boundary-Stones and Memorial Tablets*, London 1912, is supplemented by R. Borger, *Handbuch der Keilschriftliteratur*, III, Berlin-New York 1975, pp. 40–41. In any case, the new material does not change the overall picture.

39   As quoted in *Assyrian Dictionary*, 8 (K), Chicago 1971, p. 495. There are similar examples in King, op. cit. (n. 38).

40   With considerable linguistic resourcefulness, Steuernagel interpreted *gblw* as a future perfect verb. However, in the light of Proverbs 22. 28, I concur with Smith, who maintains that in the context of Moses' address, *'ašer gablū ri̇šōnīm* is an anachronism that clashes with the second half of the verse ("in the property that *will be* allotted to you etc."); see ad loc.: C. Steuernagel, *Das Deuteronomium übersetzt und erklärt* (GHAT), Göttingen 1923²; G.A. Smith, *The Book of Deuteronomy* (CB), Cambridge 1918.

The law under discussion has much closer affinity with Hebrew Wisdom literature.[41] In the Book of Proverbs we find the following:

> Do not remove the ancient boundary stones; do not encroach upon the field of orphans, for they have a mighty Kinsman, and He will surely take up their cause with you (Prov. 23. 10–11).

The parallelism between "ancient boundary stones" and "the field of orphans" is peculiar (though not impossible). The first strophe appears to preach the safeguarding of property in general, while the second strophe narrows concern to the fields of orphans.

Moreover, in the Mishnah we find the following:

> If a man put a basket beneath the vine while he was gathering the grapes, such a one is a robber of the poor. Of him it is written "Remove not the landmark of them that come up" (Prov. 22. 28, reading *'olīm* for *'olām* M. Peah VII:3). If a man will not suffer the poor to glean, or suffers one and not another, or aids one of them, he is a robber of the poor. Of such a one it is written: "Remove not the landmark of them that come up" (ibid. V:6).

This last phrase is discussed in the Talmud Yerushalmi (Peah V:6) by Rabbi Jeremiah and Rabbi Joseph, one saying that they are those who came up from Egypt, the other saying that they are those who have become impoverished (as a euphemism for those who "have come down in the world"). Their Bible text read *'wlym*, which the Mishnah interpreted to mean "the poor" (*'wl* understood as similar to the Arabic *'yl*.[42] The same variant appears in Yerushalmi Sotah IV:3:

> A man shall not marry a woman pregnant by another man, or one nursing her child by another. If he does, it is written of him: "Do not remove the boundary stones of *'ulim* set up by previous ones; do not encroach upon the field of orphans".

Here it is clear that they read *'ulim*, interpreting it as "little ones", which

---

41   For what follows, see A. Geiger, "Symmachus, the Greek Translator" (Hebrew), *Heḥalutz*, 5 (1860), p. 28; N.H. Torczyner (Tur-Sinai), *The Book of Proverbs* (Hebrew), Tel Aviv 1947, p. 52; I.L. Seeligmann, "Voraussetzungen der Midraschexegese", *SVT*, I (1953), pp. 164–167.

42   J. Barth, "Beiträge zum Lexicon der Mischna", *Jahrbuch der Jüdisch-Literarischen Gesellschaft*, 7 (1909), pp. 130–131; A. Kahane, *The Book of Proverbs with Commentary* (Hebrew), Tel Aviv 1929, ad loc.

is a perfect parallel to "orphans".[43] That is also the reading of Jerome, who translated *ne adtingas terminos parvulorum et agrum pupillorum ne introeas* apparently under the influence of his Jewish teachers.[44] This reading is undoubtedly to be preferred, both because of the context, and because of its status as *lectio difficilior*.

If these considerations are correct, they can help us assess the origin of the similar statement in Proverbs 22. 28: "Do not remove the ancient boundary stone that your ancestors set up".[45] The first strophe repeats the faulty Masoretic reading of 23. 10, in keeping with which the author explains — "which boundary stone? The one that your ancestors set up".

Another consideration in support of the secondariness of Proverbs 22. 28 is that it gives a national tinge to the general moral statement characteristic of the common Wisdom of the ancient Near East — that orphans and minors are under the protection of God. Similar universalistic admonitions are found in *The Instruction of Amen-em-opet*, which influenced the style of this collection in the Book of Proverbs.[46] There we find in chapter 7, for example, "Do not carry off the landmark at the boundaries of the arable land, nor disturb the position of the measuring-cord. Be not greedy after a cubit of land, nor encroach upon the boundaries of a widow".

This discussion leads us to a better understanding of the nature of Deuteronomy 19. 14. Here too, as in Proverbs 22. 28, a national-historical reinterpretation — "set up by previous generations" — is given to a prohibition that was originally common to all ancient cultures. If so, it would appear that this verse is the transformation into a statute of a familiar Wisdom proverb. While the removal of boundary markers in general (not just those of orphans and of the young) is a common enough transgression (see Hosea 5. 10; Job 24. 2), the statute here contains a detail that does not appear anywhere else — "your neighbor's landmark". This expression may be regarded as typical of

---

43   Cf. Job 24. 9: "They snatch the fatherless infant from the breast / and seize the child of the poor as a pledge" (following the vocalization suggested by N.H. Tur-Sinai in his *Book of Job, With a New Commentary* [Hebrew], Tel Aviv 1954).

44   M. Rahmer, *Die hebräischen Traditionen in den Werken des Hieronymus*, I, Breslau 1861, pp. 64–67.

45   See I.L. Seeligmann, n. 41 above.

46   See W. McKane, *Proverbs; A New Approach* (OTL), London 1970, pp. 369–406; and I. Grumach, *Untersuchungen zur Lebenslehre des Amenope*, Munich 1972.

Deuteronomy, for it also appears in Deuteronomy 27. 17: "Cursed be
he who moves his neighbor's landmark".

All this leads us to propose that Deuteronomy 19. 14 has recast a
wisdom tradition into the form of a statute, as a way of concretizing the
precept "You shall not covet your neighbor's house". That would
explain the differences in phrasing between Deuteronomy 19. 14 and
its presumed sources in Wisdom literature.

Proverbs 23. 10 can also help clarify the statutes in Deuteronomy 23.
25–26, while being in turn illuminated by those verses. Proverbs 23. 10
concludes with the words "Do not encroach upon the field of orphans".
the statutes in Deuteronomy 23. 25–26 make the meaning of that
admonition clear: it refers to a brief entry into the field in order to
partake of its yield.[47] The proverb admonishes that such entry,
permitted in an ordinary field, is forbidden in an orphan's field. As for
the statutes, they in turn set limits to the benefits a person may enjoy
when he enters a produce-bearing field or plot.

It appears, then, that the statutes in Deuteronomy 23. 25–26 were
not intended to *innovate* permission for wayfarers to eat from vineyards
and fields along their way.[48] Such permission is taken for granted by
these laws. It continued to be part of the unwritten common law of the
Near East down to modern times, as observed by nineteenth-century
travelers in Palestine and northern Arabia.[49] Indeed, the phrasing of
the statutes themselves bears witness to the same effect. They do not
warn the landowner against enclosing his vineyard or field. Rather,
they address the wayfarer, and set limits to his right to help himself: No
basket in the vineyard! No sickle in the standing grain! These statutes
are not for the benefit of the wayfarer; it is the property owner whom
they seek to protect.

The laws under discussion are further clarified by the Sages,
especially in the Talmud Yerushalmi (Maas. V:4):

47   We find kindred expressions in the Book of Numbers: "We will not pass through
     fields or vineyards" (20. 17), "We will not turn off into fields or vineyards" (21.22),
     both of which go on to say "(and) we will not drink water from wells".
48   Some commentators seem to have overlooked the exact purport of these verses; cf.
     Driver (n. 37 above) and A.D.H. Mayes, *Deuteronomy* (New Century Bible
     Commentary), Grand Rapids, Mich.-London 1981.
49   Ed. Robinson-E. Smith, *Biblical Researches in Palestine*, I. Boston 1856, pp. 493,
     499; C.M. Doughty, *Travels in Arabia Deserta*, New York–London 1923³, II, p.
     152 (= London 1936, II, pp. 171–172).

It is written: "When you enter your neighbor's standing grain", and so on. Now, that might be taken to apply to anyone. Therefore the Torah continues, "You must not put a sickle to your neighbor's grain". From this we learn that the verse refers only to one who has a right to put a sickle. Who might that be? Only the fieldworker. Issi ben Akaviah says: No, the verse refers to everyone. But the phrase "put a sickle" teaches us that it is only at harvest time that one is permitted to help oneself.

All the halakhot, including those formulated in the Mishnah (B.M. VII:2, 4–6) and in the Tosefta (ibid. VIII:2 ff.) are based on the interpretation that restricts the permission to eat to the laborer alone, and further curtails it to specified periods related to the time "when the job is in its final stages".

Apparently this expresses the concern of the Halakhah at the end of the Mishnaic period for the agricultural economy of the country. Following the decline in population and the impoverishment of Jewish society in Palestine after the Great War with Rome, and especially after the Bar Kokhba Revolt, the Sages sought to rehabilitate the surviving Jewish land husbandry.[50] Accordingly, a person's right to eat his fill from the produce of a field was denied, even though that right was entrenched in ancient practice. This is also evident from the fact that the statement of Issi is attributed to some apocryphal document:

> Rav said: I found a hidden scroll at the academy of Rabbi Hiyya, wherein it was written: Issi ben Judah said: When Scripture says "When you come into your neighbor's vineyard" it refers to the entry of anyone (B.M. 92a).

What is more, the interpretation according to which anyone is allowed to eat of the produce during the harvest, and from the vineyard at vintage time, is also reported by Josephus (*Antiquities*, IV. 8. 21). This then was the ancient Halakhah, which was followed during the Second Commonwealth. It already carries the restriction on the rights of the

---

50 Gedaliah Alon, *History of the Jews, etc.* (Hebrew), Vol. 1, Tel Aviv 1953, pp. 173–179; Vol. 2, Tel Aviv 1955, pp. 53–56, 66–69 = *The Jews in Their Land in the Talmudic Age*, transl. by Gershon Levi; Vol. 1, Jerusalem 1980, pp. 277 ff.; Vol. 2, Jerusalem 1984, pp. 643 ff.; 646; 659–663. Cf. also the recent discussion by M. Ayali, "When You Come into Your Neighbor's Vineyard...", *Heqer veiyun — Studies in Judaism*, ed. Y. Bahat, M. Ben-Asher, T. Fenton, Haifa 1976, pp. 25–38.

wayfarer one step beyond the statute in Deuteronomy 23. 25–26 — a restriction apparently not yet known in the Galilee in Jesus' time: witness the action of his disciples, who passed through a field, on the Sabbath, and plucked ears of grain to eat (Matt. 12. 1–8; Mark 2. 23–28; Luke 6. 1–5).[51]

It appears, then, that the early Halakhah had already begun to protect farmers from having their fields overrun by passersby, and had restricted entry and eating to harvest-time. But these restrictions may also have had another thrust, namely, the desire to bring these rulings into line with the laws governing alms for the poor. In Deuteronomy 24. 19–22, for example, sheaves forgotten in the field, olives left on the tree after the boughs are beaten, and gleanings left on the vine are set aside for the foreigner, the orphan and the widow. But if these needy ones are permitted to glean in the fields only after the harvesters, why then should the field be open to all others at any time, even if they are restricted to eating in the field only? A fortiori, their rights should not exceed those of the poor.

This logic led the Sages to restrict everyone's entry into fields under cultivation, beyond what is implied by the plain meaning of the biblical statutes. Their solution enabled the poor to glean after the harvesters, permitting them to fill their baskets, while others were permitted to pick up at harvest-time only what they could eat then and there.

Critically considered, the incongruence between Deuteronomy 23. 25–26, and 24. 19–22, stems from the fact that the statutes come from different sources.[52] The norms in Deuteronomy 24.19–22 were formulated as laws of charity for the destitute, whereas 23. 25–26 arose from a different, almost opposing motive — to protect private property, concretizing the Commandment: "You shall not covet your neighbor's house".

In Deuteronomy 24. 10–13 we read as follows:

---

51 At Luke 6.1. some manuscripts read *en sabbato deuteroproto*, apparently to emphasize that they ate after the waving of the Omer-sheaf, in accordance with the law. Thus, in this reading the Gospel stresses the propriety of their act with respect to the laws of sacrifice, while being contrary to the laws of Sabbath observance. However, the narrator is unaware of the ancient halakhah that limited to harvest-time the entry of passersby into fields. Presumably he did not know about that halakhah.

52 A different view is taken by A. Dillmann, *Numeri, Deuteronomium und Josua,* (KEHAT[2]) Leipzig 1886.

10. When you exact any sort of credit (due you) from your neighbor, you must not enter his house to seize his pledge. 11. You must remain outside while the man to whom you made the loan brings the pledge out to you. 12. If he is a needy man, you shall not go to sleep in his pledge. 13. You must return the pledge to him at sundown, that he may sleep in his cloth and bless you; and it will be to your merit before the LORD your God.

It is evident that this is not one single statute, but two which have been merged. The first, in verses 10–11, deals with a creditor's claim on a pledge, while the second, in verses 12–13, lays down rules for the daily return of certain pledges. Beside their differing content, the two statutes are incongruous. The first commands that the security be selected by the debtor from the objects within his house, while the second deals with the poor man's garment with which he covers himself day and night, as is stated in Exodus 22. 26: "It is his only clothing, the sole covering for his skin. In what else shall he sleep?" This is not something the debtor is likely to give up of his own free will nor is it necessary to enter his house since he wears it on his body.[53] Indeed, in Exodus 22. 25–26 we find only the second law, which requires the return of the garment by sundown. It appears, then, that the statute in Deuteronomy 22. 10–11 is separate and distinct. It is not concerned primarily with compassionate behavior, but with protecting a man's property from seizure — even by creditors who have a rightful claim to it.

Here, too, the reality reflected in the Book of Proverbs illustrates the background of this statute. Proverbs 20. 16 declares: "Seize his garment, for he stood surety for another; take it as a pledge (for he stood surety) for an unfamiliar woman". The same is repeated in Proverbs 27. 13. Both proverbs allow a creditor to take the guarantor's garment, without consideration for the fact that he might want to give up something else instead.

This hard-bitten attitude comes out most explicitly in Proverbs 22. 26–27: "Do not be one of those who give their hand, who stand surety for debts, lest your bedding be taken from under you when you have no money to pay". From this we learn that creditors would high-handedly enter the homes of debtors and guarantors and take as a security whatever they saw fit.

---

53   The word *we'im* at the beginning of verse 12 is, in Deuteronomy, often a sign of redaction; cf. Deut. 19. 8; 22. 2 and 20; 25. 7.

Against this background one can better appreciate the significance
of the statute under consideration. It is an "idealistic" statute. It does
not emerge from Israel's customary law in the biblical period. It is an
attempt rather to alter the existing situation and to reshape it in the
name of an ideal.[54] We have already indicated that this ideal is expressed
in the Tenth Commandment: "You shall not covet your neighbor's
house".

At the beginning of this essay we cited Maimonides' view of the
Tenth Commandment:

> This prohibition warns against developing stratagems for getting
> hold of what belongs to someone else, even if we are prepared to
> pay a high price for it. Any action of this sort is a violation of
> "You shall not covet".[55]

If in fact the statute in Deuteronomy 24. 10–11 is an exemplification
and concretization of this Commandment, then Maimonides cuts very
close to the core of the plain meaning of the biblical text. The law in
Deuteronomy 24. 10–11 is not about the acquisition of something
through theft, force or fraud, but about entering a house to attach some
item of value. Heretofore such entry had been regarded as legitimate.
According to this statute, however, a creditor who enters a debtor's
home and looks around until he finds and takes what he likes violates
the Commandment not to covet, no less than he who moves his
neighbor's boundary stones in the darkness of the night.

The four laws in Deuteronomy that speak of "your neighbor" are
now dispersed in three different places. Their present location is
undoubtedly the work of the book's editor, who arranged them
according to principles of his own — chiefly, the principle of

---

54   The unfortunate situation where a debtor's very last possession is seized is described
      in other places in the Bible as well; see I.L. Seeligmann, "Lending, Pledge and
      Interest in Biblical Law and Biblical Thought", in *Studies in Bible and the Ancient
      Near East Presented to S.E. Loewenstamm* (Hebrew Section), Jerusalem 1978, pp.
      193–195. Ben Sira also cautions against imprudent surety, but without mentioning
      the seizure of a garment (29. 18–20; verses 20–23 in the Segal edition). "Going
      surety has ruined many prosperous men / and shaken them like an ocean wave / It
      has driven influential men out of their houses / and made them wander among
      foreign nations". This reflects a new situation: emigration from Palestine for
      economic reasons during the period of Ptolemaic rule.

55   *Book of the Commandments* (n. 4 above), number 265.

association.[56] As we have seen, however, the statutes in and of themselves belong together, both in terms of their basic intent, and with regard to their style. They also belong together by reason of their casuistics, that is, the instances they deal with, all highly interrelated in Wisdom literature. As we have seen, the moving of boundary markers is mentioned together with incursion into fields in Proverbs 23. 10. And Job says of the wicked: "(They) remove boundary stones; they carry off flocks and pasture them; they lead away the donkeys of the fatherless, and seize the widow's bull as a pledge" (24. 2–3). Similarly, the Book of Proverbs speaks of the removal of a boundary stone immediately after dealing with the seizure of a pledge (22. 26–28). In Wisdom literature, the boundary-mover and the pledge-taker are placed side by side.

It may be said, then, that these four "neighbors" statutes come from the same source. A single author who stood under the influence of Wisdom literature, composed them.[57] He meant them to be interpretations of the Tenth Commandment.[58] As he understood it, "You shall not covet your neighbor's house" forbids all trespass into the realm of the other that may cause damage to his property, or to his ownership rights.

Translated by Arnold Schwartz

---

56   See A. Rofé, "The Arrangement of the Laws in Deuteronomy" (Hebrew), in: *Studies in Memory of M.D.U. Cassuto,* Jerusalem 1987, pp. 217–235.

57   Cf. M. Weinfeld, "The Dependence of Deuteronomy upon Wisdom Literature" (Hebrew), in: *Yehezkel Kaufmann Jubilee Volume,* Jerusalem 1960, pp. 89, 108. It remains to be determined, however, which wisdom circles, and the extent to which their influence was direct or mediated. See my remarks in *Tarbiz,* 32 (1962–3), pp. 110 ff., and my review of Weinfeld's *Deuteronomy and the Deuteronomic School,* in: *Christian News from Israel,* 24 (1974), pp. 204–209.

58   Interestingly enough, Maimonides in his *Book of the Commandments* (265–268) connects the laws in Deuteronomy 23.25–26, to the Commandment "You shall not covet".

3. THE DECALOGUE IN PROPHETIC LITERATURE

MEIR WEISS

The majority of biblical scholars now agree that prophetic literature shows traces of the Decalogue[1]. This claim is generally based on passages from Hosea and Jeremiah[2] in which these two prophets seem to base their prophetic rebuke upon prohibitions found in the Decalogue as it appears in Exodus 20 and Deuteronomy 5.

Hosea 4. 1–2, in which the prophet uses the words "[false] swearing, dishonesty, and murder and theft and adultery" to describe the situation as a result of which "...the LORD has a case [*rīb*] against the inhabitants of this land" (4.1), is held to be a reference to three prohibitions found in the Decalogue: The word "murder" is taken as an echo of the Sixth Commandment, the word "theft" as an echo of the Eighth and the word "adultery" as an echo of the Seventh (Ex. 20. 13; Deut. 5. 17).[3]

---

1   For reference to the Decalogue in current scholarship, see A. Toeg, *Lawgiving at Sinai* (Hebrew), Jerusalem 1977, pp. 64–80 (with bibliography), as well as the study by M. Weinfeld in the present volume.

2   See however the theory advanced by R. Knierim (n. 31, below).

3   Among modern commentators on the Book of Hosea, this is the view of Jacob, Weiser*, Wolff, Rudolph*, Mays* and McKeating. (In this and the following notes, a commentator's name alone refers to his commentary on the passage under discussion.) For full bibliographical data consult *The Bible From Within* (below, n. 7), pp. 445–451. This is also the opinion of H.B. Huffman, "The Covenant Lawsuit in the Prophets", in: *JBL*, LXXVIII (1959), p. 41; J.J. Stamm* and M.E. Andrew*, *The Ten Commandments in Recent Research*, London 1967, p. 89, n. 35; F.Ch. Fensham, "The Covenant Idea in the Book of Hosea", in: *Studies in the Books of Hosea and Amos (Papers Read at the 7th and 8th Meetings of the O.T. Werkgemeenskap in Suid-Afrika*, Pretoria 1964–1965), p. 42, etc. Those scholars whose names are followed by an asterisk(*) believe that the first two accusations ("false swearing and dishonesty") refer to the Decalogue as well. According to most, the reference is to the Third Commandment; there are a few who suggest that

Scholars maintain that the impress of the same three utterances, as well as that of two others, is also to be found in the word of God as spoken by Jeremiah in the gates of the house of the LORD (Jer. 7.9):[4]

> Will you steal and murder and commit adultery and swear falsely and sacrifice to Baal, and follow other gods whom you do not know?

The first three transgressions mentioned are the very ones found in Hosea, and the other two are held to correspond to the Third and Second Commandments respectively: "swear falsely" to "You shall not take the name of the LORD your God in vain" (Ex. 20. 7; Deut. 5. 11), "and sacrifice to Baal and follow other gods", to "You shall have no other gods beside Me.... You shall not bow down to them or serve them" (Ex. 20. 3, 5; Deut. 5. 7, 9).

To be sure, neither in Hosea nor in Jeremiah are these transgressions listed in the order found in the Pentateuch. This fact is occasionally marshalled in favor of the claim that the Decalogue came into existence later than the prophecies of Hosea and Jeremiah.[5] Alternatively, if the prophetic passages are assumed to be a reference to the Decalogue,[6] the deviation in the order is viewed simply as literary license.

Now, the order in which the crimes of murder, theft and adultery

---

it might be the Ninth. Fohrer, who finds a parallel only with respect to the last three accusations, uses this to support his opinion, once prevalent among Bible scholars, that the Decalogue as it appears in Exodus belongs to the pentateuchal source E, and was therefore not yet fixed at the time of Hosea. In his opinion, Hosea worded these five accusations as an echo of five bisyllabic prohibitions of the apodictic law, which are the source of the Sixth, Seventh and Eighth "Words" in E's Decalogue. E, of course, is held to have originated in the Northern Kingdom, where Hosea lived and worked; see G. Fohrer, "Das sogennante apodiktisch formulierte Recht und der Dekalog", in: *Kerygma und Dogma*, XI, 1965, p. 64 = *Studien zur alttestamentlichen Theologie und Geschichte (1949–1966), BZAW*, CXV, Berlin 1969, pp. 136–137. Incidentally, in his essay dealing with Jeremiah's oration at the gate of the House of the LORD ("Jeremias Tempelwort — Jeremia 7. 1–15", in *ThZ*, V, 1949, pp. 401–417 = *Studien zur alttestamentlichen Prophetie, 1949–1966, BZAW*, XCIX, Berlin 1967, pp. 191–203), Fohrer claims that in Jeremiah 7. 9, as in Hosea 4. 2, there is a reference to the Decalogue.

4   See H. Weippert, *Die Prosareden des Jeremiabuches, BZAW*, CXXXII, Berlin–New York 1973, p. 34 (n. 38 there presents a list of other scholars who make the same claim).

5   For example, this is the current position of Fohrer (see above, n. 3).

6   As they are by Wolff and Rudolph and before them, for example, Sellin.

appear in Jeremiah 7 is no ground for denying the connection between Jeremiah 7 and the Decalogue.[7] Nor is it necessary, in order to affirm that connection, to assume that the order is a random variation of the original. The relation between the two passages is chiastic: the prohibitions appearing in the second Table of the Decalogue (theft, murder and adultery) are referred to in Jeremiah first, and those of the first Table (swearing falsely and worshipping other gods) follow. In addition, the internal order of the latter group has been changed so that the reference to the Third Word of the Decalogue precedes the reference to the Second:

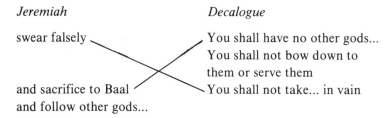

Jeremiah   *Decalogue*

swear falsely   You shall have no other gods...
                                    You shall not bow down to
                                    them or serve them
and sacrifice to Baal   You shall not take... in vain
and follow other gods...

Furthermore, the reference to the Second Commandment in Jeremiah is arranged in a manner which itself constitutes an inversion of the Decalogue passage:

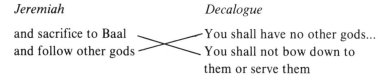

Jeremiah   *Decalogue*

and sacrifice to Baal   You shall have no other gods...
and follow other gods   You shall not bow down to
                                    them or serve them

This chiastic relationship between the two passages would seem to be violated in the first portion of the passage from Jeremiah, in which reference is made to the prohibitions of the Second Table of the Decalogue. The order (theft, murder, adultery[8]) is neither parallel to nor a precise chiastic inversion of the order in the Decalogue itself (murder, adultery, theft). However,[9] the order of these prohibitions from the Second Table of the Decalogue is reflected otherwise in Jesus'

---

7   With regard to the passage from Jeremiah, see my discussion in *The Bible From Within — The Method of Total Interpretation*, Jerusalem 1984, pp. 256–259.

8   The order in the Septuagint (*kai phoneutete kai moichasthe kai kleptete* = "and you murder and commit adultery and steal") does correspond to that of the Decalogue; see below.

9   *The Bible From Within* (see above, n. 7), pp. 257–259.

reply to the Roman who asked "What shall I do to inherit eternal life?" in Luke 18. 20: "The commandments you know, you shall not commit adultery, you shall not murder, you shall not steal, do not testify falsely, honor your father and your mother". Luke begins with the Commandment which occupies the Seventh position in Exodus and Deuteronomy, following which he mentions the Sixth, Eighth and Ninth (and finally, the Fifth) Commandments. Paul too cites the Decalogue in this order in the Epistle to the Romans (13. 9); the same order appears in Philo[10] and in Septuagint B to Deuteronomy 5. In the Nash Papyrus, "Honor your father and your mother" is followed by "You shall not commit adultery, you shall not murder, you shall not steal" in that order.[11] Thus, while Jeremiah 7 is not a chiastic inversion of the Decalogue as it appears in Exodus and Deuteronomy, it is a chiastic inversion of the Decalogue as it appears in the aforementioned sources:

Jeremiah   *NT, Philo, Nash, LXX^B*

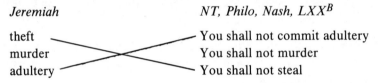

theft   You shall not commit adultery
murder   You shall not murder
adultery   You shall not steal

Chiastic parallelism between two passages is not a matter of casual variation; it is a structural convention prevalent in the Bible. Analysis of the use of this convention clearly shows that it is not merely a technical device: M. Seidel[12] has demonstrated that chiastic parallelism reflects and calls attention to a connection between two verses, and the

10   *De decalogo*, 121 ff.; *De specialibus legibus*, III, 8; *Quis rerum divinarum haeres sint*, 173.

11   Lines 18–19; see M.Z. Segal, "The Nash Papyrus", in: *Tradition and Criticism* (Hebrew), Jerusalem 1957, p. 250. For the reverse order of "You shall not steal" and "You shall not commit adultery", which appears in other sources as well, see D. Flusser, "Do Not Commit Adultery, Do Not Murder", in: *Textus*, IV, Jerusalem 1964, pp. 220–224. According to Gese, the order in which the two appear in the Masoretic text (as well as in the Samaritan Pentateuch, in a fragment of the Book of Deuteronomy found at Qumran, and in Josephus) has been altered from the original, which is that found in the Nash Papyrus and elsewhere (H. Gese, "The Structure of the Decalogue", *Proceedings of the Fourth World Congress of Jewish Studies*, I, Jerusalem 1967, English Section, pp. 155–159).

12   "Parallels Between the Book of Isaiah and the Book of Psalms" (Hebrew), *Sinai*, XXXVIII (1956), pp. 150–151 = *Studies in the Bible* (Hebrew), Jerusalem 1978, pp. 2–3 (with additional examples).

existence of this phenomenon has been verified by other studies.[13] The very structure of the verse in Jeremiah would thus seem to reflect the prophet's intention to refer, and perhaps to stress the fact that he refers, to the Decalogue (though this is admittedly not Jeremiah's central concern in the chapter). The reference, however, is not to the Decalogue as preserved in Exodus and Deuteronomy but to a variant tradition with regard to the order of the Second Table.

A similar intent is reflected in the three denunciations in Hosea 4. While they do not constitute a chiastic inversion of the Decalogue as it appears in Exodus and Deuteronomy[14] or even in the variant order to which Jeremiah 7 apparently makes reference, we do find that Septuagint B to Exodus 20 arranges the Second Table differently from the Masoretic Text: *ou moicheuseis, ou klepseis, ou phoneuseis* ("You shall not commit adultery, you shall not steal, you shall not murder"). Hosea's prophecy relates to this version in chiastic fashion:

Hosea   *LXX^B to Ex. 20*

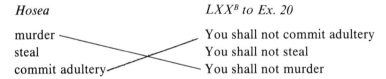

murder   You shall not commit adultery
steal   You shall not steal
commit adultery   You shall not murder

It is fairly reasonable to conclude, therefore, that these prophecies of Hosea and Jeremiah are indeed prophetic references to prohibitions of the Decalogue, each one reflecting the sequence of prohibitions in the Second Table that was current in the prophet's own time and place.

A number of scholars[15] hold that Hosea's use of the Decalogue is not confined to those prohibitions which pertain to interpersonal relationships (i.e., those found in the Second Table) and that it extends as well to Hosea's description of the relationship between God and Israel. Thus they find echoes of the First and Second Commandments of the Decalogue ("I the LORD am your God who brought you out of the land of Egypt...You shall have no other gods beside Me" [Ex. 20. 2–3; Deut. 5. 6–7][16]) in Hosea 13. 4 ("Only I the LORD have been your God ever since the land of Egypt; You have never known a God but

---

13   For example, *The Bible From Within* (see above, n. 7), pp. 95–97, 116 and n. 9, 326 f., 337, n. 85, etc.
14   See above, n. 11.
15   Such as Weiser, Rudolph, Toeg (above, n. 3).
16   See below, n. 20.

Me") and in Hosea 12. 10 ("I the LORD have been your God ever since
the land of Egypt").[17] Likewise it is occasionally suggested[18] that the
Second Commandment ("You shall have no other gods beside Me...")
influenced Hosea's formulation of God's command in 3. 1 ("Go, love a
woman... just as the LORD loves you the Israelites, but they turn to
other gods...").[19] This suggestion stems from Hosea's use of the phrase
"other gods" instead of his more usual "Baal" (or *bĕ'ālīm* — see 2. 10,
15, 19; 11. 2; 13. 1), ostensibly echoing the "other gods" of the
Decalogue.

While arriving at any such conclusion merely on the basis of a single
phrase appears farfetched,[20] and the possibility that there are echoes of
the Decalogue in Hosea 12. 10 and 13. 4 requires further study, a
clearer reflection of the Decalogue would seem to be present in a
prophetic passage which scholars have overlooked. We refer to Amos
3. 1–2, as careful analysis will reveal.

1.   Hear this word, O people of Israel,
      That the LORD has spoken concerning you
      Concerning the whole family that I brought up from the land of
      Egypt:
2.   You alone have I singled out
      Of all the families of the earth —
      That is why I will call you to account
      For all your iniquities.

Verse 1 contains two subordinate clauses. The first ("that the LORD
has spoken") is in apposition to the direct object of the main clause
("this word"). The second ("that I brought up", etc.) is a definition of

---

17   This was apparently the understanding of the Septuagint as well, since the
     translation includes the addition *anegagon se*, i.e. the verb that would have served
     to translate "brought up" (as in verse 14).
18   Wolff, Rudolph.
19   According to Rudolph, the use of the Divine Name in the quotation from God's
     word ("just as the LORD loves the Israelites") reflects the influence of the opening
     passage of the Decalogue.
20   For the expression "other gods" in the Bible, see Weippert, (above, n. 4), pp.
     215–222. Fohrer, who maintains that Exodus 20. 2 is a Deuteronomistic addition,
     also claims that "other gods" is a Deuteronomistic re-working. The ancient
     expression was that which appears in Exodus 34. 14: "another god" (*Kerygma und
     Dogma*, p. 58 = *BZAW*, CXV, p. 131; see above, n. 3).

the object of the preposition "concerning" ("you") in the first.[21] It is widely held among scholars that more than one hand wove the fabric of this verse, especially in view of a further stylistic peculiarity, namely, the fact that the reference to God in the third person in the first subordinate clause, which is appropriate to the introductory statement ("Hear this word...") in which Amos himself is the speaker, is replaced in the second subordinate clause by God's direct speech ("that I brought up") as in the body of the oracle (v. 2). A further claim against the integrity of verse 1 is that God's direct speech, which seems to begin with "that I brought up", etc., in verse 2, is interrupted by the word *lē'mōr*, a locution which never again appears in Amos as a preface to the divine word. Additional doubt is cast upon the verse by the fact that "concerning the whole family" appears to be a reflex of "of all the families" in the following verse, while "that I brought up from the land of Egypt" appears to be influenced by "And I brought you up from the land of Egypt" in 2. 10. Bolstering their claims with various assumptions regarding the ideational content of the verse,[22] scholars who question the unity of the verse generally maintain that verse 1b ("concerning the whole family", etc.) has been interpolated into the text.[23]

There is, of course, no way of proving that verse 1, as it appears in the present text is identical with the verse in its original form. More importantly, the arguments cited above against the authenticity of the present text do not undermine its structural unity. As we shall proceed to demonstrate, the "questionable" elements in the verse are not all that unusual in and of themselves, and when seen in context they are actually quite significant. The verse is actually an organic whole, and it provides verse 2 with its natural and necessary preamble.

The fundamental argument against the unity of the verse, that is, the abrupt transition from reference to God's word to that word itself, fails to convince in light of a psychological explanation for the change in grammatical person. The prophet, who sees himself as God's messenger when conveying His word, identifies so fully with his Sender

21 In the Septuagint, the phrase "concerning the whole family..." is not seen as being in apposition to "concerning you", since the translator has preceded it by the conjunction *kai* ("and").

22 See below, n. 45.

23 See the very partial list of scholars expressing this view in K. Koch et al., *Amos — Untersucht mit den Methoden einer strukturalen Formgeschichte*, I, Neukirchen-Vluyn 1976, p. 126.

that he not only speaks for Him but actually assumes His Person.[24]
This phenomenon, while common in the Bible[25] and in prophetic
literature in particular, appears in Amos only here. In fact, Amos'
prophecies are peculiarly distinguished by the clear demarcation drawn
between the words of the prophet and the words of God which he
quotes.[26] This clear separation is also found in our verse, and with
considerable emphasis. That the speaker in verse 1 is indeed the prophet
is apparent not only from the wording of the first strophe; it is clearly
denoted by the word *lē'mōr* at the end of the second clause. This word,
since it indicates that what follows is the divine oracle itself, marks the
conclusion of the prophet's preface.

Of course, this is so only if we adopt the psychological explanation
for the use of the first person in the latter part of verse 1. If we do not,
and if we take the unusual *lē'mōr* as an indication of what scholars have
posited, i.e., that verse 1b is an interpolation, then the question
immediately arises: What did the later redactor hope to achieve by
introducing the reference to God's "bringing up" Israel from Egypt?[27]
And if, as is generally suggested,[28] the aim was to elaborate upon the
theme of verse 2 ("You alone have I singled out"), why, though the
speaker in the sentence is clearly the prophet and not God (a fact of
which the interpolator could not have been unaware since the word
le'mor is clear enough), why is the clause formulated in the first person?

---

24   According to Lindblom, this change of person is typical of revelation; see J.
     Lindblom, *Die literarische Gattung der prophetischen Literatur — Eine
     literargeschichtliche Untersuchung zum Alten Testament*, Uppsala 1924, p. 77.
25   On this phenomenon, which was already noted by Moses Ibn Ezra and which he
     illustrated by quoting Psalm 81.17 (*The Poetry of Israel*, translated into Hebrew by
     B.Z. Halper, Leipzig 1924, Jerusalem 1967, p. 185), see E. König, *Stilistik,
     Rhetorik, Poetik im Bezug auf die biblische Literatur*, Leipzig 1900, pp. 248–250.
26   An expression of this concern is the frequent use of such phrases as "Thus said the
     LORD" (fourteen times), "the LORD said" (eleven times), "declares the LORD"
     (twenty-one times), etc.
27   According to Weiser, the same redactor added both verse 1b and 2. 10, in an
     attempt to mark the connection which he saw between the two sections (A. Weiser,
     Die Prophetie des Amos, BZAW, LIII, Giessen 1929, p. 118), but the solution
     which this explanation provides is by no means convincing.
28   Among recent commentators see, for example, Amsler, Wolff and Vollmer (J.
     Vollmer, *Geschichtliche Rückblicke und Motive in der Prophetie des Amos,
     Hosea and Jesaja, BZAW*, CXIX, Berlin 1971, p. 29).

One possibility is that the phrase originally read "that *He* brought up", and this route is occasionally taken by scholars.[29]

However, a further possibility presents itself. In view of the discernible references to the Decalogue in the prophecies of Hosea, and in view of the formulation of Psalm 81.11 which is a clear reference to the First Word ("I the LORD am your God who brought you up [Heb. *hamma'alĕkā*, from *he'ĕlā*] out of the land of Egypt"),[30] it appears plausible that verse 1b is a citation from the Decalogue[31] in the form in which it was known[32] to Amos and his audience.[33] Conclusive support for this theory is not lacking: verse 2b ("call you to account for all your iniquities" [Heb. *pōqēd 'āwōn 'al*] echoes the Second Commandment: "holding the children, grandchildren and great-grandchildren accountable for the iniquity of the fathers" (Ex. 20. 5; Deut. 5. 9; Heb. *pōqēd 'āwōn 'al*).[34]

Since his audience was familiar with the opening statement of the Decalogue in this form ("that *brought you up*; Heb. =*he'ĕlētī*), it is thus that Amos quotes it in his preface (and not, as in the version in Exodus

29   See A. Winter, "Analyse des Buches Amos", *ThStKr*, LXXXIII (1910), p. 338.
30   The expression "brought up" (from the land of Egypt) rather than "brought out" (see below) appears consistently in the early prophetic books and frequently in the older parts of the Bible. M.D. Cassuto attempts to prove that these two phrases are actually expressions of two meanings: *The Documentary Hypothesis and the Composition of the Pentateuch*, Jerusalem 1961, pp. 48–49. However, according to the prevalent scholarly opinion, to which Cassuto was opposed, the two versions reflect different traditions and different time periods. The generally accepted explanation is that "brought up..." is employed by E, while J, P and D generally use the phrase "brought out...". See also below, n. 33.
31   See R. Knierim, *Die Hauptbegriffe für Sünde im Alten Testament*, Gutersloh 1965, repr. 1967, pp. 205–206.
32   According to Wolff, verse 1b is a "phrase from a liturgical tradition"; cf. Mays. For the opinion of scholars with regard to the place of the Decalogue in the cult, see Toeg (above, n. 1), pp. 66–67; B. Schwartz, "Psalm 50 — Its Subject, Form and Place" (Hebrew), in *Shnaton — An Annual for Biblical and Ancient Near Eastern Studies*, III (1979), pp. 99 f. See also below, n. 33.
33   Cf. Amos 2. 10 and 9. 7. Wijngaards is convinced that the wording "brought up..." was commonly accepted in the Northern Kingdom, at the sanctuaries of Beth-El and Dan, but that it was repressed under the influence of the Deuteronomistic school due to the association which it conjured up of the calf-worship of those sanctuaries; I. Wijngaards, "הוציא and העלה — A Twofold Approach to the Exodus", *VT*, XV (1965), pp. 100–102.
34   See below.

and Deuteronomy, "that brought you out"; Heb. =*hōṣē'tī*). The intent
of the verbatim citation is to call to the mind of the listener the very
event from which Amos' contemporaries drew their confidence in their
own invulnerability, and which seemed to justify that confidence:[35]
that is, the redemption from Egypt. Amos on the contrary evokes the
memory of the Exodus in order to refute this vain belief.

Our reading of verse 1b as a direct quotation explains both the
presence and the position of the word *lē'mōr*, while at the same time
clarifying the connection between the opening verse and the body of
the oracle. In fact, it becomes evident that the preface is an organic part
of the oracle, a message dealing with God's relationship to Israel and
what that relationship implies.

Of that relationship we read in verse 2a: "You alone have I singled
out of all the families of the earth". By virtue of the use of the verb
yāda', with all its emotional connotations as expressed in a number of
its derivative forms,[36] the relationship is depicted as being intimate,
personal and emotionally charged. Moreover, this relationship is a
unique one, as conveyed by the prepositional phrase "of all the families
of the earth" and doubly stressed — by the placing of the direct object
"you" before the subject-verb (*yāda'ti*) and by the use of the adjective
"alone".

Elsewhere in the Bible, in passages referring to the uniqueness of
Israel's relationship with God, Israel is said to have been chosen from
among all peoples (Deut. 10.15) or "all the peoples of the earth" (Deut.
7. 6; 14.2). Amos here uses the word "families" because the same word
is used in the previous verse ("concerning the whole family that I
brought up", etc.). Unlike "nation",[37] "family" is apolitical. "Earth"

---

35   Cf. 9. 7.
36   As a reference to sexual relations: Gen. 4. 1; 19.5, 8; Numbers 31. 17, etc.;
      connoting special attention: Gen. 39., 6, 8; Isaiah 58.3; Nahum 1.7; Psalm 31.8 etc.
37   As has been pointed out by E.A. Speiser, "'People' and 'Nation' of Israel", *JBL*,
      LXXVII (1960), pp. 157–163, and before him by L. Rost ("Die Bezeichnungen für
      Land und Volk im Alten Testament", *Procksch-Festschrift*, Leipzig 1934, pp.
      141–205 = *Das kleine Credo und andere Studien zum Alten Testament*, Heidelberg
      1965, pp. 89–101), the noun "people" (*'am*) in its original connotation, unlike
      "nation" (*gōy*), does not carry any political implications. However, in time the
      original ethnic nuance became blurred and the word took on a national flavor, as
      evidenced by the routine interchange of *'ammim* and *goyim* so common in biblical
      style. See I.L. Seeligmann, "Researches into the Criticism of the Masoretic Text of
      the Bible" (Hebrew), *Tarbiz*, XXV (1956), p. 137.

too may well retain here its original, apolitical connotation,[38] especially since it is used in conjunction with "families". "Families of the earth" appears only twice more in the Bible, on both occasions in regard to the election of the patriarchs, Abraham (Gen. 12. 3) and Jacob (Gen. 28. 14). The possibility suggests itself that Amos refers to the community of nations, from among which God singled out Israel for a unique relationship, with the same phrase, "the nations of the earth", in order to arouse the association of the covenant with the patriarchs.[39] Additional corroboration may be found in the use of the same word, *yāda'ti*, in the same sense, "I have singled out", in connection with God's relationship with Abraham in Genesis 18. 19.[40]

If the connection between this prophecy of Amos and the traditions relating to Abraham is accepted, the words of verse 2a may be said to signify, connotatively and by association, what they do not state explicitly. For verse 2 provides an answer to the question about the nature of God's relationship with His chosen people. The answer to the

---

38   Rost (above, n. 37), pp. 128–130 (= pp. 78–79).
39   According to Schmidt, the word "family" (*mišpāḥā*) is part of the lexicon of the election tradition (W.H. Schmidt, "Die deuteronomistische Redaktion des Amosbuches", *ZAW*, LXXVII (1965) pp. 172–173). In Rudolph's opinion, Amos relates to this tradition. Wolff also points to the repetition of this expression in the stories of the patriarchs. However, he states categorically that "there is no recognizable influence from that quarter".
40   Compare Th.C. Vriezen, *Zum alttestamentlichen Erwählungsglauben*, Zürich 1953, pp. 79–80, with Mays. Recently, Vriezen has expressed the opinion that the reference is to the word of God to Jacob at Beth-El (Gen. 28. 14), since the parallels to the stories of Abraham "are not so close [to it], because of the fact that they are not tied to Beth-El" ("Erwägungen zur Amos 3.2", in *Archäologie und Altes Testament — K. Galling-Festschrift*, Tübingen 1970, p. 256). However, while we recognize the necessity of exercising caution in assuming that the reference here is to the tradition of the election of Abraham, it must be said that Vriezen's arguments against it are not convincing. The absence of a connection between the Abraham story and Beth-El is only felt in the counter-argument if we assume that such a connection should be found in Amos, and this assumption is itself quite problematic. In any case, the suggestion that "all the families of the earth" refers to the Jacob tradition is undoubtedly more far-fetched than the notion that it refers to the tradition of Abraham. Incidentally, it should be noted that in those prophecies which mention the patriarchs it is through Abraham that God's familial relationship with Israel is realized; see Chr. Jeremias, "Die Erzväter in der Verkündigung der Propheten", in: H. Donner, R. Hanhart, R. Smend, ed. *Beiträge zur alttestamentlichen Theologie — Festschrift für W. Zimmerli zum 70 Geburstag*, Göttingen 1977, pp. 206–222.

question contained in the latter half of the verse ("I will call you to account", etc.) is indirect; the associative, connotative answer found in the first clause is actually more direct. The phrase "of all the families of the earth" calls to mind the promise given to Abraham that "all the families of the earth shall bless themselves by you" (Gen. 12. 3), while "You alone have I singled out" recalls "For I have singled him out, that he may instruct his children and posterity to keep the way of the LORD by doing what is just and right" (Gen. 18. 19). For Amos, the reason God has singled out Israel is in order that Israel do "what is just and right"; this is clear from the use of the term "just and right" in his prophecies (5. 7, 24; 6. 12).

Assuming a connecting link between Amos and the patriarchal traditions concerning Abraham provides a possible answer to yet another question. When, in Amos' view, did this special, conditional relationship between God and Israel begin? Though our verse points only to a tentative reply, it would seem that Amos believes that this special relationship dates from the time of Abraham.

Much less speculative is the inescapable conclusion that "I singled out" in verse 2 and "I brought up from the land of Egypt" in verse 1 refer to two separate manifestations of God's initiative in the course of His relationship with Israel. The two phrases are not an example of one and the same idea expressed in two ways, once explicitly and once implicitly,[41] i.e., it is not the case that Amos has merely reformulated his own statement "You alone have I singled out" (in which, as we have seen, he assumes God's identity as speaker) and recast it as an utterance of God's ("I brought up from the land of Egypt"). Even if the theoretical possibility that one of the two acts is intended to be the actualization[42] or exemplification[43] of the other were admitted, it would have to be ruled out in the final analysis, since it is totally illogical for the actual event ("brought up from the land of Egypt") to precede the conceptual ("singled out") or for the example to come before the generalization. This is especially true since the former — the reference to the actual

---

41 As explained by the medieval commentators Joseph Kara and Joseph Ibn Caspi and echoed by those scholars who believe that the model for this prophecy is that of the contractual covenant, e.g., U. O'Rourke Boyle, "The Covenant Lawsuit of the Prophet Amos", *V. T.*, XXI (1971), pp. 338–362; and those who claim that 1b is an explanatory addition to 2a (see above, n. 28).

42 As is assumed by the commentators and scholars mentioned in n. 41.

43 As the connection between 1b and 2a is understood by Eliezer of Beaugency.

event, the Exodus — is contained in the preface, and the latter — the abstraction — is contained in the body of the oracle, and not the opposite. Logic compels us to conclude that, if the redemption from Egypt had been intended as the basis of this prophetic address, that topic would have been raised not in the proem but in the divine utterance itself — all the more so in the context of what appears to be a citation from the Decalogue.

Israel's unique status, as determined by Amos in this passage, is not derived from the fact that God brought Israel up from Egypt, but rather from the fact that He "singled out" Israel "alone", "of all the families of the earth"; i.e., solely from His personal, intimate relationship with Israel. Israel's uniqueness lies not in God's intervention at the beginning of its history,[44] i.e., not in its national pedigree, but rather in the affinity which exists between God and Israel. In other words, the only difference between "the whole family that I brought up from the land of Egypt" and "all the families of the earth" lies in God's having "singled out" Israel. Amos states: "...True, I brought Israel up from the land of Egypt, but also the Philistines from Caphtor and the Arameans from Kir" (9. 7); but "you have I singled out from all the families of the earth".

If this is indeed the intended reading of verse 2a, does it not follow, as maintained by many scholars,[45] that verse 1b was simply grafted on to the original preface and that it is not organically connected to the whole of the oracle? The answer is a function of the structure of the entire passage, the significance of which becomes clear through a close examination of verse 2b: "That is why I will call you to account for all your iniquities".

Full attention must be given to the linguistic design of this concluding statement. The noun *'āwōn* ("iniquity"), found in Hosea, for example,

---

44   Cf. the recent work of J.J. Stamm, "Überlegungen zu den geistlichen Voraussetzungen der Prophetie Amos", in: *Wort-Gebot-Glaube — Beiträge zur Theologie des Alten Testaments — W. Eichrodt zum 80 Geburstag*, Zürich 1970, pp. 209–225.

45   For example, R. Smend, "Das Nein des Amos", *Ev. Theol.*, XXIII (1963), p. 409; Vollmer (above, n. 28, pp. 26, 29) and others, see verse 1b (as well as verse 2. 10) as additions, since in their view, these verses express the idea that the election of Israel is connected with the Exodus from Egypt, while this tradition — so these scholars hold — was actually a northern one which Amos did not accept, as is further evident from 9. 7.

eleven times, appears in Amos only in this verse. The idiomatic expression "to call to account" (*pāqad 'al*) appears twice more in Amos, both times in the brief oracle of 3. 14. Though the direct object there, *pešā'īm* ("transgressions") is Amos' standard word for Israel's sins, the idiom *pāqad pešā' 'al* appears nowhere else in the Bible and seems to be Amos' own coinage. In our passage, on the other hand, Amos uses *'āwōn*, which is not a part of his lexicon, apparently because he required a stock phrase, a conventional idiom, a sort of quotation. As noted above, the quotation is almost certainly from the Second Word of the Decalogue.[46] Now, as we have said, the irregularities of verse 1b become comprehensible only if the verse is seen as a quotation from the opening statement of the Decalogue. Thus we have ascertained to a high degree of probability that the prophet concludes both his own introduction to the divine proclamation. and the formulation of that proclamation itself, with citations from the first two utterances of the Decalogue.

The oracle in Amos 3. 1–2 sets out to topple the nation's bastion of self-assurance by undermining its very foundation — the fact that God brought them up from Egypt, or more precisely, their perception that the Exodus created an ongoing, unconditional pact ensuring their security and immunity and acting as a guarantee that all their wrongdoing would be forgiven. For this reason the prophet addresses Israel by referring to its attitude toward the very historic event which gives this belief its credibility — the Exodus. What is more, by referring to this event with the very same formula which God Himself used in the revelation at Sinai, at least according to the version which was current in his time, Amos actually appears to be affirming, even strengthening, his listener's beliefs. His opening words serve to draw his audience to him,[47] so that they accompany him along the path he paves for them in verse 2a, not fully cognizant of his message, not yet thinking that the words "that is why" will mark a parting of the ways. The audience is caught unaware, ensnared and swept along through the second part of verse 2, only to discover at its conclusion that Amos has led them in a

---

46 See also Knierim (above, n. 31); M. Buber, *The Prophetic Faith*, New York 1949, p. 45.

47 O. Seesemann, *Israel und Juda bei Amos und Hosea*, Leipzig 1898, pp. 6–7, long ago noted the use of this rhetorical technique, characteristic of Amos, in this particular prophecy. With respect to recent scholars, cf. Buber. (above, n. 46); Smend (above, n. 45), pp. 409–410, and others.

direction totally opposite to that which they anticipated. Only then do they discover that the statement concerning their special status was made in a tone quite different from what they originally supposed: God's "singling them out" and "calling them to account", which they believed to be mutually contradictory, are now revealed by the prophet to be one and the same. If they had but thought about the formulation of the oracle, it would have occurred to them that the transition from "brought you up" to "singled [you] out" is no mere stylistic variation. They might even have realized that the quotation from the opening of the Decalogue was not meant to reaffirm their vain self-assurance but to undermine it. It was intended to allude to the fact that the very voice which proclaimed "I brought [you] up from the land of Egypt" is the same voice which declared "I will call you to account for all your iniquities".

If this elucidation of Amos' prophecy is true to its content, then we can say with reasonable certainty that there are traces of the Decalogue in the books of Amos, Hosea and Jeremiah, taking the form of veiled references to the commands which appear as the First, Second, Third, Sixth, Seventh and Eighth Commandments. Twice they appear in an order different from that found in the Pentateuch, and in all cases they deviate linguistically from the pentateuchal formulations. Some of the divergencies appear to be intentional, and must always be explained in context, in keeping with the aim of the specific prophecy. Thus we find in Jeremiah 7 that instead of general formulations based on the Decalogue ("You shall not bow down to them or serve them"; "You shall not take the name of the LORD your God in vain") the prophet refers to these prohibitions by mentioning specific offenses of which Israel is guilty: "sacrifice to Baal" "swear falsely". The latter charge refects another passage, Leviticus 19.12: "You shall not swear falsely by My name", which refers to the prohibition contained in the Third Commandment. Thus we find that there are no more than slight traces of the Decalogue in prophetic literature, that these traces are not always entirely clear, and that they are confined to three of the prophetic books in all.

Translated by Adina Ben-Chorin

4. THE DECALOGUE TRADITION CRITICALLY EXAMINED

MOSHE GREENBERG

This essay surveys traditions about the Ten Commandments in the Bible as well as in the literature of commentary that has grown up around it. My intention is to examine the biblical texts as they stand, noting the difficulties which they present, unprejudiced by the aura of sanctity that surrounds them. Such a clear-eyed approach will reveal both the uncertainties and the ambiguities attached to these few short sentences which have given rise to so much thought and discussion through the ages.

THE HEBREW NAME "THE TEN UTTERANCES" ('asereth ha-dibberoth)

When Moses repeats the Ten Commandments (Deut. 5. 6–18) he calls them "these words (*devarim*) which the LORD spoke...to your whole congregation at the mountain (Horeb) with a mighty voice out of the fire" (5. 19). Earlier, he had introduced these Commandments as "the ten words" (i.e., utterances): (*'asereth ha-devarim*, 4. 13),[1] the same expression used in Exodus 34. 28 for the text inscribed on the second set of tablets which he had hewed, "He wrote down on the tablets the terms of the covenant, the ten words". According to Deuteronomy (10. 4) these were the same Commandments as those written on the first tablets, although this is not made entirely clear in Exodus 34 (see below); and in the original account of the giving of the Commandments (Ex. 20), the name "ten words" does not appear at all.

Later on, Mishnaic Hebrew replaced *devarim* with *dibberoth*, the

---

1   The term recurs in 10.4, where the Septuagint translates it into Greek: *deka logoi* (so too in Ex. 34. 28); the origin of the English "Decalogue".

plural of *dibber*, the term specialized for divine speech.[2] This rabbinic theological term is cognate with the Aramaic *'asartei dibberaya* of the Palestinian Targumim (including the Neofiti), and corresponds to the phrase *'asra pithgamin* used by Onkelos (Ex. 34. 28; Deut. 4. 13).

THE NARRATIVE SETTING

The Torah does not provide a single clear, consistent account of the giving of the Ten Commandments. In Exodus 19.9 we read that before their proclamation, God told Moses on Mount Sinai: "I will come to you in a thick cloud, in order that the people may hear when I speak with you and so trust you ever after". To what does this refer? Ibn Ezra writes:

> In my opinion this verse alludes to the Sinaitic revelation when God spoke the words of the covenant i.e., the Ten

---

2 In Jer. 5. 13, the wicked say of the prophets of God, that "the Word (*ha-dibber*) is not in them" (so Radak, correctly, for verses 12–13 are a single utterance and God's response begins only afterwards). Rashi explains: *dibber* as "the sacred word that they tell us in the Lord's name"; Radak concurs: "i.e., the holy spirit"; likewise the Septuagint translates it *logos Kyriou* (= the word of god). Jonah ibn Janah (*Sefer ha-Shorashim*, trans. from Arabic to Hebrew by Judah ibn Tibbon, ed. W. Bacher, Berlin 1896, p. 104) adds the example: "The beginning of the word (*dibber*) of the LORD to Hosea" (Hos. 1. 2; Septuagint translates *arche logou Kyriou*, like Targum Jonathan: "The beginning of the word of God".) "The form of this noun," says Ibn Janah "is the same as that of *qitter* 'offering by fire' in Jer. 44. 21". Another example of this noun form is: "Mine are vengeance and *shillem* ('recompense')" (Deut. 32. 35). All of these are verbal nouns, properly — "speaking", "offering", "avenging". In rabbinic Hebrew, the noun *dibber* came to refer specifically to prophecy, but due to its rarity in the Bible, and the frequency of the word *dibbur* (= "speech") in rabbinic Hebrew, copyists miswrote it until *dibber* was almost consistently replaced by *dibbur* in printed texts. With the help of manuscripts we can verify the existence of the theological term *dibber* in rabbinic Hebrew. See, for example, *Torat Kohanim*, ms. Rome, vocalized text ed. Louis Finkelstein, New York 1957, top of p. 6); D. Goldschmidt, ed., *The Passover Haggadah, Sources and History* (Hebrew), Jerusalem 1960, top of p. 80; where a Genizah manuscript of the Haggadah reads *'anūs al pi ha-dibber* (see note there); *Mekhilta de R. Simeon bar Yoḥai*, ed. Epstein-Melammed, Jerusalem 1955, p. 7, lines 14–15. Concerning the plural form, *dibberoth*, see M.Z. Segal, *Mishnaic Grammar* (Hebrew), Tel Aviv 1936, p. 94. The form *middabber* appears in the *Mekhilta de R. Simeon bar Yoḥai*, p. 7, line 17. *Niddabber* refers only to prophetic speech in rabbinic usage, and it is that usage that underlies the peculiar vocalization *middabber* that occurs three times in the Bible (Num. 7. 89; Ezek. 2. 2; 43. 6) — all dealing with the word of God to the prophets. See Rashi on these verses.

Commandments...and the "trust" refers to the fact that many
Israelites said that it is impossible that an incorporeal being
speak with a man of flesh and that he remain alive. Proof of this
is [the people's confession] "We have seen this day that man may
live though God has spoken to him" (Deut. 5. 21).

And indeed Exodus 19. 19 does mention a kind of dialogue between
God and Moses, with Mount Sinai covered in smoke because the LORD
had descended upon it; amidst the blare of the horn "Moses spoke, and
God answered him in thunder (lit. 'in voice')". Rashi understands this
verse too as an allusion to the proclamation of the Decalogue: "When
Moses was speaking and proclaiming the Commandments to
Israel...the LORD helped him by granting him strength so that his voice
would be powerful and audible."

Rabbi Meyuhas b. Elijah (fourteenth-fifteenth centuries) makes an
explicit connection between Exodus 19. 9 and 19. 19:

> The LORD would dictate to Moses, and Moses would repeat the
> words to Israel, like one who reads from the Torah and Israel
> would hear both of them — as it is said earlier, "that the people
> may hear when I speak with you (v. 9)", and further on, "I stood
> between the LORD and you at that time to convey the LORD's
> words to you" (Deut. 5. 5).

However, it is not universally accepted that verse 19 refers to the giving
of the Decalogue. Nahmanides links it to the adjacent verses 20–24, in
which the LORD descends to Mount Sinai before the proclamation and
calls Moses to Him:

> And he [Moses] spoke with the Israelites to instruct them what to
> do, and Israel heard the LORD's voice which answered Moses
> and commanded him, but they did not understand what He said
> to him. God gave Moses the instructions listed in the paragraph
> "Go down, warn the people" (19. 21).

Then, after Moses goes down to the people (Ex. 19. 25), God speaks
"all these words", i.e., the Ten Commandments. It is not, however,
clear to whom He spoke. The Alexandrinus ms. of the Septuagint adds
"to Moses" (verse 20. 1) a reading that is consistent with the above
explanations. Yet verse 20. 19 reads "You yourselves saw that I spoke
to you [plural] from the very heavens", which implies that God spoke
to all of the Israelites. The people are frightened and they ask Moses to

be an intermediary between them and God, "Let not God speak to us, lest we die" (Ex. 20. 16. Here we learn for the first time that God is to speak directly to the people). Moses reassures the people, and then, in order to receive the rest of the covenant stipulations, he approaches the cloud enshrouding God (verse 17–18). Despite the appropriateness of verses 15–18 to the context, Nahmanides claims (at 20. 15) that these verses should precede the giving of the Decalogue and that the people's fear and their request to Moses should immediately follow the preparatory events of 19. 18–19[a]. After all, verses 20. 15–16 do not mention that the people were afraid of the divine voice, nor do the people request that "God not speak to us *any more*".

Deuteronomy relates that God commanded Moses to gather the people at Mount Horeb so that they might hear His words and learn to revere Him forever (Deut. 4. 10; cf. Ex. 20. 17). He spoke to them face to face from the fire (Deut. 5. 4), while Moses stood between the LORD and the people to convey His words, as the people were afraid of the fire and would not go up the mountain (Deut. 5. 5).[3] After they heard the Ten Commandments, they were afraid that "if we hear the voice of the LORD our God any longer, we shall die" (5. 22), so they request that Moses serve as the intermediary.

Unless we manipulate them, these details do not add up to a continuous, consistent story. Nahmanides' approach, for example, forces him to assume that the people drew back twice, and that they twice requested Moses to act as intermediary — once prior to the proclamation of the Decalogue (Ex. 20) and once subsequent to it (Deut. 5). The tension between Deut. 5. 4 and 5. 5 is resolved by the explanation that God gave the two Commandments "I the LORD am your God", and "You shall have no other gods" (Commandments in which He speaks in the first person), to the people "face to face", whereas Moses "stood between the LORD and you...to convey" the rest of the Commandments. (Hizzequni accordingly claims that Ex. 20. 15–17, which relates the people's fear and request for mediation,

---

3   Isaac Abrabanel enumerates the problems in these verses: If God spoke to them "face to face", then why does Moses say, "I stood between the Lord and you at that time to convey the Lord's words to you"? Another difficulty is the implicit accusation in Moses' words "for you...did not go up the mountain"; according to the narrative in Ex. 19. 12, he warned them from the outset not to go up the mountain.

"should actually follow 'keep my commandments' (20. 6), but the Torah did not want to interrupt the recitation of the Decalogue").

An unbiased reading of these narratives reveals that differing conceptions of the event have been interwoven: (a) God spoke with Moses, and the people overheard; (b) He spoke with Moses, and then Moses transmitted His words to the people; (c) God spoke to the people directly.[4] Common to them is the idea that all the people experienced the revelation at Mount Sinai; they differ only concerning the manner in which the Decalogue was received — whether from God directly or via Moses.[5]

What is the significance of this public theophany? Both Exodus 20. 17 and Deuteronomy 4. 10 say that it was intended to instil the fear of God in the hearts of the people. Another purpose was to cause the people to believe in Moses's prophecy, and to have them accept his mediation between them and God (Ex. 19. 9; 20. 16; Deut. 5. 21–24).[6] Medieval theologians perceived the latter as the main purpose:

> The Jews did not believe in Moses despite the miracles he had performed.... What then did inspire belief in him? The event at Mount Sinai. Because we heard with our own ears and saw with our own eyes the fire and the thunder and lightning. We saw Moses enter the dark cloud and heard the Voice telling him "Moses, Moses, go and tell the people thus and so". This too is the purpose of the passage (Deut. 5. 4) "Face to face the LORD spoke to you on the mountain"; likewise (v. 3) "It was not with our fathers that the LORD made this covenant but with us". Now, whence do we know that it was the revelation at Sinai that

4 Is (b) perhaps a compromise between (a) and (c)? For a detailed analysis of this problem, see Arie Toeg, *Lawgiving at Sinai* (Hebrew), Jerusalem: Magnes 1977, pp. 46–59.
5 Another divergence, namely, concerning the place where the Decalogue was proclaimed, may be concealed in this complex of traditions; cf. the apparent inner contradiction in Nehemiah 9. 13; "You came down on Mount Sinai and spoke to them from heaven". Compare also the *Baraita* of Rabbi Ishmael, at the beginning of the *Sifra*, where Ex. 19. 20 ("The Lord came down upon Mount Sinai, on the top of the mountain") and Deut. 4. 36 ("From the heavens He let you hear His voice to discipline you") are said to be an example of two verses that contradict one another. For the difference of opinion about this in rabbinic thought, see A.J. Heschel, *Theology of Ancient Judaism* (Hebrew), London 1965, II, chapters 2, 3.
6 M. Greenberg, "נסה in Exod. 20:20 and the Purpose of the Sinaitic Theophany', *Journal of Biblical Literature*, 79 (1960), pp. 273–276.

confirmed Moses as a prophet?... from the passage (Ex. 19. 9) "I
will come to you in a thick cloud, in order that the people may
hear when I speak with you and so trust you ever after". The
implication is that beforehand they had not had implicit faith in
him, of the unshakeable kind. Their belief in him was conditional,
clouded by doubts (Maimonides, *Mishneh Torah, Yesodei
Torah*, 8. 1).[7]

That the Decalogue was written by the finger of God on two stone
tablets, and that it comprised the terms of the covenant between God
and Israel, is the concept clearly expressed in the Book of Deuteronomy
(4. 12–13; 9. 10). Hence the significance of the term "the Tablets of the
Covenant", used in Deuteronomy (9. 9, 11, 15). The Exodus account is
more obscure: one must combine several verses: 24. 12 ("Come up to
Me on the mountain...and I will give you the stone tablets...which I
have inscribed to instruct them"); 31. 18 ("When He finished speaking
to him..., He gave Moses the two tablets of the Pact, stone tablets
inscribed with the finger of God"); 32. 15, 19 (the two tablets of the Pact
that Moses broke when he saw the golden calf); 34. 1 (carving two more
tablets like the first); and 34. 28 ("and he wrote down on the tablets the
terms of the covenant, the Ten Commandments"). Even after
combining these verses, there is still no definite identification of the
Commandments in Exodus 20 with the contents of the first and second
sets of stone tablets (see below for discussion on Ex. 34. 28). Only by
turning to Deuteronomy do we find a connecting link, for the Exodus
traditions are less crystallized and shaped than the tradition in
Deuteronomy.

Likewise, the epithet "tablets of the Pact" (*luḥoth ha'eduth*) is
obscure: early exegetes interpreted *'eduth* as from *'ed*, i.e., "testimony"
(Onkelos, *sahadutha*): "an eternal reminder testifying to the covenant
between God and Israel" (see Cassuto, *Commentary on Exodus*, 30–31.
18). This explanation is supported by the custom of making covenants
in the ancient Near East (see below). Other commentators rely on the
parallel phrase "tablets of the covenant" (*luḥoth ha-berith*) and regard
'eduth as coming from the root *'dy*, as in the ancient Aramaic term *'dy*
(plural construct) or *'dy'* (plural definite), meaning "covenant".[8]

---

7   Cf. Judah Halevi, *The Kuzari*, 1:87.
8   See M. Parnes, "*'Eduth, 'Edoth*, and *'Edvoth* in the Bible in the Light of External
    Evidence" (Hebrew), *Shnaton, Annual of Biblical and Near Eastern Studies*, 1,
    (1976), 235–246.

Moses breaks the first tablets in anger over the golden calf, and after conciliating God, is ordered to engrave a second set of tablets just like the first. On these latter tablets is inscribed exactly what had been written on the first (Ex. 32. 19; 34. 1, 4, 28ᵇ; Deut. 9. 17; 10. 1–4). At God's bidding a wooden ark is made for the tablets, an ark called the "Ark of the Pact" (*"'aron ha-'eduth"*, Ex. 25. 21–22) or the "Ark of the Covenant" (*"'aron ha-berith"*, Deut. 10. 1–5; Josh. 3. 6); "Ark of the LORD's Covenant" (*"'aron berith YHWH"*, Num. 10.33; Deut. 10.8). In the desert the Ark was housed in the "tent sanctuary of the Pact" (Ex. 40. 20–21; Num. 1. 50; 9. 15; 17. 22); then later in Shiloh (I Sam. 4. 3–4), and in Kiriath-jearim (I Sam. 7. 1), until David brought it to Jerusalem and placed it in the tent he pitched for it (II Sam. 6). Finally, the priests placed the Ark in the sanctuary of Solomon's Temple. The last mention of the tablets appears in this context: "There was nothing inside the Ark but the two tablets of stone which Moses placed there at Horeb" (I Ki. 8. 9). If the cherubs above the ark are God's chair, since He is styled "Enthroned on the Cherubim" (I Chron. 13. 6), then the Ark itself is the "footstool of our LORD" (I Chron. 28. 2). Accordingly, storing the tablets inside the Ark is parallel to the ancient Egyptian custom of depositing important documents beneath statues of the gods as evidence of the solemn commitment of the owners of the documents in the presence of the gods (a custom that supports the view that the "tablets of the Pact" testify to the covenant).⁹

To what does the expression "the terms of the Covenant, the Ten Commandments" in Exodus 34. 28 refer? Verses 10–26 present a short series of commandments, opening with God's declaration, "I hereby make a covenant". About this covenant, God says to Moses (verse 27): "Write down these commandments, for in accordance with these commandments I make a covenant with you and with Israel". This series includes: (1) forbidding alliances with the Canaanites; (2) forbidding molten gods; (3) enjoining the Festival of Unleavened Bread;

9   See N. H. Tur-Sinai, in *Language and Book*, (Hebrew), 3, *Beliefs and Concepts*, Jerusalem: Bialik Institute 1956, pp. 60–61; M. Haran, "The Holy Ark and the Cherubim" (Hebrew), in *Eretz Yisrael*, 5 (Mazar Volume), (1958), pp. 87–88; R. de Vaux, *The Bible and the Ancient Near East*, London: Darton, Longman & Todd 1972, pp. 147 f. However, S. Japhet maintains that the idea of the ark as God's footstool is an innovation of the Chronicler and is not an ancient concept; see her *The Ideology of the Book of Chronicles* (Hebrew), Jerusalem: Mosad Bialik 1977, pp. 71–73.

(4) firstlings; (5) the Sabbath; (6) the Festival of Weeks; (7) the Ingathering Festival; (8) pilgrimages; (9) statutes concerning the Passover sacrifice (10) first fruits; and (11) a ban on cooking a kid in its mother's milk. After noting that Moses spent forty days and nights fasting before the LORD, the text reports that "he inscribed on the tablets the terms of the Covenant, the Ten Commandments"(verse 28).

In context Moses is apparently the one who inscribed, and what he inscribed is the preceding series of commandments.[10] Yet if this is indeed the case, then we have before us another series called the "Ten Words" (*'asereth ha-devarim*)! However, since it is improbable that one designation should cover two such different series of injunctions, it appears that the end of verse 28 refers to verse 1 ("I will inscribe upon the tablets the words that were on the first tablets") and is to be detached from its adjacent context. Hence, an independent series of covenant injunctions appears between verse 1 and 28b, which is not called the "Ten Words".[11] The relationship of these two series to each other, and of both to the "record of the covenant"(Ex. 24.7) containing "all these commands" with reference to which the Sinai covenant was made according to Ex. 24. 8, is unclear. Evidently several documents called the "Words of the Covenant" were preserved by ancient tradition; the biblical narrator integrated them all into the story of the giving of the Torah, and he was unable (or did not want) to smooth over the problems caused by his conservative method — an outcome of the awe in which he held these traditions.

10   It is difficult to determine exactly the number of commandments in this series, but it is equally difficult to determine the number of commandments in the Decalogue in Exodus 20 (see below). The connection between the series of commandments in Exodus 34 and the foregoing story of the Golden Calf is pointed out in Joseph Bekhor Shor's commentary on verses 14, 18.

11   It is a widely held scholarly theory that Exodus 34. 10–26 comprises a deca-(or dodeca)-logue. This is called the "cultic decalogue"(because it deals only with the relationship between Israel and God), and is assumed to be more primitive religiously than the Ten Commandments (of Ex. 20) which is designated the "ethical decalogue". The religion of Israel is supposed to have undergone a farreaching evolution, from a level at which cultic commandments were central, to a culmination in classical prophecy, when ethics became primary. Critics of this theory point, among other things, to the fact that the ethical stance of our Decalogue is far from unique. It can be found not only in pre-prophetic parts of the Bible, but also in extra-biblical literature (see an example below). One of the first scholars to reject this theory was H. Gressmann, *Mose und seine Zeit*, Göttingen: Vandenhoeck & Ruprecht, 1913, pp. 473 ff.

In addition to the two versions of the Decalogue found in the masoretic text of the Pentateuch (Ex. 20. 2–17 and Deut. 5. 6–21;) the Samaritan Pentateuch preserves slightly differing Hebrew texts (see plate). The Samaritan text tends to reduce the differences between the versions in Exodus and Deuteronomy. For example:

Masoretic Version	*Samaritan Version, Both Books*
Ex.: Remember Deut.: Observe	Observe
Ex.: You shall not covet your neighbor's house Deut.: And you shall not covet your neighbor's wife	You shall not covet your neighbor's house
Ex.: You shall not covet your neighbor's wife Deut.: And you shall not crave your neighbor's house	And you shall not covet your neighbor's wife
Ex.: his male or his female slave, or his ox, or his ass Deut.: his field, or his male or his female slave, or his ox, or his ass	his field, his male or his female slave, his ox, or his ass
Ex.: after "you shall not murder", five "you-shall-not" 's Deut.: five "and you-shall-not" 's	four "you-shall-not" 's the fifth: "*and* you-shall-not"

The major difference between the Masoretic and the Samaritan versions is the Samaritan addition of a Commandment considered the Tenth, according to their numbering (their First Commandment is "You shall have no other gods..."). This comprises the injunction to publish the Decalogue on Mount Gerizim and to build an altar there. The Samaritan Exodus and Deuteronomy both contain the passage:

> And it will come to pass when the Lord brings you to Canaan and you possess the land (cf. Deut. 11. 29), then you shall raise up

*   See the detailed Table on the following pages.

VERSIONS OF THE DECALOGUE

EXODUS (E)   DEUTERONOMY (D)

(The superscript numbers refer to the variants listed below)

I the LORD am your God who brought you out of the land of Egypt, the house of bondage: You shall have no other gods beside Me. You shall not make for yourself a sculptured image, or any (D: any)[1] likeness of what is in the heavens above, or on the earth below, or in the waters under the earth. You shall not bow down to them or serve them. For I the LORD your God am an impassioned[2] God, visiting the guilt of the fathers upon the children, (D: and)[3] upon the third and upon the fourth generations of those who reject Me, but showing kindness to the thousandth generation of those who love Me and keep My commandments (D: *ktiv* His commandments).

You shall not swear falsely by the name of the LORD your God, for the LORD will not clear one who swears falsely by his name.[4]

Remember[5] the sabbath day and keep it holy. Six days you shall labor and do all your work, but[6] the seventh day is a sabbath of the LORD your God: you shall not do any work[7] — you, your son or daughter, your male or female slave,[8] or[9] your cattle, or the stranger who is within your settlements. **For in six days the LORD made heaven and earth, sea and all that is in them, and He rested on the seventh day; therefore the LORD blessed the sabbath day and hallowed it.**[10]	**Observe** the sabbath day and keep it holy, **as the LORD your God has commanded you**. Six days you shall labor and do all[11] your work, but[6] the seventh day is a sabbath of the LORD your God: you shall not do any work[7] — you, your son or your daughter, **and**[12] your male or female slave, and[13] **your ox or your ass,**[14] **or any of your** cattle,[14] or the stranger who is within your settlements, **so that your male and female slave may rest as you do. Remember that your were a slave in the land of Egypt and the LORD your God freed you from there with a mighty hand and an out-stretched arm; therefore the LORD your God has commanded you to make**[15] **the sabbath day.**[16]
Honor your father and your mother,[17] that you may long endure on the[18] land which the LORD your God is giving you.	Honor your father and your mother, **as the LORD your God has commanded you,**[19] that you may long endure, **and that you may fare well,**[19] in the land that the LORD your God is giving you.

[20]You shall not murder.

(D: And)[21] You shall not commit adultery.

(D: And)[21] You shall not steal.[20]

(D: And)[21] You shall not bear false (E: *šeqer*; D: *šaw*) witness against your neighbor.

You shall not covet your neighbor's **house;**[22] **you shall not covet**[22a] **your neighbor's**[24] **wife,**[23] or[25] his male or female slave, **or**[26] his ox or his ass,[27] or anything that is your neighbor's.

And[21] You shall not covet your neighbor's **wife**.[28] **And**[28a] **you shall not crave**[29] **your neighbor's house,**[30] **or his field,**[31] or his male[32] or female slave,[33] or his ox,[34] or his ass,[35] or anything that is your neighbor's.

VARIANTS

1	Q, Ds, Dg: +any		17	+ that you may fare well and N, Eg
2	N: (q n w')		18	+ good Eg
3	Q, Ds, Dg: upon		19	that you may fare well and
4	N: [š]mh			that you may long endure Dg
5	Observe Es		20	adultery, theft, murder Eg;
6	+on N, Q			adultery, murder, theft N, Dg (Philo)
7	+ on it (*bh*) N; (*bw*) Q, Eg,		21	> Q, Ds, Dg
	Dg; =Es, Ds		22	wife [N], Eg
8	+ your ox and your ass and all		22a	*ttm ?wh* N
	your N, Eg		23	house N, Eg
9	> Es		23	house N, Eg
10	N: *vyqdsyw*		24	N, Es, Eg + his field
11	Q: + *eth*		25	> Es
12	> Q, Ds, Dg		26	Es: his cattle
13	> Q, Ds, Dg		27	+ or all his cattle Eg
14	Q: and your cattle		28	house(hold) Ds
15	observe Q,		28a	> Q, Dg
16	+ and to hallow it Dg; + to		29	covet Q, Sd, Dg
	hallow it, for in six days		30	wife Ds
	YHWH made heaven and earth,		31	+or Dg
	the sea all that is in them,		32	> Q, Ds
	and He rested on the seventh		33	> Q
	day; therefore YHWH blessed		34	or Dg
	the sabbath day to hallow it Q		35	+ or all his cattle Dg

KEY TO VARIANTS

Dg = Greek Deut. (LXX) (ed. Rahlfs)
Ds = Samaritan Deut. (ed. von Gall)
Eg = Greek Exod.
Es = Samaritan Exod.
N = Nash Papyrus (plate 2 in this volume)
Q = 4Q Deut.ₘ (in "Scrolls from the Wilderness of the Dead Sea: A Catalogue of the Exhibition", *The Dead Sea Scrolls of Jordan*, University of California, 1965).
+ = added matter in source(s) indicated
> = "is missing in"

large stones and coat them with plaster and write on the stones all
the words of this Torah (Deut. 27. 2b–3. 1a).

And when you cross the Jordan you will raise these stones which
I command you this day on MountGerizim (it appears thus, as
one word; cf. Deut. 27. 4a in the Masoretic version: "Mount
Ebal") and you shall build an altar there to the Lord your God, a
stone altar, etc. (27. 5–7), that mountain west of the Jordan, by
the terebinth of Moreh, opposite Shechem (Deut. 11. 30 in the
Samaritan version).

This Commandment reflects, on the one hand, the Samaritan belief in
the holiness of Mount Gerizim,[12] and on the other hand the notion,
first attested in Hellenistic-Jewish literature (see below, essay on Philo)
that the Decalogue contains "all the words of the Torah". The Nash
Papyrus discovered in Egypt, and dating from about the second
century B.C.E. to the first century C.E., contains yet another version
of the Decalogue. Because the passage *Shema' Yisra'el* follows, it has
been postulated that the Nash text had a liturgical use (i.e., it reflects
the order of reciting the portions during prayer, see below). The Nash
Papyrus version of the Decalogue is close to the Septuagint translation
of Exodus, and it is likely that it was copied from the Hebrew version
underlying the Greek translation.[13]

There is a marked tendency among non-Masoretic texts to assimilate
the Exodus and the Deuteronomy version of the Decalogue and to
combine them. Thus, itemization of property in the Sabbath
Commandment and in "Thou shall not covet" are brought more closely
into line. The differentiated Masoretic version is evidently the older
one and the others are dependent on it.

Most of the differences between the Masoretic readings of Exodus
and those of Deuteronomy can be attributed to the Deuteronomic
context, and should be viewed as secondary to the Exodus Decalogue.
The essence of the Sabbath Commandment in Exodus (God's hallowing
the seventh day on which he rested after the six days of Creation) is
related to the initial clause of the Commandment ("Remember...to
hallow it"), inasmuch as God's rest is the sole basis for the holiness of

12   See Y. Ben Zvi, *The Book of the Samaritans* (Hebrew), Jerusalem: Yad Ben-Zvi
     1970, pp. 140–141.
13   See M.Z. Segal, *Tradition and Criticism* (Hebrew), Jerusalem: Kiryat-Sefer 1956,
     pp. 227–236.

the day ("therefore the Lord hallowed it").[14] In contrast, Deuteronomy's explanation, "so that your male and female slave may rest as you do" (cf. Ex. 23. 12), is more appropriate to that book's humanitarian attitude.[15] "Remember that you were a slave in the land of Egypt", which appears in the sequel is one of many similar mentions of the Egyptian bondage found throughout Deuteronomy's legal material (e.g., 15. 15; 16. 12; 24. 18–22). The rhetorical expansions "that you may long endure" and "as the Lord your God has commanded you", which appear in Deuteronomy's Commandments on the Sabbath and on parental honor, are typically Deuteronomic; see Deuteronomy 5. 26; 6. 18; 12. 25 ff.; 4. 23; and 20. 17. The addition of ox and ass in the list of a man's property in the Deuteronomic Sabbath Commandment is apparently taken from the Commandment "You shall not crave". Exodus begins the list of objects which "You shall not covet" with the general "house" = all the members of your neighbor's household (cf. Gen. 18. 19; Deut. 25. 9), and then proceeds to detail human and animal members in descending order of value omitting real property, reflecting perhaps a setting in nomadic life. Deuteronomy, which does include real property, places the wife first (as in Exodus) and joins house (here meaning the building) to field (a common pair, cf. Gen. 39. 5; II Ki. 8. 3, 5). In these cases, the Deuteronomic reading is obviously secondary. Ibn Ezra's note (in the introduction to the Decalogue, in his long commentary on Exodus) applies to the other changes in wording:

> The custom of the speakers of the sacred tongue (Hebrew) is sometimes to explicate matters at length and sometimes to use only so many words as are needed to make their meaning plain. Words are like bodies, their meaning is like the soul; the body is like a vessel for the soul. Hence the custom of the wise to use

---

14   It is difficult to find a reason for Deuteronomy's substitution of "observe" for Exodus's "remember", since "remember" goes with "day" in Deuteronomy (16. 3) just as "observe" goes with "day" in Exodus (12. 17), and neither book shows any preference for one or the other term. Concerning the free substitution of synonyms in parallel expressions, see S. Talmon, "Synonymous Readings in...the Old Testament", *Scripta Hierosolymitana*, 8 (1961), pp. 335–383.

15   M. Weinfeld describes the humanitarian nature of Deuteronomy in his book, *Deuteronomy and the Deuteronomic School*, Oxford: Clarendon Press 1972, pp. 282 ff. On the differences in the Sabbath Commandment, see ibid., p. 222 (for an opinion different from mine).

language that preserves the sense, and not to be concerned about changes in the words so long as their meaning stays the same.

THE DIVISION INTO TEN COMMANDMENTS

The tradition governing the division of the Decalogue into paragraphs (*parashiyot*) does not conform to the tradition of its division into Ten Commandments (see *Minḥat Shai* on Exodus 20. 4, the end). The long section in which God speaks in the first person (verses 4–6, "I the LORD... My commandments") is one paragraph — as opposed to its usual division into two Commandments, as for example, in the *Mekhilta Baḥodesh*, chapter 8 (ed. Lauterbach, vol. II, p. 262), which counts "I the LORD" as the First and "You shall have no other gods...My commandments" as the Second Commandment.[16] On the other hand, it was apparently in order to arrive at ten paragraphs that the prohibition of coveting in Exodus 20. 14 was broken into two *parashiyot*, each beginning with "You shall not covet" (in Deut. 4. 18 it is "You shall not covet" and "You shall not crave"); this, even though the accepted reckoning (e.g., the *Mekhilta*) considers them to be one Commandment.[17]

There are two sets of cantillations for the Decalogue; Hizzequni explains them as follows (at the end of his commentary on the Exodus Decalogue):

> Most of the Ten Commandments have two sets of cantillation signs. To wit: on Shavuot, which is a representation of the giving of the Torah, and the Commandments are accompanied by the [explanatory] Targum,[18] we chant the whole Commandment,

---

16   Cf. Hizzequni on Exodus 20. 14: "The Commandments 'I the LORD' and 'You shall have no other gods' also carry 'large' cantillation accents combining them into one verse, as a reminder that they were given as one utterance". Concerning the cantillation, see below.

17   Ibn Ezra, in his introduction to the Ten Commandments (the long commentary) deprecates the separation of these clauses. *Minḥat Shai* surmises that the division into paragraphs caused this "error".

18   "In Deutschland und Frankreich kannte man die Übertragung nur bei zwei sehr feierlichen Perikopen, bei der Erzählung vom Auszuge aus Aegyptien am 7 Tage Pesach (Ex. 13. 17–26) und von der Offenbarung am Sinai (Ex. 19. 20) am Wochenfeste. Es ist mit eigenartiges Targum, das das Machsor Vitry für die zwei Tage mitteilt, eine Verbindung von Onkelos mit dem Fragmenten-Targum." Ismar Elbogen, *Der jüdischen Gottesdienst in seiner geschichtichen Entwicklung*,

"You shall have no other gods", and the whole Commandment, "Remember the Sabbath", with the "enlarging" cantillation, which treats each one as a single verse since each is an individual Commandment. The Commandments "You shall not murder", "You shall not commit adultery", "You shall not steal", and "You shall not bear false witness", are chanted with the "shortening" cantillation, which breaks them into four verses, for they are four individual Commandments. In the month of Shevat, however, when one reads the Torah portion "Jethro" as a regular weekly portion, one chants "You shall have no other gods" and "Remember" in the "shortening" cantillation, so that each of them becomes four verses, while the Commandments "You shall not murder", "You shall not commit adultery", "You shall not steal", and "You shall not bear false witness", are chanted with the "enlarging" cantillation, so that they all become one verse, since nowhere else in the Bible is there a verse consisting of only two words. Only on Shavuot as I said above, are the Commandments "I the LORD", and "You shall have no other gods", chanted according to the "enlarging" cantillation, making them one verse in order to remind us that they were proclaimed in a single utterance.

The gist of this is that on the Feast of Shavuot one chants the Commandments in a versification that represents the way in which Israel heard the Ten Commandments at Mount Sinai — some very long utterances and some very short utterances. On the Sabbath for which "Jethro" (Ex. 18. 1–20. 23) is the Torah portion, one chants the Commandments according to a normalizing cantillation that breaks the passage into verses of usual length. The system that lengthens or shortens the verses is called the "upper cantillation", and the system that normalizes the verses is called "lower cantillation".[19] (*Minḥat Shai*

Frankfurt am Main 1931, p. 191.
(In Germany and France there were only two especially solemn occasions when the prescribed Torah reading was accompanied by an Aramaic translation [Targum]. These were the Seventh Day of Passover, when the story of the Exodus is read (Ex. 13. 17–26), and Shavuot, when the Scriptural portion described the revelation at Sinai (Ex. 19 and 20). For these two days, Mahzor Vitry (twelfth century) provides a peculiar translation, a combination of Onkelos with the "Fragment-Targum").
19 See the example of the two systems of cantillation in the *Encyclopaedia Biblica* (Hebrew), s.v. "*te'amim*", Vol. 3, pp. 403–404; also plate 4a and 4b below. Based

asserts that the upper cantillation is for public reading of the Decalogue and that the lower cantillation is for private reading.)

The chief difficulty and the focus of disagreement is the first paragraph ("I the LORD...My commandments"), which is stylistically uniform — entirely in the first person — yet diverse in its content.[20] Philo defines the content of the First Commandment: "to acknowledge and honour the God Who is above all" (*On the Decalogue*, 65);[21] he describes the Second Commandment as dealing with "idols of stone and wood and images in general made by human hands" (ibid., 51). Josephus too defines the First Commandment as teaching, "that God is one and that He only must be worshipped", and the Second Commandment as "a commandment to make no image of any living creature for adoration".[22] Apparently both Philo and Josephus considered "You shall not make for yourself a sculptured image" as beginning the Second Commandment. A similar division is made by Rabbi Ishmael in *Sifre Numbers* (112) commenting on "he has spurned the word of the LORD" (Num. 15. 31):

> R. Ishmael says: the Torah refers here to idolatry, as it is written, "He spurned the word of the LORD" (that is, "God's utterance"). He spurned the first utterance God made to Moses: "I the LORD am your God. You shall have no other gods beside me."

We called this "a similar division", because it is not clear whether Philo and Josephus considered "I the LORD" as part of the First Commandment. The Samaritans do not count it in, nor do most

on manuscript evidence, S. Pinsker suggested that the origin of the term "upper cantillation" was the Babylonian notation system, by contrast with the Tiberian system which is mainly under the letters. See *Liqute Qadmoniot*, Vienna 1860, pp. 33–37, and *Mavo el hanniqud ha-ashuri*, Vienna 1863, pp. 19 ff.

20   On the division of the Commandments, see articles in this volume: Mordechai Breuer, "The Division of the Decalogue into Verses and Commandments", and Gad B. Sarfatti, "The Tablets of the Covenant as a Symbol of Judaism" = *Tarbiz*, 29 (1960), especially pp. 386 f.).

21   *Philo*, The Loeb Classical Library, trans. F.H. Colson, Cambridge–Harvard University Press 1968; VII, pp. 38 and 31; see also Yehoshua Amir, "The Decalogue According to the Teachings of Philo", in the present volume.

22   *Antiquities*, III : 91; *Josephus*, Loeb Classical Library, trans. H. St. J. Thackeray, Cambridge–Harvard University Press 1961.

Christians.[23] However, the link between "I the LORD" and "You shall have no other gods", can be seen in the sequence of ideas in the following verses:

> I brought you up out of Egypt and freed you from the house of bondage... And I said to you, "I the LORD am your God: you must not worship the gods of the Amorites in whose land you dwell"... (Judg. 6. 8–10).
> You shall have no foreign god, / you shall not bow to an alien god. /
> I the LORD am your God / who brought you out of the land of Egypt... (Ps. 81. 10–11).

We see here that the mention of the Exodus from Egypt serves as a motive for the commandment adjacent to (either preceding or following) it; i.e., "because I the LORD am your God, you must not worship the gods of the Amorites"; "you shall have no foreign god...because I the LORD am your God who brought you...". According to these parallels, and following Philo, Josephus and Rabbi Ishmael, for whom the First Commandment ends with verse 3 ("You shall have no other gods beside Me"), the First Commandment should be defined as the imperative to recognize the LORD as the sole God, because He revealed Himself as "your God (= your shield and your saviour) who brought you out of the land of Egypt". Compare this verse with Hosea 13. 4: "Only I the LORD have been your God / Ever since the land of Egypt; / You have never known a [true] God but Me, / You have never had a helper other than Me". (The parallel between "God" and "helper" shows that the first half of the verse means: "Only I the LORD have been your God [who revealed Himself as your helper] since the land of Egypt"; just so we must understand the beginning of the First Commandment.)[24]

---

23   See W. Harrelson's convenient chart in *The Ten Commandments and Human Rights*, Philadelphia: Fortress Press 1980, p. 47. Compare Ibn Ezra's position in his introduction to the Decalogue.

24   Note the punctuation in *Tanakh*, Philadelphia: JPS, 1985, p. 115: "I the LORD am your God who brought you out of the land of Egypt, the house of bondage: You shall have no other gods beside me".

     The rabbinic Sages, who called the Commandment "I the LORD" (verse 2 alone) by the name "Acceptance of God's Sovereignty" counted it as the First Commandment (see n. 16 above, and the context to which it is attached; also *Mekhilta Baḥodesh*, 6). The commentators of old disagreed over the question whether verse 2, the

The Second Commandment begins "You shall not make for yourself",[25] and prohibits any sculptured images for worship. Artistic renderings for decoration (e.g., plant forms, figures of various animals for the Temple) are not forbidden, nor is the making of images of God's entourage, such as cherubim. What is prohibited is the making of images of the Deity. No distinction is made between the Israelite God and pagan gods; indeed no distinction is made between the image and the deity, i.e., there is no recognition of the symbolic value of the image as nothing more than a symbolic rendering of the (usually) invisible deity. Every sculptured image is equally forbidden, and is perceived as a deity itself; therefore, the sculptured image is "other gods", and the idol worshipper arouses God's passion by transgressing the (first) Commandment "You shall have no other gods beside Me".[26]

This prohibition is explained in Deuteronomy 4. 15–18: "since you saw no shape when the LORD your God spoke to you at Horeb out of the fire". One is forbidden to create an image (or sculpture) of the LORD because no one knows how He looks; any picture that one may draw will be false. It is implied that an idol represents (albeit here falsely) an invisible being. A distinction between the symbol and the symbolized emerges here for the first time, even though this distinction is quite infrequent in the Bible, and is absent in the Decalogue. It appears to be the product of reflection, of an attempt to find a rational explanation, overly simplistic, for the Decalogue's ancient prohibition.

This lack of distinction between the image and the deity is neither a mistake (Kaufmann's view) nor a polemical exaggeration. For the idol

---

self-description of God, is actually a commandment, or is the basis of belief from which the other commandments derive. See, e.g., Maimonides, *Sefer Ha-Mitzvoth*, positive commandment No. 1, and Nahmanides's critique thereof.

25   Sarfatti in his article in the present volume and in *Tarbiz*, 29, notes that on some representations of the Tablets of the Covenant in Italian Synagogues, the Second Commandment is "You shall not make for yourself a sculptured image".

26   That the Second Commandment is not a prohibition against art is argued by C. Konikoff, *The Second Commandment and Its Interpretation in the Art of Ancient Israel*, Genève: Imprimerie du Journal de Genève, 1973, p. 26. On the lack of distinction between the sculptured image and the deity itself throughout the Bible, and especially in biblical legislation, see Y. Kaufmann, "The Bible and Mythological Polytheism", *Journal of Biblical Literature*, 70 (1951), pp. 179–197; specifically on the Decalogue, ibid., pp. 188–189. My reservations about his comments on Deuteronomy 4. 15–18, and about his judgment that the biblical polemic distorts idolatry, appear below.

worshipper, the line between the invisible deity and the image was truly blurred. By a prescribed ritual he was able to "animate" the idol; and all worship, all acceptance of worship, and all of the deity's relationship with the worshippers were accomplished through the idol.[27] The "fetishistic" version of the prohibition found in the Decalogue is directed at a widespread and psychologically deep-rooted conception that was common among idol worshippers in the ancient world. The Second Commandment was right on the mark when it ignored the difference between the symbol and the thing symbolized. The polemic against idolatry, depicting it as man worshipping his own handiwork in wood or stone, is likewise well founded (e.g., II Ki. 19. 18; Isa. 2. 7; Ps. 115. 3–7).

Deuteronomy's innovative explanation ("since you saw no shape") may not have a precedent, but it certainly has derivatives. Isaiah 40. 18 already expands this idea to express the incomparability of God: "To whom, then, can you liken God, / What form compare to Him?" — as the introduction to the mockery of idolatry (cf. 46. 5), an idea adopted later by many to explain the Second Commandment (cf. Buber: "He should not be imagined, that is, limited to any one definite form; nor should He be equated to one or other of the 'figures' in nature, that is, restricted to any one definite manifestation".)[28] This idea contains an attractive element of intellectualization, but it lacks the holistic trenchancy of the original ancient Commandment.

The Third Commandment is ambiguous. It reads literally "You shall not bear the name of the LORD your God in vain". "Bear" is interpreted according to the fuller phrase of Ps. 16. 4 "I will not bear their names on

---

27   A.L. Oppenheim, *Ancient Mesopotamia: Portrait of a Dead Civilization*, Chicago 1977, pp. 183–193; H. Frankfort, *Kingship and the Gods*, Chicago: University of Chicago, 1948, pp. 302–306; E. Bevan, *Holy Images*, London: Allen & Unwin, 1940, Lecture 1, pp. 13–45. A critique of Kaufmann's view, richly illustrated from ancient texts, is J. Faur, "The Biblical Idea of Idolatry", *Jewish Quarterly Review* 69 (1978), pp. 1–15.

28   M. Buber, *Moses*, transl. into English, New York: Harper and Row 1958, p. 127. Josephus comes closer to the Deuteronomic idea with his explanation of the prohibition against making a sculptured image of God: "By His works and His bounties He is plainly seen, indeed more manifest than aught else, but His form and magnitude surpass our powers of description. No materials, however costly, are fit to make an image of Him, no art has skill to conceive and represent it. The like of Him we have never seen, we do not imagine and it is impious to conjecture" (*Apion*, II, 190–191).

my lips" = utter their names[29] (cf. also Ps. 50. 16). The Hebrew word *la-šaw'* can refer to lying or deceit (Ps. 144. 8, 11; cf. the substitution for *'ed šeqer* in the Exodus Decalogue, by *'ed šaw'* in the Deuteronomy Decalogue, both meaning "false witness"; Job 31. 5). It can also mean "for naught", or "in vain" (Jer. 2. 30; 4. 30; 6. 29.). The complete phrase can be understood as "Do not utter the name of the LORD falsely or in vain" — an interpretation which itself contains ambiguities. The parallelism found in Ps. 24. 4 (lit. "who has not borne my life in vain or sworn deceitfully"[30]) leads one to understand that the Third Commandment forbids using the name of the LORD in a false oath, as in Leviticus 19. 12: "You shall not swear falsely by My name, profaning the name of your God".

According to the other meaning of *la-šaw'*, however, the ancients understood the prohibition to forbid the name of the LORD in unnecessary oaths. Philo understood it in both senses: a prohibition against false oaths, as well as the habit of "some who without even any gain in prospect have an evil habit of swearing incessantly and thoughtlessly about ordinary matters...for from much swearing springs false swearing and impiety" (*On the Decalogue*, 84–91). Onkelos includes both interpretations: "You shall not swear by the name of the LORD your God frivolously, for the LORD will not clear one who swears falsely by His name." There are still other possibilities since the Hebrew verb here, *ns'* means "utter", "express" (not necessarily in an oath). The Sages expanded the scope of the Commandment to include the prohibition of any idle use of God's name; for example "Whoever says a blessing which is superfluous transgresses the Third Commandment" (Ber. 33a).

The Fourth Commandment ordains the sanctification of the Sabbath by ceasing from all work. This cessation is explained in Exodus as honoring the day because God blessed and hallowed it by resting from

29   The phrase "bear on one's lips", parallel to "rise on one's heart" (= come to mind) occurs in the Sefire Inscription III, 14–15, with the same meaning as "utter", see J.C. Greenfield, "Stylistic Aspects of the Sefire Treaty Inscriptions", *Acta Orientalia*, 29 (1965), p. 5.

30   David Kimhi in his commentary on Psalms says of this verse, "The words 'by my life', are spoken by God Himself...'His life' means 'His Name,' as in Amos 6.8: "The LORD God has sworn by Himself (lit. 'by His life')". It is noteworthy that swearing truthfully by God's name is not only permitted, it is considered an expression of commendable fear of God: Deut. 6. 13; Jer. 12. 16, Ps. 63. 12.

Creation. We can compare this reason to the one given in Isaiah 58. 13: "If you call the sabbath 'delight', / The LORD's holy day 'honored'; / And if you honor it and go not your ways / Nor look to your affairs, nor strike bargains...". The motive for the Sabbath in Exodus depends on the Creation story in Genesis 1–2, and is similar to it as well in ascribing an anthropomorphic attribute (resting) to God. Deuteronomy substitutes a humanitarian ground, one that actually refers only to a man's household, without giving a reason for his own rest: "so that your male and female slave may rest as you do" (cf. Ex. 23. 12).

Deuteronomy also adds another reason for observing this Commandment: "Remember that you were a slave in the land of Egypt and the LORD your God freed you from there...". This motive recurs frequently in Deuteronomy, and is a comprehensive one that may be compared to the opening of the First Commandment ("I the LORD"). Compare Deuteronomy 6. 21–24, where observing all of the LORD's commandments is grounded on loyalty to Him, and gratitude for His many benefactions. As Ibn Ezra puts it: "The LORD redeemed us from the house of bondage and bestowed on us this good; therefore we are obliged to fear Him".[31]

The Fifth Commandment enjoins honoring one's father and mother. As here, the other laws dealing with parent-child relations treat both parents as equals: striking or cursing a parent (Ex. 21. 15, 17; Lev. 20. 9; Deut. 27. 16), and the wayward or defiant son "who does not heed his father or mother" (Deut. 21. 18 ff.). The commandment to honor one's parents also appears next to the commandment to honor the Sabbath in Leviticus (19. 3). It bridges the first set of Commandments, which deal with the relations between man and God, and the later Commandments dealing with the relations between man and man. The ancients explained the transitional position of this Commandment in

31 Cf. my comments in *Studies in Jeremiah* (Hebrew), B.Z. Luria ed., Part II, the Society for Biblical Research in Israel (1971), pp. 32–33. On the anthropomorphism in the conception of the holiness of the Sabbath in Genesis 1–2, and in the relevant Commandment, see M. Weinfeld, "God the Creator in Genesis I and in Deutero-Isaiah" (Hebrew), *Tarbiẓ*, 37 (1968), pp. 105–112. I have already referred to Weinfeld's description of the humanitarian character of Deuteronomy (above, n. 15). In his discussion of the motives for the Sabbath in the Decalogue (*Deuteronomy, etc.*, p. 222) he does not consider the possibility that the replacement of an anthropomorphic by a humanitarian ground conforms to Deuteronomy's ideology — which he himself fully documents, pp. 191 ff.

this way: "The three of them — God, one's father and one's mother —
are partners in every person" (*Mekhilta de R. Simeon b. Yoḥai*, ed.
E.Z. Melammed, p. 152).[32] Compare this interpretation to Genesis 4. 1
and Rashi's interpretation thereof: "I have gained a male child with the
help of the LORD". Rashi explains: "When He created me and my
husband He created us by Himself, but in the case of this one we are
copartners with Him" (Compare Nid. 31a: "In every person's life there
are three partners: God, his father and his mother".)

The Sixth Commandment prohibits spilling innocent blood. Joseph
Bekhor Shor (France, 12th century) comments:

> In the vernacular, *mwrtr'*[33], that is to say, the unlawful taking of
> life. The verb applies only to such an act, whereas the terms
> *mithah* and *haregah* refer to any taking of life, lawful or
> otherwise. Note that when the Bible refers to execution by law, as
> in Deut. 13. 10, it says, "You shall take his life" (*harog tehargenu*);
> or in Lev. 20. 9 "He shall be put to death" (*moth yumath*). Hence
> there is no need for the Commandment to describe the
> circumstances at this point; the use of the word *rẓḥ* shows that
> only unlawful homicide is meant.[34]

This Commandment affirms the sanctity of human life, in the spirit of
Gen. 9. 6: "For in His image did God make man".

The Seventh Commandment prohibits adultery, defined as sexual
relations between a man and a married woman. This is the usual sense
in the Bible of the verb *nʾf*: "If a man commits adultery with a married
woman, committing adultery with his neighbor's wife" (Lev. 20. 10);
"committing adultery with the wives of their fellows" (Jer. 29. 23); "the
adulterous wife who welcomes strangers instead of her husband" (Ezek.
16. 32).[35] When a married woman willingly has sexual relations with a

---

32   Nahmanides develops this idea in his commentary on the Commandment, but
     unlike his sources, he relates to the father alone!
33   The medieval French equivalent of modern *meuntre* = "murder".
34   The use of the term *rẓḥ* for accidental homicide (Num. 35. 11; Deut. 4. 42) does not
     disprove this sound observation, since it, too, is illegal.
35   There is a semantic difference between the root used here — *nʾf* — and the verb *znh*.
     The latter means properly "to participate willingly in sexual intercourse with a man
     not one's husband", the subject being nearly always a woman, single or married.
     (When used metaphorically, the subject is usually the Israelites, and the offense —
     idolatry.) Hence, there is a measure of correspondence between the two verbs (see
     Amos 7. 17) but also a decisive difference, as when Ezekiel (23. 2–3) uses *znh* for

man other than her husband, she, too, is called "adulterer" (Lev. 20. 10). Later commentators expanded the scope of the prohibition to include all illicit sex (Joseph Bekhor Shor comments: "An adulterer is one who has relations with any of those on the forbidden list" (Lev. 18. 6–20, 20. 10–21"; see *Meor ha-Afelah*[36]). Saadiah went so far as to identify six levels of sex forbidden under this prohibition. (Ibn Ezra cites them in his long commentary.) The purpose of this Commandment is to preserve a society based on the patriarchal clan. Philo describes at length the damage to society that results from violating this Commandment (*On the Decalogue*, 121–131).

The Eighth Commandment "You shall not steal" has undergone an interesting process of interpretation. According to its ordinary usage, "steal" in this Commandment means "to take property by stealth" (Ibn Ezra) — that is, without the owner's knowledge and consent — since the biblical verb *gnb* refers, in the vast majority of instances, to theft of property, possessions. However, the Sages interpret this Commandment as referring to the theft of persons — kidnapping:

> This is a case where we derive the meaning from the context. And what is the context here? It is *nefashot*, "persons" (or alternatively, "lives"). Consequently, this Commandment, too, deals with *nefashot* (Sanh. 86a).

(If *nefashot* means "persons" then the scriptural context is, "*Do not murder*" — a person; "*Do not commit adultery*" — with a person; therefore "*Do not steal*" — a person. Alternatively, if it means "lives", as in *dinei nefashot* = "cases involving lives" = capital crimes, then the

---

fornication on the part of two (figurative) girls who are unmarried. The distinction is made even clearer by the parallelism in Amos (4. 13): "Your daughters [single] fornicate / and your daughters-in-law [obviously married] commit adultery". Ibn Ezra attempts to prove that *ni'uf* and *zenuth* are synonymous, on the basis of Jeremiah 3. 9: "She committed adultery with stone and wood". But that verse merely proves that the verb *nʼf* can have as its subject a woman as well as a man (a married woman who voluntarily has intercourse with anyone beside her husband). Jeremiah's use of the word is precise: he is comparing Israel to a married woman. Thus every act of adultery is fornication, but not every act of fornication is adultery.

36   Nethanel ben Isaiah, *Meʼor ha-ʼAfelah* (Hebrew), trans. from the Arabic by Y. Kafaḥ, Jerusalem: The Society for Preserving Yemenite Documents 1957.

context is: *Murder*, a capital crime; *Adultery*, a capital crime; therefore *Stealing* = the capital crime of kidnapping.

Although this logic is not compelling (since the immediately following Commandment dealing with false witness is not necessarily a capital crime, and has an equal claim to serve as the context of "You shall not steal") some contemporary scholars have concluded that the Eighth Commandment really does refer to kidnapping.[37] However, it seems doubtful that this Commandment should be interpreted in terms of its penalty, since it appears in a document which makes no mention at all of sanctions. It is more reasonable to take *gnb* in its usual sense as "theft of property", though in certain circumstances, it may refer to theft of persons.

This Commandment affirms the principle that every person has the right to his possessions.

The Ninth Commandment forbids testifying "against your neighbor" as a "false witness".[38] The setting is a court of law, whose verdict derives its legitimacy from the reliability of the evidence. When, in the absence of other proof, witnesses support or contradict the claims of the litigants, it becomes possible to arrive at the truth — providing the witnesses are trustworthy.

This Commandment is not the same as the talionic law of the "scheming witnesses" (Deut. 19. 16–19). That deals exclusively with cases of injury to the person.[39] The scope of this Commandment is much wider, since witnesses also play a role in civil matters (e.g., transfer of property, as in Jer. 32. 14). The thrust of this Commandment is to protect the validity and reliability of the judicial process, on which the social order depends.

The meaning of the Tenth Commandment has been, and still is, the subject of controversy, on account of the ambiguity of the verb *ḥmd* (modern scholars are often unaware that they are repeating the

---

37   A. Alt, "Das Verbot des Diebstahls im Dekalog", *Kleine Schriften zür Geschichte des Volkes Israel*, Vol 1, München: Beck, 1953, pp. 330–340; A. Phillips, *Ancient Israel's Criminal Law*, New York: Schocken 1970, pp. 130 ff.

38   Exodus has *'ed šeqer*; Deuteronomy, *'ed šaw'*, but they mean the same thing. See above, discussion of the Third Commandment. Grammatically *'ed šeqer* "false witness" describes a state of being; cf. "fell down slain" (I Sam. 31. 1 OJPS) and "went out in bands" (II Ki. 5. 2 OJPS).

39   The *Mekhilta* combines these verses, and Phillips, (above, n. 37, p. 143) understands from this combination that the Commandment deals specifically with capital cases.

arguments of the ancients[40]). Thus, the *Mekhilta de R. Simeon Bar Yohai* (ed. Epstein-Melammed, Jerusalem 1955, p. 153):

> Here it says "You shall not covet", but further on it says "You shall not crave" (Deut. 5. 18)... What is craving? When one says (text breaks off).... And what is coveting? When one exerts pressure to obtain possession.

The *Mekhilta de R. Ishmael* (ed. Horovitz–Rabin, Jerusalem 1960, p. 235; cf. ed. Lauterbach, II, p. 266) reads:

> Perhaps even the mere verbal expression of coveting is banned? No; for it says (Deut. 7. 25): "You shall not covet the silver and gold on them and *take* it for yourself." Just as there, only acting [on one's desire] is forbidden, so also here what is forbidden is only to act [on one's desire].

Levi ben Gershon (1288–1344) reinforced this interpretation with the following argument:

> The meaning of "covet" is to attempt to obtain something from one's neighbor, for example, to offer him money to divorce his wife so that he can marry her, or to sell him his male or female slave or his ox or his ass...for this is a very evil characteristic, to attempt to take away one's neighbor's possessions. We know that coveting is not just in one's heart but that it entails some action, from what is said in the Torah "You shall not covet...and *take* it for yourselves" (Deut. 7. 25). Moreover, it says "no one will covet your land" (Ex. 34. 24), which means that no one will attempt to take your land when you make a pilgrimage; and it is also said "They covet fields, and seize them" (Micah 2. 2). Hence we infer that one does not violate the prohibition if one does not actually do something in order to obtain the coveted object.[41]

40 Compare the citations given below, with Alt's argument (above, n. 37) that "covet" entails action, making it almost the equivalent of "steal". See also W. Kessler, "Problematic des Dekalogs", *Vetus Testamentum*, 7 (1957), p. 13.

41 Maimonides, in his *Book of Commandments*, negative commandment no. 266 (cf. translation by C.B. Chavel, London–New York 1967, vol. II, pp. 250 ff.) writes as follows: "If you see something desirable in the possession of someone else, and you can't stop thinking about it and craving it, you have violated the Commandment in Deuteronomy 'You shall not crave'. But if your desire for the object is so strong that you take measures to acquire it, and you don't stop importuning the owner and

Ibn Ezra presents a more balanced explanation in his commentary on
Deut. 5. 19:

> The word "covet" in the Bible has two meanings. The first is to
> seize or to extort or to take from others forcibly, as in "no one
> will covet your land" (Ex. 34. 24), for if this is not the meaning,
> then the land would be bad — but the Torah means to praise it.
> The second meaning is to crave in one's heart without acting on
> that desire, as we see in "You shall not covet your neighbor's
> house" in the Ninth Commandment (in the Exodus Decalogue,
> not counting "I the Lord" as a commandment) and "You shall
> not covet your neighbor's wife" in the Tenth Commandment....
> The proof [that "covet" here means "crave"] is that in
> Deuteronomy, where Moses explains the Torah, he substitutes
> for "You shall not covet" the words "You shall not crave".

It appears that the principles of halakhic interpretation are at work in
these commentaries, e.g., the principle that there is no superfluity or
redundancy in the Torah, so that there must be two separate meanings
for "You shall not covet" and "You shall not crave". It further appears
that the guiding principle is that the Ten Commandments have the
status of enforceable laws so that it is desirable to consider "covet" as
an overt act, removing it from the internal realm of thought and from
the problematic area of speech. However, if we confine ourselves to the
linguistic evidence, it does not, in fact, support the definition of "covet"
as "take", etc. (The opposite is true — the texts indicate that one must
complement "covet" with another verb like "take" or "seize", because
the former does *not* include this sense.) The substitution of "You shall
not crave" for "You shall not covet" indicates that "covet" = "crave".

In Micah 2. 2, the verb "covet" (*ḥmd*) is complemented by the verb
"seize". In Prov. 31. 16 a similar sequence uses the verb "resolve"
(*zmm*) followed by "acquire". Both are instances of planning followed
by action, yielding the equation *ḥmd:gzl = zmm:lqḥ* ."To covet",
therefore, means "to have thoughts (= *zmm*) of acquiring someone
else's possessions". As for the idiom "covet in one's heart" (Prov. 6. 25)
it probably differs from ordinary coveting in the same way that "say in
one's heart" differs from ordinary saying; namely, in that the former

exerting pressure on him (compare the terminology in the *Mekhilta de R. Simeon*)
to sell it to you or to exchange it for something of greater value...and you achieve
your purpose, you have also violated 'You shall not covet'."

denotes coveting in thought only while the latter denotes coveting overtly, in speech or behavior. From there it is but a short step to "attempt" or "exert pressure".

One way or the other, this is the most scrupulous of the Commandments. It aims to prevent the flagrantly evil acts enumerated in the preceding Commandments, by mastering those impulses which drive people to commit such acts.

A CRITICAL VIEW OF THE ORIGINAL VERSION OF THE DECALOGUE

Modern critics try to reconstruct a primary form of the Decalogue, on the assumption that originally the Commandments constituted a series uniform in both form and style, similar to the list of "curses" in Deuteronomy 27. 15–26 or to the list of virtues in Psalm 15. The fact that motive clauses appear only in the first Commandments, and that divergent grounds for the Sabbath are presented in Exodus and Deuteronomy, raises doubts about the originality of both. Likewise, the surprising shift in the motive clauses from first to third person with reference to God[42] and the shifts from "thou shalt not" to "thou shalt" run counter to the assumption of unity of style. Therefore recent critics suggest terse, repetitive reconstructions. Below are two examples:

I

Thou shalt not bow down before any other god.
Thou shalt not make to thyself any idol.
Thou shalt not take the name of Yahweh in vain.
Thou shalt not do any work on the Sabbath day.
Thou shalt not despise thy father or thy mother.
Thou shalt not commit adultery with thy neighbour's wife.
Thou shalt not pour out the blood of thy neighbour.
Thou shalt not steal any man from thy neighbour.
Thou shalt not bear false witness against thy neighbour.
Thou shalt not covet thy neighbour's house.[43]

42 This shift led to the traditional view that the Commandments, "I the LORD" and "You shalt have no other" were heard directly from God (Mak. 24a), whereas the rest of the Commandments were mediated to the people by Moses. See the detailed explanation by Joseph b. Simeon Kara (France, 11th–12th century) quoted in the commentary of Joseph Bekhor Shor on this verse. To be sure, such a change of pronoun occurs in other places as well (e.g., Ex. 23. 13–19; 34. 11–26), and there, too, the change serves critics as a basis for stratifying the text.

43 E. Nielsen, *The Ten Commandments in New Perspective*, Studies in Biblical Theology, 2/7, Naperville: Allenson 1968, pp. 84 f.

II

There shall not be to thee (or: Thou shalt not have) other gods.

Thou shalt not make for thyself an idol.

Thou shalt not lift up the name of Yah-weh for mischief.

Thou shalt not despise (or treat with contempt) the sabbath day.

Thou shalt not curse thy father or thy mother.

Thou shalt not kill (or take the life of) thy neighbor.

Thou shalt not commit adultery with the wife of thy neighbor.

Thou shalt not steal anything that is thy neighbor's

Thou shalt not answer thy neighbor as a false witness.

Thou shalt not covet the household of thy neighbor.[44]

There are two separate questions involved in dating the Decalogue: 1) what is the date of the text in its present form, including all of the "expansions" which are clearly tied to other parts of the Torah? (e.g., the Exodus motive for the Sabbath, tying it to the Creation story attributed to the Priestly source, Gen. chapters 1–2; or special idioms in the Deuteronomic Decalogue also appearing throughout the Book of Deuteronomy); 2) what is the date of the original as reconstructed, free of any such literary influences?

The answer to the first question depends on the dating of the assumed sources, but at any rate it is certainly not early. As for the reconstructed original version, scholars today favor a very early date, as there is nothing in it that necessitates a late one. The obligations to worship only the LORD and not to make sculptured images are as old as, and inseparable from, biblical faith. The concept of the Sabbath as a day of rest is already present in the parts of the manna story (Ex. 16) attributed to the ancient sources JE. The ethical level of the interpersonal Commandments is also reflected in ancient Near Eastern texts as early as, or even earlier than, the time of Moses. One such example is the "Protestation of Guiltlessness" of the dead, an Egyptian text from the New Kingdom (16th century B.C.E.). The deceased addresses his divine judges, each with a special declaration (the names of the deities are omitted here). The first ten lines of this declaration read:[45]

1.　　I have not committed evil.

44　　Harrelson (above, n. 23), pp. 42, 207.

45　　J. B. Pritchard, *Ancient Near Eastern Texts*, Princeton University 1950, p. 35 (the B list).

2. I have not stolen.
3. I have not been covetous.
4. I have not robbed.
5. I have not killed men.
6. I have not damaged the grain measure.
7. I have not caused crookedness.
8. I have not stolen the property of a god.
9. I have not told lies.
10. I have not taken away food.
(19.) I have not committed adultery.

The Decalogue does not reflect the prophetic ethic which would have necessitated dating it as late as the classical prophetic period. Placing first the obligations to God and balancing them with one's obligations to one's fellow is not typical of the prophetic message, which prefers the latter and deemphasizes the former. Furthermore, the main prophetic themes are absent from the Decalogue: saving the oppressed from the hand of the oppressor, aiding the poor, executing justice at the gate, etc. Therefore, neither the religious nor the ethical content of the Ten Commandments points to a late date, nor do they negate the possibility of a date as early as the birth of the nation. It seems that the expanded version of the first five Commandments, which express values specific to Israel (including the connection between living long in the land and honoring one's father and mother), bear the impress of those of the Torah's sources that were not formulated before the monarchy (P and D). Literary traces of the Decalogue in the rest of the Bible tend to confirm the early date of at least a terse form. The Commandments are echoed in the words of Hosea: "[False] swearing, dishonesty, and murder, / And theft and adultery are rife" (Hos. 4.2); "I the LORD have been your God / Ever since the land of Egypt" (Hos. 12. 10; see also 13. 4). We also see a trace in Jeremiah: "Will you steal and murder and commit adultery and swear falsely, and sacrifice to Baal, and follow other gods whom you have not experienced?" (Jer. 7. 9).

A clear echo is Psalms 81. 9–11 (which is difficult to date):

Hear, My people, and I will admonish you;
    Israel, if you would but listen to Me!
You shall have no foreign god,
    you shall not bow to an alien god.
I the LORD am your God
    who brought you out of the land of Egypt....

THE STRUCTURE OF THE DECALOGUE

The ancients already sensed that the Decalogue had a significant structure and arrangement. Thus, Philo:

> "The superior set of five... the first set of enactments begins with God the Father and Maker of all, and ends with parents who copy His nature by begetting particular persons. The other set of five contains all the prohibitions..." (*On the Decalogue*, 51).

The first five Commandments deal with matters "between a person and the Creator" (Ibn Ezra's introduction to the short commentary), and the second group of five deals with matters between a person and his fellow. The first group, furthermore, expresses special Israelite values, and therefore all its items are motivated by invoking the authority of the God of Israel. God is not mentioned in the second group, which codifies universally recognized values that do not require any grounding. The inclusion of the Commandment on honoring parents among the first five Commandments points to the special value assigned to parental authority, an authority that is affirmed and supported by God's blessing for those who honor it.[46] The distinction between the two groups of five is aptly expressed in the following, attributed to the Roman Emperor Hadrian: "The first five Commandments that the Lord gave to Israel all bear His name, while the last five Commandments which He gave to all the nations of the world do not bear His name" (*Pesikta Rabbati*, 21, ed. Ish-shalom, p. 99a; the Midrash rejects this explanation).

The Ten Commandments are said to have been engraved on two stone tablets (Ex. 31. 18; Deut. 9. 10): "...tablets inscribed on both their surfaces: they were inscribed on the one side and on the other" (Ex. 32. 15). Rectangular writing tablets made of wood and ivory have been

---

46 Because parental authority is upheld by a death sentence for those who violate it (Ex. 21. 15, 17; Lev. 20. 9; Deut. 21. 18-21), there is substance to the homily of Rabbi Judah the Patriarch: "The honor of father and mother is very dear in the sight of Him by whose word the world came into being, for He declared their honor to be equal to His own" (*Mekhilta, Ba-Ḥodesh*, Horovitz–Rabin, p. 231; cf. Lauterbach, II, p. 257). Note the sequence of maledictions in Deuteronomy 27. 15, 16. In the Code of Hammurabi (Law 195, which corresponds to Ex. 21. 15), one who strikes his parents is punished by having his hand amputated. In the same Code, Laws 192 and 193, dealing with an adopted son who rejects his adoptive parents, prescribe cutting out his tongue or his eye; in the Bible the rebellious son is punished by death.

found in Mesopotamia, including two or three diptychs and triptychs.[47] Yet the meaning of "on both their surfaces" has not yet been clarified. The widely accepted traditional explanation is that there were five Commandments written on each side (in a diptych), without consideration for the resulting quantitative imbalance. This explanation is included in an ingenious homily on the correlation of the parallel Commandments from the two sets of five:

> How were the Ten Commandments arranged? Five on the one tablet and five on the other. On the one tablet was written: "I am the Lord thy God", and opposite it on the other tablet was written: "Thou shalt not murder". This tells us that if one sheds blood it is accounted to him as though he diminished the divine image.... On the one tablet was written: "Thou shalt have no other god", and opposite it on the other tablet was written: "Thou shalt not commit adultery". This tells us that if one worships idols it is accounted to him as though he committed adultery, breaking his covenant with God.... On the one tablet was written: "Thou shalt not swear falsely", and opposite it on the other tablet was written: "Thou shalt not steal". This tells us that he who steals will in the end also swear falsely. On the one tablet was written: "Remember the sabbath day to keep it holy", and opposite it on the other tablet was written: "Thou shalt not bear false witness". This tells us that if one profanes the Sabbath it is as though he testified in the presence of Him by whose word the world came into being, that He did not create the world in six days and did not rest on the seventh day.... On the one tablet was written: "Honor thy father and thy mother", etc., and opposite it on the other tablet was written: "Thou shalt not covet thy neighbor's wife". This tells us that he who covets will in the end beget a son who may curse his real father while giving filial honor to one who is not his father (*Mekhilta de R. Ishmael*, Horovitz–Rabin, p. 234; Lauterbach, vol. II, pp. 262 f.).

By correlating the "parallel" Commandments, this homily signals how the relation of man to God is linked to the relation of man to man. By shifting the point of departure for each correlation back and forth

---

47 A photograph of three hinged ivory tablets from Assyria is found in J.B. Pritchard, *The Ancient Near East in Pictures*, 1969, p. 348, no. 803.

between the two series their equal value is emphasized. (At the same time, it is noteworthy that the homily starts its correlation more often from the second set, the social one, than from the first, including the opening and closing.)

On the surface, the Commandments are arranged in a clearly hierarchical order: matters between man and God precede matters between man and man. Even within each set of five there is a specific hierarchy: the obligation to worship God precedes the duty to honor His name, and both of these injunctions precede honoring His holy day. Finally in the first set, one must also honor one's parents. There is also a hierarchy among the five ethical Commandments: the value of life, the marriage bond (in the Masoretic version), the right to possession, reliability of public testimony, and finally the prohibition of guilty desires, which aims at safeguarding the previous four superior values.[48]

ORIGIN AND FUNCTION

The Rabbis interpreted the verse, "So Moses declared to the Israelites the set times of the LORD" (Lev. 23. 44) to mean that "each paragraph [dealing with a particular holy day] in that chapter shall be read in its due season" (Mishnah Megillah 3:6). In the Talmud to that Mishnah (Megillah 31a), the view of "others" is that on Shavuot, which is the anniversary of the giving of the Torah,[49] the prescribed public reading begins at Exodus 19. 1 — "In the third new moon"; according to Abudarham (fourteenth century Spanish authority on the liturgy) the reading continues to the end of chapter 20, encompassing the Decalogue and its narrative setting. This is the prevailing practice today, and it lends some credence to the modern theory that in ancient Israel there existed a festival of "covenant renewal" whose liturgy included the recitation of the Decalogue.

This theory draws further on the ceremonial public reading of the Torah appointed for the "assembly" to be convoked during the Feast of Sukkot of the sabbatical fallow year (Deut. 31. 11). Moreover, Psalm

---

48   The commentators discuss the meaning of the sequence of the Commandments: see, e.g., Ibn Ezra, who quotes Saadiah Gaon's explanations along with his own. Joseph Bekhor Shor provides entirely different explanations.

49   According to Jubilees, 6. 17–22, the festival in the third month has celebrated the renewal of the covenant since the time of Noah.

91 hints at a connection between the first Commandments (verse 9–11) and a holiday accompanied by horn blasts which occurred between the new moon and the *keseh* (the full moon)[50] — evidently during the first two weeks of the seventh month. These data and their implications provide the basis for the theory of a covenant renewal festival, which was also the Feast of the Ingathering and the New Year. Such a central holiday was, it is hypothesized, an opportunity for an annual reaffirmation of the principles of the covenant, and the main means for transmitting the Decalogue — which is the essence of the terms of the covenant — to the people throughout the generations.[51]

This theory touches mainly on the transmission of the Ten Commandments and their dissemination, but it does not offer any satisfactory suggestion concerning their origin. A helpful analogy might be found in the formal similarity between the Decalogue and the Rechabite regimen recorded in Jeremiah 35. 6–7:

> ...for our ancestor, Jonadab son of Rechab, commanded us:
> "You shall never drink wine, either you or your children.
> Nor shall you build houses
> or sow fields
> or plant vineyards, nor shall you own such things;
> but you shall live in tents all your days,
> so that you may live long upon the land where you sojourn."

The "sons of Rechab" know the "five commandments" (most but not all negative) given them by their ancestor, the founder, of the order. These "commandments" define the order's way of life; and accepting them is a condition of belonging to the order. The Ten Commandments constitute a collection similar in purpose: they are the Commandments of the founder of the "order" of the children of Israel as "the LORD's nation", as "His holy people", the founder being God Himself. This compilation is just one of many scattered throughout the Torah and described as a collection of stipulations — most but not all of them

---

50 For this meaning of *keseh*, see W. Baumgartner, *Hebräisches und Aramäisches Lexicon zum Alten Testament*, 3te Auflage, Lieferung II, Leiden: Brill 1974, pp. 463–464.

51 The principal fathers of this theory are S. Mowinckel and Albrecht Alt. A convenient summary of its development and a critique of the thesis can be found in J.J. Stamm and M.E. Andrew, *The Ten Commandments in Recent Research*, Studies in Biblical Theology, 2/2, Naperville, Allenson, 1967, pp. 22–75.

negative — that the Israelites must observe in order to fulfill the obligations of their consecration to God.

It is especially enlightening to compare the Decalogue to the collection found in Leviticus 19. 1–18, which opens: "...Speak to the whole Israelite community[52].... You shall be holy, for I, the LORD your God, am holy", and continues with a detailed list of the terms of consecration, with "You shall" and "You shall not" commandments, reminiscent of much of the Decalogue. Common to both collections is that they were proclaimed before the entire nation; they served as the basis for the making of the covenant, or they were included in a broader document that was the basis for the covenant between God and His people. This covenental ceremony is depicted as including a solemn ceremonial obligation on the part of the nation to observe the injunctions presented to them. Such ceremonies appear several times in the history of the Israelites: during the days of Joshua (Josh. 24), Josiah (II Ki. 23), and Ezra (Neh. 8–10). They are all similar in scale to the Sinai theophany, constituting a sort of imitation of the earlier event. It is reasonable to assume that the origin of the ceremony really does go back to the dawn of the nation (Mosaic times), and that its central point was a collection of "Constituent Rules of the Order". There is no reason to dismiss the possibility that the kernel of the Decalogue was this very collection, even though we cannot reconstruct a "mundane" account of the proclamation of the Decalogue that can serve as a "historical" replacement for the legendary versions found in Exodus and Deuteronomy.[53]

Of all such lists and collections, the Decalogue is outstanding for its scope and its suggestiveness: its terms are general and even ambiguous; it does not prescribe penalties (which would have defined and limited the scope of each Commandment); it invites explication, clarification,

---

52   Based on this expression, R. Ḥiyya drew an analogy between the nineteenth chapter of Leviticus and the Ten Commandments: "R. Ḥiyya taught: From this we conclude that this section was proclaimed to the entire assembly of Israel [like the Decalogue; see Deut. 4. 10].... R. Levi said: Because this section includes the Ten Commandments".

53   On the origin of the Decalogue as a set of rules binding a community of believers and on its subsequent role, see the instructive article by M. Weinfeld: "The Decalogue: Its Meaning and Evolution in Jewish Tradition", in *Reflections on the Bible: Studies in Memory of Yishai Ron* (Hebrew), II, Jerusalem 1977, pp. 109–121. See also Weinfeld's essay in the present volume.

or even expansion. The Decalogue is further distinctive because it evenly balances obligations to God and to man and because its choice of subjects comes close to reflecting the Torah's most important concerns.

As a result, Jewish thinkers have often regarded the Ten Commandments as the essence of the Torah. Philo's essay is entitled: "About the Decalogue, Being the Principal Laws of Moses", and in it he itemizes the individual laws of the Torah as deriving from each of the Commandments. For example:

> Under the Third he includes directions as to all the cases when swearing is forbidden, and as to the time, place, matters, persons, state of soul and body which justify the taking of an oath.... The Fourth, which treats of the seventh day, must be regarded as nothing less than a gathering under one head of the feasts and the purifications ordained for each feast...and the acceptable prayer and the flawless sacrifices, with which the ritual was carried out (*Decalogue*, 157–158). In the Fifth Commandment, on honouring one's parents, we have a suggestion of many necessary laws drawn up to deal with the relations of old to young, rulers to subjects, benefactors to benefited, slaves to masters... (*Decalogue*, 165).

And so he continues: the Sixth Commandment covers all matters concerning sexual morality; the Seventh covers laws of bodily injury; the Eighth deals with property damages; the Ninth concerns matters of breach of trust (see *On the Decalogue*, 157–172).

This perception evidently underlies the Second Temple period liturgical practice of reciting the Ten Commandments before the Shema, thereby enumerating the principles of the Torah before reciting the formula for accepting the obligation to observe them (M. Tamid 5:1). The Nash papyrus offers external evidence of the combination of these texts, apparently reflecting Jewish prayer in Egypt.

That the Decalogue was joined to the Shema is also evidenced by tefillin found at Qumran; it has been supposed that the ancient order of biblical passages in the tefillin corresponded to the liturgy in the Second Temple, as described in the Mishnah.[54] Because of the conflict

54   A.M. Haberman, "Tefillin in ancient Times" (Hebrew), *Eretz Israel*, 3 (Cassuto Volume), Jerusalem: The Society for Study of Eretz Israel and its Antiquities, and

with heretics during the first centuries of Christianity, the recitation of
the Decalogue was deleted, as related in the Palestinian Talmud:

> R. Matana and R. Samuel b. Nahman [Amoraim at the end of
> the third century C.E.] both say: the Ten Commandments should
> properly be recited every day; but now they are not read because
> of the zeal of the heretics, in order that they not be able to say that
> these [commandments] alone were given to Moses at Mount
> Sinai (Yer. Ber. I. 5, 3c).[55]

By way of compensation for removing the Decalogue, the idea arose
that it is in fact entirely incorporated in the Shema, moreover that for
that reason we recite the Shema (Yer., ibid.)! Despite the Rabbis' ban,
the Jews of Egypt continued their daily public recitation of the Ten
Commandments for many generations, and Babylonian Jews continued

the Bialik Institute, 1954, p. 174. For tefillin containing both the Decalogue and the
Shema, see R. de Vaux, J.T. Milik, *Qumran Grotte 4*, II. *Discoveries in the
Judaean Desert*, VI, Oxford: Clarendon Press 1977, pp. 52, 59–62, 74–75. Other
examples of Qumran tefillin containing the Decalogue (without the Shema) are
found in Y. Yadin, "Tefillin for the Head from Qumran" (Hebrew), *Eretz Israel*, 9
(Albright Volume) Jerusalem: Society for the Study of Eretz Israel and Its
Antiquities, 1969, pp. 60–85.

55   For interpreting *ṭinnath* in the sense of "zeal", (cf. the Syriac *tnn* "be zealous") so
that the passage would mean "because of their strict devotion to their false belief",
see L. Ginzberg, *A Commentary on the Palestinian Talmud* (Hebrew), New York:
Jewish Theological Seminary 1951, 1, p. 166. Ginzberg identifies these heretics as
"the Nazarenes and their like, who taught that their Savior had promulgated a new
religion, according to which a person had only to believe in the Creator, in reward
and punishment and similar fundamentals of faith, and to abide by the socio-ethical
Commandments of the Decalogue, but not by the ritual mitzvot of Judaism". See
Ber. 12a, and Rashi ad loc. In *Maḥzor Vitry*, ed. S.H. Horovitz, Nuremberg 1923,
Part I, p. 12, the reading is "...so that the disciples [*of Jesus*] should not say: the rest
of the Torah is not true, and the proof is that we recite only that which the LORD
Himself spoke, and which the Israelites heard at Mt. Sinai". This formulation has
been couched in terms of the ongoing polemic between Jews and Christians in the
Middle Ages. In this connection see Elazar Touitou, "Plain Sense and Apologetics
in the Commentary of Samuel ben Meir on the Biblical Moses Stories" (Hebrew),
Tarbiẓ, 51 (1982), pp. 230, 234 and n. 45. On the problem of identifying the *Minim*
mentioned in the Talmud, see G.F. Moore, *Judaism, etc.*, Harvard University
Press, Cambridge 1945, III, pp. 95 f., n.64; R. Kimelman, "*Birkat Ha-Minim...*",
in: E.P. Sanders et al, eds, *Jewish and Christian Self-Definition*, II, Philadelphia;
Fortress Press, 1981, pp. 226–244.

to write the Decalogue in their tefillin until the end of the fourth century.[56]

No doubt because of this polemic, rabbinic writings retain but few references to the centrality of the Decalogue. Nevertheless, there do remain vestiges of the ancient view that the Ten Commandments are the essence of the Torah, or that they include all of the Torah.[57] At the end of the Gaonic period, and toward the beginning of medieval times, this view resurfaced. An outstanding expression of it is the composition of *Azharot*, pityyutim in honor of Shavuot; in which the entire canon of 613 commandments is spun out of the Decalogue. An excellent example of this genre was composed by Saadiah Gaon, and appears in his *Siddur* (ed. Israel Davidson, et al, Jerusalem 1941, pp. 191-216; see also Ismar M. Elbogen, *Der jüdische Gottesdienst usw.*, Frankfurt on Main 1931, p. 218).

Jewish thinkers of the Middle Ages had no hesitation in exalting the Ten Commandments, much like Philo, as befits philosophers who seek general principles from which particulars may be derived.[58]

Translated by "In Other Words",
Moshav Shorashim

---

56   With regard to the recitation of the Ten Commandments in Egypt, see J. Mann, "Genizah Fragments of the Palestinian Order of Service", *Hebrew Union College Annual*, 2 (1925), p. 283; on the Decalogue in Babylonian Tefillin, see Haberman, above, n. 54, p. 175.

57   See A.J. Heschel, *Theology of Ancient Judaism* (Hebrew), London-New York: Soncino 1965, 2, pp. 108–110; but this interesting material must be treated critically with due regard to variations in dating. E.E. Urbach strongly denies that the Sages elevated the value of the Decalogue above the other commandments; see his *The Sages*, Jerusalem: Magnes Press 1975, pp. 360–365; but perhaps this very fact reflects the ongoing polemic on the matter.

58   A clear example is provided by Joseph Albo, *Sefer ha-Ikkarim*, III, chap. 66.

5. THE DECALOGUE ACCORDING TO PHILO

YEHOSHUA AMIR

I

In a comprehensive discussion of the impact of the Ten Commandments on the history of Jewish thought, a place of honor must be reserved for Philo of alexandria.* His *De decalogo*[1] is the earliest attempt, Jewish or non-Jewish, to make a special study of the subject. And while he himself does sometimes speak of older interpretations (probably of Palestinian provenance, as we shall see) he still remains our earliest witness for these too.

Since Philo is an innovator, it is understandable that his works frequently contain the seminal formulation of questions about the revelation at Sinai and the contents of the Ten Commandments that have challenged the exegetes of every generation since his day. A number of the issues debated by later scholars were first raised by Philo in the context of his philosophic distillation of Scripture, which represents for him the thought of that divinely inspired man and philosopher *par excellence* — Moses.[2] It is only to be expected that, along with the originality that characterizes many of the questions which Philo poses, there are also inconsistencies in his work, the usual price of being a pioneer.

To be sure, in the ongoing discussion of issues which Philo was the

---

* A German–language version of this study is included in my work *Die hellenistische Gestalt des Judentums bei Philon von Alexandria*, Neukirchener Verlag 1983, pp. 131–163.

1 *Philo* in The Loeb Classical Library, ten volumes with an English translation by F.H. Colson (hereinafter cited as "Colson"), VII, pp. 3–95.

2 On this see my study "Moses als Verfasser der Tora bei Philon", in my above-mentioned book, pp. 77–106.

first to raise, his standing has not been that usually accorded to a leading spokesman. Medieval Jewish exegetes and philosophers never mention his name, even when they are pursuing lines of thought which he first opened up. It must be assumed that these ideas came to them from their Muslim milieu, and that they were unaware that the Muslims themselves had derived them from Christians, who had in their turn been influenced in their interpretations of Scripture by the works of Philo Judaeus. However, by the time that these traditions had filtered down to the Jews of the Middle Ages, it seems that they had already shed the name of their progenitor. Consequently, whenever motifs identified by us as Philonic appear in medieval Jewish thought, we have to find out if there are any retrospective links, Jewish or non-Jewish, connecting these writers with Philo. Whenever such a question arises, it must be examined in detail, and on its own merits. We shall encounter such questions a number of times during the course of the present study.

As for the role of *De decalago* in the whole corpus of Philo's writings, I must content myself for the present with no more than a few brief words.[3] The tractate is part of a series in which he treats the Torah as a law-book; but in the *summa* of his philosophy this concept is secondary. Basically, he regards the Torah not as a code of laws, but rather as a book of philosophy. To understand its varied levels of meaning, it is not enough to take the plain sense of the text; one must move up to the level of allegory, for there is the only key with which to unlock the inner meaning of the Torah. Not that Philo means to dismiss the legal sense of the Scriptural text taken at face value; but he does intend to keep it on a secondary level.

This is something like Plato's view of the relationship between the two worlds of his philosophical system — the world of ideas and the world of phenomena. Plato does, to be sure, say that truth resides in the world of ideas alone. But that does not mean that the world of experience is false. Rather, because it is suspended between being and nothingness, it "partakes" of truth, but is not truth itself.

Something of this relative status attaches to everything that Philo derives from the plain sense of the biblical text. Consequently, one

---

3   For a more extensive treatment of Philo's series of essays on the Torah as a legal codex, see my chapter "Philo of Alexandria" in Vol. IX of *World History of the Jewish People*.

never finds the final word of Philo the thinker at this level of his exposition.

This important reservation must be kept in mind whenever we read what Philo says about the literal sense of the Bible. Nevertheless, it is a reservation that fades into the background when he does deal with the literal meaning. Hence we shall find that in the series of essays examined, the gulf between his outlook and that of the talmudic Sages becomes much narrower compared to what we find in his other writings. This is especially true of *De decalogo*, where the Alexandrian keeps silent about many of the intellectual reservations he expresses in his other works. Whereas Philo does not generally hesitate to speak of Moses as the lawgiver who legislated the laws of the Torah — to be sure, under divine inspiration — here he speaks of a supernatural character. True, he offers an "explanation" for what happened at Sinai; nevertheless he does affirm that it was a divine miracle, described as,

> entirely signs of the divine execellences... too great to be lauded by human lips... scarcely indeed could heaven and the world and the whole existing universe worthily sing their praises.[4]

This explains why those elements in his presentation of the event at Sinai which might have seemed alien to the rabbinic Sages would not in the final analysis have been found by them in his approach to the theophany. In this work they would have discovered only minor indications that Philo came to his subject from a Greek cultural millieu, causing him at times to see the biblical narrative from a rather unusual point of view.

II

Within a series expounding the entire Torah of Moses in terms of a law-book, Philo devoted a special essay to the Ten Commandments. In the first tractate of this series he questions the place in such a law-book of the Creation story and the lives of the Patriarchs. At the moment, these questions need not detain us. Then he proceeds to deal with the laws themselves, introducing them with his treatise "Concerning the Decalogue". For him, it appears, the Ten Commandments are, as to their content, in a class by themselves. After all, according to his literary design it was not the narrative per se that was the main concern

4   *Vita Mosis*, II, pp. 189–191 (Colson, VI, p. 543).

but rather the meaning of the corpus of laws. Had he not regarded the Ten Commandments as having a special status within that corpus, he would not have devoted a special essay to them. We shall therefore have to determine just what place it was that he assigned to the Decalogue within the framework of the laws of the Torah as a whole.

Philo does not offer any special explanation for his view of the Ten Commandments. It would probably not have occurred to him that his approach called for an explanation, because the biblical narrative itself testifies to the central position accorded to these laws. As he sees it, the Torah distinguishes between the two ways in which the commands of the Deity were made known to the people. For most of the laws, God made use of His prophet, that is to say Moses, to transmit His words. But the Ten Commandments were treated differently; they were pronounced by God Himself in all His Majesty.[5] In them, He addresses the people in the first person, as Philo notes,[6] apparently unaware of the distinction made by the Midrash between the first two Commandments, "spoken by the Almighty", and the rest of the Commandments, in which He is referred to, if at all, in the third person. Philo takes it for granted that they were all "heard from Heaven". So it is obvious to him that those imperatives which the LORD saw fit to transmit directly to the people must be of extraordinary importance, for otherwise the mode of transmission used for all the other mitzvot would have sufficed.

Thus, it was not the creative literary urge that made Philo include a dramatic and impressive description of the theophany in his work on the Decalogue. That would have been the sort of thing we might have expected from Josephus, but not from Philo's description of the giving of the Torah is the core of his argument. He implies that the words of the Decalogue, emanating from the Almighty Himself amidst thunder and lightning and balasts of the shofar, must be of a status loftier than all other mitzvot in the Torah.

But obvious as this appears to him in the light of his understanding of the biblical narrative, it is not at all self-evident. The most cursory glance at rabbinic literature will show that the Sages held a different view. They classified the mitzvot in a variety of ways, such as dividing them into positive and negative ("thou shalt" and "thou shalt not"); distinguishing between the scriptural and the rabbinic; or giving a

---

5   *De decalogo*, 18 (hereinafter: *Decal*), Colson, VII, p. 15.
6   *autoprosōpos.*

special status to those three mitzvot for which one has to be ready to suffer martyrdom. But they never so much as mentioned any classification by which the Ten Commandments are to be distinguished from all the rest, and put into a class by themselves. Some of the Ten belong among the 365 prohibitions, others go together with the 248 positive commands. Although the Aggadah sets the "Ten Words" in a special place,[7] the Halakhah shows no interest whether a mitzvah is included in the Decalogue or not.

This attitude seems surprising, but the reason for it is well known. Whenever there has been a tendency to elevate the status of the Ten Commandments, the tradition has shown concern lest the standing of the other commandments be diminished. We know that in the earliest formularies of prescribed prayer the Decalogue had an honored place, but was relegated to a less central position "because of the contention of the *Minim* that these Ten alone were given to Moses at Sinai".[8] The Sages taught: "Moses received the Torah at Sinai" — not just the Ten Commandments.[9] If we pay special honor to the Decalogue there is a danger that we will apear to sectarians (and perhaps even to ourselves) to be assenting in some measure to the contentions of the *minim*.

Who were these *minim* whose contentions the Sages were so bent on rejecting? And most especially — was Philo one of them? The question is far from simple. At no point does Philo offer an interpretation of Exodus 24. 12, which is the basis for the rabbinic teaching that it was not only the tablets that Moses brought down from the mountain. As for the question, how and when the rest of the mitzvot were given to Moses, Philo has nothing at all to say.

Consequently, if the Sages knew about Philo and his teachings, they would most likely have included him among the *minim* because he presents the Decalogue only as that which was revealed at Sinai. No doubt they would have judged by their own hermeneutic principle that what is not included is by implication excluded. And if the crux of the question is whether all the other mitzvot were delivered specifically at Sinai to Moses, it is highly probable that Philo's answer would not have been acceptable to the Sages.

If, however, the main issue is not *when* the other mitzvot were given,

---

7   See, e.g., *Pesiqta Rabbati*, chapters 21–24.
8   Yer. Ber. I: 5,4c.
9   Avot, I:1.

but whether they are all binding, there could not have been any disagreement between Philo and the Sages, because the special status which Philo claimed for the Ten Commandments was not intended to undermine the authority of the other mitzvot. Quite the contrary: its purpose was to establish on an unquestionably firm foundation the full authority of all the rest of the mitzvot.

This brings us to the very core of Philo's concept of the relationship between the Ten Commandments and all the other commandments. As he sees it, the relationship is not that of the primary to secondary, or of the weighty to the less important, but of the general to the particular. Or, to put it in his own terms, it is the relation of the genus to the species. If we may borrow the terminology of the halakhists, it is the relation of the initial causes *(avot)* to their consequences *(toladot)*. Or we might put it this way: the Decalogue encompasses the whole of the Torah, for all of the mitzvot simply elaborate in detail what the Ten Commandments say in compressed form. Hence we may conclude that the binding force of the mitzvot in all their detail is based *in potentia* on the authority of the Ten Commandments.

To be sure, it is possible to find a similar motif in certain midrashic statements,[10] and there is even an opinion that Philo found his concept ready-made in the aggadic tradition.[11] However, a comparison of the language of the Midrash with Philo's formulation of his idea forces one to admit that if indeed one of these sources derives from the other, it cannot be said that it was Philo who was inspired by the Midrash, which puts it this way:

> Just as at sea there are huge waves, with a host of little waves between them, so are there Ten Commandments, with a host of refinements and particular commandments of the Torah between them.[12]

The relationship between the big wave and the little wave is not the same as that between the primary cause and its consequences; and the logical relationship between a "Commandment" and the particulars embedded between its lines remains unclear in the simile quoted. Certainly there is no implication in the Midrash that these particulars

---

10 Urbach has assembled the sources for this in *The Sages, Their Concepts and Beliefs*, Jerusalem 1975, I, pp. 360 ff. Also see his study in the present volume.

11 According to Harry A. Wolfson, *Philo*, Harvard 1947, II, p. 261.

12 Yer. Sheq., VI:1, 49d.

and refinements add up to the entire 613 mitzvot. On the contrary, the Midrash sounds like the muffled echo of some traditional idea whose meaning was no longer understood; and if we did not have the text of Philo, we would have had to postulate something like it as the presumed source of the vaguely expressed talmudic idea. Consequently I am inclined to disagree with Urbach,[13] and to see a connection between Philo's idea and the Midrash; only this time Philo seems to me to be the source, rather than the recipient.

This is all the more likely when you take into account the fact that what apears in the Midrash as a stray thought, rather peripheral, is for Philo the very keystone of his entire concept of biblical legislation. He does not merely throw out an attractive suggestion about the relationship between the Ten Commandments and all the other commandments in the Torah; he goes ahead and makes this idea the basis for his work *About the Particular Laws*, which comprises four "books".[14]

In these, he looks for a place for every one of the variegated commandments under the heading of one or another of the Ten Commandments. Each of the Ten is treated as a genus, the main category under which species and sub-species of mitzvot can be grouped. However, the fact remains that this grand architectonic blueprint is not fully realized in Philo's presentation. If the Ten Commandments are the ten vessels into which Philo sought to decant all the laws found in the Torah, then it must be admitted that some of the vast quantity overflowed the intended containers, to the point where he was finally forced to provide a number of auxiliary containers for those laws which he could not fit into the Ten Commandments.[15] But this flaw in the implementation of his program does not detract from the concept of method which he set for himself as a guide for his chosen task.

An attempt of this sort — to assign each of the mitzvot to its own category, i.e., to one of the Ten Commandments — was never tried by the Sages, and one might say that it was foreign to their spirit.[16]

---

13   Urbach, above, n.10, p. 362.
14   *De specialibus legibus* (Colson, VII, pp. 101–607; VIII, pp.1–155).
15   *De virtutibus* (Colson, VIII, pp. 157–305); *De praemiis et poenis* (ibid., pp. 307–423).
16   The Sages would probably have felt that a systematic structure of the mitzvot implied placing limits on the freedom of the Divine will.

However, it may be noted that this very plan was implemented later by
Saadiah Gaon in his *azharah* beginning with the words *I am
Consuming Fire*.[17] The question whether there is a chain of tradition,
the links of which are not available to us, between the first-century
Alexandrian and the tenth-century Gaon, remains unanswered for the
time being. Later on we shall encounter other elements which Saadiah
has in conmon with Philo.[18]

For our purpose it is more important to understand what prompted
Philo to choose this method. If every one of the Torah's laws is
subordinate to one of the major categories represented by each of the
Commandments in that overriding set of principles known as the
Decalogue, then the legislation of Moses cannot be viewed as a
concatenation of individual laws, but is seen to be a well-organized
code with its inherent logical system. Its multiplicity is thus given
internal unity; or if you will, not laws but a Law — in Philo's term a
nomos.

For the normative Judaism of Judaea, this internal unity of the
Torah rested upon the unity of the God who gave it. To Philo's Greek
way of thinking this must mean an immanent unity of concept; or, to
revert to Greek terminology, an internal *logos*.

Here we put our finger on the core motifs implicit in Philo's idea of
the intrinsic nature of the Torah. As he puts it in his preface to his series
dealing with the Torah as a code of laws, this legislation differs from all
other legal codes in that it is not the territorial law of some state or
other, but rather the constitution of the universe — and that is why
Moses begins his law-book with a chapter presenting in philosophical
language nothing less than the creation of the world.[19]

At this point we might well bear in mind what Stoic philosophy had
to say about codes of law. By contrast to the codes in all the various
existing states, there was only one which the Stoics recognized as
absolutely valid — the code of that utopian state which embodies all
those, both gods and men, who bear the *logos*. The real states that we

17 The piyyut appears in *Siddur R. Saadiah Gaon*, ed. Davidson-Assaf-Joel, Mekize
   Nirdamim, Jerusalem 1941, pp. 191–216. At the end of the poem it is stated that
   "there are six hundred and thirteen letters from the beginning of the Decalogue to
   its end". As Urbach notes (above n. 10) the midrashic sources which relate the 613
   mitzvot to the Ten Commandments are later than Saadiah and probably derived
   the idea from him.
18 See below at n. 91.
19 *De opificio mundi*, 1–3 (Colson, I, p. 7).

find scattered over the face of the earth are only pale and flawed reflections of that ideal state. Only as far as their laws succeed in incorporating some measure of the perfection of the ideal state, is the wise man able — nay obligated — to regard them as states worthy of the name.

Thus the idea of *nomos* is the foundation of the ideal state which nowhere exists; and the idea itself is but the representation in human society of the *logos*. It is the *logos* which sustains the universe and pervades it. Stoic philosophy identifies it with the Godhead.

When, therefore, Philo argues that the Torah of Moses is the realization in practice of the ideal *nomos*, by virtue of which all *nomoi* in the world exist; and further, that everyone who takes this *nomos* upon himself becomes not merely a citizen of this or that state but a citizen of the world, a true *kosmopolites* — then it follows that this *nomos* must necessarily embody the *logos* on which the whole universe depends. It must be assumed, therefore, that the primary identification mark of such a *nomos* is that it does in fact embody the *logos*, i.e., that it is "logical", consistent with itself.

So then for Philo the logical character of the legislation of Moses is not merely a matter of stylistic grace designed to make the Torah more attractive, but rather an element essential for revealing the uniqueness of the Torah in the universe. Thus, a motif which the Sages could afford to leave to the playfulness of homiletic ingenuity ("along came Amos and reduced the Torah to a single commandment")[20] becomes, in Philo's scheme of things, the key to understanding the nature of the Torah.

But the chain of Philo's reasoning is not yet complete. By placing all of the mitzvot on the firm foundation of the Decalogue, he will have ensured their inner unity only on condition that he can demonstrate the inner unity within the multiplicity of the Ten Commandments themselves. Herein lies the philosophical significance attaching to Philo's speculations on the extraordinary attributes of the number ten. It is not necessary to enter here into a detailed examination of the mathematical calculations and the musicological analyses employed by Philo in order to establish the special qualities of this number. But we have to insist on the fact that, for him, these ideas are sufficient justification for declaring the number ten to be *the* perfect number,

20   Mak. 24a.

along the lines of Pythagorean philosophy.[21] The number contains all
the features on which both the system of mathematics and the musical
scale are based. This proves that the Decalogue is not a conglomeration
of disparate items, but rather a perfect whole.

In addition, we ought to consider another attribute of the number
ten which, as Philo points out, is the number of the Aristotelian
categories.[22] According to Aristotle these categories embrace every
possible content of any possible statement, and hence in terms of his
basic assumptions cover the whole of being in all its possible
manifestations. Thus, the number of the Commandments points to the
fact that they are categories embodying *ab initio* every legitimate
formulation of law which satisfies the basic requirements of *logos*.

This organization of all the laws of the Torah into categories is thus
tantamount to proof that the Mosaic law ought to be looked upon as
the practical embodiment of the law of the universe. That is exactly the
absolute status Philo claimed for the Mosaic legislation in his
introduction to the literary work dealing with the Torah as a book of
laws. (The fact that he fell short in implementing his theoretical scheme
does not detract from this fundamental principle.)

III

Another question which Philo discusses in his introduction to *De
decalogo* is this: why were the Ten Commandments proclaimed in the
wilderness? Anyone familiar with midrashic literature will recognize
this question. But the twist given it by Philo shows that his point of
view is different from that of the Sages. He puts it this way: "Why were
His laws promulgated in the depths of the desert instead of in cities?"[23]
What Philo finds surprising is that here we have a constitution that was
not laid down in a *polis*. To him, this went counter to an association
which seems to him axiomatic. After all, the purpose of a code of laws
is to regulate the shared life of a group of people. To describe such a
group, the Greek word that springs to mind is *polis*. And in the view of
Aristotle,[24] it is a *politeia* (system of laws) which converts such a group

21 *Decal.*, 20 ff. (Colson, VII, pp. 15 ff.).
22 Ibid., 30 (colson, p. 21).
23 Ibid., 2–17 (Colson, pp. 7–15).
24 Aristotle, *Pol.* 3. 3 = 1276b 1–13.

from a mob into a human society, i.e., a *polis*. In fact, when preparations were being made to found a new city (a colony) it was customary to announce the constitution or the laws by which the citizens of the new colony would live. Sometimes the task of preparing such a constitution was entrusted to a philosopher.

So it came about that the political-historical outlook of the Greco-Roman world tended to classify Moses among such philosopher–legislators. This explains why Moses, who was known by enlightened circles of the Hellenistic public as "the Lawgiver of the Jews", was also mistakenly assumed by most of them to be the founder of the city of Jerusalem.[25] The fact, then, that his code was promulgated in the desert and not in a city is unusual, and calls for an explanation.

Philo suggests four possible explanations. ("The true reasons are known to God alone".[26]) If we want to determine the relation of these explanations to the Palestinian tradition, we shall have to analyze each of Philo's suggestions in turn. In assessing them, one of the important considerations is this: does the argument disparage urban life, or conversely does it extol life in the desert?

1. Philo's first suggested reason rests on a negative view of city life per se. Among the drawbacks of the city, he dwells at length on the temples and statues honoring pagan deities. This immediately calls to mind the passage in the *Mekhilta* explaining why the LORD appeared to Moses and Aaron "in the land of Egypt" (presumably in the countryside; Ex. 12. 1) and not in the capital. It was because the latter place was full of pagan shrines, and the LORD does not appear in a place of uncleanness.[27] However, Philo's criticism of the city is not exactly the same. He denigrates it as being "full of countless evils, both acts of impiety against God, and of wrongdoing between man and man".[28]

There is no parallel in talmudic literature for Philo's denunciation of the city as the abode of vice, or (as he goes on to list in detail) of social inequality, falsehood and fraud, arrogance and extravagance. And even when it comes to matters of religion, we have to notice his

---

25   See, e.g., Menahem Stern, *Greek and Latin Authors on Jews and Judaism*, Jerusalem 1974, I, p. 26: Hecataeus, 11. 3.

26   *Decal.*, 18 (Colson, p. 115).

27   *Mekhilta de R. Ishmael, Tractate Pisḥa*, 1: "because it was full of abominations and idols"; cf. ed. Lauterbach, I, p.4.

28   *Decal.*, 2 (Colson, p. 7).

emphasis on wasteful and ostentatious display in everything connected with worship.

This was a type of criticism fairly prevalent in the philosophical literature of the time dealing with public worship, and it was not confined to the Cynics.[29] To be sure, in dealing with this aspect of the case against city life, Philo successfully integrated the Jewish point of view with the general line of criticism directed at certain cultural trends.[30] However, the general idea undoubtedly came to him from the literature of his time.

2. The second explanation proposed by Philo is also connected with criticism of city life, but this time from a different angle. Now the issue is not the suitability of the place, but rather the nature of the human group for whom the legislation is intended. Such a group, if it is to be worthy of receiving holy laws, must be in a state of purity. But the city rabble, whom Philo describes as "a motley promiscuous horde", has acquired so many flaws in its collective character that it must undergo purification.[31] Only then will such a populace be fit to hear sacred words. In order to purify such people, it is necessary to remove them from the source of their pollution, as Philo explains by means of a medical analogy. The use of such analogies was common in Greek ethical literature.

This makes it likely that what we have here is an application of hygienic advice normally prescribed for individuals. According to this method, in order to cure someone of a psychological illness it is necessary to remove him from the source of his disorder. For example, if the patient is to be weaned from some excessive appetite, he is to be placed for a fairly lengthy period under a regimen of abstinence.

In the case of the Israelites the analogue of such an ascetic regimen would be life in the desert. It follows that it became necessary as a first step to remove the Israelites from the corruption of urban life and to submit them to the rigors of the desert until their souls were prepared to receive the sacred gift in store for them.

---

29   Apparently the first to express disapproval of such ills in the religious cultus was Theophrastus, in his *Peri Eusebias*. The extant fragments of his work have been collected by Walter Pötscher in his *Theophrastos, etc.*, Leiden 1964.

30   On Philo's attitude to the social and cultural criticism prevalent in his day among many schools of Hellenistic philosophy, see I. Heinemann, *Philons griechische und jüdische Bildung*, Breslau 1932, pp. 431 ff.

31   *Decal.* 10 ff. (Colson, p. 11).

It must be admitted that apart from the parallel between asceticism and life in the desert, the elements in Philo's analogy are hardly appropriate. The narrative in the Book of Exodus does not describe the slaves who left Egypt as having been corrupted by luxury to the extent that their souls had to be brought to a state of holiness by a regime of asceticism.

The reader familiar with midrashic literature will no doubt have been reminded of a text that fits the situation much better than Philo's analogy. There is a homily on Songs of Songs 2. 5[32] which is also concerned with the need for time to elapse between the Egyptian experience of the slaves and their appearance at Mount Sinai. The reason given by this Midrash resembles the one cited by Philo: "My children have not yet achieved the radiance proper to them". However, according to the Midrash, this radiance is missing because the Israelites had become coarsened "by slaving with bricks and mortar". As a consequence, it was necessary "for My children to be cleansed and refined by three months of eating quail and manna". Here we have a Palestinian tradition which answers Philo's question as to why the Israelites had to achieve a distance from their former slave condition; but this answer is more in keeping with the biblical narrative than is Philo's.

We might perhaps assume that this Palestinian version of the matter was already current in Philo's day, and that he knew about it. But Philo was fully as prone to anachronism as were the talmudic Sages. In his mind the Egyptian Jews of Pharaoh's day were replaced by the Egyptian Jews whom he met every day of his life; especially the Jews of Alexandria, that great metropolis with its vast population, so many of whom could be called "a motley promiscuous horde of men". The blemishes of their society were those of a big city, with all the evidences of corruption characteristic of such a place. As a result of this mental shift, Philo was led to mingle the Palestinian tradition with the ethico-medical notions which he derived from his familiarity with the Stoic doctrine of the soul. Hence, his second suggested interpretation appears very similar to the first, even though its conceptual origin is altogether different.

3. The third reason proposed by Philo is this: while it is true that every code of laws is designed for ultimate use in the city, it is

---

32   *Cant. Rabbah*, II:15, in a homily on "stay me with dainties."

nevertheless wise to prepare for the regulation of city life in advance, so that when the time for implementation arrives, everything will be in readiness. This prudent rule is exemplified by the preparations customary before a ship sets sail. The vessel itself and all necessary equipment must be carefully readied so that when the time comes to lift anchor, there will be no unnecessary delays. It scarcely needs saying that this nautical example, with all its accompanying technical detail, comes to Philo quite naturally, as part of his Greek educational background.

Similarly,the strong association of a legal constitution with the life of a city, which as we have seen he takes for granted, is established in all Greek political thinking. It is worth noting that in none of the reasons advanced so far is there any evaluation of desert life as such. What we have until now is a Greek question answered in typically Greek fashion.

4. But the fourth reason is altogether different from the others, and it is the only one which Philo attributes to anybody else: "There are those who say"... Since the topic is biblical, those quoted must be Jews — in all likelihood Palestinian Jews. Conversely, just as the previous answers did not pass judgment on life in the desert, so does this one make no mention of the city. Nor is the desert cited this time as a model of the austere, ascetic life, but rather as the place of manna, quail and water gushing from the rock. Just as the question is raised in a purely biblical context, so is the suggested answer an entirely biblical one: the desert is portrayed as a place where all of life depends on miracles.

Why then was the Torah given in the desert? In order to convince us that it is a miraculous gift of heaven, just as all of life is a miraculous gift of heaven.

This way of thinking is not typical of Philo. The overwhelming concept of the power of the miracle is not an organic part of his thought. As he puts it, the reason for the miracle was that

> it was necessary to establish a belief in their minds that the laws were not the inventions of a man but quite clearly the oracles of God.[33]

As I have demonstrated elsewhere,[34] this sharp distinction between the oracles of God and the word of man is not typical of Philo, for he is

33 *Decal.*, 15 (Colson, p. 13).
34 See n. 2, above.

capable of saying in one and the same breath that the laws of the Torah are "words of God" and also "laws given by men whom God loves".[35] That can only mean that at this point Philo has yielded the floor to circles in the Land of Israel for whom miracles are a regular part of existence, an attitude not easily reconciled with his own philosophic outlook.

Nevertheless we have to face the fact that Philo does give this view a hearing, even stating quite explicitly that it "agrees very closely with the truth".[36] But if it had not been expressed by others, it is scarcely likely that he would have thought of it himself. However, since these ideas are current among those Jews for whom he feels a spiritual affinity, Philo makes room for them in his writing. After all, we are dealing with matters beyond human comprehension; and if I understand Philo correctly, he turns such ideas off with a respectful bow.

IV

Let us now see how he treats the Sinaitic event itself. Actually, in the Philonic context we cannot speak of a narrative, for although he does begin by saying that the entire people assembled, men, women and children, and the LORD of the universe caused them to hear the Ten Commandments, he is immediately impelled to break off the account and ask what is meant by "hearing". And the moment a philosopher trained to think rationally asks himself that question, he is going to find himself in difficulties. On the face of it, there are only two ways to treat the report of a miracle. One can either accept it unquestioningly, in the naive way in which people accept the wonders of mythology — or one can dismiss it on rationalist grounds. However, Philo is impelled to try to have it both ways. So he sets out to make the miracle rationally acceptable; that is, he approaches it as a physical fact, and tries to make it conform with the scientifically proven phenomena of physics.

This is not the place to utter an opinion as to the value or otherwise of such an approach, but we must trace the complicated route pursued by Philo's philosophical thinking, because it represents a method adopted by so many thinkers in medieval times. The theory which he

---

35 *Quod deterius, etc.*, 13 (Colson, II, p. 211); cf. my above mentioned book on Philo, p. 94.

36 *Decal.*, 15 (Colson, p. 13).

elaborated here for the first time is known as the doctrine of "the created voice".[37]

It is difficult to determine exactly what was Philo's role in the development of this doctrine. There are certain tentative adumbrations of the idea in the writings of two other Hellenistic-Jewish authors. True, those writers do not refer to the voice which made itself heard to the whole people at Mount Sinai, but rather to the voice that Moses heard from the burning bush. However, it is quite easy to see the resemblance between the two narratives.

First of all, Ezekiel the Tragedian says in his play about the Exodus that from out of the fire which burned in the bush but did not consume, "there shone forth divine speech".[38] There is an implication here that auditory and visual perceptions were merged. Whereas according to the plain sense of the biblical text God speaks from out of the fire — that is, the fire serves as a screen for the Deity who speaks from behind it — in Ezekiel's verses the Word itself is transmitted by the glow of the flames. This seems to be what Ezekiel means, especially in view of the fact that Josephus expresses himself in similar terms when he says that Moses was

> ... terrified at this strange spectacle, but was amazed yet more when this fire found a tongue and communed with him.[39]

If in one place it says that the fire speaks, and in another that the voice glows, then we must regard these as two complementary facets of one and the same phenomenon — the miraculous fusion of sight and sound.

If it is true that this motif was first expressed in connection with the burning bush rather than with the revelation at Sinai, which comes later in the biblical narrative, then it is a reasonable assumption that the notion did not come into being as a result of biblical exegesis. For there is no real basis for it in the story of the burning bush, while in

---

37 For a discussion of Saadiah's view of the "created voice", and the background of that view in Muslim thought, see Alexander Altmann, "Saadya's Theory of Revelation: Its Origin and Background", *Studies in Religious Philosophy and Mysticism*, Cornell University Press 1969, pp. 140–160. Surprisingly, Altmann does not take the discussion beyond the various Arabic philosophical schools back to *their* roots in the works of Philo of Alexandria.

38 Ezekiel the Tragedian, *The Exodus From Egypt*, verse 99.

39 Josephus, *Antiquities of the Jews*, II, 267.

connection with the theophany at Sinai the Bible explicitly says "All the people saw the voices" (Ex. 20. 18; in the Septuagint: "the voice").

Philo uses this verse three times as a basis for the statement that unlike human speech, God's voice is visible rather than audible.[40] The Bible does not prima facie lend itself to such an interpretation, for in the Book of Deuteronomy (4. 12) we find: "You heard the sound of words but perceived no shape — nothing but a voice". What is remarkable is that Philo was fully aware of this verse; he even quotes it elsewhere,[41] but uses it to draw from it the same conclusion as quoted above.

If we accept Philo's interpretation, the sense of Exodus 20. 18 is as follows: the sound of words, which is the voice of human beings, is audible to you as it is to the rest of mankind. But the same is not true of the voice of God, to which the latter half of the verse refers. That voice is beheld; but what you behold is not to be classified as a visible image, but rather as a voice.

In the light of such an interpretation, it is only to be expected that when Philo reaches the verse "We heard His voice from the midst of the fire" (Deut 5. 21) he will interpret it as follows:

> An astounding voice resounded from out of the fire that streamed from heaven, for the flames were transmuted into the speech familiar to those who heard it.[42]

It is worth noting that while the beginning of Philo's statement remains true to the biblical account, it is the second half which expresses the viewpoint characteristic of Hellenistic Judaism. The plain sense of the biblical text is not that the fire spoke, and certainly not that the fire was transmuted into speech, but simply that God spoke from out of the fire.

What then does Philo mean by this sort of speech, which has its source in fire, and of which one says that it is seen rather than heard? At this point Philo calls on the theories prevalent in his time concerning sight and sound. The Greeks knew that hearing results from air which reaches the ear. By analogy, they defined sound as "air given form and set in motion".[43] They compared this motion of the air to the ripples

---

40   *Decal.*, 47 (Colson, p. 31); *De migratione Abrahami*, 47 (Colson, IV, p. 159); *Vita Mosis*, II, 213 (Colson, VI, p. 555).

41   *De migratione Abrahami*, 48 (Colson, ibid.).

42   *Decal.*, 46 (Colson, p. 29).

43   Aristòtle, *Probl.*, XI. 23 = 901b 16 f.

caused on the surface of the water when a stone is thrown into it. The ear is thus simply the recipient of an activity which it did not originate, but by which it is activated.

As for sight, Philo accepted the most widely accepted theory, according to which the eye projects beams which seek out and illumine what they are looking for. That is why, according to the theory of the Stoics, the sense of sight is superior to all the other senses. For although the eye apprehends color, for example, in the same way that the ear registers sound or the sense of touch reports the solidity of an object, the sense of sight does more. In addition to recording the attributes of a thing, it apprehends the thing itself which causes us to experience these attributes.[44] Sight also enables us to have in mind, or imagine, the thing, once we have seen it. Proof of this is adduced from the Greek language, in which the word for "imagination" is derived from the word for "light",[45] as if to say that just as light reveals to the beholder not only the object seen but also the light itself, so does imagination encompass, together with the attributes of any object, the whole object itself.

This is apparently what Philo has in mind when he explains in another context that the eye is a participant in every perception by any of the other senses.[46] Thus he states that taste is visible to the eye — not specifically, of course, for that is the function of the sense of taste — but in the process of identifying the taste-bearing object. The exception to this rule is the sense of hearing, for we hear without seeing the body from which the sound emanates or seeing the sound itself. This theory can easily be backed up by reference to what was explained above: the physical aspect of sound is air, and although air is accounted a substance, it is invisible.

I have no doubt that in the Stoic original of this theory, the explanation for the exceptional nature of the sense of hearing was the one just given. But Philo seems to have misunderstood it. He took "sound" in the restricted sense of "speech", and postulated "intelligence" as the "physical" source of it. To be sure, intelligence is not visible either; but in any event, the reference to the scientific approach helped Philo explicate the background of that miracle described as part of the

---

44   StVFr, II, 54.
45   *phōs — phantasia.*
46   *De migratione Abrahami*, 51 (colson, IV, p. 161).

revelation at Sinai — the visible voice.[47] In all other sense perception there is an element of vision, but not in hearing, so that a visible voice is a contradiction in terms. Hence the miracle.

Indeed, if this voice differed from the sound familiar to us because of the way in which it was received, it follows that it must have been different in its origin as well. If sound is normally air in a particular condition, then in this specific instance the voice cannot have come from air. But since nevertheless it is still classified as a "voice", and whatever is not defined as a body of air in motion cannot be called a voice, there is no other possibility than that this phenomenon began as air, and through some miraculous process that air was transmuted into a visible entity.

Since in Stoic physics air and fire are related as the two "active" elements in contradistinction to water and earth, which are the two "passive" elements; and since the same philosophy recognizes "pneuma" (spirit), a mixture of fire and air, as the basis of all living things, it follows naturally that air made visible as in the present instance can only be fire. Thus the structure of nature leads us to conclude that if we want to conceive of the miracle (miracle though it be) in terms recognizable to us from the natural order of things, we will have to conceive of it as the metamorphosis of air into fire. When the flame bursts into speech, it declares itself thereby to be air transmuted into fire. In other words, when the voice is perceived as a fiery spectacle, we have the evidence of our eyes to prove that the air formed into sound has not retained its character as air, but has become fire.

Thus we have an explanation of the miracle in terms of a sort of physics. But once we enter the realm of physics, we cannot help being drawn further along the same line. True, the phenomenon under consideration is "the voice of the Deity", and obviously we cannot divest it of its character as miracle. Nevertheless, since it occurs in nature it cannot be exempted from subservience to the fundamental categories governing the natural order. That is to say it must be subject to causality. Therefore it is legitimate to ask what caused the transformation of air into fire. Obviously, it would have been possible to give the simple answer that this was a case of divine intervention in the order of nature. Such an answer would not have cut the Gordian knot, but at least it would have completed the chain of causality in nature by adding one supplementary supernatural link.

47 *De migratione Abrahami*, 50 (Colson, ibid.).

In the long run we shall no doubt have to arrive at such an answer —
unless we want to deny the miracle altogether, and that was certainly
not Philo's intention. But before we reach that point, there is still room
for an intermediate link in the quasiphysical chain of causation. The
longer we make that chain, the easier it becomes to accept the miracle
as somehow "rational", that is, accessible to reason. The search for
"rationality" of this sort is one of the characteristics of the supernatural
metaphysic developed by Philo.

So how then does this air in motion become fire? Underlying this
miraculous transformation Philo discerns[48] "an invisible voice"[49]
coming into being in the air "fitted with perfect harmonies". This sound
is all soul, devoid of physical substance, as Philo explains in the sole
passage where he tries to trace the origin of the miraculous phenomenon
and find cause for it. If we may be permitted to read certain fine
distinctions into these bold speculations of his , let us suggest that he
means that this sound, though it is in the air is not of it — is not itself
air. And if we may carry the distinction further, we shall have to say
that in spite of its name it is not really the voice heard later by the
people, but rather the cause of that voice. As Philo explains it, God
created

> a rational voice full of clearness and distinctness, which giving
> shape and tension[50] to the air and changing it to flaming fire,
> sounded forth like the breath through a trumpet an articulate
> voice.

If we adhere to the syntactical construction of Philo's sentence, the
sound equated with the pure soul permeating the air is presented to us
as the combined cause of both the flame and the utterance. It causes the

---

48 *Decal.*, 33 (Colson, p. 23).
49 So the ms. versions. But we shall see that the miraculousness of the voice depends
    precisely on its visibility. We ought therefore consider the possibility that instead
    of reading *aóraton*, it would be better to read *horatón*. This suggestion is put
    forward with some hesitation, because it may be that Philo actually does intend to
    preserve a distinction between *phonè* which is visible, and *ékhos* which is invisible.
    In any event, the question should be looked into.
50 This, it seems to me, is how the Greek word should be translated. In his Hebrew
    version Rokach relates the noun to the high register of the sound heard,
    miraculously in this instance. However, there is no further mention of this, whereas
    the idea that added tension changes air into fire is well established in Stoic physics,
    as we shall soon see.

fire because it "tenses" the air. Such tension is a fundamental concept in Stoic physics. According to their doctrine, the cohesive power that holds every body in nature together functions by means of sinews which bind the periphery to the core. The degree of cohesion depends on the tensile strength (*tonos*) of these sinews. This tension is to be found in the "active" elements, and of these two, in fire more than in air. It is the action of "tension", therefore, that changes the air into fire; and it is this fire that is described as the miraculous "sound".

A particular detail in Philo's description of the phenomenon corroborates the statement that in this instance fire takes over the function of air, which is normally the bearer of sound. He says that the voice sounded forth "from the midst of the fire that streamed from heaven",[51] using terminology reminiscent of an accepted definition of sound in Greek science as "a stream of air".[52] The manifestation of the sound as a voice is likened by Philo to air compressed through the funnel of a trumpet and emerging as a tone. If the bearer of this activity is pure disembodied spirit, it is obvious that the simile of the air in the trumpet cannot serve as anything more than a symbol. But, indeed, that is all we can expect when we try to give a concrete illustration of things which are abstract and immaterial. It thus appears that the added measure of rationality sought by positing the "sound" as the common source of both the fire and the voice has not really been achieved.

A more important question is, what was special about that miraculous voice which the Israelites heard at Sinai, and of which the Septuagint says "all the people saw the voice"? The simplest explanation of this phenomenon is the one given by Philo:

> Then from the midst of the fire that streamed from heaven there sounded forth to their utter amazement a voice, for the flame became articulate speech in the language familiar to the audience, and so clearly and distinctly were the words formed by it that they seemed to see rather than hear them.[53]

In order to get the full force of that last phrase one has to keep in mind the unqualified superiority which the Greeks attributed to the sense of

51   *Decal.*, 46 (Colson, p. 29).
52   Aristotle *Probl.* XI 45 = 904 a 22: *rhusis tis.*
53   *Decal.*, 46 (Colson, p. 29).

sight over all the other senses. In their opinion, nothing is so clear and distinct as that which is seen. To say that the Israelites at Sinai were more like spectators than listeners means that, although they really were listeners, the quality of their hearing was above and beyond anything that a listener usually experiences. The language was the one familiar to them, every word clear and resonant. They were amazed because they had never known it was possible for language to be so explicit. The motif of visibility is not intended to detract from the articulateness of the utterance, but on the contrary, to underscore it.

Continuing with his theme, Philo asks why the Torah says that the voice issued from the midst of the fire. His answer is that the words of God are pure, like gold refined in the fire. Just as the "visibility" of the words is a powerful symbol, so too are the flames a powerful symbol, reinforcing the reality of the utterance.

Philo probably had this last symbolic interpretation from a Palestinian source, because it sounds very much like a homily on Psalm 12.7, although he does not quote the verse here or anywhere else: "The words of the LORD are pure words, silver purged in an earthen crucible, refined sevenfold". It can be assumed that the homily did not originate with him, because if he had had the verse before him he would have used the metaphor "silver", as the Psalmist does, rather than "gold".

How does "seeing" perceive the word of God more clearly and distinctly than hearing? Here Philo points out two things. One is that, consistent with Greek theory, the two senses operate in different ways:

> For that [hearing] is but a sluggish sense, inactive until aroused by the impact of the air, but the hearing of the mind possessed by God makes the first advance and goes out to meet the spoken words with the keenest rapidity.[54]

It is instructive that the two ways of perceiving are distinguished here, not as hearing versus seeing, but rather as two modes of hearing. But when Philo comes to characterize the second mode of "hearing", he defines it in terms recognizable to us as the definition of seeing.

As for his second point, he draws our attention to the fact[55] that the strength of a sound diminishes the further one gets from its source. Of course, the same process occurs with sight as well, but it seems likely

54   *Decal.*, 35 (Colson, p. 23).
55   *Decal.*, 34 (Colson, ibid.).

that because the eye can see much farther than the ear can hear, Philo was misled into converting this relative difference into an absolute one. He declares that people distant from this voice could hear it no less clearly than those nearby. Not satisfied with that, he goes further and claims that the power of God made this voice "more brilliant in its ending than in its beginning", so that those far away could hear it even better, so to speak, than those near the source.

What these two points have in common is that "seeing" the voice is defined as nothing more than a highly amplified form of hearing.

It is important to get a proper perspective on the tension that exists between this approach and the way in which Philo interprets the same phenomena in his allegorical writings. In the latter he presents the vast distance between human speech and the divine voice in the most clear-cut terms:

> Whereas the voice of mortal beings is judged by hearing, the sacred oracles intimate that the words of God are seen, as light is seen; for we are told that "All the people saw the voice", not that they heard it. For what was happening was not an impact on air made by the organs of mouth and tongue, but virtue shining with intense brilliance, wholly resembling a fountain of reason.[56]

It follows that this is not speech at all, but something fundamentally different. It is here that Philo presents his daring interpretation of Deuteronomy 4. 12: "You heard the sound of words, but perceived no shape — nothing but a voice". In that verse, "the sound of words" refers specifically to human speech, as distinct from the divine voice which is not "the sound of words": or to use Philo's words, not "the voice dividing itself into noun and verb and the parts of speech in general".

Here the divine voice is differentiated from human speech not merely by its greater degree of clarity and tone, but most especially by its internal structure. The rules of syntax, as exposed by Aristotle and others who developed the science of grammar, are left behind by this unimaginable power, which is actually the effulgent radiance of light. In the interpretation previously quoted, Philo had stated that the Israelites heard the miraculous voice speaking "in the language familiar to them" so that they could distinguish each spoken word with marvellous clarity. But this time he tells us that they received a message

---

56 *De migratione Abrahami*, 47 (Colson, IV, p. 159).

transcending all the categories which make human speech understandable. "Understanding" in this case cannot be achieved by linguistic analysis; rather it is imparted to the beholder instantaneously as an all-enlightening radiance. We might put it this way: whereas in the first interpretation "sight" and "fire" were treated as symbolic hyperbole, the second interpretation uses "voice" in a sense quite different from its usual meaning, referring it to something that transcends analytical reason.

It is only natural that the first interpretation should be found in *De decalogo*, part of Philo's major work on the laws of the Torah. These laws are expressed in "the language familiar to us", and not in a tongue which lacks "noun and verb and the parts of speech". Any interpretation that makes the structure of language evaporate in the blinding radiance of divine light would undermine the basis of Philo's work on the laws. Therefore it suits his purpose this time to consider sight as reinforcing hearing.

But we should not harbor the illusion that this is the main thrust of Philo's thought. However great his devotion to the observance of the mitzvot as written in the Torah, he is drawn irresistibly to that vision, in the light of which the literal meaning of the words is transcended. This imbalance between the two tendencies within him can be observed when we find the visionary mode of interpretation, which properly belongs to his allegorical exegesis, twice slipping into his large work on the laws as understood literally.

One time this happens is when the Fourth Commandment, concerning the sanctity of the Sabbath, comes up. In describing the case of the man caught gathering wood on the Sabbath[57] (Num. 15. 32 ff.) Philo makes the magnitude of the man's offense vivid by saying

> ... though the echoes of the divine command about the sacredness of the seventh day were ringing in his ears, commands promulgated by God not through His prophet but by a voice which, strange paradox, was visible and aroused the eyes rather than the ears of the bystanders.

If we read carefully, we will find that the voice which essentially stimulates the eyes is not to be understood as a voice which renders the words so transparent that you seem to be seeing them, not just hearing

---

57   *Vita Mosis, II*, 213 (Colson, VII, p. 555).

them. Rather it is a voice which addresses vision, and has nothing to do with the articulation of words. Nevertheless, what is referred to here is the substance of the Commandment forbidding all manner of work on the Sabbath day. How could the wood-gatherer disregard this prohibition which must have hung before his very eyes in so striking a form?

This time Philo is not so meticulous in listing those reservations with which, in order to avoid obscuring the imperative of the Commandment itself, he hedged his words in *De decalogo*. However, a greater problem is presented by another breach in the defense he so carefully erected — a breach discernable even in *De decalogo* itself. Immediately after he has neutralized the difficulty in "All the people saw the voice", he continues as follows:

> It is the case that the voice of men is audible, but the voice of God is truly visible. Why so? Because whatever God says is not words but deeds, which are judged by the eyes rather than the ears.[58]

Here Philo let himself be carried away by this favorite concept, to such an extent that he momentarily failed to realize that he had cut the ground from under his own argument, by carrying his interpretation to such extremes. For if that which God says is not really "words", then what is the point of discussing at such length those "Ten Words" which, it now turns out, are not really what God said? Obviously Philo did not realize that what he had written could lead to so devastating a conclusion. At any rate, he could not help letting slip this problematical remark, because it accurately reflects the main thrust of his philosophy.

There remains one final question. How does Philo's intricate theory help make the divine utterance, as described in the Torah, more accessible to "reason"? The cornerstone of Philo's approach to Revelation is contained in the essential difference that he postulates between the Ten Commandments and all the other mitzvot, a difference based on the way they were made known. Whereas all the other commandments were mediated by the prophet, these Ten are distinguished by the fact that God Himself communicated them "in all His glory", and "not through the agency of a prophet"; indeed, "in the First Person".

This difference is apparent in the biblical text, read simply. In

---

58   *Decal.*, 47 (Colson, p. 31).

connection with the Decalogue, Moses is not told to "Speak to the Israelite people"; instead, we read: "Face to face the LORD spoke to you on the mountain out of the fire" (Deut. 5. 4). This verse confronts us with the miracle in all its unmediated majestic wonder, with no attempt to make it "reasonable", that is, acceptable to the intelligence accustomed to thinking in terms of rational causality.

Philo cannot accept the simple sense of the text, which he finds anthropomorphic, because "speaking" the Decalogue implies literally the use of organs of speech, such as the mouth and the tongue. Nevertheless, although he rules out the literal meaning of "speech" on theological grounds, he does not do the same to the literal meaning of "God's voice". We have already seen how he develops the concept of the divine voice, and differentiates between it and human speech. But the question remains: if we cannot say that God's voice issued from his mouth, what then is the relation between that voice and its divine source? Philo's answer is this:

> I should suppose that God wrought on this occasion a miracle of a truly holy kind by bidding an invisible sound to be created in the air.[59]

That sound is one of the things especially created for the occasion, and since Philo uses the same verb for "created" as Plato does in his *Timaeus* when he speaks of the work of the *demiurge* in fashioning the world, we can view the voice as one of those primordial items made at the time of creation, even though this one was held in reserve and not brought out until a certain later moment. To be more precise, we are not told that God "created" or "fashioned" or "made" it, but rather that He ordered that this be done; from which we can ssume that Philo intended to assure equal status for this voice with all other created things. They too, it is implied, fall into the category of "He commanded — and they came into existence" (cf. Ps. 33. 9).

However, what Philo's construction of the revelation gains in terms of metaphysics, it loses in exactly the same measure in religious value. To be sure, he succeeds in neutralizing the anthropomorphic impact of the biblical text as it stands. No longer are we attributing speech to God, but merely having Him issue a creative decree calling into being one more entity to be added to those already existing in His

---

59   *Decal.*, 33 (Colson, p. 23).

Creation. And if theology can cope with the idea of God the Creator, then the existence of this voice does not add any new metaphysical difficulty.

But now a new question arises. What assurance have we that this pure "incorporeal soul" created by divine fiat really is the voice of God? Is not the prophet also created by God? And that being so, what makes this special form of revelation superior to the way in which all the other commandments were revealed — that is, through the mediation of the prophet? On this reading, the created voice loses all the special significance for the sake of which it was introduced.

Philo has already stated explicitly what it was that he was trying to explain, namely, why it was these Commandments that "God had judged fit to deliver in His own person alone without employing any other".[60] It is obvious that Philo believes he has clarified this by means of his theory of the voice, when he speaks of "the power of God that breathed on it and spread it abroad on every side".[61] However, all of this holds good only if, and insofar as, God Himself is at work in the voice that reaches human beings. And it is exactly this immanence that Philo himself invalidates by replacing the relationship between God and His voice with the relationship between the Creator and the thing created. Yet this he feels obliged to set up because of his concern to avoid anthropomorphism.

So Philo's thinking becomes entrapped by his metaphysical-rationalistic theology, from whatever angle it is examined. Either the people really heard these fundamental Commandments, which embody all the rest of the commandments, from God Himself and not from any intermediary — in which case no possible reformulation, however sophisticated, will let us escape from the anthropomorphism of the biblical text; or else we strip the voice of its rationally insupportable identification with the Godhead — in which case the directness of the communication of the commanding Deity with the people becomes flawed. We may admit that the created voice as compared with the human voice of Moses, in speaking to the people, has the advantage of being perfectly harmonious. It is perceived with a lucid and superior kind of hearing which may well be called "seeing". But then, this superiority is merely relative; whereas divine

---

60 *Decal.*, 18 (Colson, p. 15).
61 *Decal.*, 35 (Colson, p. 23).

communication, when compared to the human kind, ought to have an absolute superiority. But this is ruled out when the voice is detached from the Godhead which is its source.

It is not because of any erroneous step in his reasoning that Philo is impaled on the horns of this dilemma, but because of the nature of his initial assumptions. Retracing the steps of his intellectual odyssey, we are justified in saying that he was bound to end up in this difficult position.

V

I shall pass over the question raised by Philo as to why the Ten Commandments are couched in the second person singular, as though addressed to one individual,[62] because the phenomenon is not peculiar to the Decalogue. On the other hand, I do want to dwell for a moment on his concluding remark, where he asks why the lawgiver, unlike most lawgivers, does not specify the sanctions that go with breaking his laws.[63] He is well aware that this omission does not hold good for laws elsewhere in the Torah. Indeed, later in his work on the mitzvot, after he has devoted several books to the detailed laws that flow from these fundamental Ten, he concludes the entire corpus with a discourse on "Reward and Punishment". In that discourse he also takes account of the admonitory sanctions listed in the Torah. But he sees this omission as a unique characteristic of the Commandments promulgated directly by the Deity. They are apodictic, a format which does not, as he explains, contain any mention of punishment. (It will be noticed that he ignores the passage about "visiting the guilt of the fathers on the children". But that exegetical flaw simply reveals to us that he did not derive his idea from the text, which gives it no support. The reverse seems to be true. Philo came to the text with the idea already formed in his mind.)

His idea is, that since God is good, He cannot be the source of evil things. Consequently, He deems it appropriate to this attribute of His to give us the Commandments, which are for the good of human beings, but to refrain from declaring the penalties in store for transgressors. So Philo does not argue here, as he does elsewhere, that since punishment is designed for the improvement of the transgressor,

62   *Decal.*, 36–43 (Colson, pp. 25 ff.).
63   *Decal.*, 176–178 (Colson, pp. 93 f.).

it is not evil but good. That point does not appear in the present context; here the assumption is that punishment is bad, though undoubtedly it is necessary. Again we are confronted with a dilemma: there is something that God cannot be the cause of, because it is evil, and it is inconceivable that God should be the cause of anything not appropriate to His nature.[64] On the other hand, it is inconceivable that God should oppose punishment, because it is necessary.

It is only with this background in mind that we can understand the sequel to this idea as expressed by Philo towards the end of *De decalogo*:

> He therefore thought right not to couple punishment with His utterances, though He did not thereby grant immunity to evil-doers, but knew that Dikē, His assessor, the surveyor of human affairs, in virtue of her inborn hatred of evil, will not rest, but take upon herself as her congenital task the punishment of sinners.[65]

First of all, we have to face up to the amazing fact, without attempting to gloss it over, that Dikē referred to here is a figure from the dramatis personae of Greek mythology, where she is a divine being, the personification of justice. According to many sources[66] she sits at the side of Zeus, father of gods and men, whose daughter she is, and supervises human affairs. To be sure, Philo scarcely dwells on this figure, and since her name is simply the Greek word for "justice", a Jewish writer might well feel free to use it as a figure of speech, a synonym for what was familiar to him as *midat ha-din* — God's attribute of justice. In his own mind he could make light of the mythological figure sitting beside the pagan god as nothing more than a borrowed metaphor with which to embellish his rhetoric, without in any way committing himself to its actual content.

Philo is not the only Hellenistic Jewish writer to speak of "Dikē, enemy of evil".[67] But he happens to be one who makes frequent use of

---

64 *Decal.*, 177 (Colson, p. 94). On the importance of this concept, see W. Jaeger, *The Theology of the Early Greek Philosophers*, Oxford 1947, pp. 49 f.

65 *Decal.*, 177 (Colson, p. 95).

66 Hesiod, op. 259; Sophocles, OC, 1382; Demosthenes, 25, 11.

67 The Septuagint (Esther 8. 12d) contains this added phrase. Cf. also IV Maccabees 4. 21; and Wisdom of Solomon 9. 4.

the expression.[68] He notes admiringly that the punishment that befell the wicked Flaccus was a sign that "Dikē who watches over the affairs of men" was on guard.[69] And he denounces the wicked who do not realize that they will ultimately suffer at the hands of "Dikē who surveys human affairs", the same pain they now inflict on others.[70] Similarly, in an even more explicit reference, he speaks of those who are not afraid of "Dikē who sits beside the throne of the ruler of all".[71] Those who built the tower of Babel should also have known that "Dikē who accompanies the God" would take her revenge on them.[72]

Dikē as the symbol of justice is therefore by no means unusual in Philo's works. That he makes use of that figure of speech in the present context is due, as has been rightly surmised, to the fact that he was thinking of a passage in Plato's *Dialogues* where she appears as the executive arm of the Deity, who enforces the rule of law in general.[73]

However, none of this touches the crucial point in Philo's use of that phraseology in this particular connection. In all the instances we have cited, Dikē stands for the chief divine authority in its special capacity of law enforcement. Almost nothing would have been changed in those citations if, instead of Dikē, the reference had been to the Deity Himself "beside whose throne she sits". The only advantage in mentioning Dikē might be that it helps the reader understand immediately which aspect of the Godhead was being referred to.

But this is exactly where the trouble lies. In our context Dikē is not a stand-in for the Deity "at the side of whose throne she sits". Quite the contrary: if for Dikē we substitute the Deity Himself, we completely destroy Philo's whole concept. His idea rests entirely on the distinction between Him and her.

In order to point this up, let us pay particular attention to Philo's twice repeated use of the word "nature". Admittedly, this word is so commonly employed by Greek thinkers that we probably should not attach too much importance to it. Nevertheless, the way in which he uses the term twice in the concluding paragraphs of *De decalogo* is instructive. First he says of God that "He judged it was most in

---

68 See G. Meyer, *Philon Index*, s.v. *dikē; misoponēros.*
69 *In Flaccum*, 146 (Colson, IX, p. 383).
70 *Quod omnis probis liber sit*, 89 (Colson, IX, p. 61).
71 *De specialibus legibus*, IV, 201 (Colson, VIII, p. 138).
72 *De confusione linguarum*, 118 (Colson, IV, p. 75).
73 Plato, *Leg.*, 716a.

accordance with His *nature* to issue His saving commandments free
from any admixture of punishment"; and then he says that Dikē "by
virtue of her *nature* has a hatred of evil".

You might say that here we have two "natures" confronting each
other, and that this opposition makes it clear why God does not do
what Dikē does. What makes this contrast all the more telling is that
Philo carefully avoids any suggestion of cooperation between God and
Dikē, who sits beside His throne. He does not say that the Deity
entrusts the execution of His just decisions to Dikē; nor does he say
that He allows her to get on with her task. What he does say is that God
knows she will see to it that the transgressor will not go unpunished.

This formulation is neither fortuitous nor casual, but is careful and
calculated. Behind it lie considerations whose thrust is to limit the
association between Goodness and the wages of evildoing; because the
punishment of the wrongdoer, necessary though it be for the existence
of an orderly world, is nevertheless something negative, especially from
the point of view of those to whom the commandments are issued.
Consequently, the threat of punishment leads to the danger that people
will obey the commandments from fear of the consequences, rather
than out of choice. From this point of view, the mention of sanctions is
likely to spoil the essence of the mitzvah. And since God does care for
the purity of motive with which the commandments are observed, He
seeks to avoid the punitive aspect as much as possible.

Unfortunately, the context did not allow Philo to introduce at this
point the matter of reward for performing the mitzvot, because then in
principle he would have had to admit that the hope of reward entails
the same danger to purity of motive as does the fear of punishment.
That would have destroyed his carefully constructed theory which we
have been scrutinizing here.

However, let us leave anthropology and get back to theology. The
question has just arisen, albeit within a limited context, of the origin of
evil. The solution suggested by Philo was, that since God Himself
cannot be the source of evil, there must be an authority dependent on
Him but not identical with Him, charged with inflicting on the world —
with His knowledge — that evil which the realities of life make
necessary. Such a force cannot be identical with Him, for that would
impair the purity of the concept of God. On the other hand, a sufficient
relationship must be preserved between God and Dikē, for otherwise
the principle of Divine unity would be impaired.

It can hardly be said that the means employed by Philo to free God from the responsibility for the necessary evil in the world is at all convincing. Certainly the problematics of theodicy are not helped very much by his attempt to justify the ways of God by making an analogy with the secular ruler. The state, he says, keeps the peace while simultaneously maintaining a department for the waging of war. The great king, he says, must be one who bestows the abundant blessings of peace and plenty on his subjects, while under him there serves a minister of war whose task it is to take all measures needed for the defense of the realm. "For indeed God is the Prince of Peace while His subalterns are the leaders in war".[74] The implication is this: in the eyes of the people, the personality of the king is linked exclusively to the beneficent aspects of the kingdom. The darker side, without which the state cannot be maintained, is entrusted to the armed forces. As for the fact that these forces serve "under" the king — are subordinate to him — this is left aside.

It must be admitted that here again Philo has touched on one of those fundamental paradoxes from which no religious outlook is immune, and with which no purely rational system can cope. He must therefore not be judged too severely for advancing so vulnerable an explanation. If there is a fault to be found, it is in the somewhat casual tone with which he appears to dismiss the problem.

VI

It does not seem to be necessary to repeat here the detailed explanations which Philo offers for each of the Ten Commandments. We shall content ourselves with a few selected points which reveal an original approach peculiar to him.

Such originality can be seen in the way he understands the Fourth Commandment; that is, in his treatment of the significance of the Sabbath. He says that what we are really celebrating when we observe the Sabbath is the cyclic orderliness of the universe, expressed by the properties of the number seven. These properties, which he works out in terms of his mathematical mysticism, cannot be gone into here. It may suffice to note that its model in the cosmos is assumed to be the "seven planets". In honor of the solar system, Philo tells us, Moses depicts the creation of the world as having taken place in six days, with the seventh day as its climax. But that is symbolic. The truth is that God

---

74   *Decal.*, 178 (Colson, p. 95).

does not need any time at all to complete His work. Philo refers the reader to his disquisition on the Creation, dealing with the sense in which we are allowed to say of God that He created the world in a fixed number of days.[75]

However, if we take the biblical account as it stands, what is there in it according to Philo that makes the seventh day special? On this point he has something unique to say. It is that when God rested from His work on the seventh day "He began to contemplate well what had been created".[76]

We should scarcely hold this to be the plain meaning of the biblical text. It was on the sixth day, not the seventh, that the Book of Genesis says "God saw all that He had made and found it very good". And the fact is that this divine "seeing" is nothing more than a summing up of all the other "seeings" that accompanied each act of creation from the first day onwards; and each "seeing" accomplished its purpose with the verdict that "it was good", or that "it was very good". But as far as Philo is concerned, the work of creation was confined to the six days, whereupon the era of contemplation took over. In this way he creates a basis for the interrelation between the two types of meaningful life as conceived by Greek ethical thought: the life of action and the life of contemplation. Certain serious reservations aside, there can be no doubt that Philo gives priority to the life of contemplation.

It follows that in his concept of God, as it emerges from the topic we have just been discussing, the attribute of contemplation has priority over the attribute of action. That is probably why, when Philo defines the seventh day as the beginning of the period of contemplation, by contrast to the preceding six, his intention was to imply that from then on God is to be thought of as a contemplative God. And if we bear in mind that time-bound expressions are mere metaphors when used in relation to God who transcends the dimension of time, then it follows that the state of contemplation is His eternal essence, and that those "six days", which in the philosophical sense are non-time, do not impair this principle.

This has direct implications for the nature of the Sabbath day as Philo conceives it, because God's rest established the model for the way

---

75 *Decal.*, 102 (Colson, p. 59); and cf. *De opificio mundi*, 13 ff. and *Legum Allegoriae*, I, 2–4 (Colson, I, pp. 13 and 147 ff.).

76 *Decal.*, 97 (Colson, p. 55).

in which human people are to rest. The act of creation set up the design for the world, which is the true *polis*, and all who inhabit it are its citizens. Now, you become a citizen of any *polis* by accepting its laws. The same applies to the *Kosmopolis*, the City-of-the-World. As with any state or city, its constitution was formulated at the time it was founded. It follows that the original design of the world determined what was to be its nature — that is to say, its laws.

All of this leads to the conclusion that the Sabbath,.with which the world was created, and which went into effect then and there, became the statute determining membership in that ideal city called the *Kosmos*. By observing the Sabbath, therefore, we are in effect following the injunction of the philosophers to the wise man:"Always follow God".[77] Thus it comes about that for Philo the Jewish Sabbath develops, paradoxically enough, into a fulfillment of the cosmopolitan imperative; while its aspect as "a sign for all time between Me and the people of Israel" (Ex. 31. 17) fades into insignificance.

How then are we obeying the injunction to "follow God" when we observe the Sabbath? By abandoning action and moving over to contemplation. It is true that because we are mere mortals we have to work all the time to provide ourselves with the necessities of life; so we cannot free ourselves permanently from the life of action. In contrast to the transition which God made at one stroke from action to contemplation, we have to follow a repetitive cycle: six days of labor and one day of contemplation. After every Sabbath this formula repeats itself. That is the meaning of the biblical verse "Six days shall you labor ... but the seventh day is a Sabbath of the LORD" (Ex. 20. 9–10).

All this gives us a clear idea of how Philo views the nature of the Sabbath. He says that we are supposed to "work for six days but rest on the seventh and turn to the study of philosophy", giving ourselves leisure "for the contemplation of the truths of nature".[78]

In order not to misunderstand this requirement we must first of all realize that in Stoic philosophy, from which Philo derives his terminology, the natural sciences culminate in the study of theology. Obviously, this is what Philo has in mind when he speaks of "nature". What we call "natural science" was to him of minor importance;

---

77   *Decal.*, 100 (Colson, p. 57).
78   *Decal.*, 98 (Colson, ibid.).

certainly it was not something which God had obliged mankind to study.

Secondly, it should be noted that the Hellenistic Jews customarily referred to the Torah as the "philosophy" of their ancestors. Consequently, we may understand Philo's requirement to study philosophy on the Sabbath as a Hellenic way of expressing the duty to study Torah on the Sabbath. We know that there were circles in Hellenistic Jewry — probably the majority — for whom the focus of this Sabbath activity was the study of halakhah.[79] No doubt the scholarly level of such study was lower than it was among the Jews of Palestine at that time. For Philo, however, and for the intellectual elite whom he represents (doubtless a small minority among the Jews of Alexandria) this Sabbath study assumed a distinctly philosophical character. That contemplation which Philo declared to be the real purpose of the Sabbath meant for him nothing less than the study of philosophy proper.

This is implied by the reference to those "truths of nature" which Philo mentions as a synonym for philosophy. However, the contemplation about which he speaks is not only metaphysical (in his terminology, "physical"). For in the rest of the sentence just quoted he goes on to speak of a person's duty on the Sabbath to examine his deeds of the past week in the light of the laws. What this means — and the point comes out clearly in many of Philo's expressions — is that the Sabbath contemplation includes ethical introspection. Physics and ethics, which for Philo are the only areas of philosophical interest, are thus declared to be the proper content of a person's contemplation on the Sabbath day.

When Philo subordinates the biblical motif of Sabbath "rest" (in the Septuagint version "cessation from work") to the motif of Sabbath contemplation, it is obvious that he is trying to cope with the prevailing Greek view, as expressed for example by Aristotle.[80] In that view, festivals are an interruption in the normal routine of work, and as such are not seen as an end in themselves. Hence, to a Greek, the Sabbath defined as a "cessation" can only be regarded as a means to something else. This is an additional stimulus for Philo to direct our attention to the positive purpose for which the cessation was instituted.

---

79   See e.g, Philo's *Hypothetica*, Chap. 7, paras. 12–14 (Colson, IX, p. 433).

80   On this subject, see Heinemann (above, n. 30), pp. 113 ff. The reference to Aristotle is to *Nicomachean Ethics* X, 6 = 1176b 35 f.

When he comes to discuss the Fifth Commandment, Philo is concerned with its position on the Tablets of the Law. There are five Commandments on each of the tablets. The first tablet is the more important of the two, since it deals with divine matters,[81] while the second pertains to the duties which one person has to the other.[82] How then does the Fifth Commandment, prescribing the honor due to one's father and mother, fit into this scheme?

Philo's answer is that it belongs on the border-line between the two groups of Commandments. True, it is inscribed on the first tablet, but it adjoins the second. The reason for this is that it really belongs to both.

> Thus one set of enactments begins with God the Father and Maker of all, and ends with parents who copy His nature by begetting particular persons.[83]

One has to examine these words carefully in order to detect their non-Jewish nuance. For even though from biblical times onward it was acceptable to speak of God as "Our Father", here we find foreign ideas creeping in by association.

In the present context the similarity between the human father and "our Father in heaven" lies in the fact that the human father also begets; except that human parents beget particular persons, whereas the Creator begets all of existence.

It must be said that the combination "Father who begets" as describing the Deity is easily recognizable as deriving from the Dialogues of Plato; and no wonder, for it very clearly reflects the traditional cosmogony of Greek mythology. Philo did not hesitate to use this Platonic turn of speech, because after all he had plentiful warrant in Jewish tradition for calling God "Father"; nor was he worried by the pagan nuance that the expression carries with it.[84] Indeed, it provides him with an opening for his statement that parents

> stand by their nature on the border-line between the mortal and

---

81   *Decal.*, 50 (Colson, 31).
82   *Decal.*, 106 (Colson, 61).
83   *Decal.*, 51 (Colson, 33).
84   There are further instances of this in Philo's works. Scholars have been especially embarassed by his use of the expression "visible gods" which he sometimes uses to designate the celestial bodies. See, for example, his *De aeternitate mundi*, 10 (Colson, IX, p. 191).

the immortal... because the act of generation assimilates them to God, the Generator of the All.[85]

To be sure, in another context Philo dwells on the danger of linking these ideas.[86] When he discusses the commandment of circumcision, he quotes several reasons for it which he had heard from other sources, and then adds two reasons of his own. One of these is that circumcision is intended to counteract the arrogance of those

> who dared imagine that, like skilled sculptors, they were able to create man, the most beautiful of living creatures, and in their braggart pride assumed godship.

These people might have realized, he goes on to explain, that the true cause of all birth is God; for they can see that there are both men and women whose intercourse does not result in the birth of children. The purpose of circumcision is to remind such people that their generative organs do not raise them to the level of the true Generator of All.

But despite all these reservations, in *De decalogo* Philo describes parents as belonging somewhere between the mortal and the immortal. On the one hand, like all human beings their lives come to an end; but on the other hand, their ability to create life endows them with a touch of the Divine.

That is why the Commandment to honor one's parents is written adjacent to the Commandments that deal with one's duties to one's fellowman; but is inscribed nevertheless on the first tablet, along with such Commandments as the belief in one God, and the ban on graven images.

This intermediate status of parents determines the position of "Honor your father and your mother". If it is possible to differentiate between those who love God and those who love their neighbor, or between the reverent and the moral, each of whom attains only half the perfection of character, then it may be said of one who keeps the Fifth Commandment that he has done his duty by both faith and ethics, and has thus achieved the fullness of virtue. For in the honoring of one's parents there is an element of honoring God, as well as honoring man.[87]

The converse is also true. One who disdains this Commandment is a

---

85   *Decal.*, 107 (Colson, p. 61).
86   *De specialibus legibus*, I, 10–11 (Colson, VII, p. 105).
87   *Decal.*, 110 (Colson, p. 63).

defective personality in both areas of human obligation, the religious and the moral.[88] At this point Philo draws a logical conclusion: if a person treats his own parents shamefully — those who bestowed on him the greatest gifts, some of them so great that they can never under any circumstances be repaid — just imagine how he will treat everybody else!

Here Philo adds another motif derived from his background in Greek philosophy. The Stoics had gathered a lot of information about the fidelity of animals to their aged. The purpose of this scientific effort was to prove that such fidelity is inborn, wisely implanted in every living thing by nature — hence by the divine *Logos* which controls nature. By internalizing this urge we adapt our individual *logos* to the all-embracing *Logos*, of which our own is a part. This adaptation, this harmonization, is the fundamental goal which Stoic ethics strives for.

Philo, however, reduces this idea to lesser proportions, and uses it for a rather superficial type of moralizing. He says that although animals should learn from us, since we are on a higher rung in the scale of creation, the least we can do is to be on guard not to fall below them in our standard of behavior, lest we might have to "hide our faces for shame".[89]

Finally, a word about the Tenth Commandment. "You shall not covet" is interpreted by Philo as a prohibition against desire. He disregards the plain sense of the biblical text, which enumerates objects of illicit desire, and sums them up with the generalization "anything that is your neighbor's". The way the Bible puts it, what makes desire wrong is that it moves you to do harm to your neighbor.

Philo too is fully aware that in principle the second tablet deals with interpersonal relations, and that the internal structure of the Decalogue is determined by the fact that the Commandments begin with "I the LORD" and conclude with "your neighbor". But when it comes to ethics, his teachers are the Stoics, whose morality is basically individual rather than social. Thus, it is the duty of the individual person to make the *logos* within him the guiding principle of his psyche. In order to do this he must gain the upper hand over his emotions and appetites, the passions that assail him and displace the *logos* from the mastery proper to it. Thus it is that of the four passions identified in Stoic doctrine,

88   *Decal.*, 111 (ibid.).
89   *Decal.*, 118 (Colson, p. 67).

namely pleasure, pain, fear and appetite, Philo tries to prove that the last is the most despicable. For by contrast to the others, to which a person may have to submit against his will, the surrender to appetite contains an element of deliberate choice. In the case of such surrender, a person is more responsible than he is for what assails him in spite of himself. To be sure, Stoic doctrine requires a person to emancipate himself from every sort of passion; but here in the Decalogue, which deals with only the most fundamental imperatives, the Deity confines Himself to the worst of all, which is desire.[90]

This approach, which changes the plain meaning of the text, has practical consequences as well for Philo — not expressed in *De decalogo*, to be sure, but made explicit in his larger work *De specialibus legibus*, where he derives from each of the Commandments the laws implicit in it. With regard to the Tenth Commandment, he finds in it the background for the dietary laws. These he explains as a set of restrictions designed to rein in men's appetites.

This association of ideas is possible only if the Commandment is shorn of its concluding words "anything that is your neighbor's". For after all, kashrut has nothing to do with issues of ownership, of "mine and thine". An animal is not forbidden as food because it is stolen goods. Eating forbidden food is classified with transgressions "between man and his Maker", not with those between man and his fellow.

This shows that in thinking about the Tenth Commandment, Philo disregarded its dimension of avoiding harm to one's neighbor, and made of it instead a rule of moral self-discipline. He thus removed it entirely from its proper context, which is the realm of interpersonal relations.

In this connection, there is something remarkable to be observed. Saadiah Gaon, who wrote a piyyut classifying the whole 613 mitzvot under one or another of the Ten Commandments,[91] also relates kashrut to the Tenth Commandment, just as Philo did! This correspondence of ideas raises a question: were there channels for the transmission of this idea between the first and the tenth century? Some submerged lines of communication through which the thought could have passed from Philo to Saadiah?

I prefer to leave that question unanswered.

---

90   *Decal.*, 142 (Colson, 77 f.).
91   See above at n. 17.

VII

There can be no doubt that, unlike the Sages of normative Judaism, Philo attributed a special status of their own to the Ten Commandments. This was not simply due to the fact that these laws were pronounced from on high; after all, the Sages could read that plainly stated in the Bible. The difference has to do with the special weight Philo assigned to the Decalogue. The possible influence of his approach on those heretics — *Minim* — from whom the Sages dissociated themselves, and the extent of such influence if any, is a question of importance in the history of religion; but one to which we cannot address ourselves here.

However, as far as Philo himself is concerned, one thing is certain: the superior status which he assigned to the Ten Commandments did not in the least induce him to make light of the other mitzvot. The hierarchy which he set up in the relationship between the Decalogue and all the other commandments was purely methodological, and had nothing whatsoever to do with the binding force of the latter. Quite the contrary: in his view the unconditional obligation that attaches to all the commandments derives from the fact that they are all anchored in these categorical imperatives — the Ten Words that were pronounced from on high to the Israelites assembled at Mount Sinai.

Translated by Yvonne Glikson

6. THE ROLE OF THE TEN COMMANDMENTS IN JEWISH WORSHIP

EPHRAIM E. URBACH

I

In the Jewish tradition the special role of the Ten Commandments is expressed visually as well as liturgically. For one thing, the two tablets of the Covenant inscribed with the Decalogue have long been used as a symbol decorating many a synagogue. For another, it is customary almost everywhere for the congregation to rise when the Ten Commandments are read from the Torah. And in various times and places, to swear by the Ten Commandments has been considered a most awesome oath.

When was it that this special status became attached to the Decalogue? What lies behind this preferential position? Has it held good for a long time? Did anyone ever question this status, and if so, why? This issue has a history, which we propose to examine in what follows.

The Torah identifies the Ten Commandments as "the terms of the Covenant". In Exodus 34. 28 we read: "He wrote down on the tablets the terms of the covenant, the Ten Commandments". In Deuteronomy (4. 13) Moses repeats: "He declared to you the covenant which He commanded you to observe, the Ten Commandments, and He inscribed them on two tablets of stone". Whereas this verse refers to the original tablets, which God himself wrote, the passage in Exodus speaks of the second tablets, written by Moses.

To be sure, in the verse in Exodus just preceding (34. 27) God says to Moses: "Write down these words, for in accordance with these words I make a covenant with you and with Israel". However, just what "these words" are, is not made explicit.[1] In the description of the covenant

---

1   Rabbi Johanan uses this verse in order to stress the importance of the oral

itself (Ex. 24. 4) before the promulgation of the Decalogue, we read: "Moses then wrote down all the commands of the LORD". But this expression, along with "the record of the covenant" in verse 7, is explained by the Tannaim as referring, not to the Ten Commandments, but rather to earlier commands given to Adam, to Noah and his descendents, and to the Israelites at Marah.[2] It was only the opening sentence of the Decalogue, "The LORD spoke all these words, saying": (Ex. 20. 1) that was interpreted by the Sages in such a way as to express the unique nature of the theophany.

> "All these words". Scripture hereby teaches that God spoke the Ten Commandments in one utterance — something impossible for creatures of flesh and blood — for it says: "God spoke all these words, saying, etc." If so, why then is it said "I am the LORD your God", "You shall have no other gods", and so on? It simply teaches that the Holy One, blessed be He, after having said all the Ten Commandments in one utterance, repeated them, saying each commandment separately.[3]

This midrash elevates the Decalogue to a special position as a historical event, but assigns it no special role in the conduct of future generations. Nowhere in the Torah, or for that matter anywhere else in the Bible, is there any directive whatsoever concerning the recitation of the Decalogue or its ceremonial use within the Sanctuary or outside it. The only rule is that everyone must observe its contents.

However, the Mishnah does tell us that in the priestly service of the Jerusalem Temple the reading of the Ten Commandmants occupied a special place. The Tractate Tamid informs us that each morning before the daily whole-offering the priest-in-charge would say to the duty-priests:

tradition: "It was only by virtue of the Oral Law that the Holy One made His covenant with Israel, as we read: 'For in accordance with these words I make a covenant with you'" (Git. 60b; and see Yer. Peah, II:17, and *Tanḥuma*, 58.3).

2   *Mekhilta de Rabbi Ishmael, Ba-Ḥodesh*, II, p. 211, and see n. 13 there; cf. ed. Lauterbach II, p. 211. Also *Mekhilta de Rabbi Simeon bar Yoḥai*, p. 220; *Midrash Tannaim*, ed. Hoffman, p. 56; and I.N. Epstein, in: *Chayes Memorial Volume*, Vienna 1933, p. 30.

3   *Mekhilta de Rabbi Ishmael, Ba-Ḥodesh*, IV, p. 218, ed. Lauterbach, II, p. 228. For varying interpretations of the phrase "Why then does Scripture say?..." see n. 12 there. The probable meaning is: "Why are the Commandments divided into ten, considering that they were spoken in but one utterance?"

"Recite a benediction!" They did so, and then read the Ten Commandments, followed by "Hear O Israel" (Shema, Deut. 6. 4–9); "If then you obey" (Deut. 11. 13–21); and the law of the fringes (Num. 15. 37–41). They recited three benedictions with the people, namely *Emet veyaziv*, the Avodah, and the Priestly Blessing [See prayer book, e.g. Singer, pp. 42, 50 and 53] (Tamid V:1).

What did the priest-in-charge mean when he said "Recite a benediction"? Certain Amoraim explain this as referring to *Ahavah Rabbah*, a thanksgiving for the selection of the people of Israel, and for granting them the Torah.[4]

The reading of the Ten Commandments in the Temple when the daily whole-offering was about to be placed on the altar constituted a reminder of the contents of the revelation at Mount Sinai, and amounted to a repetition of the covenant between God and His people. As I have tried to show elsewhere,[5] the reading of the Ten Commandments preceded the recitation of the Shema. It was added in order to emphasize the idea of the absolute oneness of Israel's God and the utter negation of the very existence of any other gods; as well as to deny absolutely the dualistic concept. This latter denial is made explicit in the first of the three benedictions preceding the Shema: "He who fashions light and creates darkness" (quoting Isaiah 45.7; see Ber. 11b).

The Nash Papyrus, containing as it does the Ten Commandments along with the first two paragraphs of the Shema, may not constitute absolute proof that it was customary to include the Decalogue in the liturgy *outside* the Temple in Jerusalem. But it does at least lend support to the idea that this was indeed the practice (plates 2 and 3).

In Deuteronomy 6, at verse 3, the Septuagint has an extra sentence, inserted just before the Shema. It reads:

> These are the statutes and laws which the LORD commanded the Israelites in the wilderness when they went out of Egypt.

This addition appears before the verse "Hear O Israel!" and follows close on the Ten Commandments in chapter 5. The most reasonable

---

4   Yer. Ber. I:8, 3c; Bavli, ibid., 11b.
5   E.E. Urbach, *The Sages — Their Concepts and Beliefs*, Jerusalem 1975, pp. 19 ff.

assumption is that the extra sentence got into the Septuagint under the influence of the liturgy, and not the other way around.[6]

The close connection between reciting the Decalogue and reading the Shema (and at the same time the difference between the two) is illuminated by the *Sifre* when it comments on Deuteronomy 6. 7–8. The biblical passage reads:

> Repeat them regularly with your children. Recite them when you stay at home and when you are away, when you lie down and when you get up. Bind them as a sign on your hand and let them serve as a symbol on your forehead, etc.

This does not make explicit what we are to repeat, or what we are to bind. The mishnah quoted from Tamid speaks only of reciting the Commandments and reading the three paragraphs of "the Shema". The *Sifre* puts it this way:

> "Repeat them regularly with your children". The passages containing those words are the ones to be repeated, not the other two paragraphs [contained in the tefillin] — "Consecrate to Me every first-born" (Ex. 13. 2) and "when the LORD has brought you"(Ex. 13. 11). I might have reasoned that, since the paragraph concerning the fringes (Num. 15. 37) *is* included in the recitation [i.e. of the Shema], even though it makes no mention of the tefillin, the paragraphs "Consecrate" and "When the LORD", which *do* mention the tefillin, ought certainly to have been included. To avoid such a conclusion, Scripture tells us: "Repeat them", meaning: Repeat these paragraphs, but not those other two. Still, if the paragraph of the fringes, which is preceded by other commandments, is nevertheless included in the recitation of the Shema, the Ten Commandments, which are not preceded by other mitzvot — ought they not have been included in the recitation of the Shema? This can be countered a fortiori: if "Consecrate" and "When the LORD" which do mention the binding are nevertheless excluded from the recitation, the Ten Commandments, which do not mention the binding, ought certainly to be excluded. On the other hand, the paragraph of the

---

6   See M.H. Segal, *The Nash Papyrus* (Hebrew), *Leshonenu* 15 (1947), pp. 227–236; also Jespen: "Beiträge zur Geschichte und Auslegung des Dekalogs", *ZAW* (1967), pp. 277–304.

fringes can prove the opposite, for it is included in the recitation even though it does not mention the binding, and the same might very well apply to the Ten Commandments. Therefore Scripture settles the matter by saying "Repeat them regularly with your children"; i.e., repeat "these words" (Deut. 6. 4–9 and 11. 13–21) but not the Ten Commandments.[7]

Slightly further on in the *Sifre* there is a passage which parallels the above and complements it. The problem this time is the binding of the tefillin.

"You shall bind them". The paragraphs containing these words are to be bound (in the tefillin) but not the paragraph of the fringes. I might have reasoned that, since "Consecrate" and "When the LORD", which are not included in the Shema, are nevertheless included in the tefillin, the paragraph of the fringes which is included in the Shema ought also to be included in the tefillin. To avoid such a conclusion, Scripture tells us "Bind them", meaning bind *these* paragraphs, but not the one dealing with the fringes. Still, if "Consecrate" and "When the LORD", which were preceded by other mitzvot, are nevertheless included in the tefillin, ought not the Ten Commandments, which are not preceded by other mitzvot — ought they not have been included in the tefillin? This can be countered by an argument a fortiori: If the paragraph of the fringes, which is included in the Shema, is nevertheless excluded from the tefillin, the Ten Commandments, which are not included in the Shema ought certainly to be excluded from the tefillin. On the other hand, "Consecrate" and "When the LORD" can be used to prove the opposite, for they are not included in the Shema, but are in the tefillin. So too, the Ten Commandments, though not included in the Shema — ought they not be included in the tefillin? Therefore Scripture settles the matter: "Bind them as a sign". Bind these paragraphs in the tefillin, but not the Ten Commandments.[8]

7 *Sifre Deut.*, XXXIV, ed. Finkelstein, p. 60; and n. 14 ibid., which quotes the explanation by David Pardo. For the usage *'eser ha-dibberoth* rather than *'asereth ha-dibberoth*, see *'Arugath Ha-Bosem*, ed. Urbach, I, Jerusalem 1939, pp. 179–180, 229.

8 *Sifre Deut.*, XXXV, p. 63. For the Decalogue in tefillin, see A.M. Haberman, Eretz Israel, 3 (1954), pp. 147 ff.; and Y. Yadin, *Tefillin from Qumran*, XQ Phyl. 1–4 (= *Eretz Israel*, 9, W.F. *Albright Memorial Volume*, p. 60).

The first passage quoted from the *Sifre* assumes the tefillin contain all four paragraphs in which the binding is mentioned, namely "Hear O Israel" (Deut. 6. 4 ff.), "If then you obey" (Deut. 11. 13 ff.), "Consecrate" (Ex. 13. 2), and "when the LORD has brought you" (Ex. 13. 11); whereas the duty of daily reading applies only to the first two of them, both of which contain the phrase "repeat regularly". Added to these two is the paragraph of the fringes *(zizit)* which speaks of remembering the mitzvot and performing them. The discussion in this first exposition revolves around the question "What justifies the inclusion of the fringes-paragraph along with the two which explicitly prescribe 'repetition' [*shinun*, which means, as David Pardo explained, being recited twice a day]?"[9] But the Ten Commandments, "which were preceded by no other mitzvot" do not come under that heading, since according to the Mishnah Tamid, they were recited only once each day. The corresponding question is asked concerning the paragraphs "Consecrate" and "When the LORD", although in their case it is not a question of repetition, since they are not formally recited at all.

The second passage quoted from the *Sifre* focuses on the question: why were the Ten Commandments not included in the tefillin "even though no other mitzvot preceded them"? To be sure, we know that in certain circles there were Jews who did write the Ten Commandments in their tefillin. But whatever arguments might have existed about that matter, the present context does not enter into polemics about it. What we have here is simply the straightforward opinion that the duty to "bind them" applies only to those paragraphs which explicitly mention the binding, and therefore neither to the paragraph of the fringes nor to the Ten Commandments.

The discussion in the *Sifre* reveals both the close connection between the Decalogue and the Shema, and at the same time the difference between them. In any event, nothing in these two expositions so much as hints at the abolition of the recital of the Ten Commandments before the reading of the morning Shema.

A reference to the custom of reading the Ten Commandments before the Shema has been preserved for us in the record of discussions by

---

9   This accords with those who say that the story of the Exodus should be recounted at night. On the other hand, see *Sifre Numbers*, CXV, ed. Horovitz, p. 126, where it is stated that the chapter of the fringes should be recited only during daylight hours. See ibid., p. 12.

certain Amoraim. As we shall soon see, they also tell us why the practice was dropped. In answer to the question, why the paragraphs "Hear O Israel" and "If then you obey" are recited every day, the Amora Rabbi Levi says:[10]

> It is because these two paragraphs contain, by inference, all Ten Commandments. Thus:
>> I am the LORD your God —
>> = Hear O Israel, the LORD is our God.
>> You shall have no other gods —
>> = The LORD is one.
>> You shall not swear falsely by the name of the LORD —
>> = You must love the LORD your God (He who loves the King will not take his name in vain).
>> Remember the Sabbath day and keep it holy —
>> = So that you shall remember.
>> Honor your father and your mother —
>> = To the end that you may long endure in the land.
>> You shall not murder —
>> = You will soon perish (He who kills will be killed).
>> You shall not commit adultery —
>> = Do not follow your heart and your eyes in your lustful urge.
>> You shall not steal —
>> = Gather in your grain (not your neighbor's).
>> You shall not not bear false witness —
>> = I the LORD am your God (the LORD your God is truth — Jer. 10. 10).
>> You shall not covet your neighbor's house —
>> = Inscribe them on the doorposts of your house (not your neighbor's).

It would appear that Rabbi Levi's midrash was spoken at a time when the Ten Commandments were no longer recited every morning, for when that practice was still followed there was no need to seek out parallels to the Decalogue in the paragraphs of the Shema. A saying by Rabbi Ba is better suited to the time when the Ten Commandments were still recited daily. He said that the Ten Commandments "are the very essence of the Shema", and that therefore one should recite a

---

10   Yer. Ber. I:8, 3c. I have omitted the explanatory elaborations.

benediction over them.[11] R. Levi too does not dispute the basic reason
for reciting the Shema morning and evening, namely: it is founded on
the Scripture "When you lie down and when you rise up".[12] His point is
that these paragraphs take the place of the Ten Commandments, the
recital of which had, by his time, been abolished.

Why had this recital been abolished? The Yerushalmi in the same
context explains it as follows:

> Both Rav Matna and Rav Samuel bar Nahmani stated that by
> rights the Ten Commandments should be recited every day. Why
> then is this not done? because of the antipathy of the Minim.[13]
> The purpose was to deny their claim that these Ten, and no more,
> were spoken to Moses at Sinai.

The coupling of these two Rabbis in this passage is not intended to
imply that they spoke at one time or place. It simply means that they
both held the same opinion, so the editor put their joint names to it.
Actually, Rav Matna was a Babylonian Amora,[14] who had studied
under Samuel of Nehardea; while Rav Samuel bar Nahmani was one of
the great Palestinian aggadists, who lived in Babylonia for a short
time.[15] There is a strong likelihood that it was he who brought to
Babylonia the tradition explaining why the daily recital of the Ten
Commandments had been abolished.

Additional evidence for this is the style in which the Babylonian
tradition is couched (Ber. 12a). It is connected with repeated efforts
which were made to revive the practice of saying the Ten
Commandments. It occurs at a point where the Talmud is engaged in
interpreting the Mishnah Tamid, with its statement "They recite the
Ten Commandments". Says the Gemara:

---

11   Yer. ibid.; and see L. Ginzberg, *Perushim ve-Ḥiddushim, etc.*, I, New York 1941, p.
      166, and his retraction, p. 225.
12   In the Yerushalmi, R. Simeon is quoted as saying, "because these verses refer to
      lying down and rising up". See Ginzberg's *Yerushalmi Fragments*, Ber., p. 30, and
      ms. Leyden. The word *tinat* has been altered to *ta'anat*, as pointed out by S.
      Lieberman in his *Yerushalmi Kifshuto*, p. 526. Compare Maimonides' *Hilkhot
      Yerushalmi*, ed. S. Lieberman, p. 22; and Ginzberg, *Perushim ve-Ḥiddushim*, etc.,
      loc. cit.
13   The reading in a Genizah fragment.
14   Also see Bacher, *Die Agada der Babylonischen Amoräer*, Frankfurt a/M. 1913, p.
      83.
15   Idem, *Die Agada der Palestinensischen Amoräer*, I, Strassburg 1892, pp. 477 ff.

Rabbi Judah quoted Samuel: People wanted to recite the Ten Commandments together with the Shema outside the Temple, but the practice had long since been abandoned because of the arguments of the Minim. (The same has been taught in a baraita: R. Nathan said, people outside the Temple wanted to read in this manner, but the custom had long been abolished because of the arguments of the Minim.)[16] Rabbah bar Rav Huna[17] thought to institute the practice in Sura, but R. Hisda said to him: The custom was set aside because of the arguments of the Minim. Amemar considered doing the same in Nehardea, but Rav Ashi said to him: It was set aside because of the arguments of the Minim.

The version in the Yerushalmi differs from that of the Bavli in two respects. It begins by saying that "by rights the Ten Commandments should be recited every day". And it closes by explaining why that is no longer the practice — "because of the antipathy of the Minim, to deny their claim that these Ten and no more were spoken to Moses at Sinai". In the Bavli, R. Judah quotes a tradition transmitted by Samuel, in the past tense: "People wanted etc." Where did that happen? Apparently in Palestine. Samuel may have heard about it from Rav Matna.

Then we are told of an attempt to revive the custom in Sura two generations later, and again in Nehardea in the time of Rav Ashi. All this is related in the past tense: "They set them aside because of the arguments of the Minim". But we are not told anything about the nature of these arguments. The fact that attempts were made in Babylonia to revive the saying of the Ten Commandments is evidence that the custom of *omitting* them was not regarded as of very long standing[18] — and also that the claims of the Minim were no longer regarded as a serious problem.

16   The sentence in parentheses is not found in ms. Munich, ms. Paris, or *Beth Nathan*; see *Dikduke Soferim*, p. 52, 389. It is possible that the name "R. Nathan" in this context really stands for "R. Matna". The phrase "R. Nathan says" is also absent from ms. Florence.

17   This is the reading in the mss. Current editions have "Rabba bar bar Hana"; see *Dikduke Soferim*, ad loc.

18   It is true that Josephus says of the Ten Commandments "these words it is not permitted us to state explicitly to the letter, but we may indicate their purport" (*Ant.*, III, 90). However, the suggestion put forward by A. Schalit in his Hebrew version of *Antiquities* (1955), Vol. II, p. 63, quoted by A.J. Heschel in his

The question, however, remains: just when was the custom abolished in Palestine? To answer that we shall have to identify those Minim who claimed that the Ten Commandments, and no more, were given to Moses at Sinai.

The accepted opinion is that they were Christians. But there is no agreement as to which Christians, and when the thing took place. There have been those who relate the dropping of the Decalogue from the formal prayers to the step taken by Rabban Gamaliel of Yavneh when he introduced *Birkat ha-Minim* into the Eighteen Benedictions.[19] However, even if it is true that *Birkat ha-Minim* intended to exclude Jewish Christians from Jewish public worship,[20] there is nothing in the circumstances of the time sufficient to justify the abolition of a deeply-rooted liturgical practice — just because some Minim held a heretical opinion. There is no basis whatsoever for the idea that there was any connection at all between dropping the Ten Commandments from the liturgy, and the beginnings of Christianity.[21] The theory that there was is grounded for the most part on Christian sources, which give primacy to the Ten Commandments over the other parts of the Torah. A careful examination of such sources shows that what they express is either a

Theology of Ancient Judaism (Hebrew), Soncino 1965, Vol. II, p. 109, must be rejected. What Josephus really means is simply that the Ten Commandments should not be *translated* literally, but rendered in terms of their content as interpreted. For example, he gives the Third Commandment as "Do not swear for an evil purpose in God's name", after the rabbinic interpretation; and not "Do not mention God's name in vain", which is the way the Septuagint has it. Incidentally, Nahmanides calls the latter the "plain meaning".

19   Already suggested by M. Joel in his *Blicke in die Religionsgeschichte*, I, Breslau, 1880. p. 36. Aptowitzer, in *MGWJ*, 73 (1929), p. 111, found this convincing, adding proof in n. 4, p. 112, from a baraita which states that R. Nathan Ha-Bavli wanted to revive the custom. What he overlooked is the fact that the mss. do not support this reading. Nevertheless, the idea that the practice was abolished by the Yavneh synod is accepted by Albeck in his *Introduction to the Mishnah, Zeraim*, Jerusalem–Tel Aviv 1957, p. 9. See also A.J. Heschel (above, n. 18) p. 110. Certainly, Matt. 25. 18 is not directed simply at the Decalogue.

20   See Yer. Ber. V:4, 3c; and Bavli, ibid., 28b–29a; also Ismar Elbogen, *Der jüdische Gottesdienst in seiner geschichtliche Entwicklung*, Frankfurt a/M 1931, pp. 37 ff.; also R. Kimelman, "Birkat Ha-Minim and the Lack of Evidence for an Anti-Christian Prayer in Late Antiquity", *Jewish and Christian Self Definition*, II, pp. 226 ff.

21   A view enunciated by Aptowitzer, "Bemerkungen zur Liturgie und Geschichte der Liturgie", *MGWJ*, 74 (1930), pp. 194 ff.

general antinomian attitude, or a strong bias in favor of commandments of a moral-ethical nature. Nowhere do we find an explicit doctrine to the effect that the Ten Commandments are beyond further elaboration and interpretation.[22]

Some have pointed to the answer given by Jesus when he was asked, "What shall I do to inherit eternal life?" (Luke 18. 20; Mark 10. 19). His reply was:

> You know the commandments *(tas entolas oidas)*: Do not commit adultery. Do not kill. Do not steal. Do not bear false witness. Honor your father and your mother.[23]

The questioner — in Luke an *archon*, in Mark just an unidentified man — replies: "All these I have observed from my youth". It is Jesus' answer to this remark that is the main point here:

> One thing you still lack. Sell all you have and distribute to the poor and you will have treasure in heaven; and come follow me.

Note that in dealing with a pagan, Jesus is ready to forgo the first five Commandments. The initial answer of the pagan shows us why the early Christians, in their efforts to win converts, concentrated on the second half of the Ten Commandments.

Before we continue our investigation into the reason why the daily recital of the Ten Commandments was dropped; and before we try to approximate the time when this happened, let us attempt to clarify

22   The point is stressed by H.M. Grant in *Harvard Theological Review*, XL (1947), pp. 1–18. In this he is followed by W.D. Davies, *The Setting of the Sermon on the Mount*, Cambridge University Press 1964, p. 281. He too relies on the quotation from R. Nathan in order to assign the abolition to the synod at Yavneh; see n. 16 above. David Flusser, *Judaism and Christian Origins* (Hebrew), Tel Aviv 1979, basing himself on the Mishnah (Ber. II:2) argues that by the time of the synod in Usha the Decalogue had been removed from the reading of the Shema, since it is not mentioned among the passages recited. But even the Mishnah in Tamid does not say that the Ten Commandments were part of the reading of the Shema. After all, you cannot speak of "the Shema" before you have come to the words "Hear O Israel". The added verse (in the Septuagint: "These are the statutes and laws, etc.") acts as a division between the Decalogue and the Shema, and it is the latter which is the topic of the aforementioned Mishnah.

23   Matt. 19. 19 adds "Love your neighbor as yourself". For other differences, see the chapter in the present volume by David Flusser: "The Ten Commandments and the New Testament".

further the original significance of the practice. We stated above that it was a sort of re-affirmation of the covenant at Sinai. But does that imply a special status for the Decalogue, setting it above all the rest of the many commandments in the Torah? That indeed would seem to be the thought underlying the following homily:

> Why were the Ten Commandments not placed at the very beginning of the Torah? This can be explained by a parable: Once a king entered a city and said to the people, "Let me be your ruler". They said to him, "Why should we? What good thing have you done for us?" What did he do then? He built a wall around the city, he brought in a supply of water, he fought their battles. After all that, he said to them, "May I be your king?" They answered "Oh yes! Yes!" So it was with the All-Present. He brought the Israelites out of Egypt, He divided the Red Sea for them, He gave them manna, He brought up the well in the desert, He assembled the quail, He fought the battle with Amalek. And then He said to them, "Shall I be your King?" And they answered "Oh yes! Yes!" (*Mekhilta de Rabbi Ishmael Ba-Ḥodesh* V; cf. Lauterbach, II, pp. 229–230).

In this tannaitic midrash the Ten Commandments are perceived as the terms of the agreement by which the Israelites accepted God's sovereignty, after He had demonstrated His power and might. But the agreement, or covenant, is seen differently by the Tannaim when they interpret the verse: "Now then, if you will obey Me faithfully and keep My covenant" (Ex. 19. 5). There, they take "covenant" to refer to one or another specific mitzvah that had been promulgated before the Ten Commandments:

> R. Eliezer says, this means the covenant of circumcision. R. Akiba says, it means the covenant of the Sabbath. But the Sages say, it means the covenant not to worship idols.[24]

It may be necessary to note that all the pre-Sinaitic narratives in the

---

24   *Mekhilta de R. Simeon bar Yoḥai*, p. 139 (= *Midrash Ha-Gadol*, on Exodus, p. 379). *Mekhilta de R. Ishmael* reads: "R. Eliezer says, this means the covenant of the Sabbath, while Rabbi Akiba says it means the covenants concerning circumcision and idolatry". However, the connection between R. Eliezer and the covenant of circumcision is supported by *Tanḥuma, Kekh-Lekha*, 20, as well as by *Pesiqta Rabbati* and *Agadat Bereshit*; see below, n. 41.

Torah take it for granted that the prohibition of idol worship was well known and long established. Suffice it to quote Genesis 35. 2: "So Jacob said to his household and to all who were with him, 'Rid yourselves of the alien gods in your midst.'".

As for the covenant of circumcision, it was not only a pact made with Abraham and his son Ishmael (Gen. 17. 10 ff.) but it is repeated at the time of the exodus in the law of the paschal offering (Ex. 12. 43). Similarly, the law of the Sabbath had been laid down at the time when the manna first fell (Ex. 16. 23).

Faithfulness to these older covenants was, then, a precondition for Israel's becoming chosen, "My treasured possession among all the peoples", worthy of the revelation that was about to take place.[25] The pre-existence of these three mitzvot, on which it was possible to base the promise "I will keep my covenant", in no way detracts from the unique significance of the Ten Commandments as the occasion for the acceptance of God's sovereignty. And if it became customary to recite them every day in the Temple before the *tamid* was offered up, and outside the Temple as well, as is evident from various sources dealing explicitly with the matter, there scarcely seem to have been any reasonable grounds for dropping the practice.

It will not do to suggest that the change came about in reaction against Philo's idea that all the mitzvot in the Torah are simply elaborations in detail of the Ten Commandments, the latter being the sources and basic principles of all the laws. There is no evidence that any Tannaim or Amoraim were aware of this idea. It shows up only in late midrashim from the eleventh century onwards, and seems to have reached them via Saadiah Gaon (tenth century).[26]

But even if we assume that Philo's idea was known in Palestine in talmudic times, resistance to it can scarcely have caused the abolition of an old custom. Philo's idea itself should not be seen as anything more than a means for the dissemination of knowledge about Judaism in the Hellenistic world.[27] It was for this purpose that condensed summations and rules-of-thumb came into being, such as the tale

---

25 This is the interpretation given by Nahmanides, unlike Rashi and Ibn Ezra. See *Midreshei Ha-Torah* by Solomon Astruc (Barcelona, fourteenth century), ed. Eppenstein, Berlin 1899, p. 115. There is a hint of this in Kasher, *Torah Shelemah*, ad loc.

26 See Urbach, *The Sages* (above, n. 5), pp. 360 ff.

27 See I. Heinemann, *Philos griechische und jüdische Bildung*, Breslau 1932, p. 354.

about the pagan who asked Hillel to teach him the whole Torah while
he stood on one foot. Hillel accepted him as a proselyte, and answered
his question by saying that the whole Torah can be summed up in the
rule: "What is hateful to you do not do unto others".[28]

But Hillel did add: "The rest is commentary. Go and study it". He did
not think for one moment that the pagan would be able to fulfill the
entire Torah on the basis of what he could learn while standing on one
foot — not without a pretty extensive commentary. All he meant to do
was to state a broad general principle, just as Rabbi Akiba was to do
some generations later when he said: "The great principle of the Torah
is, Love your neighbor as yourself": or as Ben Azzai was to do when he
responded: "An even greater principle is, 'This is the book of the
generations of man. When God created man, He made him in His own
image".[29]

These are surely great principles, but they do not reveal how they are
to be implemented. Therefore it would be a mistake to regard the
tendency towards simplification represented by Philo and those who
followed in his footsteps as something which had to be combatted by
removing the Ten Commandments from the daily prayers.

Actually, the urge to find brief formulations for the guidance of
people in ordering their lives is a general one. Those who ask for such
formulations want short, concentrated answers. Certain passages in
the Bible, in which some scholars have thought to find decalogues or
mini-decalogues, are really nothing more than attempts to satisfy this
demand — to answer the question: "How shall I order my life?" The
question can be asked in many ways. It may say: "Who shall sojourn in
Your tent? Who may dwell in Your holy mountain?" Or perhaps: "Who
may ascend the mountain of the LORD? Who may stand in His holy
place?" (Psalms 15 and 24). Or it may be formulated in mishnaic
language, like "What is the right way to which a person should cling?"
or "What is the evil way from which a person should distance himself?"
(Avot II: 1, 9). Or the question might be unasked, but the answer given
anyway, like "The righteous person shall live" (Ezek. 18. 9) or "He has
told you, O man, what is good" (Micah 6.8).

Actually, concerning the main principles of religion the rabbinic
Sages said:

28   Shab. 31a. See Urbach, *The Sages*, pp. 589, 955, n. 93. The words "This is the whole
      Torah" are not found in certain mss.
29   *Sifra, Qedoshim*, IV:12.

David reduced them to ten... Along came Micah and reduced them to three... Along came Habakkuk and reduced them to one (Mak. 24a).

It was not the purpose of these reductions to minimize the observance of the detailed mitzvot in which the general principles find expression. It is worth noting that Jesus, in his answer to the learned Pharisee who asked, "Which is the greatest commandment in the law?" said "You shall love the LORD your God... this the great and first commandment. And a second is like it: You shall love your neighbor as yourself." Here the love of God is called the greatest and first commandment, while the love of one's fellow-man is described as second to it and comparable to it; and of the two of them it is said: "On these two depend all the law and the prophets".[30]

The statement of these two principles contains nothing that could have aroused Jewish opposition. As a matter of fact there is a midrash, albeit a late one, which says practically the same thing.[31]

> Thus did the Sages say: All the mitzvot in the Torah are based on two verses: one, "You shall love the LORD your God" and the second "You shall love your neighbor as yourself". Two hundred and forty-eight positive commandments are founded on love of God; for whoever loves the LORD and loves himself will perform them. And all the negative commandments are based on love of one's neighbor, for as long as you are careful about that, you will be obeying the negative commandments. The Torah says, "You shall have one standard for the stranger and the citizen". That is why the Sages taught: "Do not to others what is hateful to you".

In my opinion, the work in which this passage occurs was written during the Gaonic period (early Middle Ages).[32] Nevertheless, it incorporates material from earlier sources, and is echoed in other compilations.[33]

---

30 Matt. 22. 35–40; Mark 12. 28 ff.; Luke 10. 25 ff. Matthew translates "might" as *duania*. Strack-Billerbeck, *Kommentar zum NT aus Talmud und Midrasch*, I, p. 907, quite correctly points to the Mishnah (Ber. IX:5) "By whatever measure (*middah*) He metes out (*moded*) to you do you thank (*modeh*) Him exceedingly (*bim'od me'od*"). See Flusser, *Judaism and Christian Origins*, above n. 22, p. 244.
31 See my edition of *Sefer Pitron Ha-Torah*, Jerusalem 1978, p. 80.
32 Ibid., introduction, p. 32.
33 See my comments, ibid., p. 80, notes 59–60.

In the light of all this, the removal of the Ten Commandments from the daily liturgy cannot be attributed to the trend to reduce the mitzvot to a few general principles; nor can it be seen as a measure against those who found everything in the Decalogue; nor can it be understood as an act of disagreement with those who interpreted the Torah allegorically.[34]

As we noted above, the reason given by the sources for the abolition was "the antipathy of the *Minim*; let them not claim that these ten and no more were given to Moses at Sinai". In all the sources examined so far we have not detected any such special enthusiasm for the Decalogue. Let us now turn to another source which does refer to an explicit claim that revelation was confined to the Decalogue. According to this idea, only the Ten Commandments were revealed, and they cannot be made the ground for any other commandments. The source in question is the *Midrash Yelamdenu*, and the view is attributed to Korah in his dispute with Moses:

> "They assembled themselves against Moses and Aaron" (Num. 16. 3): They convened meetings against them. They said: Come let us tell you what the son of Amram has been doing. All the community are holy, all of them. We were all sanctified at Sinai, as it is written "Go to the people and sanctify them" (Ex. 19. 10). When the Ten Commandments were given every one of us absorbed them from Sinai, and all we heard was the Ten Commandments. We heard nothing about priestly offerings, about the first dough (*ḥallah*), about heave-offerings (*terumah*) and tithes; we heard nothing about fringes on our garments. You made these up yourself.[35]

---

34   Such theologians as the author of *The Epistle of Barnabas* made manful efforts to discover the "true" (i.e., spiritual) meaning of the mitzvot; but these very efforts only prove that they would not deny that the mitzvot were divinely revealed. See A. Harnack, *Die Mission und Ausbreitung des Christentums*, I, Leipzig 1924, p. 275; and G. Alon, "Halakhic Elements in the Epistle of Barnabas" (Hebrew), *Tarbiz*, 11 (1940), pp. 23–38, 223 = *Meḥqarim*, I, pp. 295–312. Even a gnostic like Ptolemaeus, contemporary of Irenaeus, who interpreted the halakhot of sacrifices, circumcision, the Sabbath and Passover as mere abstract allegories and symbols, could not bring himself to deny their divine origin; see his *Epistle to Flora* in Epiphanius, *Panarion*, 33. 3.

35   Quoted in *Yalqut Shim'oni, Qorah*, 247.

This argument — that the Israelites were given only ten commandments and all the rest were invented by Moses — is quoted for the first time in amoraic midrashim. It is not mentioned at all in tannaitic literature. When Josephus tells the story of Korah he sticks to the biblical narrative, attributing Korah's revolt to the simple lust for power.[36] He does attribute that lust to Korah's great wealth, a motif found also in the Yerushalmi:[37] "Rav said, Korah was a man of great wealth. He had discovered Pharaoh's treasures between Migdol and the sea." However, in the same context we also read:

> Rav said: Korah was an unbeliever. What did he do? He went and made cloaks entirely of *tekhelet* and then went to Moses and said: Moses our teacher, does a tallit entirely of *tekhelet* require fringes? Moses answered: It does, for it is written "You shall make tassels on the four corners of your cloak". Korah asked further: Does a house full of Torahs require a mezuzah? Moses answered: It does, for it says "You shall write them on the doorposts of your house." Then Korah asked: What is the law concerning a patch of discoloration the size of a groat on the skin? Moses answered: "Unclean". And if the discoloration spreads to the entire body? "That is clean". At that point Korah declared: The Torah is not from heaven; Moses is no prophet, and Aaron is not a high priest.

However, the attribution of this second midrash to Rav is not at all certain. In parallel passages where Rav is quoted about Korah's great wealth, the rest is attributed to other Amoraim, or is given anonymously.[38]

---

36   *Antiquities*, IV, 14; see S. Rappaport, *Agada und Exegese bei Flavius Josephus*, Wien 1930, p. 36.

37   Yer. Sanh. XI:1, 27d; quoted in the name of Rav in *Midrash Ha-Gadol* on Numbers, ed. Rabinowitz, 1967, p. 265. For a variant version, see Pes. 119a and Sanh. 110a, where the attribution is to R. Hama bar Hanina. In *Eccl. Rabbah* V;12, on the verse "Riches hoarded by their owner to his misfortune", Rabbi Joshua says: "This refers to Korah". See *Gen. Rabbah*, VII:11, p. 528; and M. Baer: "The Rebellion of Korah and Its Causes in Rabbinic Aggadah" (Hebrew), *Studies in Memory of Joseph Heinemann*, Jerusalem 1981, pp. 9 ff., and see p. 87, n. 83.

38   The phrase "Rav said" (*amar rav*) is stylistically unusual. Actually, in *Yerushalmi Fragments*, p. 260, it is abbreviated as ר"א which may well have been intended as ד"א (= *davar aḥer*); and in the *Midrash Ha-Gadol* the quotation from Rav is followed by "and Resh Laqish said, the verse 'riches hoarded by their owner to his

Those who argued that the Torah was not a divine revelation
certainly did not mean to include the Ten Commandments. After all,
Korah's point was that "the whole community are holy" — they had all
stood at Sinai and heard the declaration "I am the LORD". What he was
attacking was those mitzvot not explicitly spoken at Sinai. He began by
mocking mitzvot in detail, and ended by accusing Moses and Aaron of
acting solely in their own selfish interests, under the guise of
transmitting God's will.[39] The polemical nature of these arguments is
strikingly obvious. They are directed against those who claim exclusive
authority for their interpretations, and proceed to describe the resulting
commands and prohibitions as the word of God. Since only the Ten
Commandments were revealed, all the rest has no leg to stand on.

People who use such arguments are equated with the followers of
Korah by the authors of the midrash. That means that they, too, will
come to a bad end. At the same time, it was found necessary to drop the
daily repetition of the Ten Commandments, so that everyone might
understand that these were not the only commands given at Sinai. But
there was not the slightest intention of detracting from the special
status of the Decalogue. The matter is summed up by Resh Laqish,
commenting on Deuteronomy 10. 2:

> "I shall give you the tablets of stone, the teaching and the
> commandment which I have written for their guidance".
> "The tablets" — that means, the Ten Commandments.
> "The teaching" — that means the rest of the Torah.
> "The commandment" — that means, the Mishnah.

misfortune' refers to the riches of Korah, who fell because he trusted in his wealth.
For you find that the Holy One commanded Moses concerning the fringes on the
garment, whereupon Korah stood up and, vaunting his wealth, made two hundred
and fifty cloaks... and declared 'Moses is no prophet, the Torah is not revealed,
there is no resurrection of the dead'". It is fairly certain that the text beginning with
the words "you find that the Holy One, etc." is an anonymous addition. It occurs in
Tanḥuma, Qorah, II:4; in *Num. Rabbah*, postscript II; ibid., XVIII:1. See also
ibid., XIV, on Prov. 18. 19; *Midrash Ha-Gadol*, ibid., p. 101, and *Midrash
Proverbs*, 11. 17. It is noteworthy that in Sanh. 109b as well, the phrase "On ben
Peles was saved by his wife" lacks the attribution to Rav in ms. Florence. See
Dikduke Soferim, 177, letter ש.

39   See *Midrash Tehillim*, ed. Buber, X:15, p. 14, and the parallel passages listed by
     Ginzberg in *Legends of the Jews*, VI, n. 567. See also *Pitron Ha-Torah*, above n.
     31, pp. 162–163, and n. 90; also M. Baer, *"The Riches of Moses in Rabbinic
     Aggadah"* (Hebrew), *Tarbiẓ*, 43 (1973), pp. 77 ff.

"Which I have written" — that means, the Prophets and the Hagiographa.

"To guide them" — that is the Talmud.

This teaches us that all of them were given to Moses at Sinai.[40]

We have no way of finding out whether the *Minim* who held that only the Decalogue was revealed constituted a specific sect; but we have reason to believe that they were contemporaries of Rabbi Matna and Rabbi Samuel bar Nahmani, and that it was on their account that the Rabbis felt compelled to discontinue the reading of the Ten Commandments as part of the daily morning service. They saw a danger that such an idea would undermine all the other commandments, including the mitzvah of circumcision. This idea was probably behind the question — and it was asked not only by applicants for conversion — "If God so loved the mitzvah of circumcision, why was it left out of the Ten Commandments?"[41]

For such doubts about circumcision there is no early Christian source. On the contrary, the obligatory nature of the rite is accepted without question in Luke 1. 59 and 2. 21; while John 7. 22 explicitly states that it is a mosaic law going back even earlier, to the patriarchs — and that it supersedes the Sabbath.[42] All the spokesmen of the Judeo-Christian sects stressed the fact that Jesus was circumcised. In the argument over circumcision within the early church, neither Paul nor Barnabas urges the abolition of circumcision of the flesh simply because it is not mentioned in the Ten Commandments.[43]

Hadrian's ban on circumcison, although it was not originally intended as an anti-Jewish measure, became one of the causes of the Bar Kohhba Revolt.[44] Many Jews let themselves be martyred rather

---

40 Ber. 5a; *Lev. Rabbah* XXII:1, p. 496.

41 In *Pesiqta Rabbati*, one account names the questioner as Aquila the Proselyte, and quotes the answer in the name of R. Eliezer. But in the same source in the next incident it is a Roman matron who asks, and R. Jose ben Halafta who gives the answer. In *Tanḥuma, Lekh Lekha*, para 20, as well as in *Aggadot Bereshit*, XVIII, p. 36, the questioner is King Agrippa, and the answer is again attributed to R. Eliezer.

42 The argument in John 7. 23 ("If on the Sabbath, etc.") is paralleled by the statement of R. Eleazar ben Azariah in Shab. 132a.

43 Acts 15. 1–5; see H.J. Schoeps, *Theologie und Geschichte des Juden-Christentums*, Tübingen 1949, pp. 138 ff.

44 See S. Lieberman, "Persecution of the Jewish Religion" (Hebrew), *Salo Baron*

than violate this commandment. In this connection the *Sifre* quotes
Rabban Simeon ben Gamaliel:

> Every mitzvah which Jews were prepared to defend with their
> lives during the Hadrianic persecutions is now observed openly.
> But mitzvot which they were not willing to defend with their lives
> — these are now rather indifferently observed.[45]

The emphasis on open, rather than surreptitious, observance is
significant. The fact is that not everyone was prepared to risk his life for
the sake of circumcision. There is clear-cut evidence that, not only at
the time of the Hadrianic persecutions, but also much earlier when the
Seleucid monarch Antiochus forbade the practice,[46] there were Jews
who "drew" their foreskins in order to conceal the fact that they were
circumcised. A person who did that was called a *mashukh*. Following
the Bar Kokhba War, the Sages were disagreed on whether such an
individual was duty bound to have himself circumcised again.

> Rabbi Judah says: The *mashukh* should not be circumcised
> because it is dangerous. They answered him: There were many
> such who underwent the procedure in the days of Koziba (*Bar
> Kokhba*) and then begat children without mishap.[47]

So not everyone took the risk of defying the decree. A baraita rules that
a kohen who is a *mashukh* is allowed to partake of *terumah*.[48] And the
Amora Rav Huna is quoted as saying, "By the law of the Torah a
mashukh may eat *terumah* but he is barred from doing so by a rabbinic
ordinance".[49] It stands to reason, therefore, that the number of those
who attempted to hide their circumcision was not inconsiderable.
There are even traditions dating from the fourth century which ascribe
the act to Adam,[50] to the Israelites after Joseph's death,[51] and to

Festschrift, Jerusalem 1979, III, p. 214; M. Herr, "Causes of the Bar Kokhba
Revolt" (Hebrew), *Zion*, 43 (1978), p. 6 and accompanying bibliography, n. 25.

45   *Sifre Deut.*, XXIII, p. 141. See Shab. 130a: "Every mitzvah which they undertook
joyfully, like circumcision, etc." In *Tanḥuma, Tazria*, V, the matter is explained as
referring to the expense involved in performing the mitzvot, and rejoicing therein.
46   See I Macc., 1.15; Josephus, *Antiquities*, XII, 241.
47   Tos. Shab. XV, p. 71; Lieberman, *Tos. Kif.*, ibid., p. 251.
48   Tos. Yev. X:2, p. 31; also *Gen. Rabbah*, XLVI:13. p. 470.
49   Yev. 72a. The Yerushalmi quotes Rabbi Jonathan as saying that this was a penalty:
"according to Rav, the Sages made a prohibitory ordinance". See *Tos. Kif.*, p. 93.
50   Sanh. 38b.

Achan.[52] It was said that priests who officiated at the altar were included, not to speak of royalty of David's line,[53] especially Jehoiakim.[54]

It is possible that in the conditions of mortal danger created by the Hadrianic decrees, there were Jews who justified the act of *meshikhah*, or even of omitting the mitzvah altogether, on the ground that it is not mentioned in the Ten Commandments. It was probably to counteract such arguments that the following was said:

> Great is circumcision, for it is the equal of all the other mitzvot combined; as Scripture says: "Moses took the blood and dashed it on the people and said, 'This is the blood of the covenant which the LORD now makes with you concerning all these commandments'" (Ex. 24. 8).[55]

In this saying, the blood of the covenant which God made with his people is equated with the blood of the covenant of circumcision.[56]

In the light of some of the deviant opinions we have just quoted, the de-emphasis of the Ten Commandments in the daily prayers becomes explicable. The Commandments may have been played down at a time when a tendency had appeared in Eretz Israel to minimize the importance of mitzvot not mentioned in the Decalogue — including even the commandment of circumcision. And if this surmise about the time and the reason for dropping the Ten Commandments from the regular liturgy is correct, it may also help explain the later attempts in Babylonia to revive the practice.

---

51 *Yalqut Shimoni* on Jeremiah, 284, quoting *Yelamdenu.*

52 Sanh. 44a.

53 *Tanḥuma, Lekh Lekha,* 20.

54 *Lev. Rabbah,* XIX:6, p. 436, where parallels are noted. See Strack-Billerbeck, above n. 30, IV, p. 33.

55 Appears as an addendum in the Yerushalmi version of the Mishnah, Nedarim, III (37d). In the Leyden ms. it is added in the margin; in the Tosefta, ibid., it occurs as a baraita; in the Mishnah mss. Cambridge and Kauffmann it is a postcriptum. See S. Lieberman, *Tos. Kif.,* on Nedarim, p. 424, and J.N. Epstein, *Introduction to the Text of the Mishnah* (Hebrew) Jerusalem 1957, p. 450.

56 In his fourteenth century commentary on Nedarim (31b) Rabbenu Nissim of Barcelona wonders about this. "After all, the verse refers to the blood of the sacrifice, not that of circumcision. However, since the Torah as a whole is called 'covenant' and circumcision is also called 'covenant', the commandment can be equated in importance with all the other commandments taken together". See Kasher, *Torah Shelemah,* XIX, p. 267, letter ב.

The vicissitudes which the Ten Commandments underwent did not, however, diminish their status or the esteem in which they were held. The Amora R. Abbahu was of the opinion that the sole biblical extract that requires a blessing both before and after it is recited is — the Decalogue.[57] Palestinian and Babylonian Amoraim present long lists of things which are to be read because of some resemblance to the Ten Commandments,[58] or that are held in special esteem because in some way they symbolize the Ten Commandments.[59]

What is more, the custom of reciting the Ten Commandments every day was revived centuries later, and not only in Babylonia, but also in synagogues of Palestinian Jews in various places. In a document giving us a glimpse of the prayer customs of such Jews in the synagogue of the Palestinians at Fustat (Cairo) for weekdays and New Moons, there is a rubric instructing the worshippers to take out of the Ark, after the morning prayers are over, a special scroll called *sefer al-shir* and to read the Ten Commandments from it.[60] Additional light was thrown on this when Jacob Mann published Genizah fragments of the Palestinian liturgy, which contained the Ten Commandments right after the blessing which concludes the "Verses of Song", just before *Barkhu*.[61]

There are grounds for supposing that Rav Hai Gaon was familiar with this custom.[62] In any event, he mentions in passing that he disapproved of it. Once he was asked why we do not read the passage about the additional Sabbath offering from a Torah scroll. His response was:

> If you want to raise objections on behalf of ancient customs no longer practised, the list will be a long one. You may ask why we no longer recite the Ten Commandments, as was done in the

---

57   Yer. Meg., III:7, 74b; and *Penei Moshe*, ad. loc.

58   Yer. Meg., V:2, 75a: "Let them (read) no less than ten verses; Hizkiah says, corresponding to the Ten Commandments". In the Bavli, ibid., 21b, R. Joseph is cited as the authority for this. He is also the one quoted as saying that the ten verses of sovereignty (*malkhuyot*) correspond to the Ten Commandments (R.H. 32a). See Yer. Sheq. II:4, 46d; and *Arugat ha-Bosem*, I, pp. 217 ff.

59   See *Sefer Hizhir*, ed. Y.M. Freimann, 1873, 42a: "Observe how precious the laws are to the Eternal, for he made their sum equivalent to the Ten Commandments...". See *Leqaḥ Tov* on Exodus, 72a, and *Menorat Ha-Maor*, ed. Enelow, IV, p. 182.

60   See Mann, *The Jews in Egypt and in Palestine under the Fatimid Caliphs*, I, p. 221.

61   See Mann's articles in *HUCA*, II, p. 299, and IV, p. 288.

62   *Oẓar Ha-Geonim* ad Megillah, entry 250, p. 67.

ancient Temple. Someone else may ask why we do not read the story of creation, as was once done — and so on... The answer is that we ought to conduct ourselves in accordance with what the leading authorities of our own time have ordained. It is not for us to deviate from the norms they have set.

In spite of this statement of his there were deviations in his own time, not only in the recitation of the *ma'amadot*[63] but also by the introduction of the Ten Commandments. After Hai's time as well, there were attempts to put the Decalogue back into the liturgy. In the thirteenth century Rabbi Solomon ibn Adret of Barcelona was asked his opinion about a proposal "to introduce the reading of the Ten Commandments at morning service in the synagogue". [64] His reply was in the negative. However, his younger contemporary Jacob ben Asher wrote in his code of Jewish law and practice (*Tur*): "It is a good thing to recite the biblical chapters about the binding of Isaac, the descent of the manna, and the Ten Commandments" as part of one's prayers.[65] In his commentary on the same code, Joseph Caro (*Beth Joseph*, sixteenth century) remarked that the removal of the Ten Commandments from the rubric of daily service because of the *Minim*

> applied only to public prayers; but in private devotions, where the problem of the Minim does not apply, it is good to repeat the Commandments, for this will be a daily reminder of the revelation at Mount Sinai, and will help to strengthen one's faith.

63 See my article *"Mishmarot u-Ma'amadot", Tarbiẓ*, 42 (1973), pp. 313 ff.

64 *Responsa of Ibn Adret*, I, no. 184, and III, no. 289. In this connection it is worth noting that in Spain it was customary to take an oath by the Ten Commandments. Ibn Adret was asked, as he says, "about the custom in your city to keep a folio in the court of the Gentiles, on which are inscribed the Ten Commandments in our script. The document is illustrated with a human figure wearing the sort of cloak normally worn by Jews. ...The question is whether it is permissible to swear an oath on this document; or whether it is forbidden because of the human figure with which it is illustrated". Ibn Adret replies that "if the document was written by a Jew, one may swear by the Ten Commandments written thereon, etc." The use of a Torah scroll (which of course contains the Decalogue) for oath-taking is first mentioned by the Gaon Rav Sar Shalom, who quotes Rav Yehudai Gaon as his authority; see B.M. Levin, *Oẓar Ha-Geonim, Nedarim*, p. 10. About the custom of Spanish Marranos to swear by the Ten Commandments, see Beinart, *Conversos on Trial*, Jerusalem 1981, p. 283, n. 196; also Lieberman, *Tosefta Kifshutah* on Nedarim, p. 402, n. 34.

65 *Tur Oraḥ Ḥayyim*, 1, and comments ad loc. by *Bet Yosef, Bayyit Ḥadash*.

In Caro's own code, the *Shulkhan Arukh*, he repeats Jacob ben Asher's "it is a good thing". Moses Isserles of Cracow (sixteenth century) in his gloss on the *Shulkhan Arukh*, inverts the emphasis: "Only in private is one permitted the daily repetition of the Commandments. But it is forbidden to recite them at congregational prayer."

This restrictive attitude did not appeal to his contemporary Solomon Luria, who wrote in a responsum:

> I have resumed the practice of reciting the Ten Commandments aloud before the *Barukh She-amar* even though the Rambam (*read*: Rashba) wrote in a responsum that one should not do so, citing as his proof Berakhot, chapter one... Nevertheless, it seems to me that the Decalogue should be given a set place as part of the *yoẓer*, the same as the Shema. Even so did Rashi explain the matter. As for saying the Ten Commandments every morning in honor of the Torah and in honor of the Creator who inscribed these words in heavenly script on the two tablets of stone — this seems to me to be a great mitzvah. The "Tur", Rabbi Jacob ben Asher, wrote that it is a good thing to repeat them. My practice is to recite them just before *Barukh She-amar*.[66]

The urge to keep alive the memory of the ceremonials of the ancient Temple produced from time to time the desire to revive ancient practices. No doubt this lay behind the reintroduction of the custom of reciting the Ten Commandments, as they had been recited of old when the daily *tamid* was offered up. To this nostalgic motivation new reasons were now attached, such as Caro's "It will be a daily reminder of the revelation at Mount Sinai, and so will help to strengthen one's faith".[67]

II

What should be read from the Torah on Shavuot? Talmudic sources differ about this. The Mishnah (Meg. III: 5) says: "On *'aẓeret* one reads 'seven weeks'" (Deut. 16. 19). But the Tosefta (ibid., VI:5) adds "Some say 'In the third new moon'" (Ex.19 1). The Yerushalmi says "There are some authorities who prescribe 'In the third new moon'" (ibid.,

---

66 Luria's *Responsa*, no. 64; see *Ateret Zeqenim* on the opening paragraph of the Shulhan Arukh; and the Malbim, *Arẓot ha-Ḥayyim*, Warsaw 1860, para. 5.
67 *Bet. Yosef*, see n. 65, above.

III:7), while the Babylonian Talmud (ibid., 31a) puts the matter thus: "Nowadays, when we observe two days, we read both passages, but in reverse order". That is to say, in the Babylonian diaspora, where the festival is extended to two days, the chapters in Exodus containing the Ten Commandments are read on the first day, and the section in Deuteronomy containing the calendar of festivals is read on the second day.[68]

In the Torah itself there is no explicit connection between the festival of Shavuot and the Giving of the Torah. A baraita does state that "the Commandments were given on the sixth of the month" (i.e. Sivan; Shab. 86b), but diligent students of the Scriptures were not satisfied to let the matter rest there. They sought — and found — a biblical hint at the connection between the fiftieth day of the Omer and the day when the Torah was given:[69]

> An aggadic midrash asks: Why does Scripture attach the festival of Shavuot to a process of counting off days, something that does not hold good for any other festival? The reason is, that when the Israelites were told they were going to be freed from Egypt they were also told that they would be receiving the Torah fifty days after the Exodus, as it is written: "When you have freed the people from Egypt, you shall worship (*ta'avdun*) God at this mountain" (Ex. 3. 12). Now, that *nun* in *ta'avdun* is superfluous; but it is the symbol for fifty, and it means that after fifty days have passed you will worship God, for then you will receive the Torah. So the Israelites eagerly began to count off the days, saying "One more day has passed", for it seemed to take a long time, so eager were they to receive the Torah. Thus it came about

68 As late as the twelfth century we still find Maimonides writing: "On Shavuot one reads 'Seven weeks etc.' but it is a widespread custom to read 'In the third New Moon' on the first day of the festival". On the other hand, the *Tur* says (*Oraḥ Ḥayyim*, para. 494): "On the first day we read from the portion 'Jethro heard' [i.e., 'In the third New Moon']." Apparently Maimonides is hinting at the fact that custom had prevailed over the prescribed procedure.

69 This midrash is quoted in *Shibolei ha-Leqet*, 236. Joseph Bekhor Shor (France, twelfth century), in his commentary on Lev. 22. 15, attributes the same midrash to his father. It is also hinted at in *Mekhilta, Beshallaḥ*, p. 75: "'For it was near' (Ex. 13. 17): That is, the thing which God had promised Moses was near at hand, namely 'When you have freed the people from Egypt you shall worship God at this mountain'". Cf. Lauterbach I, p. 170; also see *Pesiqta de Rav Kahana*, ed. B. Mandelbaum, p. 185, and the parallels listed there.

that the counting of the days and weeks from Passover to Shavuot became a permanent practice for all generations.

In this midrash, which has its roots in older aggadic literature, the counting of the Omer has been converted into a counting of the days in anticipation of receiving the Ten Commandments; and the Feast of Shavuot, originally celebrating "the first fruits of the wheat harvest", has become "the Time of the Giving of our Torah". Furthermore, the chief observance of the day has become the reading of those chapters of the Torah which describe the revelation at Mount Sinai. As the *Pesiqta* puts it:

> The Holy One, blessed be He, said to Israel: My children, do you read this chapter every year, and I in turn will count it in your favor as though you were standing in my presence at Sinai and accepting the Torah.[70]

The phrase "standing in my presence" takes it for granted that the congregation rose to its feet when the Ten Commandments were read on Shavuot — and apparently also on those Sabbaths when they are part of the regular cycle of Torah readings. We do, in fact, have clear-cut evidence that this was indeed the custom. Nevertheless, this practice too became the subject of debate, something like the dispute over the inclusion of the Decalogue itself in the daily prayers. A question about the matter was directed to Maimonides:[71]

> Regarding a community whose Rabbis and lay leaders had for many years followed the custom of remaining seated while the Ten Commandments are read from the Torah during congregational prayer. Long before, this community had been rather unlearned, but when a great Rabbi took over he introduced proper instruction, and took measures to rectify certain communal practices. Among these, it had previously been customary for everyone to rise when the Ten Commandments were read from the Torah in public, out of respect. This learned Rabbi, of blessed memory, changed that custom, and instructed the people to remain seated — in fact he forbade them to rise, and for generations after his time that remained the custom. When he

70 *Pesiqta de Rav Kahana*, p. 204.
71 *Responsa of Maimonides*, ed. A.H. Freimann, no. 46, p. 46, and addenda, p. 359; also the collection edited by J.Blau, no. 263, p. 495.

was asked about this, he published a responsum, signed by his own hand, grounding his opinion on the fact that the Sages of old had discontinued the reading of the Ten Commandments along with the Shema because of the Minim, and their claim that the Ten Commandments are superior to the rest of the Torah ... — — Now there has come to the city in question a newly appointed Rabbi, who hails from a place where it is customary to rise for the reading of the Ten Commandments. As far as scholarship is concerned, he does not begin to compare with the aforementioned learned Rabbi. But he has started to rise for the reading of the Decalogue, and some of the congregation are following his example. The leaders of the community have said to the new Rabbi: It is not seemly for us to abandon the custom of our fathers, and their fathers before them... we cannot substitute the custom of the place you come from... all the more so since the Halakhah supports our position... for the Sages long ago abolished the practice of reciting the Commandments with the Shema, even in a sitting position, because of the contentions of the Minim. And especially since, if we stand, we are making a distinction between these Ten and the rest of the Torah, and behaving like Karaites, who stand when the Torah is read. In answer to these arguments the new Rabbi quotes Exodus 19. 16, which, speaking of the Israelites when they heard the commandments at Sinai, says: "They *stood* at the foot of the mountain".

The newly appointed Rabbi relies on the fact that in Baghdad the custom is to stand. The question put to Maimonides is whether this Rabbi has the right to change the established *minhag* of the community, and whether his scriptural citation proves anything.

It is clear from the question itself that it originated in a community where the much older custom had been to rise for the reading of the Decalogue, but that several generations ago an outstanding Rabbi had changed this practice. His reasoning had been based on the classical sources, which show that the reading of the Ten Commandments with the Shema had been discontinued in ancient times because of the contention of certain Minim that these commandments had a status superior to others. It is also possible that this learned Rabbi knew that communities of Palestinian Jews in Egypt in his own day still followed the ancient custom.

It is not surprising that Maimonides in his reply supports the view of the deceased Rabbi — that is, to remain seated. "The proofs he adduced are sound", he writes, "in the opinion of those qualified to judge". Maimonides' judgment is a dogmatic one, based on theoretical principles. He disagrees with his questioners about the Karaites,[72] for they were no the *Minim* that the ancient Rabbis had in mind. The ones they meant, he says, were "Sadducees and Boethusians". The real issue in the matter under discussion was "to reject anything that might lead to the belief that some of the Minim held, namely, that the only divinely revealed part of the Torah is the Ten Commandments", or alternatively, that "some parts of the Torah are of a higher degree of importance than others". Rising for the reading of the Torah might lead to questioning the eighth principle of faith enunciated by Maimonides in his commentary on the Mishnah (Sanhedrin, X):

> We are to believe that the entire Torah as we now have it is the same Torah that was given to Moses, and that all of it emanated from the Almighty; that is to say, that it was transmitted to Moses by means of what we, using human terms, metaphorically call "speech". The nature of that transmission is known to no one but the person who received it, peace be upon him.

These words effectively nullify any distinction between the various rabbinic versions of the way in which the Ten Commandments were heard by the Israelites. They wipe out any difference between the saying: "All Ten Commandments were spoken in one utterance",[73] and the saying "Moses spoke all but the first two; they alone were actually heard in God's voice".[74] What is more, they negate all differences between such verses as "The descendants of Ham: Cush, Mizraim, Put and Canaan" (Gen. 10. 6), or "His wife's name was Mehetabel daughter of Matred (Gen. 36. 39), on the one hand — and on the other, "I am the

---

72 The Karaites customarily stand whenever the Torah is read. For Rabbinite opinion on this, see *Tur, Oraḥ Ḥayyim*, 146, and *Shulḥan Arukh* Ibid., para. 4.; also *Responsa* of Rabbi Menahem Azariah da Fano (sixteenth century), no. 92.

73 See n. 3, above.

74 Hor. 8a; Mak. 24a; *Cant. Rabbah*, I:2. See Aptowitzer, *Derashah in Praise of the Torah* (Hebrew), *Sinai*, 27 (1940), pp. 148 ff., also my article *Rabbinic Exegesis, Origen's Commentaries and Jewish-Christian Polemics* (Hebrew), *Tarbiẓ*, 30 (1960), p. 155.

LORD your God" (Ex. 20. 2) and "Hear O Israel, the LORD is our God, the LORD alone" (Deut. 6. 4). To quote Maimonides again:

> It is all divinely inspired, all of it is the perfect Torah of the LORD teaching true holiness.[75]

Maimonides' reply to the question of rising for the Ten Commandments is guided more by his basic theological principles than by any responsiveness to the actual issue of standing or sitting.[76] But in actual practice, it was customary in various communities, even in Maimonides' own Egypt, for the congregation to stand during the reading of the Ten Commandments.[77] And this held good in most Jewish communities. When they stood up and heard the words "I the LORD am your God", they did not feel quite the same as when the reader chanted "His wife's name was Mehetabel". They felt rather, in the words of the *Pesiqta*, "as though they were standing again at Mount Sinai and receiving the Torah anew".

Translated by Gershon Levi

75   See Maimonides, *Commentary on the Mishnah, Neziqin*, ed. Kapah., pp. 214–215.
76   See I. Twersky, *Introduction to the Code of Maimonides*, 1980, p. 133.
77   See Elijah Hazzan, *Neveh Shalom*, Alexandria 1894, 9a, para. 23.

7. "OBSERVE" AND "REMEMBER" SPOKEN IN ONE UTTERANCE

EZRA ZION MELAMMED

1. HOW WERE THE TEN COMMANDMENTS GIVEN?*

The Talmud (Hor. 8a = Mak. 24a) says:

> It was taught in the academy of Rabbi Ishmael that the Commandments "I am the LORD" and "You shall have no other gods" (Ex. 20. 2–3) we heard directly as spoken by the Almighty.[1]

One might very well ask, does not the Torah say "God spoke *all* these words" (Ex. 20. 1)? The answer to this question can be found in the *Mekhilta de R. Ishmael*:

> It simply teaches that the Holy One, blessed be He, after having spoken all the Ten Commandments in one utterance [i.e., in one continuity, without any pauses] then went back to the beginning, and repeated them one at a time (*Baḥodesh*, IV, ed. Horovitz-Rabin, p. 218; cf. ed. Lauterbach, II, p. 228).

It was then, when they heard the first two Commandments repeated, that the people pleaded with Moses (Ex. 20. 16) "You speak to us and we will obey, but let not God speak to us lest we die". So Moses mediated the rest of the Commandments to the people.

The Bible commentator Hizkiah ben Manoah (Hizzequni, probably France, thirteenth century) remarks:

> Everything in the Torah from "All the people" up to "may not be

---

*   *Dibberoth* (Commandments) plural of *dibber* (Jer. 5. 13). In rabbinic Hebrew the term becomes *dibbur*, just as *shillem* (Deut. 32. 25) becomes *shillum* (Hos. 9. 7). A different opinion holds that *dibberoth* is plural of *dibberah* (cf. Eccl. 3. 18).

1   Variant readings: "They heard".

exposed on it" (Ex. 20. 15–23) really belongs after "keep my commandments" (verse 6); the reason it is not placed there is so as not to interrupt the Ten Commandments.

Earlier in his commentary, Hizzequni had quoted Rashi, based on the Midrash, and noted:

> That is to say, at first the Holy One spoke all Ten Commandments simultaneously and in one utterance, so that the Israelites simply did not understand. That He repeated them a second time means that the Explicator went over them singly, enunciating each Commandment by itself, so that the Israelites might understand. The first two — "I am the LORD" and "You shall have no other" — these the Holy One spoke a second time, but the people were unable to bear the sound any further, as we read in verse 16: "They said to Moses, you speak to us and we will obey, but let not God speak to us lest we die". Our Sages put it this way: "'I am' and 'You shall have no other'" — these we heard directly from the mouth of the Almighty". Moses then took up the recitation from, that point onward, reciting each Commandment separately. This interpretation is also supported by the style of the language: the two beginning Commandments are couched in the first person — "*I* am", "keep *My* commandments", while all the rest are in the third person.

When the Decalogue is repeated in the Book of Deuteronomy (5. 6) Hizzequni adds:

> From the opening words of the Decalogue up to "keep my commandments" there is not the slightest difference between the Ten Commandments in Exodus and those in Deuteronomy, because the Holy One Himself enunciated them both times, as we explained in our commentary on Exodus; and when Moses came to repeat them in the present chapter he did not want to vary a single syllable. As for the rest, which Moses had originally mediated to the people, the change of a word here or there is of no concern, since the meaning remains unchanged. As a general rule, whenever a matter is repeated in Scripture with a change of language, the meaning remains unchanged.

This last remark is a summary of what the twelfth-century Spanish scholar Abraham ibn Ezra had said:

The grammarians of biblical Hebrew tell us that Scripture sometimes explains the matter at hand fully, and at other times uses short and simple words, the meaning of which is obvious. Know that words are like bodies, and meanings are like souls.[2] Now, the body is to the soul as a vessel is to its contents. Therefore it is the judgment of the linguists in every language that one should be careful of the meaning, but not too concerned about the use of synonyms... For example, when Abraham's servant met Rebekah, he said "Please let me sip a little water" (Gen. 24. 17), and when he described the meeting to her family, he reported, "I said to her, 'Please let me drink a little water" (verse 45)... The Ten Commandments as written here [in Exodus] are the words of GOD, with nothing added or left out; they alone were written on the tablets. In this I disagree with Saadiah Gaon, who said that "Remember" was on one set of tablets, and "Observe" on the other.

It is appropriate at this point to quote M.D. Umberto Cassuto, who writes in his commentary on Exodus (p. 173):

The problem of the relationship between the Decalogue in Exodus and the one in Deuteronomy is not very serious, provided we do not regard the two as isolated and independent documents, the way most scholars do, but rather view them within their context. In the Book of Exodus, we read that God declared the Ten Commandments to the Israelites while they stood at Mount Sinai. In the Book of Deuteronomy, Moses reminds the Israelites forty years later of what had happened at the mountain. Now, the literary convention of the ancient east, followed also in biblical literature, was to avoid verbatim repetition when describing how someone quoted words or events already set forth. In such instances it was customary to introduce certain variations and verbal substitutions. In chapter 24 of Genesis, when Abraham's servant is telling his story to the family of Bethuel, he does not quote his dialogue with Abraham, and his encounter later with Rebekah, in the precise words with which they were reported earlier in the same chapter. The same applies in the case of the Decalogue. When Moses recalls God's words,

2   Ibn Ezra repeats this idea when he comments on the Decalogue in Deuteronomy.

he does not quote them literally, word for word. Consequently there is no reason for surprise at the variations in form; quite the contrary, it would be surprising if everything were repeated with exact literal precision.

Ibn Ezra, in the commentary quoted above, calls our attention to the differences between the two Decalogues:

> There are some difficult questions regarding this.... In the Fourth Commandment it is said "For in six days the LORD made heaven and earth, etc... therefore the LORD blessed etc.". Now we read this chapter in Exodus first, and the version in Deuteronomy later... and from "Remember the Sabbath day" until the end of the Commandments there are all kinds of changes. In Exodus the Fourth Commandment says "Remember the Sabbath day" while in Deuteronomy it says "Observe" and goes on to add "as the LORD your God commanded you". Also, in Exodus it says "or your cattle" while Deuteronomy adds "your ox or your ass". The most difficult question concerns the reason given for the Sabbath. Exodus says "For in six days the LORD made heaven and earth" and adds "therefore did the LORD bless the Sabbath day". These verses do not appear at all in Deuteronomy. Instead, a different reason is given: "Remember that you were a slave in the land of Egypt" concluding with "therefore the LORD your God commands you to observe the Sabbath day".

Before we take up these questions, let us try to explain the origin of the midrash which says that all ten of the Ten Commandments were uttered in one breath, and then repeated one at a time. In my opinion, the midrash was drawing an analogy between instruction received directly from God, and the instruction received from a teacher in the Beth ha-Midrash, the House of Study. In olden times, the method was to study the section of the Mishnah as a unit, and then to enter the academy to learn the meaning of the chapter, taking up one halakhah at a time. The Talmud relates that Rabbi Mesharshaya said to his sons:[3] "Whenever you intend coming in for your lesson with your teacher, revise the subject first and then enter the presence of your teacher" (Hor. 12a).[4]

---

3   There are textual variations in the sources. In what follows, such variations will be
     noted in this translation as "Var." unless they have a bearing on the substance.
4   Var.

Facsimile of The Nash Papyrus

פפירוס נאש

(העתקה)

1 [אנכי י]הוה אלהיך אשר [הוצא]תיך מארץ מ[צרים מבית עבדים לוא]

2 [יהיה ל]ך אלהים אחרים ע[ל פ]ני לוא תעשה [לך פסל כל]

3 [תמונה] אשר בשמים ממעל ואשר בארץ [מתחת]

4 [ואשר במי]ם מתחת לארץ לוא תשתחוה להם [ולא תעבדם]

5 [כי] אנכי יהוה אלהיך אל קנוא פק[ד עון אבות]

6 [על בני]ם על שלשים ועל ר'בעים לשנאי [ועשה חסד]

7 [לאלפים] לאהבי ולשמרי מצותי לוא ת[שא את שם]

8 [יהוה א]להיך לשוא כי לוא ינקה יהוה [את אשר]

9 [ישא את שמ]ה לשוא זכור את יום השבת ל[קדשה]

10 [ששת ימי]ם תעבוד ועשית כל מלאכתך וביום [השביעי]

11 [שבת ליהוה] אלהיך לוא תעשה בה כל מלאכה [אתה ובנך]

12 [ובתך ו]עבדך ואמתך שורך וחמרך וכל ב[המתך]

13 [וגרך אשר] בשעריך כי ששת ימים עשה י[הוה]

14 [את השמי]ם ואת הארץ את הים ואת כל א[שר בם]

15 וינח [ביום] השביעי על כן ברך יהוה את [היום]

16 השביעי ויקדשיו כבד את אביך ואת אמ[ך למען]

17 ייטב לך ולמען יאריכון ימיך על האדמה [אשר]

18 יהוה אלהיך נתן לך לוא תנאף לוא תרצח לו[א]

19 [תג]נב לוא [תענ]ה ברעך עד שוא לוא תחמוד [את ?]

20 [אשת רעך ול]וא תחמוד את בי[ת רעך שד]הו

21 [ועבדו ואמתו וש]ורו וחמרו וכל אשר לרעך [...]

22 [? ואלה החק]ים והמשפטים אשר צוה משה את [בני]

23 [ישרא]ל במדבר בצאתם מארץ מצרים שמ[ע]

24 [ישרא]ל יהוה אלהינו יהוה אחד הוא וא[הבת]

25 [את יהוה א]ל[ה]יך בכ[ל ל]בבך וגו'].

Text of the Nash Papyrus

2. *"REMEMBER" AND "OBSERVE" IN ONE UTTERANCE*

Heading the list of differences between the two versions of the Decalogue is the opening word of the Sabbath Commandment — in Exodus "Remember" and in Deuteronomy "Observe".[5] The rabbinic Sages commented (R.H. 27a; Shevu. 20b): "It has been taught, 'Remember' and 'Observe' were pronounced in a single utterance, something which the [human] mouth[6] cannot utter nor the ear hear".[7]

In the context where this tradition is reported in the tractate Shevuot, the Talmud regards the two verbs as interdependent, and is able to draw a conclusion therefrom:

> The two words were pronounced in one utterance, as Rabbi Ada bar Ahavah taught: "Women are in duty bound to sanctify the Sabbath [*i.e. to recite kiddush*] by decree of the Torah, for Scripture says both "Remember" and "Observe" — all who are required to observe are required to remember; and women, since they are included in 'observe' are included in 'remember'. However, in the case of false oaths, what halakhic conclusion can be drawn from the substitution of *lašeqer* [= falsely] for *lašaw* [= in vain][8]

The variation in the Fourth Commandment, along with a number of similar instances, is also considered by the *Mekhilta de R. Ishmael*:

> "Remember the day of the Sabbath to keep it holy". "Remember" and "Observe" were both spoken in one utterance. "Every one that profanes it shall be put to death" (Ex. 31. 14) and "On the Sabbath day two he-lambs" (Num. 28. 9) were both spoken in one utterance. "You shall not uncover the nakedness of your brother's wife" (Lev. 18. 16) and "Her husband's brother shall unite with her" (Deut. 25. 8) were both spoken in one utterance.[9] "You shall not wear cloth combining wool and linen" (Deut. 22. 11) and "You shall make [woolen] tassels on the four corners of your garment" [even linen] (ibid., verse 12) were both spoken in[9]

5 Similarly, in the law of Passover: "Remember this day" (Ex. 13. 3), but "Observe the month of Abib" (Deut. 16. 1).
6 Var.
7 Var.
8 Synonyms for "falsely", used respectively in Ex. 20. 7 and Lev. 19. 12.
9 Var.

one utterance. This is a manner of speech impossible for creatures of flesh and blood. As it is written (Ps. 62. 12) "God has spoken one utterance, which we have heard[10] as two". It is also written, "Behold, my word is like fire" (Jer. 23. 29). (*Baḥodesh*, VII, ed. Horovitz-Rabin, p. 229: cf. ed. Lauterbach, II, p. 252).

H. S. Horovitz, who edited the text of the *Mekhilta*, makes the following comment. "In the case of 'Remember' and 'Observe' the intent is not the same as in the other instances listed. For in the former instance, both are versions of the same Commandent. Note the language in the *Mekhilta de R. Simeon bar Yoḥai*, But in the examples that follow, such as 'Everyone who profanes it etc.' the idea is to provide the warning necessary whenever a punishment is to follow".

In the *Midrash ha-Gadol* on Exodus (ed. M.M. Margoliouth, p. 412) in a passage taken over by the *Mekhilta de R. Simeon bar Yoḥai* (ed. Hoffman, p. 107; ed. Epstein–Melammed, 148) we find:

> "Remember" and "Observe" were spoken for one and the same purpose, something impossible for the [human] mouth to speak or ear to hear. Thus, Scripture says, "God spoke *all* these words "and it is also written, "God has spoken one utterance, which we have heard as two".

There is no manuscript extant for this particular chapter in the *Mekhilta de Rabbi Simeon bar Yoḥai*, which makes it difficult to determine whether the source used by the *Midrash ha-Gadol* was the *Mekhilta de R. Simeon bar Yoḥai*, or that of Rabbi Ishmael.

In the *Midrash ha-Gadol* on Deuteronomy, (ed. S. Fish, p. 111) we find a concise summary of this passage as it occurs in the *Mekhilta de Rabbi Ishmael*, with all the details precisely in place.

The following is a quotation from the *Sifre* on Deuteronomy (ed. L. Finkelstein, p. 265):

> The Commandments "You shall not wear cloth combining wool and linen" and "You shall make tassels on the four corners of the garment" were both uttered simultaneously; "Remember" and "Observe" were both spoken simultaneously; "Everyone who profanes it" and "On the Sabbath day two he-lambs" [to be sacrificed] were both spoken simultaneously; "Do not uncover

---

10   The biblical text reads "I have heard".

the nakedness of your brother's wife" and "Her husband's brother shall unite with her" were both spoken simultaneously; "Every daughter who inherits" and "No inheritance shall pass over from one tribe to another" (Num. 36. 8–9) — both were spoken simultaneously; something impossible for flesh and blood, to say two things at the same time, as it is written: "God has spoken two utterances, which we have heard as one".

Louis Finkelstein has called attention to the fact that this extract does not belong to the body of the work, but has been added from another source. In support of this statement, it may be added that Hillel did not have this passage in his text. We quote the Yerushalmi:

"In vain" and "falsely" were spoken in one utterance, something which no ear can hear nor mouth can utter. "Anyone who profanes it" and "[sacrifice] on the Sabbath day two he-lambs" were both spoken in one utterance; "Do not wear linen and wool" and "Make tassels on the corners" were both spoken in one utterance; "No inheritance shall pass over" and "every daughter who inherits" were spoken in one utterance — something which no mouth can utter nor ear can grasp. Thus does Scripture say: "God has spoken one thing, and we have heard it as two". And further: "Behold, My word is like fire" (Yer. Shevu. III, 34d).

Note: The Yerushalmi makes no mention of "Remember" and "Observe"!

The same subject comes up elsewhere in the Yerushalmi, namely in Nedarim, III, 37d, albeit the details are listed in somewhat different order: false oaths, profaning the Sabbath, the brother's wife, the tribal inheritance, the tassels on the garment. In this instance, too, there is no mention of "Remember" and "Observe" in our basic version (the Leyden manuscript) of the Yerushalmi, except that whoever revised that text in the process of preparing it for the printing of the *editio princeps* added in the margin the phrase from the Bavli about the two versions of the Fourth Commandment (a procedure he followed in many other instances) and the printer dutifully incorporated it into the text.[11]

Two questions arise in connection with this topic as dealt with in the

11 See my article in *Tarbiz*, vol. 3.

Yerushalmi. First, *šaw'* (in vain) and *šeqer* (falsely) were not spoken simultaneously; one is in the Decalogue, and the other is in the Holiness Chapter (Lev. 19). The Bavli puts it accurately: *šaw'* and *šeqer* are one and the same.

Secondly, with regard to inheritance by daughters, mentioned in both *Sifre* and the Yerushalmi: the two verses cited do not contradict one another; rather, one explains the other:

> Every daughter among the Israelite tribes who inherits a share must marry someone from a clan of her father's tribe, in order that every Israelite may keep his ancestral share. Thus no inheritance shall pass over from one tribe to another, but the Israelite tribes shall remain bound each to its portion (Num. 36. 8–9).

If there is any contradiction here, it is contained within the first sentence: "Every daughter who inherits — in order that every Israelite may keep his ancestral share."

In *Exodus Rabbah* as well (28. 4) a similar tradition omits mention of "Observe" and "Remember":

> The Commandment "Remember the Sabbath day" co-exists with the command "on the Sabbath day [sacrifice] two yearling he-lambs", and the Commandment "Do not uncover the nakedness of your brother's wife" with the law beginning "If brothers dwell together". All these were spoken at the same time, which is why Scripture stresses: "The LORD spoke *all* these words".

So we discover that the discrepancy between "Remember" and "Observe" is not even mentioned in Palestinian sources, such as the Talmud Yerushalmi, the *Sifre* on Deuteronomy, the Midrash *Exodus Rabbah*. Actually, according to the plain sense, there is no real difference between "Remember" and "Observe". On the other hand, the two verbs are treated as different in the Babylonian Talmud, and in the *Mekhilta de R. Ishmael*. In the latter work, it is worth noting, "many of the Sages quoted are disciples of Rabbi Ishmael, including quite a number of Babylonians".[12] This is the source of similar passages

12   Quoted from J.N. Epstein, *Introduction to Tannaitic Literature* (Hebrew), ed. E.Z. Melammed, Jerusalem 1957, p. 570.

in *Midrash Ha-Gadol* (perhaps also in the *Mekhilta de R. Simeon bar Yoḥai*).

With regard to the discrepancies enumerated by the Midrash, it is in order to cite the Babylonian Talmud (Hul. 109b).[13]

> Yalta once said to Rabbi Nahman: For everything that the Divine Law has forbidden to us, it has permitted one exception to the rule: it has forbidden the eating of blood, but permitted liver; it has forbidden intercourse during menstruation, but permitted to us the blood of purification; it has forbidden the fat of cattle, but permitted the fat of wild beasts; it has forbidden us swine's flesh, but permitted us the brain of the *shibbuta* fish;[14] it has forbidden the married woman, but permitted us to marry a divorcee during the lifetime of her former husband; it has forbidden the brother's wife, but permitted levirate marriage; it has forbidden the non-Jewess, but permitted the captive woman. Now then, I want to eat meat with milk! Where do I find the exception? Rabbi Nahman said to the butchers: "Give her roasted udders!"[15]

3. TREATMENT IN THE CLASSIC COMMENTARIES

Rashi (France, 1040–1103) gives a condensed summary of the *Mekhilta de R. Ishmael* on the Sabbath Commandment in Exodus:

> "Remember" and "Observe" were spoken in one utterance, the same as "You shall not wear cloth combining wool and linen" and "Make tassels"; or "The nakedness of your brother's wife" taken with "Her husband's brother shall unite with her".[16] This is the meaning of the verse "God has spoken one utterance, which we have heard as two".

When he gets to the Decalogue in Deuteronomy, Rashi has this to say:

> "No other gods, before me" — meaning, wherever I am, which is to say, in the whole universe. Another explanation: as long as I endure.

13   See *Diqduqe Soferin*, ad loc.
14   Var.
15   Rashi: "Give her a spleen on a spit"; see Tosafot, ad loc.
16   The *Mekhilta de R. Ishmael* has these two in reverse order.

The first comments is original with Rashi; the second is derived from the
Mekhilta de R. Ishmael.[17] And at this point, Rashi writes: "As for the
Ten Commandments, I have already explained them". Nevertheless, he
proceeds to comment on the differences between the version in Exodus
and the one in Deuteronomy. With regard to the topic we are discussing,
he writes:

> "Observe": But in the first version it says "Remember". Both
> were spoken in one utterance, as one word,[18] and heard as one.[19]

Abraham ibn Ezra (Spain, 1089–1164) has this to say:

> The Ten Commandments as recorded in the Book of
> Deuteronomy are the words of Moses... And when God had said
> "Remember", all those who heard understood the meaning to be
> "Observe" as though the two words were spoken at the same
> time.

Nahmanides (Spain, 1194–c.1267), when he comments on the
Decalogue in Exodus, says:

> Here we read "Remember the Sabbath day", while in
> Deuteronomy it says "Observe the Sabbath day". Our Sages
> noted the difference, and said, " 'Remember' and 'Observe' were
> spoken in one utterance". But they did not concern themselves
> with the other differences in language between the two
> Decalogues. In this case, they wanted to point out that
> "Remember" is a positive commandment; we are to remember
> the Sabbath day to keep it holy, and not to forget. Whereas
> "Observe" (*šamor*) they viewed as a negative commandment. For

17 In this commentary on the Decalogue in Exodus, Rashi offers only the second of
these interpretations and goes on to say: "So that no one can say, idolatry was
forbidden only to that generation".

18 The idea suggests itself that the phrase "in one word" has been inserted into the
original text of Rashi, because *tebhah* in the Talmud usually means "a written
word". However, in Hullim 91b it means simply a "a word", viz.: "The Israelites
mention God's name after two words (*Shema Israel*), while the ministering angels
do so only after three words (*Holy, holy, holy*).

19 Rashi takes the same line on "As He commanded you" (see below). On adultery he
says "The term applies only with respect to a married woman". He had said the
same thing in Exodus, only there he offered proof. On Rashi's repetition, see *Siftei
Hakhamim*.

wherever in Scripture we find "take care" (*hišamer*), equally with "lest" or "do not", that constitutes a negative commandment. In the present case, we have an admonition to "keep" (*šamor*) it holy, and not profane it. Now, it would not have been proper for Moses to alter God's words, from a positive to a negative command. ...And I wonder why, if "Remember" and "Observe" were both spoken by the Almighty, how is it that the latter was not inscribed on the first set of tablets. To me, it seems probable that on both the first and the second tablets, the word inscribed was "Remember", and Moses [in Deuteronomy] explained to the Israelites that "Observe" had been spoken along with it. This is what the Sages really meant.

When Nahmanides gets to Deuteronomy, he writes:

If you follow the plain sense, "Observe" does duty for "Remember". If you follow the homiletic interpretation of the Sages, it means they were spoken in one utterance.

Samuel ben Meir (*Rashbam*, France, ca. 1085–1158), in his commentary on Exodus, writes:

"Remember the Sabbath day": Remembrance always refers to past events, as in "Remember days of old... when the Most High gave nations their homes" (Deut 32. 7-8). Here too, "Remember the Sabbath day" i.e., out of the six days of creation, as Scripture goes on to say, "for in six days the LORD made heaven and earth". Consequently, the text here reads "Remember" — in order to sanctify it by resting from your labors; "therefore did the LORD bless the Sabbath day", as I explained in my commentary on Genesis.

Rashbam believes that the whole account of the Creation in Genesis is intended to serve as an introduction to the Sabbath Commandment in the Decalogue. This is his explanation:

Here is the essence of the plain meaning, in accordance with Scriptural usage. Scripture usually anticipates by telling us something that we don't really have to know for itself, but which will clarify something that will come up later on.[20] Thus, we read

---

20   Rashbam uses *lefanav* as the equivalent of Aramaic *leqaman* ("later on").

"Shem, Ham and Japhet... and Ham was the ancestor of Canaan" (Gen. 9. 18). This is because shortly thereafter (verse 25) we read "cursed be Canaan". If we had not been told who Canaan was, we would not understand why Noah cursed him. ... So too with this entire story of the work of Creation. Moses gave it as an introduction to the Torah, to enable us to understand what the Holy One said at Sinai: "Remember the Sabbath day to keep it holy ... for in six days He made ... and on the seventh day He rested". That explains why the Torah says "It was evening and it was morning, the *sixth* day, i.e., the sixth day of the third month which the Holy One was to speak of when He gave the Torah. This was why Moses described the creation of the world to the Israelites, so that they would know that the Word of God is true.

In commenting on the Decalogue in Deuteronomy, Rashbam says:

"Observe": In my commentary on Exodus I have already explained why it says "Observe" here, while there it is "Remember".

Apparently the copyists left something out in Rashbam's commentary on Exodus, because the text as we have it says nothing about "Observe". Hizzequni, whom we quoted earlier, says in his commentary on Exodus:

The term "Remember" includes the idea of observance, so that when "Remember" was spoken, everybody understood it to mean "Observe" as well, as though they had been spoken simultaneously.

When he reaches Deuteronomy he writes:

In the Commandments in Exodus, when He wants to remind the Israelites about the Sabbath, which He had already given to them at Marah, the appropriate word is "Remember". But here in Deuteronomy, when the Commandments are being repeated forty years later for the benefit of those who did not hear them the first time, the appropriate word is "Observe" since the matter was not new to them.

Our final quotation is from *Or Ha-Hayyim* (Hayyim ibn Attar, Morocco-Palestine, early eighteenth century) at the end of his commentary on the Ten Commandments in the book of Exodus:

It may well be that God said only "Remember" except that to discerning people, one word implies the other. So that when God said "Remember", he meant for us to make a conscious effort to avoid errors in the observance of the Sabbath. From the subsequent context one might derive the idea that we are also commanded regarding "six days shall you labor". Perhaps that is what Moses meant when he said "Observe" — that that too is included in "Remember". I offer this merely as a possible interpretation.

4. REASONS FOR THE SABBATH COMMANDMENT

The rabbinic Sages do not take notice of the two different reasons for the Sabbath Commandment. The question is examined by the Maharal of Prague (ca. 1525–1609) in his commentary on Rashi, called *Gur Aryeh*. After discussing what Nahmanides wrote about Rashi, and taking account of the criticisms of Elijah Mizrahi (d. 1526) on Nahmanides, Maharal writes:

> Thus, the question remains: Why should this discrepancy between "Remember" and "Observe" be treated differently from other discrepancies, such as "For in six days the LORD created" versus "You shall remember that you were a slave in the land of Egypt?" Why did the Sages not say in this connection as well, that the two different reasons were spoken in one utterance? It seems however, and this is the real point, that they only drew this inference when the essence of the Commandment was involved. Certainly, anything in the Decalogue in Deuteronomy which simply offers an alternative reason, or an additional explanation, is no cause for question. Clearly, Deuteronomy has the purpose of adding clarification, but when all is said and done the essence of the Commandment remains unchanged.

In the same vein, Rashi comments on Deuteronomy 5. 15: "Remember that you were a slave, and that God freed you in order that you might become a servant to Him, and keep His commandments". Not a word about the shift in motive from Creation to Emancipation.

Other commentators, however, are drawn up short by the shift. Ibn Ezra, on the Exodus Decalogue, notes:

> Later, it will not be necessary for Moses to repeat the reason given here, namely that in six days God created Heaven and

earth. He takes care of that in Deuteronomy, when he says: "As the LORD your God commanded you", as though to remind them of the Commandment in Exodus, reading from "Remember" to "and he hallowed it". But since the Commandment here ordains rest for the manservant and the maidservant, and does not explain why, Moses gives the explanation when he repeats the Ten Commandments: God commands you to give your slave rest, so that you may remember that you were a slave in Egypt just like him, and God redeemed you.

As Ibn Ezra sees it, "You shall remember that you were a slave" is not a reason for observing the Sabbath, but rather a reason for allowing one's servants to rest on that day.

Consistent with this explanation, Ibn Ezra writes in Deuteronomy:

"That your servant may rest" — Moses adds an explanation of "your manservant and your maidservant" saying, "Remember that you were a slave, and give rest to your slave; that is why your God commanded you". The reason given is in explanation of the slave's rest.

Ibn Attar follows his own line in dealing with the reason for the Sabbath as given in Deuteronomy:

Should you ask, why did Moses leave out the Creation theme when he repeated the Fourth Commandment? That theme is the fundamental reason for the existence of the Sabbath; but not the reason for our obligation to observe it. That reason, says Moses, is grounded in the duty to believe, as our Sages taught, and as I have explained in another context. For the Exodus from Egypt revealed the faith in the Creator of the universe. That is what Moses was saying when he wrote, "Remember that you were a slave ... and the LORD brought you out". That is, you saw that He is the ruler of the whole universe, thus confirming the words of the original Fourth Commandment: "For in six days the LORD created heaven and earth".

5. *AS THE LORD YOUR GOD COMMANDED YOU*

In the Deuteronomic version of the Decalogue, the Fourth Commandment (the Sabbath) and the Fifth Commandment (honoring one's parents) contain the added phrase "as the LORD your God commanded you". With regard to the Sabbath Commandment, Rashi explains: "As He commanded you earlier, at Marah"(Ex. 15. 23 ff.). As for the Fifth Commandment, Rashi's comment is: "Honor of father and mother was also ordained at Marah". These explanations of Rashi's are derived from the *Mekhilta de R. Ishmael* (p. 156; cf. ed. Lauterbach, II, p. 94); and *Mekhilta de R. Simeon bar Yoḥai*, (p. 154):

> "There He laid down for them a statute and an ordinance" (Ex. 15. 25) — "Statute" refers to to the law of the Sabbath; "ordinance" refers to the honoring of one's parents. So said Rabbi Joshua.[21]

Rashbam explains the added phrase differently:

> "As the LORD your God commanded you": That is, for the reason given earlier, in the original version of the Ten Commandments in the Book of Exodus; namely, "for in six days the LORD made heaven and earth etc.". The phrase "as the LORD ... commanded" is added only to the Sabbath Commandment and to the one calling for honor of one's parents, because only these two are positive commandments, while the other eight are all negative admonishments, so that in their case the words "as he commanded, etc." would have been inappropriate. Take note of the scriptural usage, for example Deuteronomy 7. 11: "Which I command you this day *to do*" — nowhere do we find "I command you *not* to do".[22]

It is in the same vein that Hizzequni says, "It is appropriate to write 'As the LORD your God commanded you' in connection with the Commandments 'Observe' and 'Honor' since both of them are positive commandments".

This explanation is adoped by David Hoffman in his commentary on Deuteronomy (*Das Buch Deuteronomium,* Berlin 1913, Erster Halbband, s. 73):

> Mit כאשר צוך וגו' wird teils auf schriftliche, teils auf mündliche

---

21   The *Ba'al ha-Turim* points out that the numerical value of the final letters of the Hebrew words for "as the LORD your God commanded you" equals 245, which is the sum of the letters of Marah!

22   Rozin's question (*Zophnat Pa'neah* on Lev. 4:2 "(Commandment of the LORD which shall not be done") is not valid. The passage does not read "which He commanded you not to do". See the remarks of D.Z. Hoffman immediately below.

erlauterungen zum Sabbatgezetze hingewiesen. Ebenso ist dieser
Zugab in v. 25 [sic! 16?] zu deuten. Dass nicht noch bei anderen
Geboten des Dekalogs dies hinzugefürgt wird, rührt daher, weil
alle anderen Gebote in negativer form (mit לא) ausgedrückt sind,
wozu כאשר צוך nicht passt. אנכי ist wieder kein Gebot, sondern
eine Ankündigung.

(The phrase "As the LORD commanded etc." refers to elucidations of
the Sabbath Commandment, some of them written, some of them
orally transmitted. The use of the same additional phrase in verse 16
should be understood in the same way. The fact that these words do not
appear in any other Commandments of the Decalogue can be attributed
to the fact that they are all worded negatively (using לא) and in such
sentences they would be out of place. As for the opening words of the
Decalogue — "I am the LORD, etc." — they are not a commandment,
but rather a proclamation).

6. *YOU SHALL NOT COVET — NOR SHALL YOU CRAVE*

A more important variation as between the Decalogue in Exodus and
the version in Deuteronomy concerns the Commandment "You shall
not covet":

Exodus	*Deuteronomy*
You shall not covet your neighbor's house.	You shall not covet your neighbor's wife.
You shall not covet your neighbor's wife,	Nor shall you crave your neighbor's house,
nor his manservant, etc.	his field, his manservant, etc.

The *Mekhilta de R. Ishmael* deals with this discrepancy in the following
manner (p. 234; cf. ed. Lauterbach, II, p. 264):

> Rabbi Judah says: One verse reads "You shall not covet", while
> the other reads "You shall not crave". How can these two
> Scriptures be reconciled? One of them must be understood as an
> admonition not to seek profit from the act of an adulterer.

This midrash presents difficulties. After all, both versions of this
Commandment deal with *coveting* one's neighbor's wife. The difficulty
has been commented on, and the suggestion has been made that this
midrash has been misplaced (see Horovitz-Rabin, ad loc.).

I venture to suggest that a lacuna has somehow intruded into the text after the words "How can these two Scriptures be reconciled?" and that the words following really belong to "You shall not commit adultery". This would conform to the homily attributed in the Babylonian Talmud to Rabbi Simeon b. Tarfon (Shevu. 47b).

The discrepancy between Exodus and Deuteronomy is dealt with by the *Mekhilta de R. Simeon bar Yoḥai* (p. 153) in the following manner: "'You shall not covet' — and further on it says 'You shall not crave', the purpose being to make one culpable for craving as a separate offense, and for coveting as a separate offense".

The *Mekhilta de R. Ishmael* (ed. Horovitz-Rabin, ibid.; ed. Lauterbach, II, p. 265) combines the "field" of Deuteronomy with the other particulars mentioned in Exodus, to build a sequence of the type general-particular-general:

> When Deuteronomy says "his field", it specifies a particular item which can be acquired and disposed of [so that the law applies to everything of that nature, and only of that nature].

However, the Sages paid no attention to the variation in the order of the particulars. But Hizzequni did, and it is interesting to note how his comment reflects the realities of life in his day (perhaps also in ours):

> At this point Moses arranges the sequence according to the way young men behave: first they desire to have a wife, and after that a house; then a manservant, a maidservant, fields and vineyards. But in Exodus the Torah sets matters forth in the order recommended by the wise, who first acquire a house, then a wife, then a manservant and a maidservant, and then an ox and an ass.

7. YOUR CATTLE — YOUR OX, YOUR ASS, ALL YOUR CATTLE

Again, Exodus and Deuteronomy differ. Here too, the discrepancy gives the Midrash opportunity for an exposition of the type general-particular-general. The Mishnah (B.Q. V: 5) reads:

> The laws concerning animals, such as help in loading and unloading, the ban on cross-breeding, the prohibition to work them on the Sabbath, and so on ... apply not only to an ox, but to any other animal, as well as to non-domestic creatures, to fowl and the like.

In discussing this, the Bavli (B.Q. 54b) adduces scriptural proof for each specific law, thus:

The law of loading and unloading can be derived from the Sabbath law, since both refer to "ass"; similarly with the law of muzzling, since both refer to "ox". But how do we know that the terms used in the Sabbath law are intended to have general application? This we know from a tradition transmitted by Rabbi José in the name of Rabbi Ishmael:[23] The Decalogue in Exodus reads "Your manservant and your maidservant and your cattle", while the Decalogue in Deuteronomy[24] reads "Your ox and your ass and all your cattle". But surely your ox and ass are included in "All your cattle"?[25] Why then are they sepcified? To let us know that just as non-domestic creatures are included in this context, so too are they in other contexts. Thus we have a general — "Your cattle" — in the Exodus Decalogue, followed by a particular — "your ox and your ass" in the Deuteronomy Decalogue. The rule is: When a general term is followed by a specific thing or things, the general term applies only to the specified particulars, so that the law would apply only to your ox and your ass, but not to anything else. However, the Commandment in Deuteronomy goes on to sum up with a repetition of the general term — "and all your cattle". This brings into play a different rule, namely: When a general term is followed by a specification, which is then summed up by a general term, the particular(s) specified serve, not to limit, but purely to illustrate the general term. In the present case, the particulars are examples of living creatures; therefore the law includes all living creatures.

In this passage, the tradition is attributed to Rabbi José, citing Rabbi Ishmael. The same tradition occurs in a different context in the *Mekhilta de R. Simeon bar Yoḥai* (p. 186), where the subject is the law of negligence for leaving an open pit uncovered, "so that an ox or an ass falls into it" (Ex. 21. 33):[26]

Rabbi José says, in the name of Rabbi Ishmael: Here Scripture says "ox or ass", and in the Sabbath Commandment it says[27] "ox

23   Tos. B.Q., 6. 19.
24   Var.
25   Var.
26   Note the remarks of J.N. Epstein, above n. 12, on this passage.
27   The ms. shows a scribal erasure at this point.

or ass". Just as there it means every sort of cattle, or beast or fowl, here too in the context of torts, it means every sort of cattle, beast or fowl.

In the *Mekhilta de R. Ishmael* (*Nezikin*, chap X; cf. ed. Lauterbach, III, p. 74) the attribution to R. José is omitted. Also, this same tradition can be found, but in reverse order, in *Midrash Tannaim* on Deuteronomy (p. 22, taken verbatim from *Midrash ha-Gadol*):

> R. José says in the name of R. Ishmael: Here [in the Sabbath law] Scripture says "your ox and your ass", and there [in the law of torts] it says "an ox or an ass". Just as there it means every sort of cattle, beast or fowl, here too, in the context of Sabbath rest, it means every sort of cattle, beast or fowl.

I suggest, albeit with some diffidence, that what we have here is a text that has been tampered with by someone insufficiently learned. After all, the Talmud as quoted above makes the Sabbath law the basis from which the principle governing torts is derived — and not the other way around!

On this variance between the two Decalogues Ibn Ezra also has a brief comment: "'Your ox and your ass and all your cattle' — particular terms followed by a general one. Earlier [in Exodus] there was only a general term. Taken together, both versions thus come to the same thing".

8. *THAT IT MAY GO WELL WITH YOU*

In Deuteronomy, the Fifth Commandment has the added words "that it may go well with you". Ibn Ezra comments: "There are some who say that this is an intimation of the world-to-come". On the other hand, Obadiah Sforno (Italy, sixteenth century) writes: "That it may go well with you even in this world, as the Sages say: 'These are the commandments which yield fruit in this life, and continue to yield fruit in the world-to-come as well: honoring father and mother, etc. etc.' " (Peah, I:1). The comment by Ibn Ezra derives from a rabbinic teaching about the law of freeing the mother bird (Deut. 22. 6–7):

> "That you may long endure and that it may go well with you": The first phrase refers to that world which endures forever — the life of eternity; the second phrase describes the same world,

which is altogether good.[28] (Hul. 142a; Qid. 39b; see also Tos. Hul., concluding words).

About this extra phrase in the Fifth Commandment in Deuteronomy there is a discussion in the Babylonian Talmud:[29]

> Rabbi Hanina b. Agul asked Rabbi Hiyya bar Abba: Why is there no mention of goodness (*tov*) in the Ten Commandments in Exodus, but there is in the Decalogue in Deuteronomy? He answered: Before you ask me that, better determine whether goodness really is mentioned in the Decalogue in Deuteronomy, because I am not sure that it is![30] Why not go and ask Rabbi Tanhum b. Hanilai, who is a disciple of Rabbi Joshua b. Levi, the expert on Aggadah? So he went to see Rabbi Tanhum, and this is the answer he got: "I never heard Rabbi Joshua say anything about that question, but I did hear this from Rabbi Samuel b. Nahum: ... 'It was because the first set of tablets were destined to be broken.'" [The question is then asked] What difference does that make? The answer given by Rav Ashi was: God forbid that goodness should be absent from Israel [even for a time]!

What this midrash implies is that the phrase was not really an addition, but was spoken with the original Commandment, and left off the first tablets because they were destined to be broken.

Hizzequni offers an entirely different explanation. The phrase is indeed an addition! "In the first set of Commandments the letter *tet* does not appear. Therefore the phrase is added, so that the entire Hebrew alphabet will be represented".

What the *Midrash ha-Gadol* (quoted also by *Midrash Tannaim*) says on this point is rather surprising:

> The second edition of the tablets was greater than the first; for the second included "goodness", as it is written, "that it may go well (*yittav*) with you", whereas that phrase is not present in the first tablets.

---

28   Mss. Munich, Rome B, and *Or ha-Torah* derive this homily from the law of the mother-bird.
29   The text given here is based on mss. per my edition of Baba Qama, translated into Hebrew with commentary, Tel Aviv, Dvir-Masada.
30   See Tosafot, B.B. 113a, beginning *tarvayhu*.

Quite possibly this statement is not derived from any midrashic source, but is the work of the compiler of the *Midrash ha-Gadol* himself.

9. PARALLELS TO THE DECALOGUE

The strong affinities between the Holiness Chapter (Leviticus 19) and the Ten Commandments are the subject of the following passage in *Leviticus Rabbah* (25. 5; ed. Margoliouth, p. 557):

> Rabbi Hiyya taught: This chapter was read at the Septennial Assembly. And why? Because most of the essentials of the Torah depend on it. Rabbi Levi said, because it contains the essence of the Ten Commandments, thus:

Decalogue	*Leviticus 19*
I the LORD am your God	I the LORD am your God (v. 2)
You shall have no other ...	Do not make... molten gods (v. 4)
Do not ... take in vain	Do not swear falsely (v. 12)
Remember the Sabbath ...	Keep my Sabbaths (v. 3)
Honor your father and mother	Each one revere his mother and father (v. 3)
You shall not murder	You shall not stand upon the blood of your neighbor (v. 16)
You shall not commit adultery	Do not degrade your daughter (v. 29)
You shall not steal	You shall not steal (v. 11)
You shall not bear false witness	Do not go about as a talebearer (v. 16)[31]
You shall not covet	Love your neighbor (v. 18)

Midrash Tanḥuma quoted this tradition without attribution. It was apparently the source from which Hizzequni drew his comment.

10. THE TEN COMMANDMENTS EVERY DAY

When describing the ancient Temple service, the Mishnah tells us (Tamid, V:1):

31   See comment of Margoliouth ad loc.

> The priest-in-charge said to those on duty: Recite one
> benediction! They did so. Then they recited the Ten Command-
> ments; the Shema (Deut. 6. 4–9); "If then you obey" (Deut. 11.
> 13–21); and the law of the fringes (Num. 15. 37–41).

The Talmud Yerushalmi (Ber. III:3c) takes up this Mishnah, and after
discussing which were the "benedictions", continues:

> Both Rav Mathna and Rav Samuel bar Nahmani[32] stated that by
> rights the Ten Commandments should be recited every day.[33]
> Why then is this not done? Because of the ill-will[34] of the *Minim*.
> It became necessary to deny their claim that these Ten were all
> that were given to Moses at Mount Sinai.

Something similar is recorded in the Talmud Bavli (ibid. 12a):

> Rabbi Judah quoted Samuel as saying that people wanted to
> recite the Ten Commandments along with the Shema outside the
> Temple[35] but the practice had long been given up because of the
> misrepresentations (*ta'aromet*) of the *Minim*. (Gloss by Rashi:
> To prevent them from telling the unlearned that the rest of the
> Torah is untrue; and arguing that only what God spoke at Sinai
> should be read to the people. *He adds*: The Minim were the
> disciples of Jesus).[36]

The Yerushalmi also has the following (Ibid., I, 8, 3c):

> Why do we recite these two[37] paragraphs every day? Rabbi
> Simon says, because they speak of "lying down" and "rising up".
> Rabbi Levi says, because these two paragraphs contain, by
> inference, all the Ten Commandments [By taking phrases from
> the Shema (Deut. 6. 4–9) and *Vehayah im Shamo'a* (11. 13–21),
> one can get the following parallels:

32 Var.
33 That is, in public, before the Shema.
34 *tinat*; so ms. Leyden, *Yerushalmi Fragments* (p. 30) the *Arukh*, etc. In ms. Leyden
    the word has been corrected by another hand, to read *ta'anat* ("arguments",
    "claims"), a reading adopted by the Venice edition.
35 Rashi: They wanted to include it in the reading of the Shema.
36 So the Venice edition, s.v. *ovedei avodah zarah*.
37 Mss. Leyden, Rome, and *Yerushalmi Fragments* read "two". This conforms to
    Rabbi Simon's comment. But for Rabbi Levi, one would have to understand
    "three", because his homily includes the law of the fringes.

(*Decalogue*)	(*Shema*)
I the LORD am your God	Hear O Israel, the LORD is our God
You shall have no other gods	The LORD alone
You shall not swear falsely by the name of the LORD	You must love the LORD (He who loves the King will not misuse His name)[38]
Remember the Sabbath day	so that you shall remember
Honor your father and your mother	so that you may long endure in the land
You shall not murder	you will soon perish (he who kills will be killed)
You shall not commit adultery	do not follow heart and eyes in your lustful urge[39]
You shall not steal	You will gather your grain (not your neighbor's)
You shall not bear false witness	I the LORD am your God (The LORD your God is Truth: Jer. 10.10)
You shall not covet your neighbor's house	Inscribe them on the doorposts of *your* house

In connection with the Fourth Commandment, Rabbi Judah says, "This Sabbath Commandment equals all the other commandments of the Torah put together, as we read (Neh. 9. 14) 'You made your holy Sabbath known to them, and ordained for them mitzvot, statutes and Torah' ". In connection with the Seventh Commandment, Rabbi Levi says, "The heart and the eye are the two panderers who lead man to sin, as we read (Prov. 23. 26) 'My son, give me your heart, and let your eyes watch my ways'. The Holy one says: if you give me your heart and your eyes, I will know that you belong to me.[40] On the Ninth Commandment, the Talmud asks: "What is meant by 'Truth'? Rabbi Abun says, the Truth is that He is the Living God and King of the universe. Rabbi Levi says, in this Commandment the Holy One tells us: "If you bear false witness against your neighbor

38   Var.
39   Taking in the whole verse.
40   Var.

I treat you as though you had testified that I did not create heaven and earth".[41]

It is noteworthy that in nineteenth-century Sephardic prayerbooks the Shema is printed accompanied by the Ten Commandments, with each Commandment in its appropriate place as assigned by the tradition quoted above.

11. SENTENCES AND CANTILLATIONS

There are two distinct ways of breaking the Decalogue up into sentences:

A. One way treats each Commandment as a unit, resulting in ten sentences, as follows: 1) I the LORD. 2) You shall have no other.[42] 3) You shall not swear falsely. 4) Remember. 5) Honor. 6) You shall not murder. 7) You shall not commit adultery. 8) You shall not steal. 9) You shall not bear false witness. 10) You shall not covet.

B. The other method uses short sentences. The longer Commandments are broken up into several verses, while the very terse Commandments are combined, with this result: 1) I the LORD. 2) You shall have no other.[43] 3) You shall not make. 4) You shall not bow down. 5) But showing kindness. 6) You shall not swear falsely. 7) Remember. 8) Six days shall you labor. 9) But the seventh day. 10) For in six days. 11) Honor. 12) You shall not murder; you shall not commit adultery; you shall not steal; you shall not bear false witness. 13) You shall not covet.

These differences in verse arrangement are accompanied by corresponding differences in cantillation — and sometimes even by different vowelling. The cantillation that goes with method A is more dramatic, and full of vocal flourishes. It is known as "the upper mode" (*ta'm ha-'elyon*). In the ordinary copies of the Pentateuch, intended for use in the synagogue or home, the body of the text usually shows method B, with a Decalogue appended to Exodus and Deuteronomy displaying method A, for the convenience of those who are to read the

41 Part of this is missing in *Yerushalmi Fragments*.
42 That is the way it is in Saadiah's Bible, and in the text used by Jacob b. Habib. The copies of the Pentateuch in use today cantillate "I the LORD" and "You shall have no other" as one sentence.
43 The Leningrad manuscript (edited by A. Dothan) shows "I the LORD" and "You shall have no other" as one sentence.

Ten Commandments in public. However, full Hebrew Bibles frequently print the two systems in combination in the body of the text, so that one word usually displays two different cantillation signs, and sometimes there are even conflicting vowels. This has led to no small amount of confusion.

The author of *'Eyn Ya'aqov* (Jacob b. Habib, 1460–1510) in his commentary on the Aggada of the Yerushalmi (Sheq. VI) writes:

> In books written by expert scribes and punctators we find the Ten Commandments written with two sets of vowels on some words, and two sets of cantillations. For example, in the Second Commandment, the *nun* of *panay* is written with both a *qames* and a *patah* (פָּנַי).[44] The same thing happens with the Sixth and Seventh Commandments — double vowels and two sets of cantillation signs. In addition, in those Commandments every *taw* is written both soft and hard — looking self-contradictory. Now the real reason for all this is well known: there are two different ways of reading the Ten Commandments. One applies when an individual reads them by himself. He does not have to take care to keep each Commandment as a unit, so that the Second Commandment, which is a long one, he reads as several verses, and the same holds good for "Remember the Sabbath day". As for the last four Commandments, which are short, the individual puts them all into one verse. However, one who reads at public worship must read each Commandment as a separate entity, whether it is long or short. This makes it inevitable that there will be variations in both the cantillation and the vocalization. A proof of this is the fact that the First Commandment does not have two systems of vowels and cantillations, because it is short, and it is proper to read it as one verse.

The Italian Rabbi Jedidiah Norsi (early seventeenth century), in his work *Minhat Shai*, starts his comment on the Decalogue by quoting the above remarks of Jacob b. Habib, and after discussing them proceeds to quote Menahem da Fano (Italy, 1548-1620) on Torah-

---

44   Several years ago it was reported that the French ambassador in Jerusalem asked a
      Bible scholar why there were two vowels on the *nun* of *panay* — and was unable to
      get an answer!

readers who attempt to read *both* vowels on the same letter. "It is a grievous error, and he who does this is to be silenced, and he will be held to account" [presumably in the afterlife]. Menahem later quotes Hizzequni (see below) on the separation of the shorter Commandments into distinct verses; and cites the Zohar on the subject:

> Were it not for the fact that the cantillations punctuate with a marked pause after "Thou shalt not!" (steal, etc.) we would have had to treat the prohibitions as absolute; whereas there are circumstances when it is permissible to mislead (lit. = *steal the mind*), such as asking a witness an innocent-sounding question in order to get at the truth. "You shall not" (pause) "steal" — sometimes you shall!

This is reminiscent of the treatment in the Talmud (B.M. 30a) of Deut. 22. 1: "If you should see ... and you should remain indifferent" — sometimes you *should* remain indifferent!

The interested reader will find a thoroughgoing study of the "upper mode" of cantillating the Ten Commandments in *Havanat Hamiqra*, by Wolf Heidenheim, the nineteenth-century scholar of the liturgy.

When is it in order to use this "upper mode"? Hizzequni writes the following:

> Most of the Ten Commandments are equipped with two different cantillation signs. On Shavuot (which is a sort of re-enactment of the Sinaitic revelation, and when the Commandments are read at public worship along with the Targum) the whole of the Commandment "You shall have no other" is read with the more expressive cantillations, and so too is "Remember the Sabbath day"; so that each of these is treated as a single verse, each Commandment by itself; and the four short "Thou shalt not"s are read with the simpler cantillation, yielding four verses for the four Commandments. But when the Book of Exodus is read as part of the annual cycle, and the turn of Exodus 20 rolls around, "You shall have no other" and "Remember the Sabbath" are chanted the simple way, each of them becoming four verses. On that occasion, the Commandments "You shall not murder", etc. are read with the more expanded cantillation, and become one single verse, since the whole Bible does not contain any two-word sentences, apart from these "shall-nots." And as I have already explained, for Shavuot there is also available a more elaborate

cantillation for "I the LORD" and "You shall have no other", combining these two Commandments into one, as a mark of the fact that they were both spoken in one utterance.

Hizzequni makes no mention of the procedure for reading the Decalogue in Deuteronomy. One must assume that it is handled in the same way as the Commandments in Exodus.

However, the reverential emotion of those who read the Torah at public services has brought it about that it is customary among Sephardim and Oriental Jews to use the "upper mode" even on ordinary Sabbaths. The same holds good for Hasidim as well. Those Yemenite communities that follow the Sephardic rite do likewise. However, there are many Yemenite communities who read the Decalogue in the "lower mode" even on Shavuot.

12. SUMMARY

We began this study with a discussion of the midrash which says that the Ten Commandments were spoken in one utterance. Further examination revealed that as far as the Sabbath Commandment is concerned, the idea that "Remember" and "Observe" were spoken together is not even mentioned in the Yerushalmi. We also discovered that the traditional commentaries are at odds as to the meaning of this midrashic phrase.

Note was taken of Rashbam's doctrine that the Creation story is intended purely as a backdrop for the Fourth Commandment. Then we went on to discuss the variances between the two Decalogues in the Pentateuch. Finally we discussed the relationship of the Ten Commandments to the Shema, and ended up with a discussion of the special cantillation mode designed for reading the Ten Commandments at public worship.

May we conclude with the hope that the Ten Commandments will find their way into the hearts and minds of all mankind.

Translated by Gershon Levi

8. THE TEN COMMANDMENTS AND THE NEW TESTAMENT

DAVID FLUSSER

That Christianity is a daughter religion of Judaism; that the Hebrew Bible, along with the New Testament is part of Holy Writ for all churches and denominations; and that Jesus and his disciples were Jews thoroughly familiar with the Jewish Scriptures — all this goes more or less without saying. Included in the legacy of Christianity from Judaism is a high regard for the Ten Commandments. Indeed, from the time of the earliest Fathers of the Church, Christians assigned an even more exalted position to the Decalogue than Judaism did.

The reason for this is to be found in the mounting tension between the new religion and the Jewish way of life. Gentile Christians were not required to observe the many commandments of the Jewish Torah; and in order to draw a clear distinction between the two religions, Christians reasoned that their teachings were superior to those of Judaism. Some of them went so far as to claim that the Jewish Torah had been superseded.

Ultimately, the attitude of what became the Catholic Church was expressed most clearly in one of its principal hymns — the *Pange Lingua*, composed by Thomas Aquinas in the thirteenth century. The hymn describes how Jesus partook of his last Seder, observing the laws of the Torah to the letter. Then, when it was time to break the matzah and distribute it to the participants, he surrendered himself to be eaten by his disciples. When he said "This is my body", he transmuted the bread into his flesh. In the same way, he turned the wine into his blood. By that act he created a new sanctity. "The old document had to give way to the new form of worship." In this poetic fashion the great Catholic thinker expressed one of the important motifs characterizing the attitude of the Church to the Jewish Bible. The full authority of the latter had been set aside by the coming of Jesus and his death on the

219

cross. The mitzvot dealing with the ritual observances of Judaism and
its forms of worship were no longer binding on Christians. More than
that, and as time went on, and under varying circumstances, it became
actually forbidden to observe those Jewish commandments.

In the present paper we do not propose to study the fluctuations in
this attitude over the years. But one thing we do wish to point out. The
high valuation which Christians assigned to the Ten Commandments
was at no time affected by changes of attitude to the "Old Testament".
Quite the contrary. It was exactly the broad general character of the
Decalogue, by contrast to the detailed mitzvot of Judaism, that
recommended it to Christians.

For Christians, the Ten Commandments are the words of the Living
God, and their authority remains undiminished. This, despite the
difficulty created by the Fourth Commandment, which deals with the
observance of the Sabbath. That challenge was at first met by
interpreting the Commandment in an abstract way, as meaning
faithfulness to God; and then, at a later period, as referring to Sunday,
after Constantine had made the first day of the week the Christian
Sabbath.[1] But because, among other reasons, the Sabbath is mentioned
in the Decalogue, which is binding on Christians, modern times have
seen the rise of Sabbatarian sects who keep the seventh day.

It is not part of our present task, I regret to say, to deal with the
importance of the Ten Commandments in ancient Judaism, even
though a fresh look at that subject holds promise of some interesting
conclusions, in the light of recent advances in New Testament and
Patristic studies, as well as in Judeo-Christian and Gnostic sources.
However, we shall touch here only lightly on that area. So too, we shall
not go into the question of the order of the Sixth and Seventh
Commandments, a matter to which we have already devoted a brief
study.[2]

---

1   Texts on the subject of the weekly day of rest — Shabbat or Sunday — from the
     birth of Christianity up to the last of the Church Fathers, have been collected and
     explained by Willy Rordorf in *Sabbat und Sonntag in der Alten Kirche*, Zurich
     1972.
2   In what follows it should be remembered that the sequence "You shall not murder >
     You shall not commit adultery" was not the only order of the Commandments
     known during the Second Commonwealth. The opposite arrangement (adultery >
     murder) was also extant. The former sequence is represented by the masoretic text
     and by the text of Deuteronomy found at Qumran (and not yet published). The

The fact is that the New Testament does not use the term "Ten Commandments" even once; and that the references to them that do occur are confined to the last five — the socio-ethical Commandments ("between one person and another"). Even then, these five are not mentioned as a unit, except in one recurring passage which is interesting in itself, and deserves our special attention.

The passage occurs in Matthew (19. 16–22); Mark (10. 17–22) and Luke (18. 18–23). It describes an encounter between Jesus and a "rich man".[3] The man asks Jesus "Master, what good shall I do that I may gain eternal life?" That is how the question is put in Matthew 19. 16. But in Luke (18. 18) and in Mark (10. 17) the questioner asks "Good master, what shall I do?" etc. This form of address ("My good Rabbi") is characteristic of Greek style, but is unnatural and artificial in Hebrew or Aramaic.[4] Consequently,the wording of the question in Matthew is to be preferred — "Rabbi, what good shall I do?" Luke the Greek, and in his footsteps Mark, were misled by their Greek sense of language. Hence their use of the phrase "My good Rabbi", even though this usage is completely out of place in the Hebrew environment of Jesus himself.

This peculiar form of address, derived as it is from Greek speech, had a distorting influence on the way Jesus' reply is recorded in Luke (18. 19) and in Mark (10. 19). They have him saying to the rich man, "Why do you call me good? God alone is good." Whereas in Matthew he gives a straightforword answer to the question, "Rabbi, what good shall I

latter sequence occurs, not only in the Septuagint, but also in the Nash Papyrus, and in *Antiquitates Biblicae* (11. 10–11), which has to be sure, survived only in Latin translation, but which was originally in Hebrew. See Flusser, "Do not Commit Adultery, Do not Murder", *Textus*, IV, Jerusalem 1964, pp. 220–224.

3   Only in Matthew 19. 19 and 22 is the rich man called "young". But in both Luke and Mark the rich man says "All this have I observed *from my youth*". In my opinion this latter reading is to be preferred.

4   See the hesitant handling of this by V. Taylor, *The Gospel According to St. Mark*, London 1957, p. 425; and by E. Klostermann, in: *Das Markusevangelium*, Tübingen 1971, p. 101. The attempt on the part of both these scholars to justify this reading is the outcome of the widely held, but erroneous, assumption that Mark is the oldest of the three synoptic gospels, and that Matthew and Luke are both derived from it. See Kenneth E. Bailey, *Through Peasants' Eyes: More Lucan Parables*, Grand Rapids, Mich. 1980, p. 162. We do not regard as relevant to the issue fragment no. 11 of the extra-canonical *Gospel According to the Hebrews*, since that pseudepigraphical work is a derivative of the Greek text of Matthew. Probably the judgment nearest to the mark is that of W. R. Farmer, in his *The Synoptic Problem*, London 1964, p. 160.

do?" He says, "Why do you ask? There is one that is good." Matthew uses the masculine gender; that is, the translator of the underlying Hebrew text assumed that Jesus was referring to God.

Now we can undertand that it was not only the Greek *Sprachgefühl* of Luke (and following him Mark) that caused the distortion of the preceding question. If Jesus had actually answered by saying "There is only One good", he would have been evading the question that had been asked.

It seems probable that the Greek translator of the original Hebrew text misunderstood. When Jesus had said "There is only one good", he had meant the Torah and the commandments. He was not referring to God. This becomes clear the moment we read on. "You know the commandments", he says (Luke 18. 20; Mark 10. 19); or, if we follow the reading in Matthew (10. 16 ff.): "Rabbi, what good shall I do?"... "Why do you ask me what is good? There is only one good. If you would enter life, keep the commandments".

The thrust of this exchange is perfectly clear in Hebrew. The misunderstanding arose from the fact that there is no differentiation in the Hebrew language between the masculine gender and the neuter. The ancient translator thought that when Jesus said "The good is one", he meant God. But the continuing narrative makes it clear that he meant the Torah.[5] Not only that, but the rich man's query echoes the question implied by Micah (6. 8): "He has told you, O man, what is good, and what the LORD requires of you." In addition, Jesus' answer, as we have interpreted it, reflects a well known midrash on Proverbs 4. 2: "For I give you good instruction — forsake not my teaching".[6] Even the turn of phrase "there is only one good" (lit. "there is none good but one")[7] reminds one of the midrash in Avot VI.3 on the same verse: "there is none good but Torah".

In the light of this, we may understand the encounter as follows: Question: "What good thing shall I do so as to merit eternal life?"and

---

5   My friend Robert Lindsay agrees with me on this, but is willing to go further, and
    postulate that both Luke (18. 19) and Mark (10. 18) preserve an erroneous
    translation of Jesus' original words; and that their reading should be, "What do
    you mean, 'good'"?

6   Add *Midrash Tehillim* 90a to the citations given by Strack–Billerbeck, I, p. 803.

7   By referring to ancient rabbinic sources we believe that we have been able to
    reconstruct the original words of Jesus. Matthew reads: "One is the good". Luke
    and Mark read: "There is none good but one, the Lord".

Jesus answers "Why do you ask me about the good? You know the commandments:[8] Do not murder; do not commit adultery;[9] do not steal; do not bear false witness,[10] honor your father and your mother".[11]

So then, the rich man wants to achieve eternal life — and Jesus refers him to the commandments of the Torah. The connection between the Torah and eternal life had long been taken for granted. It is expressed in the ancient benediction which is recited after reading from the Torah: "Thanks be to Him who gave us the Torah of truth, and so implanted eternal life within us".[12] Besides, the phrase "Torah of life" appears in Ben Sira (Wisdom of Jesus Son of Sirach) 17. 11, where we read: "He bestowed knowledge upon them, and allotted to them the Law [Torah] of life". It so happens that the Hebrew original of that sentence is not among those that have been discovered. However, we do have the Hebrew for another passage that uses the phrase: "He placed in his [Moses] hand the commandment, the Torah of life and understanding" (45. 5). Thus we see that the exchange between the rich man and Jesus corresponds nicely with ideas that were already prevalent among Jews at that time.

Notice that Jesus mentions the last five Commandments of the Decalogue. In the synoptic gospels, the list ends with the Commandment to honor one's father and mother. The fact that this, the Fifth Commandment, comes at the end of the list makes it seem likely that it was added to the text later on. Someone saw fit to append it to the original words of Jesus because fundamentally it too is a socio-ethical

---

8   The last sentence comes from Luke and Mark. According to Matthew, 19. 17–18, Jesus says, "If you want to enter life, keep the Commandments", and the other asks "Which?" and Jesus goes on to specify. It is obvious that the text in Matthew has been expanded.

9   Luke (18. 20) quotes the two Commandments in inverse order, in accordance with the Septuagint, see above, n. 2.

10   In the gospels, only the first Greek word of the Commandment in Ex. 20. 12 appears. When the same matter comes up in the Sermon on the Mount (Matt. 5. 33) a different Greek word is used ("Do not swear falsely"). At this juncture Mark (10. 19) adds: "Do not defraud". Note the variant readings; and see W. R. Farmer, loc. cit. (n. 4, above).

11   Here Matthew (19. 19) adds at the end, "you shall love your neighbor as yourself". As we shall see, this addition is significant.

12   About the antiquity of this benediction and its original meaning see D. Flusser, *Sanctus und Gloria in Abraham unser Vater*, Leiden 1963, pp. 141–143).

rule, even though in the Hebrew Bible it is included in the first half of the Decalogue.[12a]

In the New Testament it is not only Jesus of Nazareth who quotes from the second half only of the Decalogue. Paul does the same thing. In his Epistle to the Romans he says:

> Owe no one anything, except to love one another; for he who who loves his neighbor has fulfilled the law. The commandments: "You shall not commit adultery, You shall not kill, You shall not steal, You shall not covet", and any other commandment, are summed up in this sentence: "You shall love your neighbor as yourself." Love does no wrong to a neighbor; therefore love is the fulfilling of the law (Rom 13. 3-10).

Here we see that "Love your neighbor" is perceived as a general rule, the detailed implementation of which is set down in the second half of the Decalogue. Love of one's fellowman is also seen as the broad general principle of the Torah in Paul's Epistle to the Galatians, 5. 14.

One might have thought that Paul's stress on the second half of the Decalogue came from his ambivalence towards the ritual observances of Judaism — were it not for the fact that the same thing can be found in the Epistle of James (2. 8–11), a document thoroughly Jewish in spirit, committed to the continued observance of the Jewish Halakhah. Indeed, there are those who claim — correctly in my opinion — that the Epistle of James is a polemic against Paul's critical attitude to the mitzvot. Despite this, James too quotes only the second half of the Decalogue:

> If you really fulfil the royal law, according to the scripture, "You shall love your neighbor as yourself", you do well. But if you show partiality, you commit sin, and are convicted by the law as transgressors. For whoever keeps the whole law but fails in one point has become guilty of all of it. For he who said "Do not

---

12a For the whole question of the Jewish and early Christian *Gattung* based on the second half of the Decalogue, the definition of Christian ethics in the oldest Christian apology, written by Aristides, is of extreme importance (see there, 15. 4–5). This passage too is based on the second half of the Decalogue, mentions the love of one's neighbor, and quotes the Golden Rule (in its negative formulation). As in the passage about the rich young man (Matt. 19. 18–19 and parallels) the duty to honor one's father and mother is also included in the apology of Aristides.

commit adultery", said also "Do not kill". If you do not commit adultery but do kill, you have become a transgressor of the law.[13]

It is important to note that in this Epistle, too, the second half of the Decalogue is related to one all-encompassing principle — love of one's neighbor.[14] In addition, another Jewish idea is expressed, namely that violating one commandment is the equivalent of violating them all.[15] At the same time, the author of James confined this idea to the second half of the Ten Commandments. What he says is based on the following midrash:

> You might have thought that a person is not guilty unless he transgresses all these commandments; therefore does the Torah say "You shall not murder, You shall not commit adultery, You shall not steal, You shall not bear false witness, You shall not covet" (Ex. 20. 13), in order to make one liable for each commandment separately. That being so, why does Deuteronomy join all these commandments together, saying "You shall not murder *and* you shall not commit adultery *and*, etc." (Deut. 5. 17)? It is to teach us that they are all interrelated. When a person breaks one of them, he will end up by breaking them all.[16]

This midrash rests, of course, on one of the differences between the two texts of the Decalogue. In Exodus, each of the five concluding "Thou shalt nots" stands alone, while in Deuteronomy they are all joined

---

13 The command to love one's neighbor is designated here "The Royal Law". Rabbi Akiba called that command "The Great Summary of the Torah", and, as we shall see, Jesus called it that too. It would seem, then, that the Greek phrase simply adjusts the Hebrew idiom to the Greek way of thinking. It can be assumed that the Greek phrase in James 2. 8 came into being in Hellenistic-Jewish circles.

14 In the passage quoted above from Romans (13. 8–10) we find, after the Tenth Commandment, the words, "And if there is still another commandment, etc.". At this point there is an important observation to be made: when Jesus answers the rich man, Matthew (19.19) adds to the second half of the Decalogue the verse "You shall love your neighbor as yourself".

15 See, for instance, M. Dibelius, *Der Brief des Jakobus*, Göttingen 1957, p. 135; and especially Yitzhaq Baer, "The Historical Foundations of the Halakhah" (Hebrew), *Zion*, 27 (1962), pp. 127–128. Baer might well have included *James* along with the other sources he refers to. Parallels in Hellenistic-Jewish literature can be adduced: e.g. Philo, *Legatio ad Gaium*, 115–117, and IV Macc. 5. 20.

16 *Mekhilta de R. Simeon bar Yoḥai* on Ex. 20. 14, ed. Epstein–Melammed, Jerusalem 1955, p. 154.

together by the conjunctive *waw*. Hence, "they are all interrelated. When a person breaks one, he will end up by breaking them all".

This is exactly what is stated in the Epistle of James (2. 10–11). The resemblance to the midrash will be even stronger if we read verse 11 thus: "For he who said 'Do not commit adultery' said '*and* do not kill' ", and so on.[17] To be sure, in the light of the Greek text, the translation we offered above seems preferable. But, even so, the fact remains that in the background of James stands the midrash just quoted.

We have seen, then, that in the synoptic gospels as well as in the other books of the New Testament, it is the second half of the Decalogue that is quoted, usually coupled with the command to love one's neighbor.[17a] The latter is called "the royal law" in James (2. 8). The Epistle to the Romans (13. 8–10) says that whoever loves his fellowman has fulfilled the rest of the Torah, and that the commandment to do so sums up the second half of the Decalogue. In Galatians (5. 14) Paul says, without reference to the Decalogue, that the whole Torah is fulfilled in the commandment "Love your neighbor as yourself."

So we see that these passages in the New Testament say two things

---

17   *James* adheres to the order of the Septuagint.

17a A link between the Golden Rule and the second half of the Decalogue is offered in an instructive excerpt from an early Jewish-Christian work preserved in the writings attributed to Clemens Romanus. These writings consist of two works, both of which are reworkings of the same source, which in turn emanates from the Jewish-Christian sect called "Ebionites". The excerpt is found in both reworkings, and can be seen in *Die Pseudoklementinen*, ed. B. Rehm, I, *Homilien*, Berlin 1969, p. 118 (*Hom.* VII, 4, 3–4); and II, *Recognitionen*, Berlin 1965, p. 253 (*Rec.* VIII, 56, 7–8). The first of these works quotes the Golden Rule in the positive form, while the second gives it in the negative version. The context makes it appear that the original source had it in the negative. The text speaks of "one unique saying as transmitted to the God-fearing Jews", namely "What we do not want done to us, we will not cause to be done to others; if you do not want to be killed, do not kill anybody; if you do not want anybody to commit adultery with your wife, do not commit adultery with anyone else's wife; if you don't want anything of yours stolen, do not steal anything that belongs to someone else". This passage, then, is independent evidence of the tradition linking the command to love one's neighbor — represented here by the Golden Rule — and the second half of the Decalogue. We have seen that tradition in Romans 13. 8–10; in James, 20. 8–11, and in the episode of the rich man, as told in Matthew 19. 18–19. Here it appears in a Jewish-Christian composition, and from all appearances does not derive from the passages in the New Testament. The mention of God-fearing Jews in connection with the Golden Rule may be an indication that the entire excerpt was derived by the Jewish-Christian author from a Jewish source.

about the sentence that commands love of one's neighbor. On the one hand, it is presented as a summary of the whole Torah; and on the other hand, it is called a summary of the second half of the Decalogue. The first of these approaches is reflected in the teaching of the Jewish Sages, insofar as their words have come down to us. Rabbi Akiba, in his well-known comment on "You shall love your neighbor as yourself" (Lev. 19. 18), says: "This is the great general rule of the Torah" (*Sifra Qedoshim*, II).[18] Even though the term "great general rule" (*kelal gadol*) does not, in and of itself, necessarily mean "summary", Rabbi Akiba probably meant just that.

In any event, there is the famous reply of Hillel to the pagan: "What is hateful to you, do not do to anyone else — that is the whole Torah, and all the rest is commentary [*perusha* = specifying the details] — go and learn it." According to *Aboth de Rabbi Nathan* (version b, 26, ed. Schechter, Vienna 1887, p. 53) this Aramaic sentence, commonly called "The Golden Rule", is attributed to Rabbi Akiba, who calls it "the great general rule of the Torah".[19]

So it developed that in Judaism the Golden Rule became another form of the biblical "Love your neighbor as yourself"; indeed, it is appended to the Aramaic Targum of that verse — a verse that was perceived in certain circles as a summary of the entire Torah.

In the New Testament as well, the following occurs as a teaching spoken by Jesus: "Whatever you wish that men would do to you, do so to them; for this is the law and the prophets" (Matt. 7. 12). Here we find the "great general rule of the Torah" as the Golden Rule stated in positive terms, as against the negative formulation attributed to Hillel, Akiba and the Targum. The positive form of the rule can also be detected in the Book of Jubilees (20. 2). According to that ancient work, Abraham instructed his children and his posterity

> to observe the way of the LORD, to act righteously, to love each his neighbor, and to behave towards all men as one treats oneself.

There can be no doubt that here we have the Golden Rule in its positive form attached to the biblical command to love one's neighbor, even

18 See S. Safrai, *Rabbi Akiba ben Joseph* (Hebrew), Jerusalem 1971, p. 219.
19 For what follows, see D. Flusser, "A New Sensitivity in Judaism" in *Judaism and the Origins of Christianity*, Jerusalem 1988, pp. 469–492. = HTR 61 (1968) pp. 107–127. The citation from the Book of Jubilees is based on Klaus Berger, *Das Buch der Jubiläen*, Gütersloh 1981.

though the Ethiopic text is unclear, because the Ethiopian translator, or perhaps his predecessor the Greek translator, did not understand the original Hebrew of the Book of Jubilees.

It should be observed that this passage in Jubilees sees the command to love one's neighbor — taken together with the Golden Rule — as an expression of "the way of the LORD"; to be sure, not the sole expression because it has Abraham adding other commandments. But in any event, this evidence from Jubilees is of considerable importance, because it expresses the idea that love of one's fellowman is one of the prime essentials of "the way of the LORD". On the other hand, we have seen — so far only on the basis of quotations from the New Testament — that the verse commanding love of one's neighbor was also thought of as summarizing the second half of the Ten Commandments. Apparently, then, there were two different views of the verse about loving one's fellowman — two views that existed side by side.

(It is interesting to note the following from an old Hebrew translation of *Tales of Sanbar* (ed. Morris Epstein, Philadelphia 1967, p. 296). Towards the end of the story, the hero advises the king, "What you yourself hate, do not do to your neighbor; and love your people as yourself." So runs one group of mss.; and it is clear that we are dealing with a translation from some other language. In a second group of mss. the Golden Rule and the quotation about loving one's neighbor have been corrected to conform with the classical biblical and talmudic formulations — with the Golden Rule quoted in the Aramaic formulation of Hillel: "What is hateful to you do not do to your fellowman, and your shall love your neighbor as yourself.")

In order to be clear about this, we must bear in mind that during the Second Commonwealth there were those who believed that the entire Torah could be expressed in two of its most sweeping imperatives. The first of these is Deuteronomy 6. 5: "You shall love the LORD your God", covering the commandments between man and God; while the second is Leviticus 19. 18, "You shall love your neighbor as yourself", which covers man's duties to his fellowman. So we find Jesus saying, in answer to the question "What is the great summary[20] in the law?"

---

20   Because of his inability of find a suitable Greek word for the Hebrew *kelal*, the author, working from a Hebrew original, always falls back on the Greek equivalent for "commandment". Paul, however, was able to overcome this linguistic difficulty, as can be seen from a glance at the Greek text of Romans, 13.9, and of Galatians 5.14.

You shall love the LORD your God with all your heart and with all your soul and with all your mind. This is the first great summary. And a second is like it, you shall love your neighbor as yourself.[21] On these two summaries depend all the law[22] (Matt. 22. 37–40).

When Jesus said that the two great general rules in the Torah are like one another, he was right on the mark. Both commandments begin with the word *ve'ahavta* ("you shall love"). And when he said that the whole Torah depends on these two teachings, he was right in line with Jewish tradition; the *Sifra* uses the identical phrasing when it says of the Holiness Chapter (*Qedoshim*, Leviticus 19, which incidentally includes the second of Jesus' two rules): "Most of the essentials of the Torah depend on this chapter." And when he said that the whole Torah depends on these two general rules, he was in a sense echoing Hillel the Elder, who taught that the Golden Rule is "the whole Torah; the rest is commentary (specification)" — that is to say, the entire Torah is encapsulated in the Golden Rule, while the remaining commandments spell out the details of that one great general rule. In those days, as we know, *perush* meant "giving the particulars".[22a]

The earliest text we have in which these two great rules are quoted side by side is the Book of Jubilees, a work written originally in Hebrew about the year 150 B.C.E.[23] In chapter 36 of that book we find Isaac adjuring his sons with a great oath. The latter phrase is especially instructive, because Haninah the Vice-High Priest is quoted as saying that "the whole world depends" on the command to love one's neighbor; and that the entire people was placed under oath at Mount Sinai to observe it.[24] The exact phrase "a great oath" occurs in the parallel

---

21 In the gospels, the question is put to Jesus by someone. Perhaps that is the way it really happened.

22 The author of the gospel adds, "and the prophets".

22a See Chaim Rabin, *The Zadokite Documents*, Oxford 1954, p. 24 (to C. D. 6. 14).

23 See my article in *HTR* cited above (n. 19). For the present discussion, the words attributed to Noah in Jubilees 7. 20 are especially important.

24 *Aboth de Rabbi Nathan*, version B, 26, ed. Schechter p. 53. The entire text of this passage is in an unsatisfactory condition. Perhaps, instead of "the whole world depends on it", we should read "the whole Torah depends on it". In any event, it does seem likely that the latter was the original wording, because it conforms to the many passages we have cited in the present article. Nevertheless, it is possible that Rabbi Haninah the Vice-High Priest deliberately changed the traditional wording,

saying by Rabbi Simeon ben Eleazar: "It was with a great oath that this command 'You shall love your neighbor as yourself' was uttered".[25] On the other hand, we have already seen that the selfsame Book of Jubilees (20. 2) regards love of neighbor as an important aspect of the "way of the LORD" followed by Abraham.

Thus we learn that the two great rules of the Torah — love of God and love of man — are already juxtaposed in this pseudepigraphical work, dating without doubt from the second pre-Christian century. These are the very rules of which Jesus was to speak some generations later. Apart from this, the same two rules appear yoked together again in another extra-canonical work — *The Testaments of the Twelve Patriarchs*. This is a book which purports to record the last words of each of Jacob's twelve sons.[26]

In addition, the two great principles of love of God and love of man, along with the Golden Rule, are given explicitly as a definition of "the way of life" at the beginning of *The Teaching of the Twelve Apostles* (*Didache*), an early Christian work which is based on a still earlier, pre-Christian Jewish source (commonly named "The Two Ways"). All of these writings come from that trend of thought out of which the Essene sect emerged.

In the light of the foregoing, the question arises: where did Jesus get the idea of the two great general principles, with their implications for our understanding of the Ten Commandments? Was it from the Essene school of thought, or from the Pharisaic-Rabbinic world-outlook? So

because he wanted to stress that love of one's fellowman is a matter "on which the whole world depends". Comp. Matthew 5.18, and corresponding passages in rabbinic literature.

25   *Aboth de Rabbi Nathan*, version A, chapter 16. ed. Schechter, p. 64; cf. Goldin, *The Fathers According to Rabbi Nathan*, New Haven, 1955, p. 86.

26   *Testament of Dan*, 5.3; *Issachar*, 5.2 and 7.6; *Zebulun*, 5.1 and *Joseph*, 11.1. For what follows, see D. Flusser, "There Are Two Ways", in: *Judaism and Christian Origins* (Hebrew), Tel Aviv 1979, pp. 235–252. Apart from the *Testaments of the Twelve Patriarchs* in Greek (and fragments of their original Hebrew and Aramaic that have turned up at Qumran and in the Genizah) there has also survived in Hebrew a medieval translation of a variant version of the *Testament of Naphtali*, taken from the Latin or Greek. This is readily apparent the moment one reads the opening chapter, where the two Great Rules are presented as quotations: "I command you to fear only the Lord, to worship Him and to cleave to Him... and that no one shall do to his fellowman what he does not want done to himself". Here the love of man is expressed by the Golden Rule, translated into Hebrew.

far we have found the latter trend stressing only one great rule — love of neighbor, or the Golden Rule, as the distillation of the whole Torah. To be sure, we now have a late rabbinic text[27] which resembles what Jesus said about the two great rules. But we have no assurance that the document in question is not derived, however indirectly, from the New Testament. We will get back to this document later, because, among other things, it is important for the study of the Ten Commandments.

It seems reasonable to suppose that it is merely by chance that rabbinic literature has preserved only one view, namely that the all-encompassing principle of the ethics of the Torah is love of man. It is even possible that the other point of view, which marches under the banner of *two* great principles, did not find expression in the rabbinic sources that have come down to us simply because of the great authority of Rabbi Akiba. He followed the line of those who taught that love of one's neighbor encompasses love of the Creator. After all, the Sages themselves drew a distinction, dividing sins into those committed against God, and those committed against one's fellowman (Mishnah Yoma, VIII:9).[28] In addition, it is clear that Jesus was following a rabbinic style of hermeneutics when he juxtaposed two verses that begin with the word *ve-ahavta* ("you shall love", Matt. 22. 36–40). Besides, love of God and love of man are placed side by side elsewhere in rabbinic teaching. The tractate Avot, for example, teaches that one should "Love the Eternal, and love humankind" (Av. VI:1 and VI:6).[29]

Even if we did not know that the idea of two Great Rules existed, we would have been able to deduce it from *The Testaments of the Twelve Patriarchs*, where we find such combinations as: "Love the LORD and your neighbor" (Issachar 5.2); "I have loved the LORD with all my might and in the same way I have loved all men as though they were my own children" (ibid., 7. 6); 'Keep the commandments of the LORD and show mercy towards your neighbors, and compassion towards all" (Zebulun, 5. 1), and the like. So the apparently innocuous statement in Avot, "Be a disciple of Aaron, loving the Eternal and loving humankind", may actually be an indication that there were those among the Sages who held explicitly to the doctrine of the "two Great

---

27   *Sefer Pitron Torah*, ed. E.E. Urbach, Jerusalem 1978, pp. 79–80. See Urbach's comments ad loc.

28   Josephus says that the Zealots tried to outdo one another in violating the laws, whether between man and God, or between man and his fellow (*Wars*, VII, 260).

29   The phrase "loving mankind" occurs as early as Hillel the Elder (Avot, 1.12).

Rules" in the Torah, both of which begin with the word *ve-ahavta* —
you shall love the LORD your God, plus another "you shall love" —
your neighbor as yourself.

Getting back to the Ten Commandments, let us recall the words of
Jesus himself.[30] In that connection, the incident of the rich man (Matt.
19. 18–20) is important because Jesus quotes the second half of the
Decalogue as an example of the mitzvot to be kept. The command to
love one's neighbor is added by the author of Matthew.

A different situation is reflected in the first part of the Sermon on the
Mount (Matt. 5. 17–48 and its parallels). It is true that the author of the
Gospel according to Matthew broadened the subject by adding matter
from other sources. (I believe that this applies, for example, to the
reference to divorce in Matthew 5. 31–33). But taken as whole, the
passage constitutes a single entity; and a sound supposition is that it
was spoken by Jesus on one particular occasion.

Following his introduction, in which Jesus explains his homiletic
method (Matt. 5. 17–20), he goes on to discuss the Commandments
"You shall not kill" and "You shall not commit adultery".[31] Then he
quotes, "You shall not swear falsely, but shall perform to the LORD
what you have sworn". The first words of that sentence derive from the
Holiness Chapter (Lev. 19. 12). We have already had occasion to quote
that code, and not by chance, because of its close affinity to the Ten
Commandments. Jewish thinkers in antiquity were well aware of this
connection, and that is why the Jewish literature of the times often has
excerpts from Leviticus 19 intertwined with verses from the Ten
Commandments.

The same thing happens here, in the Sermon on the Mount. The
language of the sentence about oaths may be reminiscent of the Holiness
Chapter. But the intent is to speak of the Commandment "You shall

---

30   The topics that follow have been dealt with in some detail in my *Judaism and the
      Origins of Christianity*, referred to above (n. 19); see "There are Two Ways" (pp.
      235–252) and "The Treatment of the Torah in the Sermon on the Mount" (pp.
      226–234). The German original of the latter essay, under the name "Die Tora in der
      Bergpredigt" was published in my *Entdeckungen im Neuen Testament, Bd 1*,
      Neukirchen, 1987, pp. 21-31. See now D. Flusser and Sh. Safrai, "Das
      Aposteldekret und die Noachitischen Gebote", in: *Wer Tora vermehrt, mehrt
      Leben*, Festgabe fur H. Kremers, Neukirchener Verlag, 1986, pp. 173–192. These
      three essays also contain matter which has been discussed above.
31   We omit here the question of divorce, as not being relevant to the present context.

not bear false witness against your neighbor" — part of the second half of the Decalogue.

After disposing of the matter of false oaths (Matt. 5. 33–37) Jesus takes up "An eye for an eye, a tooth for a tooth" (Ex. 21. 24). Why he chose to deal with this particular subject at this point (Matt. 5. 38–42) is a question which does not belong here. But finally he reaches his goal — the verse "You shall love your neighbor as yourself" (Matt. 5. 43–48). Once again we have been given a lesson on a topic from the second half of the Decalogue, connected to the verse which mandates love of one's fellowman.

In this instance there can be no doubt that Jesus too realized the connection between the command to love your neighbor and the last half of the Decalogue. It should be kept in mind that that command comes in the section *Qedoshim* (Leviticus 19) "upon which all the main essentials of the Torah depend", and which resembles the Ten Commandments in many respects. As a consequence of this affinity between the Holiness Chapter and the Ten Commandments, there is always the possibility of verses from the former creeping in to any discussion of topics from the latter. Besides, as we have already noticed, when matters of social ethics are being dealt with, it is not necessary to quote the Commandments in their entirety, or in exact order. One has, so to speak, freedom of maneuver in this area. That is why we find in Matthew, after the introduction (5. 17–20), a discussion of "You shall not kill" and "You shall not commit adultery", plus a variant of the Commandment "You shall not bear false witness"; whereupon Jesus brings up the matter of "An eye for an eye" and then concludes, quite logically, with "You shall love your neighbor as yourself".

Now let us examine certain aspects of the matter before us. The entire subject deals with commandments between man and his fellowman, summed up by the rule to love one's neighbor, at which the entire discourse had been aimed. However, in his introduction, Jesus had spoken of the whole Torah, with all its major and minor commandments. Consequently, he takes the same line in the present context as he took when he defined the Golden Rule, saying "This is the whole Torah" (Matt. 7. 12). That is exactly the same point of view we have seen in the Epistles of the New Testament, as well as in a Jewish-Christian compilation.[32] It is the same view as that expressed by Hillel

---

32   See n. 17a above, and cf. also n. 12a above.

and Akiba. On the other hand, there is an occasion when we find Jesus summing up the whole Torah by the use of *two* Great Rules — the love of God and the love of man (Matt. 22. 32–40, and the parallels). As we have seen, this idea too can be found in Jewish sources.

In the opening remarks of the Sermon on the Mount, Jesus says that he has come to fulfil the original meaning of the Torah. "For it is easier for heaven and earth to pass away than for one iota or dot of the Torah to become void".[33] Even the smallest portion of the Torah keeps the world going, so that it would be dangerous to discard even the least of the mitzvot:

> Whoever then relaxes one of the least of these commandments and teaches men so, shall be called least in the kingdom of heaven; but he who does them and teaches them shall be called great in the kingdom of heaven.

Jesus requires of his disciples that they observe the mitzvot even more strictly than the scribes. From what follows we learn that it is the ethical mitzvot that he is talking about. It is these that he means when he speaks of "the least of these commandments". That is why in this sermon of his he moves as a general rule from the minor instance to the major — a rabbinic method of interpretation called *qal va-homer* (a fortiori) — at least with respect to those mitzvot connected with the second half of the Decalogue. The argument goes like this: the Commandment reads, to be sure, "Do not kill"; but "whoever loses his temper shall suffer Gehenna". To be sure, the Commandment reads "You shall not commit adultery"; but "whoever looks at a woman lustfully has already committed adultery with her in his heart". And although the Torah merely forbids taking a false oath, Jesus believes that one should not take any oath at all. "Let what you say be simply 'yes' and 'no'; anything more comes from evil".[34] One might well say

33   The original form of this saying is not preserved in Matt. 5. 18, but rather in Luke 16. 17. The latter, however, forgot to mention the *yod* ("jot").

34   Jesus was apparently familiar with the midrash on Leviticus 19. 36, which asks, "Why does Scripture say 'You shall have an honest balance ... and an honest *hin* (liquid measure)'? [To teach] that your 'no' be an honest 'no', and your *hen* (yes) be an honest 'yes' ". Bacher refers to the corresponding words of Jesus in *Die Agada der Tannaiten*, Vol. 2, 2, Strassburg 1890, p. 418. From the parallel saying of Jesus, and from the use of the word "honest", it is apparent that the midrash deals, not merely with abstract principles of truthful speech, but specifically with honesty in business dealings and legal negotiations.

that the whole sermon is an expression of Jesus' Hasidean (pietistic) approach. In point of fact, the part of the sermon we have been discussing comes very close to the Hasidean school of thought of those times.

On the other hand, there is a great affinity between our subject and a Jewish work which we now know about.[35] The resemblance is so strong as to make it appear that there is a direct connection between that Jewish work and Matthew 5. 17–48.

The composition in question is generally spoken of as "The Two Ways". It underlies the early Christian work, in Greek, called *Didache*, also known as *The Teaching of the Twelve Apostles*. When the *Didache* first appeared scholars assumed, quite rightly, that the first six chapters were a Christian reworking of a Jewish original. In the meantime we have learned, thanks to the discovery of the Dead Sea Scrolls, that there is no need to reconstruct that hypothetical original. It turns out that *The Two Ways* itself has survived, albeit in a bad Latin translation. That text had been known all along, but we had to recover *The Manual of Discipline* from the Qumran Caves in order to realize what had happened. The strong affinity between the *Manual* and *The Two Ways* made it clear that the latter had originated within those Jewish circles in which the Essene sect of the Judean Wilderness took shape.

The work itself is based on the dualistic concept which teaches that there are two alternative paths in the world — "the path of life and the path of death, the way of light and the way of darkness. Over these preside two angels, the one of righteousness and the other of evil, and great is the difference between these two ways". The first four chapters deal with the way of life, while the fifth chapter deals with its opposite, the way of death. Chapter six, a short one, is the conclusion.

Immediately after the words just quoted, we find the following definition:

> The way of life is this: First, you shall love the LORD your Maker, and secondly, your neighbor as yourself. And whatever you do not want to be done to you, you shall not do to anyone else. And the interpretation of these words is: Do not kill, do not commit adultery, do not bear false witness, do not fornicate, do not steal, do not covet what belongs to your neighbor.

35 My article "There Are Two Ways", referred to in n. 30 above, deals with this work. Now see also my studies on the Sermon on the Mount, above, n.30 and below, n. 47.

This definition of the right way of life in *The Two Ways* is highly instructive. It consists of the two Great Rules, the first of which is love of God, and second is love of one's neighbor. The second rule appears here in two forms, namely, the verse in Leviticus, and immediately following, the Golden Rule.

As we noted above, the two Great Rules had already been alluded to in chapter 36 of the Book of Jubilees. We also observed that in the selfsame book (20. 2) Abraham instructs his descendents to keep the way of the LORD, to love their neighbor and to follow the Golden Rule. Hence we see that in this passage in Jubilees, as in *The Two Ways*, there occurs both the motif of "the way of the LORD", and the command to love one's neighbor, combined with the Golden Rule. The author of *The Two Ways* quotes the two Great Rules, and then proceeds to describe the path of life itself by saying "the interpretation of these words is —" quite like Hillel the Elder, who appended to the Golden Rule: "The rest is interpretation" (*perusha* = specification). As noted above, Hillel meant that the entire Torah is a specification of the Golden Rule while the author of *The Two Ways* uses the term in a derivative sense. He intends to spell out the meaning of the two Great Rules here and now.

The manner in which he treats "the way of life" is rather complex. He makes use of a wide variety of sources and traditions. Then, after expounding the ethical doctrines of the circles in which he moved, he can be briefer about the way of death, listing the evil characteristics which are to be avoided. In his entire discussion it has been clear from the very outset that great importance attaches to the second half of the Decalogue. All of its five "Thou shalt nots" 's are listed in chapter 5 (and in chapter 2). But in chapter 3 (6–7), on which we shall focus later, the prohibition of false witness is missing; while in chapter 2, the prohibition of false oaths has been added to the list, despite the fact that it comes from the *first* half of the Decalogue. Curiously enough, that commandment also appears in the Sermon on the Mount (Matt. 5. 33).

The second half of the Decalogue is especially prominent in the interesting passage in *Didache*, 3. 1–6. Apparently this passage was at one time a separate document.[36] However, it is difficult to determine its

---

36   The passage is followed by a new topic (*Didache*, 3. 7–10), beginning with language which is in fact a Greek translation from the *Manual of Discipline* (4. 3–4) giving a list of desirable characteristics of the person: "A spirit of humility and slowness to

original form, because as it appears at present in *The Two Ways* it is heavily influenced by the list of transgressions recorded in chapter 5 of the *Didache*.[37] Nevertheless, one might venture to suggest that the original treatment, before the topic had been reworked, ran something like this:

> My child, flee from all evil and from everything that resembles it. Be not prone to anger because anger leads to murder. Be not covetous, because coveting leads to adultery. My child, be not a diviner, because this leads to idolatry. Do not be a liar, for lying leads leads to theft; nor one who complains, for that leads to blasphemy.

If I am right in my attempted reconstruction of this passage, then it, too, deals specifically with the second half of the Decalogue. All that is missing is the Commandment against false witness.

The entire passage in the Jewish *Two Ways* is important not only for the history of the Decalogue, but also for the prehistory of the so-called "Noachide commandments" — the precepts which are binding on all mankind (based on Gen. 9. 1–7). The list of sins in *Didache*, 3. 1–6 is as follows: murder, adultery, idolatry, theft, blasphemy. The connection with the second half of the Decalogue is clear enough. But on the other hand, precisely these same five sins form a list of basic transgressions quoted as well in *Sifra* to Leviticus 18. 4 (see also Yoma 67b.). At the same time, the list comprises five of the seven Noachide precepts. Thus, one of the stages in the development of the idea of the Noachide precepts is preserved in *Didache*, 3. 1–6.

The matter we are discussing is very important, not only because it touches on the Ten Commandments, but also because it rests on traditions, or to be exact, sources which underlie that part of the Sermon on the Mount on which we have focused (Matt. 5. 17–48). For the sake of comparison, let us set the parallels side-by-side:

---

anger, great compassion and eternal goodness". In *Didache* 3. 7–8, this list appears verbatim, and in the same identical sequence as in the *Manual of Discipline*.

37 For a more detailed analysis of the matter, see my *Judaism and Christian Origins* (Hebrew) above n. 26, pp. 249–252; and also my *Judaism and The Origins of Christianity* (English, above, n. 19) pp. 494–508.

Didache	*Matthew 5*
evil and everything resembling it	the least of these commandments
anger leads to murder	everyone who is angry with his brother — to Gehenna
coveting leads to adultery	who looks at a woman lustfully has already committed adultery with her in his heart.

So the Sermon on the Mount and the passage in *The Two Ways* are both linked to the second half of the Decalogue. And they have something else in common. *The Two Ways*, in its opening words, quotes "You shall love your neighbor as yourself". Jesus, at the conclusion of the whole passage (5. 47–48) quotes the very same verse.

This part of *The Two Ways* (3. 1–6) is devoted to one idea, namely that one must avoid anything *resembling* evil, because it always leads to evil itself. "My child, flee from all evil, and from everything resembling it". It is an idea that recurs frequently in the teachings of the Jewish Sages.[38] Thus, for example, Tractate *Yir'at Ḥet'*:

> Keep far from whatever leads to sin; far from [moral] ugliness and whatever resembles ugliness. Recoil from the slightest trans-gression, lest it pave the way to a graver one. Rush eagerly to perform the slightest mitzvah, for it will lead you to greater ones.

This throws light on the well-known apothegm, "Be as careful of an unimportant mitzvah as of an important one".[39] In its original meaning, this was an alternative form of the counsel, "Keep your distance from all that is ugly, or that even resembles it".

This reference to "unimportant mitzvot", in the sense of moral preventatives or safety precautions, also appears in the opening remarks of the Sermon on the Mount (Matt. 5. 17–20). That introduction can be summed up, if you like, in the words "My child, flee from all evil and

---

38   See Gedaliah Alon, "The Halakhah in the Teaching of the Twelve Apostles (*Didache*)", in his *Studies in Jewish History* (Hebrew) I, Tel Aviv 1978, pp. 297–302. See also the German study, quoted above, n. 30.

39   The term "easy" (*qalot* = lightweight) puts in its earliest appearance among the antagonists of the Pharisees. The Essene writer who interprets Psalm 37.7 attacks the Pharisees "for they have chosen the *qalot*" (*DJD*, VII, p. 43).

from everything that resembles it!" The sentence is a kind of definition of the particulars of the topic as a whole, as dealt with in *The Two Ways*, (3. 2–6) a work constructed in a series of ethical *a minori* statements. In this it resembles the Sermon on the Mount, except for the concluding sections of the latter (Matt. 5. 21–37). Also Matt 5. 11–20 is an introduction to statements *a minori* (Matt. 5. 21–37).

Apart from that, we have already noted the astonishing resemblance between the treatment of the Commandments "You shall not kill" and "You shall not commit adultery" by Jesus in the Sermon on the Mount, and by the author of *The Two Ways*. Hence we may conclude that not only is the resemblance between the two introductions no mere accident, but more — that there is an actual literary link between *The Two Ways* and the Sermon on the Mount.

To summarize: it seems likely that if we knew more about the streams of Jewish thought during the Second Commonwealth, the picture we have pieced together would probably not turn out so complex and so incomplete. We have been dealing with two ideological and literary phenomena, both interconnected. The first of these is the concept that all the commandments of the Torah can be subsumed under one all-inclusive rule, or perhaps two. Those who said "one rule" pointed to "You shall love your neighbor as yourself" –– in other words, the Golden Rule. Those who said "two rules" encompassing the whole Torah pointed to "You shall love the LORD your God" plus the rule that is worded like it, "You shall love your neighbor as yourself". These two approaches find indirect expression as early as *The Book of Jubilees* (chap. 20.2 and chap. 37, especially verses 7 and 8).

The second phenomenon is the emergence of the idea that love of one's neighbor is spelled out in the second half of the Decalogue, which deals with transgressions against one's neighbor. These last five of the Ten Commandments, with no mention of the love of neighbor, are dealt with in the Jewish source underlying the *Didache* (3. 1–6) as well as in Mark (10. 19) and Luke (18. 20). But Matthew (19. 19) adds to Jesus' words the verse about loving one's neighbor.

The combination of the second half of the Decalogue with the commandment to love one's neighbor also occurs in the Sermon on the Mount (Matt. 5. 17–45); in Romans (13. 8–10) and in James (2. 8–11), as well as in a Jewish-Christian document.[40] To be sure, the Jewish

---

40   See above, notes 17a and 12a.

source of the *Didache* begins by defining the good way in terms of the two Great Rules in the Torah, combined with the Golden Rule. However, one of the chief components of that Jewish work is the second half of the Ten Commandments which, as we have observed, were customarily expressed in condensed form by the command to love one's neighbor.

This survey leads to the conclusion that during the Second Commonwealth there existed a *Gattung* of a homily based upon the last five of the Ten Commandments, accompanied by the verse "You shall love your neighbor as yourself", or by the Golden Rule. It is clear that this *Gattung* was the product of a specific religious approach, one close to that of Hillel the Elder (Shab. 31a) and of Rabbi Akiba (*Sifra*, *Qedoshim*, IX:12). We may safely assume that in accordance with the anthropocentric standpoint which characterizes Hillel and his school, the norm of loving God is included in the norm of loving one's neighbor.

We have put forward a number of hypotheses; but they are almost inescapable, given the nature of the material at hand. And there is an additional consideration. The notion that all the mitzvot in the Torah are embedded in the Ten Commandments[41] must have led to the idea that the last five of those Commandments are summed up in the command to love one's neighbor. I think it likely that this idea was at one time far more current than we might be led to believe if we were to rely only on the sources that have come down to us. No doubt the idea lost ground because of the danger that the Decalogue might be overvalued at the expense of all the other mitzvot. It seems probable that the notion that all the commandments are inherent in the Decalogue originated both in the very nature of the matter and in the general tendency of Judaism, for we have a similar idea in the statement that all the essentials of the Torah depend on the Holiness Chapter (*Qedoshim*); or on the two Great Rules; or even on the one Great Rule — to love one's neighbor.

In all the sources at our disposal there is, to be sure, a missing link.

---

41   See especially E.E. Urbach, *The Sages*, Jerusalem 1975, pp. 360 ff; and the chapter by Yehoshua Amir in the present volume. About the idea that the Decalogue implies all the particular commandments, see the parable in *Pesiqta de Rav Kahana*, 12.8, ed. B. Mandelbaum, New York 1962, p. 209; English translation by W. G. Braude and J. Kapstein, London 1975, pp. 233–234, and n. 31 there. See also C. Thoms und S. Lauer, *Die Gleichnisse der Rabbinen*, vol. 1, Bern 1986, pp. 187–188.

We might have expected that during the Second Commonwealth there were people who held that the *first* five Commandments contained all of man's duties to God, capable of being summarized in the verse "You shall love the LORD your God"; just as the second five Commandments, dealing with man's duties to his fellowman, can be summarized in the verse worded like it, namely, "You shall love your neighbor as yourself". In any event, it cannot be denied that there were in fact those who believed that all the mitzvot in the Torah are embedded in the Ten Commandments. There were also, as we have seen, those who took the whole Torah to be an extension of the love of one's neighbor; and others who thought that the whole Torah was an expansion of the *two* great "Thou shalt love" principles.

Apart from this, let us bear in mind something else. Our sources have preserved the opinion that the verse "You shall love your neighbor as yourself" not only contains the essence of the Torah, but is also the distillation of part two of the Ten Commandments.

It is clear, then, that most of the proposed building-blocks we have used to reconstruct the opinions of the ancients actually did exist. Nothing is so obvious as that people should have tried to match up the first five Commandments, taken in order, with the last five. Of course, those who held with Hillel and Akiba that there is but one all-inclusive principle — love of one's neighbor — believed that the whole Torah was derived from that principle. Interestingly enough, it is that doctrine, not the other, which predominates in the New Testament. From that doctrine emerges the literature which stresses the importance of the second half of the Ten Commandments, linked to the verse "You shall love your neighbor as yourself", or to the Golden Rule.

The area of conjecture in our preceding discussion would shrink, or perhaps vanish altogether, if we could be sure that a passage in a certain medieval midrashic compilation is based on older material originating in antiquity; and if we were convinced that this compilation was not influenced by the New Testament, however indirectly. The compilation in question is called *Sefer Pitron Torah*, a miscellany dealing with *Qedoshim*, the Holiness Chapter.[42] The critical passage reads as follows:

> The verse 'You shall love your neighbor as yourself' is the general rule underlying all the negative commandments addressed to the

---

42   This work was first published, with commentary and indices, by Ephraim E. Urbach, see above, n. 27.

individual. Because so long as you love your neighbor as yourself, you will obey.[43] 'You shall not take the name ... in vain' and 'You shall not kill' and 'You shall not commit adultery' and 'You shall not steal' and 'You shall not bear false witness' and 'You shall not covet'. You will have obeyed all the commandments of that sort. This is what the Sages said: All the mitzvot in the Torah are based on two verses. One is 'You shall love the LORD your God'; and the other is, 'You shall love your neighbor as yourself'. Two hundred and forty-eight positive commandments are founded on love of God; for whoever loves God and loves himself will perform them. And all the negative commandments are based on love of one's neighbor, for as long as you fulfil that commandment you will be obeying all the negative commandments. It includes the stranger, of whom the Torah says, 'You shall have one law for the stranger and the citizen'[43a]. That is why the Sages taught: 'Do not to others what is hateful to you'.

Here we have a midrash, one of whose central motifs is the doctrine of the two Great Rules. "The Sages say, 'All the commandments in the Torah are based on two verses'" and so on. Even though the doctrine of the two Great Rules is compatible with the rabbinic *Weltanschaung*, we have not so far found it enunciated so explicitly in ancient rabbinic literature. But the idea does appear in other Jewish sources of the Second Commonwealth period, and as the editor of *Pitron Torah* quite rightly points out, is also referred to by Jesus (Matt. 22. 34–40 and parallels).

Was the author of this late midrash indirectly influenced by what Jesus said? It is possible; but in my opinion unlikely. Take, for example, the fact that this midrash links "You shall love your neighbor as yourself" with the second half of the Decalogue. There is nothing like that in the words attributed to Jesus; but you *will* find the idea not only elsewhere in the New Testament, but also in the Jewish source underlying the *Didache*.

But even if we are willing to assume that *Pitron Torah* incorporates an ancient midrash which has somehow disappeared from other rabbinic sources, we must nevertheless grant that what we have is not the midrash in its original form. The text before us contains an

---

43   My friend Menahem Kister suggests the emendation "you will *not* perform", i.e. these are the negative commandments.

43a   "The stranger" refers to the proselyte.

interesting innovation. The author claims that the first general Rule — love of God — includes all the positive commandments; while the second Rule — love of neighbor — encompasses all the negative commandments. This idea is based on the assumption that the love of God is itself a positive command, whereas the love of one's fellowman is grounded essentially on not behaving badly towards him.

Is it possible that this idea was at one time part of the presumed original midrash? I find it difficult to accept the notion. Nevertheless, it is possible that the idea of equating the two Great Rules, each in turn, with the positive and negative commandments respectively, arose at some intermediate stage. After all, it is a fact that all the commands in the second half of the Decalogue begin with the word *lo'* (You shall not). Furthermore, as we have seen, the command to love one's neighbor was already thought of during the Second Commonwealth as the essence of the second half of the Decalogue, in which sense it is quoted in the late midrash we have been discussing.

It was his adherence to this idea that impelled the author of our midrash to co-opt the third Commandment ("You shall not take the name of the LORD your God in vain") into the second half of the Decalogue, even though it does not belong there; because after all it too is a negative commandment, beginning with *lo'.* Consequently, even though it is a logical assumption that our text represents the reworking of a presumed older midrash, it remains problematic to assess the stages through which that reworking passed.

In any event, the passage in *Pitron Torah* fills a lacuna in our knowledge, and buttresses the conclusions we arrived at on the basis of other evidence. For example, one is struck by the fact that this midrash ends by quoting the Golden Rule verbatim in Hillel's Aramaic. Nevertheless, despite the valuable new information provided by the publication of this hitherto unknown text, we still lack any evidence for one link in the development of the ideas involved. The idea that "You shall love the LORD your God" is the summation of the *first* half of the Decalogue — about that even our "new" document says nothing explicit.

Our discussion of the Ten Commandments in the New Testament has opened up a wide variety of topics. We have touched on many ethical ideas and literary forms in the Judaism of antiquity. We have seen how the Jewish Sages sought an answer to the question: What constitutes the fundamental essence of Jewish teaching? This kind of investigative study has many aspects, and an exhaustive treatment of it is not to be expected in this context. The same applies to the role of the Ten Commandments in the teachings of Judaism. Let it be said only that we have taken the first modest step in investigating this subject; and let us hope for future opportunities to continue with these studies.

In the literature of antiquity there are two additional important references to the idea of the two Great Rules.[44] In each case, the author seems to have gotten the idea from some earlier source.

The first of these authors is Philo. Writing about the Sabbath Commandment (*De specialibus legibus*, II. 63) he says that there are two major principles (*kephalaia*) from which flow innumerable truths. The first principle is to relate to God through reverence and piety; and the second principle is to relate to people through love of man, and of righteousness. Each of these principles branches out into a multiplicity of divisions, all of them of real importance.

Clearly, this passage is evidence for the existence of the doctrine of the two Great Rules. But it is doubtful that Philo himself was aware of all the elements that went into the making of this homily. It seems likely that he had heard it from some preacher, and remembered only its theological content. Interestingly enough, he calls the two Great Rules "supreme *kephalaia*". That Greek word is the closest translation of the Hebrew *kelal* (general principle). Paul uses the same Greek root in Romans 13. 9, when he says that the verse "You shall love your neighbor as yourself" is the summing up of the last five of the Ten Commandments.

In Matthew 22. 36, the Hebrew phrase *kelal gadol ba-torah* is rendered as "the great commandment in the law". Clearly, the translator did not use the exact Greek word, as Philo and Paul did, to render the Hebrew for "rule" or "general principle". Perhaps he deliberately avoided it. Anyone familiar with the simplistic style employed by the translators of the original gospels from Hebrew into Greek will readily understand why, to take the present instance, the translator could not render the Hebrew word *kelal* as *kephalaion*. That word was simply too highflown for him!

The other author who shows some knowledge — second-hand, from

---

44   For a bibliography of recent research on the two Great Rules, see. J. Becker, *Die Testamente der zwölf Patriarchen*, Gütersloh 1974, p. 94.

all appearances — of the idea of the two Great Rules, is Lactantius, a Latin Church Father. His chief work, *Divinae Institutiones*, was written around the year 300 of our era. His own knowledge of the Scriptures, both Jewish and Christian, was quite faulty, but he made use of some important sources, and his quotations from them are very valuable.

One of the most rewarding of these quotations occurs in Book 6 of his work, chapter 9. 1 and chapter 10. At this point it is fairly obvious that Lactantius is based on an original Christian work whose author was an excellent thinker, thoroughly familiar with Greek philosophic thought. He grounds his argument in favor of love of one's fellowman on the doctrine of the Stoics concerning the brotherhood of man. It is even possible that the author of the source used by Lactantius was not a Christian at all, since his writing contains no distinctly Christian elements. He could have been a Hellenistic Jew, but it seems more likely that he really was a Christian who drew on Hellenistic-Jewish sources.

In the sixth book of his major work, at the beginning of chapter 9, Lactantius writes that "the premier chapter[45] of the Law (Torah) is to know the LORD Himself, to hearken to none but Him, and to worship Him alone".[46] Then, at the beginning of chapter 10, he writes: "I have said what we owe to God. Now I shall state what we must bestow on man, even though whatever you do for man is done for God, since man is the image of God".

Here then is an echo of the two Great Rules, and the line of reasoning is very interesting. We are given the idea that the commandments

---

45   *primum caput* (The Greek source used by Lactantius probably had Philo's term — *kephalaion*). The word can mean either "chapter" or "head" or "summary".

46   These words are connected with Jesus' answer to Satan (Matt. 4. 10; Luke 4. 8): "For it is written 'You shall worship the LORD your God, and him only shall you serve' ". The verse goes back to Deut. 6. 13 and 10. 20: "You shall fear the LORD your God, you shall serve him". In both these places a major manuscript of the Septuagint reads "You shall serve him *alone*". This rendition was not invented; it came from a Hebrew text used by the translator. That same text was followed by the author of the Hebrew original of *Antiquitates Biblicae* (24. 14), and has also left its traces on Josephus (*Ant.*, III, 91). It was also the wording used by the High Priest and the congregation at the conclusion of the *Avodah* portion of the liturgy (see Ismar Elbogen, *Der jüdischer Gottesdienst in seiner geschichtliche Entwicklung*, Frankfurt on Main 1931, p. 56). Hence, the source used by Lactantius need not necessarily have been the gospel. It could just as easily have been a Jewish source.

between man and his fellow actually have a bearing on one's relationship to God. How you treat any other person is really a function of your attitude to the deity, since man is created in God's image. We have assumed that it was this idea which led the Jews — as well as the early Christians of Jewish extraction — to include the Great Rule of Love of God within the second Great Rule, the Love of Man, and to concentrate on the second half of the Decalogue, which is summed up in the Great Rule "Love thy neighbor". Here we find our hypothetical conjecture put in explicit terms by the author on whom Lactantius drew. And if perchance that author was not expressing his own original idea, then we will be driven to the conclusion that it reached him via the thought-world of Jewish Aggadah.

If the source of Lactantius' quotation was not Christian but Judeo-Hellenistic; or even if its real author actually *was* a Christian, but an accomplished philosopher familiar with Judeo-Hellenistic literature — in either case it becomes understandable how the theoretical foundation for the doctrine that love of neighbor encompasses the entire Torah should find its way into the writings of the Church Father called Lactantius.

In any event, what he says and what Philo Judaeus says both throw light on the two Great Rules in the Torah.[47]

Translated by Gershon Levi

47　For the Decalogue in early Christian Literature, see now W. Rordorf, "Beobachtungen zum Gebrauch des Dekalogs in der vorkonstatinischen Kirche", in: *The New Testament Age — Essays in Honor of Bo Reicke*, Mercer University Press, Macon 1984, pp. 437–492. For the Sermon on the Mount see now D. Flusser, "A Rabbinic Parallel to the Sermon on the Mount," *Judaism and The Origins of Christianity* (n. 19, above) pp. 494-508.

9. THE DECALOGUE AND MAN AS "HOMO VOCATUS"

NATHAN ROTENSTREICH

I

Judah Halevi, writing in the eleventh century, in *The Kuzari*, says the following:

> The first of the Ten Commandments enjoins belief in Divine Providence. The second commandment forbids the worship of any but the One God, or the association of any being with Him; and prohibits the representation of Him in statues, forms and images, as well as any personification of him (*Kuzari*, I, 89).[1]

However, if we examine the wording of the Commandment we see that it does not enjoin belief in God as an entity, but deals rather with what may be called God's authority to command Israel, and to set before them what Yehudah Halevi calls "the very essence of the mitzvot" (*Kuzari*, I, 67).[2]

This authority is grounded, not on the fact that the world is created, and is therefore dependent on the Creator; nor on the contingent nature of all creation. The authority to command is grounded, rather, on an historical event — God's act in liberating Israel from Egyptian bondage. That is to say, by bringing Israel out of a geographically and spiritually alien land, and freeing them from the bondage of spiritual and social dependence, He established His right to make demands on them.

The exodus from Egypt is referred to again when the Ten Commandments are repeated in Deuteronomy; not only at the beginning (Deut. 5. 6) but also in connection with the Sabbath Commandment (5. 15): "Remember that you were a slave in the land of Egypt, and the LORD your God freed you from there."

1 Compare *The Book of Kuzari*, transl. Hartwig Hirschfeld, New York 1946, p. 54.
2 Ibid., p. 53.

It is obvious that there is a difference between grounding the Commandments on Creation, and grounding them on the exodus from Egypt. Creation is the universal, all-embracing source of authority, while the Exodus was an act confined to the Jewish people — an historical rather than a cosmic event. But the fact that the opening of the Decalogue refers to the exodus, rather than to the creation of the world, can be explained: the Ten Commandments were addressed to the Jewish people.

The Ten Commandments are a quintessential expression of One who commands, calling out directly to the one who is commanded. In this context we shall designate the latter *Homo Vocatus* — "the one who is called". Such a person is of course a rational being, for otherwise he would not be able to understand the call, or be capable of receiving the Torah at Mount Sinai, along with the teaching and instructions of which it consists. But it does not suffice to say that man is a rational being — *Homo Sapiens* — for rationality can take a number of directions, from man's mere ability to speak, up to his capacity for independent reasoning, exemplified by such things as his ability to think logically in accord with laws of identity and non-contradiction. Reason is also manifested when the ability to decipher is trained on nature and natural phenomena, and in similar activities.

The Ten Commandments direct man towards the imperative that is addressed to him; that is to say, the fact that man is a rational creature is a condition for his absorbing and fulfilling the command. Within the bounds of this relationship between man as a called creature, and God as the One who calls him to a way of life, the Supreme Being who brought the slaves out of Egypt is closer to the experience of *Homo Vocatus* than He is as Creator of the world who exerts power over the entire universe.

In a certain sense, it may be said that the status of *Homo Vocatus* leads to a degree of historization of the authority of the call, or of the guiding commandment. Historization in this context does not mean that the matter under consideration is time-bound, transitory. It means rather being anchored in an historical event — an event which is seen as engendering and establishing the body of Jewish history. "Engendering" refers to the temporal framework, the starting-point in time; "establishing" deals with the content, the substance of the call. The summons addresed to the individual Israelite is anchored in just such an establishing act.

II

It is worth noting at this point that the prohibition against having other gods appears as the Second Commandment, even though it would seem more logical for the assertion of God's uniqueness to precede the assertion of His role as the One who brought Israel out of bondage. Yet the fact remains that that is not the order. The line is not from the broad to the restricted, but from the restricted — an historical event — to the assertion of monotheism in the strict sense, negating all pseudo-divine reality apart from the reality of God, and prohibiting any representation of Him in statue or image. The first assertion is the monotheistic proclamation of God's unity and uniqueness; the second denies the possibility of representing Him in statues or images, which are by their nature secondary, and as such not on the level of exalted uniqueness. For if a reality can be represented by a statue or an image, it is no longer a reality whose essence lies in its difference from any other reality; and that applies all the more to that which is, as it were, a visual reflection of a reality exclusive and unique.

We see, then, that the structure of the Decalogue leads from the status of God in history to His status in the domain of Being at large. Even here, however, the emphasis is not on God's act as Creator of the world, but on the uniqueness of His essence, and on the impossibility of comparing it to any realms of being which might possibly be thought of as being on His level.

The prohibition of embodiment or representation in likenesses or graven images is related to the fact that such representations were common in neighboring beliefs and religions. That is to say, they apprehended the transcendent as capable of being represented in the visual realm. The Commandment totally denies that possibility, because of the singular nature of the reality which has a unique status, and is *sui generis,* and cannot be realized, as it were, or presented in any statue or image.

However, if we seek to understand the progression from the First Commandment to the Second, we might say as follows: When the person (or Israelite) is confronted with the call contained in the Commandment, and the authority to address him at all derives from God's status as the One who brought the Israelites out of Egypt — a fundamental question arises. What is God's status over and above His role as liberator from Egypt? The question is asked, keeping in mind the fact that His status is grounded, not on the act of creation, but rather on His uniqueness as Being or Existent. It is a uniqueness that finds expression in the impossibility of comparing Him to any other being. That impossibility is reflected in the impossibility of formulating His status in terms of any domain of reality which is in any way close to man's world, or within his capacity to grasp. Now, the visual domain is one aspect of man's experience, and therefore is excluded.

The historical experience of the Exodus from Egypt leads to the conclusion that it deals with something that is beyond normal experience — as if to teach us that it would be a mistake to think that one can pass from one kind of experience — the Exodus — to another sort of experience, one in the visual realm. The Commandment asserts that such a passage is not possible; the attempt to achieve it is forbidden. The prohibition is stated explicitly by the Commandment; but implicit in it is also an assertion of God's unique status. The Commandment goes on to speak of Him as an impassioned God, who visits the guilt of the fathers upon the children, but who also shows mercy to the thousandth generation. This sets the status of God within man's experience: that is to say, His uniqueness is also expressed through reward and punishment. In other words, the experiential expression of His uniqueness is not only something to be contemplated, nor is it reflected in the domain of the visual, but is to be found in His judgmental status. Judgment does not stand on its own and is not self-justifying; it is grounded, rather, on God's ontological status.

The combination of this status with the judgmental status is one of the essential thrusts characteristic of the Decalogue, and indeed of the biblical conception as a whole. Here we come upon the notion that *Homo Vocatus* is *ipso facto* man the judged, in the concrete sense of judgment — namely, that he is subject to reward and punishment.

So we can say that the progression from the First Commandment to the Second is a movement from experience to an ontological assertion, with experience at times general and at times individual, for punishment and reward are events within the realm of the individual. Experience corresponds to the position of God as the One who established the people's history: the One who oversees the actions of men. The actions in question are those related to the Divine, and those concerned with the relations between man and his fellowman, the subject dealt with in the subsequent Commandments.

III

In this context we may ask: What is *Homo Vocatus* called upon to do by the First Commandment? It would appear that the First

Commandment calls on him to affirm that a historical event — the Exodus from Egypt — was an act of God. The Exodus was no neutral event, for it was essentially a bringing out, and a bringing out of this particular people. But when we come to the Second Commandment, *Homo Vocatus* is confronted not merely with an invitation to affirm, such as is implicit in the assertion about the liberation from Egypt, but with a direct demand. The statement of God's uniqueness is a demand to recognize His exclusiveness which, as we have indicated, does not admit representation or embodiment. These lead beyond mere affirmation as such, while the demand in the Commandment corresponds to God's exclusive status. The drawing of a distinction between the exclusiveness of the existent and the ban on depicting or embodying it, takes into account the possibility — perhaps also the inclination — to give concrete expression to the abstract. The purpose of the Commandment is to forbid the acting out of that inclination, indeed to root it out completely. What is prohibited is a blurring of the distinction between the legitimate status of uniqueness, and the trespass beyond the bounds of that status. The other side of the coin of such violation of the abstract boundaries of God's status is — moral transgression.

In this sense the Third Commandment extends the range of the prohibition, but this time not by dealing with the possibility of violating the frontiers of divinity. Now its focus is, as it were, within that domain itself. The transgression is the taking of God's name in vain. That has several meanings. One of them is the use of God's name unrelated to a sincere avowal of Him, but rather to serve other purposes and concerns. Whereas the Second Commandment prohibited the blurring of distinctions *between* levels of reality, the Third Commandment prohibits the blurring of distinctions *within* the domain of the unique reality, while drawing no conclusions about its uniqueness.

The affirmation of uniqueness cannot be uttered absent-mindedly, for its meaning cuts deep. That is to say, such affirmation may not be made a cover for inclinations and interests other than the affirmation itself. The Commandment does not formulate this in an abstract way: it does not forbid affirmation other than the affirmation of His uniqueness. Its prohibition applies to the possible expression of non-affirmation, which constitutes the taking of God's name in vain.

It may also be said that the Commandment is not only about overt conduct; it applies to motives as well. That is to say, *Homo Vocatus* is commanded not only about his visible behavior, but also with respect to his inner thoughts. If that is so, then we have touched on one of the major problems of human morality: the extent to which there is a correspondence between actual behavior and its underlying psychic and spiritual motivations.

IV

It may be asked why the Fourth Commandment singles out the Sabbath from the whole drama of Creation; for the Commandments make no mention of the events that preceded the Sabbath, although it was the last act in the Creation story. An answer to this question — an answer which is consistent despite its various aspects — may be found in the description of how the Sabbath came into being. Firstly, out of all the elements in the Creation story (except for living creatures), only of the Sabbath is it said: "God blessed the seventh day". Blessing is not only a matter of saying "It is good". It also assigns meaningful content capable of gladdening or elevating the one who hears the blessing, or the one who utters it, or the one to whom it is addressed.

Blessing is related to sanctification, one of the meanings of which is setting aside or singling out. In this case a day is singled out, removed from the round of ordinary days, and given a special status. The blessing is not given to the ordinary, but to that which is distinctive. The distinctiveness, seen from the perspective of activity, resides in the fact of completion, described in human terms as "He rested".

This status of the Sabbath is in several respects significant from the point of view of the Commandment addressed to *Homo Vocatus*. Memory is one such respect. Remembering is not only a matter of acknowledging that an event took place in the past, even though that event is the very source of authority for the Commandment itself. Remembering is a constant return, a continual going back to a specific occasion. In this instance the occasion is not related to the individual and his people, but to the cosmos and its processes. The remembrance itself can be called "imitation". Man imitates the act of God, so to speak. Just as God rested on the Sabbath, so too is man called upon to rest on that day. Given his human status, his resting cannot possibly be cosmic. It is human resting, which is to say, cessation of human labors. It is nonetheless imitation of a sort, in the sense of transferring the model of God's action into the narrow realm of human behavior.

Thus, the Commandment addressed to *Homo Vocatus* has its origin in remembering, and is expressed by abstaining from work. The relationship is that of a remembrance that sustains the bond between man and God; the abstention from work translates this relationship into human behavior. The remembrance as such can remain a matter of inner motivation, whereas the abstention from work is an external manifestation of this, obtruding into real life.

Another probable reason for the singling out of the Sabbath from the sequence of days in Creation is the fact that, just as the Commandments as a whole are directed to the people of Israel — and this is pointed up in the First Commandment — so the Commandment related to the Sabbath and formulated as a ban on work is addressed to the Israelite, for whom the setting apart of the Sabbath provides reason and anchorage for his way of life. The commitment expressed by accepting this Commandment finds expression in what can be characterized as an imitation of God, whereas the previous Commandments dealt with God's status, and required of man the affirmation of His uniqueness. That affirmation does not of itself lead to the kind of behavior which constitutes the active attachment of *Homo Vocatus* to the One who calls on him to act.

So far we have offered some comments on the Commandments which have to do with God's status and man's relationship to it. The Commandments which follow have to do with the human realm proper. First we must consider the difference in formulation between the first of these Commandments in the human realm, dealing with the relations between children and their parents, and the remaining commandments, all of which are couched in the negative, and formulated as prohibitions. We shall consider whether there is a built-in reason for this difference in formulation — this too in the light of the status of man as *Homo Vocatus*.

V

One expression of the call addressed to *Homo Vocatus* takes the form of restraint on his conduct and his drives. We may even go so far as to say that, underlying the formulation of the Commandments dealing with the interpersonal realm is the assumption that the first step towards achieving behavior consonant with the principles that should guide it, is the imposition of restraint on man's instinctual urges. The underlying assumption is, that since such urges exist they must be contended with either by restraint or by redirection. A well-known problem in ethical theory is, to what extent does a prohibition imply a positive command. Or put differently, to what extent is prohibition, which is expressed as a restraint, a prior and necessary condition for behavior which constitutes a response to a positive command. A positive command itself, it may be pointed out, may also imply restraint, as for example in the formulation of Kant's imperative — that one should treat every person as an end, not merely as a means. It may be said that we cannot undertake to act on the basis of positive principles if we do not first restrain the urge to treat others only as means. Putting it another way: were it not for the existing drive to treat others as nothing more than means, it would have been unnecessary to formulate the positive demand to treat every person as an end in himself. Therefore, even when the formulation is not in the negative, a negation is implicit in the command.

VI

Beginning with the Fifth Commandment, we come to the area of man's relations with his fellowman. These Commandments, except for the one concerning honor of parents, are formulated negatively, as prohibitions. We have said that the Commandments impose restraints in the realm of man's relationship to his fellow, and that the restraint is expressed in a negative statement which prohibits certain behavior. To be sure, the positively worded command also contains an element of restraint; but because it is worded positively it directs that restraint towards obligatory conduct. In the present instance, the obligatory conduct is honoring one's parents. Here we can distinguish between the aspect of *paying* honor, which is behavioral, and *feeling* honor, which is emotional.

It may be noted further that when restraint is formulated negatively — as a prohibition — *ipso facto* it includes mutuality. For a prohibition such as that against murder applies to A in relation to B, as well as in relation to people in general, just as it applies to B in relation to A, and to people in general in relation to any one particular person. The command to honor one's parents, by contrast, is not mutual, but refers to children vis-à-vis their parents. A relationship of honor, whether demonstrated or felt, is by its nature not reciprocal, for the concern parents have for their children does not necessarily involve honor, while the relationship of children to their parents involves — or should involve — honor.

It may be asked — and the question arises, of course, only against the background of cumulative human experience — why is the relationship of children to their parents couched positively, instead of being formulated as a restraining prohibition? This derives perhaps from the consideration that the lives of men within the domain of family are not anonymous, but consist of a host of intertwined daily bonds. Fathers and mothers are by their very nature specific individuals within the context of relationship to their children. This context is specific, and replete with detailed everyday components. It is a context and a framework that cannot be generalized and made to refer to the relationship between any individual and all other individuals. That relationship stems from the fact that any one individual belongs to the context of individual men; whereas a system of specific relationships is composed of fragments which, joined together, form a whole that calls for an even more specific relationship. The positive relationship called for in the Commandment to honor one's parents is thus more specific than is the conduct involved in, e.g., murder, theft and the like.

In the literature on ethics we find disagreement among philosophers regarding the nature of positive relationship. The specific question is, whether honor is to be preferred to love, both being positive relationships. Many have pointed out that love cannot be commanded, whereas honor can be, at least more so than love. Kant has taught us that the law is to be obeyed out of respect for it, not adhered to out of love of it.

It is worth noting in this connection that respect includes not only positive relationship and attachment, but also distance and separation. When a person respects or honors someone, he honors him in accordance with his status and authority. Respect does not entail the closeness that is expressed in love which, as we have said, is more emotional. In the relationship of children to their parents we notice therefore that respect — in all its aspects — entails both closeness and distance. This seems more compatible with what we may call the objective status of parents vis-à-vis their children. In other words, parental authority is revealed more clearly in a relationship of respect than is likely to be revealed in a relationship of love. In this context, authority appears to be the decisive factor, for authority concerns the warrant to demand particular behavior, whereas love is a free awakening that does not necessarily entail a demand. The authority of parents derives from their status as such, and is in no way conditional on their behavior or on the nature of the demands they make on their children.

We can summarize and say that the positive command applied to the relationship of children towards their parents is anchored in the fabric of everyday relations between parents and children. The fullness of the content of this relationship does not permit abstraction to a general setting of interpersonal relationships, as is the case in the Commandments that follow. What all of these Commandments as a group share is restraint on human behavior, though this restraint takes a different form in a specific and defined system as opposed to an anonymous and abstract system. The additional clause "that you may long endure on the land" underscores the fact that this Commandment, which is anchored in the relationship between children and their parents as such, is also a Commandment whose observance entails reward. This is a combination that recurs frequently in the Bible, though in the present context it may have another implication, namely that when children who honor their parents become parents themselves, their children will have to give them the respect and honor which they were required to give to their own parents.

VII

The negative formulations of the subsequent Commandments, all of them couched as prohibitions, are of course connected to the web of interpersonal relations. The prohibitions place restraints on conduct that might otherwise be harmful. The assumption is that there are human drives and urges that can lead to behavior which would be injurious. The Commandments specify these kinds of injury, whether they are rooted in drives to wreak physical or property damage, or in pleasure-seeking desires, the satisfaction of which is calculated to inflict injury on others. The prohibitions specified do not refer to the public domain, but are restricted to the relations between man and his fellowman. Moreover, as was stated above, that fellowman is not identified in terms of his relationship to the one who commits, or is liable to commit, the transgression. He is considered, rather, in terms of the place he occupies in the broad general context of inter-human relations. In this regard, we can say that the Commandments are concerned with the relations between man and God, and between man and his fellowman; but not with the intermediate domain of the relations between the individual and the public domain. This will lead us to a final comment by way of summary.

VIII

One of the shortcomings of the above explication of the Ten Commandments is that it does not consider the traditional commentaries on the subject. This is intentional, but derives also from an inadequate familiarity with the relevant traditional sources. However, there is one issue that must not be omitted, and that is, the nature itself of "commandment" or "mitzvah" — for the Ten Commandments are mitzvot par excellence. The call to man is, as it were, an objective parallel to man's nature and his capacity to respond. The reference here is to the distinction between rational commandments and traditional commandments, as that distinction was formulated by Saadiah Gaon; a distinction which was to become central to Moses Mendelssohn's interpretation of Jusaism.

The Ten Commandments would seem to fall into the category of the "traditional", but not merely in the terminological sense of the word. Their source of information is, if we may put it that way, in speech, or the Word. There is an essential bond between the Commandment (*dĭbbĕr*) and the word of God. The Ten Commandments as given have a structure which we have sought to explicate, and structure is one of the distinguishing marks of what is called discourse. In this instance it is discourse which, while related to the Word of God, has at the same time a rational structure and argument whose meaning we can at least attempt to formulate. We have here, then, something which is at one and the same time both traditional and rational — although possibly the distinction between traditional and rational cannot be applied to something so central as the Decalogue.

Moses Mendelssohn, when talking about the state, said that man is by nature subject to obligation; for if it were not so, no agreement or contract entered into by him would be binding.[3] Here we may say that the difference between a conception of man as by nature under obligation, and a conception of man as called, is that the category of man's natural status is not applicable to the latter; for in being called, man is in a position of correlation with the God who commands or imposes the obligation. Nature is not a datum that springs forth by itself; it is rather a constituent in that correlation, and as such contains a readiness, as it were, to respond to the call implicit in the status of being called.

Mendelssohn is thus correct in saying that in divine religion there is no difference between action and thought, since the act is commanded

---

3 *Jerusalem*, by Moses Mendelssohn, transl. Allan Arkush, with introduction and commentary by Alexander Altmann, Hanover N.H. Brandeis University 1983, p. 36.

only as a token of conviction.[4] Nevertheless, we can say that men can be impelled to perform actions, but can only be induced to engage in reflection.[5] However, here we encounter the contrast between action and contemplation, without considering the fact that there are other types of thought, such as that which is the foundation for being called, and which responds to the call when it is understood (as opposed to speculative thought or vision, like metaphysics which deals with the Supreme Being or the Cause of Causes or other such traditional subjects). As we have observed, the First Commandment, the one that deals with the status of God, does not deal with His metaphysical status, and therefore does not invite speculation in the metaphysical sense of the term. It deals rather with the relationship obtaining between men — i.e., the people of Israel — and the One who brought them out of Egypt.

As we know, Mendelssohn argued that Judaism does not claim to be a revelation of eternal truths on which man's happiness depends, and therefore is not to be described as a revealed religion in the usual sense.[6] The divine book given us through Moses was intended as a book of laws comprising commandments and a way of life, while at the same time it is also replete with rational truths and religious doctrines which are so intimately connected with the laws that they form an indivisible whole.[7]

This description of his seems more applicable to the structure of the Ten Commandments than is his sharp distinction between unexplained statutes (to be accepted on faith) and rational directives. At the same time it is doubtful whether the distinction between body and soul can help us to see the structure of the Ten Commandments.

The question that must be asked is: What is the meaning of "eternal truth"? The reference to the Exodus from Egypt is not a reference to a being that exists eternally and of itself, but rather to an event and to the One who brought it about; an event that took place within historical time. "Eternal" in this context may mean that the truths of the statement about the liberation from Egypt can never lapse, because ever since that event took place it has irrevocable force from which specific

4	Ibid., p. 73.
5	Ibid., p. 119.
6	Ibid., p. 97.
7	Ibid., p. 99.

conclusions ensue. These conclusions impose obligations on man, who is in a correlative position with God. A distinction must be drawn, then, between "eternal" as a status of being, and "eternal" as referring to the binding force of the assertion contained in the First Commandment.

For that reason we cannot follow Mendelssohn when he goes on to say that ancient Judaism has no books of dogma, no articles of faith.[8] It can be argued, rather that the statement about the relationship between the people and its liberation from bondage, as well as with the One who brought them out of bondage, is a statement in which the idea that man has a vocation is based on faith. The same holds good with regard to such other principles as God's uniqueness, and the prohibition against blurring the boundaries between Him and any other being.

Even the command to observe the Sabbath is not based on any utilitarian consideration, such as man's need for a day of rest. That Commandment is anchored rather in the cosmic status of the Sabbath, a status derived from the very act of Creation.

In the light of this, we must re-examine the distinction proposed by Mendelssohn:

> The lawgiver was God, that is to say, God not in his relation as Creator and Preserver of the universe, but God as Patron and Friend by covenant of their ancestors, as Liberator, Founder and Leader, as King and Head of this people....[9]

This distinction has a certain basis in the First Commandment, but it cannot be maintained as a whole with respect to any of the subsequent Commandments.

We have considered the interpretation of Judaism as presented by Moses Mendelssohn, whose influence on the Judaism of recent generations is universally acknowledged. In doing so, our purpose has been to stress the fact that the Decalogue is, if we may put it so, a document of faith consisting of diverse components. Nevertheless, it has structure, and from the standpoint of structure it is a sort of synthesis of its various elements. Taken together, the Ten Commandments provide an insight into the integral character of Judaism.

Translated by Arnold Schwartz

8   Ibid., p. 100.
9   Ibid., p. 127.

10. THE TEN COMMANDMENTS
AND THE ESSENCE OF RELIGIOUS FAITH

SHALOM ALBECK

1. *THE INHERENT PROBLEM OF THE TEN COMMANDMENTS*

The high point of all the miraculous events recorded in the Bible is the revelation of God on Mount Sinai before all Israel; and the main element in that biblical account is the declaration of the Ten Commandments. Moses himself testifies to this "...ever since God created man on earth, from one end of heaven to the other, has anything as grand as this ever happened, or has its like ever been known? Has any people ever heard the voice of a god speaking from out of a fire, as you have, and survived?"[1]

God's purpose in His revelation to the people was to give them the Torah and the mitzvot so that they would experience Him, revere Him, and keep His commandments. Even so, one who reads the account may well ask why such an extraordinary phenomenon was necessary, and why God Himself in all His power and glory spoke the Ten Commandments. In what respect do those Commandments differ from all the other teachings given to Israel through Moses and the prophets, and expounded in the Torah? To this we might add the observation that most of the Ten Commandments are kept by other peoples even though they did not hear them at Sinai. Indeed, it is universally accepted that no society could exist without regard to such basic imperatives as "Honor your father and your mother", "You shall not murder", "You shall no commit adultery", "You shall not steal", "You shall not bear false witness against your neighbor", or "You shall not covet...".

A further difficulty can be noted. The Ten Commandments are

---

1   Deut. 4. 32–33.

teachings which people could have arrived at through reason and good sense, while there are many other laws which are not dependent on reason and which were not explicitly promulgated at the time. For example, laws about how to worship God, what sacrifices may be offered and how they are to be offered, what festivals to observe and how to observe them; indeed, the entire corpus of laws which deal with God's special relationship with Israel. Furthermore, some of the teachings included in the Decalogue were repeated by Moses at various times in a somewhat different form, while others were taught and even observed before the revelation at Sinai.

We might add to the above a further question which relates to the literary style of the Ten Commandments. They are not positive declarations but rather negative commands. We do not find here anything like "You shall love the LORD your God with all you heart..."[2] but we do have "You shall have no other gods before Me". We do not have anything like "You shall love your neighbor as yourself",[3] but rather the negative laws, "You shall not murder; You shall not commit adultery; You shall not steal; You shall not covet". These considerations might seem to detract from the very special place which the Decalogue appears to assume in the biblical record of the Divine revelation at Sinai.

Subsequent generations did not apparently find any unique significance in the Ten Commandments. In the Bible they are referred to only rarely. As far as the talmudic Sages are concerned, the Assembly at Sinai refers to the time when the whole Torah was given, not just the Ten Commandments. The Sages extended the meaning of the Decalogue by attaching to each command all the explanations and laws which are related to it, so that in effect the entire Torah was given together with the Ten Commandments. Thus we find, "Hananiah the nephew of R. Joshua says: Between each pair of Commandments were inscribed the letters of the Torah".[4] *Canticles Rabbah* has a similar teaching: "Hananiah the nephew of R. Joshua says: Between each pair of Commandments were written the other sections and minutiae of the Torah".[5] The same point is made in Targum Pseudo-Jonathan which paraphrases Exodus 24.12 with "And I will give you the tablets of stone

2   Ibid., 6. 5.
3   Lev. 19. 18.
4   Yer. Sheq. VI:1; Sotah VIII:3.
5   V:14.

in which are included the rest of the Torah".[6] Similarly R. Moses the Preacher in his *Bereshit Rabbati* expresses the view that the Ten Commandments include all the Torah, i.e. all the six hundred and thirteen commandments.[7]

The uniqueness of the Ten Commandments is diminished not only when it is taught that the rest of the Torah is included in them; the special character of the Ten Commandments is somewhat blurred by the fact that the very words with which they are given were not always known. This might be gathered from the talmudic record:

> R. Hanina b. Agil asked R. Hiyya bar Abba, "Why is the word 'good' not included in the first Commandments [in Exodus 20] in relation to the fifth Commandment, while in the latter Commandments [in Deuteronomy 5] the term 'good' is found?" To this R. Hiyya replied, "Instead of asking why the word 'good' is found in the latter Commandments, why not ask if that word is in fact found there at all? Now in truth, I don't know whether it is found there. You should go and ask R. Tanhum".[8]

A comment by the Tosafists throws some light on the curious anecdote and suggests, "Sometimes the rabbis were not completely knowledgeable in the biblical verses. Thus we find (B.Q. 54b) a question like, 'Why is the word "good" not included in the First Commandments...'?".[9]

We are left then with the task of understanding the special significance which (in spite of all that has been said) the Torah ascribes to the Ten Commandments. We have to find the meaning of the unique divine revelation on Mount Sinai and see why it exercised such extraordinary influence in history. To do all this it is necessary to explain the Ten Commandments in the light of their deeper meaning as indicated in the teachings of the Sages, who fashioned the special character of Jewish religious faith; and especially the Jewish concept of God which distinguishes Israel from other peoples.

It seems that the Ten Commandments reveal something of the essence of the spiritual God, understandable to men only in the form of his attributes.

The Bible describes the phenomena which occurred before the revelation in the following words: "... there was thunder and lightning

---

6   Jonathan, ad loc.
7   Ed. Ch. Albeck, p. 8; see also note to line 16, and *Torah Shelemah*, XVI, pp. 203 ff.
8   B.Q. 54b–55a.
9   B.B. 113a.

and a dense cloud... and a very loud blast of the horn; and all the people who were in the camp trembled... the sound of the horn grew louder and louder".[10]

Now none of this is a description of God's physical revelation to man. God does not appear to the prophets in this way. When, for example, God appeared to the prophet Elijah, the Bible tells, "...And behold the LORD passed by, and a great strong wind rent the mountains, and broke in pieces the rocks before the LORD; but the LORD was not in the wind; and after the wind an earthquake; but the LORD was not in the earthquake; and after the earthquake a fire; but the LORD was not in the fire; and after the fire a still small voice".[11] Maimonides observes, "The prophets experience their prophecy only in a dream at night, or in a deep trance, as we read (Num. 12.6), 'I make Myself known to him in a vision, I speak with him in a dream.'"[12] At Sinai also God revealed Himself in total silence as is suggested in the following Midrash:

> R. Abbahu said in the name of R. Johanan: When God gave the Torah no bird twittered, no fowl flew, no ox lowed, none of the Ofanim stirred a wing, the Seraphim did not say, "Holy, Holy," the sea did not roar, the creatures spoke not, the whole world was hushed into breathless silence, and the Voice went forth, "I am the LORD your God."[13]

We may infer from this that the fire, the cloud, and the voice of the horn were merely agencies used to put the people in an appropriate mood of awe for the great event of the revelation of God's Commandments. A similar purpose was served by the three days of preparation. For the fire, the cloud and the sound of the horn are not regular manifestations of nature, but extraordinary phenomena. Experiencing them, the people were more likely to be filled with spiritual awe, and become more open to receive the Commandments and to observe them afterwards. And so the Bible summarizes the same point:

> When you heard the voice out of the darkness, while the mountain was ablaze with fire, you ... said, "The LORD our God has just shown us His majestic presence and we have heard His voice out of the fire.... Let us not die, then, for this fearsome fire

10   Ex. 19. 16–19.
11   I Ki. 19. 11–12.
12   Maimonides, *Hilkhot Yesodei HaTorah*, VII:2.
13   *Exodus Rabbah*, XXIX:9.

will consume us.... You go closer and hear all that the LORD our God says; then you tell us everything...". [God answers:] "They did well to speak thus. May they always be of such mind, to revere me and follow my Commandments".[14]

II. *I THE LORD AM YOUR GOD. YOU SHALL NOT MAKE FOR YOURSELF A GRAVEN IMAGE*

From what has been said so far we may conclude that God is not perceived through the phenomenal context of the Sinaitic revelation but rather in the Commandments themselves. These begin with the words, "I the LORD am your God who brought you out of the land of Egypt, out of the house of bondage". Even for those who hold that this is the first of the Commandments and is actually a command to believe in God,[15] it shows something of the nature of the God who otherwise cannot be understood because of His immaterial and spiritual essence. This attribute is not associated with fire, clouds or thunder, but with the redemption of Israel from Egypt. The additional words "out of the house of bondage" underline the teaching that He is a God who is a merciful and compassionate God who redeemed Israel from slavery. He is the God of Israel because He is their benevolent ruler, and not because He is the Creator of heaven and earth and a mighty power in the world.

This teaching — that the people must recognize Him as their God and accept His sovereignty over them because of His kindness to them — is emphasized in the following midrashic exposition:[16]

> Why were the Ten Commandments not recorded at the very beginning of the Torah? The rabbis explain the reason with the following parable. A stranger came into a city and said to the inhabitants, "I will be your king." The people answered, "What have you ever done for us, that you should be our king?" So he proceeded to do many things for the benefit of the city and the people. He built a defense wall, he brought in water to the city and he defended them against their enemies. Then he said to them again, "I will be your king." And the people immediately

14 Deut. 5. 20–26.
15 See Maimonides, *Book of Commandments*, First Positive; and Nahmanides ad loc.
16 *Mekhilta de R. Ishmael; Ba-Ḥodesh*, V, ed. Horovitz-Rabin, p. 219; cf. ed. Lauterbach, II, pp. 229–230.

agreed. In the same way, God delivered the Israelites from Egyptian slavery, and He parted the Red Sea; He gave them manna from heaven, the water and the quail; and He fought for them against Amalek. Then He said to them, "I will be your king" and the people immediately agreed.

As soon as He brought the people out of Egypt and was accepted as their God, He commanded, "You shall have no other gods beside Me. You shall not make for yourself a graven image, nor any likeness...". It appears from this that it is prohibited to make any graven image or likeness even as an aid to the worship of God. The interpretation of Joseph Bekhor Shor on this is worth noting. He comments:

> Do not say, "I will not serve other gods, but since our God is a hidden God who cannot be seen, I will make myself some graven images and likenesses which I will keep handy, and I will worship them in God's name. In that way I should be able to remember God all the more"... Now to prevent this grievous error, the Bible warns, "You shall not make for yourself". And if others make them for you ? "You shall not bow down to them, nor worship them...". The same prohibition is emphasized in another biblical text: "You saw no shape when the LORD your God spoke to you at Horeb..." (Deut. 4. 15).

From this explanation we should be able to understand another of God's attributes and that is His absolute spirituality. His unique incorporeality means that he cannot even be symbolized by any other existence and cannot be worshipped by means of any material symbol or image. Nor can we associate with His spiritual essence any other essence, not even if it is a beneficial agency in the world and separate from Him.

III. YOU SHALL NOT TAKE THE NAME OF THE LORD YOUR GOD IN VAIN

Another divine attribute, relating to God's essence, which He has revealed to the world, is His truth. The prophet declares, "But the LORD God is the true God, He is the living God and the everlasting King; at His wrath the earth quakes, and the nations are not able to abide His indignation".[17] Rashi comments on that verse, "Why do we

---

17   Jer. 10. 10. Rashi's comment is based on *Tanḥuma, Ḥuqath*, IV; see Buber's comment there, V.

call God, the true God? Because He is living and eternal, and is therefore able to fulfil his word. But a human being will say that he will do something, and then he dies, or becomes ill, or is reduced to poverty, and is unable to carry out what he promised to do". So we can say that the basis of Truth, in relation to God, is his eternity. The rabbis teach, "The seal of the Holy One Blessed be He is Truth",[18] and this Third Commandment, "You shall not take the Name of the LORD your God in vain" is the consequence of this Divine attribute.

Now the term "in vain" is very much like the term "falsely". Indeed, the Ninth Commandment which reads, "You shall not bear false witness against your neighbor" is repeated in Deuteronomy (5. 17) in the words, "Neither shall you bear false witness against your neighbor", as if the Hebrew words *šeqer* and *šaw'* are interchangeable, with the same meaning. However, the rabbis suggest a slight difference in the following:

> R. Dimi said in the name of R. Johanan: One who swears "I will eat" or "I will not eat", and fails to carry out his oath, has sworn falsely (*šeqer*), for an oath relating to the future which is not fulfilled is called *šeqer*. The Bible warns against such an oath with the prohibition, "You shall not swear falsely (*šeqer*) by My Name".[19] If he swears, "I have eaten" or "I have not eaten", and his statement is untrue, then his falsehood is called *šaw'*, for an oath which relates to the past which is untrue is called *šaw'*. The Bible warns against such an oath in the text, "You shall not take the Name of the LORD your God in vain (*šaw'*)".[20]

The Mishnah however, has a different exposition. "What is a false oath (*šaw'*)? If one swears that something known to everyone is the opposite to what it is. For example, if he takes an oath that a block of stone is made of gold, or that a man is a woman...".[21] However, in the Jerusalem Talmud we find that a false oath (*šaw'*) is defined as an oath about the truth which is already obvious to everyone:

> Hezekiah says: A man who swears that two plus two equals four is punished by flagellation because of his vain oath (*šaw'*).... R.

---

18 Sanh. 64a; and *Minḥat Yehudah* on *Genesis Rabbah*, ed. Theodor-Albeck, p. 971.
19 Lev. 19. 12.
20 Shevu. 20b.
21 M. Shavu. III:8.

> Samuel bar Nahman said: There were twenty four towns in the
> south which were destroyed because of the widespread practice
> of swearing about things which were manifestly true (*šaw*).[22]

According to these explanations, the reason for the prohibition in the
Third Commandment against taking the Name of God in vain (*šaw'*), is
because such an oath expresses disrespect for God's Name, and one
who is guilty of such an offense cannot accept the yoke of God's
supreme sovereignty.

But it is also possible to argue that even in the case of a man swearing
about something which is manifestly true there is an element of
falsehood. For normally, a man does not swear at all unless others
might have some doubt about the truth of what he is saying. But on
something which is clearly known to everyone he would not take an
oath. Therefore, when this fellow jumps in with his oath his listeners
suspect that he is really swearing about something else, and not about
the thing which is already known to everyone. It is this misrep-
resentation of the situation on his part which is a form of falsehood.
According to the following midrash[23] the Third Commandment implies
a warning against oath-taking with an element of falsehood:

> Another explanation: Why is the verse "You shall not take the
> name of the LORD your God in vain" recorded at all in the
> Scriptures, when we have the verse "You shall not swear by My
> name falsely" (Lev. 19. 12)?[24] The answer is, that from the latter
> verse we can understand the prohibition against taking a false
> oath. But how would we know that one should not even take it
> upon himself to swear falsely? Therefore the verse "You shall not
> take the name of the LORD your God in vain" is necessary.

Since man ought to cleave to the ways of God , which includes the
attribute of truth, it must follow that man has to keep far from
falsehood. This is part of what Ibn Ezra says on the Commandment we
are discussing, "The reason for mentioning God's name in an oath is to
emphasize to man that just as God's name is Truth, so should his own
words be true; and that if he does not fulfill his word then it is as if he

---

22   Yer. Shavu. III:8.
23   *Mekhilta de R. Ishmael, Ba-Ḥodesh*, VII; ed. Horovitz-Rabin, p. 227; cf. ed.
     Lauterbach, II, p. 248.
24   Lev. 19. 12.

had denied God Himself". Jospeh Bekhor Shor makes a similar observation:

> A man should not say, "Since God does not want us to swear by any other god, I will always invoke His name, whether my case is true or false". For the verse comes to warn us, "You shall not take the name... in vain", since God is Truth and one may not invoke His name except to establish the truth.

The Jerusalem Talmud makes the connection between God in His attribute of Truth and the prohibition against falsehood, in the following comment:

> The Bible declares, "You shall not bear false witness against your neighbor.... I am the LORD your God". It is also written, "The LORD is a God of Truth". What does this latter text mean ? R. Abbun said: It means that He is the living God and King of the Universe. R. Levi taught: God said, "If you bear false witness against your neighbor it is as if you testified falsely against Me, that I did not create heaven and earth".[25]

One keeps away from falsehood not only by the avoidance of swearing on oath or by not taking the name of God in vain, but in other ways as well. The Bible warns, "You shall not bear false witness against your neighbor". Now a witness is not allowed to take an oath, yet he is still forbidden to make a false statement, even without an oath. Other biblical prohibitions in the same class are, "Keep far from a false matter"[26] and "You shall not deal deceitfully or falsely with one another".[27]

These other ways are not mentioned in the Ten Commandments, and the commandments do not contain a comprehensive prohibition against speaking anything which is not true, because there are "falsehoods" of a kind which are not really prohibited. Examples of this class are nonsense statements, or hyperbole, or deviations from the truth for the sake of the higher value of peace between man and his fellow. Such "falsehoods" are unavoidable if a man follows the teaching of the Sages that he should always be involved in the day-to-day life of his

25   Yer. Ber. I:5.
26   Ex. 23. 7.
27   Lev. 19. 11.

community.[28] These are in any case situations where there is no danger that anyone will be misled by the "false" statements because everyone knows, say in a situation of nonsense or hyperbolic talk, that the speaker does not mean to be taken literally. However, when it comes to a situation where people are going to believe what one says, then one has to take care to speak only that which is true. This will usually apply in the situation where the speaker takes an oath since in such a case people are certainly inclined to believe that what he says is the truth.

IV. THE CHARACTER OF THE FIRST THREE COMMANDMENTS

Since the human mind can only understand something of God's attributes but not His essence, God reveals aspects of these Divine attributes in the first three Commandments, because only the activity of these attributes can be seen in the real world. This enables us to learn something about divine worship resulting from the Divine nature. In brief, the kind of worship of God which is implied in the Ten Commandments can be understood rationally from our grasp of the teachings about the divine attributes. The Ten Commandments themselves include no specific ordinances about divine worship. There is no command to pray to Him, or to offer sacrifice to Him. No mention is made of devotion to God, or to any particular religious world view, or of any decree which cannot be derived by reason from His attributes. In fact these Ten Commandments contain only prohibitions without any positive laws at all. A man may love God and be devoted to Him in his own way. A man is free to worship God and to pray to Him as best he can and in accordance with his own temperament, provided that it can be established that nothing in that man's chosen way contradicts the attributes of God, but on the contrary, all his religious worship of God derives from his understanding of God's attributes. These will certainly include his recognition that God benefits those who love Him, that God is uniquely One, that He has no bodily form, that He is eternal and that He is the total Truth.

As we have already indicated, these first Commandments contain only prohibitions and no positive ordinances connected with the worship of God. Laws dealing with pilgrimages or sacrifices, for example, have absolutely no place in these Commandments. The same characteristic is found in the later Commandments, and particularly in those dealing with man's relationship with his fellow. This will be explained below.

28   Ket. 17a.

V. *REMEMBER THE SABBATH DAY TO KEEP IT HOLY*

"Remember the Sabbath day to keep it holy... but the seventh day is a Sabbath of the LORD your God: you shall not do any work...". This Commandment also illustrates a divine attribute. The reason for the Sabbath, according to this text in Exodus 20, is because... "in six days the LORD made heaven and earth and sea and all that is in them, and He rested on the seventh day". God is here described as the Creator who "rested". Now since man is taught to follow in God's ways, and to cleave to Him by imitating Him, so man too should work for six days and rest on the seventh.

However, in the text of the Ten Commandments as repeated in Deuteronomy 5. 14 the reason for the sanctity of the Sabbath is ... "so that your male and female slave may rest as you do. Remember that you were a slave in the land of Egypt and the LORD your God freed you from there". It might seem that the two reasons given for sabbath observance in Exodus and in Deuteronomy are in the nature of cause and effect. Why did God create heaven and earth in six days? Why did He rest on the seventh day? And why are we told all this in the Torah? Surely, since God could have created the Universe in a split second He did not need six days. Again, He does not need rest. What then is the whole purpose of this part of the biblical record?

The answer to all these questions is seen in the repetition of the Commandments when the concept of human freedom is emphasized. As free men we must not labor constantly as the slaves did in Egypt. We are all meant to be servants of God, and not the servants of servants. To remind himself of this truth, man has to rest on the seventh day. In that way he can imitate the sovereignty and freedom of God who also "rested" from his work on the seventh day, and there is no power which can force Him to work. Reference to the Exodus from Egyptian slavery underlines this important concept.

We can therefore conclude that whether we follow the reason given in Exodus or the one in Deuteronomy, the purpose of the Sabbath is to instill the teaching of *imitatio dei*. God created the world in six days and rested on the seventh, in order to teach man how he should live in freedom, and how he should relate to his own servants and even to his animals, to whom as well he should be merciful and upright, as God is to his creatures. For in order to follow in God's way he has to treat other men as if they were free men and to relate to them in uprightness. This point will be explained later on. Meanwhile, we can summarize this section by posing the question and giving the answer: How should men behave in their own lives? Only as free human beings. This is an important teaching, and Bible emphasizes the critical nature of human freedom by saying that God delivered Israel from slavery "with a strong hand and an outstretched arm".

This entire message is explained in the following midrash:[29]

> "He rested on the seventh day". Is He then subject to such a thing as weariness? Is it not written: "Creator of the earth from end to end, He never grows faint or weary"?[30] And also: "He gives strength to the weary"?[31] And then, "By the word of the LORD the heavens were made".[32] How then can Scripture say "He rested on the seventh day"? It simply means that God allowed it to be written about Himself that He created the world in six days and then rested, as it were, on the seventh. Now by the logic of *a fortiori* you must reason: If He for whom there is no weariness allowed it to be written that He created the world in six days and rested on the seventh, how much more should man of whom it is written, "But man is born unto toil"[33] rest on the seventh day.

This Commandment about the Sabbath is promulgated as a negative command. That is, we are given a prohibition against working on the holy day but no positive ordinance about what a man should do on the Sabbath. Even the command to make the Sabbath day holy seems to be fulfilled by refraining from work on that day, and we are not told how to sanctify the day with positive action. It would seem then, and in accordance with what has been stated above, that provided a man behaves in a spirit of true freedom, and follows the ways of God with reason and with knowledge, then he can be left to make the day holy in accordance with his own circumstances and ability.

VI. HONOR YOUR FATHER AND YOUR MOTHER

Although the Fifth Commandment dealing with honor to be given parents is also couched as a positive command, i.e., "Honor your father and your mother", yet it contains no more positive instruction than does the Sabbath law. That is, we are not told what to do in order to

29   *Mekhilta Ba-Ḥodesh*, 7, ed. Horovitz-Rabin, p. 230;, cf. ed. Lauterbach, II, p. 255.
30   Isa. 40. 28.
31   Ibid., 29.
32   Ps. 33. 6.
33   Job 5. 7.

honor our parents. This mitzvah is placed in the middle, between those Commandments which deal with man's relationship to God and the others which are between man and his fellow man. On the surface this Fifth Commandment belongs to the latter group.

The Jerusalem Talmud[34] classifies honor due to parents as a kind of repayment of a debt:

> R. Abbin says: If in the performance of a law which in fact is no more than a repayment of an obligation the Torah still promises "that you may long endure and that it may go well with you"[35] how much more so is there a reward in the performance of a command which involves financial loss or even danger. R. Levi disagreed and said: The law involving a repayment is greater than the law in which there is no repayment.

And giving honor to parents belongs to the class of repayment because (to quote the comment of *Pene Moshe*) "everything a man can do for his father and mother is no more than a return for all the good they have done for him in bearing him, raising him and educating him".
We can learn from the following talmudic exposition about another of the divine attributes, an attribute which is revealed to man in the Fifth Commandment, in order that man may imitate Him. This attribute is humility:

> Ulla said: What is the meaning of the verse "All the kings of the earth shall praise you, O LORD, for they have heard the words you spoke" (Ps. 138. 4)? When the peoples of the world heard the first two commands "I am" and "You shall have no other", they said: "Their God is concerned only for Himself." But as soon as they heard "Honor your father and your mother", they changed their minds about the first commands, and admitted their truth.[36]

The first sign of haughtiness is egotism, since the conceited or haughty man thinks only about himself. All his thoughts and deeds are concentrated on his own person. This makes him arrogant and domineering. But a humble man possesses the opposite qualities. Therefore His chief concern is to spread peace and friendship among all. The Talmud calls haughtiness, *gasut ruah* — and the Sages strongly

34   Peah I:1.
35   Deut. 5. 16.
36   Qid. 31a.

condemn it.[37] Similarly, at the end of the second chapter of Tractate Sukkah we read, "The worst kind of human failing is haughtiness" (Rashi explains: *gasut ruaḥ* is haughtiness which leads to a desire to lord it over others). In contrast, the Bible praises the humble with the words, "But the humble shall inherit the land, and delight in abundant well-being" (Ps. 37. 11). Further, R. Johanan said (Meg. 31a) "In every passage in Scripture where you find the greatness of God, there you will also find a reference to His humility.... An example of this is in the text, 'He upholds the cause of the fatherless and the widow' (Deut. 10.18)." Now since God's law to honor parents does not deal with His own honor, but with the honor of others, it shows something of the Divine humility and His peace-loving nature. Accordingly, it follows that this quality of humility should be imitated by man. It is even fitting that this Fifth Commandment with its teaching of humility is the first of the social Commandments with their emphasis on righteousness, because in a sense humility is at the heart of all social justice.

It is noteworthy that the Sages suggest a comparison between honoring parents and honoring God. So we read in the Yerushalmi:

> R. Simeon bar Yohai says: The Commandment to honor parents is a very important one, since God gives it priority even over His own honor. Thus it is written: "Honor your father and your mother" (i.e., with all your ability) while elsewhere Scripture merely says, "Honor the LORD with your wealth".[38]

Another tradition[39] reads:

> Rabbi Judah says: The honoring of one's father and mother is very dear in the sight of Him by whose word the world came into being. For He declared honoring them to be equal to honoring Him, fearing them to be equal to fearing Him, and cursing them to be as serious as cursing Him. It is written, "Honor your father and your mother"; and correspondingly it is written, "Honor the LORD with your wealth". Scripture thus puts honoring one's parents on an equal footing with honoring God. It is written, "You shall each revere his mother and his father"[40] and

---

37 Sot. 4b ff. See Meiri, ad loc. and Maimonides on the Mishnah, Avot IV:4.
38 Prov. 3. 9.
39 *Mekhilta Ba-Ḥodesh*, 8, p. 231; cf. ed. Lauterbach, II, pp. 257–258.
40 Lev. 19. 3.

correspondingly it is written, "Revere only the LORD your God".[41] Scripture thus seems to place the fear of parents and the fear of God in an equal category of importance.

The command to honor one's parents is a natural law which people would always observe even if it were not included in the Ten Commandments or anywhere else in the Torah. As Rabbi Judah observed,[42] "Although a person honors both parents, he loves his mother more than his father.... And although one can fear both parents, he frequently fears his father more than he fears his mother...". Further, the ethic to honor one's parents is universally observed; even non-Jews are faithful to this precept, although they did not experience the Revelation at Sinai. A good example of this is told in the wonderful talmudic stories about Damah bar Netina, a gentile from Ashkelon.[43]

That being so, why was the law expressly stated in the Ten Commandments? The comment of Bekhor Shor is appropriate here.

> God says, although I have commanded that I alone am to be worshipped, glorified and honored, nevertheless you are to show all honor to your mother and your father, and do not forget all that they have done for you. They gave you birth, they nurtured you until you were grown up, and all their concern was centered on your well-being. I know that if you honor them and give them their recompense, then you are all the more likely to honor Me, for all the good which I have bestowed on you.

The text of the Commandment provides a motive for its observance. "...that you may long endure upon the land which the LORD your God gives you". Now this statement is not a promise of direct reward for fulfilling the Commandment, no more than the other Commandments carry a statement of reward for their observance. What it means rather is that one who honors his parents in their old age by caring for their well-being in fact lengthens their years. At the same time he provides his own children with an example, showing them how the Fifth Commandment is to be obeyed. Then in the time of his own old age, his children in their turn will care for him in the same way, and so add to the years of his own life. This interpretation matches the comment of

41 Deut. 6. 13.
42 *Mekhilta*, ibid., p. 232, ed. Lauterbach, II, p. 259; Qid. 30b–31a.
43 Qid. 31a; Yer. Peah I:1.

Joseph Bekhor Shor who says, "When you observe this commandment, your own children will honor you and support you in your old age, so that you will live to the maximum number of your years."

Another reason for this Commandment may by given. It is the only one of the Ten which is given as a positive command; all the others (with the exception of the First) are negative commands. Perhaps we can understand it in the following way: Parents generally train the child how to behave from the beginning. Now if he honors them, then he is likely to respect all their teachings, including of course those relating to social behavior. Consequently, this command to honor parents becomes a starting point for the observance of the last five Commandments which deal with man's relationship to his fellow. The opposite will also be true: one who shows no respect for his parents is less likely to heed the other Commandments. This thought provides a link between honoring parents and honoring God, because the honor and fear of God is also a prerequisite for the observance of His commandments.

R. Moses the Preacher taught,[44]

> The good deed of honoring parents is as great as the study of Torah. In the case of the latter, it is written "For thereby you shall have life and shall long endure" (Deut. 30. 20); and in connection with honoring one's parents the Bible promises, "that you may long endure" (Ex. 20. 12). The similarity of the two promises shows a connection between the two values of Torah study and honoring parents, and thus emphasizes that a person who honors his parents is also assured of life in the world to come, even though he may not be learned in the Torah.

From what has been said we can see something of the twofold nature of this command. It is among the first five Commandments relating to the

---

44   *Bereshit Rabbati*, ed. Albeck, p. 146, and similarly regarding honor due to students of the Torah. The Talmud (Ket. 111b) expounds Deuteronomy 4. 4: "'But you, who held fast to the LORD your God, are all alive today,' Is it then at all posibble to hold fast to God? But what it means is that one who marries his daughter to a scholar of the Torah, or does business on behalf of Torah scholars, or benefits them from his own property, is likened to one who holds fast to the Divine Presence. The same explanation applies to Deuteronomy 30.20: "Choose life... by loving the LORD your God, heeding his commands, and holding fast to Him'". Cf. *Sifre Deut.* 49, ed. Finkelstein, pp. 114–115.

service of God, while it is also a mitzvah which belongs to the last five which deal with man's relationship to his fellow.

VII. THE DIVINE ATTRIBUTES IN THE COMMANDMENTS WHICH MAN SHOULD EMULATE

The five Commandments of the second group all relate to man's social behavior:

> You shall nor murder. You shall not commit adultery. You shall not steal. You shall not bear false witness against your neighbor. You shall not covet your neighbor's house: you shall not covet your neighbor's wife, or his male or female slave, or his ox or his ass, or anything that is your neighbor's.

Here God reveals His attribute as the God of righteousness and justice. As in the first Commandments, here too God relates to His world in this way as a partial revelation of the Divine mystery which it would otherwise have been impossible for the human mind to grasp, since man can only understand something about God through His actions, and here He is revealed as concerned with practical righteousness. Now, just as the first Commandments reveal Divine attributes which men are to follow, these latter Commandments which emphasize Divine righteousness and justice are also attributes of God which man must try to emulate in his own life in order to come as close as he can to God. Social justice like the attributes mentioned earlier is not an inner experience like love and compassion, but a religious concept which leads to action, and from which detailed behaviour can logically be derived.

The Ten Commandments do not explicitly state that man must walk in the ways of God and be like unto Him. But that is spelled out elsewhere in Scripture: "After the LORD your God shall you walk, and Him shall you fear, and His commandments shall you keep, and unto His voice shall you hearken; Him shall you serve, and to Him shall you cleave".[45] Again, "You shall keep the commandments of the LORD your God and walk in His ways".[46] The Sages offer the following interpretation of these verses:[47]

45   Deut. 13. 5.
46   Ibid., 28. 9.
47   Sot. 14a.

R. Hamma b. Hanina said: What is the meaning of the text,
"After the LORD your God shall you walk?" Is it at all possible to
walk in the path of the Divine Presence? Does not the Bible
describe God as a "consuming fire"? The answer is that our verse
means that we should follow the Holy One Blessed be He in the
following manner: Just as He clothes the naked, in accordance
with what is written, "And the LORD God made for Adam and
for his wife garments of skins and clothed them", so you should
clothe the naked. God visits the sick as it is written, "And the
LORD appeared unto him [Abraham during his indisposition] by
the terebinths of Mamre" — so you too should visit the sick. The
Holy One blessed be He comforts the mourners as it is written,
"And it came to pass after the death of Abraham, that God
blessed Isaac his son", — so you too should comfort the bereaved.
God even buries the dead, as it is written, "And He buried him
[Moses] in the valley" — so you too should bury the dead.

A similar teaching is found in the following rabbinic passage:[48] "Abba
Saul explains the word *veanvehu* (I will glorify Him (Ex. 15. 2) — Be
like Him (Rashi: *veanvehu = ani vahu*, i.e., I and He: I will make
myself godly by cleaving to His ways). Just as he is gracious and
compassionate so you too must be gracious and compassionate".

A further example of this teaching is found in connection with the
text, "To love the LORD your God, to walk in all His ways, and to
cleave unto Him",[49] on which the Midrash offers the comment:[50]

To walk in all His ways, means to emulate the ways of the
Omnipresent: "The LORD God is merciful and gracious".[51] And
it is written: "It shall come to pass that whosoever shall call on the
name of the LORD shall be delivered".[52] Now how can one
possibly know the name of God to call upon Him? The answer is
that since God is called merciful, so you too be merciful. As God
is called gracious, be you also gracious, as it is written, "The
LORD is gracious and full of compassion".[53] God is called

48   Shab. 133b.
49   Deut. 11. 22.
50   *Sifre Deut.* 49, ed. Finkelstein, p. 114; see Maimonides, *Mishneh Torah, De'ot* I:6;
     and *Guide*, I:54.
51   Ex. 34. 6.
52   Joel 3. 5.
53   Ps. 145. 8.

righteous as it is written, "For the LORD is righteous, He loves righteousness",[54] so you too be righteous. God is called merciful as it is written, "For I am merciful, says the LORD" (Jer. 3. 12), so you likewise be merciful.

Now our treatment of the subject is not found explicitly in the Ten Commandments. But in the Book of Deuteronomy, Moses explains those Commandments in the way we have indicated above, so that man should know how to follow in the ways of God. We shall explain why those principles are not included in the Commandments themselves, and why the last Commandments emphasize only these five prohibitions, to the exclusion of all other social laws.

VIII. THE CONCEPT OF JUSTICE IN THE TEN COMMANDMENTS

Justice is correct behavior towards one's fellow man and towards the community, and right behavior of the community towards the individual. Of course since it is impossible to lay down detailed descriptions of applied justice in every single situation, we have to concern ourselves with general principles. We can only attempt to judge a particular action or a new occurence by comparing it with another which has something in common with it, and which has already been evaluated as just or unjust. It is possible to compare two cases only if there is a broad principle which can cover both situations; but then the case can also be decided according to the principle, instead of by comparison. A principle is always arrived at by conceptualizing the common elements of similar cases, elements which are characteristic and constant, and not accidental and variable. Therefore the reason for every decision is the selfsame principle of which the case is a particular and a consequence. It follows, that a decision according to the principle should be made, and there is no need to compare the case to a similar one, which is governed by the same principle.

Now the fact of the matter is that most human actions are really very complex and contain elements which are subsumed under a variety of different and even opposing principles. This makes the assessment of a person's actions very difficult, since the act would belong to different values and therefore end up with different assessments according to its different elements. At times it is not even possible to decide which principle is the main factor in a person's action and which one is

54   Ps. 11. 7.

relatively unimportant, in order to make the judgment in line with the chief principle. Further, it may be difficult to discover any overriding or comprehensive ethical value which can embrace the varied principles which are involved in the particular act, so we are then unable to arrive at the point where we can properly judge a man's conduct.

It is maintained here that the last five Commandments, dealing with interpersonal relations, illustrate the decisive world view whenever opposing principles are involved. On the basis of this world view we can judge every specific social act. These same fundamentals can even enable us to lay down the very principles by which we assess what is just and what is unjust, what is permitted and what is prohibited, when a man is guilty and when he is innocent. These fundamentals cannot be arrived at by logic or common sense, or by comparing them with similar or overriding concepts. In fact, since they cannot be grasped merely through logic or common sense, such concepts might be accepted by various peoples at different stages of history in many different ways, with the result that there would be different ethical values. Since the fundamentals in these Commandments are abstract principles they do not lay down (let alone explain) how one should behave. However, the fundamentals in the Commandments do say how to carry out human behaviour; how an action would be just and morally right. It is just like the pigment which is mixed in with any matter and gives that matter its distinctive color. Let us explain this a little further.

IX. YOU SHALL NOT COMMIT ADULTERY; YOU SHALL NOT MURDER

Take for example the Commandment, "You shall not commit adultery". Rashi explains,[55] "Adultery is only with another man's wife". However, Ibn Ezra disagrees and comments, "There are many who think that adultery can be only with another man's wife... but the matter is not so.... The word *ni'uf* (adultery) is the equivalent of *zenuth* (whoredom)". According to this, any illicit sex relationship is *ni'uf* (adultery) and is prohibited in the Commandment. But to know exactly what is an illicit sex relationship within the terms of the prohibition one would have to know all the sex laws which belong to the subject. For example, sex with one's brother's wife is always prohibited. But what happens if his brother dies childless? Then the surviving brother has the

---

55   Ex. 23. 13; Deut. 5. 17.

duty to marry the widow. From the simple law "You shall not commit adultery" it is impossible to know what is sexually prohibited and what is permitted. Even on the assumption that this ban only prohibits sex with another man's wife, we would have to know much more about the legal marital status of the particular woman in question. Perhaps after all, she is not really the legal wife of another man.

So we see that this prohibition does not teach us any of the detailed laws on the subject and should be understood only as a fundamental principle of the kind we have discussed above. In this respect the purpose of this law is to make a determination between conflicting rules, when it is impossible logically to prefer one rule to the other. The Commandment is a fundamental principle which has no logical basis and cannot be derived rationally from any other concept by way of analogy or deduction. Therefore many cultures and philosophies (Plato for example) do not prohibit categorically acts of adultery or sexual relations between relatives. It is thus a social and ethical ideal for the people of the Torah, which decides between conflicting rules, although in certain circumstances the prohibition against acts of adultery is also found among other nations and cultures. The idea that this Commandment is a fundamental ethical concept deciding between conflicting rules, with no rational derivation, and therefore unique among civilizations, is expressed by the Sages in the saying: "The God of the Israelites hates whoredom".[56]

An example of how this Commandment can be the deciding factor in a situation where a man's act falls between two conflicting considerations is the following case:[57]

> R. Judah said in the name of Rav: There was a man who was so infatuated with a woman that he became seriously ill because of his unsatisfied passion. His family sought the advice of a doctor who said, "There can be no cure for him until he has sex with her." Whereupon the rabbis ruled, "It were better that the man die rather than submit the woman to intercourse with him." Another suggestion was made that she be permitted to stand naked before him, but the rabbis objected again and said, "It were better that he be left to die." Finally, the suggestion was made that the woman be allowed to speak with him behind a

56   Sanh. 93a; 106a.
57   Ibid., 75a.

screen. But the rabbis protested even at this and would not give their permission. There were two opinions about the circumstances of the case. One opinion held that the woman in question was a married woman, while another opinion held that she was an unmarried woman. Now if she were a married woman then there is good reason for the rabbis' attitude even though the man was sick to death. But what if she were single? Why all the fuss and the objection of the rabbis? After all, couldn't they see that they could save the man's life? R. Pappa said, the rabbinic strictness was to avoid shaming the lady's family. R. Aha the son of R. Ikka said that the rabbis remained firm in order to prevent licentiousness among Jewish maidens.

The rabbis opposed such practices, and their decisions received their sanction from the fundamental principle of the Sinaitic Commandment.

The same argument applies to all the other Commandments. Each one is the source and the rationale for the principles and the laws governing man's relationship to his fellow man. In situations of doubt each Commandment can provide a fundamental teaching from which the final decision can be made, and each can contribute its special tone to the concept of justice as revealed on Mount Sinai.

Consider the Commandment, "You shall not murder" from this point of view. Clearly it is a prohibition against killing another person. But there are situations in which the law not only permits killing another but commands it, since even the Torah lays down the death penalty for certain offenses. Hence the Commandment cannot be taken as a practical instruction directing one how to act, since it is devoid of all the laws which, in certain situations, provide the sanction for taking life. And besides, the prohibition of murder is not specific to the Ten Commandments but is common to all civilisations. The only way in which we can read the Commandment, then, is to take it as a fundamental principle which gives its special quality to the concept of the sanctity of life.

In this way we can also understand the Mishnah:[58] "A High Court which sentences a man to death once in seven years is called a murderous court.... R. Tarfon and R. Akiba said: If we had been members of such a court we would never have given a death sentence". This is because in any case of doubt due to conflicting principles one should be guided by the fundamental teaching not to shed blood.

58   M. Mak. I:10.

This guided teaching also informs the rabbinic ruling[59] that nothing is allowed to stand in the way of saving a life except for the prohibitions against idolatry, sexual immorality and murder. Similarly we have the ruling[60] that one may cure a disease in all circumstances except where the cure involves idolatry, sexual immorality or murder. Or the teaching that if one were ordered to transgress a law or be killed, he should rather transgress the law in order to save his life, except if he be ordered to commit one of three offenses: idolatry, sexual immorality or murder.[61] The rabbis also taught that "The Temple was destroyed and the Divine Presence parted from Israel on account of the crime of murder".[62] In other civilizations there is also a prohibition against murder, but this prohibition is not a decisive principle when rules conflict, or in cases of doubt, or when killing appears necessary.

X. THE FUNDAMENTAL PRINCIPLE OF JUSTICE

It is of course true that all civilized peoples recognize the validity of the concepts of justice and the laws which regulate social behavior. But they accept them as a result of common sense and reason and not because these five Commandments represent a higher concept which stands above reason, nor because they are absolute in their authority to decide in every situation when principles conflict. This point is apparently indicated in the Midrash which offers the following:[63]

> The other nations were invited to receive the Torah in order to prevent any future complaint that, had they been offered the Torah they would have accepted it. But when the offer was made they refused the opportunity. God went to the Edomites and asked them if they were prepared to accept the Commandments. "What is in them?" they asked, and when He gave them as an example, "Thou shalt not murder" they immediately refused and said, "Killing is our very way of life which we inherited from our ancestor Esau!"... God then invited the Amonites and Moabites to receive the Commandments, but when they heard the command "Thou shalt not commit adultery" they too refused the Torah, saying "How can we possibly take these Commandments

59   Yoma 82a.
60   Pes. 25a.
61   Sanh. 74a.
62   Shab. 33a.
63   *Mekhilta de R. Ishmael, Ba-Hodesh*, 5, p. 221; cf. ed. Lauterbach, II, pp. 234–236.

when our very origins are from acts of incest?"... When God offered the Torah to the Ishmaelites they too wanted first of all to know what they would have to keep, and when they were told "Thou shalt not steal" they rejected it saying, "The chief blessing given to our ancestor permits us to live by robbery!"... Finally, God went to the Israelites and they immediately cried out, "All that the LORD hath spoken we will do and will hear!" R. Simeon b. Eleazar said: If these people cannot even keep the seven universal Noachide laws which they were commanded and which they accepted, how much less would they have been able to keep the other laws of the Torah!

We might learn from this that Israel alone recognized the validity and authority of these Commandments as the ultimate value in any conflict of values. The other nations have different priorities and a different world outlook. Israel is different in this from any other nation, as a separate people, "a kingdom of priests and a holy nation".[64] Because, as was already explained, only they accepted these commandments as ultimate principles of justice, as imitation of God in his attributes.

We conclude, therefore, that the Ten Commandments are absolute and ultimate; they cannot be deduced from broader principles or derived by analogy from other principles. Therefore we cannot look for reasons for their observance in, say, their importance for social stability, or for man's happiness, or for the sake of the security and prosperity of the nation, because these would then be higher values. For example, take the case of two men: one old, wicked and rich; the other young, of excellent character, but so poor that he is starving. Is it then permitted to kill the wicked old man and take his money to support the young man, and so open up the possibility of increasing happiness in the world? There may be an argument for doing so. But the answer of the Decalogue is a clear "no!" The categorical imperative "Thou shalt not murder" sweeps aside and invalidates all rationalizations to the contrary. In the same way the prohibition "Thou shalt not commit adultery" is the decisive fundamental in the case of the man whose life was in danger because of his love-sickness. An argument was in fact adduced to the effect that the woman should submit to having sex with him. His life might be saved, and being an unmarried woman she would not suffer too much thereby. But the law of the Decalogue stands

64   Ex. 19. 6.

unmoved against such reasoning. The reason that these Commandments stand as a world view is that they manifest the attributes of God as the God of Justice, and nothing else.

The purpose of the Decalogue is seen in God's revelation of His divine attributes, and in the description of Himself as the God of Justice. The laws of the Decalogue, then, are not dependent on any other factor. Furthermore, a divine revelation which is devoid of the principles of righteousness and justice, applicable in the affairs of man, would only be a cause for fear of those supernatural forces which are removed from the world of man and whose terrible powers are unknown because they are rare and unusual. At the very best such a revelation could excite an emotional irrational relationship to the revealing power like religious experience or sexual love; but it would have no practical application to any real life situation. Forces which give rise to such emotions really have nothing to distinguish them from demonic forces. We therefore emphasize the special character of the Sinaitic revelation in which the divine attributes of righteousness and justice are made known. These obligate all who love God to follow in their pattern.

XI. THE NATURE OF THE LAST FIVE COMMANDMENTS

We have already explained that the fundamentals of justice enumerated in the Ten Commandments are stated as absolute values, and are not a series of detailed laws. Obviously it is quite impossible for the Commandments to regulate from the outset all the laws required to cover the countless situations in which a person can find himself at different times and in different circumstances. These fundamentals which are in the Ten Commandments therefore have no detailed content at all. All men are at liberty to act in accordance with the particular demands of time and place, and each one in accordance with his circumstances, ability and temperament. There is only one rule, and that is that his actions pass the unequivocal test by the standard of justice. Every act has to have the stamp of justice.

Justice is a social concept and is therefore only present in human relationships. It is in more frequent demand in those situations where there are difficulties with limited resources and no possibility for magnanimity; and especially when there is jealousy, rivalry, scarcity and controversy among men. Still, that is the whole purpose of Torah; to be a practical guide to man; and as the Sages observe — the Torah was not given to angels. So R. Joshua ben Levi offers the following thought:[65]

> The angels protested to God saying, "You have a magnificent treasure [the Torah]. Why give it away to ordinary men of flesh and blood?" God persuaded Moses to answer the angels. Moses asked, "The Torah which You propose to give us, what is in it?" God replied, "I am the LORD your God who brought you out of the land of Egypt." Turning to the angels, Moses challenged them, "Did you ever live in Egypt? Were you ever the slaves of Pharaoh? Of course not! So what relevance has the Torah for you?" Again Moses asked what is written in the Torah and when God replied, "You shall have no other gods beside Me" Moses asked the angels, "Were you ever made to live among heathen peoples with their false gods? So what is this law to you?" When Moses asked God about a further Commandment he was told, "Remember the Sabbath day to keep it holy". Addressing the angels he said, "Since you don't labor during the week what significance can the Sabbath rest possibly have for you?" Moses was then told about the law against taking a false oath in God's name, and he argued that since the angels are never involved in business dealings the Commandment is hardly applicable. Then he challenged the angels about the Commandment, "Honor your father and mother". He said to the angels, "But you have no father and mother". And what about the other Commandments: "You shall not murder; You shall not commit adultery; You shall not steal". "Do you have any jealous angels? Do you have any sex-drives, any acquisitive passions? Surely then these Commandments are revelant only to man, and not to you"!

We see that there are no positive laws in these latter Commandments. They are given as negative laws. They do not teach a person what he should do. This he decides for himself, but they teach him how to do it correctly by avoiding injustice. The Commandments insist that what he does shall be just. And for this purpose they are more effective when they are couched as negative prohibitions. It is not only the five social Commandments which are stated in this way; nearly all the first Commandments which speak of man's relationship to God are similarly worded. Those Commandments do not tell man how he should worship

65   Shab. 88b–89a.

God, or love Him, or fear Him. In those matters every man will follow
his own pattern according to his nature and ability. The
Commandments do however exhort one to avoid doing what is
prohibited, because breaking the prohibitions would distance him
from God and His attributes as revealed in the Ten Commandments.
And it is the same thing with respect to the last Commandments. There
is no law here for example, that a person must keep his promise, or
restore loans, or repay debts. We do not read that one must use his
possessions for the benefit of society, or for the glory of God. There is
no positive law that man must be involved in social welfare, or influence
others in that direction. There is not even a general teaching that a
person limit his activity to those things which are his own business. The
negative Commandments stress that one should not harm his fellow in
any way and keep away from his fellow's business. He should not even
covet that which does not belong to him, lest he find ways of taking
what he covets even if it is for the welfare of society.

The single exception to all these negative Commandments is the
Fifth, "Honor your father and your mother". It is possible to explain
this exception by suggesting that in a way it is a foundation-principle
for the other Commandments. One is obligated to honor his parents
because they train him to behave properly. To the extent that he honors
them he has respect for the rest of their teaching, and so he can fulfill
the law of God and keep close to His will.

XII. THE GENERAL NATURE OF ALL THE COMMANDMENTS

There is another feature of the Ten Commandments, in addition to
what has already been described; that is, they were promulgated to the
entire people of Israel. In general, whenever laws are proclaimed they
are first given to the leader for him to transmit to the people. Or the
ruler will himself impose laws on the people in the first place, since that
is after all one of the functions of leadership. For their part, the people
are then under the compulsion to obey the laws or suffer the
consequences.

However, the Ten Commandments were given directly to every
individual Israelite without any intermediaries, priests, kings or other
leaders who could impose the Torah on the people. There is not even
any mention of rulers, leaders or judges to compel and to punish.
Nahmanides observes in this context, "All the Ten Commandments are
promulgated in the singular; thus '... the LORD *thy* God who brought
thee out ...' and not in the plural form with which the entire record of
the revelation is introduced, viz. 'You [plural] have seen that I spoke to

you [plural] from the heaven.... You [plural] shall surely hearken...'
(Ex. 19. 4–5). For God spoke to each individual and commanded each
one, so that no individual can take cover behind a sinful majority".[66]

Again, in the words of the *Leqaḥ Tov*, "Why were the Ten
Commandments proclaimed in the singular? To tell you that every
Israelite has to feel that the Torah was given to him and that he
personally has to observe it. It is not good enough for him to say that he
can get by with its observance by others".[67] Further, no one can shift his
personal responsibility and claim that he will only obey the orders of
the leaders who are supposed to know best. The Ten Commandments
will not permit the individual to hide behind blind obedience to a leader
who orders him to do anything against them, even if it is with good
intentions or for the benefit of society.

This point about individual responsibility underlies the commentary
on the text, "For I the LORD your God am an impassioned God,
visiting the guilt of the parents upon the children, to the third and
fourth generations of those that reject me". The Talmud comments:[68]

> R. Jose the son of R. Hanina said: Moses imposed four rulings
> on Israel. Then four prophets arose who annulled them.... Moses
> said of God that he visits the guilt of the parents upon the
> children. But the prophet Ezekiel came and annulled it and said,
> "The person who sins, he alone shall die."[69]

The Mosaic text now is understood to mean that only when the
children and grandchildren themselves sin, is the guilt of the parents
added to their own guilt, since in that situation the children have
willingly followed in the sins of the fathers. There is therefore a clear
personal responsibility on their part.

That the Ten Commandments were given to each individual is an
aspect of the Decalogue which is in a way related to what has been said
above about them being couched in the negative rather than the
positive. Action is the responsibility of each individual which should not
be enforced on him by his superiors. In that respect too, as we have
already seen, the emphasis is more clearly on the behavior of the
individual.

These two conclusions are clearly implied in the talmudic aggadah:

66   ad Ex. 20. 2.
67   *Leqaḥ Tov*, ed. Buber, p. 134.
68   Mak. 24a.
69   Ezek. 18. 20.

R. Abdimi bar Hama bar Hasa said: We may infer from the words, "They stood at the foot (*betaḥtit*, literally 'under') of the mountain", that the Holy One Blessed Be He held the mountain over their heads and said to them, "If you accept the Torah, well and good; otherwise this place will be your grave." R. Aha bar Jacob added: This provided the people with a defense, since if in the future they should be accused of not keeping the Torah, they could reply that they had accepted it under compulsion, and not of their own free will. Rava said: Nevertheless, a later generation in the days of Ahasuerus confirmed their willing acceptance of the Torah (cf. Esther 9. 27).[70]

From the words of R. Aha and Rava we can observe the tendency to stress the place of the individual and his personal choice in his own right.

From all that has been said we can conclude that the Ten Commandments represent an educational and ethical ideal by which the individual Jew may be trained. Those who are influenced by these teachings will live differently from those who are not brought up with them. The great influence of the Decalogue was not limited in any particular class or vocation in life. The Ten Commandments served as directives to everyone, whatever his economic or social group, whether he lived in prosperity or in poverty.

As a result of the extraordinary influence of the Ten Commandments in sensitizing the conscience of the people of Israel in accordance with their ideals, the Jews were trained to cleave to the attributes of God. Those ideals were so infused into the nature of the Jewish people as to become recognizable elements of their national character. But the Ten Commandments were also absorbed into the rest of the Torah so that they were not regarded as something separate or unique. The talmudic Sages and their successors actually read into the Decalogue the principles of all the laws of the Torah and taught that they were all given on Sinai together with the Ten Commandments. The observance of the Ten Commandments became a matter of habitual practice — a sort of second nature — to the Jew, who could not think of any other way to live, and therefore needed no emphasis, exposition or special attention.

Translated by Chaim Pearl

70 Shab. 88a.

11. DIVIDING THE DECALOGUE INTO VERSES AND COMMANDMENTS

MORDECHAI BREUER

A. *CANTILLATION OF THE OPENING WORDS (EXODUS 20. 2)*

There are two alternative systems of cantillation for the Ten Commandments. The first system, known as "the lower cantillation", divides the Hebrew text into verses, in the usual way. The second system, known as "the upper cantillation", treats each Commandment as a unit. In manuscripts of the Bible and in most printed editions, these two systems are displayed simultaneously, both on the same word, and in most instances even on the same letter. This is the way the cantillation signs (tropes) are applied in the two systems:

In the upper cantillation, each Commandment is one complete verse. This applies not only to those Commandments that are of normal verse length, such as "You shall not swear falsely" (Ex. 20. 7), but also to the very long ones, like "You shall not have" (ibid., 3–6) or "Remember the Sabbath day" (ibid., 8–11); as well as to the very short ones, like "You shall not murder", etc.

In the lower cantillation, by contrast, each verse is of normal length, so that the two long Commandments divide into four verses, while the four short Commandments are combined into one single verse.

As for those Commandments which are themselves of normal verse length, there ought to be no difference at all between the two systems of cantillation. Indeed, that is exactly the situation for three such Commandments: "You shall not swear falsely"; "Honor your father and your mother"; and "You shall not covet". Each of these is one single verse in both systems. Whether regarded as a verse or as a Commandment, the result is the same.

However, there is one Commandment that is exceptional in this respect, namely the First: "I am the LORD your God". It is formulated as a normal verse; yet it has two or three different sets of tropes. Two of these were in use during the time of the Masoretes, while the third came into being at a later period.

Of these two earlier sets of tropes, one ended the Commandment with a *silluq* (full stop; see plate 5a), the other with an *etnah* (demi-stop; plate 5b). During the masoretic period these two sets served side by side, as witness ancient manuscripts that were written at that time[1] (see plate 5c).

There can be no doubt at all about the syntactical meaning of these two sets of tropes. The use of the *silluq* combination is meant to convey that the Commandment "I am the LORD" is to be treated as a separate and independent verse; whereas the *etnah* clause creates a longer verse which includes the Commandment "I am the LORD", with the first verse of the Commandment "You shall have no other", in the framework of the lower cantillation.

It was perfectly clear at the time the early manuscripts were written how these two sets of tropes were to be distributed between the upper cantillation system and the lower. The ancient scribes customarily wrote the accent for the lower cantillation first, and placed the sign for the upper cantillation after it on the word. In this instance they wrote the *etnah* before the *silluq*, and the accompanying *munah* before the *merkha* (plate 5c). Therefore the *etnah* clause is part of the lower cantillation system,[2] while the *silluq* arrangement belongs to the upper cantillation.

Another proof of this rests on the inner structure of the trope-clusters. The verse marked by the *etnah* comes to its end with the phrase "You shall have no other gods beside Me (*'al panay*)". But the word *panay* bears a *silluq* only in the lower cantillation. Consequently, the *etnah* clause can belong only to the lower cantillation system, which means that the *silluq* cluster belongs to the upper cantillation.

However, the very fact that the First Commandment has a dual cantillation system raises some difficult questions. After all, it is

---

1   Ms. Leningrad, B 19a; British Museum, Or.4445; mss. Sassoon 507 and 1053.

2   This is also proven by ms. Sassoon 507, where a marginal note beside the beginning of the First Commandment reads: *"Anokhi–ta'ama' qadma'"*. The same ms. has a similar note at the beginning of most verses in the lower cantillation, such as *"Remember — ta'ama' qadma'"*; *"Six days — ta'ama' qadma'"*. In all of these notes, the phrase refers to the lower cantillation.

formulated as an ordinary sentence, and should therefore have been given the tropes of an independent verse in no matter what system of cantillation. As a Commandment, it should have been treated as a unit in the upper system; as a verse in the lower system, it should have been treated the same way. One set of tropes, ending in a *silluq*, would have sufficed.

This question became more acute as time went on, and the First Commandment acquired a third set of cantillations, a cluster ending in a *revi'a*. Had this cantillation been adopted in its entirety, the result would have been as shown in plate 5d. However, the full *revi'a* clause for this sentence is nowhere to be found. The various versions display it only partially. To take some of the later ones: the 1526 Venice edition of *Miqra'ot Gedolot* shows Exodus 20. 2 as in plate 5e and the same sentence in Deuteronomy 5. 5, as in plate 5f. Certain Sephardic manuscripts have the arrangement shown in plate 5O.[3]

All of these reveal the penetration of the *revi'a* clause into the Commandment "I am the LORD your God". But this penetration was only partial, because the sentence was already provided with two sets of cantillations, the *etnah* clause and the *silluq* clause; and the imposition of a third set presented a problem. That is why in one place (plate 5e) only the *revi'a* itself, the dominant element in the clause, has intruded, and is marked above the word *'avadim*; while in another place in the same edition (plate 5f) the *revi'a* clause has found its way onto every word where room was still left, that is to say, *hoz'etikha me'erez mizrayim* and *'avadim*. These words were already marked with the *etnah* and *silluq* clauses; but both of those are placed below the words, leaving the space above free for elements of the *revi'a* clause.

In the third version, that of the Sephardi manuscripts, most of the *revi'a* clause has penetrated the second half of the sentence, attached to every word not already signed with more than one trope, i.e., *'asher hoze'tikha me'erez mizrayim*. On these words, the *silluq* clause and the *etnah* clause share identical tropes, leaving room for additions. But all these arrangements have one thing in common: they leave no space on the words "I am the LORD your God" to insert the customary elements

---

3   In the Hebrew Bible edited by Snaith, London 1952, based on Sephardi manuscripts, this is the cantillation. The same holds good for the Ginsberg Bible, except that there the systems are separated, with the *etnah* and *revi'a* systems attributed to the Palestinians, and the *silluq* to the Babylonians.

אָנֹכִי֙ יְהוָ֣ה אֱלֹהֶ֔יךָ אֲשֶׁ֧ר הוֹצֵאתִ֣יךָ

מֵאֶ֤רֶץ מִצְרַ֙יִם֙ מִבֵּ֣ית עֲבָדִ֔ים: לֹֽא־יִהְיֶֽה־לְךָ֛ אֱלֹהִ֥ים אֲחֵרִ֖ים עַל־פָּנָֽי:

לֹֽא־תַעֲשֶׂ֨ה־לְךָ֥ פֶ֣סֶל ׀ וְכָל־תְּמוּנָ֗ה אֲשֶׁ֤ר בַּשָּׁמַ֙יִם֙ ׀ מִמַּ֔עַל וַאֲשֶׁ֥ר בָּאָ֖רֶץ

מִתַָּ֑חַת וַאֲשֶׁ֥ר בַּמַּ֖יִם ׀ מִתַּ֣חַת לָאָ֑רֶץ: לֹֽא־תִשְׁתַּחְוֶ֥ה לָהֶ֖ם וְלֹ֣א תָעָבְדֵ֑ם כִּ֣י

אָֽנֹכִ֞י יְהוָ֤ה אֱלֹהֶ֙יךָ֙ אֵ֣ל קַנָּ֔א פֹּ֠קֵד עֲוֺ֨ן אָבֹ֧ת עַל־בָּנִ֛ים עַל־שִׁלֵּשִׁ֥ים וְעַל־

רִבֵּעִ֖ים לְשֹׂנְאָֽי: וְעֹ֤שֶׂה חֶ֙סֶד֙ לַאֲלָפִ֔ים לְאֹהֲבַ֖י וּלְשֹׁמְרֵ֥י מִצְוֺתָֽי: לֹ֥א

תִשָּׂ֛א אֶת־שֵֽׁם־יְהוָ֥ה אֱלֹהֶ֖יךָ לַשָּׁ֑וְא כִּ֣י לֹ֤א יְנַקֶּה֙ יְהוָ֔ה אֵ֛ת אֲשֶׁר־יִשָּׂ֥א אֶת־

שְׁמ֖וֹ לַשָּֽׁוְא:

זָכ֛וֹר֩ אֶת־י֥וֹם֙ הַשַּׁבָּ֖ת לְקַדְּשֽׁ֑וֹ: שֵׁ֤שֶׁת יָמִים֙ תַּֽעֲבֹד֒ וְעָשִׂ֖יתָ כָּל־מְלַאכְתֶּֽךָ:

וְי֙וֹם֙ הַשְּׁבִיעִ֔י שַׁבָּ֖ת ׀ לַיהוָ֣ה אֱלֹהֶ֑יךָ לֹֽא־תַעֲשֶׂ֣ה כָל־מְלָאכָ֡ה אַתָּ֣ה ׀ וּבִנְךָֽ־

וּבִתֶּ֡ךָ עַבְדְּךָ֣ וַאֲמָֽתְךָ֩ וּבְהֶמְתֶּ֙ךָ֙ וְגֵרְךָ֔ אֲשֶׁ֖ר בִּשְׁעָרֶ֑יךָ: כִּ֣י שֵֽׁשֶׁת־יָמִים֩ עָשָׂ֨ה

יְהוָ֜ה אֶת־הַשָּׁמַ֣יִם וְאֶת־הָאָ֗רֶץ אֶת־הַיָּם֙ וְאֶת־כָּל־אֲשֶׁר־בָּ֔ם וַיָּ֖נַח בַּיּ֣וֹם

הַשְּׁבִיעִ֑י עַל־כֵּ֗ן בֵּרַ֧ךְ יְהוָ֛ה אֶת־י֥וֹם הַשַּׁבָּ֖ת וַֽיְקַדְּשֵֽׁהוּ:   כַּבֵּ֣ד

אֶת־אָבִ֖יךָ וְאֶת־אִמֶּ֑ךָ לְמַ֙עַן֙ יַאֲרִכ֣וּן יָמֶ֔יךָ עַ֚ל הָֽאֲדָמָ֔ה אֲשֶׁר־יְהוָ֥ה אֱלֹהֶ֖יךָ

נֹתֵ֥ן לָֽךְ:   לֹ֥א תִּרְצָֽח: לֹ֥א תִּנְאָֽף: לֹ֥א

תִּגְנֹֽב: לֹֽא־תַעֲנֶ֥ה בְרֵעֲךָ֖ עֵ֥ד שָֽׁקֶר: לֹ֥א תַחְמֹ֖ד בֵּ֣ית

רֵעֶ֑ךָ   לֹֽא־תַחְמֹ֞ד אֵ֣שֶׁת רֵעֶ֗ךָ וְעַבְדּ֤וֹ וַאֲמָתוֹ֙ וְשׁוֹרוֹ֙ וַחֲמֹר֔וֹ וְכֹ֖ל

אֲשֶׁ֥ר לְרֵעֶֽךָ:

Plate 4

The Decalogue: Exodus 20.2-14 Showing Upper and Lower
Cantillations Combined

בטעם העליון	בטעם התחתון
אָנֹכִי יְהֹוָה אֱלֹהֶיךָ אֲשֶׁר הוֹצֵאתִיךָ	אָנֹכִי יְהֹוָה אֱלֹהֶיךָ אֲשֶׁר הוֹצֵאתִיךָ
מֵאֶרֶץ מִצְרַיִם מִבֵּית עֲבָדִים׃ לֹא	מֵאֶרֶץ מִצְרַיִם מִבֵּית עֲבָדִים לֹא־
יִהְיֶה־לְךָ אֱלֹהִים אֲחֵרִים עַל־	יִהְיֶה לְךָ אֱלֹהִים אֲחֵרִים עַל־
פָּנָי לֹא תַעֲשֶׂה־לְךָ פֶסֶל ׀ וְכָל־	פָּנָי׃ לֹא־תַעֲשֶׂה לְךָ פֶסֶל וְכָל־
תְּמוּנָה אֲשֶׁר בַּשָּׁמַיִם ׀ מִמַּעַל	תְּמוּנָה אֲשֶׁר בַּשָּׁמַיִם מִמַּעַל
וַאֲשֶׁר בָּאָרֶץ מִתַּחַת וַאֲשֶׁר בַּמַּיִם ׀	וַאֲשֶׁר בָּאָרֶץ מִתַּחַת וַאֲשֶׁר בַּמַּיִם
מִתַּחַת לָאָרֶץ לֹא־תִשְׁתַּחֲוֶה	מִתַּחַת לָאָרֶץ׃ לֹא־תִשְׁתַּחֲוֶה
לָהֶם וְלֹא תָעָבְדֵם כִּי אָנֹכִי יְהֹוָה	לָהֶם וְלֹא תָעָבְדֵם כִּי אָנֹכִי יְהֹוָה

אֱלֹהֶיךָ אֵל קַנָּא פֹּקֵד עֲוֺן אָבֹת עַל־בָּנִים עַל־שִׁלֵּשִׁים וְעַל־רִבֵּעִים

לְשֹׂנְאָי	לְשֹׂנְאָי׃ וְעֹשֶׂה חֶסֶד לַאֲלָפִים וְעֹשֶׂה חֶסֶד לַאֲלָפִים

לְאֹהֲבַי וּלְשֹׁמְרֵי מִצְוֺתָי׃ לֹא תִשָּׂא אֶת־שֵׁם־יְהֹוָה אֱלֹהֶיךָ

לַשָּׁוְא כִּי לֹא יְנַקֶּה יְהֹוָה אֵת אֲשֶׁר־יִשָּׂא אֶת־שְׁמוֹ לַשָּׁוְא׃

זָכוֹר אֶת־יוֹם הַשַּׁבָּת לְקַדְּשׁוֹ	זָכוֹר אֶת־יוֹם הַשַּׁבָּת לְקַדְּשׁוֹ׃
שֵׁשֶׁת יָמִים תַּעֲבֹד וְעָשִׂיתָ כָל־	שֵׁשֶׁת יָמִים תַּעֲבֹד וְעָשִׂיתָ כָל־
מְלַאכְתֶּךָ וְיוֹם הַשְּׁבִיעִי שַׁבָּת ׀	מְלַאכְתֶּךָ׃ וְיוֹם הַשְּׁבִיעִי שַׁבָּת
לַיהֹוָה אֱלֹהֶיךָ לֹא תַעֲשֶׂה כָל־	לַיהֹוָה אֱלֹהֶיךָ לֹא־תַעֲשֶׂה כָל־
מְלָאכָה אַתָּה וּבִנְךָ וּבִתֶּךָ עַבְדְּךָ	מְלָאכָה אַתָּה ׀ וּבִנְךָ וּבִתֶּךָ עַבְדְּךָ
וַאֲמָתְךָ וּבְהֶמְתֶּךָ וְגֵרְךָ אֲשֶׁר	וַאֲמָתְךָ וּבְהֶמְתְּךָ וְגֵרְךָ אֲשֶׁר
בִּשְׁעָרֶיךָ כִּי שֵׁשֶׁת־יָמִים עָשָׂה	בִּשְׁעָרֶיךָ׃ כִּי שֵׁשֶׁת־יָמִים עָשָׂה

יְהֹוָה אֶת־הַשָּׁמַיִם וְאֶת־הָאָרֶץ אֶת־הַיָּם וְאֶת־כָּל־אֲשֶׁר־בָּם

וַיָּנַח בַּיּוֹם הַשְּׁבִיעִי עַל־כֵּן בֵּרַךְ יְהֹוָה אֶת־יוֹם הַשַּׁבָּת וַיְקַדְּשֵׁהוּ׃

כַּבֵּד אֶת־אָבִיךָ וְאֶת־אִמֶּךָ לְמַעַן יַאֲרִכוּן יָמֶיךָ

עַל הָאֲדָמָה אֲשֶׁר־יְהֹוָה אֱלֹהֶיךָ נֹתֵן לָךְ׃

לֹא תִרְצָח׃ לֹא תִנְאָף׃ לֹא תִגְנֹב׃	לֹא תִרְצָח לֹא תִנְאָף לֹא תִגְנֹב
לֹא־תַעֲנֶה בְרֵעֲךָ עֵד שָׁקֶר׃	לֹא־תַעֲנֶה בְרֵעֲךָ עֵד שָׁקֶר׃

לֹא תַחְמֹד בֵּית רֵעֶךָ לֹא־תַחְמֹד אֵשֶׁת רֵעֶךָ

וְעַבְדּוֹ וַאֲמָתוֹ וְשׁוֹרוֹ וַחֲמֹרוֹ וְכֹל אֲשֶׁר לְרֵעֶךָ׃

Plate 4
The Decalogue: Exodus 20,2-14 Showing Upper
and Lower Cantillations Separated

אָנֹכִי יְהוָה אֱלֹהֶיךָ אֲשֶׁר הוֹצֵאתִיךָ מֵאֶרֶץ מִצְרַיִם

מִבֵּית עֲבָדִים

a. Upper cantillation, <u>silluq</u> cluster:
First Commandment as a complete verse

אָנֹכִי יְהוָה אֱלֹהֶיךָ אֲשֶׁר הוֹצֵאתִיךָ מֵאֶרֶץ מִצְרַיִם

מִבֵּית עֲבָדִים

b. Lower cantillation, <u>etnaḥ</u> cluster:
First Commandment part of verse

אָנֹכִי יְהוָה אֱלֹהֶיךָ אֲשֶׁר הוֹצֵאתִיךָ מֵאֶרֶץ מִצְרַיִם

מִבֵּית עֲבָדִים

c.   <u>Silluq</u> and etnaḥ shown together
in ancient manuscripts

Plate 5
Original masoretic punctuation

אֽנֹכִי יְהוָה אֱלֹהֶיךָ אֲשֶׁר הוֹצֵאתִיךָ מֵאֶרֶץ מִצְרַיִם

מִבֵּית עֲבָדִים

d.   Full revi'a cluster (hypothetical)

אָֽנֹכִי יְהוָה אֱלֹהֶיךָ אֲשֶׁר הוֹצֵאתִיךָ מֵאֶרֶץ מִצְרָיִם

מִבֵּית עֲבָדִים

e.   Incipient revi'a cluster:
     (Miqra'ot Gedolot, Venice 1526, Ex. 20.2)

אָֽנֹכִי יְהוָה אֱלֹהֶיךָ אֲשֶׁר הוֹצֵאתִיךָ מֵאֶרֶץ מִצְרָיִם

מִבֵּית עֲבָדִים

f.   Partial revi'a cluster:
     (Miqra'ot Gedolot, Venice 1526, Deut. 5.6)

אָֽנֹכִי יְהוָה אֱלֹהֶיךָ אֲשֶׁר הוֹצֵאתִיךָ מֵאֶרֶץ מִצְרַיִם

מִבֵּית עֲבָדִים

g.   Old Sephardi manuscripts

Plate 5
Development of the *revi'a* cluster

of the *revi'a* clause. For these words already have two sets of tropes —
one above the words, one below. There is no room left.[4]

In two of the three versions we have referred to — the Venice
edition's version of Exodus 20. 2 (plae 5e) and the Sephardi
manuscripts (plate 5f) — the *revi'a* clause has not been able to dislocate
the pre-existing systems. Consequently, even after having entered the
second half of the Commandment, it appears only as an addition to the
earlier *silluq* and *etnah* systems, but does not displace either one. The
result is, three cantillation systems in the second half of the
Commandment.

However, the situation is different for the same Commandment in
Deuteronomy 5. 6 (Venice edition, plate 5f). There the *etnah* system
has really been reduced by the penetration of the *revi'a* cluster; so much
so, that the *etnah* itself has completely disappeared. It seems probable
that the punctator of this passage could not envisage three tropes —
silluq, etnah and *revi'a* — on a single word. So he got rid of the *etnah*,
leaving the other two. After all they were more firmly entrenched by
virtue of the tropes that preceded them — the *geresh* group before the
revi'a and the *merkha* before the *silluq*. The *etnah*, by contrast, had
nothing in the second half of the Commandment to support it. This led
the punctator to retain only the *silluq* and the *revi'a*. And although the
etnah was much older, and the *revi'a* comparatively new, he chose to
"clear out the old to make room for the new" (Lev. 26. 10).

The three cantillation systems that have come to mark the First
Commandment in recent centuries have been discussed at some length
by those Jewish scholars who dealt with the Masorah and the biblical
text. The outstanding names in this connection are those of Menahem
di Lonzano (sixteenth century, Turkey), author of *Or Torah*; Yedidiah
Norzi (sixteenth century, Italy), author of *Minhat Shai*; Solomon

4   It is equally possible that the punctators who introduced the *revi'a* system did not
     feel the lack of the *pazēr* cluster at the beginning of the Commandment, because all
     they were after was to round out the *revi'a* musically, by the *geresh* and its
     attachments. They failed to notice that it should also be completed syntactically by
     the *pazēr* and company. Something like that happened in the story of Reuben
     (Gen. 35. 22–23) where the *etnah* system is completed musically, but not
     syntactically. See the notes by Rabbi H. M. Brecher in the appendix to the Yehoash
     Bible. If this is so, then the error of those who introduced the *revi'a* was something
     like the error of the grammarians of early modern times, such as di Lonzano, Norzi,
     Dubno and Heidenheim, whom we shall discuss later; see note 6.

Dubno (Poland and Holland, 1738–1813), author of *Tiqqun Soferim*; and Wolf Heidenheim[5] (Germany, 1757–1832), editor of the well-known Rödelheim prayerbooks. By the time these scholars had come on the scene, the old manuscript versions had fallen into disuse, and these men were for the most part familiar only with the two systems displayed by the printed Hebrew Bible of 1526. Nevertheless, the influence of the three systems of cantillation described above was still discernable. However, since it did not seem reasonable that the opening Commandment should bear three systems of cantillation, it became necessary to decide which two to use; and then to determine which of them belonged to the upper cantillation, and which to the lower.

However, the truth of the matter is that these questions need not have arisen even though the manuscript version had been forgotten. The *revi'a* cluster is visibly flawed on its own terms; and the lateness of its origin is apparent on the very face of it. Even without the evidence of the manuscripts one can see that this cluster appears in fragmented form in all the various versions, whereas the *silluq* and *etnah* forms are complete in all or most of the versions. This in itself proves that the *revi'a* cluster is a late intrusion, for it has been able to penetrate only the second half of the Commandment.

Nevertheless, although this logic is quite conclusive, it never occurred to the scholars who dealt with the subject. There are historical reasons for this. Medieval works on the Masorah concerned themselves only with the musical aspect of the tropes; they paid no attention to the syntactical rules by which the tropes are governed. Hence not everybody realized that the *zaqef* on the word *'elohekha* can subdivide only the clause governed by the *etnah*, while if a clause governed by a *revi'a* is to be subdivided, that must be done by a *pazer*. Consequently, they failed to sense the absence of the *pazer* from the cluster that is dominated by the *revi'a*. They assumed that the *zaqef* that served as a subdivider in the *etnah* clause played that role in the clause ending with a *revi'a*.[6] In

---

5   In his Pentateuch edition *Me'or 'Eynayim*, at the end of Exodus.

6   If the suggestion put forward in n.4 is correct, the grammarians were not wrong about the meaning of the tropes, for this indeed was the intention of the punctators who introduced the *revi'a* clause. They too thought that the *zaqef* of *'elohekha* could serve in a *revi'a* combination. Nevertheless, what we have said here is quite correct, for no punctator who was leading up to a *revi'a* would insert a *zaqef* at this point, unless he found one already there. See also n.8, below. However, it is possible that a punctator who found a *zaqef* already in place — as part of the *etnah*

this way three sets of cantillation came into being, each of them fully represented at least once in the *Miqra'ot Gedolot* of Venice, 1526.

Thus, we have the *silluq* clause in both Exodus and Deuteronomy (plate 5a); the *etnah* clause in Exodus (plate 5b); and the *revi'a* cluster — partially in Exodus (Plate 5e) fully in Deuteronomy (Plate 5g).[7]

Viewed thus, the *etnah* clause no longer has primacy. On the contrary, the *revi'a* clause is the superior one, since it is represented partially or in full in both of the Pentateuchal versions of the Ten Commandments, whereas the very existence of the *etnah* clause is attested in only one place.

However, this entire approach derives from a purely musical understanding of the rules of cantillation. For in fact, the *revi'a* cluster, created by scholars, is an artificial blending of two distinct sets of tropes. From a musical point of view, it looks like a complete *revi'a* clause, but in actuality it is the result of cross-breeding. The Commandment begins with an *etnah* clause — and ends with a *revi'a* system.[8]

What is more, the *revi'a* system causes difficulties not only from a stylistic point of view, but also from the point of view of interpretation. There can be no doubt as to its syntactical significance. It creates a verse which includes the Commandment "I am the LORD", plus the whole of the Commandment "You shall have no other gods". But it cannot be recited either in accordance with the upper or the lower cantillation; for the latter requires verses of normal length, while the former requires each Commandment to be a distinct and separate unit; whereas the *revi'a* system creates one *long* verse which includes *two* Commandments.

This question was raised by a number of scholars, and the only answer they were able to come up with was this: the first two Commandments are in a class by themselves, for "we heard them directly from the mouth of the Almighty" (Mak. 24a); as though to say "I am the LORD" and "You shall have no other gods" were spoken "in

clause — might make the mistake of thinking that the *zaqef* could also serve a *revi'a* clause, so he failed to fill in that clause. This shows that the *revi'a* was superimposed on the *etnah* clause only at a late date.

7 To be exact, not quite fully; a *munah* on the word *'asher* is still lacking.

8 This *revi'a* system violates another of the tropsal rules: it forms a verse with a *zaqēf* before a *segol*.

one utterance (*dibbur*)"⁹ and may therefore be considered "one Commandment (*dibber*)", hence it is appropriate to recite them as one verse, as is done with the other Commandments in the upper cantillation.

This explanation will help us understand the several treatments afforded to the three tropal systems that have become attached to the Ten Commandments since the invention of printing. We will note two main classifications: that of di Lonzano, Norzi and Dubno, on the one hand, and of Heidenheim on the other.

According to the former, the *silluq* system is designated the lower cantillation, and one of the other two systems is called the upper cantillation. Di Lonzano and Norzi¹⁰ give this role to the *etnah* system, while Dubno assigns it to the *revi'a* system. The rationale is this: the *silluq* system creates a verse of normal length, while the *etnah* (or alternatively the *revi'a*) system creates a long verse which incorporates both the Commandment "I am the LORD", and the Commandment "You shall have no other gods" — because those two were heard "directly from the mouth of the Almighty".

However, these solutions cannot be correct. It is hard to understand how di Lonzano and Norzi could have made their proposal. It cannot be recited, because it produces a sentence with two *etnah*'s (*'avadim* and *leson'ai*) — an obvious impossibility. But Dubno's method is also problematic because, as we have already pointed out, the *revi'a* clause in this context is an artificial creation, a cross between an *etnah* clause and a full *revi'a* clause. It can scarcely be called the representative of the upper cantillation.

An additional difficulty applies to all these methods. All of them

---

9　In his commentary on Exodus (20. 13) Hizzequni writes: "For both the Commandments 'I am the LORD' and 'You shall have no other' there is a grand chant, such as to make them into one single verse in memory of the fact that 'they were spoken in one utterance'". The meaning of that last phrase in this context is not the usual one — not "simultaneously", as in the dictum "Observe and Remember were spoken in one utterance". Here it means, "in one declaration", as though two Commandments were delivered as one Commandment, since these two "we heard directly from God". Hence it is fitting for them to be put together into one verse in the upper cantillation, which then resembles the verses of that system, in which each verse is one Commandment.

10　In his commentary on Exodus, di Lonzano directs the reader to follow the *etnah* system at that point, and to use the *revi'a* in Deuteronomy. But when he gets to Deuteronomy he changes his mind, and calls for the *etnah* system there as well.

show the upper cantillation combining two Commandments into one
verse — something directly contrary to the very purpose of the upper
cantillation. The latter was created with the sole aim of dividing the
passage into *ten* Commandments, treating each one as a unit. These
solutions leave us with only nine.

Nevertheless, the approach of these methods has been accepted by
most editions of the Hebrew Bible, as well as by most Jewish
communities. It is also referred to in the later halakhic literature.[11] At
the same time it should be pointed out that the line followed by di
Lonzano and Norzi, which utilizes the *etnah* clause in the upper
cantillation thereby creating two *etnah*'s in one verse, has generally
been rejected in favor of the method proposed by Dubno: the *silluq* in
the lower cantillation, the *revi'a* in the upper.

A fundamentally different method was followed by Wolf
Heidenheim.[12] It found acceptance in only a small number of editions
of the Bible, and in a limited number of communities.[13] Nevertheless, it
has one overriding virtue: it can solve most of the problems mentioned
above.

Heidenheim accepted the *silluq* clause in both the lower and the
upper cantillation. In the lower system it results in a sentence of normal
verse-length, while in the upper it creates a verse consisting of the
Commandment "I am the LORD". That puts the Commandment in the
same class as "You shall not swear falsely", "Honor your father", or
"You shall not covet". All of these are of normal verse-length, so that
one set of tropes, a *silluq* clause, can serve for both upper and lower
cantillation.

On top of these, Heidenheim also accepted the *etnah* and the *revi'a*
systems — but not as intended for actual reading in either the upper or
the lower cantillation. In his opinion they were designed only as
reminders that "I am the LORD" and "You shall have no other" were
heard "directly from the Almighty". The *revi'a* combination attaches
these two Commandments in toto to one another, in conformity with
the teaching of Nahmanides to the effect that these Commandments

---

11   *Shulḥan Arukh, Oraḥ Ḥayyim*, 494: 1; *Mishnah Berurah*, ibid., para.3 and
     commentary; *Shulḥan Arukh Ha-Rav*, ibid.
12   Heidenheim based his method on analysis of Hizzequni ad Exodus 20. 13.
13   Heidenheim's approach was known only in Germany, and in Pentateuchs printed
     in that country.

were heard directly from the Almighty.[14] The *etnah* combination attaches the verse "I am the LORD" to the first verse only of "You shall have no other gods beside Me". This agrees with the teaching of Maimonides, who held that it was only these two verses which were heard directly.[14]

However, Heindenheim's method also suffers from being somewhat forced. It does not seem reasonable to suppose that the Ten Commandments were supplied with additional cantillations, over and above the lower and the upper systems; additional cantillations which were not intended for use, but merely as "reminders".

It is hardly necessary to add that this version does not conform to the original masoretic system of cantillation, for the Bible manuscripts antedating the advent of printing show no trace of the *revi'a* clause at all, while the *etnah* clause serves them as the lower cantillation. There can be no doubt that it was intended for actual reading, not as a mere "reminder".

This leaves us still facing the two questions which we raised at the beginning of our discussion. The Commandment "I am the LORD" resembles in length the Commandments "You shall not swear falsely", "Honor your father and your mother", and "You shall not covet", in that it is not longer or shorter than an ordinary verse. Consequently, one set of cantillations would have served it, the *silluq* clause. What then actuated the ancient manuscripts to add the *etnah* clause to the *silluq*? And why did the still later versions add still another arrangement, the *revi'a* clause?

B. THE TWO MASORETIC TROPE ARRANGEMENTS: THE SEMANTIC DIFFERENCE[14a]

It seems that we can find an explanation for all this if we bear in mind the general relationship between the upper and the lower cantillations. From what we have said above, it is clear that only the divisions of the lower cantillation deserve to be called "verses", in the usual meaning of the term. The full stops indicated by the upper cantillation do not

---

14 See Maimonides, *Book of Commandments*, positive commandment no.1 and negative commandment no.1. Also Nahmanides and Joseph Teitchik, *Lehem Setarim* (*Megillat Esther*), Venice 1608.

14a This chapter deals only with tropes in manuscript versions. Later versions will be dealt with in chapter E.

properly speaking mark off verses at all, but Commandments. Consequently, we see that the lower cantillation divides the entire passage into twelve *verses*, while the upper system divides it into ten *Commandments*.

However, even though these are two different ways of dividing up the text, there is no disagreement in principle between them. Rather, they complement one another. One who divides the passage into twelve verses must also admit that it consists of ten Commandments, for this is stated explicitly in the Bible (Ex. 34. 28; see also Deut. 4. 13 and 10. 4) "He wrote down on the tablets the terms of the covenant, the Ten Commandments".

Similarly, he who divides the section into Commandments will admit that it is also appropriate to divide it into verses, like all other sections of the Torah. Consequently, we are entitled to expect complete agreement between the upper cantillation and the lower; that is to say, that the verses of the latter can be read as Commandments in the upper cantillation; and that the Commandments of the upper cantillation lend themselves to reading as verses, if one switches to the lower cantillation.

This is exactly what happens from "You shall not swear falsely" to the end. That portion includes eight verses in the lower cantillation, and eight Commandments in the upper. The relationship between them is, that one unit of the one set comprises an exact number of units of the other. Thus: one verse includes four complete Commandments ("You shall not murder, etc.") while one Commandment comprises four complete verses ("Remember the Sabbath day"). Or one complete verse corresponds to one complete Commandment (as in "You shall not swear", "Honor", "You shall not covet"). So that the division into verses fits the division into Commandments; only full Commandments combine to form one verse; and only full verses combine in one Commandment.

But the situation is different in the text between "I am the LORD" and "My commandments". There we find four verses, according to the lower cantillation, and two Commandments according to the upper. But the divisions do not match. The first verse contains one Commandment and part of another (from "I am the LORD" to "beside Me") while the Second Commandment includes part of a verse plus three other complete verses ("You shall have no other" to "commandments"). This relationship between verses and Commandments not only runs counter to the rule enunciated above, but is also contrary to all logic. For in this arrangement, the phrase "you shall have no other gods" is attached to "I am the LORD" and separated from "You shall not make", in terms of the division into verses; and is attached to "You shall not make" and separated from "I am the LORD", in terms of the division into Commandments. The result is, that in the verse system it is the conclusion of what precedes it; but in the system of Commandments, it becomes the introduction to what follows. But this is a totally unacceptable state of affairs. The verse system and the Commandment system of division ought to be guided by one single principle. It is not reasonable that the Commandment enunciated by the Almighty should be contradicted by the verse-system set up by Moses.

Consequently, we are forced to the conclusion that the upper and lower cantillations for the beginning of the Decalogue, from "I am the LORD" to "My commandments", not only do not complement one another, but actually disagree with one another. The disagreement affects the division into verses as well as the division into Commandments. The first verse according to the lower cantillation runs from "I am the LORD" to "beside Me", while according to the upper cantillation the first verse can run no further than "house of bondage". So too with regard to the division into Commandments; in the upper system the First Commandment runs from "I am the LORD" to "house of bondage"; whereas in the lower system the First Commandment can comprise no less than "I am the LORD" to "beside Me".

This disagreement between the two systems can be viewed as a disagreement about verse-division, or a disagreement about interpretation. Its consequences are many, not only related to divisions of the text, but also to the calculation of the number of the mitzvot, and to defining which were the words "heard directly from the Almighty". But first let us try to understand what issue is at stake as between the two systems.

The meaning of the lower cantillation system cannot be in doubt. It combines "I am the LORD" and "You shall have no other" into one verse, because these two statements are addressed to the mind and heart, and encompass the whole faith of Israel. The opening words declare that the LORD is God. The rest forbids us to accept any other as God.

Thus, these two directives are two sides of the same coin: "I am the LORD your God", therefore "You shall have no other gods beside Me".

This is the way the Sages interpreted Exodus 12. 12: "I, the LORD" —
"there is no other" (Mak. 21a).[15] That is why "other gods" are mentioned
here in contrast to "the LORD your God". For the other gods spoken of
in this context are not simply idols made by human hands, but include
all alien deities and every power, even immaterial, which men accept as
godly, from angels on high and the hosts of heaven to the spirits which
dwell in the northernmost mountains. All these are called "gods", and
they stand in opposition to "The LORD God". Therefore they can be
spoken of as "other gods"; so to speak, other than the LORD.

On the other hand, "You shall not make for yourself a sculptured
image" prohibits a specific act — the making of a statue or likeness for
purposes of worship. Since such objects are the work of human hands,
they do not stand in opposition to the LORD. Of them it is written (II Ki.
19. 18) "They are not gods, but man's handiwork of wood and stone". If
you do refer to them as "gods", borrowing the term from those who
worship them, you do not call them "other gods", for the LORD is the
Creator of all things in heaven and on earth, and with respect to Him,
man's handiwork is not "other".[16]

This is doubtless the meaning reflected by the lower cantillation, for
it includes "I am the LORD" and "You shall have no other" in one verse;
while "You shall not make" is the opening of a second verse.

The meaning of the upper cantillation is somewhat uncertain. It may
be that it does not differ in principle from the lower cantillation, but
thinks that belief in God rejects not only the belief in spirits ("other
gods") but also rejects the making of images and likenesses for the
purpose of worship. For the LORD who took us out of Egypt and
revealed Himself to us at Mount Sinai is not corporeal nor the likeness

---

15   Similarly in the Passover Haggadah: "I the LORD — I and none other". This
      midrash is a sort of summary of the first two sentences of the Ten Commandments.
      The Maharal, in his commentary on the Haggadah, also takes this line. "When it
      says 'I the LORD and none other' it means, other gods". Even so, the Maharal did
      not notice the connection between this midrash and the opening of the Ten
      Commandments, because in another context (*Gevurot ha-Shem*, Chap. 55, end) he
      vigorously rejects the explanations of Maimonides and Nahmanides for "you shall
      have no other", adopting instead the interpretation of the *Mekhilta*, namely, that
      this is a ban on possession.

16   The distinction between "other gods" and idols is explained well by Nahmanides in
      his comment on Exodus 20. 2. See also his comment in the *Book of
      Commandments*, negative commandment 1.

of anything corporeal. Hence, His very Godhead negates the possibility of making any image — neither the image of another god, nor any image that is intended to symbolize Him. It is stated explicitly (Deut. 4. 15) "Since you saw no shape when the LORD your God spoke to you at Horeb out of the fire". It is obvious, then, that God's divinity negates the worship of other gods or idols. Consequently it is appropriate to place the opening phrase, which teaches belief in the LORD, alongside the admonitions connected with false worship, thus: "I am the LORD your God"; therefore "You shall have no other gods beside Me", and "You shall not make for yourself a sculptured image", and "You shall not bow down to them or serve them".

However, it is possible that the upper cantillation actually disagrees with the lower as to the meaning of the text. It may read "I am the LORD" not simply as the basis for the prohibition of false worship, but as the basis for all the Commandments, and indeed the foundation of the entire Torah; because the principle that the LORD is God not only rules out idolatry, but also has a positive side: it makes it obligatory to accept His sovereignty, and that is the basis for accepting the authority of His commandments. This idea is expressed in the *Mekhilta* (n.17) by a parable:[16a]

> Once a king occupied a province. His officers said to him: Impose some decrees on the inhabitants. But he answered, No! After they have accepted my authority I will promulgate my decrees. For if they do not accept me as their ruler, how can I expect them to obey my laws? In the same way, God said to Israel, "I am the LORD your God — You shall have no other gods. It is I whose sovereignty you accepted when you were in Egypt". When they said to Him, "Yes!" He continued: "Now then, just as you have accepted Me as your Ruler, you must also accept My decrees; You shall have no other gods beside Me".[17]

16a   *Baḥodesh*, VI. ed. Lauterbach, II, pp. 237 ff.

17   According to this interpretation of the *Mekhilta*, the purpose of the declaration "I am the LORD" is to indicate acceptance of God's sovereignty, as a preliminary to acceptance of the yoke of the mitzvot. But the *Mekhilta* itself contains another interpretation (ibid., V; ed.Lauterbach, II, p. 231): "'I am the LORD thy God" — why is this said? For this reason: at the sea He appeared to them as a mighty hero, as it is said: 'The LORD is a man of war' (Ex. 15. 3). At Sinai He appeared to them as an old man full of mercy, as it is said: 'They saw the LORD of Israel, etc.' (24. 10). And after they had been redeemed what does it say? 'And the like of the very heaven

On this reading, "I am the LORD" is an introduction, not just to the prohibitions connected with idolatry, but also to all the other Commandments. Consequently, it is proper to read the opening words of the Decalogue as a separate statement: "I am the LORD your God who brought you out of the land of Egypt, etc." It follows therefore that "You shall have no other"; that "you shall not swear falsely"; that you shall "Remember"; and so on.

Thus we find ourselves with three interpretations of the opening words of the Decalogue. According to the lower cantillation, "I am the LORD" is intended only to forbid belief in other gods; according to the upper cantillation, it is either the basis for prohibiting all idolatry, or is the basis for all of the mitzvot in the Ten Commandments.

Any one of these three interpretations fits the plain sense of the biblical text quite nicely, so that there is no way of deciding in favor of one of them over the others. At least two can be supported by reference to passages in other parts of the Torah. For example, in Deuteronomy 6. 12–15, after Moses has repeated the Ten Commandments, he says:

> Take heed that you do not forget the LORD who freed you from the land of Egypt, the house of bondage.... Do not follow other gods, any gods of the peoples about you, for the LORD God in your midst is an impassioned God.

The wording of these passages is reminiscent of the language at the beginning of the Ten Commandments, from "I am the LORD" to "those who reject Me". It makes explicit the antithesis expressed by the lower cantillation between "the LORD who brought you out of the land of Egypt", on the one hand, versus "do not follow other gods" on the other.

---

for clearness' (ibid.). Scripture therefore would not let the nations have an excuse for saying that there are two [divine] powers. 'I am the LORD thy God'. I am He who was in Egypt, and I am He who was at the sea; I am He who was at Sinai... I am He who was in the past, and I am He who will be in the future; I am He who is in this world and I am He who will be in the world to come". According to this, the statement "I am the LORD" is intended to stress the unity of God, and to negate any idea of dualism. Consequently, *Anokhi* expresses the principle that precedes the prohibition "You shall have no other", but it is not the declaration of God's sovereignty, which is the foundation of all the Commandments. This interpretation agrees with the first one suggested above for the upper cantillation. It is also in accord with the interpretation of the lower cantillation.

However, interpreting the verse in accordance with the upper cantillation, at least in terms of the second alternative proposed above, can also be supported by pointing to those passages where the Torah introduces — or concludes — any commandment with the words "I am the LORD your God", especially when coupled with "who brought you out of the land of Egypt".

A good example is Leviticus 18. 2–6 where the phrase is repeated four times. Similarly in Leviticus 19, where the words recur over and over in relation to many commandments not connected with idolatry, the whole concluding with language strongly reminiscent of the opening of the Decalogue:

> You shall have an honest balance, honest weights, an honest *ephah* and an honest *hin*. I am the LORD your God who brought you out from the land of Egypt (Lev. 19. 36).

Here we have an almost verbatim repetition of the opening sentence of the Ten Commandments, not as a basis for forbidding idolatrous practices, but as a fundamental rationale for obeying all the mitzvot.

The alternative interpretation of the upper cantillation is not without some support from elsewhere in the Torah. Leviticus 19. 4 reads "Do not turn to idols or make molten gods for yourselves; I am the LORD your God". The latter phrase, an abbreviated form of our opening Commandment, occurs here specifically in the context of idolatry, not only as a matter of false belief, but also as a ban on making idols.

Since the plain text admits of any of these interpretations, and each of them can be supported by other passages in the Torah, it becomes unnecessary to decide between them. Indeed, it may be the intention of the biblical text to express all these meanings simultaneously, as though following the principle "Both these and those are the words of the Living God". Consequently, the Masorah did not decide in favor of one interpretation, but accepted at least two of them, expressing them by the twofold cantillation of the sentence "I am the LORD your God".

All that remains for us is to investigate the effect that these different interpretations have on the calculation affecting the number of the mitzvot, and the division of the Decalogue into Ten Commandments.

C. DIVIDING THE DECALOGUE INTO TEN

Let us consider the various possible divisions, beginning with those that can be attributed to the cantillation signs. In the upper cantillation of the Masorah — as shown in the ancient mss. — the First

Commandment runs from "I am the LORD" to "bondage", and the
Second from "You shall have no other" to "My commandments".
Thus, the First Commandment deals with belief in God, while the
Second forbids idolatrous worship. Alternatively, if "I am the LORD" is
an introduction to the whole Decalogue, the First Commandment
asserts the sole sovereignty of God, and the Second imposes the "yoke"
of His commandments.

This reading is followed by the *Mekhilta*,[18] as well as by the Targum
Pseudo-Jonathan, and since it is the only version expressed by the
cantillation — not by inference but explicitly — it is generally taken to
be "the traditional Jewish arrangement of the Commandments",[19]
while all other systems of division are accounted foreign, not acceptable
to Jewish authorities.

However, it is apparent from everything that has been said so far that
this opinion is unfounded. After all, there can be no doubt that the
masoretic "lower cantillation" divided the Decalogue differently, and
the lower system is no less "traditional" than the upper. It is also
apparent that the division of the Hebrew text into "paragraphs"
(*parashiyyot*) was based on a different method of dividing up the
Decalogue. The Hebrew displays ten such paragraphs, open or closed.
The first is "I am the LORD". The second is "You shall not swear
falsely", while the last two separate paragraphs are "You shall not
covet your neighbor's house", and "You shall not covet your neighbor's
wife, etc." (so, in Exodus; in Deuteronomy, "You shall not covet" and
"You shall not crave").[20] These paragraphs do not conform to the
upper cantillation, which reads "You shall not swear falsely" as the
Third Commandment, and does not treat the last "covet" (or "crave")
as the beginning of a separate Commandment.

A different approach is apparently represented by the later
punctators, who introduced the *revi'a* system into the opening sentence.
Their point of departure was, that all those verses in which the Divinity
speaks in the First Person constitute one Commandment. That would
make the First Commandment run all the way to "My
commandments". Its contents would resemble that of the first two

---

18   *Baḥodesh*, section 8; ed. Lauterbach, II, pp. 262 f.
19   So M.D.U. Cassuto in his comment following the Ten Commandments.
20   This was the arrangement as Maimonides had it, according to the Ben Asher
      manuscript, and ms. Leningrad.

Commandments as per the upper cantillation in the original masoretic version.

This approach runs contrary to the division dictated by the upper cantillation of the Masorah, but it does harmonize nicely with the interpretation on which that tradition is based. For, according to this reading as well, the admonition "You shall have no other" is not connected to the preceding sentence, but rather to the admonitions that follow. In addition, this approach can be seen as conforming to the division of the *parashiyyot*.

As for the division indicated by the masoretic lower cantillation, the matter is not entirely clear. It may be that it intends the First Commandment to go as far as "beside Me", while the Second would run from "You shall not make" to "My commandments". That would make the First Commandment contrapose the belief in the LORD to the belief in other gods, and have the Second Commandment add the ban on making images, or worshipping them; and conclude with the reward and punishment connected with these laws.

However, we cannot be certain that the lower cantillation of the Masorah intended the Commandments to be apportioned in this way. It is possible that the system meant to punctuate in such a way that the First Commandment would comprise everything that refers to God in the first person. If that is so, then the First Commandment would run from "I am the LORD" to "My commandments". Its first verse would end with "beside Me", and the First Commandment would embrace everything designated by the previous system as the first two Commandments.

It seems that the manner of parsing the Decalogue in accordance with the lower cantillation was also acceptable to the Sages. It is implied in a midrash attributed to Rabbi Ishmael,[21] which states that the ban on idolatry was "the first pronouncement spoken to Moses by the Almighty, (namely) 'I am the LORD your God — you shall have no other gods beside Me'". This way of putting it conforms especially to the assumption that the First Commandment runs from "I" to "beside Me".

Both of the above readings of the lower cantillation are in disagreement with the interpretation given by the upper cantillation, in that both of them connect "You shall have no other" to the preceding

---

21 *Sifre Numbers*, Section 112; ed. Horovitz, p. 121.

words rather than to what follows; and only the second of the two conforms to the traditional paragraph divisions.

But all the systems mentioned so far assume that the sentence "I am the LORD, etc." is part of the Decalogue. If that be granted, then we have presented all possible ways of dividing the Commandments; and every one of them can be supported by the syntax of the cantillation signs.

However, there is no proof that this assumption is correct. Perhaps that opening sentence is not one of the Ten Commandments at all, but rather an introduction to the whole Decalogue. It may be that the First Commandment is "You shall have no other gods," and the Second is "You shall not make for yourself a sculptured image" to "My Commandments". On that reading, the First Commandment forbids belief in other gods, while the Second prohibits the making of idols and the worship of them, concluding with the reward and punishment connected with these two prohibitions.

It is also possible according to this reading of the text to say that all the verses which speak of God in the first person constitute one single Commandment, from "You shall have no other" to "My commandments", with its first verse ending at "beside Me", and its content including what was previously counted as two Commandments.

Both ways of understanding the text according to this reading conform to the interpretation of the masoretic upper cantillation. In both of them the admonition "You shall have no other" relates to the prohibitions following, and not to the preceding words. However, with respect to the division of the Ten Commandments, they do not fit in with the upper cantillation or with the *revi'a* clause. Nor, it goes without saying, do they conform at all to the masoretic lower cantillation. However, it seems that the second alternative can be seen as conforming to the paragraph divisions.

These, then, are all the possible ways of dividing up the Decalogue so as to arrive at the number "Ten". There is no doubt that the Masorah recognized as least two of these ways: the system of the upper cantillation, and one of the possible alternatives for the lower cantillation. If we assume that the paragraph divisions and the lower cantillation system did not have an identical purpose, we can add a third method, one of the possible derivatives of the paragraph division. Apparently it was one of these systems that was adopted by the more recent punctators.

We are led to conclude that there is only one system that cannot possibly be attributed to the Masorah, namely the one that treats the sentence "I am the LORD, etc." as outside the Decalogue, and reads "You shall have no other gods beside Me" as the totality of the First Commandment. That system is clearly rejected by the Masorah; it does not conform to either the upper or the lower cantillation, nor does it agree with the paragraph divisions. It was also not accepted by the later punctators.[22]

Every single one of the systems we have described creates some difficulty. Consequently, it is hard to choose between them on the basis of logical considerations. Let us survey the difficulties involved, for which purpose it will be convenient to divide them into three types: those that can be harmonized with the paragraph divisions, ending the First Commandment with "My commandments"; those that end the First Commandment with "beside Me"; and the masoretic upper cantillation, which ends the First Commandment at the word "bondage".

Those systems which include in the First Commandment everything up to "My commandments" count the twice-repeated "You shall not covet" (or alternatively "You shall not covet — You shall not crave") as two separate Commandments. This is readily acceptable for the Deuteronomic version of the Decalogue, where a distinction is made between "coveting" your neighbor's wife and "craving" his property — "his house, his field, his male or female slave, his ox, his ass, or anything that is your neighbor's". The two admonitions differ in both their language and their content, so that it is appropriate to count them as two separate Commandments.

But things are different in the Exodus version. There we read:

> You shall not covet your neighbor's house: you shall not covet your neighbor's wife, or his male or female slave, or his ox or his ass, or anything that is your neighbor's.

Here no distinction is made between "coveting" his wife and "coveting" his property. Quite the contrary; the wife is enumerated along with the

---

22   Currently this is the preferred theory of Bible scholars. But it would never have found acceptance if they had not first deleted, as a late insertion, everything in the Commandment from "you shall not bow down" to "My commandments". By doing so, they also eliminated the problem inherent in this method of dividing the Decalogue.

possessions over which the man has the right of ownership. Therefore the two "you shall not covet" commands, alike in language and content, can scarcely be separated. They relate to one another as general to particular: do not covet the house, and everything in it. That makes it difficult to see these two admonitions as two separate Commandments.

That problem does not arise in those systems which end the First Commandment at *'al panay* ("beside Me"). They simply take the repeated "You shall not covet [or crave]" as one Commandment. However, these systems are confronted with a different problem: they do not keep the Commandments sufficiently separate. In their reading, the First Commandment prohibits the attribution of divinity to any alien god, while the Second Commandment prohibits the making of idols. But the Second Commandment goes on to say "You shall not bow down to them or serve them". Logically, that prohibition applies to the "alien gods" mentioned in the First Commandment as well as to the idols mentioned in the Second. Similarly, the reward and punishment mentioned in the Second Commandment would appear to apply to everything spoken of in both Commandments. This blurs the division of the text into two Commandments, leaving the first two commingled from "You shall not bow down".

None of these difficulties exist if one follows the upper cantillation, ending the First Commandment at "bondage". In this system, all the laws concerning idolatry are gathered together in the Second Commandment, and all the coveting and craving included together in the Tenth Commandment. That may be why this system became standard in the Jewish tradition, and is the one familiar to all Jews.

However, it cannot be denied that this system has its difficulties as well. The very idea that the sentence "I am the LORD your God who brought you out of the land of Egypt, the house of bondage" constitutes an entire Commandment in itself, is hard to conceive. It is not couched as a command or an admonition, as all the other Commandments are. Consequently, it is much easier to see it either as part of a Commandment, or as a general introduction, as do all the other systems described here.

D. COUNTING THE COMMANDMENTS

The differences between the upper and the lower cantillations left their mark, it seems, on the disagreement among early authorities respecting the number of mitzvot in the passage from "I am the LORD" to "My commandments". Maimonides[23] counts five: "I am the LORD", "You shall have no other", "You shall not make", "You shall not bow down", "You shall not serve them". Nahmanides, on the other hand, sees only two: "I am the LORD", and all the admonitions against idolatry, which should be accounted one mitzvah.[24]

A different line is taken by the *Halakhot Gedolot* and expounded by Nahmanides.[25] In this view, "I am the LORD" ought not be accounted one of the 613 mitzvot. For one thing, it is the basis for all the mitzvot; for another, it is not worded as a mitzvah.

Similarly, "You shall have no other" ought not be considered a mitzvah by itself; for, as the *Mekhilta* points out, this admonition is connected with what follows: "You shall not make". The latter forbids the manufacture of the idol, while the former forbids you to have it in your possession.[26] Accordingly, the *Halakhot Gedolot* counts only two mitzvot here: one which forbids you to make or possess an idol, and a second which forbids you to worship it or any other god.

This difference of opinion arises from differences in the interpretation of a midrash attributed to Rabbi Hamnuna (Mak. 23b) on the verse "Moses charged us with the Torah" (Deut. 33. 4). The homily says that Moses charged us with 611 commandments (the numerical value of the letters of *Torah*), while God Himself gave us two additional commandments: "'I am the LORD' and 'You shall have no other gods beside Me'. These we heard directly from the Almighty". Thus we have a total of 613 commandments.

This homily is the point of departure for the difference of opinion cited above. The midrash says explicitly that "I am the LORD" and "You shall have no other" comprise two commandments. But which two ? Only "I am the LORD" and "you shall have no other", says Maimonides; no, says Nahmanides, the second includes all the admonitions concerning idolatry. The third opinion is that of the *Halakhot Gedolot*: "You shall have no other" plus "You shall not make" is one; "You shall not bow down to them or serve them" is the other.

But the truth of the matter is, that this difference of opinion flows

---

23   *Book of Commandments*, positive commandment 1, negative commandments 1, 2, 5, 6.

24   Ibid., negative commandment 1.

25   Ibid., positive commandment 1.

26   *Baḥodesh*, VI:2, ed. Lauterbach, II, pp. 238 f.

directly from the difference between the lower cantillation and the upper. Maimonides follows the lower cantillation, which joins "I am the LORD" and "You shall have no other" in one verse, forming one Commandment on one theme. So that when the Talmud says "I am the LORD and you shall have no other" it means to indicate this verse, which contains both phrases. And since it says that this verse contains two commandments, that proves that "I am the LORD" is one, and "You shall have no other" is the second. Therefore, the other admonitions concerning idolatry must be considered additional commandments, emanating from Moses.

As against this view, Nahmanides interprets according to the upper cantillation. In this reading, "I am the LORD" stands alone, with all the prohibitions concerning idolatry subsumed under "You shall not have." Consequently, when the Talmud says "I am the LORD and you shall have no other", it refers to the two Commandments that begin with those words. And since the Talmud says that these two Commandments add up to only two mitzvot, it is reasonable to conclude that the Commandment "I am the LORD" is one such mitzvah, and the Commandment "You shall have no other" is the second.

According to the *Halakhot Gedolot*, "I am the LORD" is just a sort of introduction to the Decalogue, and should not be counted as one of the 613 mitzvot. So when R. Hamnuna in the Talmud speaks of "the two commandments 'I am the LORD' and 'You shall have no other'", he must mean two mitzvot in the second sentence. If one includes in the Commandment nothing but "You shall have no other", there remains only one. If one says the Commandment includes all the admonitions connected with "You shall have no other gods", there will be at least three mitzvot — against deifying alien gods, against making images, and against worshipping them. So *Halakhot Gedolot* is compelled to go along with the *Mekhilta*, and to interpret "You shall *have* no other", not in its plain sense (belief in other gods) but in a derived sense (possession or maintenance of them). That attaches the ban to "You shall not make" (manufacture of them). Now we can say that the Commandment "You shall have no other gods" consists of only two mitzvot: one, possession and manufacture; two, bowing down and worshipping.

All this makes it clear that the author of *Halakhot Gedolot* reads the passage according to the upper cantillation, as Nahmanides does; but unlike Nahmanides, he does not follow that system for separating the Commandments. He does not include "I am the LORD" as one of the

613 mitzvot, and it stands to reason that he does not include it as one of the Ten Commandments, either. For him, the Ten Commandments begin with "You shall have no other gods beside Me", and that First Commandment continues up to "My commandments". This is the last of the possible methods, discussed above, of dividing the Decalogue into ten. It can be matched with the paragraph divisions, but not with the punctuation of the cantillation signs.

We have mentioned the interpretation given by the *Mekhilta*, that has "You shall have no other" refer to the maintenance of idols. Only the *Halakhot Gedolot* follows this line, while Maimonides and Nahmanides both say that the prohibition forbids one to attribute divinity to alien gods.[27] There can be no doubt that this is the plain sense of the text.

It may be pointed out now that this difference of opinion is rooted in the semantic difference between the lower and the upper cantillations. The lower system combines "I am the LORD" with "You shall have no other", placing in one verse belief in the LORD against belief in alien gods. Consequently, "You shall have no other" must be understood in its plain sense, as dealing with matters of belief.

But the upper cantillation calls for a full stop at *'avadim*, separating "You shall have no other" from the preceding sentence, and attaching it to "you shall not make for yourself". To be sure, this does not settle the issue: "You shall not have" can still be taken in its plain sense of belief, while "You shall not make" can be seen as dealing with the making of idols. But it is also possible to say that "have" and "make" belong together and both deal with the same subject — idols: the owning of them and the making of them.[28]

In the light of all this, we can understand the three-way difference of

27 According to Nahmanides, the interpretation of the *Mekhilta* is the individual opinion of R. José, but the Sages take the passage in its plain sense (see *Sifra* ad Lev. 19. 4).

28 The connection between the upper cantillation and the *Mekhilta* can be shown from the *Mekhilta* itself. The latter first says that *Anokhi* marks the prior acceptance of God's sovereignty, which is followed by the acceptance of His mitzvot; and then immediately interprets "You shall have no other" as a prohibition against possessing an idol. There can be no doubt that these two statements are interdependent; for if the connection between "I am the LORD" and "You shall have no other" had not first been broken by the upper cantillation, it would not have been possible to interpret the second statement as a prohibition against possession.

opinion about the meaning of the Commandment "You shall have no
other gods beside Me" between Maimonides, Nahmanides and the
Halakhot Gedolot. Maimonides follows the lower cantillation. He
must therefore adhere to the plain sense of the text. The other two
interpret in terms of the punctuation of the upper cantillation, which
leaves the meaning of the Commandment uncertain.

But since Nahmanides counts only one mitzvah in this Commmandment, he has to follow the plain sense of the text; for only if this
Commandment forbids belief in alien gods is it possible to include in it
the admonitions not to make or worship them — so that we end up with
only one mitzvah.

As against this view, the author of *Halakhot Gedolot*, for whom this
Commandment contains two mitzvot, is forced to interpret it as the
Mekhilta does — a prohibition against possession. Only thus is it
possible to include manufacture along with it, leaving bowing down
and worshipping as a separate matter, and thus arriving at two mitzvot
within this Commandment.

Just as the author of *Halakhot Gedolot* was forced to depart from
the plain sense of the Commandment "You shall have no other", so too
was he constrained to interpret the Talmud in a sense other than the
obvious. The Talmud says that "I" and "You shall not have" we heard
"spoken by the Almighty". From the context it seems that these two are
the two mitzvot that were heard directly. But the *Halakhot Gedolot*
would have us force the meaning: to be sure, these two sentences were
spoken by the Almighty; but the two mitzvot that were heard were
"You shall have no other gods", and "You shall not serve them", both
of which are included within one of the Ten Commandments.

This forcing of the sense of the Talmud is not present in the
interpretations of either Maimonides or Nahmanides. Both of them
agree that *Anokhi* and *Lo yiheyeh* are two separate statements, and are
also the two Commandments "spoken by the Almighty". The difference
between them is this: according to Maimonides, *"Anokhi* and *Lo
yiheyeh* is a way of referring to a *single verse* in the lower cantillation;
according to Nahmanides, it is a way of referring to *two Commandments* in the upper cantillation.

E. DEVELOPMENT OF THE POST-MASORETIC CANTILLATION SYSTEMS

Let us return to the double and triple cantillation of the Commandment
"I am the LORD your God who brought you out of the land of Egypt,
the house of bondage". As we pointed out above, there were two

systems during the time of the Masoretes — the *etnaḥ* clause in the lower cantillation, and the *silluq* clause in the upper cantillation. But unlike all the other duplicate systems in the Ten Commandments, these two do not complement one another. On the contrary, they represent differing approaches. The *silluq* clause represents the method which sees the words just quoted as both the first verse and the first Commandment in its entirety. The *etnaḥ* system, on the other hand, stands for the view that combines those words with "You shall have no other gods beside Me", to form the first verse — and the First Commandment or part of it.

We may now be better able to understand the development at a later stage of the *revi'a* system. It seems likely that both punctators and Torah-readers sensed the contradiction between the *silluq* and the *etnaḥ* systems. They therefore changed the latter into a *revi'a* system. These two correspond to one another: both of them combine *Anokhi* and *Lo yiheyeh* into one verse or one Commandment. The difference is that the *etnaḥ* system combines *Anokhi* only with the words "You shall have no other gods beside Me", a combination obscured by the *silluq* system; while the *revi'a* arrangement joins *Anokhi* to all the prohibitions concerning alien gods. This can be harmonized with the *silluq* system, since the *revi'a* can be assigned to the upper cantillation, where it can create the Commandment that includes *Anokhi* and everything connected with idol-worship; and the *silluq* can be assigned to the lower cantillation, performing the function of closing the first verse of the long Commandment created by the *revi'a* system.

And so it came about that the whole meaning of the cantillation systems was reversed, putting the upper below, and the lower above. Originally the *etnaḥ* combination had been read in the lower cantillation, and the *silluq* in the upper; and the two contradicted each other. Now the *etnaḥ* system disappeared from the lower cantillation, its place taken by the *revi'a* clause of the upper cantillation, while the *silluq* moves from the upper system to the lower. And now the two systems no longer contradict one another!

However, the punctators who introduced this change did not follow through with the necessary conclusion. They should have seen that the *revi'a* system represents that view which includes *Anokhi* and *Lo yiheyeh* and all its corollary prohibitions in the First Commandment. To keep the count of ten, that view calls for the division of the "covet" (or "crave") Commandment into two. So they should have added a *silluq* to the *etnaḥ* of *re'ekha* (the first "covet"). But this necessary completion of the *revi'a* system was never made — a further proof of the late origin of the *revi'a* system.

This helps us understand the treatment afforded by the grammarians to the three-fold cantillation of the sentence *Anokhi*. They noticed that the *revi'a* system was contradicted by the cantillation of "You shall not covet". But they did not conclude that additional signs should be added to that Commandment. They were after all grammarians, not punctators. They could resort to interpretive skill, but not to tampering with the punctuation. So they abandoned the plain sense of the *revi'a* system, and gave it a new meaning.[29] Its purpose, they said, was not to create one Commandment out of *Anokhi* plus all the prohibitions of *Lo yiheyeh* — but rather to ally the two Commandments which, according to Nahmanides, were heard directly from the Almighty. So the problem of the Tenth Commmandment was solved.[30]

This ultimately became the method adopted by most Jewish communities. The *silluq* system is read in the lower cantillation, where it renders *Anokhi* as a complete verse. The *revi'a* system is made for the upper cantillation. It conjoins the Commandment *Anokhi* to the Commandment *Lo yiheyeh*, because these two were the two Commandments heard directly from the Almighty. But there is no system in the upper cantillation (the "Commandment" cantillation) which renders the Commandment *Anokhi* as a separate unit, and the Commandment *Lo yiheyeh* as a separate unit.

There is no doubt that this arrangement cannot be right. Not only does it contradict the manuscripts (which show no trace of the *revi'a*) but it does not even give a proper explanation for the system of the later punctators who introduced the *revi'a* system. It does not seem at all reasonable that a system which is to be read in the upper cantillation should do nothing more than combine Commandments, rather than create the framework for a Commandment. But a grammarian who is

---

29　This meaning of the *revi'a* system had been mentioned by Hizzequni in his commentary on the Decalogue, and it was adopted by all the grammarians.

30　Later on di Lonzano reverted to the *etnaḥ* instead of the *revi'a*; but it was not the same *etnaḥ* system which the punctators had replaced by the *revi'a*. He restored an *etnaḥ* which took the place of the *revi'a*, because for him it had the same meaning. It was to be read in the upper cantillation, and to couple "I am the LORD" with the Commandment "You shall have no other". And because this use of the *etnaḥ* clause violates the rules of the tropes (it places two *etnaḥ* before a *silluq*) Dubno came along later and put the *revi'a* system back in place.

not a punctator has no other way of harmonizing the *revi'a* system with the tropes of "You shall not covet".

All of this enables us to understand the method adopted by Heidenheim. He accepted the explanation of the grammarians as far as the *revi'a* system is concerned; but it led him to a conclusion that had not occurred to anyone before him. He decided that their way of solving the problem raised by the *revi'a* could also be applied to the *etnah* system. For it is possible to say that the *etnah* is not intended to create a verse that includes *Anokhi* and *Lo yiheyeh*, but rather to conjoin the two verses which, according to Maimonides, were the two "that we heard from the mouth of the Almighty". As a result, not only is it possible to harmonize the *revi'a* system with the tropes of "You shall not covet", but it is also possible to harmonize the *etnah* system with the system of the *silluq*.[31]

This interpretation of Heidenheim's is nothing but a logical conclusion of the interpretation given by the grammarians to the *revi'a* system, but it has the effect of undermining the balance between the various trope arrangements. For the Masorah and the later punctators were united in recognizing only two tropal systems: either the *silluq* and the *etnah*, or the *silluq* and the *revi'a*. Thus, one of these combinations could be read for the lower cantillation, and one for the upper. But Heidenheim recognized three tropal systems, and it is impossible to actually read more than two.

That is why he introduced a novel idea:[32] only one system — that of

---

31 This interpretation of the *etnah* clause never entered the minds of the grammarians who preceded Heidenheim, because to them the *etnah* system was part of the upper cantillation, serving to yoke two Commandments together; cf. n. 30. So Heidenheim's innovation had two aspects. He explained the *etnah* clause as a coupling of "I am the LORD" with "You shall have no other". Furthermore, he treated it the way the grammarians before him had treated the *revi'a* system — not as a means of creating verses, but as a means of yoking verses together.

32 From the way he puts it, it seems that Heidenheim would have come to the same conclusion even if he hadn't been forced to. He vigorously attacks the very idea that the upper cantillation divides the Decalogue into only nine Commandments; he also proves that Hizzequni says the upper cantillation was introduced purely as a reminder. However, his proof from Hizzequni is weak; and the very idea of a cantillation system with no function except to "remind" is rather forced. It therefore seems likely that he would not have made bold to suggest his idea, had he not noticed that all three sets of cantillations for the opening sentence of the Decalogue could be harmonized. And since it is not possible to read them all in the upper and lower cantillations, he had to relegate two of them to the category of "reminders".

the *silluq* — is for purposes of reading, in *both* upper and lower
cantillations. In the upper, it marks off the Commandment *Anokhi*. In
the lower, it concludes the *verse Anokhi*. As for the systems of the
etnaḥ and the *revi'a*, they were not intended for purposes of actual
reading, but only as instructive reminders. The *revi'a* serves to conjoin
the two *Commandments* which, in the view of Nahmanides, are those
which "we heard from the mouth of the Almighty". The *etnaḥ* serves to
conjoin the two *verses* which, in the view of Maimonides, are those
which we heard by Divine pronouncement. The fact is obvious that
these two systems are not intended to mark off verses or
Commandments, which is their normal function; but rather to *join*
verses or Commandments which were heard directly in the Divine
voice. They therefore have no place in actual reading — neither in the
upper cantillation nor in the lower.

Without a doubt this interpretation also leaves something to be
desired. However, it seems that Heidenheim distanced himself from the
original intent of the tropal Masoretes even more than the grammarians
who preceded him. The latter at least followed the opinion of the later
punctators, who read the *silluq* system for the lower cantillation, and
the *revi'a* for the upper. They merely misinterpreted the meaning of the
revi'a system; no longer was it seen as a system creating the
Commandment "I am the LORD" to "My commandments", but rather
as a system joining together the *two* Commandments "I am the LORD"
and "You shall have no other".

Heidenheim, on the contrary, seems to have been unaware of the
intent of either the Masoretes or of the later punctators. For whereas
the Masorah read the *silluq* system in the upper cantillation and the
etnaḥ system in the lower cantillation; and the later punctators read the
silluq in the lower cantillation, and the *revi'a* in the upper —
Heidenheim followed neither of them. Instead, he read the *silluq* for
both upper and lower. What is more, he interpreted the *etnaḥ* and the
revi'a systems incorrectly. No longer were they systems for creating
verses or Commandments, to be read in either the lower or the upper
cantillation. Now they were transformed into systems for connecting
verses or Commandments, and were transformed into nothing more
than "reminders".

In terms of the original meaning of the *etnaḥ* and the *revi'a* systems,
this approach is misconceived. But more than that, it is logically
unacceptable. It is not at all reasonable to suppose that the Masoretes
or the punctators of the biblical text would leave us sets of tropes that

had no tropal function, and were not meant to be used in reading but were nothing more than tokens of remembrance.

In summing up this discussion we must also take note of an astonishing phenomenon that has been exposed. The Masorah left us two sets of tropes for the Commandment *Anokhi*, but in the course of time these two were altered so as to become unrecognizable. First they were "corrected" by the punctators, and then they were "explained" by the grammarians. But the correction made for confusion, and the subsequent explanations confounded matters even more.

This strange phenomenon stems from the fact that the Masorah left us two sets of tropes that contradict one another in their understanding of the text. The explanation of this is, that the two systems come from two different sources. The lower cantillation originated in the Land of Israel, while the upper system came from Babylonia. So we have here one more point of disagreement between the "Westerners" (Palestine) and the "Easterners" (Babylonia). As a rule the Masorah decides in favor of one or the other — usually in favor of the West. But in this instance it let the two systems stand side by side, and so both of them entered the Tiberian Masorah.

Once we realize that the two systems come from two different sources, we need no longer be surprised at the contradictions between them. It seems that the Palestinian scholars differed from those in Babylonia on two matters. The former were accustomed to read the Ten Commandments in the lower cantillation, dividing the Decalogue into regular verses; while it was the Babylonian custom to read with the upper cantillation, marking off the Commandments. In addition to this disagreement — which is actually nothing more than a difference in custom — they also differed in the way they interpreted the opening passage. In the Land of Israel they held that the first verse included "I am the LORD" and "You shall have no other gods beside Me". Consequently they read the *etnaḥ* (a pause) in the lower cantillation. But in Babylonia they thought that the sentence "I am the LORD, etc." stood by itself, as the first *verse*, as well as the First Commandment. Consequently they read it with a *silluq* (full stop) using the upper cantillation.

The punctators and the grammarians were apparently unaware of all these developments. Confronted as they were by two tropal systems, they took it for granted that both of them came from the same source, and that the difference between them could only be functional, namely, that the lower system divided the text into verses, and the upper into

Commandments. But it was inconceivable to them that there should be a difference in interpretation between the systems.

This is what caused the whole sequence of errors that were made in cantillating the Commandment "I am the LORD your God". The punctators were confronted by the *etnah* series, which is contradicted by the *silluq* series. Had they but known that these two systems came from different sources, they would have let the contradiction stand. But they thought that both systems came from the same source, so the contradiction had to be solved. Thus they were forced to substitute the *revi'a* system for the *etnah* system. This "correction" resolved the contradiction, but, as usually happens with correctors, they left the job unfinished. Their emendation had upset the number of Commandments, and they should have added to the tropes of "You shall not covet" in order to restore the balance. This they neglected to do.

Their corrected version reached the commentators[33] and the grammarians[34] who now found themselves facing the *etnah* system of the Masorah and the *revi'a* system of the punctators. Both these systems conflict with some other tropal system. The *etnah* system conflicts with the *silluq* system, while the *revi'a* system is in conflict with the cantillation of "You shall not covet". There is, however, a fundamental difference between these conflicts. That between the *etnah* and the *silluq* is a difference between the lower and the upper cantillations. But the dissonance between the *revi'a* system and the cantillation of "You shall not covet" is a contradiction within the upper system itself. For in that Commandment, upper and lower are identical.

The grammarians could have deduced from this that the *revi'a* clause was a mistake[35] because there is no way of reconciling it with the tropes of the Commandment "You shall not covet", whereas the conflict between the *etnah* and the *silluq* systems can readily be explained as the reflection of two differing interpretations that emanated from two different sources.

But this never occurred to them, because they had no idea that the lower and the upper cantillations had originated independently of each

33   Such as Hizzequni; see above, notes 9, 12, 29 and 32.
34   Such as di Lonzano, Norzi, Dubno and Heidenheim; see above, notes 4, 10, 30, 31 and 32.
35   They could also have deduced this from the syntax rules of the tropes (cf. n. 8). But as we have already explained, they were not familiar with those rules.

other. They took it for granted that the entire complex of tropes for the Ten Commandments had been transmitted by a single masoretic tradition. Just as it was impossible that there should be an inner inconsistency in the upper cantillation system, so it seemed to them impossible that the upper and the lower systems should contradict one another.

This has always been the way of commentators who confront an inconsistency in the text they are interpreting, but who refuse to admit that the text itself comes from divergent sources. They are forced to "explain" away the contradiction. They are likely to propose far-fetched and unreasonable interpretations, just so long as the contradiction appears to be resolved.

This is what happened in the present instance. The grammarians noticed that the *etnah* system was contradicted by the *silluq* system, and that the *revi'a* arrangement was in conflict with the cantillation of "You shall not covet". Had they but known that the *etnah* and the *silluq* came from two different sources, the difficulty would have disappeared, while the conflict between the *revi'a* system and the tropes of "You shall not covet" would have been seen to be due to the mistaken introduction of the former. But since they did not recognize the fact that they were dealing with two different sources, they were unable to see this. They therefore had to invent "solutions" to the inconsistency, first by interpreting the *revi'a* system as a device for coupling two still separate Commandments, thus restoring the total number to Ten; and later by Heidenheim's idea that the *etnah* system coupled separate verses without uniting them, thus resolving the conflict between it and the *silluq* system.

All this led to the forced explanation that the upper cantillation *joined* Commandments together — the reverse of its original function; or that the Masorah left us purely theoretical tropal systems — designed not for use but as reminders. These explanations were offered in spite of their questionable nature, because the alternative — that what looked like inconsistency was really two different approaches — never entered into consideration.

This harmonizing method, which solves inconsistencies by means of ingenious interpretation, was especially justifiable in relation to the cantillation of the Ten Commandments. That is because the semantic difference between the *etnah* and the *silluq* systems gives rise to differences in dividing the Decalogue into its ten components. However, only one such system of division became the norm among Jews everywhere — the one represented by the *silluq* clause. So it never occurred to them that Jews had ever divided the Ten Commandments in any other way. It was even less conceivable to them that such "alien" divisions had found a place in the Masorah itself. As a consequence, they would have been unable even to consider the idea that the different cantillations came from different schools of thought, which disagreed about how the Ten Commandments should be divided.

F. SYNAGOGUE CUSTOMS OF CANTILLATION

In relatively modern times a variety of customs have developed in the various Jewish communities. Ashkenazim are accustomed to read the upper cantillation only when reading the Ten Commandments on the festival of Shavuot, whereas Sephardim use that system for every public reading of the Decalogue.[36] Still other procedures were followed at the time of the Masoretes.

In this connection, reference should be made to the two-fold cantillation in the episode of Reuben and Bilhah (Gen. 35. 22–23).[37] The two double cantillations — in this passage, and in the Ten Commandments — were treated in different ways by masoretic circles. There are three distinct methods of handling the situation.

One such method is reflected in the number of verses given by the Masorah for each book of the Bible. The numbers recorded for the Books of Exodus (1209) and Deuteronomy (955) are correct, if the Ten Commandments are read in 12 verses — that is, according to the lower cantillation; while the total for the Book of Genesis (1534) is also correct if we read the episode of Reuben as two verses — again, in accordance with the lower cantillation. So that all these numbers follow the lower cantillation.

A second method reflects the masoretic totals for each of the weekly pericopes. For the ones containing the Ten Commandments, *Yitro* (in Exodus) totals 72 verses, while *Va-Ethanan* (in Deuteronomy) comes

36 Sephardic and Ashkenazic customs are explained by Dubno and Heidenheim. However, not all Sephardim adhere to the same custom, and such differences await further study. In any event, to the best of my knowledge Ashkenazi customs are pretty firmly established. They adhere to the lower cantillation, except on Shavuot. Hasidim, who follow the "Sephardic" liturgy, always use the upper cantillation for public reading.
37 I rely here on the reading in ms. Sassoon 507. Ms. Leningrad is not entirely clear at this point.

to 119. These figures are correct if the Decalogue is read as 10 verses — that is, according to the upper cantillation; while the figure for the pericope in Genesis containing the Reuben story is correct (154) if we read that episode as two verses — that is, in the lower cantillation.

A third method is reflected in the old Bible manuscripts. In the Ten Commandments they show the tropes of the lower cantillation written in before those of the upper cantillation; but the reverse in the episode of Reuben. The explanation for this inconsistency seems to be that the punctators always wrote in first the system that they preferred in practise; so that it would appear that for the Decalogue, they followed the lower cantillation, but for the Reuben story, the upper.

That is how it came about that we inherited three different customs for reading those biblical passages that have dual tropes. The Masoretes who calculated the number of verses in each of the biblical books always followed the lower cantillation. Those who added up the verses of the weekly *parashiyyot* read the Ten Commandments in the upper cantillation, and the Reuben story in the lower. As for the punctators of the Tiberian manuscripts, they did the exact opposite: they read the Ten Commandments in the lower system, and the Reuben story in the upper.

But why did both of them treat the Reuben story differently from the Ten Commandments? We know that both the Palestinians and the Babylonians were accustomed to make a difference in the way these passages were treated. The "Westerners" (Palestinians) read the Ten Commandments in the lower cantillation, and the Reuben story in the upper. The "Easterners" (Babylonians) did the exact opposite. The result was, two contradictory sets of customs.

It seems that the calculation of the number of verses in the weekly *parashiyyot* was made in the Babylonian academies. After all, the very division of the Torah into weekly pericopes was a Babylonian custom. Obviously, then, the number of verses in the *parashiyyot* always corresponds to the Babylonian custom — in the Decalogue as well as in the Reuben story. But the punctators of the manuscripts followed the Palestinian custom, true to the Tiberian tradition. It was only natural that they should enter the tropes in the Palestinian manner.

However, a special importance attaches to the custom which is reflected in the number of verses reported for each book of the Bible. These numbers are apparently older than the similar numbers calculated for the weekly pericopes — just as the books themselves are older than their division into weekly scriptural lessons. And since the

numbers given for the whole books always agree with the lower
cantillation, this proves that that system reflects the more ancient
custom of reading the Torah. There is also an intrinsic reason for
coming to the same conclusion, for it is only the lower cantillation that
is faithful to the plain sense of the text, and the usual biblical style. The
opposite is true of the upper system: in the Ten Commandments it
fashions inordinately long and short verses, while in the Reuben episode
it matches the midrashic sense rather than the obvious one. Since the
Scripture was almost always chanted in accordance with the plain
sense, we can assume that in this case too, the lower cantillation alone
was followed.

There is another reason for believing that the lower system is the
older one: its very name. It was referred to in the early masoretic period
as *taʿama qadma* ("the ancient trope")[38] in connection with both the
Reuben story and the Ten Commandments. We are therefore justified
in concluding that it was the earliest tropal system, long in use.

The same conclusion is mandated as well by the grammar of the
tropes. The lower system always adheres to their syntactical rules,
while the upper cantillation violates those rules in a number of places.
And in those passages it is obvious that the upper system was grafted
onto the lower at a later period.

This phenomenon is especially apparent in the Reuben passage. The
silluq formation of the lower cantillation is complete in all respects
throughout the verse; whereas the *etnah* formation of the upper
cantillation is complete only in the section from *"vayyelkh"* to *"Israel"*.
That leaves the opening clause of the verse with tropes that are
grammatically consistent only with a *silluq* arrangement. So it turns
out that the relationship of the upper system to the lower in the Reuben
passage is exactly that of the *reviʿa* to the *etnah* in the Ten
Commandments. And just as the *reviʿa* in the Decalogue is without
doubt a late intrusion, so is the upper cantillation in the story of
Reuben and Bilhah.

The same sort of thing can be detected in various places in the Ten
Commandments. In the Commandment "You shall have no other" it
would have been appropriate for the *etnah* of the upper cantillation to
have been placed under the word *"la-ʾareẓ"*, or under *"taʿovdem"*; and

---

38   This is the designation used in ms.Sassoon 507, also found in the Reuben episode;
      cf. n. 2, above.

in the Sabbath Commandment, it should have been attached to "your settlements". It seems likely that the tropes were assigned in the way that they were in order to align the upper cantillations to the lower in the concluding part of the Commandment.[39] All of this makes it apparent that the upper cantillation was a late intrusion.

From all of this we can learn something important about the order of division of the Ten Commandments. We have already mentioned the received opinion about the so-called "traditional" division, according to which "I am the LORD your God who brought you out of the Land of Egypt" stands by itself as the First Commandment. However, as we have shown, this is not the only arrangement known to the Masorah, even though it really is reflected in the *Mekhilta* and in Targum Pseudo-Jonathan. This arrangement was transmitted only in the upper cantillation system, which reflects the customs of Babylonian Jewry. But there is a different tradition, reflecting the custom of Palestinian Jewry, and extending the First Commandment at least as far as "any other gods beside Me". This, it seems, was the *original* scheme of the Masorah!

One other point about the later custom in reading the Ten Commandments. We have already mentioned the difference between Ashkenazic and Sephardic customs. Be it noted that both these traditions find a place for both the upper and the lower cantillations — and still the traditions differ. The difference can be explained in the light of what has been said above. The Sephardic tradition is influenced to a greater extent by the Babylonian. Therefore they usually follow the upper cantillation — as did the "Easterners". The lower cantillation finds a place only in private reading. The Ashkenazim, on the other

---

39 In the Sabbath Commandment in Exodus, this explanation is less satisfactory, because if the word "settlements" had been given an *etnah*, the upper cantillation would have been similar to the lower from "you shall do no work" to "settlements". But the number of words in this passage is only half the number from "For in six days" to the end of the Commandment. This may be why they preferred to equalize the upper and lower cantillations in the concluding part of the Commandment. It should be pointed out that in the Deuteronomic version ("Observe") the upper cantillation is also inexact. The second "your God" ought to have been given a *zaqēf*; perhaps it was given a *revi'a* in order for it to match the cantillation of the Exodus version. But even if this explanation is inexact, the fact remains that the upper cantillation was inserted in a number of places contrary to the normal syntax of the tropes. This is additional evidence of its late origin.

hand, were influenced more by the Palestinian custom, so they generally read in the lower cantillation. Only on Shavuot do they give expression to the upper cantillation.[40]

There is something to be said in favor of this custom of the Ashkenazim. For it is the accepted rule that the Ten Commandments are no holier than all the other commandments in the Torah; they were all, as the saying goes, given by the same shepherd, and written down in the Torah given at Sinai. And yet there *is* a difference; for all the mitzvot were first transmitted as oral Torah to Moses alone and written in the Torah later on; while these Ten were spoken to the whole people of Israel gathered in sacred assembly, and only later inscribed in the written Torah, along with all the other commandments.

It appears then that these two aspects of the Ten Commandments are reflected in the two systems of cantillation that have come down to us. It seems that they were first spoken at Sinai as Ten Commandments, and as such were subsequently written on the tablets, as a lasting memorial of that event: "He declared to you the covenant which He commanded you to observe, the Ten Commandments, and He inscribed them on two tablets of stone" (Deut. 4. 13). However, when the Ten Words were·later inscribed in the Torah, they were sanctified again as the Written Torah and divided into verses like all the rest of the Word of God.

All this is expressed in the Ashkenazi custom. On Shavuot they read the Ten Commandments as at the revelation at Sinai — hence they divide the words into Ten Commandments, using the upper cantillation. But when the annual turn of the Decalogue in Exodus and Deuteronomy comes around, they read the passage in the normal manner, divided into verses like all the rest of Scripture.

Translated by Gershon Levi

40   Compare n. 36.

12. SOME COMMENTS ON THE CANTILLATION
OF THE TEN COMMANDMENTS

AMNON SHILOAH

I

For the Ten Commandments both in Exodus (30. 2–17) and in
Deuteronomy (5.6–21) there are two sets of cantillation signs. One is
called "the lower cantillation", and the other is known as "the upper
cantillation". There is one other biblical verse where that peculiarity
appears (the episode of Reuben and Bilhah, Gen. 35. 22) but that is not
relevant to our present topic.

One result of having two different sets of cantillations is that there
are two different ways of dividing the text into verses, and in some
instances two different vowels for the same letter. Thus, the
Commandments have nine verses in the upper cantillation, but thirteen
in lower. The First and Second Commandments make up one long
verse in the upper system, and five verses in the lower. The Third
Commandment is the same in both. The Fourth Commandment is read
as one verse in the upper but as four in the lower cantillation. For the
Fifth Commandment there is no difference between the two. The
Sixth, Seventh, Eight and Ninth are treated as separate verses in the
upper cantillation, but are read together as one verse in the lower. The
Tenth Commandment is the same in both systems.

The upper cantillation is responsible for creating some very long
sentences — the longest in the Bible — side by side with the three
shortest verses in the Hebrew Scriptures. It also stands to reason that
the existence of the two systems would give rise to different ways of
reading the Ten Commandments, and to varieties of chanting them.
Indeed, to the best of our knowledge the double cantillation is the cause
of varying customs which are still observed in various Jewish
communities with respect to the public reading of the Ten Commandments.

The topic of the upper cantillation in general is dealt with elsewhere

331

in this volume. Here we will focus principally on the musical aspects of the subject. The question we shall consider is this: does the special way of intoning the Commandments on special occasions derive purely from the special arrangement of the verses, in their unusual length and brevity? Or perhaps from the multiplicity of elaborately melismatic cantillation signs characteristic of the upper system? Or is it possible that the change to the upper cantillation is more substantive, and reaches beyond the musical rendition of the signs, which after all are not in themselves unique?

An examination of the literature dealing with the cantillation signs reveals that the upper cantillation gets scant mention. The main focus is on the detailed exposition of the categories into which the signs are divided. When the upper cantillation does get mentioned, it is only in the context of "variations in the musical motifs", such as those at pauses in the reading, and at the conclusion of biblical books; special renditions for the Days of Awe, or for dramatic passages such as the Song of the Sea; and so on.

Such variations are to be found in all communities. They can be described and understood by reference to the standard basic systems, of which there are two categories: the cantillation for twenty-one of the biblical books, and the distinct system for Psalms, Proverbs and Job. In practice, however, the renditions vary according to the nature of the books: their content and the liturgical circumstances under which they are read; as well as in relation to the local musical traditions, and the individual interpretation offered by each reader.

However, it must be emphasized that the wide variety of individual interpretations and local traditions is subordinate to one overriding principle: faithfulness to the correct phrasing, which is fixed by the disjunctive and conjunctive accents. In other words, the written text and its meaning, its exact phrasing and emphases — these values are given, not to be altered or deviated from. They dictate the chant and the cadence. The truth is that the biblical chant is not determined by musical standards, but is derived from, and subordinate to, the punctuational values already determined by the function of the cantillation symbols.

As for the musical aspect itself of the cantillation signs, it is based on two components: melody and cadence. The melodic component is expressed by using tonal patterns which interpret the various cantillation symbols. Some of these patterns are more or less exactly defined, others not so. Actually, it is only in the Ashkenazic tradition that a system developed in which each symbol is assigned a particular melody. But even in this tradition, the same tonal pattern is sometimes used for several different symbols. In all other traditions there is no fixed pattern, and the melodic motif can be very simple — that is, simply putting emphasis on the disjunctives. At the same time, the melodic component can be trilled and elaborated at will, even when there is no indication of this in the cantillation sign. The music was influenced by the local styles of singing; hence the differences between the various traditions. But the rhythmic component which is based on the principle of flowing and retention is governed by the disjunctive and conjunctive accents; hence the remarkable underlying similarity in this respect between all the traditions. When there are variations in this component, they derive for the most part from the particular solemnity of the reading. The more solemn the reading, the slower the pace and the longer the retention. Trilled and embellished reading also affects the pace at which it is read, as well as the length of the pauses.

In the light of these principles, let us explore one of the possible explanations for the use of the upper cantillations in the public reading of the Ten Commandments. According to this explanation, the upper system bestows an added measure of solemnity on the reading by virtue of its large number of superlinear symbols, most of which represent rich melodic patterns. They appear in close proximity to one another, which makes for a rendition more elaborate and more stately.

However, it is possible to observe even at this stage of our discussion that there are some traditions which do not require a perceptible musical difference when chanting the Ten Commandments in the upper cantillation. This is true of those traditions which are simple to begin with, such as those of the Jews of Yemen and of Morocco. The Sephardic tradition, on the other hand, seems to be the one offering the greatest freedom, even allowing for different musical readings of the same symbol. In that tradition special musical patterns evolve which give prominence to the solemn stateliness appropriate to the reading of the Ten Commandments.

II

In his volume of Responsa *Sha'arei Tefillah*, Rabbi Solomon Hanau[1]

---

1   Solomon Zalman Hanau (1687–1746), Hebrew grammarian, son of a hazan. His *Sha'arei Torah* appeared in 1718, with an appendix on cantillation entitled *Sha'arei Zimrah*. His *Sha'arei Tefillah* appeared in 1725.

is asked for a ruling about the correct way to read the Ten Commandments. In his long and reasoned answer he comes to the following conclusion: "It is clear that the proper way is to read in accordance with the lower cantillation at all times. At no time whatsoever should the upper cantillation be used". At the very beginning of his responsum he notes that the Sephardim do customarily chant in accordance with the upper cantillation, in connection with which custom he takes issue with Rabbi Menahem di Lonzano, author of *Or Torah*.[2] According to Hanau, di Lonzano wrote that on one occasion, when he was sitting with a group of scholars, a question was raised concerning the dual cantillation signs for the Ten Commandments. Various opinions were expressed, until finally Rabbi Menahem explained that the upper cantillation was intended for the public reading of the Commandments at congregational worship, while the lower signs were for the individual to use in his private reading. Hanau proceeds to say: "This statement was made by Rabbi Menahem without any supporting evidence whatsovever."

Rabbi Jacob Emden[3] disagrees with Hanau's conclusion that the lower cantillation should be used exclusively, and expresses surprise at the latter's attack on the Sephardi custom:

> Let me ask why he rejected the tradition of these Sephardic sages in Israel, and went on to villify and castigate them, saying that their words were mere speculation, just fantasy without rhyme or reason or proof.

Among the interesting arguments that Emden adduces in this polemic of his, there is one of a musical character:

> It is plainly self-evident that the upper cantillation contains a higher range of melody as well as louder sounds, whereas the lower system has lower tones that can barely be heard. Note also that those cantillation signs which call for raising one's voice

---

2   Born 1550, apparently in Constantinople; died in Jerusalem, before 1624. Linguist, poet and kabbalist, he was close to the mystics of Safed. Best known for his *Shetei Yadot* (Venice 1618), containing *Or Torah*, which was also printed separately (Amsterdam 1659).

3   Rabbi and halakhic authority (1697–1776); also studied kabbalah as well as secular subjects and knew several languages. He wrote some 50 books, of which his *Lu'aḥ 'Eres* deals with the language of the Prayer Book and includes comments on Hanau's *Sha'arei Tefillah*.

have been placed above the letters, like *zarqa, pazēr, zaqēf gadol, qadma v'azla,* and so on. When he comes to these, the reader raises his voice.

In support of his description of the upper cantillation, Emden quotes the Zohar and its commentaries. Finally, he presents a bold defense of the Sephardic *minhag* for the reading of the Ten Commandments, and gives full backing to Rabbi Menahem di Lonzano. He acknowledges, "In this matter the tradition of the Sephardim is ancient, straightforward, and quite correct." In his summation, Emden writes:

> Reverting to the tortuous words of Rabbi Hanau, who called the Sephardic custom pure fantasy without reason, so that the question of reading in public according to the upper cantillation remains unanswered... how can he presume to give a decision when he is one of those with no capacity to taste that which is sweeter than honey.[4] The fact is that the upper cantillation is appropriate for public reading, so that the Commandments sound something like they did when promulgated at Sinai; whereas when they are read in private, one need not be particular about this. Besides, it is difficult for the average person to master the proper way of rendering long and short sentences, and to handle the patterns of speech which differ from one person to another. But when it comes to congregational worship, the matter is in the hands of an expert reader.

There can be no doubt that Emden is talking about reading the Torah with a special melody of a grand and stately nature, suitable for the re-enactment of the revelation at Mount Sinai.

III

At first glance, this argument seems to be a tempest in a teapot. What can it really matter whether the reading is public or private? However, a number of elements in the debate are calculated to give us some interesting insights into the situation at that time, as well as a more substantive explanation for the reading of the Ten Commandments in the upper cantillation.

---

4   Apparently a reference to the midrash: "He who reads the Scripture with relish and song, of him the Song of Songs says (4. 11): 'Honey and milk are under your tongue'" (Canticles Rabbah, IV :23).

The points to which we should direct our attention are these: the reliance on Rabbi Menahem di Lonzano as spokesman for the Sephardim, and as a halakhic authority in the matter of the emphasis to be placed on the musical nature of the upper cantillation signs; the decision by Emden that the Sephardic tradition of reciting the Ten Commandments in an especially stately manner is an old and correct tradition; and finally, his decision that the upper cantillation is proper for public reading "so that the Commandments sound something like they did when promulgated at Sinai".

We know that di Lonzano had close relations with the kabbalistic circles that flourished at that time in Safed, and was much influenced by them. He was also a talented musician, who knew a good deal about musical theory and played several instruments. He composed a number of liturgical poems (piyyutim) and set them to Turkish tunes. In a collection of hymns which he published in Constantinople about the year 1575, he prefaced an apology and an explanation:

> The Lord above knows, and let all Israel now know that I have not published hymns set to tunes of the Ishmaelites in order for frivolous people to make merry with fife and drum at their drinking bouts,[5] after the fashion of those songs composed for drinkers of strong drink. But I have chosen Ishmaelite melodies because I find them to be the expression of a broken and contrite heart. It occurred to me that perhaps in this way my uncircumcised heart might be humbled, and I might gain atonement for my sins (cf. Lev. 20. 41).

In addition to this purpose of intensifying religious emotions and experience by means of music, Lonzano has another reason, which he mentions in his work *Shetei Yadot* (para. 142. 11):

> The reason that I composed most of my songs to Ishmaelite tunes was because they call for raising the voice to high and intensive levels more than any others.

That is to say, he found these melodies suitable for singing the LORD's praises with a maximum of power and intensity. Di Lonzano was careful to choose those tunes which were suitable for religious occasions, and to reject those which were inappropriate — something

5   An allusion to Isaiah 5. 12.

which his contemporary, the gifted poet Israel Najarah failed to do.[6] Di Lonzano criticized Najarah for not choosing his musical modes with care, and for including some which were not necessarily suited to the mood of humility.

Lonzano also condemned Najarah for his unabashed metaphors and outspoken language in the hymn which the latter wrote celebrating the Torah as a marriage contract (*ketubah*) between the Holy One and the Jewish People. This hymn is sung in trembling awe before the open ark on Shavuot in hundreds of Jewish communities shortly before the solemn reading of the Ten Commandments. In language taken from the Song of Songs, the *"Ketubah for Shavuot"* describing the nuptials between God and *Kenesset Israel*, begins as follows:

> My Beloved went down to His garden, His spice-bed,
> To embrace the noble princess,
> To enfold her in His tabernacle of peace
> A palanquin King Solomon made him.
>
> He abandoned seraphim and ophanim,
> Leaving His horsemen to ride free,
> And reclined between the breasts
> Of the beloved gazelle,
> On his wedding day,
> The day of his heart's joy.

In the light of all this, we can assume that it was not by chance that Rabbi Hanau referred to the halakhic decision of Menahem di Lonzano, nor was it purely coincidental that Jacob Emden stressed the priority of the Sephardic custom, and connected it to the revelation at Mount Sinai as well as to the Zoharic comments on the significance of the upper cantillations. It would appear, then, that the Sephardim — who generally allowed a certain measure of freedom in the musical interpretation of the biblical cantillation signs — were the only ones, as far as we know, who added a special degree of stateliness and musical elaboration to the reading of the Ten Commandments.

The element of emotional experience and rhetorical flourish in reading the scriptural text as it is practiced in Sephardic congregations

---

6   See Joseph Yahalom, "Rabbi Israel Najarah and the Revival of Hebrew Poetry in the East After the Expulsion From Spain" (Hebrew), *Pe'amim*, 13, pp. 96–124.

finds clear-cut expression in Judah Halevi's *Kuzari*, in words which the author puts into the mouth of the Ḥaver.[7] In a passage in which Halevi, great poet that he was, enumerates the uniquely Jewish virtues of reading the Bible according to the cantillations, he speaks of the effects of softening the voice or amplifying it, of the expression of question, of wonder, of inducement, of threat or supplication which ordinary folk do not know how to convey. In summing up this exposition Halevi declares triumphantly: "A person who strives for these effects will undoubtedly forgo the rules of poetic meter."

The Torah reader is expected to breathe life into the written word of Scripture, enabling it to reverberate in the consciousness of the congregation and to be absorbed by them, all in accordance with his own feeling for the Word and his rhetorical and musical ability to communicate. He gives expression to the range of his emotion and experience by making skilled use of the factors of musical sound and timing: by controlling the pitch, dynamic, duration and tempo. He also adds decorative flourishes without, of course, interfering with the process of expressing the Scriptural text in accordance with the rules of phrasing laid down by the conjunctive and disjunctive accents.

We can assume that the special way in which Sephardim chant the Ten Commandments to this very day was influenced by the underlying approach presented here; as well as by the attempt to make palpable something of the overwhelming experience of the Sinaitic revelation, in which the factor of sound played so important a role. This factor attracted a lot of attention in midrashic and kabbalistic literature. The sound that emanated from the Almighty, it was said, was accompanied by flashes of light, and the sound flew through the air in circles until it reached the ears of the Israelites.[8]

> The Holy One, praised be He, wanted everyone to recognize His unity and His uniqueness, and to know that there is none beside Him. What did He do? When He revealed the Torah He silenced the whole universe, and hushed both the upper world and the lower world. No sound was heard in space other than His voice.

7 *The Book of Kuzari*, translated by Hartwig Hirschfeld, New York 1946, Second Discourse, para. 72.
8 The midrashic references at this point are based on Ginzberg's *Legends of the Jews*, III, Philadelphia 1919–1938, pp. 95 to 97 ff; and on Kasher's *Torah Shelemah*, Part XV, New York 1943, pp. 97 ff.

No bird sang, no winged creature flew, no ox lowed; the angels did not fly, the Seraphim stopped singing "Holy, Holy, Holy". When the Holy One promulgated the Torah at Sinai He showed the Israelites extraordinary wonders by means of His Voice. He would speak, and the sound would reverberate throughout the world. The Israelites would hear the voice coming to them from the south, and would rush in that direction to receive it. Then it would divide itself into seventy voices and the seventy tongues of mankind.

Thus, this voice spoke to all the peoples of the world, to each in its own language. It spoke to all the human race, to each person in terms of his ability to understand. "Old people heard it in their own terms, young people in theirs. The voice was different for each person".

The matter of "seeing the sounds" (Ex. 20. 15) aroused a good deal of comment. Philo has this to say:

...from the midst of the fire that streamed from heaven there sounded forth to their utter amazement a voice, for the flame became articulate speech in the language familiar to the audience, and so clearly and distinctly were the words formed by it that they seemed to see rather than hear them.[9]

Nor was the voice of Moses, in all its powerful grandeur, absent from this spectacular symphony of sound and fire. In every corner of the Israelite encampment his voice was heard:

Now the voice of Moses was heard by those both near and far, for the Holy One gave him the power and the strength, helping him transmit the words in voice and volume and melody just as he heard them.

It seems that these passages, describing in brilliant colors a spectacular scene of "sound and light" at Sinai, left their mark on the special way of reading the Ten Commandments customary among Sephardic Jews of eastern countries. It also seems highly likely that a variety of influences emanating from kabbalistic circles in the sixteenth and seventeenth centuries were at work, making for a reading of dramatic grandeur. This assumption is supported by the fact that singing was much cultivated in these circles, and that it flourished because of their

---

9   Philo, *De decalogo*, 46 ff., transl. Colson, Loeb Classics, VII, pp. 29 ff.

widespread influence. We have already had occasion to mention the great love Menahem di Lonzano had for melancholy Turkish melodies, and his sincere belief that the selective use of such melodies was capable of exalting the prayer experience and the worship service. Since Solomon Zalman Hanau who rejects his opinion, and Jacob Emden who approves it, both speak of him in connection with the reading of the Ten Commandments, we may perhaps assume that the elaborate melody reserved for reading the Decalogue took shape at approximately that time.

IV

Support for this conjecture may be found in the practice of certain Sephardic Torah readers, though it is admittedly rare even in their own special tradition. The widely accepted way of chanting by well-trained Sephardic readers is to retard at certain words and accents in the rendition of the Ten Commandments. The elaborations of greatest length and emphasis occur when stressing the word *lo'* (Thou shalt not) in the Sixth, Seventh and Eighth Commandments. This is the climactic moment, which raises the emotional tension to its highest level.

However, this solemn rendition, which takes about twice as long as does the reading of the same verses in any other tradition, pales into insignificance when compared with the virtuosity displayed by a number of highly skilled Sephardic readers. These latter borrowed special melodic patterns from Turkish and Arabic musical artistry, and adapted them to the general content of the Commandments, to isolated words, or even to associated ideas which these words or sentences arouse.

The art music of the Persians, Turks and Arabs is based on a well defined set of modes. Each of these modes has its characteristic tonal scale, its sequence of development of fragments from that scale, its preferential notes constantly recurring, special melodic patterns, and various other components into which there is no need to go at the moment. What is important here is, that in music theory as well as in practice these cultures attributed to their musical modes the power to exert all kinds of influences on man's psyche — and even on his physical state. They even related them to various cosmological theories.

This gives us added insight into the criticism levelled by Menahem di Lonzano against his contemporary Israel Najarah. Di Lonzano charged that Najarah was not sufficiently discriminating in selecting the musical modes most suitable for prayers of supplication, and for helping a person achieve the proper feelings of humility and contrition. It is in this spirit that we should understand the various modes used in reading the Ten Commandments as practiced in the Jewish communitities of eastern countries.

A well-known Sephardi cantor, a Jerusalemite thoroughly versed in traditional Turkish music, explained to the writer how the oriental modes are adapted to the reading of the Ten Commandments:

> When the reader comes to the passage "visiting the guilt of the fathers upon... those who reject Me", he modulates; the expression "those who reject me" is distasteful, provoking a shift to a low and doleful mode called *avitsh*. Immediately afterwards, at the words "those who love Me and keep My commandments" he moves to a more festive mode, called *suznak*. The next Commandment speaks of punishment once again, so that a sad mode is called for. For the Fourth Commandment the reader chooses a mode evocative of Passover and Sukkot. The Commandment to honor one's parents is chanted in the mode called *ṣaba*, one of the loveliest and most captivating of the modes, the one which is sung at the Sabbath service when a Bar Mitzvah is being celebrated. For the short "Thou shalt not's" the reader executes rapid transitions to doleful modes. Finally, on arriving at the Tenth Commandment, he reverts to the special mode for Shavuot in order to stress the fact that this passage is also read on that festival, which celebrates the Giving of the Torah.

Despite the fact that a reading of this quality demands of the hazan a high degree of skill and a wide knowledge of musical theory, it is not supposed to be used as an occasion for the display of artistic virtuosity.[10] The purpose of all this intricacy is solely to add feeling and solemnity. All the elaborate prolonging at certain words, all the ornamentation and flourishes which characterize the public reading of the Decalogue, as well as the Song of the Sea, are considered exceptional even by Sephardi cantors themselves. The selfsame cantor whose description of the special modes for these readings has just been quoted, added the following words:

10 Even among the few cantors still living who read the Ten Commandments in the manner described above, there are some who are bent on showing their artistic ability, although they may not admit it.

Our tradition enjoins us not to add too much, not to stray too far from the norms accepted as appropriate for the particular passage, There are cantors who permit themselves to introduce excessive flourishes, in the manner of Arabic readers of the Quran. Such cantors are not approved of by most of us Sephardim. Apart from the Song of the Sea and the Ten Commandments, we do not elaborate any biblical reading.

It has been our purpose in this brief essay to show that from a purely musical standpoint the reading of the Ten Commandments in the upper cantillation was given a special flavor of stateliness most particularly among the Sephardim. The Sephardi manner of Torah reading, by nature freer and more expressive than that of the other traditions, was consequently more open to the development of a unique style of reading the Song of the Sea and the Ten Commandments, two mighty events in the history of the People of Israel.

Translated by Shalom Bronstein

13. THE TEN COMMANDMENTS IN THE LITURGICAL POETRY OF ELEAZAR KALLIR*

AHARON MIRSKY

It is customary to view the liturgical poetry (piyyut) composed in the Land of Israel between the sixth and eighth centuries as a versification of the oral tradition. It puts into rhyme and meter the teachings of the Sages, drawn from homilies and legends based on Talmud and Midrash. However, piyyut is not simply the compilation of versified midrashim. The poet (paytan) approaches his task with his theme already formed in his mind, and chooses such midrashic material as conforms to his preconceived idea. Just as the builder arranges his building-blocks in accordance with his blueprint, so does the paytan draw on his largely aggadic sources to construct the edifice which he has in mind.

Eleazar Kallir put the Ten Commandments into verse with great imagination and a polished poetic style. He perceived the Decalogue and the theophany at Sinai in the way the Sages had — as the raison d'être of the universe, the culmination of the process of Creation.[1] He was inspired by the Sinaitic revelation and its principal message, the Ten Commandments, returning to that theme again and again.

To the Sages, biblical passages of supreme importance were by their very nature couched in language of supreme beauty and profundity. This was a view which Kallir shared as well.

---

* The nature of the subject limits the possibilities of translation, particularly with regard to the literary analysis of this highly structured and intricate poetic form. The reader with access to the Hebrew will undoubtedly want to consult the original of this study, of which the latter half is represented here only by brief selection and synopsis. The translations of excerpts from the poetry are intended to give some flavor of its content, but do not pretend to convey anything of its form.

1   *Genesis Rabbah* 1. 4.

It was on the basis of Rabbinic interpretations of Scripture that paytanim fashioned their rules of poetics. For example, the Sages had held that each blessing in Scripture was not a new beginning, but was linked to a preceding benediction, going back in an unbroken chain to the Originator of all blessing.[2]

When Kallir sat down to versify the Ten Commandments[3] he followed this method of the unbroken chain, or garland. He began with the first word of the Decalogue, *Anokhi*, relating it to an earlier *Anokhi* in the biblical text, thus linking the Decalogue to an antecedent subject. His proem[4] to this piyyut on the Decalogue ends with the lines:

> He spoke the culmination with "*Anokhi*"
> Therefore He opened with the word "*Anokhi*".

Commentators are not agreed as to which antecedent *Anokhi* the paytan had in mind. Some say he was alluding to God's culminating promise to Jacob (Gen. 36. 3–4):

> I (*Anokhi*) am the God of your father.... I (*Anokhi*) will go down with you to Egypt and I (*Anokhi*) will bring you back.[5]

Others, however, suggest that the paytan meant to refer to the culmination promised in Abraham's crucial vision "between those pieces" (Gen. 15. 17) when God promised him "I will pass judgment on the nation they will serve" (ibid., verse 14). That promise having been fulfilled by the Exodus, the Israelites are reminded of it by the opening word of the Ten Commandments as though to say, the LORD has kept His promise, now do you keep His commandments.[6]

We are accustomed to thinking of poetry as the expression of emotion, rather than as the voice of such scholarly matters. But there need be no cause for wonder. The paytanim of Eretz Israel were learned in the tradition; their poetry throbs with knowledge of Torah. Their readers too were highly knowledgeable. That is why the emotion must be sought between the lines of lofty concepts.

In the lines just cited Kallir also offered an answer to the question:

---

2   *Deuteronomy Rabbah* 11. 1.
3   In the piyyut "I the Creator" quoted below.
4   Beginning with "The Holy One appeared from Paran".
5   See comment by Heidenheim in his *Mahzor for Shavuot*, Rodelheim 1802, frequently reprinted.
6   One of several interpretations offered in *The Mahzor*, Amsterdam 1640.

"Why do the Commandments begin with *Anokhi*?" Questions of that sort were common in the world of the Midrash.[7] Indeed, the Midrash asks this very question about the word *Anokhi*, and offers a reason for its place at the beginning of the Ten Commandments.[8] This too is included by Kallir in his piyyut.

It is a characteristic of Kallir's poetry that he elaborates widely on whatever theme he is dealing with, as he does for example in his *silluq* for the Sabbath of Sheqalim.[9] There he uses the theme of the day to expatiate on everything quantified, everything connected with weights and measures (mishqal). He does the same thing in the other great *silluqim* for the other special Sabbaths preceding Passover, expanding on the central theme in a manner achieved by no other paytan. But before we examine how he worked this out in his composition on the Ten Commandments, we shall explain another characteristic related to it in his paytanic creations.

Kallir thought of the Ten Commandments as ten units within a single whole; and even though they were not all spoken "in one utterance", they were all revealed in one theophany, and all of them have the same purpose. Thus the poet poured them all into the mold of a single idea, its thrust maintained from start to finish. That thrust, that central idea, is that the Ten Commandments point to the existence of the Creator.

This concept, as it developed over time, gave a new aspect to the Ten Commandments, depending on the capacity of the individual to grasp the meaning of the Torah. Kallir treated this piyyut as he did his others, weaving into it comments and explanations of the Sages. In this fashion he made the Decalogue over, so to speak, as though it were a decree freshly issued. His readers were to feel that they were standing again at Sinai, and hearing the divine words in accordance with their ability to comprehend them.

Kallir presents the Ten Commandments as a narrative, in which God relates how he gave the Decalogue to Israel, and enumerates the Commandments one at a time, briefly giving the reason for each. For the First Commandment, the poet offers a reason different from the

---

7   Such as "Why does the Torah begin with the letter *beth* (*Genesis Rabbah* I: 10). In the same context there is an explanation for the fact that the Decalogue begins with an *aleph*. Kallir incorporated this idea into one of his piyyutim.

8   *Pesiqta Rabbati*, ed. M. Friedmann, 1880, pp. 105b–106a.

9   Its opening line is "Then you beheld".

one given in the Book of Exodus, where it is grounded on the fact that God is the Redeemer from Egyptian bondage. Kallir refers instead to God the Creator:

> I, the Creator, known as El Shaddai,
> Called "Halt!" to my creation long ago.

The Second Commandment is linked to the First, thus:

> When they, My servants, took Me as their King,
> "None other shall you have" was My command.

Similarly, the Sabbath is presented as a testimony that God created the world. This is based, not on the Fourth Commandment in Exodus chapter 20, but on a passage in the *Mekhilta* commenting on a later verse:

> "It shall be a sign for all time between Me and the people of Israel. For in six days the LORD made heaven and earth, and on the seventh day he ceased from work".[10] Whoever observes the Sabbath bears witness to Him who commanded and the world came into being, that He created His world in six days and rested on the seventh.[11]

The paytan chose to stress this reason for the Sabbath because it links up with the preceding Commandments.

The Commandment to honor one's parents is associated with honoring the Creator, an idea found in the Talmud (Qid. 30b). The prohibition against murder is related to the destruction of God's handiwork, so that the murderer is seen as one who defaces His image.[12] In a sense, then, this poem offers a rationale for the Commandments. Regarding the Fifth Commandment, something similar was said by Abraham ibn Daud (twelfth century, France) when he pointed out that reverence for parents leads to reverence for the Creator.[13]

For some of the Commandments the paytan offers not so much a ground as a prudential reason.[14] For example:

10   Ex. 31. 17.
11   *Mekhilta*, ed. Horovitz-Rabin, p. 341; ed. Lauterbach III, p. 200.
12   Ibid., Horovitz-Rabin, p. 233; Lauterbach, II, p. 262.
13   In his *Emunah Ramah*, concluding chapter.
14   See Heinemann, *Rationale of the Mitzvot*[5] (Hebrew) Jerusalem 1966, pp. 31–32.

Avoid adultery, even when in doubt,
Lest certain punishment become your lot.
Steal not, and with abundance you'll be blest.[15]

Another unifying device, this time one of form and style, was created by Kallir in order to tie the Ten Commandments into one single whole. He has God speak in the first person throughout. In the biblical text, only the first two Commandments are in the first person; according to rabbinic interpretation, this is because these two were spoken to Israel directly by God. In the next three Commandments, God is referred to in the third person. The Sages explain that these Commandments were mediated to the Israelites by Moses. The last five Commandments do not mention God at all. However, Kallir wanted to put all the Commandments on an even footing, stressing that they are all divinely ordained, whether heard directly or not. He therefore poetized them all in the First Person, avoiding the third person altogether (see the extract quoted below).

In pursuit of his purpose to treat the Decalogue as a unity, and to make it clear that God Himself spoke all these words, Kallir used other means as well. He built the structure of his poem in such a manner as to make this point. In the *qerovah* of which the piyyut we are studying is a part, there are three piyyutim that come before it,[16] and another that follows it.[17] These piyyutim are written in rhyming stanzas, four lines to a stanza, each with its own distinct and different rhyme. But the central piyyut, the one presenting the whole Decalogue in nineteen lines, departs from this form. It sustains a single rhyme throughout — the syllable *-dai*. The suggested meaning, based on the possessive pronominal suffix in Hebrew, is "mine own".[18] This indeed is the meaning of most of the verses,[19] and where it is not explicit, it is implied.[20]

There is evidence that this choice of rhyme was deliberate, in order to suggest that it was God Himself who spoke all these Commandments

---

15   See the poem quoted, in extenso below.
16   "The earth quivered and roared", "From the mountain to his habitations" and "The Holy One appeared from Paran".
17   "Then in foursquare Hebrew letters".
18   See "The Meaning of Rhyme in Spanish'Hebrew Poetry" (Hebrew) *Leshonenu*, 33 (1969), pp. 154–156; 165–170.
19   See the Hebrew text below.
20   Ibid.

to Israel. The envoi consists of six short staccato lines, all of them faithful to the *-dai* rhyme scheme, in which it is clearly God who addresses His people as "My survivors" (*seridai*).[21] In this fashion Kallir reveals his intention — to represent in a single poem the Word of God.

Another indication that the poet attributed special importance to this poetized Decalogue is his use of a device which is absent from the poems with which it is surrounded, fore and aft. It is a device which he may have learned from the Talmud, the source of much paytanic technique, such as opening and closing mannerisms, and the weaving together of linked themes and words. In the present instance he had before him the following homily by two Palestinian Amoraim:

> R. Samuel bar Nahmani said, in the name of R. Johanan: Whenever a Psalm was particularly precious to David, he began with *Ashrei* and concluded with the same word, as in Psalms 1–2 (treated as a unit) which begins "Happy is the man" and ends "Happy are all who take refuge in Him".[22]

The Tosafot[23] interpret this to mean that *Ashrei* is cited merely by way of example; but the principle intended is that any opening word or phrase is repeated at the close. This is what Kallir did in his poem. He began with "I, the Creator, known as El Shaddai", and closed with the words "There is no other one but El Shaddai".

Kallir composed a long series of poems about the Ten Commandments, the core of which is the piyyut "I the Creator, known as El Shaddai", which gives the entire Decalogue in condensed form. It is followed by a chain of piyyutim of equal length, one for each of the Ten Commandments. The chain is begun by a poem on the verse just before the Commandments (Ex. 19. 25 "Moses went down to the people") and is concluded by a poem on the verse just after the Commandments (20.15: "All the people witnessed the thunder and lightning"). All of these twelve poems are bound together by tercets, which finalize the theme and introduce the next one.

In these poems the paytan reaches the apex of his expressive powers. His overture[24] hymns the praises of the Torah and sings its beauty in

---

21   Based on Joel 3. 5.
22   Ber. 9b–10a.
23   Ibid., 10a, s.v. "Every *parashah*".
24   Beginning with the line "He came down bearing statutes".

terms based on Psalm 19.[25] The tone is intensified in the following verses, describing the wonders of nature at the theophany, and creating the mood in which the Commandments should be heard.

At this point the poet was able to expand on his theme, for he had twenty-two letters at his disposal — that is, one line for each letter of the Hebrew alphabet, alternately from *aleph* to *taw*, and from *taw* to *aleph*. He not only versifies; he interprets. Thus, in the Torah, the First Commandment speaks of God as the One "who brought you out of the Land of Egypt". But Kallir speaks of Him as the Creator, following the midrashic comment that the Liberator and the Creator are One and the Same.[26]

On this model the poet deals with the remaining Commandments, preceding each with other references to its theme in the Scriptures. For example, he begins the Fourth Commandment by elaborating on Genesis 2. 1: "The heaven and earth were finished, and all their array". His method is to substitute allusive synonyms for the original biblical terms; thus the verse just quoted emerges as something like "The end and goal of all that He had fashioned, whether in the upper realms or here below".

He pays due attention to the sequence of sounds, and is particularly fond of alliteration, a device for which there is ample precedent in the biblical text.[27] He is particularly fond of this device at the beginning of a piyyut.[28] And as the end of a stanza approaches, he is ready to make more explicit reference to the words of the Bible — in this instance, he brings in the manservant and the maidservant. The body of the poem is filled with praises of the Sabbath and its halakhot.

★

A similar treatment is given to each of the other Commandments. The opening and the closing strike the biblical chord; the body of the poem echoes the whole range of the tradition. And because Kallir regarded the Decalogue as a single unit he had to tie all these poems together. This he did by using the Hebrew alphabet acrostically,

---

25 A phrase-by-phrase comparison shows how skilfully this is done.
26 Cf. *Exodus Rabbah* V: 14.
27 See B.M. Levin, *Paired Words in Scripture* (Hebrew), Haifa 1926.
28 Good examples are the *qerovot* for *Sheqalim* and *Haḥodesh*.

weaving like a loom to and fro, alternating between *aleph* to *taw* and *taw* to *aleph*. In addition, at the end of each poem he introduces the theme (i.e., Commandment) of the poem to follow.

Anyone familiar with the ouvre of Kallir knows that he was capable of an intricate and sometimes baffling allusive style. But when he came to the Ten Commandments, which are fundamental to Judaism and are expressed in plain language that everyone can understand, the paytan chose a simpler style, so as to reach the minds and hearts of the widest possible circle of his fellow-worshippers.

What follows is the original Hebrew of three of the thirteen poems printed in the original Hebrew of this study (pp. 280–290) plus an approximation of their content in English. The Hebrew follows the text of Wolf Heidenheim's *Mahzor for Shavuot, Qerovot for the Second Day*. Of all the printed versions, his is the most exact. In the apparatus provided in the Hebrew of this volume (pp. 290–300) I have listed *variae lectiones* derived from a number of Ashkenazic manuscripts of the liturgy. In the case of the first piyyut herein, I have also used a Genizah manuscript. But even where the ms. readings are superior to those given by Heidenheim, I have retained his version, which is so widely accepted.

Kallir used a meter of three beats per line. Consequently, readings that conform to that pattern are to be preferred. I have drawn attention to such instances in the apparatus referred to above.

It should also be noted that printed versions of the liturgy have suffered distortions at the hands of the censors. The reader who refers to the apparatus will find the correct readings.

I wish to express my thanks to the Schocken Library in Jerusalem, and to its director, Prof. J. Katzenstein, who arranged for me to have access to their manuscripts of the liturgy; and to the Institute for the Reproduction of Hebrew Manuscripts, where I was able to see the Taylor-Schechter manuscript.

Translated by Neil Berns

FROM A QEROVAH FOR THE SECOND DAY OF SHAVUOT

אָנֹכִי בְּשֵׁם אֵל שַׁדַּי

פַּצְתִּי מֵאָז לְעוֹלָמִי דַּי

וּבְבָשָׁן בֶּאֱרָתִּיו בְּפֵרוּשׁ לִידִידַי

כְּשֶׁקִּבְּלוּ עַל מַלְכוּתִי עֲבָדַי

צִוִּיתִי לֹא יִהְיֶה לְךָ אֵל אַחֵר מִבַּלְעָדַי 5

לֹא תִשָּׂא שֵׁם לַשָּׁוְא וְתִנָּקֶה עָדַי

זָכוֹר וְשָׁמוֹר כִּי הֵם שְׁנֵי עֵדַי

כַּבֵּד אוֹמְנֶיךָ כִּי כְבוֹדָם כְּבוֹדִי

לֹא תִרְצַח מְתֹאַר מַעֲשֵׂה יָדַי

לֹא תִנְאָף אַף בְּסָפֵק פֶּן תֵּעָנֵשׁ בְּוַדַּאי 10

לֹא תִגְנֹב וְתִתְבָּרֵךְ עַד בְּלִי דַי

לֹא תַעֲנֶה עֵדוּת שֶׁקֶר בְּעֵדַי

לֹא תַחְמֹד כִּי אִם מַחֲמַדַּי

אֵלֶּה הֵם סוֹדַי

מוֹרִי שְׂרִידַי 15

מוֹעֲדֵי פְּקוּדַי

סָהֲדֵי מְעִידַי

כִּי אֵין בִּלְעָדַי

וַאֲנִי אֵל שַׁדַּי.

ובכן וירד משה מן ההר אל העם

אִתּוֹ מִצְוֹת וְחֻקִּים

בָּאֵר הֵיטֵב חֲקוּקִים

גְּמוּלֵי חָלָב מְנִיקִים

דַּדֵּימוֹ חָכְמָה מְפִיקִים

הַשֶּׁפַע מְקוֹר מַיִם חַיִּים מְזֻנָּקִים 5

וּמִנֹּפֶת צוּפִים וּמִדְּבַשׁ מְתוּקִים

זֹהַר לָעֵינַיִם מַבְהִיקִים

חֶבֶשׁ לָעֲצָמוֹת מַשִּׁיקִים

טוֹבִים יְשָׁרִים וְצַדִּיקִים

יְקָרִים מִפְּנִינִים וּמִכָּל־חֲשׁוּקִים 10

כְּתָב אֶצְבַּע שׁוֹכֵן שְׁחָקִים

לְנוֹצְרֵימוֹ מֵחֵטְא מְנַקִּים

מַצְדִּיקִים לְכָל בָּם עוֹסְקִים

נִדְבָּרֵימוֹ בַּסֵּפֶר נֶחְקָקִים

סוֹפְרֵימוֹ בְּצֶדֶק מְחֻקָּקִים 15

עֵץ חַיִּים הִיא לַמַּחֲזִיקִים

פְּאֵר לִוְיַת־חֵן וַעֲנָקִים

צְדָקוֹת מְלֵאִים וְלֹא רֵקִים

קְדוּמִים טֶרֶם יְסוֹד אֲפִיקִים (נ״א אֲרָקִים)

רוֹם וָעֹמֶק אֵל בָּם הֵקִים 20

שִׁמְעָם לְשׁוֹשַׁנַּת הָעֲמָקִים
תּוֹצְאוֹתָם לְחֵךְ מַמְתַּקִים

מַמְתַּקִים דִּבְרֵי אֱלֹהִים
לְאוֹמְרֵי אֵין כָּמוֹךְ בָּאֱלֹהִים
25 וַיְדַבֵּר אֱלֹהִים.

תִּתּוֹ קוֹל עֹז אֶל אֵלִים
שֶׁלְהֲבוּ לַפִּידֵי גֶחָלִים
רָצוּ בְרָקִים קַלִּים
קוֹלוֹת הִרְעִימוּ גַּלְגַּלִים
5 צָרַח שׁוֹפָר מִמְּעֵלִים
פִּצְמָה רְקוּעַת שְׁעוּלִים
עַמִּים אֲחָזוּם בֶּהָלִים
סַעַר צִירִים וַחֲבָלִים
נְהִי כַּיּוֹלֵדָה חָלִים
10 מְרַצְּדִים הָיוּ מְגֻבָּלִים
לְבָנוֹן וְשִׂרְיוֹן כַּעֲגָלִים
כַּרְמֶל וּבָשָׁן כְּמוֹ אֵילִים
יַחַד תָּבוֹר וְכָל־תְּלוּלִים
טֹרְחוּ בְגֹבַהּ וְנִמְצְאוּ פְּסוּלִים
15 חַי רָם רוֹאֶה שְׁפָלִים
זֶה סִינַי כַּדָּךְ לֹא הָכְלִים
וְהִטָּה אֵלָיו זְבוּלִים
הֶעֱטִירוּ עֲנָנִים וְעַרְפַלִּים
דָּר בּוֹ בְּשִׁנְאַן אֶרְאֶלִּים
20 גְּאוֹן קוֹלוֹ הִשְׁמִיעַ לְנִדְגָּלִים
בִּסְבִיב הָהָר נִגְבָּלִים

בְּנַעֲשֶׂה וְנִשְׁמַע דָּת מְקַבְּלִים
אָזְנָם שָׁם רֹאשׁ מִלִּים
אָנֹכִי שְׁמַע לִכְלוּלִים

25 לִכְלוּלִים הִשְׁמַעְתָּ מֶלֶךְ
מְפוֹצֵץ הָרִים קוֹלֶךְ
אָנֹכִי ה׳ אֱלֹהֶיךָ

I, the Creator, known as El Shaddai,
Called "Halt!" to My Creation long ago,
And made My true Name known to my beloved
When they, My servants, took Me as their King.
"None other shall you have" was My command.
Speak not My name in falsehood or in vain.
The Sabbath rest remember and observe.
Honor your parents, and so honor Me.
Do not kill any in Mine image made.
Avoid adultery, even if in doubt,
Lest certain punishment become your lot.
Steal not, and with abundance you'll be blest.
Bear no false witness 'gainst your fellowman.
Covet but how to live by my commands.
These My counsels,
O My survivors!
These My holy days,
There is no other,
Only El Shaddai.
"Then Moses went down from the mountain to the people".
He came down bearing statutes, laws, commands,
Engraved on tablets and full well explained,
Offering nourishment to one and all
Like infants feeding at their mother's breast.
These tablets flow with wisdom, living waters,
Sweeter than drippings of the honey-comb,
Bring light to man's eyes, healing to his bones.
Replete with righteousness, they offer man
More precious gifts than the most treasured jewels.
With His own finger He who dwells on high
Wrote words to keep man free of any sin.
All those who study them are rendered just;
Who speak them are inscribed in Heaven's book.
A tree of life to all who hold it fast,
Its words are glory and an ornament,
Replete with goodness, no word meaningless,
More ancient far than the primeval deep.
The LORD established in them height and depth,
Proclaimed them to the Lily of the vale;
Their fruit is very sweetness on the tongue.

Sweet are His words to those who do proclaim:
"Among the mighty there is none like Thee!"
He spoke in thunderous tones, and flames flared up;
Fleet bursts of lightning flashed across the sky,
The heavenly spheres gave voice in harmony,
With shofar's clarion call from highest heights.
Ridges sprang up across the continents;
Nations were overcome with fear and trembling,
A veritable storm of pangs and pains,
Moaning like woman in the throes of birth.
The very mountains leapt up in the air,
Lebanon and Sirion like youthful calves;
Carmel and Bashan dancing like young rams,
Mount Tabor joining in with all the hills.
Each of them sought the honor of God's law,
But not one there proved worthy of that role.
The mighty Everlasting One on high,
For whom the humble have a special place,
Settled His glance on Sinai's lowly Mount
And bent the heavens down unto its crest.
He crowned it with dark clouds and heavy mists
And came, surrounded by His heavenly hosts.
His chosen heard His great majestic voice
As, girded round beneath thè mount they stood.
"We will obey and hear His holy law!"
They spoke, and heard the first of His Commands:
"I am the LORD!" He told that noble band.
Unto that noble band You spoke Your words,
Showering sparks like hammer on the rock:
"I AM THE LORD YOUR GOD!"

Stanzas translated by Gershon Levi

14. A POEM ON THE DECALOGUE
ATTRIBUTED TO SAADIAH GAON

JOSHUA BLAU

In his book on Judeo-Arabic literature, Moritz Steinschneider deals in two separate places with a liturgical poem on the Ten Commandments that has been attributed to Saadiah Gaon.[1] He mentions the poem on page 63, at the end of the section devoted to the works of Saadiah; and then again, in a more important entry on page 285, in a chapter that deals with works by anonymous authors.[2] As always, the great bibliographer manages to give us all the essentials in a few spare lines:

> Paraphrases of the Ten Commandments, some in rhyme, making use of Targum and Midrash. Apparently intended for use on Shavuot, they are of a fairly early date. Over time, differing versions have developed, and it will require careful examination of all mss. and editions to establish age and authorship.

He then proceeds to scrutinize the version attributed to Saadiah Gaon.

Subsequent research has indeed added many details (see below) but has not been able to improve on this clear and succinct summary. Quite the contrary: additional study has sometimes managed to obscure the picture somewhat. For example, in his fairly recent work on Jewish liturgy, Elbogen has even accepted the view that Saadiah is the author of this piyyut.[3]

It should be obvious that this poem cannot have been written by

---

1   M. Steinschneider, *Die arabische Literatur der Juden*, Frankfurt 1902.
2   Not only does one entry fail to mention the other; there is even a partial repetition of the contents. Sometimes even Homer nods!
3   Even the Hebrew translation by Y. Amir, edited and completed by Y. Heinemann, Tel Aviv 1972 (!), pp. 241–242, repeats this attribution. Incidentally, the statement there that these piyyutim deal with the 613 mitzvot does not apply to our piyyut.

Saadiah, certainly not in the version known in our time in the synagogues of the Moghreb.[4] Neither the language nor the content permit such an attribution. Linguistically, the poem is an example of the postclassical Judeo-Arabic characteristic especially of Northwest Africa from the sixteenth century onwards. In orthography, structure and vocabulary it is far more colloquial than the classical Judeo-Arabic of which the works of Saadiah are a shining example. To be sure, our piyyut contains many literary elements, but it is basically written in a Moghrebi dialect.[5]

Even more alien to Saadiah's style is the anthropomorphism that characterizes this piyyut. The Gaon was scrupulous in avoiding expressions that depicted God as seated upon His royal throne. Thus, when he had to translate Psalm 9. 5 ("Thou sattest upon the throne") he renders it "You did place Your throne". He renders Isaiah 6. 1 as though it said, "I saw the light of the LORD seated upon a throne". But in the North African version of our piyyut there are two echoes, in the Fourth Commandment, of the well-known Quranic expression that speaks of God seated upon His royal throne. Even if we were to decide for one reason or another that our poem had Saadianic origins,[6] we would still be forced to conclude that it had undergone such far-reaching changes that it no longer reflected either the Gaon's outlook or his literary style.

What is undoubtedly the most important assemblage of bibliographical data about Saadiah is included in Henry Malter's work on the Gaon.[7] It lists not only such additional information about piyyutim on the Ten Commandments as had come to light since Steinschneider, but also some that had been available in his time. Nevertheless, even Malter does not give us an unequivocal picture of the status and provenance of the piyyut we are discussing. He does point up[8] the doubts expressed by Zunz, who wondered whether our piyyut really should be ascribed to Saadiah, or should rather be seen as

---

4   As we shall see, both the language and the content of the piyyut have indeed changed with the passage of time.
5   See the concise and accurate description of the language of the piyyut by D. Z. Baneth in the *Bulletin (Yedi'ot) of the Jewish Palestine Exploration Society*, XII (1946).
6   This however is not our opinion; see below.
7   H. Malter, *Saadia Gaon, His Life and Works*, Philadelphia 1921, pp. 406–408.
8   Ibid., p. 407.

a composition reworked in terms of Saadiah's Arabic translation of the Bible.[9] Malter agrees with Zunz that the various versions of our poem seem to have developed out of a similar work on the Ten Commandments by the Gaon himself. But the material provided by Malter's own bibliography clearly indicates a different conclusion; that is to say, the connection of our piyyut with Saadiah does not go back to its origin and its subsequent branching out into different versions, but rather the reverse. In the process of proliferating into varying versions our piyyut became linked with the name of the Gaon. This is the way Malter begins the discussion:

> *Tafsīr al-'Ashar al-Kalimāt*, a rhetorical paraphrase of the Ten Commandments, which exists in various recensions in several mss. and editions enumerated by Steinschneider, AL., p. 285, no. 87. To these are to be added the fragment no. 2861, 12a, in Neubauer and Cowley's *Catalogue*,[10] and another one in the collection of the British Museum.[11] In both fragments the work is ascribed to one Eleazar b. Eleazar, who is otherwise unknown,[12] while another ms. in the library of Paris[13] ascribes it to the Karaite Kirkisani, a younger contemporary of Saadiah.

Examination of the above-mentioned recensions reveals that, despite the differences between them, they all stem from one common source. To be sure, it is possible that identity of theme and dependence on the same midrashic sources might cause even independent piyyutim to bear a resemblance to one another. But it is difficult to imagine that such a strong resemblance in content as we find here can be purely coincidental. Some of the shared elements that point to a common source are the enumeration, in connection with the Third Commandment, of the ancients who mentioned God's name; the playing up of the number seven in the context of the Fourth Commandment; and reference to the ten things created by father and

---

9   L. Zunz, *Literaturgeschichte der synagogalen Poesie*, Berlin 1865, p. 96.

10   It comes from the Genizah, and consists of only one leaf, page 37b of the ms.

11   London, Or. 10391/3. I was able to find this and other bibliographical details with the help of the Institute for Microfilmed Hebrew Manuscripts at the National and University Library of the Hebrew University.

12   Actually, the above-mentioned Bodleian manuscript calls him "one of the scholars", without further identification.

13   No. 755/2.

mother in connection with the Fifth Commandment. This applies even to the Paris manuscript ascribed to Kirkisani[14] which differs most widely from the version ascribed to Eleazar b. Eleazar and the version ascribed to Saadiah Gaon, yet resembles them enough to rule out the possibility that the resemblance is mere chance.

It is the latter two versions that are closest to one another. In order to demonstrate this, let us look at the introductory lines, as preserved in the detached Genizah leaf attributed to Eleazar b. Eleazar, compared with the corresponding passage in the version ascribed to Saadiah, as published by W. Eisenstädter.[15]

Eisenstädter Version	*Genizah Ms.*
	תפסיר אלעשר כלמאת לבעץ' אלעלמא
	יערף ר'[!] אלעזר בר אלעזר זכרו
	לברכה
אול אבתדא כלאמנא ופתח פמנא ונטק	אבתדא כלאמנא ופתח אפואנא
לסאננא אלואג'ב עלינא אן נסבח ונמג'ד	אלואג'ב עלינא אלדעא ואלשכר קדאם
לרבנא אלד'י כ'לק אלדניא... (הרבה)...	אלאהנא אלד'י מן ג'מ'ע אלאםם
לד'לך אלואג'ב עלינא (חזרה !) אן	אכ'ת[ה]ארנ]א
נמג'ד ונשכר לרבנא אלד'י מן ארץ' מצר	ומן ארץ' מצר
כ'רג'נא ומן בית אלעבודית אפדאנא	אכ'רג'נא ומן בית אלעבודיה אפ[ד]אנא
ופי וסט אלבחר גרק אעדאנא ואלי טור	ופי וסט אלבחר גרק אעדאנא ויום

14   The ms. gives the name *Yūsuf al-Ma'ōr al-ma'rūf bil-Qirqisānî*; but obviously Ya'qūb al-Kirkisānî has been confused with the blind *Yūssuf al-Baṣîr* (a euphemism, like *al-Ma'ōr*, for the sightless).

15   "*Tafsīr al-'ashar al-kalimāt taṣnīf Rabbina Sa'adia al-Fayyūmī alayhi as-salām*; The Ten Commandments in Arabic, by our master Saadiah Gaon of blessed memory: edited and translated into Hebrew and German by me, Moses Benjamin Eisenstädter", Vienna 1868. Passages more or less identical in both texts are printed bold; those reflecting different word order are underlined. The text is more or less identical with that printed in Moghrabi prayer-books, reproduced and translated into French by I. Morali, *Dissertation homilétique sur le décalogue recitée dans les Synagogues d'Algérie le premier jour de Pentecôte, oeuvre de R. Saadia Gaon*, Algiers 1913.

סיני קרבנא ואלמן ואלסלואן	אלסבת והב לנא ואלמן ואלסללוי
אטעמנא ומן ג'מיע אלאמם	אטעמנא ואלי טור סיני קרבנא
אתצפאנא	
ובתוראֿת ובשראיע פצ'לנא	ואלתוראה ואלשראיע ורת'נא
אללה הו איל	ובסת
אבאינה...	מאיה ות'לת' עשרה
	אטעמנא ואלי טור סיני קרבנא

Nevertheless, there are considerable differences between the version ascribed to Eleazar b. Eleazar (or Eliezer; see below) and the one attributed to Saadiah, as the latter has been preserved in North Africa. Linguistically, the former is in a much more literary style than the latter. At the same time, the former is free of the anthropomorphic expressions mentioned above, such as *istawā ʿalā kursihi* ("He sat upon His throne").

How are we to explain the fact that our piyyut, in its various manifestations, was ascribed to different authors? It seems clear that the real author was Eleazar b. Eleazar. For it is easy to see how the work might be attributed, even in error, to such well-known figures as the Rabbanite Saadiah or the Karaite Kirkisani; but who would be interested in assigning it to an unknown like Eleazar b. Eleazar? Even the Genizah fragment can only identify him as *baʿḍ al-ʿulamā* "one of the scholars"! There is even some uncertainty about his exact name. The Genizah fragment calls him Eleazar b. Eleazar, while most of the manuscripts (which are Yemenite in origin) give his father's name as "Eliezer". We are driven to assume, therefore, that the author of our piyyut was this Eleazar. The librarians of the Institute for the Reproduction of Hebrew Manuscripts were entirely right when they catalogued under "Eleazar ben Eliezer"[16] not only those versions of the piyyut explicitly ascribed to him, but also those attributed to Saadiah Gaon.

But I think it probable that it was not only the fame of Saadiah Gaon that caused our piyyut to be ascribed to him, after the name of the

---

16   The manuscripts that ascribe our piyyut to Eleazar b. Eliezer are of Yemenite origin, such as J.T.S. New York, mic. 4400/6, sixteenth (?) century, pp. 51a–58a; ibid., mic. 3110, seventeenth century, pp. 190b–197a; ms. Sassoon 365 (328), pp. 444–460, seventeenth century (mentions only R. Eleazar, without giving his father's name); and a similar ms. Sassoon 371 (327), eighteenth century, pp. 352–363.

original author had been forgotten.[17] There was the additional fact that the piyyut contains verses from the Torah rendered in Saadiah's Arabic. Thus, the First Commandment in the piyyut[18] reads *ana 'llāhu 'lladhī akhrajtukum min balad Miṣr wa-min bait al-'abudiyya* — almost identical with Saadiah's translation of Exodus 20. 2.[19] In the long Fourth Commandment, there are only four places where there is a variation in the translation.

Saadiah's translation	*The Maghrebi piyyut*
אד'כר יום אלסבת וקדסה סתה	אד'כרוא יום אלסבת וקדסוה, סתת
איאס תעמל (!)²⁰ ותצנע ג'מיע	איאם תכ'דם ותצנע ג'מיע צנאיעך
צנאיעך	ופי אליום סבת עטלת לאללה הו
ואליום אלסאבע סבת (!) ללה רבך לא	רבך לא תצנע פיה שיא מן אלצנאיע
תצנע שייא מן אלצנאיע אנת ואבנך	אנת ואבנך ואבנתך ועבדך ואמתך
ואבנתך	ובהימתך וגריבך אלד''י פי מחלך
עבדך ואמתך ובהאימך וצ''יפך (!)	לעלהם
אלד''י פי מחלך²¹ לאן אללה כ'לק פי	יוג'דון ראחת מת'לך לאן פי סתת
סתה	איאם כ'לק אללה אלסמואואת
איאם אלסמאואת ואלארץ' ואלבחאר	ואלארץ'
וג'מיע מא פיהא ואראחהא (!) פי	ואלבחר וג'מיע מא פיה ואסתראח
אליום	פי'' אליום אלסאבע.
אלסאבע.	

In view of the fact that Saadiah's translation was extremely popular among the Arabic-speaking Jews of the Muslim world, it is easy to understand that it would find its way into the text of our piyyut, and just as easy to understand that people would readily identify the

17 Some manuscripts of our piyyut which mention no author: *Yemenite*: ms. Kauffman, Budapest, A7/2, seventeenth century, pp. 265–274; Margolit Collection, Bar Ilan, Ramat Gan, three nineteenth century mss., 356/2, 488/1, 500/1; *Eastern*: Bodleian 289, nineteenth century; British Museum Or. 10346/2, eighteenth century, both of them resembling the Yemenite mss; *Moghrabi*: the northern one reflecting, as expected, the version attributed to Saadiah Gaon; for example, Margolit Collection 279, with a long introduction.

18 I follow the text published by Eisenstädter.

19 For Saadiah I have used *Keter Torah Tāj*, Jerusalem 1894.

20 Exclamation marks call attention to differences between the two versions.

21 In the piyyut a short sentence from the Ten Commandments in Deuteronomy has been added, in a version differing from Saadiah's translation.

biblical quotations as Saadianic, as would assume that the whole piyyut was his.

To sum up: a well-founded Yemenite tradition ascribes this Judeo-Arabic piyyut on the Ten Commandments to the otherwise unknown paytan Eleazar b. Eleazar (or Eliezer). Since the surviving manuscripts date from the sixteenth century, it follows that our piyyut is at least four to five hundred years old. The name of the author did not mean a thing to those who read the piyyut or heard it recited; and they soon forgot who he was. Karaites attributed the piece to Kirkisani; Rabbanites assumed that it had been written by Saadiah, on account of the biblical quotations which conform to his popular *Tafsīr*.

Translated by Gershon Levi

15. THE TEN COMMANDMENTS IN SPANISH AND YEMENITE LITURGICAL POETRY

YEHUDA RATZABY

The Ten Commandments are the very foundation of Judaism, the source from which all the other commandments flow, both those between man and God and those between man and man. With the flourishing of the piyyut in the Jewish world, piyyutim about the revelation at Mount Sinai and the significance of the Ten Commandments were written in their honor. At first these piyyutim were recited by the person called up to the Torah for the reading of the Ten Commandments. As the genre developed, *qerovot* were composed and inserted into the *Amidah*, as well as *azharot* which detail the positive and negative commandments.

Before the emergence of its own native paytanim, Jewish Spain was satisfied with Babylonian and Palestinian piyyutim. But when the poetic geniuses Ibn Gabirol and Judah Halevi finally emerged in Spain, they too created works like those of their predecessors. Ibn Gabirol wrote his *azharot*, and Judah Halevi his *rehuta* "Moses descended".[1] Both modelled their piyyutim, especially from a structural point of view, on the *azharot* of Saadiah who influenced not only them but also their predecessors Joseph ben Abitur and Isaac Ibn Gikatilla. In fact, this influence becomes a chain reaction. Ibn Gabirol, who was influenced by Saadiah, in turn influenced the composers of *azharot* who succeeded him. Thus, Saadiah Gaon's work had an effect on future generations through the poetry of Ibn Gabirol.

It should be pointed out that there are few separate piyyutim solely for the Ten Commandments, either in Spain or Yemen. The reason can perhaps be traced to the *azharot* which became the piyyutim of the day.

---

1   See below, notes 37 ff.

363

Because the Ten Commandments received detailed attention in the
azharot, it seemed superfluous to the paytanim to dedicate special
poems to them alone. They preferred rather to poetize the spectacular
event of the promulgation of the Torah in which both the upper and
lower worlds participate — the Shekhinah and the angels on one side,
Israel on the other. But since our subject is the Ten Commandments,
we must exclude from our discussion the piyyutim for Shavuot which
speak of the revelation at Mount Sinai, and praise of the Torah, but do
not treat the Ten Commandments themselves.

Of all the Spanish poets, the efforts of Ibn Gabirol and Judah Halevi
in the composition of piyyutim for Shavuot are outstanding. Ibn
Gabirol's *azharot* are distinguished by their literary grace and fluent,
lucid style. It is not surprising that they displaced the other *azharot* in
the liturgies of Eastern communities. They also captivated later poets,
who attempted to imitate them. Judah Halevi, more than any other
Spanish poet, enriched the festival of Shavuot with his piyyutim.

All the poems of Spain based on the Ten Commandments are
marked by the commonly accepted structure of early Hebrew liturgical
poetry, and show no traces of the forms of Arabic poetry. And although
they are cast in unalloyed biblical language, paytanic expressions of
earlier liturgical composers occur here and there.[2]

As I have said, piyyutim on the Ten Commandments are rare in
Yemenite poetry as well. The admiration that the Jews of Yemen
accorded the sacred poetry of Spain caused them to include it as a fixed
part of their liturgy to the exclusion of their own piyyutim. Like other
Eastern communities, they too integrated the *azharot* of Solomon ibn
Gabirol into the morning service of Shavuot. Thus their paytanim
found no reason to compose *azharot* of their own. Their oeuvre contains
scattered poems that tell the story of the giving of the Torah, or
mention the Ten Commandments. The revelation at Mount Sinai is
recalled in historical poems whose subject is a chronology of the
patriarchs, the Exodus from Egypt and Israel's wanderings in the
desert;[3] It also appears in Sabbath hymns which take special note of the

2 For example, Judah Halevi calls idolatry *shimẓah*, following Yannai; the reference
   is to Ex. 32. 25. Another example is the phrase *geluyat mezaḥ* in the poem quoted
   below (n. 40).
3 In *Ḥafeẓ Ḥayyim, An Anthology of Yemenite Poetry*, Jerusalem 1953. I list the
   following poems that mention the revelation at Sinai: pp. 100–102, 205, 429, 479,
   543, 548, 569, 572, 592 and 612.

Fourth Commandment,[4] as well as in piyyutim for the festival of Shavuot.[5]

In their reading of the Torah, the Jews of Yemen have a special melody for the Ten Commandments, used as well for the Song of the Sea and the Death of Moses. It is an honor to be called up as the *mevarekh*[6] of the Ten Commandments, and many bid for the opportunity. Formerly, there was a special piyyut-blessing[7] widely accepted in Yemenite communities. In the eighteenth century, however, Rabbi Yihye Sālih (*"Mahariẓ"*), the leading sage of Yemen at that time, ruled that the traditional recitation of piyyut-blessings was a mistaken practice, since no benediction containing the name of God not mentioned in the Talmud should be said. He based his ruling on the authority of Asher ben Yehiel, Isaiah Horowitz, *Pri Ḥadash* and *Sefer Hamanhig*.[8]

We offer herewith a survey of piyyutim on the Ten Commandments in the poetry of Spain and Yemen, presented according to the chronological order of their composers.

ISAAC IBN GIKATILLA

Isaac ibn Gikatilla belongs to the second generation of Spanish poets. His *azharot* for Shavuot have been published by M. Zulai.[9] In his *azharot* for the negative commandments, Ibn Gikatilla included the last five Commandments in a single verse:

> Be not false to your people, nor covet or desire what belongs to another. Be not treacherous, nor murder, nor commit adultery, nor steal secretly. Take not in vain the name of God your Maker, Creator. Let not your mouth cause your flesh to sin.

בְּעַמְּךָ לֹא תַעֲנֶה שֶׁקֶר וְלֹא תַחְמוֹד וְלֹא תִתְאַו כָּל שֶׁלַּחֲבֵרֶיךָ
בָּגוֹד לֹא תִבְגּוֹד לִרְצוֹחַ וְלִנְאוֹף וְלִגְנוֹב בְּמַחְתָּרֶיךָ

---

4 For example, in *Ḥafez Ḥayyim*, p. 512: "At Sinai he uttered the Fourth Command/ Remember and keep the Seventh Day".

5 E.g. ibid., p. 528, in a poem by Shalem Shabazi: *Yom Mattan Torah*.

6 In the Yemenite community, *mevarekh* refers both to the person called to the Torah, and to the portion he reads.

7 "He Who Appeared To Moses At Sinai". See my article on a Yemenite liturgical manuscript in *Maḥanayim*, n. 39, pp. 93–96.

8 See *Tiklāl* (The Yemenite Prayer Book), III, Jerusalem 1894, p. 88b.

9 *Tarbiẓ*, 20 (1948), pp. 163–176.

בְּשָׁוְא לֹא תִשָּׂא אֶת שֵׁם עוֹשַׁךְ יוֹצְרֶיךָ
אַל תִּתֵּן אֶת פִּיךָ לַחֲטִיא אֶת בְּשָׂרֶיךָ[10]

The Second Commandment, forbidding idolatry is presented thus:

Truly, have no strange god, mak neither idol nor image.[11]

Similarly, the prohibition of labor on the Sabbath:

For good reason do not work on Shabbat and the first and last
days of Pesah for their holiness is special.[12]

The influence of Saadiah on Ibn Gikatilla is especially evident in the
techniques employed by the latter.[13]

JOSEPH IBN ABITUR

Joseph ibn Abitur, dubbed "Ben Shatnas", was one of the great sages
and paytanim of Spain. The composer of hundreds of piyyutim, his
poetic oeuvre serves as a connecting link between the compositions of
Babylonia and those of Spain. Most of his piyyutim are *azharot* for
Shavuot. M. Zulai has established[14] that the composer of the *azharot*
published by Neubauer[15] was Joseph ibn Abitur.

Like those of Ibn Gikatilla, Ibn Abitur's verses maintain one rhyme
per stanza, conclude with biblical phrases, and are garlanded together.[16]
Two passages from his *azharot* present the Commandment "Honor thy
father and mother", and "Remember the Sabbath day":

כּוּלָם כְּאֶחָד לְהַלְווֹת וּלְהַחֲיוֹת אָח בְּעֵת מַחְסוֹר
כִּיבּוּד אָב וָאֵם וּמוֹרָא וְהִידּוּר וְצֶדֶק לֶאֱמוֹר
כְּתָב לִלְמוֹד וּלְלַמֵּד וְלִשְׁמוֹר וְלַעֲשׂוֹת וְלִגְמוֹר
אַתָּה צִוִּיתָה פִיקּוּדֶיךָ לִשְׁמוֹר[17]

* * *

10   Ibid., p. 168, lines 145–148.
11   Ibid., p. 167, line 102.
12   Ibid., p. 170, line 201.
13   The alphabetical acrostic, the rhymed quatrains, the biblical verses at the end of
      stanzas, all woven together in a garland.
14   *Tarbiz*, 20 (1948), p. 162.
15   *J.Q.R.*, o.s., 4 (1894), p. 708.
16   Following Saadiah; cf. *Siddur Rav Saadiah Gaon*, Jerusalem 1941, pp. 157 and
      191. Ibn Gabirol did the same in his *azharot*; see his "Your God Is a Consuming
      Fire"; and see D. Yarden, *The Sacred Poetry of Solomon Ibn Gabirol* (Hebrew),
      Jerusalem 1973, pp. 372–391.
17   *J.Q.R.*, ibid.

לִשְׁמוֹר לְהִיזָּהֵר מֵחֲמִשָּׁה אֲשֶׁר בַּמִּקְדָּשׁ סְפוּרִים
לִשְׂמוֹחַ וּלְהִתְעַנֵּג וּלְקַדֵּשׁ בַּיַּיִן בְּמַאֲמָרִים
לְלַמֵּד בֵּן דָּת וּלְשַׁנֵּן וְלָשׂוּם דְּבָרִים
אֶת תְּבוּנַת מֵישָׁרִים[17]

SOLOMON IBN GABIROL

The *azharot* composed by Ibn Gabirol for Shavuot won a place in the liturgies of Spain and Yemen, and displaced the *azharot* of earlier paytanim. Since these *azharot* are divided into positive and negative commandments, the Commandments included in the Decalogue are distributed in the same way. And as the subject of the *azharot* is the enumeration of the commandments, the paytan does not expand upon the content of each one, but rather suggests it briefly. The first Commandment, for example, is coupled with observance of the Sabbath,[18] as demonstrated in the following line:

לְעַנֵּג יוֹם מְנוּחָה / בְּהַשְׁקֵט וּבְבִטְחָה[19]

The limitations of rhyme and rhythm preclude the paytan from presenting the Commandments in the order in which they appear in the Bible; rather he places them where it is poetically most convenient. Thus for the negative commandments, as when he combines the prohibition "You shall not take the name of the LORD your God in vain" with the prohibition "Do not raise a false report" (Ex. 23. 1):

וְסוּר מִשְּׁמַע שָׁוְא / וּמֵהַאֲמֵן בַּשָּׁו / וְלֹא תִשָּׂא לַשָּׁוְא / שְׁמוֹתַי הַיְקָרִים[20]

The quatrain structure on which the *azharot* of Solomon ibn Gabirol are built has become known to us through the works of Dunash ibn Labrat, the pioneer of Spanish Hebrew poetry;[21] of Isaac ibn Kaprun,[22] and of others. Ezra Fleischer has shown that the origin of this structure is in the early piyyut.[23] The first three lines of the quatrain share a single

---

18 Bialik-Ravnitzky, *the Liturgical Poems of Solomon Ibn Gabirol*, II, Tel Aviv 1925, p. 136, line 23.

19 Ibid., p. 137, line 57.

20 Ibid., p. 143, lines 201–202.

21 See for example his poem in Schirman, *The Hebrew Poetry of Spain and Provence*, I, Jerusalem-Tel Aviv 1960, pp. 34–40.

22 Ibid., p. 43–48.

23 See his article "*Garlanded Strophes in Early Piyyut*" (Hebrew), in: *Hasifrut*, n. 2, pp. 194 ff.

rhyme that changes from strophe to strophe while the fourth contains a rhyme of its own which connects and unites the strophes of the poem from beginning to end.

A composition for the positive commandments, also written by Ibn Gabirol,[24] is composed of quatrains, each containing a distinct rhyme. The fourth line of every strophe is a biblical verse, the last word of which serves as a rhyme for the verse and as a link in the chain connecting it to the next strophe.[25] The strophes are arranged in alphabetical order. The positive Commandments in the Decalogue are scattered throughout the verses, appearing where it is convenient for the poet. For example:

שְׁמוֹר שַׁבָּת מֶחַלְּלוֹ וְקַדְּשָׁתּוֹ בַּיַּין מִלְּהַבְזוֹת
אַשְׁרֵי אֱנוֹשׁ יַעֲשֶׂה זֹּאת[26]

This is based on the saying in the Talmud (Pes. 107a): "Kiddush is made only over wine."

Ibn Gabirol makes an effort to group the Commandments according to elements they have in common. For example, the Fifth Commandment is coupled with Leviticus 19. 3.[27] because both deal with the parental relationship; and these two are combined with the commandment to free the mother bird from the nest, because the reward for both commandments is long life:

חַיֶּיךָ יַאֲרִיכוּן וַעֲסָקֶיךָ תַּגִּיעַ בְּמִשְׁלַח הַקֵּן וְכִבּוּד הוֹרִים ומוֹרָאָם
וְהָיוֹתְךָ נָקִי שָׁנָה אַחַת וְתַפְרִיחַ כְּגַן רָטֹב[28]

ISAAC OF BARCELONA

Isaac b. Reuben al-Bargeloni[29] was a contemporary of Alfasi. He served as Rabbi in Dania, and is also known as a paytan.[30] His piyyutim and *azharot* won the enthusiastic admiration of Alharizi.[31]

---

24 Yarden, n. 16 above, sec. 119, pp. 372–391.
25 In the use of this form Ibn Gabirol was influenced by Saadiah Gaon (see above, n. 16).
26 Yarden, n. 16 above, p. 376, lines 23–24.
27 "You shall each revere his mother and his father."
28 Yarden, n. 16 above, p. 377, lines 28–29.
29 After his city.
30 Some ten of his compositions have survived; see Davidson, *Thesaurus of Medieval Hebrew Poetry*, IV, Index of Piyyutim, p. 418.
31 Alharizi, *Taḥkemoni*, ed. A. Kaminka, Warsaw 1899, sec. 3, p. 41.

He composed *azharot* for Shavuot in the manner of Saadiah; that is in quatrains each containing a separate rhyme. The fourth line that concludes each strophe is a biblical verse which rhymes with the strophe. The strophes are arranged in triple-alphabetical order, two letters to every strophe. Each line begins with a letter of the alphabet. This structure is divided into two sections — the positive and the negative commandments. The paytan integrated his name acrostically twice into the first section.

The first alphabetical series is conceived as a sort of introduction, a mystical interpretation of the giving of the Torah: God betrothes His daughter the Torah to the Jewish People: Moses serves as the best man. The acrostic at the end of the series spells *Yiẓḥaq*. In these verses the paytan prays that the People of Israel may merit redemption and the renewal of its ancient glory.[32] In contrast, the *azharot* for the negative commandments speak exclusively of the prohibitions except for the first and the last three strophes.[33] The first is an appeal to the congregation to hearken to the admonitions. The last is a prayer for redemption and the rebuilding of the Temple.

DAVID IBN PAKUDA

As the *azharot* of Ibn Gabirol gradually won over the communities of Spain, David son of Eleazar ibn Pakuda, a prolific paytan in twelfth-century Spain, decided to preface them with a *reshut*. It is composed in the quatrain form like the *azharot*, and the name of the composer is embedded at the beginning of the strophes, "I am David ben Eleazar Pakuda, Ḥazaq!" This *reshut* has a special virtue: each of its strophes concludes with an integrated verse that ends with the word " Elohim". It tells of the revelation at Mount Sinai and details the Ten Commandments. The paytan preserves the order of the Commandments in the Torah, and dedicates a separate strophe to each one. Take for example the prohibition of idolatry and the Command to honor one's parents:

נְטוֹשׁ זָר וּפְסְלוֹ / וְצֵא תֹאמַר לוֹ / הַיַעֲשֶׂה לוֹ / אָדָם אֱלֹהִים[34]

עֲגֹג אוֹמְנִים / בְּטוּב מַעֲדַנִּים / וְתַאֲרִיךְ שָׁנִים / לִפְנֵי אֱלֹהִים[35]

---

32   *Rinna Viyeshua*, Leghorn 1862, Part 2, 101b.

33   Ibid., 127–128.

34   *Tiklāl*, III, 47a.

35   Ibid.

Ibn Paduka's *reshut*, like the *azharot* of Ibn Gabirol, was accepted as a part of the liturgy of Spain and Yemen, and was placed as an overture to the *azharot* on the positive commandments.

The strong resemblance between Halevi's *Yom beqol hamulah*[36] and Ibn Pakuda's *reshut* bears witness to the influence of one piyyut on the other. It can be assumed that it was Halevi who influenced Ibn Pakuda. The resemblance between them is twofold — both thematic and structural. Thematically, both contain a detailed list of the Ten Commandments according to their order in the Bible; structurally, the verses of both are quatrains with a separate internal rhyme in which the fourth line is a biblical quotation ending with the word *elohim*. Ibn Pakuda was careful not to employ the same quotations as Halevi, so that all but one of the biblical passages he uses are different. Like Halevi, Ibn Pakuda too incorporated his name acrostically at the beginning of the stanzas. Surprisingly enough, it was his work rather than that of Halevi which won a place in the Spanish liturgy.

JUDAH HALEVI

Perhaps the best known of the Spanish poets, Halevi composed a number of piyyutim for the festival of Shavuot,[37] yet only three of them are dedicated to the Ten Commandments. The first of these, "The man of God came down",[38] is the most distinguished work about the Ten Commandments written in the Spanish period. The use of this phrase in a piyyut about the Ten Commandments is connected with the fact that the section containing the Decalogue begins with the verse "The LORD came down" (Ex. 19. 20) although thematically those words belong to verse 14.

This piyyut is a *rehuta* with a fivefold alphabetical acrostic bearing the signature "*Yehuda bar Shemuel Halevi Haqatan*". Its structure is a unique tour de force. The form is basically Saadianic, but the embellishments are Halevi's own. The first stanza is composed of ten lines, arranged in alphabetical order from aleph to yod. The words *vayēred* and *vayōred* alternate as anaphorae at the beginning of the ten lines. The first line, beginning with *vayēred*, refers to Moses; while the

36   See below, n. 44.
37   See *The Poetry (diwan) of Judah Halevi*, ed. H. Brody, Berlin 1911; republished 1971 by Gregg International (England) with additions, notes, etc., by A. M. Habermann, III, pp. 65–115.
38   Ibid., para. 49, pp. 97–105.

second, which begins with *vayōred*, refers to the Torah. Thus, the recurring alternation is a dual one — both structural and thematic. The odd lines — first, third, etc. — are original with the poet, while each of the even lines is a biblical phrase. What all the lines have in common is that they are all allusions — the odd ones to Moses, the even ones to the Torah. Moses is, for example, "The man of God" (Deut. 33. 1); "the man set on high" (II Sam. 23. 1), "a loyal man in the House of God" (Num. 12. 17), and so on. The Torah is "the blessing of the heavens above" (Deut. 22. 13), "the word fitly spoken" (Prov. 25. 11), and so on.

This technique of allusion is maintained in the second stanza, which is based on the first word of Exodus 20 — *vayedabber* (He spoke). God is referred to as "My Cup and my Portion", "Redeemer of His sons". The Torah is alluded to as "Nectar of honey", "words of pleasantness". This elaborate method is carried through for every verse of the Decalogue, and one step further. For even as the poet began with the verse that precedes the Ten Commandments, so he concludes with the verse that follows them: "All the people witnessed the thunder and lightning" (20. 15).

Throughout the length of the *rehuta*, each two lines are paired by their own rhyme, determined by the last word of the biblical quote (aa bb cc dd ee). Each such ten-line stanza is followed up with a brief tercet, which takes off with the concluding word of the stanza to which it is attached, and ends with a phrase from Exodus 19, whose final word serves as the rhyme for the entire stanza, and whose opening word becomes the anaphora for the next stanza, which carries forward the alphabetical acrostic (*kaph* to *tav*) and follows the same twofold system of rhyme (ff gg hh ii jj), and then appends a tercet, as before.

Following these two sections, each of which comprises a short stanza and a long stanza, there are ten sections similarly constructed, one for each of the Ten Commandments. The first word of each Commandment serves as an anaphora at the beginning of each pair of lines in the long stanza.[39] By contrast, the last line of the short tercet concludes with the opening verse of the next Commandment, which then serves as the anaphora of the following stanza.

For example, the last line of the second section is the verse "I the LORD am your God", whereupon *"Anokhi"* ("I") becomes the anaphora for the following section. That section concludes with the words "You

---

39   Thus: *Anokhi*, repeated five times; and so on.

shall have no other" — which then becomes the anaphora for the
Second Commandment.

The large and small stanzas are linked together in an unbroken
chain. The lines of the large stanzas form an alphabetic acrostic, with
the alphabet completed every two stanzas — making six complete
alphabets. Here, for example, is the stanza for the Commandment
"You shall not commit adultery":

לֹא תִנְאַף אֲזֶלֶת וְטֹפֶפֶת לְהַרְבּוֹת חֲלָלֶיהָ
בְּבֵיתָהּ לֹא יִשְׁכְּנוּ רַגְלֶיהָ
לֹא תִנְאַף גְּלוּיַת מֵצַח כַּלְּעֵנָה אַחֲרִיתָהּ
דַּרְכֵי שְׁאוֹל בֵּיתָהּ
לֹא תִנְאַף הַמְכֶרֶת בִּזְנוּנֶיהָ עַמִּים שְׁאוֹל וּמָוֶת יְגוּרֶנָּה
וְטוֹב לִפְנֵי הָאֱלֹהִים יִמָּלֵט מִמֶּנָּה
לֹא תִנְאַף זְעוּמַת שַׁדַּי כָּל בָּאֶיהָ לֹא יְשׁוּבוּן מִתַּחְתִּיוֹת
חַדָּה כְּחֶרֶב פִּיוֹת
לֹא תִנְאַף טֹרֶפֶת נְפָשׁוֹת בְּמוֹקְשֶׁיהָ לְהַקְרִיב אֵידָם
יוּקָשִׁים בְּנֵי הָאָדָם
אָדָם — לֹא תַחְמֹד לְזֵנֵב דִּבְרֵי שֶׁקֶר זָנוֹב
בְּקִנְאָתְךָ לְחֵיל עָשִׁיר כִּי יָנוֹב
לֹא תִגְנֹב[40]

This structure, which combines the beginnings of the Commandments
through anaphorae in garlanded verses, was widespread in Palestinian
and Babylonian piyyutim; Halevi simply continued an ancient poetic
tradition; and it is interesting that this very old traditional form of
piyyut continued to exist in Spain until his time (twelfth century). But
although the paytan adopted the structure of his predecessors, his
biblical language, bright and lucid, is characteristic of the Spanish
school. From this point of view, the poet's style converges smoothly
with the biblical insertions.

The fixed fivefold strophe framework for all the Commandments,
both long and short, moved the paytan to include matters only remotely
connected to the Commandments. For example, in the First
Commandment he celebrates God's power in creating and directing the
world.[41] In the Third Commandment he expatiates on God's creative
power, and His mercy for His creatures — both in this world and in the

---

40   Brody, n. 37 above, III, p. 103, lines 111–123.
41   Ibid., p. 48, lines 29–32.

world to come.[42] Sometimes Halevi contents himself with the presentation of the Commandment in one strophe, and dedicates the other strophes to thematically related ethical directives. The Commandment "You shall not bear false witness" is not included until the last strophe of the stanza. The rest of the strophes deal with the fraudulent, the quarrelsome, the slanderous — whose words should not be answered; here the warning is to avoid deceitful speech, and not to talk to excess. The last Commandment, "You shall not covet" speaks exclusively in terms of property, despite the detailed list presented in the Torah. For the Second Commandment, on the prohibition of idolatry, the paytan chose biblical excerpts that deride dumb idols.[43] The Seventh Commandment "You shall not commit adultery" is based on the strange woman of Proverbs 7.

Another piyyut that enumerates the Ten Commandments is a section from the *qerova* " 'Eder Hayaqar".[44] Its verses are quatrains, and the last line of each is a part of a biblical verse concluding with the word "Elohim". The name of God in fact draws all the strophes together and alludes to the verse "God spoke" (Ex. 20. 1) which is at the beginning of the Ten Commandments. The verses are signed in an acrostic "Yehuda Qatan Ḥazaq Amen". In this piyyut the paytan gives a condensed presentation of the Ten Commandments, in the order in which they appear in the Torah. For example:

אָב וְאֵם בְּעֶדְנָה	חִישׁ כַּבֵּד נָא
וְשֵׂיבָה אֱלֹהִים	כִּי עַד זִקְנָה
תִּרְצַח וְחוּסָה	זְכוֹר לֹא לְמַשָּׂא
בְּצֶלֶם אֱלֹהִים[45]	עַל יְצִיר נַעֲשָׂה

Halevi's third piyyut on the Ten Commandments is *"Yaḥid Nimẓa"*.[46] This poem consists of five strophes in girdle-like form; the first three strophes have separate internal and external rhymes while the rhyme of the fourth is shared by all the strophes. The initials of the strophes spell the paytan's name: Yehudah. Here as well Halevi summarizes the Ten Commandments in the order in which they appear in the Bible:

---

42   Ibid., p. 100, lines 57–65.
43   Isa. 40. 19–20; Ps. 115. 4–8.
44   Brody, n. 37 above, pp. 108–109.
45   Ibid., p. 109, lines 17–20.
46   Ibid., pp. 110–111.

אֱלֹהֶיךָ וְאֵין בִּלְעָדָי   וַיֹּאמֶר לִי אָנֹכִי
עֲשׂוּהוּ מַעֲשֵׂה יָדָי   וּפֶסֶל לֹא תַעֲשֶׂה כִּי
אַל יִשְׂאוּ לַשָּׁוְא יְלָדָי   וּשְׁמִי בְּקֶרֶב מַלְאָכִי
שָׁמוֹר כְּדָתוֹ וְעִנְיָנוֹ   וְאֶת יוֹם הַשַּׁבָּת לְקַדְּשׁוֹ

וְגַם לֹא לִשְׁפֹּךְ דַּם נְקִיִּים   דָּתִי לְכַבֵּד הָאָבוֹת
דּוֹחָה מֵאֶרֶץ חַיִּים   וְסוּר מְבַּת תָּצוּד לְבָבוֹת
וַעֲנוֹת שֶׁקֶר כַּגּוֹיִים   וְאַל יַשִּׂיאֲךָ הוֹן גְּנֵבוֹת
לַחְמֹד בֵּית רֵעוֹ וְהוֹנוֹ[47]   וֶאֱנוֹשׁ אַל יְנַקֵּשׁ נַפְשׁוֹ

LEVI IBN ATTABBAN

Levi ibn Attabban, a contemporary of Moses ibn Ezra and of Judah
Halevi, composed many piyyutim for the festivals, including four for
Shavuot.[48] Their subject is the revelation at Mount Sinai and the giving
of the Torah; the treatment is midrashic. In two of them[49] he lists the
Ten Commandments concisely according to their biblical order. His
hymn "Two lights are they — our reason and the Law" is structured as
a girdle poem. In the first two stanzas the paytan proclaims praises of
the Torah, and in the last stanza he prays for the redemption of Israel.
The middle two stanzas consist of a list of the Ten Commandments:

יוֹם נִגְלָה בְּסִינַי / אֵל רָם וְנִשָּׂא
אָנֹכִי אֲדֹנָי / שָׂח לַעֲמוּסָה
לֹא יִהְיֶה לְךָ אֵל / אַחֵר לְמַשָּׂא
לֹא תִשָּׂא שְׁמִי שָׁוְא / וּזְכֹר לְדוֹרוֹת
יוֹם שַׁבָּת לְהַלֵּל / בּוֹ יָהּ בְּשִׁירוֹת

אָב וָאֵם תְּכַבֵּד / וַחְקֹר כְּבוֹדָם
הִשָּׁמֶר וְהַרְחֵק / לְךָ מִשְׁפָּךְ דָּם
וּלְנוֹאֵף וְגוֹנֵב / שְׂמַח בְּאָבְדָם
יֹאבַד עֵד שְׁקָרִים / עוֹבֵר עֲבֵרוֹת
גַּם חוֹמֵד, וְיוּבַל / לְיוֹם עֲבָרוֹת[50]

The second piyyut, "That Day When They Received the Law",[51] opens

47   Ibid., p. 110, lines 9–16.
48   *Poems of Levi Ibn Attaban*, ed. Dan Pagis, Jerusalem 1968, nos. 41–43, 48; pp.
        114–120, 125–127.
49   Ibid., nos. 43, 48.
50   Ibid., pp. 126–127.
51   Ibid., no. 47.

with the story of the revelation at Mount Sinai and concludes with a plea for salvation. The Ten Commandments are concentrated, as in the previous piyyut, in the middle of the poem, and are pronounced by God to all of Israel:

רָם אֲנִי עַל כֹּל / וּמוֹשֵׁל בַּכֹּל / וְנַעֲלֶה עַל כֹּל / אֱלֹהִים ה'
יַחֲדוּ לְשֵׁם אֵל / כִּי אֵין כָּאֵל / כִּי מִי אֵל / מִבַּלְעֲדֵי ה'
עֵקֶב שְׁבוּעָה / וְדוֹבֵר תּוֹעָה / תָּבוֹא רָעָה / מֵאֵת ה'
קַדְּשׁוּ אֶת יוֹם / שַׁבָּת, פִּדְיוֹם / תִּמְצְאוּ מִיּוֹם / עֶבְרַת ה'
בִּכְבוֹד הוֹרִים / הֱיוּ נִזְהָרִים / כִּי מְאֹד יְשָׁרִים / דַּרְכֵי ה'
חֲדַל מֵרוֹצְחִים / וְנוֹאֲפִים וְלוֹקְחִים / גְּנֵבָה וְחוֹמְדִים / תּוֹעֲבַת (?) ה'
זֶרַע כְּשֵׁרִים / דְּחוּ עֵד שְׁקָרִים / וְתִהְיוּ יְקָרִים / בְּעֵינֵי ה'
קִנְיַן יְדִידִים / וּבָתִּים וְשָׂדִים / אַל תִּהְיוּ חוֹמְדִים / יִרְאוּ אֶת ה'[52]

The formal similarities between this piyyut and certain compositions by David ibn Pakuda and Judah Halevi[53] are not to be ignored. All three are composed of quatrains in which the final line concludes with the fragment of a verse ending with the name of God. In Pakuda and Halevi the name is *Elohim*: Ibn Attabban uses *Adonai*. Moreover, the acrostics used by Pakuda and Ibn Attabban are very similar to one another.[54]

It is difficult to tell who of these three influenced whom since they were contemporaries. But perhaps the source of influence should be identified as Judah Halevi, the foremost of the company.

ABRAHAM IBN EZRA

Abraham ibn Ezra did not compose any piyyutim on the Ten Commandments, but his piyyut "The fiery law",[55] a paean of praise of the Torah, explicitly mentions the first two Commandments:

יוֹם נִגְלָה אֵל עַל הַר סִינָי   זִכְרוּ וְצָהֲלוּ רַעְיוֹנַי
פָּתַח: אָנֹכִי יי'   לְעֵינֵי כָל עַם אֱמוּנַי
אֱלִיל הַשְׁלִיכוּ[56]

52   Ibid., pp. 124–125.
53   See above, n. 36.
54   See above, paragraph on Ibn Pakuda.
55   *The Sacred Poetry of Abraham Ibn Ezra*, ed. Y. Levin, Jerusalem 1980, Part II, Entry 445.
56   Ibid., p. 532, lines 19–21.

In the final stanza of another piyyut on the giving of the Torah,[57] Ibn
Ezra describes the Ten Commandments which, according to the
Midrash, fly in the air like sparks of fire and return to become engraved
in the stone tablets of the Covenant.[58]

ISAAC KIMḤI

In the Mahzor of Carpentras,[59] the *azharot* of Solomon ibn Gabirol are
supplemented by the *azharot* of Isaac Kimḥi,[60] rabbi and paytan of the
thirteenth century. The *azharot* of Ibn Gabirol are part of the morning
service, while those of Kimḥi are for the afternoon prayer. Both
structurally and metrically, Kimḥi's *azharot* are written in the wake of
those of Ibn Gabirol. The verses are quatrains each with its own rhyme.
The rhyme of the last line, which binds the stanzas together is -*nim* (Ibn
Gabirol uses -*rim*). The acrostic signature built in to Kimḥi's *azharot*
for the positive commandments is *Ani Yitzḥaq Qatan Qimḥi*. The
composer's full name, both in Hebrew and the vernacular, is indicated
in the rubric at the beginning of the *azharot: Rabbi Isaac Kimḥi son of
Rabbi Mordecai, known as Maestre Petit of Nîmes.*

One could cite numerous lines by Kimḥi which show the influence of
Ibn Gabirol.[61-63] But that influence is most unmistakable if we place
side by side the summaries by the two poets for their *azharot* on the
positive commandments. First, Kimḥi:

אֵלֶּה הַחֻקִּים / בְּהִירִים כִּשְׁחָקִים / וְכִרְאִי מוּצָקִים / חֲזָקִים וַחֲסוּנִים...
בְּתַח כִּנּוֹר נָעִים / וְצַלְצֵל וּמְנַעְנְעִים / וְעֹלוּ מוֹשִׁיעִים / בְּצִיּוֹן שַׁאֲנַנִּים
וְיֶאֱתֶה עָם שָׂשׂוּי / בְּכָל פֵּאוֹת בָּזוּי / לְמִגְדַּל הַבָּנוּי / אֲשֶׁר אֵלָיו פּוֹנִים[64]

Compare Ibn Gabirol's version:

אֵלֶּה הַתּוֹרוֹת / יְסוֹדוֹת נִבְחָרוֹת / וְלָהֵנָּה פֹּארוֹת / כְּסַנְסִנֵּי תְמָרִים
יְמַהֵר אֵל עֶלְיוֹן / לְקַבֵּץ עָם אֶבְיוֹן / וְיִבְנֶה עִיר צִיּוֹן / וְעֵמֶק הַפְּגָרִים ...
וְאָז כָּל עָם שׁוֹגֵג / בְּרָעָה יִתְמוֹגֵג / לְקוֹל הָמוֹן חוֹגֵג / בְּשִׂמְחָה וּבְשִׁירִים[65]

---

57   The opening of this poem is lifted from an early piyyut that used to be recited on
     Simhat Torah; see Davidson, *Thesaurus*, n. 30 above, Aleph, entry 8188.
58   *The Sacred Poetry of Abraham Ibn Ezra*, n. 55 above, II entry 455.
59   *Festival Prayers According To The Rite of Carpentras*, Amsterdam 1759.
60   The positive commandments are on pp. 98–104; the negative on pp. 113–124.
61   Ibid., 100b.
62   Ibid., 120b.
63   *Tiklāl*, n. 8 above, Part III, 55b.
64   *Festival Prayers*, etc. n. 59 above, 104.
65   *Tiklāl*, n. 8 above, III 56b.

JOSEPH BEN ISRAEL

The oeuvre of the two poets Joseph and Shalem of Mashta, who initiated the flourishing Yemenite poetry of the seventeenth century, contains some poems about the Ten Commandments, either partially or in their entirety. Joseph ben Israel based two poems on redemption and the Temple Service, arranging the Ten Commandments in their biblical order. Both are written in the same meter and their openings are almost identical.[66] At the beginning is a prayer for the final redemption. Then he describes the ingathering of the exiles and renewal of the Temple sacrifices. On Yom Kippur the High Priest enters the Holy of Holies. There he will hear the voice of God speaking with him as He spoke on Mount Sinai when He pronounced the Ten Commandments. Here the poet turns to a presentation of the Commandments; for example:

בְּיוֹם כִּפּוּר עֲבוֹדָתוֹ מְרֻבָּה / וְיִכָּנֵס לְתוֹךְ חַדְרֵי חֲדָרִים
וְיִשְׁמַע קוֹל אֱלֹהִים עֵת יְדַבֵּר / כְּמוֹ דְּבַר עֲשֶׂרֶת הַדְּבָרִים
תְּחִלָּתָן אֲנִי הָאֵל אֲדֹנָי / וְאֵין אַחֵר כְּמוֹתִי בַּיְצוּרִים
וְלֹא יָסוּר לְבָבְךָ מִשְּׁמוֹעַ / וְלֹא יִהְיֶה לְךָ אֱלֹהִים אֲחֵרִים
וְלֹא תִזְכֹּר שְׁמִי שֶׁלֹּא לְצֹרֶךְ / וְלֹא תַרְגִּיל לְשׁוֹנְךָ בַּשְּׁקָרִים
וְהִזָּהֵר בְּסוֹד שַׁבָּת בְּרֵאשִׁית / אֲשֶׁר בּוֹ יִשְׂמְחוּ זֶרַע יְשָׁרִים
לְאָבִיךָ וְאִמֶּךָ תְּפַרְנֵס / וְזוֹ מִצְוָה יְדוּעָה בַּסְּפָרִים
וְלֹא תִרְצַח לְכָל נֶפֶשׁ בְּעָרְמָה / וְלֹא תִנְאַף לְכָל גּוּפוֹת אֲסוּרִים
וְלֹא תִגְנֹב נְפָשׁוֹת לַעֲבָדִים / אֲשֶׁר לִי הֵם בְּמִצְרַיִם קְנוּיִים
וְעֵד שֶׁקֶר יְהֵא חַיָּב בְּנַפְשׁוֹ / וְכָל מַעֲשָׂיו וְעֵדוֹתָיו אֲסוּרִים
וְלֹא תַחְמֹד לְכָל בַּיִת וְאִשָּׁה / וְלֹא תַחְמֹד שְׁוָרִים וַחֲמוֹרִים[67]

The two poems by Joseph ben Israel became favorites among Yemenite Jews, and are among the most widely sung. One of them[68] has even been sung on an Israeli recording.[69]

SHALEM SHABAZI

While Joseph ben Israel presented the Ten Commandments in Hebrew, Shalem Shabazi brought them to the Jews of Yemen in their colloquial

---

66   "I ask the LORD Who made the heavenly orbs", and "I ask the LORD to send us His Messiah".
67   *Tiklāl*, no. 8 above, pp. 19–20.
68   "I ask the LORD Who made the heavenly orbs".
69   See my *Songs of Yemen*, Hakibutz Hameuhad, Tel Aviv 1982.

Arabic. In the girdle poem "My LORD Shed Light On Moses",[70]
written in Judeo-Arabic, the poet tells of the glorious event of the
giving of the Torah on Mount Sinai:

אמר פי אלכרי ואלכפר נאהי / די יכרה
קאל אנא אללה רבך מדימא / אעבדני

מן מצר אכרגתך
פי אלבחר סיירתך
באלאמם פצֿלתך ...

בר בסבתך לאנה מקדס / יום סאבע
ואכרם אלואלדין לא תנחס / כן קאנע
תם ולא תזן ותסרק ותנדס / פי צֿאיע
ען ספך אלדמא כן לזימא / לא תדני

ליס תחלף אתאם
זור תשהד כלאם
ואלמנא הו חראם[71]

In the second poem, "My LORD Shed Light Upon My Soul and Mind",
the poet details the first two Commandments, the first in Arabic and
the second in Hebrew:

אול אלקול אנא אללה. אלעאלי אלוחדאני
[דיבור ראשון אני האל, העליון היחיד]
לֹא יְהֵא לָךְ אֱלֹהִים אֲחֵרִים / אַכְזָרִים
אַל תְּכַחֵשׁ וְתִבְטַח בְּזָרִים / נֶעְקָרִים[72]

SAMUEL ADANI

The reference to the Ten Commandments has endured in Yemenite
poetry until our own generation. At the end of the nineteenth century
there lived in Aden a wise and scholarly man by the name of Samuel
Yeshua Adani. His work *Naḥalat Yosef* (Jerusalem 1907) is a sort of
encyclopedia of Torah, science and poetry. He also wrote liturgical
poems for all the festivals. The *seliḥot* that he composed for Yom
Kippur are based on the 613 commandments, after the model of Ibn

70   The diwan *Ḥafez Ḥayyim* (n. 3 above), pp. 178–180.
71   Ibid., p. 179.
72   Ibid., p. 180.

Gabirol's *azharot*. He presents the revelation at Mount Sinai in a poem for Shemini Atzeret,[73] and enumerates the Ten Commandments in two poems: one for Shavuot,[74] and a girdle poem that revolves around the giving of the Torah. The poet devotes two stanzas to the Ten Commandments:

מֶלֶךְ צוּר פָּתַח וְאָמַר / אֲנִי אֵל יָחִיד לְבַדִּי

הוֹצֵאתִי אֶתְכֶם בְּמַאֲמַר / בְּכֹחִי וְעֹצֶם יָדִי

אָנֹכִי בּוֹרֵא וְגוֹמֵר / כָּל מְצוּאִים לִי יְהוֹדוּ

לֹא תַעֲשֶׂה פֶּסֶל וְצוּרָה

וְלֹא תַעֲבֹד לְשׁוּם כָּל נִבְרָא

כִּי יִהְיוּ לְךָ לְזָרָה

לֹא תִשָּׂא שֵׁם אֵל הַנִּפְלָא / לַשֶּׁקֶר אִם תִּשָּׁבְעֶנָּה / כִּי הוּא זֶה עָוֹן פְּלִילָה

וְיוֹם שַׁבָּת זָכוֹר וְשָׁמוֹר / לֹא תַעֲשֶׂה בוֹ כָל מְלָאכָה

כִּי יוֹם זֶה קָדוֹשׁ וְטָהוֹר / לְהָנִיחַ לְךָ בְּרָכָה

וְכַבֵּד הוֹרִים וְתִשְׁמֹר / לְמַעַן יַאֲרִיךְ יָמֶיךָ

לֹא תִרְצַח נֶפֶשׁ יְקָרָה

לֹא תִנְאַף עִם אִשָּׁה זָרָה

לֹא תִגְנֹב מִכָּל גּוּבְרָא

לֹא תַעֲנֶה עֵד שָׁוְא חָלִילָה / לֹא תַחְמֹד בְּלִבְּךָ הַזּוֹנֶה / בְּהַבְלֵי רִיק תעתּוע וְכִסְלָה[75]

NATHAN BEN ISAAC

The last to invoke the Ten Commandments in his works is our contemporary Nathan ben Isaac.[76] His poem "I will praise the highest God, of hidden might" is composed as a *ma'aneh*[77] to the poem "I will praise the Rock my Creator and Shield"[78] by Sarum Alliwani (Halevi). The subject of the poem is the giving of the Torah. After a description of the hosts of angels who descended with the Shekhinah on Mount Sinai, and of the tribes of Israel who stood at the foot of the

73 "The Lord Appeared From Teman", *Naḥalat Yosef*, 52, entry 16.

74 "Hark, The Awesome Deed", ibid., 50, entry 9.

75 Ibid., 60, entry 34.

76 Died in Israel in 1960.

77 The genre is known in Arabic as a *jawāb*, and adheres to the form of the original to which it is a response. This type of poem originated in Spain whence it made its way to Yemen. This particular example has not yet been published. The manuscript is in the possession of Mr. Ratzon Halevi.

78 See the diwan *Ḥafez Ḥayyim*, no. 3 above, entry 19, pp. 125–126.

mountain, the poet presents the Ten Commandments. Here are two
injunctions, concerning the Sabbath and parental honor:

שַׁבָּת שָׁמוֹר גַּם תִּשְׂמַח / בּוֹ תָרוּחַ / נֶפֶשׁ יְהַדְּרוֹ
בְּכָל לְבוּשׁ גַּם רֵיחַ / גַּם שִׂיחַ / תּוֹרָה יְעַטְּרוֹ
עֶבֶד וְאָמָה יָנוּחַ / יַרְוִיחַ / יוֹם זֶה יְעַטְּרוֹ
קוֹלוֹת בְּשִׁירוֹת יַשְׁבִּיחַ / יַצְרִיחַ / לָאֵל יְפָאֲרוֹ
יִבְרַח בְּיוֹם זֶה מַדִּיחַ / מָשִׁיחַ / לִתְהוֹם יְהַשְׁפִּלוֹ
כָּבוֹד לְאָב / וָאֵם וְרָב
אָח נֶאֱהָב / גָּדוֹל וְשָׂב.

ADDENDA

1. After I wrote the above, the Yemenite manuscript of a *divan* (an
anthology of medieval poetry) came into my hands (a photostat by
permission of Ratzon Halevi). An examination of the poems reveals
that the Ten Commandments served as a subject of *hallelot* and *ḥaduiot*
as well.[79] In the *hallel*, which begins "I will praise Him who gave us the
Ten Commandments", the poet enumerates the first five Commandments, each of which contains the Tetragrammaton; while the last five,
which do not contain the name of God, he mentions without detail.

Another *hallel* is written in Aramaic, and it opens "I will praise the
LORD above". This *hallel* devotes a separate strophe to each
Commandment: the first half of each is an Aramaic translation of the
opening of the Commandment; the second half is a paraphrase, as
demanded by the rhyme scheme. Here are the first two
Commandments:

קדמותא אנא ה' אלהך דאפיקתך מגו פלחי צלמיא
תנייתא לא יהוי לך אלה אחרן בר מני מעובדי עובדיא

The wedding song "Beloved since the Mount of Myrrh/ trusted me with
the Good to Keep", details the Ten Commandments by their opening
words.

2. Among the poets of Yemen who wrote of the Ten Commandments,
Abraham ben Halfon must be mentioned. It is believed that he lived in
the fourteenth century. A much later document asserts that he was a
Yemenite, and the majority of his poems are preserved in Yemenite

---

79   A *hallel* is a dialogue in rhymed prose which guests and host recite antiphonally at
     feasts celebrating a mitzvah (circumcision, wedding, etc.). A *haduyah* is a
     processional chanted when accompanying a bridegroom at a wedding.

sources. One of his sacred poems, "Remember Ancient Words",[80] was composed for Shavuot, as we can see by the words in its second verse "Today is the day of revelation on Mount Sinai".

The first two stanzas are devoted to a description of the revelation, while in the remaining strophes the poet presents the Ten Commandments in his own words, independent of biblical expressions. Here are the first three injunctions:

דִּבֶּר אֲנִי הוּא אֵל יִשְׂרָאֵל / וּבַעֲבוֹדַת זָר אַל תִּתְגָּאֵל
וְלַשָּׁוְא לֹא תִשָּׂא אֶת שֵׁם הָאֵל / כִּי אֲנִי בּוֹחֵן לֵב וּכְלָיוֹת
וַאֲנִי יוֹדֵעַ מַה לִּהְיוֹת[81]

Here as well, we sense the influence of the *azharot* of Ibn Gabirol. At the end of the piyyut the paytan encourages all of Israel to keep the festival of Shavuot and to grow strong in study of the Torah. In his conclusion he prays for retribution on the kingdom of Ishmael, and for the redemption of the Jewish people and the ingathering of the exiles.

Translated by Ora Viskind

---

80 *Ziyunim, Essays in Memory of I.G. Simḥoni*, Berlin 1929, pp. 71–72.
81 Ibid., p. 71.

16. THE TABLETS OF THE LAW
AS A SYMBOL OF JUDAISM

GAD B. SARFATTI

1. THE TABLETS OF THE LAW ON SYNAGOGUE ARKS

Whoever enters a synagogue today, whether in Jerusalem or in some other city in Israel or in the Diaspora, will almost certainly see the two Tablets of the Law above the Ark and on them, in abbreviated form, the Ten Commandments. The shape of the Tablets and the version of the Decalogue appearing on them are everywhere the same. The Tablets depicted in this form are also commonly found on various sacramental objects, on prayerbooks and Pentateuchs, even on the emblems of associations and commercial enterprises. The symbol of the Tablets indicates the sacredness of the object or book, or the special Jewish character of the association or enterprise.

These Tablets appear as two adjacent rectangles, taller than wide, with the upper side of each of them not straight, but rounded. The Commandments themselves are so arranged that there are five on each Tablet. The short Commandments (Sixth, Seventh and Eighth) are presented in their entirety, while for the others, only the first two words appear. When the Tablets are represented on a very small scale, the Hebrew letters א,ב,ג, etc. appear as ordinal numbers in place of the Commandments themselves. We will not be mistaken if we say that this form has become the principal symbol of Judaism, and especially Judaism in the religious sense.

For example, examining Rachel Wischnitzer's *Synagogue Architecture in the United States*,[1] we find the Tablets of the Law in the pictures of 18 Arks,[2] while mention is made of the Tablets in the descriptions of

1 Rachel Wischnitzer, *Synagogue Architecture in the United States*, Philadelphia 1955.
2 Ibid., figs. 14, 17, 19, 28, 37, 43, 46, 53, 55, 56, 67, 68, 80, 113, 114, 119, 138, 146.

11 more synagogues.[3] In the pictures of eight synagogues it is not clear whether or not the Tablets appear on the Ark, and it is conceivable that in some of these they are in fact not present.[4] The book shows further that the Tablets are displayed on the exterior of ten synagogues.[5]

Wischnitzer also tells a very characteristic story. In 1850 a round window was installed above the Ark in the Anshe Chesed Synagogue in New York. The Ten Commandments were painted on the window, each Commandment on a separate pane, rather than in the usual format. The Tablets of the Law with the Commandments were regarded as so essential a symbol of the synagogue that the innovation sparked vigorous opposition. So much so, that a committee was appointed to examine the *halakhah* and determine whether the Commandments could "remain as they are painted in a circle on stained glass or whether it is against the *din*, and ought to be fixed in the usual way on two Tablets". Needless to say, the committee's conclusion was that "there is nothing in the laws which prescribes any particular form: consequently, it is not against the *din* to have them fixed as they are at present".

Nonetheless, a year later another committee was appointed with the task of seeing to it that the Commandments would be arranged on two tablets in accord with customary practice.[6]

A second example, closer to us in time, but also attesting to the unmediated feeling that the Tablets of the Law on the Ark are an indispensable symbol, comes from Jerusalem. Beautiful Ark doors from a synagogue in Correggio, Italy, made at the beginning of the last century, were installed in a Jerusalem Synagogue.[7] Discovering that these doors were without Tablets of the Law, the worshippers in this synagogue decided to adorn the doors with a set of Tablets made of plastic, even though this "ornament" certainly marred their beauty.

---

3   Ibid., pp. 11, 16, 25, 26, 28, 37, 39, 49, 54, 58, 98.
4   Ibid., figs. 34, 48, 74, 98, 115, 132, 140b, 144.
5   Ibid., figs. 59, 60, 79, 84, 87, 88, 93, 118, 137, 139a.
6   Ibid., p. 54. Throughout the book the Tablets are considered the main symbol in the synagogue. Second to the Tablets, in terms of time of appearance, importance, and frequency of occurence, is the Magen David. The Menorah sometimes appears as a symbol, but only in later synagogues, and then as the fruit of quasi-archeological scholarship. In isolated cases the Burning Bush (fig. 112), the Pillar of Fire (fig. 125), symbols of the twelve tribes (figs. 107, 126), and the crown (fig. 153) also appear.
7   The Hapoel Hamizrahi synagogue on Ethiopia Street; see Nahon (n. 116 below), p. 135.

Since when have the Tablets of the Law been an indispensable decoration on synagogue Arks, and a symbol of Judiasm? Furthermore, since when have the Tablets been depicted in the fixed, almost hallowed, form of two adjacent rectangles with rounded tops?

Our examination shows that up to the end of the Middle Ages, Jews did *not* use the Tablets as a symbol, and did not even depict them in drawings. As for antiquity, we rely on the researches of Goodenough, who makes no mention of them whatsoever in his monumental study, *Jewish Symbols in the Greco-Roman Period.*[8] The symbols in use in that period were the menorah, the censer, the Ark of the Covenant, the *megillah*, lulav, etrog and shofar — that is, objects seen and used by Jews regularly in ritual, or objects from the days of the Sanctuary that were still alive in the memory of the people. But who had seen the Tablets of the Law? The Holy Ark had not been extant in the Second Temple; and even in the First Temple the Tablets were enclosed within the Holy Ark and no one dared look at them. Furthermore, since it was forbidden to copy the form of any of the ritual objects of the Temple,[9] it is unlikely that anyone even thought of making a likeness of the Tablets, whose sacredness far exceeded that of any other object. And what is more, the Tablets contain the Ten Commandments, and the Sages ruled against the practice of reciting the Ten Commandments in the morning service along with the Shema[10] (and also apparently excluded them from the phylacteries[11]). That being the case, they certainly would not have consented to the special prominence given the Decalogue by inscribing it on representations of the Tablets.

It should be noted, however, that there are a considerable number of Jewish Bible manuscripts, written in Spain from the thirteenth century onwards, which begin with two illuminated pages that describe the utensils of the Temple, including that Ark of the Covenant and the Tablets inside it. Cecil Roth offers a list of 19 such manuscripts,[12]

---

8   E.R. Goodenough, *Jewish Symbols in the Greco-Roman Period*, New York 1953–1956; see especially vol. 4, part 6.

9   Maimonides, *Mishneh Torah*, Book VIII, 7:10.

10   See Mishnah Tamid V:I; Yer. Ber. I:5; also J. Mann, *HUCA*, 2 (1925), pp. 282–284; 4 (1927), pp. 288–89.

11   See Mann, *HUCA* 4 (1927), pp. 290–292; Barthélemy and Milik, *Qumran*, I, Oxford 1955, pp. 72–76; Habermann, *The Scrolls From The Judaean Desert* (Hebrew), Tel Aviv 1959, pp. 22–23.

12   Cecil Roth, "Jewish Antecedents of Christian Art", *Journal of the Warburg and Courtauld Institutes*, XVI (1953), pp. 24–44.

including one from Toledo, 1277,[13] one from Perpignan, 1299,[14] a manuscript from the Estense library[15] and one from the Ambrosian Library,[16] both the latter from the fourteenth century. These illuminations show the Tablets within the Ark as two rectangular forms each bearing an abbreviated version of five Commandments. Within this listing, Roth also includes a Bible from the Firkovitch Collection in Leningrad, which was apparently written in Egypt in 929.[17] Here too an illuminated page depicts the Tablets, among other implements of the Tabernacle, as two rectangles inside the Ark of the Covenant. In Roth's view, this book is "the tenth-century prototype of the series of illustrations of which we have evidence in Spain and Provence from the thirteenth century onwards; the tradition thus goes back for upwards of three hundred years earlier than the first European evidences".[18]

Roth even believes that this manuscript is a link between the medieval tradition in Europe and earlier illustrated manuscripts from Palestine, which have been lost. One of the clearest and most magnificent examples of this tradition is found on page 32 of the Sarajevo Haggada.[19] The picture offers an imaginary reconstruction of the Sanctuary: in the middle is the Ark of the Covenant standing on three legs (not four, in an attempt of sorts to depict perspective), and on it are cherub wings. The front section of the Ark has been removed so that it is possible to see the Tablets inside it and the Commandments inscribed on them.

Joseph Gutmann also deals with the Spanish iconographic tradition of depicting the implements of the Sanctuary and offers a list of 21 manuscripts of the Bible (which is identical only in part with Roth's listing) that represent this tradition.[20] He holds, however, that there is

13   V. Antonioli Martelli-L. Mortara Ottolenghi, *Manoscritti Biblici ebraici decorati*, Milano 1966, p. 77, pl. 24.
14   *Encyclopaedia Judaica*, vol. 4, col. 977.
15   Antonioli-Mortara, n. 13 above, p. 78, pl. 26.
16   Ibid., p. 80, plate I.
17   Bezalel Narkiss, *Hebrew Illuminated Manuscripts*, Jerusalem 1969, p. 42, pl. 1a.
18   Roth, n. 12 above, p. 28.
19   *Sarajevo Haggadah* Tel-Aviv–Jeruslaem 1944.
20   Joseph Gutmann, "The Messianic Temple in Spanish Medieval Hebrew Manuscripts", in: Joseph Gutmann (ed.), *The Temple of Solomon*, Missoula, Montana 1976, pp. 125–145.

no connection between these illuminations and the art of ancient Palestine. In his view, they express the world-view of the Jews of Spain and their messianic hopes. Roth's idea of an uninterrupted iconographic tradition from talmudic times in Palestine to medieval Spain is appealing, but Gutmann's considered opinion appears more reasonable.

Coming back to our present concern, it should be stressed that in all the pictures mentioned, the Tablets of the Law are only one among the many objects of the Tabernacle or Sanctuary; they have no special status as a symbol.

When rectangular Tablets of the Law appear in Jewish manuscripts not as an appurtenance of the Tabernacle but in a picture of the giving of the Law at Mount Sinai (as in the Rothschild Siddur[21]) it must be asked to what extent this reflects the influence of the Spanish tradition. In the picture of the giving of the Law in the "Tripartite Mahzor",[22] we see Moses holding the Tablets, which are attached to one another and are inside a frame, like a Christian diptych, but are rectangular and inscribed with abbreviated versions of the Commandments, as in the Spanish manuscript tradition. In the upper portion of the picture in the Regensburg Pentateuch as well, Moses receives two inscribed rectangular Tablets, but in the bottom part of the picture they are joined together, again like a diptych.[23]

According to *Baraita di-Melekhet ha-Mishkan*, and to the Babylonian Talmud[24], the Tablets were square in shape — "six in length, six in breadth, and three in thickness" — not the shape we are accustomed to. The Yerushalmi differs on this, and gives the Tablets a rectangular shape — "six *tefah* in length and three in breadth".[25] Ish-Shalom believes that two words have been dropped from the Jerusalem Talmud's description, and suggests that it be amended to correspond with the Babylonian text.[26] In any event, the details

21 Narkiss, n. 17 above, p. 144, pl. 52.
22 Ibid., p. 108, pl. 34.
23 Ibid., p. 98, pl. 29.
24 *Baraita di-Melekhet ha-Mishkan*, ed. Ish-Shalom, Vienna 1908, p. 40; B.B. 14a; *Numbers Rabbah* 4:21.
25 Yer. Sot. VIII:3, 22c; Yer. Taan. IV:5: 68c; see also Ginzberg, *Yerushalmi Fragments*, New York 1909, p. 183, lines 11–12; *Tanḥuma*, ed. Buber, *Ki Tissa* 20, p. 120; and *Tosafot* ad Menahot 99a.
26 *Baraita di-Melekhet ha-Mishkan*, n. 24 above, p. 43.

recounted in the Talmud and the Midrash about the material of which
the Tablets were made and the way the Commandments were inscribed
on them are so astounding[27] that they must obviously be viewed as
aggadah. It should not be mistakenly thought that here, as in some
other places, the Sages describe some ancient object or occurrence, but
are really referring to something close to them in time. In the works of
the Geonim we find it said that the size of the Tablets was 136 fingers by
28 fingers, the fingers being the fingers of God, whose little finger, that
is one quarter of a square finger, is as large as the entire world.[28]

   As we have seen, the principal location for the Tablets is the Ark. But
the many illustrations of ancient Arks all show them without that
symbol. It is absent from the Arks shown on coins of the Bar-Kokhba
rebellion,[29] from pictures in ancient synagogues (Beth Alpha, Naaran,
Dura Europos), from the Beth Shearim catacombs,[30] and from the
gold cups in the Jewish catacombs in Rome.[31] That is also the case in a
later period. Many illustrated medieval manuscripts (mahzorim,
haggadot) depict synagogue Arks[32]; an Ark from Cairo in the thirteenth
century was found in the *Genizah* and reconstructed;[33] we have pictures
of the synagogue in Worms (1034) and in Ratisbon (thirteenth
century).[34] There is no hint of the Tablets of the Law on any of these.
Similarly despite all the decorations adorning the magnificent
synagogues of Spain, and all the texts that serve as decoration, we do
not find the Ten Commandments among them.[35] The Jews of Yemen,

27 S. Krauss assembles some of the sources in his book, *Antoninus und Rabbi*, Vienna
    1910, pp. 9–10.
28 *Oẓar ha-Geonim*, Eruv. 11; the same passage appears in *Bereshith Rabbati*, ed. H.
    Albeck, Jerusalem 1940, p. 43; see Albeck's comment, ad. loc.
29 Reifenberg, *Coins of the Jews* (Hebrew), Jerusalem 1948, pl. 12, and his comments.
30 E.L. Sukenik, *The Beth Alpha Synagogue* (Hebrew), Jerusalem, 1932, pp. 22–34;
    Mazar, *Beth She'arim* (Hebrew), Jerusalem 1958, pp. 85–87, 122, pl. 34, and the
    literature cited there; Goodenough, no. 8 above, vol. 4, pp. 111–112, illustrations
    there and in vol. 3.
31 Goodenough, ibid., vol. 3, illustrations on pp. 964–978; Landsberger, *HUCA*, 19
    (1945), p. 362.
32 Goodenough, n. 8 above, vol. 4, p. 122; illustrations on pp. 75–77. See also the ark
    in Rothschild ms. 25, and the one in *Sefer Minhagim*, reproduced in *Tarbiẓ*, 28
    (1959), p. 196, fig. 1a.
33 S. Kayser and G. Schoenberger, *Jewish Ceremonial Art*, Philadelphia 1955, p.22.
34 *The Legacy of Israel*, Oxford 1927, figs. 43, 53.
35 See F. Cantera Burgos, *Sinagogas españolas*, Madrid 1955.

who were untouched by European influences, do not recognize the
Tablets as a symbol to this day. In fact, when they first saw the Tablets
on well-known Pentateuchs, with the Commandments indicated by
Roman numerals, some Yemenite Jews thought they were a Christian
symbol![36]

Furthermore, the idea that the Ten Commandments embody the
entire Torah in the form of general rules, while the rest of the Torah
simply develops them in detail, is an idea foreign to the Talmud and
Midrash, as Ginzberg points out.[37] It was Philo who first formulated
this notion. In his work on the *Special Laws*, he divided them into
categories, each of which was seen as being derived from one of the Ten
Commandments. Saadiah adopted the idea, and listed the
Commandments in that way in the *azharot* he composed.[38] The concept
was inherited from the Geonim by Moses ha-Darshan, who buttressed
it with *gematria*:

> The Tablets encompassed the 613 commandments, corresponding
> to the 613 letters from *Anokhi* [the first word of the Decalogue]
> to *re'ekha* [the last word], no more, no less.[39]

But Tannaim and Amoraim, as we have already noted, tried to deny
any privileged status to the Ten Commandments, a stance that was
given clear and vigorous expression by Maimonides:

> There is no difference between such verses as "The descendents
> of Ham: Cush, Mizraim, Put and Canaan" (Gen. 10. 6) or "... his
> wife's name was Mehetabel daughter of Matred" (Gen. 36. 39),
> on the one hand; and on the other, "I the LORD am your God"
> (Ex. 20. 2) and "Hear O Israel! The LORD is our God, the LORD
> alone" (Deut. 6. 4). For all are divine words, all the Law of the
> LORD which is perfect, all pure, holy and true.

He defines one "who believes there is in the Torah an essential part

36 For this piece of information it is my pleasant duty to thank Rabbi Joseph Kafah.
Neither Samuel Krauss in his *Synagogale Altertümer*, Berlin 1922, nor Israel
Abrahams in *Jewish Life in the Middle Ages*, London 1896, mentions the Tablets
of the Law as a symbol among Jews.

37 L. Ginzberg, *The Legends of the Jews*, Philadelphia 1909–1938, vol. 6, pp. 49–50.

38 *Siddur Rav Saadiah Gaon*, Jerusalem 1941, pp. 191–216.

39 *Bereshith Rabbati*, p. 76; also p. 8 and the parallels Albeck cites in both places.
That the Decalogue is a summary of the Torah is also the view of Abraham bar
Hiyya, *Higgyon ha-Nefesh*, Leipzig 1860, pp. 35b–37a; cf. Rashi ad Exodus 32. 19.

and a peripheral one" as a heretic. [40] For this reason, too, ancient Judaism could not have elevated the Tablets of the Law, and the Commandments inscribed on them, to a place of supreme eminence.

We have already noted that Tannaim and Amoraim tended not to stress the uniqueness of the Ten Commandments, "because of the arguments of the sectarians" (Ber. 12a). There is perhaps a vestige of a more ancient practice in the Nash papyrus,[41] and later reference to it is found in the words of Nahshon Gaon as cited in the *Arukh* (s.v. *tafel*) about a scroll "on which is written from *Anokhi* to *re'ekha*". In contrast to the Jews, the Samaritans did often write the Decalogue by itself, and engraved it on stones that they set in their houses of worship, somewhat like mezuzot.[42]

2. THE TABLETS IN CHRISTIAN ART

Since we have not found early representations of the Tablets among the Jews, let us turn to Christian art, and look for such representations in sculpture, painting and illuminations. An examination of these works discloses a division into three geographic areas corresponding to the three forms in which this object was realized. In the East, and in Byzantine art in general, the form in which the Law is represented is that of a scroll; in Italy up to the sixteenth century — two rectangular Tablets; in France — the diptych, from which developed the familiar form of rectangular Tablets with rounded tops, which at a certain point supplanted all the other forms. The correspondence, of course, is not absolute, and it is meant only to indicate the setting in which a particular form arose, or in which it became dominant.

a. THE SCROLL

In some of the oldest works we see (in clear contradiction to the biblical text) Moses receiving not tablets, but a parchment scroll. This apparently is a Byzantine tradition which made its way into the earliest illuminated European manuscripts,[43] and also reached Rome. The

---

40   *Commentary on the Mishnah, Ḥelek*, the eighth article of faith.

41   See M.Z. Segal, *Leshonenu*, 15 (1947), pp. 27–36.

42   Yitzhaq Ben-Zvi noted this in some of his writings on the Samaritans; see also J.A. Montgomery, *The Samaritans*, Philadelphia 1907.

43   "The West received most of the biblical motifs devised in the East, learning of them through trade, pilgrims, and monastic institutions", *Enciclopedia Italiana* s.v. "Bibbia", p. 920.

following are some of the works of art which depict the giving of the Law in this fashion:

1. A relief on a wooden panel of a door of the Santa Sabina church in Rome, A.D. 430.[44] (plate 6c).
2. A mosaic in the Byzantine church San Vitale in Ravenna, sixth century.[45]
3. A relief on a memorial stone in Constantinople, seventh century.[46]
4. An illustration in the manuscript of Kosmas Indikopleustes, eighth or ninth century (a copy of an original manuscript of the sixth century).[47]
5. A miniature in the Grandval Bible, French art of the ninth century.[48]
6. A miniature in the Vivian Bible,[49] resembling the preceding one (plate 6a.).
7. A picture in the Vatican collection, an exemplar of Italian-Greek art of the fourteenth century.[50]

In all of these, Moses is seen alongside the figure of a hand, extended from a cloud in the sky, giving him a scroll. This figure of a hand, which Christian art later replaced, without a qualm, with a full picture of the Creator, calls to mind the hand that restrains Abraham at the Akeda as depicted in the Beth Alpha mosaic.[51] Jews dared to portray this physical detail because of its origin in the verse: "the king could see the hand as it wrote" (Daniel 5. 5).[52] This verse exempted the hand from

---

44 *La Bibbia nell' Arte*, Firenze-London 1956, fig. 94.
45 Edizioni Alinari, Firenze, No. 18219.
46 *La Bibbia nell' Arte*, n. 44 above, 113.
47 E.L. Sukenik, *The Synagogue of Dura-Europos* (Hebrew), Jerusalem 1947, p. 60.
48 *La Bibbia nell' Arte*, n. 44 above, 112. But in the Ashburnham Pentateuch of the seventh century (ibid., 119), the giving of the Law is shown with God not giving Moses anything substantial, and what Moses has in his hand on the right side of the miniature is the "book of the covenant" mentioned in Exodus 24.7; this is written in the picture itself: *hic moyses edificabit altare ex lapidibus et leget populo librum federis.*
49 W. Kohler, *Die Karolingischen Miniaturen*, Berlin 1930, 1, pl. 71.
50 Alinari, n. 45 above, 38149.
51 Cf. "What did the Holy Blessed One do? He extended his right hand and took hold of Isaac's head", *Yalkut*, Genesis, 101; see also *Pirke de Rabbi Eliezer*, 31, and David Luria ibid. 40.68. Cf. also "And the King of Glory extended his right hand and saved him from the fiery oven", *Pirke*, 26, and Luria, ibid.
52 The "hand of God" appears often in Ezekiel. See, for example, Ezekiel 37. 1; 40.1.

the rule "for no man shall see Me and live" (Ex. 33. 20). From Scripture, the hand found its way into the Aggadah: "He prayed and there emerged the figure of a hand reaching out to him the leg of a golden table," (Taan. 25a); and from the Aggadah it passed into visual representation. An interesting detail in all of these pictures is that the hand is always a right hand, in accord with the phrase *mimino eshdath lamo* (Deut. 33. 2) as understood by the Vulgate: *in dextera ejus ignea lex* ("in his right hand was a fiery law").

The giving of the Law may also have been depicted in Dura Europos, in a picture that has been partly obliterated,[53] and which has been given a variety of interpretations by scholars. In any event, in the light of what we have seen so far, Kraeling erred by filling in the picture with two Tablets in Moses' hand;[54] a scroll would seem to be the proper completion of this picture. Another picture from Dura Europos shows a bearded man reading from a parchment,[55] and there are some who take this too to be Moses.

This surprising deviation from the biblical text — "When he finished speaking with him on Mount Sinai, He gave Moses the two Tablets of the Pact, stone tablets inscribed by the finger of God"(Ex. 31. 18) — is readily understood once we bear in mind that the ancients were neither historians nor archeologists. They depicted things as they themselves saw them and did not look for historical truth. That was a general phenomenon, but we will limit our examples of it to Dura Europos.

The Ark of the Covenant appears there in several pictures as the Holy Ark of the synagogue[56] (the chest in which the scrolls of the Law are kept) even though the description of the Ark in Exodus is quite detailed. Furthermore, the clothing shown belongs to the time and place of the synagogue, and there is no attempt to portray clothing appropriate to the biblical era and geographical setting. Solomon's Temple and the Tabernacle are drawn in Hellenistic style, without any account taken of what is said about them in the Bible. On the picture we referred to above, Sukenik correctly commented: "The picture shows Moses descending from Mount Sinai, his face radiant. In his hand he holds a scroll, not stone tablets. Just as the painter dressed him in

53   Sukenik, n. 47 above, p. 68, fig. 23.
54   C. Kraeling, *The Excavations at Dura Europos*, Final report, VIII, Part I, The Synagogue, Yale 1956, p. 230, fig. 60.
55   Sukenik, n. 47 above, p. 67, pl. 7.
56   Kraeling, n. 54 above, p. 98; Goodenough, n. 8 above, vol. 4, p. 115.

PLATE 6

a. "The Giving of the Law", miniature from the Vivian Bible

b. "The Giving of the Law", bronze panel from the door of San Zeno, Verona

c. "The Giving of the Law", wooden panel from the door of Santa Sabina, Rome

PLATE 7

a. "The Giving of the Law", capital of a column from the Doges' Palace, Venice

b. Beato Angelico, "Moses", from "The Community of
the Prophets", Orvieto

c. Andrea di Buonaiuto, "Moses", from "The
Victory of Thomas Aquinas", Florence

PLATE 8

b. Ambrogio Lorenzetti, "Moses", from "Entrance of Jesus into the Temple", Florence

a. Domenico di Niccolo , "Moses", mosaic from the floor of the Cathedral of Siena

PLATE 9

a. "The Giving of the Law", relief from the baptismal font in San Frediano, Lucca

b. Lorenzo Ghiberti, "The Giving of the Law", bronze panel from the door of Baptistery, Florence

PLATE 10

a. Justus van Gand, "Moses", Urbino

b. Cosimo Tura, "The Madonna and Child",
London

c. Raphael, "Moses", from "The Dispute
on the Sacrament", Rome

PLATE 11

a. "A Group of Augustine's Pupils", miniature from ms. of "De Civitate Dei",
Florence

b. "The Synaogue", statue on the facade of
Nôtre Dame, Paris

c. "The Giving of the Second Tablets",
miniature from the "Bible Moralisée"

PLATE 12

Guido Reni, "Moses", Museo Borghese, Rome

PLATE 13

a. The Tables of the Law on the Ark of the Synagogue, Conegliano Veneto, now in Jerusalem

b. The Ark of the Law, the Synagogue, Carmagnola

c. Title-page of the "Rules of the Levantine Fraternity" of Venice

garments of his own time, so too did he place a parchment scroll in his hand, for in his time that is what the Law was written on".[57] Since the sacred object they were familiar with, the object that contains and concretizes the Law, was the scroll, when they came to depict the giving of the Law they naturally showed it as a scroll, rather than as stone tablets, which for them could only have been an historical reconstruction without any meaning.

A further impetus to picture the giving of the Law in this way undoubtedly lies in the fact that, according to the literal text of the Bible, Moses gave the people the Tablets he had received from God as well as the Book of the Law that he wrote at His behest.[58] The distance between "received from His hand" and "wrote at His behest" is not great — and certain verses from the prophets that speak of a scroll have in fact been interpreted as alluding to the giving of the Law.[59] One such verse is from Ezekiel (2. 9): "As I looked there was a hand stretched out to me, holding a written scroll". Another is from Zechariah (5. 1): "I looked up again, and I saw a flying scroll". But a real key to understanding the pictures we have mentioned is found in a midrash that seeks to reconcile the biblical text, which speaks of Tablets, and the popular conception, which imagines a scroll. A homily by Joshua b. Nehemiah says of the tablets: "They were miraculous objects: capable of being rolled up, but made of sapphire".[60]

Hence, the scroll gained the status of a sacred symbol among Jews, and it is as such that we find it in many Jewish drawings. As late as the Nüremberg Haggadah the giving of the Law is still depicted with Moses standing atop a mountain holding a Torah scroll in his hand.[61]

---

57   Sukenik, n. 47 above, p. 67.
58   See, for example, the beginning of Nahmanides' commentary on the Pentateuch.
59   Eruv. 21a.
60   *Canticles Rabbah*, 5. 12, Pesaro edition, 1519.
61   According to David Kaufmann (*REJ*, 38, 1899, pp. 74–102) the illumination in this Haggadah is not derivative from what was contemporary Christian art. He calls this "une deuxième exemplaire de la Haggada de Nüremberg", and describes the illustration of the giving of the Torah in the following terms: "Au pied du mont, Moïse agenouillé, les mains croisées, dans l'attitude de la prière. Sur l'haut de la montagne, Moïse debut déploie la Tora, dont les rouleaux sont terminés en boules dorées; elle est ouverte à la section du Décalogue" (ibid., p. 99).

A picture of this sort also appears in the Nüremberg Haggadah. It seems to me that the man at the foot of the mountain is not a second picture of Moses, but of Joshua, who "stayed at the bottom of the mountain", according to Ibn Ezra (ad Ex.

The scroll as symbol passed from the Jews to the Christians,[62] even though their Scriptures were in the form of a book, not a scroll. That explains its presence in the pictures we have mentioned above. Interestingly, as late as the thirteenth century, in "The Baptistry" (San Giovanni Church) in Florence, in the mosaics of "The Creation of Adam", and "The Creation of Eve", which still show a Byzantine influence, the Creator is depicted with a scroll in His hand.[63]

There are Byzantine works of art, however, in which the Tablets appear as tablets, and not as a scroll. That is so in a miniature from the Bible of Leo the Patrician (Vatican) depicting the giving of the Law, which is from approximately the tenth century:[64] the same hand that appears in the previously mentioned pictures, here holds out a rectangular tablet to Moses — while Moses receives it with his garment covering his outstretched hand, for fear that the sacred object might touch his bare flesh.[65] This detail also appears on the Santa Sabina

---

24. 13; 32. 17). Christian art often depicted him that way. (A figure at the bottom of the mountain apart from the rest of the people also appears in the giving of the Law as depicted in the Sarajevo Haggadah, and he is Joshua). In one Haggadah described by Moïse Schwab (ms. 1388, Bibliothèque Nationale, Paris, *REJ*, 45, [1912], pp. 112–132), Moses is said to be shown with marble Tablets in his left hand. The photograph accompanying the article is not clear, and it is hard to judge by it, but the possibility exists that he is holding not tablets, but a parchment scroll.

62   Goodenough, n.8 above, vol. 4, p. 144, n. 332, fig. 116.
63   Alinari, n. 45 above, 58091.
64   A. Grabar, *Byzantine Painting*, Geneva 1953, p. 170.
65   Cf. the statement by R. Johanan (Shab. 14a; see also *Tractate Soferim*, ed. Higger, p. 136) "He who holds an unwrapped Torah scroll will be buried without shrouds". Perhaps the real reason for refraining from touching the Torah scroll is its sanctity, just as Moses, shown in these pictures, did not touch the Tablets of the Law because of their sanctity, and "what applies to the Tablets applies to every holy book" (Maimonides, *Hilkhot Sefer Torah*, 10:10). Apart from R. Johanan's statement, the ruling of contamination is meant to prevent direct contact with sacred writings, because they "make the hands unclean" (M.Yadayim 4: 6); it is explained there that they cause defilement because of their holiness. The reason proposed in the Gemara (Shab. 14a), having to do with storing *terumah*, is intended as a plausible substitute for the real one. The Sages preferred not to be explicit about matters of supreme sanctity as the grounds for halakhot. So, for example, they explain the practice that kohanim remove their shoes when they bless the people in the synagogue by referring to the possibility that they might be distracted by the breaking of a thong in a sandal (Sot. 40a) — when the real reason is probably the fact that the ritual recalls the ancient sanctuary, where the priests served barefoot.

door, in the miniature by Kosmas Indikopleustes, and in a memorial stone from Constantinople. Another detail in this miniature is also found in a number of other works, namely: Moses is barefoot. Here it would seem that the artists saw a parallel between the revelation at the burning bush and that on Mount Sinai.[66]

We also see rectangular Tablets in a Greek picture of Moses in the Vatican Collection.[67] And in a thirteenth-century Ashkenazi mahzor in the Bodleian Library, an angel offers two separate oblong Tablets.[68] However, Moses is not shown in that picture.

b. TWO TABLETS

Alongside the tradition that depicted the Tablets as a scroll, there developed another tradition that depicted them literally as two Tablets of rectangular form. That is what is found almost always in Italy beginning in ancient times, down through the Romanesque and Gothic periods, and up to the sixteenth century. The last, or one of the last, appearances of these rectangular Tablets is the most magnificent of them all: Michelangelo's statue "Moses". Following is a list of works of this type:

1. On a Roman sarcophagus, ancient Christian art from the fourth or fifth century.[69]
2. "The Giving of the Law" on a baptismal font in the Church of San Frediano in Lucca, twelfth century (plate 9a).[70]
3. "Moses", a statue in the cathedral in Santiago, Spain, late twelfth century.[71]

The following are from the fourteenth century:

4. "Moses" in the painting "San Tommaso" by Franceso Traini, in Pisa.[72]
5. "Moses" in the painting "Jesus Comes to the Temple" by Ambrogio Lorenzetti, in Florence (plate 8b).[73]

---

66   Sukenik, n. 47 above, p. 68.
67   Alinari, n. 45 above, 38105.
68   Z. Efron and B. Roth, *Jewish Art* (Hebrew), Tel-Aviv 1957, p. 26.
69   Alinari, n. 45 above, 29878.
70   Ibid., 18867.
71   Marques de Lozoya, *Historia del Arte Hispanico*, 1, Barcelona 1931-1934, p. 427, illus. 522.
72   Alinari, n. 45 above, 8862.
73   Ibid., 45737.

6. "Moses" in the painting "The Victory of Thomas Aquinas" by Andrea di Buonaiuto, in Florence (plate 7c).[74]

The following are from the fifteenth century:

7. "Moses" in the "The Assembly of Prophets" by Beato Angelico, in the cathedral of Orvieto (plate. 7b).
8. "The Giving of the Law" on the capital of a pillar in the Doges' Palace in Venice (plate 7a).[75]
9. "The Giving of the Law",[76] a bronze relief by Ghiberti on the door of "The Baptistry" in Florence (plate 9b).
10. "Moses", a mosaic by Domenico di Nicolò on the floor of the Cathedral in Siena (plate 8a).[77]
11. "The Giving of the Law", a relief by Bellano in the Church of Sant' Antonio in Padua.[78]
12. "The Giving of the Law", a painting by Benozzo Gozzoli in the cemetery of Pisa.[79]
13 "The Giving of the Law", a painting by Cosimo Rosselli in the Sistine Chapel in Rome.[80]

The following are from the sixteenth century:

14. "The Giving of the Law", a mosaic by Domenico Beccafumi on the floor of the cathedral in Siena.[81]
15. "Moses", a statue by Michelangelo in the Church of San Pietro in Vincoli, in Rome.[82]

In the first picture in this group (the Roman sarcophagus) we again see the hand of the Creator giving the Law to Moses. Here it is one Tablet that is given. It is conceivable that the artist's intention was to depict the two Tablets, one on the other, and therefore we see only one Tablet. The artist still refrains from depicting any more of the Creator than His hand, here too a right hand, while the left hand is extended to prevent Abraham from sacrificing Isaac. The other pictures already show a full image of the Creator.

74   Ibid., 6690.
75   Ibid., 38767.
76   Ibid., 3332.
77   Photographs, Edizioni Brogi, Florence 13472.
78   Alinari, n. 45 above, 38997.
79   Ibid., 8815.
80   Ibid., 7642.
81   Ibid., 9005, 9006.
82   *La Bibbia nel'Arte*, n. 44 above, 118.

In the relief on the baptismal font in the Church of San Frediano, where Moses is down on his knees stretching out his hand to receive the Tablet — here too we only see one Tablet. He is barefoot and keeps his hand covered with his garment, details we have already seen in other works.

Beginning with the third picture (The Santiago Cathedral), the two tablets are separated, and in most instances are each in one hand of God who is giving them, or of Moses who is receiving or holding them.

Two instances in which the Tablet has an unusual form should be noted. One is the painting by Beato Angelico (plate 7b) in which the Tablets are rectangular, each of them with a small hole near the upper edge into which Moses inserts his finger. This picture is unique in another way as well, for here the Tablets bear a Hebrew inscription, namely the beginning of the Decalogue on the left tablet (!) and the continuation on the right. The letters are distinct, but the odd shape of some of them and the way they are divided into lines indicate that the artist did not know the Hebrew alphabet. We shall return to this later.

The second special instance is the relief by Bellano (Church of Sant' Antonio in Padua) who adds two triangular extensions on the sides of the tablets, a very common detail in ancient Roman art (*tabula anseata*).

These unusual representations reinforce the notion, which in fact needs no reinforcement, that there was no fixed tradition of representing the Tablets. The artists read the biblical text and depicted the Tablets as they imagined them, usually in a simple rectangular shape, and sometimes with minor changes.

c. THE DIPTYCH

In their third manifestation the Tablets are rectangular in shape with the upper edge rounded. In that shape they appear frequently in French art. We can cite, for example, from the twelfth century:

1. "Moses and the Copper Serpent", a medallion in the window of the Church of Saint Denis.[83]
2. "Moses and the Copper Serpent", a painting on a portable altar from Stavelot.[84]
3. "Moses", a statue on the (destroyed) gateway to the Church of Saint Bénigne in Dijon.[85]

83   E. Mâle, *L'art religieux de XII siècle en France*, Paris 1928, p. 156.
84   Ibid., p. 161.
85   Ibid., p. 217.

4. "Satan Emerging from the Golden Calf", a capital from Vézelay.[86]
    Examples from the thirteenth century:
5. "The Synagogue", a statue in the cathedral of Strasbourg.[87]
6. "The Synagogue" a, statue in the cathedral of Reims.[88]
7. Miniatures in the *Bible Moralisée* (plate 11c).[89]
    From the fourteenth century:
8. "Moses", a statue by Claus Suter in "The Prophets' Well", near
    Dijon.[90]

Outside of France we find two old examples of this form of the Tablets,
both of them works of art that show French influence:
9. "The Giving of the Law", a bronze relief on a door of the Church
    of San Zeno in Verona, eleventh century (plate 6b).[91]
10. "Moses", a statue at one of the gates of the Cathedral of Burgos,
    thirteenth century.[92]

What is the origin of this form?

True, this is the usual shape of the ancient Oriental stele,[93] not only
of the Mesha Stone but also of many ancient stelae throughout the
Near East — but that is of no importance here for, as we have seen,
there is no continuous tradition from ancient times with respect to the
shape of the Tablets. It is inconceivable that medieval European artists
would use ancient Egyptian or Assyrian stelae as their model. We must
therefore seek another explanation.

---

86 Ibid., p. 371.

87 L. Réan, *L'Art religieux du moyen-âge*, Paris 1946, illus. 88.

88 A. Michel, *Histoire de l'Art*, 1, Paris 1906, p. 173.

89 Le Conte A. de Laborde, *La Bible moralisée illustrée*, 1, Paris 1911, pls. 52, 54, 55.

90 L. Réan, n. 87 above, 114b. This statue combines two approaches: Moses holds the
    Tablets in his right hand, and a scroll in his left.

91 Alinari, n. 45 above, 12664. At the bottom of the relief we see the blossoming of
    Aaron's rod, Numbers 17. 21; Aaron's rod is shown in the center, as Rashi too
    describes it, and there are a total of twelve rods, unlike what the Vulgate has:
    fueruntque virgae duodecim absque virga Aaron. The art of this church displays
    French influence; see, e.g., Mâle, n. 83 above, p. 175, n. 4. Also worthy of note here
    are the head-coverings worn by the figures in the relief — hats that were worn
    typically by the Jews of Europe.

92 De Lozoya, n. 71 above, vol. 2, p. 170, illus. 175; he notes that these works were
    influenced by French Gothic art.

93 J.B. Pritchard, *The Ancient Near East in Pictures Relating to the Old Testament*,
    Princeton 1954, illus. 246, 274, 306, 321, 447, 450, 454, 470, 475, 477, 490, 491, 493,
    499, 519.

If we compare the Tablets that appear in the works we have mentioned here with those of the previous section, we will notice another difference in addition to the change in form from simple rectangle to rectangle with rounded upper side. In the examples previously cited, the Tablets were represented as separate, such as one in each of Moses' hands, or resting one on the other; but now we find them, side by side, near each other. These two features always appear together: separated rectangular Tablets or adjacent round-topped rectangular Tablets. Furthermore, in this new form, the Tablets are not only adjacent, they are actually joined.

In the relief on the portal of the Church of San Zeno (plate 6b), God holds one tablet and Moses the other, but the Tablets remain joined. In virtually all of the works we have cited, Moses holds the Tablets in just one hand, the way one would hold an object that is of one piece. There is also a third detail: the Tablets now usually have a frame, and in statuary and reliefs there is a prominent frame around each Tablet.

All of these signs indicate that this a familiar form, namely that of the diptych.[94] The diptych originated in antiquity as two wooden tablets with waxed surfaces that were used for writing upon. The two tablets were joined together. With some variations, the diptych lasted down through the Middle Ages. In the days of the Roman Empire it was sometimes made of expensive material, such as ivory, and consuls would give it to friends as a present upon entering office. The consul's portrait or some other picture was engraved on the outer side of the two tablets of these "consular diptychs". Several dozen of these have survived, because the Church used them in the Middle Ages for binding books or for recording lists of names, such as necrologies or the names of high officials in the clergy. Alongside the ancient diptychs, the Church also made use of others, which it had artists make. These were decorated with pictures of religious subjects. In Byzantine culture the diptych served as a double picture for ritual use. In such instances, the picture was not engraved on the outer side of the tablets, but on the inner side. These sacramental diptychs later also spread to Europe, and were disseminated especially by Gothic art. From the thirteenth century

---

94   See Daremberg Saglio, *Dictionnaire des Antiquités grecques et romaines*, Paris
      1877, s.v. "Diptychon", p. 271, and s.v. "Consul", p. 1474; *Enciclopedia Italiana*,
      s.v. "Dittico"; Cabrol Leclercq, *Dictionnaire d'Archéologie Chrétienne et de
      Liturgie*, 4, Paris 1920, s.v. "Diptyque".

onwards European painting made extensive use of the diptych as the form for pictures having two compartments.

A great deal of iconographic material and important information on the Tablets of the Law in the form of diptych has been assembled by Ruth Mellinkoff.[95] She maintains that the symbol predates the twelfth century, and that it probably originated in England.[96] The earliest example known to us, she says, is in an English manuscript from Canterbury attributed to the years 1025–1050.

The origin of the diptych as the shape of the Tablets lies in its use as a writing tablet. A miniature in a manuscript of *De Civitate Dei* depicts a group of Augustine's disciples listening to their teacher,[97] holding various sorts of writing materials — books, tablets, scrolls (plate 11a). The figure third from the right holds a diptych identical in all respects with the Tablets of the Law in ancient miniatures. In depictions of the Tablets of the Law it is sometimes possible to see the hinge that joins the two pieces, as in the diptych in *De Civitate Dei*. Such hinges can be seen in a French manuscript dated about 1280.[98] Mellinkoff further informs us that Augustine in one of his works repeatedly used the Latin equivalents for *tablets* and *diptych* as interchangeable when referring to the Tablets of the Law".[99]

Waxed tablets were used for writing as late as the thirteenth century.[100] A fifteenth-century retable has been preserved in Oña, Spain, which depicts God revealing Himself to Moses and dictating the Law to him; Moses is writing it down with a quill on a diptych.[101]

It is thus not at all surprising that artists began to depict the Tablets of the Law in the form of a diptych, for the two are closely related: there

95   Ruth Mellinkoff, "The Round-topped Tablets of the Law: Sacred Symbol and Emblem of Evil", *Journal of Jewish Art*, 1 (1974), pp. 28–43.

96   Ibid., p. 30. See the pictures of Jews wearing the Jewish badge in the form of the Tablets of the Law in manuscripts from the thirteenth century, ibid., illus. 19, and *Encyclopaedia Judaica*, 4, col. 63.

97   Parchment manuscript, eleventh-twelfth centuries, England, School of Canterbury; Firenze, *Biblioteca Laurenziana, Pluteo*, 12. 17.

98   Mellinkoff, n. 95 above, illus. 1; *Encyclopaedia Judaica*, 12, col 400.

99   Mellinkoff, n. 95 above, p. 36. In the Mishnah, a diptych is called a *pinkas* with "two *levaḥim*". On the plural form of *luaḥ*, see E. Kimron in *Leshonenu*, 40 (1976), p. 147.

100 M. Cohen, *La Grande invention de l'Ecriture*, 2, Paris, 1958, p. 157.

101 See Chandler Rathfon Post, *A History of Spanish Painting*, 5, Cambridge, Mass., 1934, fig. 109.

are two Tablets, just as there are two panels to the diptych; writing is inscribed on the Tablets, and the diptych is an object often written upon; what is more, the diptych served as a sacred object in Church and as such it was fitting that it also serve as another sacred symbol. And above all, this was a common form and almost naturally presented itself to the eyes of the artists.

The diptych was made at first of two rectangular boards, but even in ancient diptychs the upper side of each board often tended to be rounded;[102] or the tablet itself was rectangular, but the picture on it was contained in a round-topped frame.[103] Needless to say, the gothic diptych bore the pointed arch characteristic of that style.[104]

That was the shape that became the new format for the Tablets of the Law. In time this format overcame all others for depicting the Tablets, and from the sixteenth century onwards it is almost impossible to find Tablets represented in any other fashion. After its origin in the diptych was forgotten, this form came to be considered the "true" form of the Tablets, such that even when the two Tablets were depicted as separated, each of them was given the form of a round-topped rectangle.

This form is so widespread and well-known that there is no need to cite examples./We shall mention only Raphael's "Disputa" in the Vatican, in which Moses is shown holding dipytch-shaped Tablets[105] (plate 10c). But before that, Justus van Gand painted the Tablets in that form in the picture "Moses",[106] which is in the Palazzo Ducale in Urbino (plate 10a). The Commandments appear on those Tablets in Hebrew letters in the form customary among Jews, and as far as I know it is the earliest such example in Christian art. The painting was done around 1475.

102 See, for example, W.F. Volbach, *Elfenbeinarbeiten der Spätantike und des frühen Mittelalters*, Mainz 1952, figs. 1, 2, 38, 51, 52, 62.

103 Ibid., figs. 6, 16, 21, 36, 40, 43, 58, 63, 64, 66, 109, 137, 146, 147, 150, 153, 154, 157, 252.

104 See, e.g., Victoria and Albert Museum, *Catalogue of Carvings in Ivory*, London 1929, part 2, pls. 1, 25.

105 There are Hebrew letters on the Tablets, some of them faulty, which do not make sense. By contrast, in Raphael's "Isaiah", in the Church of Sant' Agostino in Rome, a biblical verse is clearly legible. In the "Transfiguration" (Vatican) Raphael painted Moses to the right of Jesus, with the Tablets in his hand. Only a corner of the Tablets is visible, but it can be seen that the top is rounded and that the Tablets have "ears"; a long thread extends from the "ear" that is seen in the picture.

106 *La Bibbia nell' Arte*, n. 44 above, 226.

The diptych also appears in pictures of the Tablets with certain slight changes of form. In some works we see only one round-topped Tablet — presumably a closed diptych.[107] But odder than that are those pictures in which the Tablets appear as several round-topped tablets, joined along one of the long edges, usually five in number like the number of books of the Law. We have moved from diptych to polyptych! Tablets in this form have been placed in the hand of a sculptured woman who represents the Synagogue on the facade of the Church of Nôtre Dame in Paris (plate 11b) and are shown in that form in a fourteenth-century manuscript of the history of the world by Rudolf Mems.[108]

The diptych form also penetrated Hebrew iconography. In the Birds' Head Haggadah (Southern Germany, c.1300) we see Moses receiving the law in diptych form from the hand of God, and handing it over to the people in the form of a five-panel polyptych.[109] On page 30 of the *Sarajevo Haggadah* Moses is standing on Mount Sinai holding a diptych — and thus the "new style" of the diptych encounters the old iconographic tradition of rectangular Tablets, which are depicted there on page 32, as we have noted above.

3. THE TABLETS AS A SYMBOL OF JUDAISM

Among the examples mentioned in the previous section were two similar sculptures, examples of thirteenth-century French art, which adorn the cathedrals of Strasbourg and of Reims, and symbolize the Synagogue in the form of a woman whose appearance clearly expresses dejection and humiliation. A veil covers her eyes, which refuse to see the true faith, and she leans with one hand on the broken staff of a banner, while in the other hand she holds the Tablets of the Law. In contrast to her there stands another woman, the Catholic Church, upright, with a crown on her head, in one hand a cross and in the other the chalice of the Eucharist.[110] It was thus that the Christians made the Tablets into a distinct symbol of Judaism. But even earlier, Henry III,

---

107 Mellinkoff, n. 95 above, p. 34.
108 *Synagoga*, catalogue of exhibition of Jewish objects held in Regensburg, 1960–1961, no. D 152.
109 Narkiss, n. 17 above, p. 96, pl. 28.
110 In addition to the pictures cited in the previous notes, see the pictures and explanations in *The Legacy of Israel*, n. 34 above, figs. 2, 3. This subject was very common in the Middle Ages, and is found in other sculptures beside those mentioned here. See P. Hildenfinger, *REJ*, 47 (1903), pp. 187–196.

who ruled England from 1216 to 1272, issued a decree in the early years
of his reign about the special badge Jews had to wear on their clothing:
"Every Jew will bear on his chest on his outer garment, wherever he
goes or rides, both inside the city and outside, the shape of two white
tablets made either of linen or of parchment".[111] And Edward I, in the
third year of his reign, 1275, ordered "that every one of them above the
age of seven will wear on his outer garment a badge of yellow cloth in
the shape of two tablets, six fingers long, and three fingers wide".[112]

We see, then, that the Tablets of the Law were used as a symbol of
Judaism by Christians several hundred years before they were used as
such by the Jews themselves. There are two reasons for this. First, as we
have already indicated, Jewish tradition did not tend to regard the
Tablets and the Commandments as an epitome or symbol of the faith.
Secondly, and more importantly, there had been no inner need within
Judaism for a particular form or object to symbolize it. As Goodenough
has observed with respect to the Greek and Roman period he studied,[113]
Jewish symbols were introduced mainly as imitations of Gentile
symbols. And we ourselves are witness to the fact that it was only with
the establishment of the State of Israel, taking its place among the
nations of the world, that the need was felt for a symbol (the menorah)
on official documents and government buildings comparable to that of
other countries. The only reason, too, that a state flag was created is
that all other countries have a flag!

The statues in Strasbourg are very instructive on this point. After the
artist placed the cross and the chalice in the hands of one of the figures
as symbols of Christianity, he needed something to place in the hands
of the other, to symbolize Judaism. The Tablets of the Law answered
his purpose.

Above we mentioned the Nüremberg Haggadah, in which Moses is
shown on Mount Sinai, a Torah scroll in hand. Other medieval

111 Tovey, *Anglia Judaica*, Oxford 1738, p. 79: *quod omnes Judaei deferant in
     superiori indumento suo ubicumque ambulaverint aut equitaverint, infra villam
     vel extra, quasi duas tabulas albas in pectore, factas de lineo panno vel de
     percameno.*
112 Ibid., pp. 202, 205: *quoddam signum deferat, ad modum duarum tabularum.*
     Another edict of Edward I decrees: *quod omnes Judei regni nostri tabulas deferant
     in indumentibus suis exterioribus.* See: B.L. Abrahams, *JQR*, 8, p. 360.
113 Goodenough, n. 8 above, vol. 4, p. 67.

haggadot should also be mentioned. As we have noted, the Sarajevo Haggadah, which was produced in Spain in the thirteenth or fourteenth century, includes a picture of Moses atop Mount Sinai holding two Tablets in the form of a diptych.[114] The Bezalel Museum in Jerusalem has a Haggadah written in the Rhine region in the fourteenth century in which (typical of Ashkenazi haggadot of that period) a bird's beak replaces human facial features in pictures of human beings. In this Haggadah the giving of the Law is depicted as a hand extended from the sky giving Moses a half-closed diptych,[115] that is, two round-topped rectangular Tablets joined along one edge and somewhat overlapping, with Moses handing the people five Tablets of the Law, that is, a five-panelled polyptych.

The Tablets first appear as a symbol among Jews, however, only in the fifteenth century, and then on Arks in Italy. The history of the symbol is intertwined with that of the synagogue Ark. Up to the end of the Middle Ages, Arks resembled chests that were used for everyday purposes. The most beautiful and elaborate Arks were very much like the chests in the homes of the wealthy and the nobility, differing from them only in the biblical verses decorating them.[116] The Ark was not yet an architectural element of the synagogue. It was a furnishing — no more than that. What *was* an architectural element was the bimah, the place from which the Law was read.[117] The Holy Ark gained in importance and became a distinctive architectural element of the synagogue only during the Italian Renaissance.[118] It was then that the need was felt to adorn the Ark with a sign that would declare its essence and purpose. The Tablets of the Law were enlisted for that.

Another reason for the link between the Ark and the Tablets is the parallel between the synagogue as a "minor sanctuary"[119] and the ancient Temple. Since the place for keeping the Scrolls of the Law

114 D.H. Müller and J. Schlosser, *Die Haggadah von Sarajevo*, Vienna 1898, vol. of illustrations, p. 30.
115 D. Goldschmidt, *Haggadah shel Pesah*, Jerusalem 1960, pl. 14.
116 See notes 32–34 above. We can add to that list the Ark from Modena, dated 1472 (*Legacy of Israel*, no. 34 above, fig. 65), and many others; this tradition is also reflected in later Arks, such as that from Siena of the seventeenth century; see S.U. Nahon, *Israel Argosy*, 6, Jerusalem 1958, p. 128. See also G. Loukomski, *Jewish Art in European Synagogues*, London 1947, p. 31.
117 *Legacy of Israel*, n. 34 above, figs. 10, 43, 53.
118 Jacob Pinkerfeld, *Italian Synagogues* (Hebrew), Jerusalem 1954, p. 65.
119 Ezek. 11. 16; Meg. 29a.

(what the Mishnah calls the *tebhah*)[120] is called the "Holy Ark",[121] after the golden chest made by Moses; and the curtain hanging in front of it is given the biblical name *parokhet* — then it follows that the Tablets of the Law should be inside it, and if not them, at least a representation of them.

A Holy Ark from Urbino,[122] which is now in the Benguiat Collection in the United States, bears the date 1451. The Tablets are depicted on the inner side of its doors. It is certainly not by mere chance that this early example of Jewish Tablets of the Law comes from the same city where we found one of the earliest examples of Tablets by Christians inscribed in Hebrew, namely, the Tablets in the picture of Moses by Justus van Gand (plate 10a). The painting was made but twenty years later than the Ark, and the letters are of the same form in both. It is reasonable to surmise, then, that this Ark served as model for the Christian artist.

If we return now to the writing on the Tablets by Beato Angelico (plate 7b), it is evident that this artist did not have such a model to copy from; hence the uncertainty of his lettering. This would seem to suggest that when Angelico, who died in 1455, painted that picture, Jewish examples were not yet available, or were so rare that he did not have occasion to find one. Subsequently, Christian painters would write the Commandments in Hebrew, and the Tablets in synagogues served them as models, or else they asked to be taught by a Christian scholar. In the first instance, they divided the Commandments according to the Jewish tradition; in the second instance, according to Catholic practice — about which more below.

The Commandments are also written on the inner side of the doors of the fifteenth-century Ark from Leghorn, which resembles the Urbino Ark. They are also written that way on the Ark that was in the Great Synagogue of Leghorn (end of sixteenth century, destroyed in World War II); in an Ark from Sermide[123] (1543, in the form of a *piyyut*, two rhymes per Commandment); in an Ark from the Scuola Cases in

---

120 In the Mishnah the word has both a sacred and a secular meaning.
121 II Chron. 35. 3. On the holiness of the Ark in the synagogue, and the Karaites' opposition to it, see the texts cited by Lieberman in *Sheqi'in*, Jerusalem 1939, p. 9; and in *Midreshei Teman*, Jerusalem 1940, pp. 24–25.
122 Kayser-Schoenberger, n. 33 above, p. 22, fig. 1; see also U. Nahon, in the Jewish-Italian weekly *Israel*, Adar 5719.
123 S. U. Nahon, n. 116 above, p. 127.

Mantua (latter half of eighteenth century);[124] and in an Ark from Conegliano Veneto,[125] in which the Tablets also appear atop the front (plate 13a). It is only in the sixteenth century that we find the Tablets crowning the Ark. If we examine Jacob Pinkerfeld's book on synagogues in Italy, and take the date of each synagogue's construction as the date of its Ark (which is not always the case) we will find that Tablets of the Law crowned a Holy Ark in 1515 in the Scuola Catalana in Roma,[126] and later in the Luzzatto Academy in Venice (1538);[127] "Il Tempio" Synagogue in Rome (before 1550);[128] the Sephardi synagogue in Padua (c. 1550);[129] Scuola Spagnola in Venice (1555);[130] and the synagogue in Casale Monferrato (1595).[131] The practice, however, was far from being general.

Summarizing the material in Pinkerfeld's study, which describes synagogues built over a period of four centuries — from the beginning of the sixteenth to the end of the nineteenth — we find the Tablets in the pictures of 11 Arks,[132] but there are 15 Arks without the Tablets on them.[133] As for the shape of the Tablets, it is in most instances the usual round-topped form, except for four instances in which they are given the form of a book[134] (that is, two rectangles) or are delimited by non-straight lines.[135]

The Tablets passed as symbol from the Ark to all other sacred objects. We see them first of all embroidered on the *parokhet* and the *kapporet* (a short curtain hung above and in front of the *parokhet*) — that is, still in association with the Holy Ark — and later, on Torah scroll covers, crowns, finials, trays, amulet cases, *mizrah* pictures and the title pages of holy books.[136]

---

124   Ibid., p. 130.
125   Ibid., p. 126; this Ark is now in the Italian Synagogue in Jerusalem.
126   Pinkerfeld, n. 118 above, fig. 22.
127   Ibid., fig. 12.
128   Ibid., fig. 21.
129   Ibid., fig. 36.
130   Ibid., fig. 13.
131   Ibid., fig. 45.
132   Ibid., figs. 12, 13, 21, 22, 26, 30, 36, 40, 45, 61, 80.
133   Ibid., figs. 5, 7, 11, 18, 25, 50, 51, 53, 54, 57, 65, 66, 73, 75, 79.
134   Ibid., fig. 21.
135   Ibid., figs. 30, 40; see also the Ark from Cento; Nahon, n. 123 above, p. 137.
136   Many examples can be found in Kayser–Schoenberger, n. 33 above, and in issues of *Mitteilungen der Gesellschaft zur Erforschung jüdischer Kunstdenkmäler zu Frankfurt a/M.*

Along with the influence of Italian art on other parts of Europe, the form of Italian synagogues spread to other parts of the Diaspora.[137] The Tablets as symbol were also copied everywhere, until they took their place throughout the Jewish world. They were found all over, from the Sephardi synagogue in London (1701)[138] to the wooden synagogues of East Europe.[139] Examining Loukomski's book on synagogue art in East Europe, as we did Pinkerfeld's work, we find the Tablets of the Law on 25 Arks,[140] and only 19 Arks without them.[141] As for the situation today — we have commented on that at the beginning of this essay.

The reader will find many pictures of Holy Arks from Italy in the book by Umberto Nahon on Jewish ritual objects from Italy now found in Israel.[142] There are Holy Arks without the Tablets, others with the Ten Commandments written on the inner side of the Ark doors, others that are crowned by the Tablets, and some which bear the Commandments on both the inside and the exterior.

4. *"ENGRAVED ON THE TABLETS"*

Let us now consider the form of the Commandments themselves, as they appear on the Tablets both in Christian art and among Jews. In addressing this question, we must first note that the biblical passage containing the Decalogue (Ex. 20. 2–17) does not divide of itself into ten separate, distinct statements; even less does it fall into ten "imperatives" (*praecepta,* "Commandments"). Buber, for example, shows how it is possible to find 12 commandments here, and even more than that can be listed.[143] To reach the number 10 it is necessary to group verses together. And since that can be done in a variety of ways, a number of different approaches have developed. The main points of disagreement are the following:

---

137   See Loukomski, n. 116 above, p. 34.
138   *Legacy of Israel*, n. 34 above, fig. 76.
139   *Ha-enşiklopedya ha-ivrit*, s.v. "Bet Keneset", p. 652.
140   Loukomski, n. 34 above, pp. 32, 40, 94, 108, 125, 127, 129, 130, 131, 132, 133, 134, 152, 154, 156, 158, 159, 160, 165, 168.
141   Ibid., pp. 35, 67, 90, 95, 98, 106, 108, 109, 151, 153, 155, 156, 157, 158, 159, 160, 165, 168.
142   S.U. Nahon, *Italian Arks and Synagogue Furnishings in Israel* (Hebrew), Tel Aviv 1970. Some of the Arks mentioned in notes 123 et seq. also appear here.
143   M. Buber, *Moses*, transl. into English, New York, Harper and Row, 1958, p. 132.

1. Is verse 2, "I am the LORD..." a Commandment in and of itself? Or is it the introduction to the others?
2. Do the precepts, "You shall not have...", "You shall not make...", and "You shall not bow down..." (3–6) constitute one Commandment, or separate Commandments?
3. Do the last two precepts, "You shall not covet" (17) constitute one or two Commandments?

Three principal ways of dividing the Commandments have developed over time:

1. The accepted Jewish division.
2. The division made by Philo, and by Calvin, according to which "You shall not make" is the Second Commandment.
3. The division of Augustine, and following him, of the Catholic Church, according to which "You shall not swear falsely..." is the Second Commandment, and "You shall not covet" divides into two Commandments.[144]

There is one uniform tradition on this in the Talmud and Midrash, reaching from the Tannaim to the late Midrashim.[145] It will therefore suffice if we cite the earliest of them which is the *Mekhilta (Baḥodesh* 8; ed. Lauterbach, II, p. 262):

> How were the Ten Commandments arranged? Five on one tablet and five on the other. On the one tablet was written: "I am the

---

144 B. Jacob, "The Decalogue", *JQR*, ns, XIV (1923–24), pp. 141–187.

145 The division of the Commandments is dealt with in Yer. Ber. I:5; Leviticus Rabbah, 24. 5; *Tanḥuma*, ed. Buber, *Qedoshim*, 3; *Pesiqta Rabbati*, 20–21; *Tanna debe Eliyahu*, 24; *Targum Yerushalmi* on the Pentateuch; *Midrash 'Aseret ha-Dibberot*; and *Pesiqta Ḥadata*. Louis Ginzberg, *Legends of the Jews*, p. 43, n. 234, states that this is the only division known to rabbinic literature. See also Saadiah's *Midrash on the Ten Commandments*, quoted by Kasher in *Torah Shelemah*. This tradition is reflected in several passages of *Piyyute Yannai*, Berlin 1938, pp. 369, lines 45, 57; p. 372, line 136; page 374, line 1, and elsewhere. Ibn Ezra alludes to a different approach in his comment on Exodus 20. 1: "Some say that 'I am the LORD' is not one of the Ten Commandments. Of these, some count 'You shall not have' as the First Commandment, and 'You shall not make' as the Second; while others (keep these two together but) count 'You shall not covet your neighbor's house' as the Ninth, and 'You shall not covet your neighbor's wife' as the Tenth". When Ibn Ezra gets to the Decalogue in Deuteronomy, he makes his own position clear: "It appears to me that 'I am the LORD' introduces the One who commands... and that the number Ten is arrived at by separating 'You shall not covet your neighbor's house' from 'You shall not covet your neighbor's wife' ".

LORD thy God." And opposite it on the other tablet was written: "Thou shalt not murder."...On the one tablet was written: "Thou shalt have no other god." And opposite it on the other tablet was written: "Thou shalt not commit adultery." ...On the one tablet was written: "Thou shalt not take." And opposite it on the other tablet was written: "Thou shalt not steal." ... On the one tablet was written: "Remember the sabbath day to keep it holy." And opposite it on the other tablet was written: "Thou shalt not bear false witness." ...On the one tablet was written: "Honor thy father," etc. And opposite it on the other tablet was written: "Thou shalt not covet thy neighbor's wife".

Apart from this division, the Sages also arranged this chapter in another way, distinguishing between what was said by God directly to Israel and what was said by God to Moses and repeated by Moses to Israel. The root of that, apparently, is the use of the first person in the first group, as opposed to the third person in the rest of the Commandments. On that, the Talmud says: "Rabbi Ishmael taught: 'I am the LORD your God' and 'You shall not have' — these we heard from the mouth of the Almighty" (Hor. 8a; see also *Sifre Numbers*, 111).

So among the Sages we see a division into Ten Commandments, and a subdivision into two groupings.

Philo and Josephus have a different division.[146] They seem to take "I am the LORD" as a preface, and "You shall not have" as the First Commandment, and therefore for them "You shall not make" is the Second Commandment.

It is surprising that the division of the Hebrew text into closed and open portions does not correspond to the division presented in the Midrash. The section from "I am the LORD" to "My commandments" is continuous (possibly reflecting the teaching of R. Ishmael); while "You shall not covet your neighbor's house" and "You shall not covet your neighbor's wife are separated.[147]

---

146 It is clear that for Philo, "I am the LORD ... you shall have no other" is the First Commandment (*De decalogo*, 53–65); and "You shall not make" is the Second (ibid., 66–81). This also holds good in his survey of the first Tablet (ibid., 51) and in his heading for Book I of *De legibus*, and ibid., III, 13–20, and IV, 21 ff. Josephus follows the same pattern (*Ant.*, III 91–92, and 138).

147 To be sure, Kittel's *Biblia Hebraica*, based on ms. Leningrad, does not show the two precepts "You shall not covet" as separate paragraphs; nor do the early

As for cantillation signs, they present a complex problem.[148] As we know, the Commandments in present-day Pentateuchs have two sets of cantillations, called "upper" and "lower". According to S. Pinsker, this is a combination of two different traditions, the upper being Babylonian, the lower, Palestinian. In other words, one is "Eastern" and one "Western".[149]

In addition to these two, there is also a third set of signs, such that the word *'avadim* (verse 2) is triply noted. One symbol, the *silluq*, is appropriate to a reading of the passage verse by verse, without attempting to create ten statements. A second symbol, *revi'a*, fits the approach according to which the section is read as a continuity up to "My commandments", in accord with the open and closed portion markings and the teaching of R. Ishmael. The third symbol, an *etnah*, indicates that the verse ends with "before Me". According to this third cantillation style, "You shall not make" begins a new verse, and it thus accords with Philo's division of the Commandments.

According to Porat,[150] Philo's division reflects the Tiberian identification of verses, while the division generally accepted among Jews follows the Babylonian verse arrangement.

As for the Christians, since the time of Augustine they have accepted a division according to which everything from "I am the LORD" to "My commandments" comprises one Commandment, making "You shall not swear" the Second Commandment, and splitting the double "You shall not covet" into two prohibitions (in accord with the open and closed portion division!). Augustine justified this arrangement, and pointed out the relationship obtaining among the first three Commandments, and that among the subsequent seven. The first

   editions of Maimonides' *Code* (*Hilkhot Sefer Torah*, VIII), although the separation has been added in later editions. *Minhat Shai* says they *should* be written as separate paragraphs, and suggests that this is what led the Church to treat them as two separate Commandments.

148 See *Minhat Shai*; also Geiger, *Urschrift und Uebersetzungen der Bibel*, Breslau 1857, p. 373, n. 8; W. Heidenheim, *The Pentateuch Explained* (Hebrew), Roedelheim 1815, note at the end of Exodus; Pinsker, *Analects of Antiquity* (Hebrew), Vienna 1860, pp. 35–37; idem, *Introduction to Vocalization* (Hebrew), Vienna 1863, p. 46. Cf. Hebrew Bible, ed. C.D. Ginsburg, London 1926.

149 In a Genizah fragment (T.S. D 1/46, Cambridge) the Commandments appear twice, each time with a different set of cantillation signs, corresponding to Ginsburg's division. I owe this information to Prof. Yisrael Yeivin.

150 M.Y. Porat, *Bet Miqra*, I (1956), pp. 100–102.

group refer to the relationship between man and God, and the others between man and his fellow man. For that reason, Catholic tradition held that the first three Commandments were written on one Tablet, and the subsequent seven on the other.[151] This view was undoubtedly influenced by Jesus' statement in Matthew (22. 36) that the foremost commandment is "Thou shall love the LORD thy God", and that the second is "Thou shalt love thy neighbor as thyself". The Catholics made the two Tablets parallel to these two commandments.

That was the practice among Catholics and Lutherans. The division followed by the Greek church, the Calvinists and the Anglicans, however, is the same as Philo's.[152]

Finally, mention must be made of the revolutionary approach that finds the Decalogue not here but in Exodus 34. 14–26. That is the view of a fifth-century Greek writer; of Goethe, Wellhausen and many others after him.[153]

After the artist had painted or sculpted the Tablets, and was about to write the Commandments on them, he first had to decide which tradition he would follow. He would also have to decide how he would shorten them, for he did not have space enough to write them out in full. Sometimes he would leave the Tablets blank, or write strange imaginary signs on them that were meant to signify Hebrew;[154] or simply write a general inscription, such as *Lex Domini*.[155] Some of the first artists to deal with the subject wrote the Commandments in Latin, sometimes in keeping with Augustine's division, but without paying precise attention to the correct formulation. They adopted one of two possibilities: either they wrote on each Tablet the beginning of the Commandments belonging to it, or continued on the second Tablet what they had begun on the first. The first option was taken by Traini in his painting of San Tommaso.[156] He wrote on the first tablet: *Non adorabis deos alienos*, and on the second tablet: *Honora patrem et*

151 Augustine in Migne, *Patrologia Latina*, III, p. 620, 644; ibid., Rabanus Maurus, CVIII, pp. 95 ff., 863 f.
152 *Encyclopaedia Britannica*, s.v. "Decalogue"; see also *Encyclopaedia Espasa*, 17, p. 1181; and *Encyclopaedia Miqra'it*, s.v. *dibberot*.
153 Ibid., loc. cit.; Buber, *Moses*, n. 143 above, p. 119; Wellhausen, *Prolegomena*, New York 1957, p. 393.
154 See plate 8b herein, and n. 73 above.
155 See n. 84 above.
156 See n. 72 above.

matrem. Non occides. Non furtum facies, etc. The second course was followed by Andrea di Buonaiuto:[157] On the first tablet, he wrote: *Non habebis deos alienos non facies tibi sculptile neque omnem similitu*, and on the second Tablet, continued: *dinem quae est in caelo de super et quae in terra deorsum non adorabis neque coles.*

It is interesting to note that in his picture of Moses on the mosaic in the cathedral of Siena, Domenico di Niccolò wrote on the Tablets the verse (Ex. 34. 14) regarded by Wellhausen and his followers as the beginning of the Decalogue.[158] On the first Tablet we read, *noli adorare deum alienum*, and on the second: *domini zelotes nomen ejus Deus est aemulator.*

We find another deviation in the Greek picture of Moses in the Vatican Collection.[159] Here Moses holds the Tablets one atop the other, such that it is possible to read only one of them, and there we find in Greek the verse from Deuteronomy 6.5, in keeping with the words from Matthew referred to above.

By distinction from these examples, there are instances in which the Commandments are written in Hebrew. We have already mentioned the painting by Beato Angelico,[160] and that by Justus van Gand[161] — the first to show a faithful copy of the Hebrew text. That form is also found on the Tablets of the Law adorning the chair on which Jesus' mother is seated in a painting by Cosimo Tura (1430–1495).[162] Other instances in which we find the Hebrew letters are the painting "The Religions" in the Library in Venice,[163] and "The Golden Calf"[164] in the Doges' Palace, also in Venice. The Hebrew version is also found in Rembrandt's painting "Moses":[165] Here the second Tablet begins with "You shall not murder", and the Commandment "You shall not covet" is not split into two. In Venice the Commandments in St. Moses' Church are written in Hebrew almost in their entirety.[166] There the

157   Plate 7c herein.
158   Plate 8a herein.
159   See n. 67 above.
160   Plate 7b.
161   Plate 10a.
162   Plate 10b, National Gallery, London.
163   By G. De Mio, photo G. Böhm, Venice, no. 1210.
164   By Andrea Celesti, Alinari, n. 45 above, 18271.
165   Staatliches Museum, Berlin.
166   Alinari, n. 45 above, 18511.

second Tablet begins with "Honor your father", in keeping with the Catholic tradition. In Guido Reni's (1575–1642) "Moses" [167] the second Tablet also begins with "Honor your father and your mother"; and "You shall not covet your neighbor's house" is separate from "You shall not covet your neighbor's wife". But the Commandments written in Hebrew and divided between the tablets in the Christian manner, appear for what seems to be the first time in "The Transfiguration" painted by Sebastiano del Piombo, which was completed in 1519 in the Church of San Pietro in Montorio, in Rome. Hebrew letters and a division in the Catholic style can also be found in a much later work: the wooden door of one of the gates of the cathedral in Florence,[168] although a decorative wreath of flowers covers them and not all the letters are visible.

In contrast to the variety of approaches found among Christian artists, the Hebrew tradition is very stable. Here the division of the Commandments is naturally that laid down in the Talmud and Midrash, and the differences relate only to the extent of abbreviation. The Commandments on the second Tablet, save for the last, which is always written as "You shall not covet", do not need to be shortened; but the longer Commandments on the first tablet passed through a number of versions before settling down to the form customary today, which cuts them down to the first two words at the expense of presenting meaningful sentences. Generally speaking, the earliest examples exhibit a tendency to write full sentences, and subsequently the sentences become increasingly abbreviated, probably because their routine use eliminated the need for a comprehensible version. The Fifth Commandment, for example, was written at first "Honor you father and mother", "Honor your f. and m.", "Honor your father" — until today's version was reached — "Honor". The other Commandments traveled a similar route.[169]

There are also pictures of the Tablets of the Law that abbreviate the Scriptural text less than is customary, and present an "extended"

---

167 Plate 12 herein, Museo Borghese, Rome.
168 Porta dei Canonici.
169 See, e.g., the first Tablet in the Ark from Urbino. An even more abbreviated form is found on an amulet case from Italy. See *Mitteilungen*, n. 136 above, nos. 3–4, fig. 125. On the Ark from Chodorov (ibid., nos. 7–8, fig. 29) the Commandments are to be read as a continuity from one tablet to the other. The same applies to a tray for a Torah Scroll, from Poland (Kayser-Schoenberger, n. 33 above, fig. 55).

version of the Commandments. Such a version is found, for example, on the Holy Ark in the Spanish synagogue in Amsterdam. This synagogue was dedicated in 1675.[170]

The synagogue in Cavaillon was built in 1772 and incorporated parts of an earlier sixteenth-century structure.[171] On the inner side of the doors of its Holy Ark are written twelve, not ten Commandments, in the following format:[172]

I the LORD am your God	Honor your father
You shall have no other	You shall not murder
You shall not make for yourself a sculpted image	You shall not commit adultery
You shall not bow down to them	You shall not steal
You shall not swear falsely by the name	You shall not bear false witness against your neighbor
Remember the Sabbath day	You shall not covet your neighbor's house

Twelve Commandments divided in the same way are also found in an Italian manuscript of 1385.[173]

It appears, then, that the form of the Commandments on Holy Arks (and on ritual objects in general) went through a number of phases before arriving at today's fixed form.

Here we may note a very interesting phenomenon. In several examples of Jewish Tablets of the Law we find a division that differs from that of the Sages, and in which the Second Commandment is "You shall not make" rather than "You shall not have".[174] That is the situation in the following instances:

---

170   *Encyclopaedia Judacia*, 2, cols. 897–898. My thanks to Prof. Z. Werblowsky, who drew my attention to this Ark in his letter of Nov. 1960.

171   *Encyclopaedia Judaica*, 5, col. 261.

172   My friend U. Nahon called my attention to this variant from Cavaillon, and copied it for me when he was there. Dr. Nahon was an expert in everything connected with synagogues, and encouraged me in the writing of this essay, adding copious notes and comments. May his memory be blessed for that as well.

173   An illuminated ms. of the Bible, Italy 1385, British Museum. See frontispiece in *Jüdisches Lexikon*, 1, Berlin 1927.

174   My gratitude to Prof. Meir Weiss for calling my attention to this. Nevertheless, I must acknowledge that it had already been pointed out in Porat's essay, n. 150 above.

1. The cover page of a book entitled *Regolatione della fraterna del K.K. de Leuantini per maritar Donzelle*, printed in Venice, most probably in 1689 (plate 13c).[175]
2. A Holy Ark from Conegliano Veneto, on the Tablets on its exterior and on those on the inner side of the doors, completed in 1701 (plate 13a).[176]
3. A Torah scroll covering from Rome, 1729.[177]
4. A Torah scroll crown from Modena, 1750, now in the synagogue of Kibbutz Yavne.
5. A Torah scroll crown from Ceneda, 1755.[178]
6. An Italian ark-curtain, 1760, in the possesion of the Bezalel Museum.
7. A Torah scroll crown, one of the ritual objects of the Jewish community of Florence, 1762.
8. A Holy Ark from Carmagnola in the Piedmont, eighteenth century (plate 13b).
9. Pomegranates and a Torah crown in the Italian Synagogue in Jerusalem, apparently eighteenth century.
10. An amulet case, in the Italian Synagogue in Jerusalem, eighteenth century.

These examples came to light almost by chance, and a systematic investigation would no doubt reveal many more. On the basis of the findings, it appears that the phenomenon began around the first half of the eighteenth century in various parts of Italy. An exception, from an earlier period, is the piyyut on the Holy Ark in Sermide,[179] which dates from 1543.

"You shall not make" also appears as the Second Commandment on ritual objects of the Jews of Kurdistan. At an exhibit on Kurdistan Jewry at the Israel Museum in 1981–1982, there were four "synagogue Tablets", silver trays 10–16 cm. in size, from Iraqi Kurdistan, on which the Ten Commandments were engraved. On one of them, "You shall not make" appears as the Second Commandment,[180] while the others

175 The late Rabbi Sabato Toaff informed me of this book, and sent me a photocopy.
176 See n. 125 above.
177 Now in the possession of the Italian Synagogue in Jerusalem.
178 This item too is now in possession of the Italian Synagogue in Jerusalem.
179 See Nahon, n. 116 above.
180 Shifra Epstein et al, *The Jews of Kurdistan*, etc. (Hebrew), Israel Museum, Jerusalem, Catalogue 216, 1981, p. 254, no. 1739.

present the usual division. It may well be, however, that these trays are imitations of similar objects that reached Kurdistan from other countries, for, as we have already said, depictions of the Tablets of the Law were not characteristic of Jewish communities outside of Europe. Indeed, the former Sephardi Chief Rabbi of Israel, the late Rabbi Isaac Nissim, once told me that the Jews of Iraq did not know that symbol. Another indication of outside influence is the fact that one of the trays[181] is decorated with the *fleur de lis* of the kings of France!

"You shall not make" as the Second Commandment is also found on a silver tray inscribed with the Commandments in the synagogue of Corfu, and on a *parokhet* from 1886 in the Spanish synagogue in Ancona.[182]

S.H. Weingarten has commented that those who regard "You shall not make" as the Second Commandment apparently believe that "I am the LORD" is not a Commandment, for it does not command, but sets the ground for "You shall not have", which is the First Commandment.[183] That is also the view of the author of *Halakhot Gedolot*, as cited by Duran.[184] Weingarten also cites from another work by Duran:

> Perhaps it should be said that "I am the LORD" and "You shall not have" are one Commandment, for they have one concern, which is the recognition of God and the abandonment of deities that are not He... and if that is so, then the Second Commandment would be "You shall not make", a warning about making images, and "You shall not bow down to them or serve them" are specifications of the negative command "You shall not have", and are not to be counted.[185]

I do not know how to explain the appearance of this division of the Commandments. It is the same as that of Philo, Josephus, and of one of the cantillation systems — but this eighteenth-century phenomenon should not be linked to such an early source, as long as intermediate points have not been established. It is also the division of the Calvinists, but how can we consider Christian influence on such an internal Jewish matter, especially one on which there is a talmudic-midrashic tradition?

181   Ibid., no. 1738.
182   Reported to me by Dr. Nahon.
183   S.H. Weingarten, *Bet Miqra*, 4, 59 (1974), pp. 549–571.
184   Simeon bar Ẓemah Duran, *Zohar ha-Raki'a*, Vilna 1879, p. 67.
185   Idem, *Tashbeẓ*, Amsterdam 1741, 70a; cf. the view of Ibn Ezra, n. 145 above.

It is also difficult to account for it by referring to the view of single individuals, such as Abraham ibn Ezra and Simeon bar Zemah Duran. The question awaits an answer.[186]

5. CONCLUSION

As we have seen, in early times Jews did not recognize the Tablets of the Law as a Jewish symbol. They do not appear on any picture known to us until the Middle Ages. Christian art, whose motifs included Moses and the giving of the Law, depicted the Tablets in a variety of forms. From Christian works of art the Tablets passed to Jewish illuminated manuscripts in approximately the thirteenth century, and from there to Arks in the fifteenth century as a symbol of Jewish belief — in contrast to the symbols of Christianity to be seen in churches. Furthermore, it appears that Christians preceded Jews in employing the Tablets of the Law as a symbol of Judaism. Then, however, the new symbol spread quickly, acquiring a sort of sanctity and achieving permanent status on certain objects, and above all on Holy Arks.

The impulse to make use of religious symbols came from the cultural setting in which Jews found themselves, as well as from synagogue architecture and the form of the ritual objects inside them, which became increasingly rich and ornate. Since there was no longer reason to oppose giving prominence to the Decalogue, such as had existed in the early centuries of the Common Era, the Tablets of the Law came to serve as such a symbol. The people took to the symbol for understandable reasons. Apart from the self-evident one: the nature of the Commandments as general rules upon which the body of the Law depends, and which have a special place in the Law for having been given in a situation of unmatched exaltation — there are other reasons as well:

1. The Tablets as symbol bring Judaism as a religion into prominence. That was very desirable, especially at certain times and in certain places in the Diaspora, when the national element in Judaism began to be forgotten or was felt to be a disturbing factor.
2. The symbol of the Tablets brings into prominence that ideational and moral aspect of Judaism which the nations of the world also acknowledge and hallow — by distinction from the halakhic

---

186 Peculiarly enough a study guide issued for the Ministry of Education in 1973 by Moshe Ilan and others states with finality (p. 90) that "You shall not make" is the Second Commandment.

aspect, which the nations of the world found reason to oppose and mock.

3.   The Tablets remind one of the exalted moment of God's revelation to the nation as a whole, and that memory could uplift the people's spirit and console them during the long years of Exile — especially given the fact that the peoples among whom the Jews lived recognized that occasion and acknowledged the honor paid the Jewish people at that moment.

It seems to me that in recent times only one other symbol offers the Tablets of the Law any competition, and that is the Magen David, the Shield of David. In many instances, the Magen David was regarded as the exact parallel of the cross, and therefore it was engraved on tombstones, a place where Christians place a cross, and the organization parallel to the Red Cross was called the Red Magen David. However, since the Zionist movement adopted the Magen David as its symbol, and that symbol thereby entered the country's flag and the uniform of its soldiers, a feeling has been created among the people that the Magen David symbolizes the Jewish national element, while the Tablets symbolize the Jewish religion. It is fortunate that when the leaders of the nation sought to establish a symbol for the state, they chose one whose roots in the nation's history reached further back than either of these two — the Menorah, the seven-branched candelabrum. Even though they chose an erroneous representation of it, carved by an anonymous Gentile artist on Titus' arch, rather than as it is represented in many ancient pictures from Palestine[187] — in any event, the Menorah is the object which, in its actuality or its representation, accompanied the Jewish people from Mount Sinai to the present.

As compared with the Menorah, the Tablets of the Law are a symbol that arrived relatively late and, as it were, from outside. Even its shape was fashioned by Gentile artists. Nevertheless, it is not surprising that despite this, it has been brought almost into the holy of holies. For that is the way of a living organism. It absorbs into itself whatever serves its own life process.[188]

Translated by Arnold Schwartz

187   See Isaac Halevi Herzog, in *Scritti in Memoria di Sally Mayer*, Milano-Jerusalem 1956, pp. 95–98, Hebrew section.

188   This essay is a revised version of my article in *Tarbiẓ*, 29 (1960), pp. 370–393. The subject had been dealt with previously by Israel Abrahams, "The Decalogue in Art", *Studies... in Honour of Kaufman Köhler*, Berlin 1913, pp. 39–55; Abrahams' conclusions do not differ substantially from my own.

17. ILLUSTRATIONS OF
THE TEN COMMANDMENTS IN
THE THIRTEENTH CENTURY MINUTE MAHZOR*

BEZALEL NARKISS

Moshe Spitzer
In Memoriam

The Tablets of the Law are normally represented in Hebrew medieval manuscripts as two parallel rectangles, on which the opening words of each of the Ten Commandments may be written. Such Tablets sometimes appear in scenes of the revelation on Mount Sinai when Moses receives them from God, for the most part in illuminated manuscripts of German origin.[1] In the case of illuminated manuscripts of Spanish origin, the Tablets are presented within the Ark of Testimony as an implement of the Sanctuary.[2]

*   My thanks to my students Naomi Feuchtwanger and Yael Zirlin for their extensive help in editing and preparing this article. Likewise, I thank my friends at the Library of the Jewish Theological Seminary of New York, Professor Menahem Schmelzer and Dr Evelyn Cohen for their enlightening comments. This translation does not include most of the Hebrew texts; their connotations can be consulted in the published original.

1   For example in Archbishop Laud's Mahzor, Bodleian Library, ms. Laud Or. 321, fol. 127v, see B. Narkiss, *Hebrew Illuminated Manuscripts,* Jerusalem 1969, plate 27; plate 15 herein; Regensburg Pentateuch, Israel Museum, ms. 180/52, fol. 154v, see Narkiss, ibid., plate 29; the Tripartite Mahzor, II, British Library, Add. ms. 22413, fol. 3; see Narkiss, ibid., plate 34. Also in the Double Ashkenazi Mahzor, Dresden Volume, Sächsische Landesbibliothek, ms. A. 46a., fol. 202; and G. Sed-Rejna, *Le mahzor enluminé,* Leiden 1983, p. 59, fig. 40.

2   For example the display of the Sanctuary implements appears at the beginning of Catalonian Bibles from the thirteenth to the fifteenth centuries. For a list of such manuscripts, see Narkiss, ibid., second ed. in Hebrew, Jerusalem 1984, notes 53–57; also the article by T. Metzger in *Bulletin of the John Rylands Library,* LII (1966), pp. 397–436; LIII (1970–1971), pp. 175–185. See examples in B. Narkiss, *Hebrew Illuminated Manuscripts in the British Isles: Catalogue Raisonné,* 1, *Spanish and Portuguese Schools,* Jerusalem-London, text volume, pp. 101–104,

At times the Tablets appear by themselves adjacent to the text of the giving of the Law.[3] Their rectangular shape has its source in Jewish thought, although it first appears in Christian art, as for example in the early seventh century Ashburnham Pentateuch.[4] Earlier in the Middle Ages, and in the early Christian art, a rolled scroll appears in the depiction of the giving of the Law, alluding to the midrashic conception that at Sinai Moses received the entire Torah in the form of a scroll. The Tablets, according to the *Midrash Rabbah*, "were a miracle, they were rolled, made of saphire but in a scroll".[5]

A different depiction of the giving of the Law, whose source is the same *Midrash Rabbah*, is found in the *Birds' Head Haggadah*, an Ashkenazi Haggadah originating in Franconia in the late thirteenth century, and now part of the collection of the Israel Museum of Jerusalem (plate 14).[6] The illustration appears in the outer margin beside the piyyut *Dayyenu*, which mentions the Giving of the Torah. The upper corner of the page shows Moses standing on Mount Sinai and receiving the two Tablets, with round tops, from the hand of God, while at the foot of the mountain Moses appears again, wearing a typical pointed Jew's hat, handing five Tablets to the Children of

plate volume, figs. 310, 326, 335, 442. See also the Temple façade in the Sarajevo Haggadah, National Museum of Sarajevo, fol. 32; see Narkiss, *Hebrew Illuminated Manuscripts*, Jerusalem 1969 and 1984, plate 10.

3   For example, an illustration to Exodus 31. 18, in the First Joshua ibn Gaon Bible of Tudela (Spain) from 1300, now in Paris Bibliothèque Nationale, ms. hebr. 20, fol. 58; see B. Narkiss and G. Sed-Rajna, "La première Bible de Josué ben Abraham Ibn Gaon", *Revue des études juives*, CXXX (1974), pp. 4–15, pl. VIII.

4   Paris, Bibliothèque Nationale, N.A.L. 2334, fol. 76, see Oscar von Gebhardt, *The Miniatures of the Ashburnham Pentateuch*, London 1883, pl. XX; E. Revel-Neher, "La double page du Codex Amiatinus et ses rapports avec les plans du Tabernacle dans l'art juif et dans l'art byzantin", in *Journal of Jewish Art*, 9 (1982), p. 16, fig. 12; cf. G. Sed-Rajna, *Le mahzor enluminé*, Leiden 1983, fig. 58. On the rectangular shape of the tablets, see Gad B. Sarfatti in the present volume. Prof. Sarfatti bases the rectangular shape of the tablets on *Baraita di-Melekhet ha-Mishkan*, VI (ed. Ish-Shalom, Vienna 1908, p. 40) and B.B. 14a; *Exodus Rabbah* end of *Ki Tissa*; *Num. Rabbah*, 4. 21; Yer. Sot. VIII: 3 and Taan IV:5; and the Tosafot on Men. 99a. On the round-topped shape of the tablets, see R. Mellinkoff, "The Round-Topped Tablets of the Law: Sacred Symbol and Emblem of Evil", *Journal of Jewish Art*, I (1974), pp. 28–43.

5   *Cant. Rabbah* 5. 12, where R. Joshua b. Nehemiah expounds Cant. 5. 14. See L. Ginzberg, *Legends of the Jews*, 6, Philadelphia 1949, pp. 49–50, n. 258.

6   Ms. 180/57, fol. 23, see Narkiss, *Hebrew Illuminated Manuscripts*, Jerusalem 1969 and revised Hebrew edition, Jerusalem 1984, plate 28.

Israel, each Tablet representing one of the five books of the Pentateuch.

In Archbishop Laud's Mahzor, an Ashkenazi manuscript from approximately 1260, now in the Bodleian Library at Oxford (plate 15),[7] the illustration of the giving of the Law appears at the top of a decorated page (127v), which includes the piyyut for Shavuot *Adon Imnani* ("The Lord trained me", Davidson, *Thesaurus of Mediaeval Hebrew Poetry*, I, Aleph, no. 484). On the left side above an arched gate is a featureless angel holding two rectangular Tablets, while on the right side a rolled-up scroll with a handle is poised to fall into the outstretched hands of three kneeling people with birds' and animals' heads, wearing Jews' hats.[8]

In the Worms Mahzor from Würzburg in Franconia, 1272, in the National and University Library, Jerusalem (plate 16), the giving of the Torah is portrayed around an arched gate that circumscribes the same piyyut for Shavuot.[9] At the top of the page, which was partially cut off by a later bookbinder, the two rectangular Tablets of the Law are shown, painted green with a red border; to their right a huge shofar comes down from the sky, and to their left a figure, apparently Moses, kneels. Above the arch of the gate, enclosed by posts on both sides as well as underneath the gate, appear ten people either kneeling or standing, wearing Jews' hats and long robes. Each of them holds an open scroll on which one of the Ten Commandments is inscribed. All ten of the figures have bird faces and gesture in conversational attitudes.

A different iconographical concept is expressed in another manuscript from Franconia, also of the late thirteenth century. This Minute Mahzor includes several text illustrations, among which nine of the Ten Commandments are depicted. This manuscript is now in the Library of the Jewish Theological Seminary in New York and was

---

7   Ms. Laud Or. 321, fol. 127v, see Narkiss, ibid., pl. 27.
8   On the phenomenon of distortion of human figures by using the heads of animals and birds in Ashkenazi illumination of the thirteenth and fourteenth centuries, see B. Narkiss, "On the Zoocephalic Phenomenon in Medieval Ashkenazi Manuscripts", in: *Norms and Variations in Art, Essays in Honour of Moshe Barasch*, Jerusalem 1983, pp. 49–62, plates LXXII–LXXX.
9   Ms. 4°781/1, fol. 111; see *Facsimile Edition of The Worms Mahzor*, ed. M. Beit-Arieh, Jerusalem-London 1985. The tops of the tablets have been cut off and it is impossible to tell whether they were square or round. See also Narkiss, *Hebrew Illuminated Manuscripts*, plate 26.

acquired as a gift by Louis Bamberger in 1928.[10] Its minute dimensions in comparison with the giant mahzosim mentioned above are approximately 120 x 85 mm. Its present binding is very recent. The contents resemble the giant Ashkenazi Festival mahzorim including piyyutim and prayers for the special Sabbaths, Holy Days and Festivals. It opens with the piyyut for Shabbat Bereshit, *El Nissa* ("A soaring God", Davidson, I, Aleph, no. 3945), and ends with the *Selihot* preceding the Days of Awe. It includes prayers and piyyutim for Shavuot as well. The entire manuscript is decorated with pen drawings and colored paintings, some of which illustrate the texts they accompany. The illustrations of the Ten Commandments embellish the prayers for the festival of Shavuot.

The manuscript lacks a colophon which would have given us the scribe's signature, place and date. However, based on its artistic style, and on comparison with other manuscripts, it is possible to date it to the late thirteenth century in the area of Franconia in central Germany.[11] The piyyutim and the sequence of the prayers are not in

10   Now numbered ms. Mic. 8972, first described by the late Alexander Marx, Librarian of the Jewish Theological Seminary, as exceptional among sixty manuscripts acquired by the gift of Louis Bamberger. See A. Marx, *Bibliographical Studies and Notes on Rare Books and Manuscripts in the Library of the Jewish Theological Seminary of America*, edited with an introduction by Menahem Schmelzer, New York 1977, pp. 100–101. Joshua Bloch placed it in Austria, approximately 1300, and called it *A Hebrew Hymnal*, see J. Bloch, *The People and the Book*, Catalogue of an exhibition at the New York Public Library, New York 1954, no. 26, pp. 56–58; see also T. Freudenheim, *Illuminated Hebrew Manuscripts from the Library of the Jewish Theological Seminary of America*, Catalogue of an exhibition at The Jewish Museum, New York 1965, p. 28.

11   The manuscript is on vellum consisting of IV + 203 folios (201 numbered + folios 84A, 107A, which are blank and unnumbered) + V folios; measuring (117–122) x (85–86) mm., text space (70–72) x (47–49) mm. Written in dark brown ink, in round Ashkenazi script, mainly 19–20 lines per page (at times between 25 and 29 lines in smaller script). Ruling by plummet 1+1 vertical and 20 horizontal lines, pricking distinguishable only in inner margins; it can be assumed that those on the outer margin were cut off by a later binder. Bound in 20 quires of 12 folios each, except for I[10], IX[10], X[4], XI[10], XII[10], XIII[16], XIV[8], XV[10], XVI[10], XVII[8], XVIII[10], XIX[10], XX[2+1]. No quire catchwords remain, except for some remnants of a pen-drawn dog (fol. 22v) and cut-off letters or drawings (fols. 34v, 58v, 178v). All the quires (aside from I) are marked at the top in Arabic numerals by a later binder. Blank pages: 1v, 58v, 79v, 84Ar and v, 98v, 107Ar and v, 131v, 167v, 201r and v. Newly bound in 1982 by Raphael Podeh, replacing earlier binding of red leather on which was stamped in gold: "Prayer Book Austria 1300". The new binder moved

chronological order according to the yearly cycle, as is usual in the larger Festival mahzorim, which were intended for the cantor's use in conducting the services in Ashkenazi synagogues of the thirteenth and fourteenth centuries.[12] In the absence of exhaustive research on the choice of prayers and piyyutim that were current in various congregations in the different areas of Germany, it is difficult to pinpoint the exact origins of the selection found in the Minute Mahzor before us. Among the piyyutim it contains, some of which have not yet been published, there are both rare and unique examples, apparently selected according to the personal taste of the anonymous patron. Because it is a personal prayerbook, not meant for the use of the cantor in the synagogue, the difficulty of determining its place of origin by the nature of the piyyutim it contains is even greater. Thus, its provenance and date of composition must be sought for by means of other internal evidence.

There can be no doubt that this tiny Ashkenazi Mahzor was written before 1325 or 1331 for in those years the deaths of the owner's father and mother were noted.[13] It can be assumed that the manuscript was

some folios around, the most important of which is the exchange of the former fol. 1 with fol. 2. On fols. 200v–201v are lists of births and deaths. Those from the years 1325 to 1331 are from Germany, while the others are from Italy, from the years 1521, 1523, 1543, 1555, 1582. Illustrations of the manuscript include:

A. Five fully decorated pages (fols. 1v, 66v, 70v, 94, 110); only the first is a text illustration.

B. Ten partially decorated pages, containing text illustrations (fols. 44v, 144v, 118, 119v, 121, 122, 123v, 125, 126v, 128). Aside from the first, all are illustrations of the Ten Commandments.

C. A few initial words embellished with gouache (fol. 2) and watercolor (fols. 17, 33, 61v, 65v, 66v, 149, 151, 156).

D. Some initial letters written in alternating colors: red, yellow, green, and many letters surrounded by a wriggly line, characteristic of Ashkenazi decoration of the thirteenth and fourteenth centuries.

E. Zoömorphic letters (for example, fols. 61v, 104, 135v).

F. Scribal pen drawings, among them animals (e.g. fol. 58v), a dragon (64v), a lily (44v).

12   See Ezra Fleisher, "Prayer and Piyyut in the Worms Mahzor", introductory volume to the Facsimile of the Worms Mahzor, ed. Malachi Beit-Arieh, Jerusalem 1985. See also Gabrielle Sed-Rajna, Le mahzor enluminé, Leiden 1983.

13   On fol. 220v in round Ashkenazi script is inscribed: "Death of my father R. Samuel bar Gad of Keham(?), of blessed memory, was on the Sabbath, 26 Sivan in the year five thousand and eighty-five [6. 7. 1325] and death of my mother Rebecca, of

written around 1295, due to its similarity to and association with a similarly sized diminutive manuscript which contains a calendar beginning in that year. The calendar was acquired by Alexander Marx, librarian of the Jewish Theological Seminary in New York, along with the Minute Mahzor and two other similarly minute manuscripts, all of them the donation of Louis Bamberger.[14] The tiny calendar manuscript includes specifications of the festivals (fols. 11–12) beginning in the year 1295 (the 267th 19-year cycle Anno Mundi, which began in the year 5055 of that calendar) and goes as far as the year 1541 (cycle 279, ending in 5301 A.M.). It also contains the calendrical work *Iggul d'Rav Naḥshon* ("The cycle of Rav Nahshon", fols. 1–12). Its dimensions, codicological components, and style of script are identical with those of our Minute Mahzor.[15] It is even possible that the calendar manuscript with the *Iggul D'rav Naḥshon* was originally a part of the Minute Mahzor since it is marked "quire 21" which follows the twenty quires of the Mahzor. Taking into

blessed memory, was on the eve of 15 Tevet in the year five thousand and ninety-one Anno Mundi" (12. 26. 1331).

14　See the description by A. Marx in *Bibliographical Studies etc.* (note 10 above) p. 101.

15　Ms. Mic. 4246, made of vellum, consisting of I+1+12+1+I folios (the last two pages are numbered 13 and 14 even though they are part of the binding). Measuring 117 x 75 mm., text space mostly 48 x 72 mm. (except for the calendrical table which takes up the entire area of the page, on fols. 1, 11v, and 12v). Written in light and dark brown ink in round Ashkenazi script, usually 19 lines per page. Ruling by plummet 1+1 vertical and 20 horizontal lines. Pricking discernable only in inner margins. Bound as a single quire of 12 pages, which is wrapped in four additional folios, two of parchment and two of paper. Marked as quire 21 in Arabic numerals on the first wrapping parchment page, apparently as the continuation of quire 20 of the Minute Mahzor, whose library number is Mic. 8972. Seventeenth-century binding made of white parchment on cardboards. Without a colophon, but with notes by the original scribe at the end of the composition (fol. 11): "Here endeth the Iggul of R. Naḥshon, May God guard me as the apple of His eye (a rhyme in Hebrew)...". At the end of the calendar (fol. 12v): "Completed praise be to Him who dwells atop the world...". On pp. 13 and 14 is a list of births from the seventeenth century (1616, 1617), and the city Vercelli (Italy) is mentioned on the last page (fol. 14). The manuscript's embellishments include scribal decorative drawings in a style similar to the Minute Mahzor: plant decorations at the end of the *Iggul D'Rav Naḥshon* (fol. 11) and at the side of the calendar (fol. 11v); a grotesque with human and goose heads on both sides of the scribe's note at the end of the calendar (fol. 12v). In addition, some letters of the calendar and the text are written alternately in red and brown ink.

account the inscriptions of deaths, births and list of owners found at the end of the two manuscripts, we may conclude that they became separated as early as the seventeenth century.

Another manuscript, similar to these two in terms of dimensions and form, includes "Rules of Ritual Slaughter by Rabbi Yehuda of Salzburg". On it as well, the quire mark 22 is found, which would place it after the calendrical work by R. Naḥshon.[16] A fourth manuscript, similar to these three, contains a list of the Torah readings for Sabbaths and Festivals and may be designated *Pisqei Parshiyot* as the scribe calls it.[17] In light of their identical small dimensions and similar codicological components, we may agree with Alexander Marx that they are all part of a single group of common origin.[18] The calendar, which begins in 1295, may thus represent the earliest date for the four manuscripts, and the obituary date of the owner's father (1325) may be the latest.

The ink drawings which decorate the four manuscripts are similar in style and were clearly done by the scribe who copied the text. Some details are written in red ink on the calendar tables. An inverted fleur-de-lys is found at the end of the calendar manuscript (fol. 11), and on its verso is a foliage interlace. Grotesques of human and goose heads are drawn on the last page after the calendar (12v) on either side of the scribe's note. At the end of the *Laws of Ritual Slaughter* there is an illustration of a slaughtered ox (fol. 10v) and at the end of the table

16   Jewish Theological Seminary, ms. Mic. 4356, vellum, consisting of 1+10+1 folios. Its dimensions and text space are the same as those of the previous two manuscripts described in notes 11 and 15. Bound in a single quire of ten folios, marked as quire 22 on the original first page, apparently as a continuation of the above-mentioned manuscripts. The only decoration which appears at the end of the text (fol. 10v) is a sketch of a slaughtered ox. Alexander Marx notes in his description (p. 101), that Rabbi Judah of Salzburg in Austria was perhaps the student of Rabbi Isaac of Vienna, of *Or Zaru'a*. Perhaps this was one reason why the origin of this entire group of manuscripts was attributed to Austria.

17   At the top of the page: "With God's help I begin the schedule of Torah readings". The manuscript, Mic. 4340, is of the same format as the three preceding manuscripts presented in notes 11, 15, 16, consisting of 1 + 14 + 1 folios, bound in a single 14 folio quire. Fols. 9 and 14 were separately attached. A single decoration, a drawing of a foliage scroll framed by an inverted cone, is found at the end of the manuscript (fol. 14v). It is similar in style to the drawings in the Minute Mahzor, the Calendar Manuscript and the Rules of Slaughter. Some initial letters are in red ink.

18   See A. Marx's description (n. 10 above), p. 101.

of Torah readings appears a drawing of a foliage scroll within an inverted cone (fol. 14v).

The outlines of the rough drawings, alternately widening and narrowing, apparently drawn with a scribe's quill, are characteristic of all four manuscripts. This kind of drawing is recognizable in all the illustrations and decorations of the original of our Mahzor although in them, watercolor or gouache was sometimes added. The Minute Mahzor contains in addition many pen drawings and wriggles surrounding the initial words as well as forming space-fillers in empty lines and line-ends. Among the decorations are the fleur-de-lys (fols. 44v, 45) and dragon (fol. 64v), similar to the drawings of the calendar manuscript (fols. 11, 12v).

The writing and drawing style is reminiscent of some manuscripts from the area of central Franconia in the late thirteenth century, as for example the Worms Mahzor from Würzburg, dated 1272,[19] and a mahzor ornamented with pen drawings made, it seems, in Bamberg in 1279 and now in the Library of the Jewish Theological Seminary in New York.[20]

This is not the place for a detailed description of all the decorations of the Minute Mahzor. Its plan of ornamentation has been detailed in note 11 above, and aside from nine illustrations of the Commandments, to be treated in the following discussion, there are two illustrations deserving attention, namely, those on folios 1v and 44v.

The drawing on fol. 44 (plate 17b) depicts a dove sitting on the shoulder of a crowned heraldic red eagle. It serves as an illustration for the piyyut "Thou didst bear the Dove on eagle's wings," (Davidson, II, Yod, no. 2050). The eagle, symbolizing God, bears the dove who symbolizes the people of Israel. The picture is related to the ingathering of the exiles in the time of the Messiah, and is known from a similar picture on an ancient clay lamp, as Avigdor Klagsbald has shown.[21]

Although it appears at the beginning of the Minute Mahzor, the illustration on fol. 1v relates to the Ten Commandments and piyyutim

19   See n. 9 above.
20   Bamberg Mahzor, Jewish Theological Seminary, New York, ms. Mic. 4843; see B. Narkiss, *Hebrew Illuminated Manuscripts*, second Hebrew ed., Jerusalem 1984, illus. 48.
21   See Ex. 19. 4, and *Targum Jonathan* to Cant. 2. 14; cf. Victor A. Klagsbald, "Clay Lamps With Biblical Scenes", *Journal of Jewish Art*, 3–4 (1977), pp. 112–129.

for Shavuot. The full page panel is divided into two: in its upper register is depicted the battle between the legendary wild ox — Behemoth — and the Leviathan, and in its lower half, the hunt for the doe (plate 17a). These two illustrations complement each other in representing the Jewish concept of history. The "beloved doe" symbolizes the Jewish people hunted down by the nations of the world while the battle between the two mythological beasts symbolizes the war of Gog and Magog, the end of days, and the beginning of the messianic era. The struggle between the wild ox and the Leviathan is also connected with the tabernacle in paradise, made from the hide of the Leviathan, under whose shade the righteous are to feast upon the flesh of these two beasts. Thus it is often the illustration used to accompany the piyyut for the morning service of the Feast of Sukkot, "I crown with wreaths of praise" (Davidson, I, Aleph, no. 3301).[22] In our Minute Mahzor this battle between Leviathan and the legendary Behemoth is used as an illustration for the piyyut which opens the book, i.e., the *yotzer* for Shabbat Bereshit "I will sing with glee for the elated God" (Davidson, I, Aleph, no. 3945).[23]

The hunt for a doe or deer most often illustrates the piyyut "A beloved doe, a gift of Sinai" (Davidson, I, Aleph, no. 2960) recited at the morning service of the Second Day of Shavuot. Indeed, that is where one finds it in a number of large thirteenth-and fourteenth-century Ashkenazi mahzorim.[24] Actually, the illustration of the battle

22 For example in Mahzor Lipsiae, Leipzig University Library, ms. V.1102, vol. II, fol. 181v; see E. Katz and B. Narkiss, *Máchsor Lipsiae*, 68 Facsimile plates and Introductory Volume, Leipzig 1965, facsimile page no. 57 and pp. 80–81, 99. On this subject see the following two articles by J. Gutmann: "When Kingdom Comes: Messianic Themes in Medieval Jewish Art", *Art Journal*, 27 (1967), pp. 171–173; idem, "Leviathan, Behemoth and Ziz: Jewish Messianic Symbols in Art", *Hebrew Union College Annual*, 39 (1968), pp. 219–230; reprinted in J. Gutmann (ed.), *No Graven Images* (New York), pp. 232–248. See also L. Roussin, "The Beit Leontis Mosaic: An Eschatological Interpretation", *Journal of Jewish Art*, 8 (1981), pp. 6–19.

23 The main section of the piyyut *El Nissa*, which deals with the battle between Leviathan and the wild ox (identified in the piyyut with Behemoth), describes the act of Creation. For a commentary on this section, see E.E. Urbach, *Sefer Arugat Habosem*, (Hebrew), II, Jerusalem 1947, pp. 205–206. See also J. Schirmann "The Battle Between Behemoth and Leviathan", *Proceedings of the Israel Academy of Sciences and Humanities* (English), 4, Jerusalem 1970, pp. 327–369, especially appendix B.

24 For example, in the Worms Mahzor of 1272, Jerusalem, Jewish National and

between the two giant primordial creatures is connected with the festival of Shavu'ot. The hymn *Aqdamut Millin*, which is the overture to a series of Aramaic piyyutim and Targum versions of the Ten Commandments, contains an even more vivid account of the battle of the titans than we find in the piyyut for Shabbat Bereshit. Indeed, this piyyut also describes the feast of the righteous in paradise.[25]

It may well be that folio 1 in our Minute Mahzor is not in its original place. A single detached page might have become attached to the beginning of the manuscript, next to the piyyutim that deal with the festival of Shavu'ot. As it happens, it fits in well, not only because of the battle between the Leviathan and the wild ox, but also because of the hunt for the beloved doe, and the gift to Israel at Sinai.[26]

The illustrations of the Ten Commandments that appear in the Minute Mahzor are included in the evening prayers for the first day of Shavu'ot, and are placed after the piyyut *Aqdamut Millin* (Davidson, I, Aleph, no. 7314), a *reshut* for the *Targum* of the Ten Commandments, composed by Rabbi Meir bar Isaac Nehora of Worms in the eleventh century. After that introduction comes a series of piyyutim, each of which deals with one of the Ten Commandments, an arrangement popular in many German communities of the thirteenth and fourteenth centuries.[27] It should be pointed out here

University Library, ms. 4°781/1, I, fol. 130v (previously 170v), and in the Tripartite Mahzor of about 1320, II, British Library, ms. Add. 22413, fol. 49. See Sed-Rajna, *Le Mahzor etc.* (n. 1, above) pp. 20, 58, figs. 7, 8.

25　Translated by J. Schirmann (see above n. 23): "Our portion from of old, which God set aside as a gift / The sport of Leviathan and the ox from the lofty mountain / When the one is interlocked with the other, they grapple together / Behemoth gores powerfully with his horns / The fish leaps against him attacking mightily with his fins / His Creator sacrifices him with his sword / With pride he prepares a meal for the righteous and a banquet".

26　Before the recent rebinding of the manuscript in 1982, folio 1 was inserted as folio 2 in the first folioed quire. The piyyutim for the festival of Shavuot which open with *Aqdamut Millin*, start on folio 108 at the beginning of quire XI, also of ten folios. In this quire no text is missing, and at the beginning there is an added single folio (the unfoliated 107A). Perhaps the single sheet (now fol. 1), on which the battle between Leviathan and the wild ox and the hunt for the doe are depicted, was inserted in this quire between fol. 107A and fol. 108.

27　The collection of Aramaic piyyutim for Shavuot in our Mahzor is almost completely parallel to that of Mahzor Vitry; see S. Hurwitz, second edition, Nürnberg 1923, pp. 305–309, 335–343. It is also parallel to other festival mahzorim from the same area, for example those in *Maehsor Lipsiae*, Leipzig University Library, ms.

PLATE 14

וְלֹא נָתַן לָנוּ
אֶת הַשַּׁבָּת דַּיֵּנוּ

אִלּוּ נָתַן לָנוּ
אֶת הַשַּׁבָּת
וְלֹא קֵרְבָנוּ לִפְנֵי
הַר סִינַי דַּיֵּנוּ

אִלּוּ קֵרְבָנוּ לִפְנֵי
הַר סִינַי
וְלֹא נָתַן לָנוּ
אֶת הַתּוֹרָה דַּיֵּנוּ

אִלּוּ נָתַן לָנוּ
אֶת הַתּוֹרָה

Moses receiving the Law: Birds' Head Haggadah Franconia, late 13th century.
Jerusalem, Israel Museum, Ms. 180/57, fol. 23

PLATE 15

Moses receiving the Law in the form of a scroll: Archbishop Laud's Mahzor, about 1260.
Oxford, Bodleian Library, Ms. Laud, Or. 321,fol.127v.

PLATE 16

Moses receiving the Law: Worms Mahzor, Würzburg, 1272.
Jerusalem, National and University Library, Ms. 4° 48171, fol. 111

PLATE 17

a. Battle of Leviathan and The Wild Ox;
and Hunt for The Gazelle; from the Minute 13th
century Mahzor, fol. 1v

b. The Dove on the Eagle's Shoulder,
fol. 44v

c. The Rescue from the Fiery Furnace, illustrating the Second
Commandment, fol. 114

[Illustrations from the Minute 13th Century Mahzor
New York, Jewish Theological Seminary, Mic. 2872]

PLATE 18

a. The Jew's Oath, illustrating the Third Commandment;
from the Minute Mahzor, fol. 118

b. Sabbath in a Jewish home, illustrating the Fourth Commandment;
from the Minute Mahzor, fol. 119v

PLATE 19

a. The Binding of Isaac, illustrating the Fifth Commandment;
from the Minute Mahzor, fol. 121

b. Benaiah Slays Joab, illustrating the Sixth Commandment; from the Minute Mahzor, fol. 122

PLATE 20

a. Joseph Serving Potiphar's Wife, illustrating the Seventh Commandment;
from the Minute Mahzor, fol. 123v

b. The Thief, in the Act, Being Tried and Hanged; illustrating the Eighth Commandment;
from the Minute Mahzor, fol. 125

PLATE 21

a. The False Witness in Court, illustrating the Ninth Commandment; from the Minute Mahzor, fol. 126v

b. Adam, Eve and the Serpent in the Garden of Eden, illustrating the Tenth Commandment;
from the Minute Mahzor, fol 128v

that the artist's source of inspiration was not the Ten Commandments themselves, but rather this collection of Aramaic piyyutim related to the Ten Commandments. These piyyutim interpret the Commandments homiletically, making use of the biblical stories and of genre scenes from everyday life. Each unit, except for the first, opens with the Commandments in Hebrew followed by an illustration which is succeeded by the Aramaic piyyut related to this particular Commandment. The unit ends with the *Targum* of the Commandment. The next Commandment in Hebrew is then attached at the end of the unit as a sort of caption introducing the illustration to the following Commandment.

The illustrations are normally on panels within the text space. A few of the illustrations are pen drawn, painted with various shades of red, green and yellow, while others are plain drawings, tinted lightly with water colors. The sequence of each unit is not followed in the First Commandment, "I the LORD am your God" (Ex. 20. 2) which, understandably, is not accompanied by an illustration.

The illustration for the Second Commandment, "You shall not make for yourself a sculptured image.... You shall not bow down to them" is depicted in a full page (fol. 114v; plate 17c). It depicts the rescue of Hananiah, Mishael and Azariah from the furnace into which they were thrown by Nebuchadnezar for refusing to bow down to the golden idol that he had set up (Dan. 3). The picture appears before the piyyut which opens with the words: "Hananiah, Mishael and Azariah making the name of the Blessed Holy One known to all",[28] and

---

V.1102, I, fols. 64–177. See the list by Elijah Katz of Bratislava,"Mahzor Lipsiae: Detailed Contents of Both Its Parts"(Hebrew), in E. Katz and B. Narkiss, *Machsor Lipsiae: 68 Facsimile Plates:* in the *Introductory Volume*, pp. XI-XII. On the wide selection of Aramaic piyyutim for Shavuot, see M. Ginsburger, "Aramäische Introduktionen zum Targumvortrag an Festtagen", *ZDMG* 54 (1900), pp. 113–124; idem, "Les Introductions araméennes à la lecture du targoum", *Revue des études juives*, 73 (1921), pp. 14–26, 186–194. My thanks are due to the late Alexander Scheiber of Budapest who brought these articles to my attention. See also J. Heinemann, "Remnants of the Poetic Works of Early Translators" (Hebrew), *Hasifrut*, 4 (1974), pp. 362–375, especially p. 336: and A. Tal, "A Liturgical Poem for Pentecost" (Hebrew), *Leshonenu*, 38 (1974), 4, pp. 257–268. See also Ezra Fleischer, "Prayer and Piyyut in Mahzor Worms" in the introductory volume to Mahzor Worms, edited by M. Beit-Arieh, Jerusalem 1985, pp. 22–24, notes 89–95.

28 So too in *Mahzor Vitry*, ed. Hurwitz, p. 337, and in *Machsor Lipsiae*, I, fols. 169–170.

describes the events. The upper part of the panel portrays Hananiah, Mishael and Azariah, wearing long garments and pointed Jews' hats, their hands bound behind their backs. On the right the diminutive crowned figure of Nebuchadnezar is seated on a throne and between them stands his gigantic bodyguard. The lower half of the panel portrays the three figures inside a furnace, their names written beneath them, and above them the angel Gabriel with the head of an eagle, who spreads his wings over their heads, his name inscribed above.[29] To the right sits Nebuchadnezar, taken aback by the fire that bursts out in his direction. The image of Nebuchadnezar's idol and the trial of Hananiah, Mishael and Azariah, who would not worship the idol, appears in one of the earliest Hebrew illustrated manuscripts known to us — Rashi's commentary on the Bible written in Würzburg in 1233.[30] From an iconographic point of view there is little similarity between the picture in the Würzburg manuscript and our Minute Mahzor. The golden statue is missing in our mahzor and the angel does not stand beside the youths, but in both manuscripts Nebuchadnezar's figure is tiny compared to the others. The reason for this strange size is found in the Midrash, which describes him as a dwarf or baby.[31] The piyyut is written in very dramatic style and includes a colloquy among the three youths and Nebuchadnezar who is called "the dwarf". The speech of each of the participants is followed by the expression "said Hananiah", "said Mishael", "said Azariah", and "said the dwarf".[32]

The illustration for the Third Commandment (fol. 118; plate 18a)

29   On the phenomenon of human beings and angels with bird and animal heads, see S. Ameisenowa, "Animal-Headed Gods, Evangelists, Saints and Righteous Men", *Journal of the Warburg and Courtauld Institutes*, 12 (1949), pp. 21–45; B. Narkiss, "On the Zoocephalic Phenomenon in Medieval Ashkenazi Manuscripts" (n. 8 above) pp. 49–62, plates LXXIII–LXXX.

30   Munich, State Library, Cod. Heb. 5, vol. II, fol. 209. See J. Gutmann, *Hebrew Manuscript Painting*, New York 1978, plate 17. On the manuscript in general, see Th. Metzger, "Le manuscrit enluminé Cod. Hebr. 5 de la Bibliothèque à Munich", *Études de civilisation médiévale (IXe–XIIe siècles): Mélanges offerts à Edmond-René Labande*, Poitiers 1974, pp. 537–552.

31   "The Dwarf of Babel" as a nickname for Nebuchadnezar appears in *Pesiqta d'Rav Kahana*, ed. S. Buber, Luck 1868, p. 112a; and in ed. B. Mandelbaum, New York 1962, p. 230. See also *Pesiqta Rabbati*, ed. M. Ish-Shalom, Tel Aviv 1963, p. 144a; and Nebuchadnezar as a naked baby, riding on a lion bridled by a snake in *Machsor Lipsiae*, II, fol. 67; and my introduction thereto, p. 98, pointing to its origin in Shab. 150a.

32   See note 91 in Ezra Fleischer's Introduction to Mahzor Worms (n. 21, above).

"You shall not take the name of the LORD your God in vain" (Ex. 20. 7) represents the taking of an oath — an actual event in German-Jewish community life. A Jew is depicted wearing a pointed hat, sitting before a stand called "the reader's tower" on which a Torah scroll lies open. His left hand holds one of the staves of the scroll and his right is raised, palm open, in the gesture of an oath. The picture is enclosed in a frame in the shape of a trifoil arch, which may symbolize the synagogue. It becomes apparent in the succeeding pictures that many of the illustrations are in fact genre paintings describing the Jew's life in his community, and this is one such illustration. The cantor's pulpit, or "tower" as it is called in thirteenth to fifteenth-century Germany, is familiar to us from many other Hebrew manuscripts of that period, and in all of them it looks like a tilted tablet atop a pillar supported by a base. In some of the pictures a book is shown on the stand; in others, a Torah scroll. Usually a reader wrapped in a *tallit* is depicted standing before them, as for example, in the Birds' Head Haggadah, which is close to our Minute Mahzor in time and place of composition.[33] I do not know of another similar "oath" picture in a Hebrew medieval illuminated manuscript, and it may thus be the artist's own invention, fashioned according to his personal experience in the synagogue of his community. The piyyut that the picture illustrates enumerates all the sights that Moses saw when he went up Mount Sinai,[34] and has nothing to do with the taking of oaths in the synagogue. On the other hand, a different piyyut for the Third Commandment opening with the words: *Aria veganvei* not in our Minute Mahzor but found in Mahzor Vitry deals explicitly with false oaths and the punishment they incur.[35] The commentator in Mahzor Vitry explains that while God will not exonerate the swearer of false oaths, the terrestrial court punishes by flogging and exonerates him.[36] The piyyut mentions the false oaths of

---

33   The Birds' Head Haggadah in the Israel Museum, Bezalel Division, Dept. of Judaica, no. 180/57, e.g., fols. 32, 33v and 40. See M. Spitzer ed., *The Birds' Head Haggadah: Facsimile of the Manuscript and an Introductory Volume*, Jerusalem 1967.

34   The piyyut opens with the words: "Moses the Prophet spake: When I did go aloft". See *Mahzor Vitry*, ed. Hurwitz, pp. 339–340.

35   *Mahzor Vitry*, ed. Hurwitz, p. 339. Another piyyut listed in Davidson, I, Aleph, no. 5566, which appears in the Worms Mahzor (fol. 151v), also describes biblical figures who were punished for false oaths. See Ezra Fleischer's Introduction to the Worms Mahzor, note 93.

36   The commentaries on the Aramaic piyyutim for the Ten Commandments can be

the judges and also of the simple Jew, whose punishment is the same as that of Gehazi, infected by the leprosy of Naaman (II Ki. 5. 1); the commentator adds, "I did not know that a false oath could cause such a thing". The fact that the drawing does not illustrate the piyyut found in our Minute Mahzor may lead us to assume that it originated in an illustration for another piyyut, and that the artist of the Minute Mahzor copied the picture from a manuscript in which it was related to a piyyut on the Third Commandment, which spoke of false oaths.

On the panel for the Fourth Commandment "Remember the Sabbath day and keep it holy" (Ex. 20. 8), the artist depicts Sabbath eve in a Jewish home (fol. 119v; plate 18b). This too is a genre painting of everyday life and makes an important contribution to our knowledge about the specific objects used for the Sabbath in the Jewish home in the thirteenth century. The illustrations relate to the piyyut *Earth and Heaven*[37] which tells of the preparation of special dishes, of fine wine and elaborate clothing, and of candle lighting, an act by which the woman honors the Sabbath. In the illustration the lady of the house is depicted on the left side, standing dressed in a red cloak with a white ermine border dotted with black, on her head a headdress and veil. She lights the special Jewish Sabbath lamp, the so-called "Juden Stern," with a long candle. Here the candelabrum appears in cross-section, hanging from the ceiling, and the arms of oil spouts extend from within its wide round body. From the bottom of the lamp hangs a vessel to catch oil droppings. Lamps of this kind are found for the most part in Hebrew illuminated manuscripts from Germany.[38] On the right side of the panel the couple is depicted at the Sabbath table, which stands on two triangles serving as legs. Each of them holds a large red goblet, perhaps of painted wood as in the Birds' Head Haggadah.[39] Above the table on which are two loaves of bread covered

---

found in *Mahzor Vitry* in the corpus of the piyyutim, ed. Hurwitz, pp. 310–334. On the interpretative literature to the Aramaic piyyutim see Menahem Schmelzer, *Sources and Studies*, I (Hebrew), New York 1978, especially the introduction on pp. 169–176; also: Israel Ta-Shma, "The Commentary on the Aramaic Piyyutim in Mahzor Vitry", (Hebrew) *Qiryat Sefer*, 57, 3–4 (1982), pp. 701–708.

37   Not listed by Davidson. See *Mahzor Vitry*, p. 340, and *Machsor Lipsiae*, I, fols. 171–172.

38   For example in the Erna Michael Haggadah, Israel Museum, ms. 180/58; see B. Narkiss, *Hebrew Illuminated Manuscripts*, plate 38.

39   See, for example, fol. 26v and the Introductory Volume to the *Birds' Head Haggadah*, pp. 40-41.

with a cloth, hangs the flowing Sabbath lamp. Both the man and woman are dressed in red garments trimmed with ermine, a symbol of the Jew's feeling of majesty on the Sabbath. The man wears a pointed hat, the woman a headdress and veil. Her dress is white, though only its sleeves can be seen.

The Sacrifice of Isaac is the subject of the next panel, which deals with the Fifth Commandment "Honor your father and your mother" (Ex. 20. 12). This time the illustration relates directly to the text of the piyyut "Isaac said to his father Abraham:" "How beautiful is the altar which you have built for me, O father" (Davidson, I, Aleph, no. 5812).[40] Abraham stands in the center of the picture (fol. 121; plate 19a) with an outline frame and raises the knife above Isaac lying on the painted altar. Above them a crowned angel with a bird's head spreads its wings. A ram appears to the right behind Abraham, its horns caught in a tree. The inscriptions that surround the figures form two arches, thus emphasizing the two parts of the picture. To the left the inscription relates in Aramaic Isaac's words: "God, tell him not to slaughter the kid", as they appear at the end of this piyyut (fol. 122; plate 19b). In the center are the words of the angel; "Do not raise your hand against the boy or do anything to him", and at the right — "Here is the other ram caught in the thicket by his horns". The similarity to the Sacrifice of Isaac in the Birds' Head Haggadah is not complete[41] although certain details like the angel with the bird's head suggest that perhaps the two share a common iconographic source.

The choice of subject illustrating the Sixth Commandment "You shall not murder" (Ex. 20. 13; fol. 122; plate 19b) is most interesting. The artist chose to represent Benaiah the son of Jehoiada killing Joab the son of Zeruiah at the order of King Solomon (I Ki. 2. 28-34) for murdering in cold blood "two men more righteous and honorable than he... Abner the son of Ner, the army commander of Israel and Amasa son of Jether, the army commander of Judah". Here as well the artist made use of the Aramaic text of the piyyut which represents the deeds of Joab as an example of murder without the permission of King David.[42] Abner is represented as a sinner, but the paytan concludes in a

---

40   *Mahzor Vitry*, ed. Hurwitz, p. 341; *Machsor Lipsiae*, I, fols. 172–172v.

41   See fol. 15v and the facsimile referral to n. 38 above.

42   "Adonijah ben Haggith summoned up his strength" (Davidson, I, Aleph, no. 3197); *Mahzor Vitry*, ed. Hurwitz, pp. 341–342; *Machsor Lipsiae*, vol. I, fols. 173–173v. See E.E. Urbach, "The Fate of Joab in the Midrash" (Hebrew) in: *Dov*

tone of sympathy for Joab in the spirit of the Bible and Midrash: "The children of Israel mourned and cried over the death of Joab ben Zeruiah".

The texts that appear alongside the characters depicted are based on the piyyut, which describes Joab's attempts to escape from Benaiah during a dramatic argument with Solomon. King Solomon sits on the right, a crown upon his head, and at his side is written "Remember Abner and Amasa", which is an abbreviation of a line in the piyyut. To the left stands "Benaiah the commander", who decapitates "the hero Joab" with a big sword. Both men are surmounted by Aramaic inscriptions based on the piyyut. Despite the connection between the illustration and the text of the piyyut, I am not aware of similar iconography in any other medieval Hebrew manuscript. Perhaps the artist himself created such an iconography, inspired by the piyyut while using a conventional rendering of decapitation by sword.

The Seventh Commandment "You shall not commit adultery" (Ex. 20. 13) illustrates the piyyut "Joseph was assailed by lust" (Davidson, II, Yod, no. 2161)[43] concerning "the righteous Joseph" who did not submit to the seduction of Potiphar's wife. The panel depicts Joseph wearing a pointed Jew's hat, as he offers Potiphar's wife a large white glass. Above the glass hangs a large pitcher (fol. 123v; plate 20a). To the left is the "friend" of Potiphar's wife. Both women are seated on chairs in a garden. Passages taken from the piyyut are written on both sides of the arched frame surrounding the panel. Potiphar's wife is quoted as regarding Joseph as a "nurseling lamb", ready to do her bidding. To the right an inscription puts words into her mouth: "Arise, O slave, show your courage, gird your sword and serve me as a slave". In her hand is a glass goblet (according to the commentary in Mahzor Vitry it was an ivory goblet) into which a drink is poured by Joseph. Nothing in the appearance or movements of either Joseph or the wife

---

Sadan Jubilee Volume, Jerusalem 1977, pp. 44–54. He explains the rabbinic praise of Joab whose house, according to Rav "was open to the poor" (Yer. Mak. II : 7). The piyyut deals with other rebels against David, beginning with his son Adonijah. It should be noted that the illustration of the battle between David and Adonijah, showing the heroes as two medieval knights, appears at the beginning of the First Book of Kings in a Hebrew Bible from Lorraine (France), 1286, now in the Bibliothèque Nationale, ms. hébr. 4, fol. 249v; see G. Sed-Rajna, "The Illustrations of the Kaufman Mishneh Torah", *Journal of Jewish Art*, 6 (1976), fig. 24.

43   In *Mahzor Vitry*, ed. Hurwitz, p. 342; and in *Machsor Lipsiae*, I, fols. 174–174v.

of Potiphar recalls the well-known colorful medieval descriptions in which Potiphar's wife is pictured in her bed, holding on to Joseph's garment, as told in the Bible (Gen. 39. 11–13) and elaborated upon in Midrash. Indeed, even the piyyut itself does not mention seduction; rather, it is entirely devoted to Joseph's beauty and attractiveness, a source of amazement for Potiphar's wife and her neighbors, who were incapable even of tasting the wine he served them "because they were driven to gaze upon his beauty", in the words of the commentator of Mahzor Vitry.

"You shall not steal" (Ex. 20. 13) is the title of the panel that illustrates the Eighth Commandment in our Mahzor (fol. 125; plate 20b). It appears at the head of the piyyut on this theme,[44] which concludes, unlike the picture before us, with the divine punishment of the thief. Here, however, the thief is depicted at the right, inside a trifoil arch; he opens the lock of a box and removes red-colored objects. Inscribed above are the words "You shall not steal". The same thief is pictured on the left, his hands bound behind his back; he stands before the judge, wearing a typical hat, who sits holding a staff in his hand. To the right of the thief within the frame is a sketch of a scaffold. Clearly what we have here is another genre painting which the artist took at least partially from the reality familiar to him, rather than an illustration of the text of the piyyut.

In the opinion of the late Alexander Scheiber of Budapest, this is an illustration of the well-known story of "Rabba's staff" (Ned. 25a).[45] The Talmud tells of a man who denied that he owed money to his neighbor, claiming that he had already paid the debt. When the two came before Rabba, the latter suggested that the debtor take an oath. The debtor went and put all the coins that he owed into a hollow staff. When he arrived at the court he said to the lender: Hold this staff in your hand until I swear. Then he went and swore on the Torah that he had returned to the lender everything he had borrowed from him. The lender in his rage broke the stick, and the coins spilled out onto the floor.

I am not sure that Professor Scheiber's opinion is correct in this case, because according to the Talmudic story, it was the lender who

---

44   *Machsor Lipsiae*, I, fols. 174v–176v; missing completely in *Mahzor Vitry*; Davidson, I, Aleph, no. 26.

45   A. Scheiber, "Mikszáth Targytörteneti Kapcsolataihoz v. Birtokszerző Mondák", in *Folklór és Targytörténet*, 2, Budapest 1977, pp. 302–303 with illustration.

held the staff and broke it, rather than the judge as our picture shows. In addition, our picture shows a thief taking objects from a box, rather than borrowing coins. It should be noted that there was a fairly long inscription to the side of the seated judge, but it has been erased and is now completely illegible, even under ultraviolet light; perhaps it contained the solution.

The picture for the Ninth Commandment, "You shall not bear false witness against your neighbor" (Ex. 20. 13), also seems to reflect a genre scene from life (fol. 126v; plate 21a). To the right sits a judge with a hat on his head and to the left stand two people in short jerkins who seem to be peasants; their hats hang from their shoulders rather than resting on their heads, in honor of the judge. The leftmost of the two raises his hand, apparently to bear witness. The picture is a crude sketch, on a blank page, and precedes the piyyut "Beware of false oaths and vile slander" (Davidson, I, Aleph, no. 2185).[46]

The illustration for the Tenth Commandment "You shall not covet" (Ex. 20. 14) is the most interesting of all the miniatures (fol. 128v; plate 21b). It shows Adam and Eve, each under a separate tree, naked and covering themselves with leaves. The leaves of the tree under which Eve stands are green, and between its branches a red bird spreads its wings, similar to the angels portrayed elsewhere in our Minute Mahzor. The tree under which Adam stands is withered. It can be assumed that the living green tree symbolizes the Tree of Life while the dried-up tree represents the Tree of Knowledge, from which Adam and Eve ate, thus losing their immortality in Eden. In the center the serpent stands erect on his tail and injects his venom, through his red tongue, into the fruit that Eve holds in her hand. An inscription stretches the length of the snake's body and beneath it penetrating into the ground. The serpent contains the entire text of the Tenth Commandment, which extends further on the page.

The representation of Adam and Eve on either side of the Tree of Knowledge, with the serpent intertwined on it, is commonly found in both Jewish and Christian art of the early Middle Ages. But this uncommon iconography showing two trees should be investigated as to its literary and artistic sources.

---

46 In *Machsor Lipsiae*, I, fols. 175v–176v; it does not appear in *Mahzor Vitry*. The piyyut appears in some manuscripts in connection with the Third Commandment, "You shall not swear falsely"; for example, in the Palatine Library, Parma, ms. De Rossi 804. See Ginsburger, above n. 27, p. 21.

The piyyut for the Tenth Commandment, which appears directly after the illustration, mentions the fruit that Eve desired only at its beginning; and the serpent is completely absent. The piyyut deals with the seductive power of women, presented in the very opening:[47] "Woman is our woe, she is full of shame; because of her Adam was driven out of the Garden of Eden". The entire piyyut is a venomous diatribe against woman in general, beginning with Eve who introduced death by eating from the Tree of Knowledge, drove men from their homes and filled graves with them, and ending with women of the paytan's own day, who bare their arms and emit sparks from their eyes, and from the day they are born display their charms for the seduction of men. In short, "woman is Satan", killer of many men, among them Lot, Samson, and Absalom! Only a few men know how to guard themselves from women, such as "Boaz, who recoiled from her, Joseph who fled from her and Solomon (of the thousand wives!) who distrusted her". The fact that not even one honest woman exists and that falsity is always on a woman's lips is proven by, of all people, the righteous matriarch Sarah who denied that she had laughed.

Understandably, the seduction of Eve by the serpent and her lust for the fruit of the Tree of Knowledge could have been the source that inspired the paytan to write such an accusatory piyyut. However, the piyyut seems to have little to do with the Commandment "You shall not covet". Its subject, the danger posed by women, is more appropriate to the Seventh Commandment "You shall not commit adultery". Perhaps, then, it was inserted in relation to the Tenth Commandment in our Minute Mahzor by mistake. Indeed in Mahzor Vitry this piyyut is paired with the Seventh Commandment.[48] The scribe of our Mahzor may have used a similar recension of Mahzor Vitry as a model for his text of piyyutim.

---

47   Appears in *Mahzor Vitry*, ed. Hurwitz, p. 343, in a slightly different version and a bit longer. Not listed in Davidson.

48   See ibid., ed. Hurwitz, p. 334, where the commentary to this piyyut is associated with the Seventh Commandment. The numbering of the piyyutim in the manuscript used by Hurwitz is wrong. The error occurred at an earlier stage; above the commentary to the Fifth Commandment, the scribe wrote "Fourth Commandment", and so on until the Seventh, above which is written: "Sixth Commandment". Since the commentary to the piyyutim for the Eighth and Ninth Commandments is missing in *Mahzor Vitry*, the title "Seventh Commandment" appears above that of the Tenth Commandment. See also note 95 in the introduction by Ezra Fleischer to the piyyutim of the Worms Mahzor (above n. 27).

This view, of woman as the originator of sin is well known in medieval literature and thought, whether Jewish, Moslem or Christian. Such warnings against the seductive power of women are found in earlier literature as well, and of course in the Bible. Even so, the comparison of woman to the devil greatly resembles the traditional Christian concept of the Middle Ages, which exercised a strong influence upon Jewish attitudes. Perhaps Christian homiletics influenced the Jewish paytan. This influence is also noticeable in the depiction of the two trees, the green and the dry. The source for the Tree of Knowledge and the Tree of Life of course is biblical (Gen. 2. 9; 3. 1–7). The identification of the Tree of Knowledge as a dry tree, symbolizing death, has its source in Jewish Hellenistic literature which influenced Christian literature in the fourth century, as can be seen for example in "The Book of Adam and Eve".[49] The idea of the Tree of Knowledge as a dead dry tree was quite widespread in the Middle Ages, when it acquired additional symbolic significance as the "Tree of Death", juxtaposed with the "Tree of Life".[50]

In the medieval Christian art and literature, both early and late, there are many representations of the search by various people for the Tree of Life in the Garden of Eden as a remedy for death, beginning with Seth the son of Adam. There are likewise many pictures of the two trees, the Tree of Knowledge and the Tree of Life growing in the Garden of Eden, with Adam and Eve sheltered in their shade.[51] Rarer are representations of the green tree after the Primal Sin. The erect serpent injecting its venom into the fruit is also described in "The Book of Adam and Eve" (section 19).[52] In the same passage Eve swears by God's throne, by the Cherubim and by the Tree of Life to give the fruit

---

49   *The Book of Adam and Eve* which incorporates *The Apocalypse of Moses*; see R.H. Charles, *The Apocrypha and Pseudepigrapha of the Old Testament*, Oxford 1969, II, pp. 134–154.

50   E.g., The medieval Midrash *Tanna d'vei Eliyahu Rabba*, ch. 5: "Do not read עצמות (bones) but rather עץ מות (tree of death), the tree from which the Holy One Blessed be He told Adam not to eat". See also M.R. Bennett, "The Legend of the Green Tree and the Dry", *The Archaeological Journal*, 83 (1926), pp. 21–32; R.J. Peebles, "The Dry Tree, Symbol of Death", *Vassar Medieval Studies*, New Haven 1923, pp. 59 ff.; Z. Ameisenowa, "The Tree of Life in Jewish Iconography", *Journal of the Warburg and Courtauld Institutes*, 2 (1938/39), pp. 326–345.

51   For examples, see "Baum", in Kirschbaum (ed.), *Lexikon der Christlichen Ikonographie*, I, Freiburg 1968, cols. 264–268.

52   In "The Apocalypse of Moses", section XIX; see Charles, Apocrypha etc. II, p. 146.

to Adam as well. It is possible that the red bird in the green tree is a depiction of a Cherub in the Tree of Life.

In conclusion, the treatment of the Ten Commandments by the artist of the Minute Mahzor stems first and foremost from his familiarity with the text of the piyyutim and their midrashic interpretations of the biblical text. These are the primary literary sources of the artist's originality. His two major artistic sources are: contemporary Christian art of the Middle Ages, and local Jewish genre illustrations. Parallel works appearing in the Middle Ages are mostly of biblical subjects such as the Sacrifice of Isaac (fol. 121) or Adam and Eve (fol. 128v). Aside from these, there are illustrations originating from the Midrash, as for example: the wild ox and Leviathan as the meal of the righteous, and the hunt for the doe (fol. 1v); Nebuchadnezar the dwarf who throws the youths into the furnace (fol. 114v) and Joseph before Potiphar's wife and friends (123v). Most of the illustrations can be considered genre paintings based on the artist's personal experience and knowledge of quotidian life in his community. Among these genre illustrations are: the oath taken on the Torah scroll (fol. 118), the Sabbath evening, complete with special lamp and clothing (fol. 119), the box from which the utensils are stolen, and the scaffold (fol. 125), the false witness and his garment (fol. 126v). Details testifying to familiarity with the Jewish and Christian environment in fact appear in each one of the illustrations — for example, the furnace and the throne in the picture of Hananiah, Mishael and Azariah (fol. 114v), and on the accessories in Potiphar's garden like the pitcher and glass (fol. 123v). The decapitation of Joab by Benaiah (fol. 122) is probably based on Christian martyr paintings, which appear in many medieval illustrated manuscripts.

The artist who created these drawings was undoubtedly knowledgeable, imaginative and quite original. It is, however, doubtful whether the illuminator of the Minute Mahzor was the inventor of its illustrations. If he had been, he would have taken care to coordinate the illustrations with the piyyutim they illustrate. The fact is that three of the drawings, those of "You shall not take the name of the LORD your God in vain" (fol. 118), "You shall not steal" (fol. 125) and "You shall not covet" (fol. 128v) are not suited to the text of the piyyut they accompany. In the case of "You shall not take the name of the LORD your God in vain" the picture is an illustration of a piyyut that does not even appear in the Minute Mahzor and the piyyut that does appear is not illustrated at all. In the case of "You shall not steal" the terrestrial

trial depicted in the picture blatantly contradicts the heavenly trial and punishment of which the paytan speaks. In the case of "You shall not covet", although the piyyut does mention Eve, it concentrates more on the subject of "You shall not commit adultery" than "You shall not covet".

It must be that the piyyutim and the various illustrations appeared in some other manuscript which the scribe illuminator of the Minute Mahzor had before him. He chose the pictures that seemed to him most appropriate, even though they did not always match the text.

It may therefore be assumed that the illustrations for the Aramaic piyyutim were executed at an earlier time, and our artist used them as a model. Besides, the style of the decorative illuminations and of the figures in the illustrations show that the artist of our Minute Mahzor was none other than the scribe himself. He remains anonymous; and it must be admitted that his artistic ability in sketching and coloring was less than outstanding.

I have offered these comments relating to the Ten Commandments because this examplar of medieval Jewish art seems to me both interesting and out of the ordinary. We have a great many drawings and illustrations for piyyutim in the Jewish art of the Middle Ages, especially in German mahzorim, but I know of no others that resemble those in the Minute Mahzor in the Library of the Jewish Theological Seminary in New York. I hope that the description presented here will stimulate scholars and students to seek out and to publish descriptions of additional examples of art applied to the Ten Commandments.

Translated by Ora Viskind

GLOSSARY

(Some words of Hebrew origin treated as loan-words in English)

Aggada (aggadists): Non-legal portion of rabbinic tradition.
ahavah: Paragraph in the liturgy (lit.= "love").
Akeda: The binding of Isaac.
amidah: Central portion of the liturgy.
Amora (-im): Talmudic Sage after mid-third century.
avodah: Prayer for restoration of the Temple.
baraita: Tannaitic Tradition not included in the Mishnah.
Bavli: The Babylonian Talmud.
etrog: Citron used on Sukkot.
Gemara: Discussion of the Mishnah (combined = Talmud).
genizah: Storage of worn books; esp. the one in Cairo.
Haggadah (-ot): Special prayerbook for Passover seder.
Halakhah (-ot; -ist): Legal part of rabbinic tradition.
kohen: Priest; of the tribe of Aaron.
lulav: Palm frond used on Sukkot.
Magen David: The six-pointed star.
mahzor (-im): Festival prayerbook.
matzah: Unleavened bread.
menorah: Seven-branched candelabrum.
mezuzah (-ot): Small enclosed parchment placed on doorpost.
Minim: Sectarians; possibly early Christians.
Omer: The seven weeks from Passover to Shavuot.
paytan: Composer of liturgical poetry.
piyyut (-im): Liturgical poem.
Seder: Ceremonial meal on Passover eve.
Selihot: Penitential prayers.
Shavuot: Pentecost
Shema: "Hear O Israel." Core of Jewish prayer.
shofar: Ram's horn trumpet.
Sukkot: The feast of Tabernacles.
tallit: Prayer shawl.
Tanna (-im; -itic): Sage before the third century.
tefillin: Phylacteries.

KEY TO TALMUD AND MIDRASH

GENERAL INDEX

Abarbanel 14 86
Abraham 39 227
Abrahams, I. 389
Abudarham 114
accentuation 6
  see cantillation
Achan 181
Acts of the Apostles 36 40 ff.
Adam 162
Adani, Samuel 378
adultery 2 13 20 104
agriculture 61
Agrippa 179
ahavah rabbah 163
Akiba 40 174 225 234 240
Albeck, H. 170 388 389
Albo, L. 119
Alexandria 133
Alfasi 368
Alharizi 368
allegory 122 176 181 143
Alon, Gedaliah 61 176 238
alphabet 206
Alt, A. 3 29 46 106 115
Altmann, A. 136 257
Ambrosian Library 386
Amir, Y. 98 240 355
Amsterdam 414
anaphora 370 f.
Ancona 416
A.N.E.T. 110 113
Angelico, Beato 396
Anglicans 411
Anshe Chesed 384
anthropomorphism 146 356
antinomianism 171
Antiochus 180
Antiquitates Biblicae 245
Antonioni-Mortara 386

aoraton 140
apodictic 10 16 148
Aptowitzer, V. 170 188
'aqdamut 44 428
Aquila 179
Arabic poetry 364
Aristides 224
Aristotle 130 137 141 143 155
Ark of the Covenant 3 22 28 385
Arks from Italy 415
Arugath ha-Bosem 165 182
Asa, King 37 39
asceticism 133
Ashburnham Pentateuch 391 420
Asher b. Yehiel 365
Astruc, Solomon 173
Augustine 408
avikh 341
Avodah 163
Ayali, M. 61
azereth 26 34
azharot 26 119 128 363

Bacher, W. 168 234
Baer, M. 178
Baer, Y. 225
Baghdad 187
Bailey, R.E. 221
Bamberg Mahzor 426
Baneth, D.Z. 356
Bar Hiyya, Abraham 389
Bar Kokhba 61 179 388
Barnabas 176 179
Barnes, M. 88
Bartholemy-Milik 385
Baumgartner, W. 115
Beaugency, Eliezer of 78
Beccafumi (Siena) 396
Becker, J. 244

444

PUBLICATIONS OF THE PERRY FOUNDATION FOR BIBICAL
RESEARCH THE HEBREW UNIVERSITY OF JERUSALEM

י׳ אבישור / עיונים בשירת המזמורים

ב׳ אופנהיימר / הנבואה הקדומה

א״א אורבך / חז״ל — פרקי אמונות ודעות

ש׳ אליצור / פיוטי ר׳ אלעזר בירבי קילר

י״נ אפשטיין / מחקרים בספרות התלמוד ובלשונות שמיות (כרכים א–ג)

י׳ היינימן / התפילה בתקופת התנאים והאמוראים — טיבה ודפוסיה

מ׳ ויינפלד / משפט וצדקה בישראל ובעמים

ז׳ ויסמן / מיעקב לישראל — הסיפורים על יעקב ושילובו בתולדות אבות האומה

י׳ זקוביץ / חיי שמשון

ש׳ יפת ור״ב סולטרס / פירוש רבי שמואל בן מאיר (רשב״ם) לקהלת

י׳ ליוור / פרקים בתולדות הכהונה והלוייה

ש״א ליונשטם / מסורת יציאת מצרים בהשתלשלותה

י׳ ליכט / פירוש על ספר במדבר (א–י)

ע״צ מלמד / מפרשי המקרא (שני כרכים)

ב״צ סגל (עורך) / עשרת הדיברות בראי הדורות

ע׳ פליישר / היוצרות בהתהוותם והתפתחותם

ע׳ פליישר / תפילה ומנהגי תפילה ארץ־ישראליים בתקופת הגניזה

י׳ יהלום / שפת השיר של הפיוט הארץ־ישראלי הקדום

ש״א ליונשטם (עורך) / מחקרים במקרא

ח״י קאסאווסקי / אוצר לשון תרגום אונקלוס (קונקורדנציה)

מ״ד קאסוטו / פירוש על ספר בראשית

מ״ד קאסוטו / פירוש על ספר שמות

מ״ד קאסוטו / ספרות מקראים וספרות כנענית (שני כרכים)

מ״ד קאסוטו / תורת התעודות

ש׳ קמין / רש״י — פשוטו של מקרא ומדרשו של מקרא

א׳ רופא / סיפורי הנביאים

ח׳ רביב / מוסד הזקנים בישראל

U. Cassuto / Biblical and Oriental Studies (two vols.)

U. Cassuto / From Adam to Noah

U. Cassuto / From Noah to Abraham

U. Cassuto / Exodus

U. Cassuto / The Documentary Hypothesis

U. Cassuto / The Goddess Anath

H. Reviv / The Elders in Ancient Israel

A. Rofé / The Preophetical Stories

E.E. Urbach / The Sages (two vols.)

M. Weiss / The Bible from Within

M. Weiss / The Story of Job's Beginning

DATE DUE

DEC 2 2 1997			
8/10/07			